COMPASS

A manual on human rights education with young people

Written by

Patricia Brander
Rui Gomes
Ellie Keen
Marie-Laure Lemineur
Bárbara Oliveira
Jana Ondrácková
Alessio Surian
Olena Suslova

Drawings by

Pancho

Edited by

Patricia Brander
Ellie Keen
Marie-Laure Lemineur

Project coordination and final editing: Rui Gomes

Project assistant: Natalia Miklash

This manual was produced under the guidance and support of a reference group, composed of:

Dr Elie Abouaoun
Mr. Anatoliy Azarov
Ms Patricia Brander
Ms Ellie Keen
Ms Corina Michaela Leca
Ms Marie-Laure Lemineur
Ms Brigitte Mooljee
Ms Louise Nylin
Ms Bárbara Oliveira
Ms Eunice Smith (Unesco)
Mr. Alessio Surian
Ms Olena Suslova
Mr. Wim Taelman
Mr. Andrew Yurov

– 2nd edition –

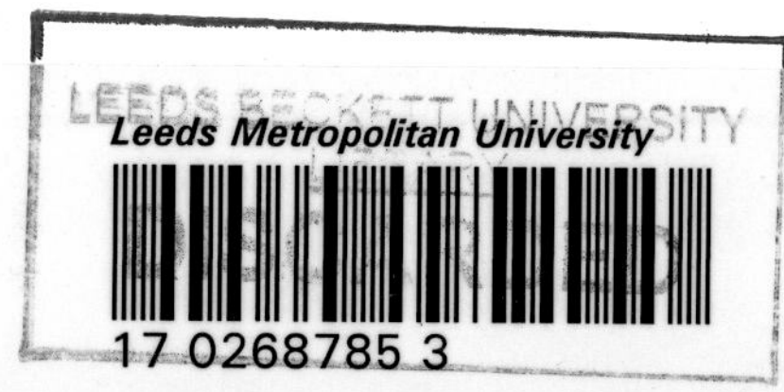

French edition:
"Repčres" - Manuel pour la pratique de l'éducation aux droits de l'homme avec les jeunes
ISBN 92-871-4595-3

Russian edition:
"КОМПАС" - учебник по правозащитному образованию молодежи
ISBN 92-871-4596-1

Design: Art Factory
Drawings: © "Pancho"
Photos: page 132 © MTI (Nelson Mandela)
page 132 © David King Collection (Evgenia Ginzburg)
page 133 © MTI (Martin Luther King)
page 133 © MTI (Mahatma Gandhi)
page 134 © Gamma Press (Daw Aung San Suu Kyi)
page 134 © Tibet Information Network (Ngawang Sandrol)

First published in May, 2002 in 3000 copies,
2nd edition, May 2003 in copies 3000.

Council of Europe Publishing
F-67075 Strasbourg Cedex

ISBN: 92-871-4880-5

Printed in Hungary

Table of Contents

Acknowledgements

Words of thanks, recognition and appreciation are owed to:

- The members of the Reference Group, for their commitment, generosity and support to the writers;
- Sunduss al-Hassani, Henrike Eisfeld, Dariusz Grzemny, Dilwar Hussain, Dr Mónika Mádai, Ivan Ivanov, Yael Ohana, Tavs Qvist, Györgyi Tóth and Arjos Vendrig for commenting and suggesting texts;
- Jeroen Schokkenbroek, from the Directorate General of Human Rights of the Council of Europe, for careful reading and useful suggestions;
- Nadia Banno Gomes, Teresa Cunha, Laura De Witte, Deepak G. Naik, Eugen Gherga, Erzsébet Kovács, Anna Rogowska, Nana Saginashvili and many others for their pertinent remarks and useful suggestions;
- The Division of Human Rights, Peace, Democracy and Tolerance at Unesco for motivation and useful advice;
- Youth organisations, national youth councils, the Foundation for Human and Humanitarian Rights (Lebanon), the Charles Malik Foundation and many other organisations, for submitting reference materials;
- Users and readers of the draft texts on the Internet – including those who are sceptical about the value of this manual;
- Members of the Human Rights Education Associates' Global Human Rights Education List for comments and suggestions for the title;
- The Monitoring Group of the Human Rights Education Youth Programme for support and ideas;
- All those who have, sometimes involuntarily, contributed to the shaping of the contents;
- Michael Hughes, from The British Council, Budapest, for being more than a proofreader.

The International Union of Railways and, in particular, Inter Rail for their financial support through the Solidarity Fund for Youth Mobility.

We apologise for any omission and regret that we were not able to include all materials and suggestions received.

It has become almost commonplace to speak about the world as a global village. Globalisation is generally associated with increased possibilities and risks, for trade, co-operation and communication. But the true challenge of globalisation remains the development of a universal conscience that puts human rights, pluralist democracy and the equality of all human beings as the most important values that we may share.

The Council of Europe and the European Convention on Human Rights were created as a response to some of the worst forms of war and barbarity that humankind has ever experienced. The Convention and other instruments that were subsequently developed – against torture, for social rights, etc. – provided inspiration and support to individuals and non-governmental organisations who have fought injustice, oppression and discrimination. Much has been achieved. But much progress remains to be made; too many rights of too many people in Europe are still violated, ignored or suppressed.

The conventions on human rights are achievements that we share as Europeans; they orient us in times of uncertainty and change. Preserving and honouring them is the highest duty for every state in Europe.

However, human rights cannot be defended by legal texts only. They need to be protected and taken care of by everyone, young people included. This manual provides young people with opportunities to understand and speak human rights. It also provides youth leaders, teachers, educators, professionals and volunteers with concrete ideas to motivate, engage and involve young people to take action for human rights in their own way, in their own community.

This manual does not provide solutions. There are no ready-made solutions to poverty, discrimination, violence or intolerance. It does not contain answers to all questions about human rights either. What the manual does provide is an opportunity for those venturing into human rights education to explore these themes in a manner that is creative, involves young people and is, in itself, human rights education.

Like a *COMPASS*, this manual indicates different ways and directions in a journey through human rights. Like a *COMPASS*, it can and should be used anywhere in Europe by anybody interested in human rights, democracy or citizenship.

If it is true that we seem to have entered the 21st century through a gate of fire, it is reassuring that many young people and youth organisations, teachers and educators, are ready to take up the challenge of education for and through human rights.

This manual is a contribution and tribute to their action.

Walter Schwimmer

Introduction

Welcome to *COMPASS*, the manual on human rights education with young people!

We hope that it will provide you with the ideas, inspiration and motivation to venture into the field of human rights education with young people. *COMPASS* has been produced within the framework of the Human Rights Education Youth Programme of the Directorate of Youth and Sport of the Council of Europe, which was launched in 2000 on the occasion of the 50th anniversary of the European Convention on Human Rights. The programme aims to put human rights at the centre of youth work and thereby to contribute to the bringing of human rights education into the mainstream.

Human rights education – meaning *educational programmes and activities that focus on promoting equality in human dignity* – is of incalculable value in shaping a European dimension of citizenship meaningful to all Europeans. Developed in conjunction with other programmes of the Directorate in Youth and Sport of the Council of Europe – intercultural learning, participation, empowerment of minorities and of young people from minority backgrounds – human rights education has the potential to be a catalyst for action and a source of synergies. Those involved in non-formal education in youth work should be able to consider the evolution, practice and challenges of human rights, with regard to their universality, indivisibility and inalienability, and what these mean to the young people of today.

The Directorate of Youth and Sport, especially through the European Youth Centres and the European Youth Foundation, has acquired an undisputed reputation for expertise in developing educational approaches and materials suitable for use both in formal and non-formal contexts as well as in different cultural environments. Its work with multipliers, the impact of projects such as the "*all different – all equal*" youth campaign, and its long-term training programme have all contributed to the development of projects that make their impact first and foremost at grass-roots level while being pre-eminently European.

Recent events, both in Europe and other places of the world, threaten the foundations of a culture of peace and human rights. They show that a more visible, explicit and conscious approach to human rights education is needed urgently.

In this context, the Human Rights Education Youth Programme aims to:

- bring Human Rights Education within the mainstream of youth work practice;
- value and develop Non-Formal Education with young people as a form of Human Rights Education;
- value young people and youth organisations as a fundamental resource for Human Rights Education and civil society in Europe;
- promote a broad understanding of Human Rights Education while respecting the diversity of youth and social-cultural realities in Europe today;
- develop new associative networks and synergies with partners in the non-formal and the formal educational fields;
- pursue and achieve the maximum "multiplying effect" by involving practitioners and partners at national and local level;
- provide practitioners across Europe with new educational tools and networks for youth activities based on Human Rights Education;
- integrate accumulated experience in intercultural and non-formal education, youth participation and research;
- take into account innovations in educational approaches and media.

A compass for practitioners of human rights education

COMPASS is central to this programme, which also includes support to local pilot projects, national and regional training courses and specific activities related to different forms of violence. Instead of "another" manual or venturing into new approaches or proposals for human rights education, the central aim of this publication is to make human rights education accessible, usable and useful to educators, facilitators, leaders, teachers, volunteers and trainers who are active in

educational activities with young people. It is, in many ways, a modest (yet ambitious) answer to the question that many concerned activists and educators pose: "HOW do we do it?"

Experiences acquired during the educational activities of the 1995 European youth campaign against racism and intolerance "*all different – all equal*" revealed that the success of European educational projects of this kind depends on:

– the provision of appropriate and accessible educational methodologies and tools, such as the Education Pack "*all different – all equal*";
– the availability of such materials in the national languages of the users;
– the existence of trainers and multipliers who can act and disseminate at national, regional and local levels.

COMPASS is a response to these needs. It is published by the Council of Europe in English, in French and in Russian and translation and adaptation to other languages and contexts is encouraged. The organisation of national and regional training courses should help trainers and educators to become familiar with the manual and to make sure that it reaches the schools, associations and youth groups at the local level. *COMPASS* only has meaning as a book for encouraging action.

An open and participatory production process

Producing *COMPASS* has proven to be a huge task. Its thematic scope is vast – human rights education concerns literally all aspects of life today – its geographical and cultural scope is extremely diverse. There are wide differences in the working environments and educational contexts of the potential users, both within and between non-formal and formal education. From the outset, the following issues became problematic:

– Is it possible to respect the intrinsic universality of human rights at the same time as addressing specific situations and cultural diversity across Europe?
– Is it really possible to use the same manual and methods across different countries?
– Is there anything in human rights or human rights education that is specific to Europe?
– Is it realistic to attempt to produce one manual that would be suitable for formal and non-formal educational environments?
– How much should users already know?
– Is it still possible to be innovative in this field?
– Will the manual's target group be prepared to use it?
– Is there any point in producing something specifically for human rights education with young people?

It was not possible to answer all questions and dispel all concerns and risks. What was called for was a production process that could either provide answers or take the concerns into account. The final product should, in fact, be the result of contributions and expertise from:

– human rights education;
– intercultural learning;
– youth work;
– pedagogy and didactics;
– human rights organisations.

Reference Group and Production Team

A *Reference Group* was constituted on the basis of an open call launched by e-mail and the Internet. The group's task was to serve as a support to the writers. The group also defined the outline of contents and general educational approaches and secured insights and perspectives from other materials and experiences.

The Reference Group was composed of:

– Dr Elie Abouaoun, Lebanon, *Nouveaux Droits de l'Homme-International*
– Mr. Anatoliy Azarov, Russian Federation, *Moscow School of Human Rights*
– Ms Patricia Brander, Denmark, consultant, experienced with the "*all different - all equal*" Education pack
– Ms Ellie Keen, United Kingdom, *Human Rights Education Associates* and *Amnesty International*

- Ms Corina Michaela Leca, Moldova, *SIEDO - The Independent Society for Education and Human Rights*
- Ms Marie-Laure Lemineur, Spain and France, consultant experienced with the *United Nations University for Peace (Costa Rica)*
- Ms Brigitte Mooljee, United Kingdom, *Citizenship team* at the *Department of Education and Employment*
- Ms Louise Nylin, Sweden and USA, consultant with the *UNDP* and with the *People's Decade for Human Rights Education*
- Ms Bárbara Oliveira, Sweden and Mozambique, consultant, former youth co-ordinator with *Amnesty International* in South Africa
- Ms Eunice Smith, *Division of Human Rights, Peace, Democracy and Tolerance, Social and Human Sciences sector at Unesco*
- Mr. Alessio Surian, Italy, *European Federation for Intercultural Learning*
- Ms Olena Suslova, Ukraine, *Women's Information Consultative Centre*
- Mr. Wim Taelman, Belgium, *Flemish Association for Human Rights Education*
- Mr. Andrew Yurov, Russian Federation, *Youth Human Rights Movement, Advisory Council of the European Youth Centre and European Youth Foundation*
- Ms Nancy Flowers, USA *, consultant, *Human Rights Education Resource Center, University of Minnesota*
- Ms Jana Ondrácková, Czech Republic *, human rights education programme developer and co-ordinator at the *Czech Helsinki Committee*
- Ms Vedrana Spajic-Vrkaš *, Croatia, Faculty of *Philosophy of Croatia University of Zagreb*

The Reference Group met in April 2001 at the European Youth Centre Budapest in what was a very intensive and fruitful meeting. The meeting produced the outline of *COMPASS*' contents and structure, including the main themes that should be explored. Ideas for the process of production and testing of activities were also brought forward. The Production Team members, the group of eight people who authored the texts for *COMPASS*, were also part of the Reference Group. Other members of the group served as advisors and supervisors for the writers during the production phase; their work was voluntary.

The Production Team members divided the work among themselves in a way that would secure maximum "cross-fertilisation" of ideas and experiences, a realistic calendar and a clear identification of tasks and responsibilities. Sections and activities had writers and proofreaders in order to make sure that each text was read and commented on by at least two or three people before it even went to the rest of the team. The team held three meetings, in May, June and September 2001.

Testing and finalising

The final drafts of the texts were placed on the Internet and users of the HRE Youth Programme, as well as members of the Trainer's Pool of the Directorate of Youth and Sports, could have access to them, make comments and suggest improvements. Although the time the texts were posted was short, the process was innovative and participatory.

Youth organisations, national youth councils and other partners of the Directorate of Youth and Sport were asked to provide references for human rights educational materials available in their country and language. The level of response was very varied and some lists were quite long; it was therefore decided to keep the references for the electronic version of *COMPASS* and for the HRE Resource Centre.

Particular attention was paid to involving or consulting youth organisations with specific expertise in the themes of the Manual. Their comments and suggestions were always useful.

The decision on the title – more than 20 suggestions for titles were received – was also highly participated, especially as a result of an announcement through the Human Rights Education Associates list (list members could indicate preferences). In order to secure consistency of styles and coherence of approaches and contents, the various authors' work was given to a team of three final editors. Ellie Keen took responsibility for chapters 1, 3 and 4, Marie-Laure Lemineur for the background information on the themes and Patricia Brander worked on the activities and related texts. Rui Gomes, Programme and Training Administrator at the European Youth Centre Budapest, and coordinator of the project, did the final editing.

* *was invited but could not attend the meeting.*

What is in COMPASS?

The Production Team received from the Reference Group a mandate to be as complete and comprehensive in the contents as possible (so that anyone and everyone can find their matters of concern or work in the Manual) while producing a manual which:

- users don't have to read in its entirety to be able to use it - a facilitator should be able to run an activity without having to read material that is not directly relevant to their context or situation;
- contains a minimum of supplementary information for those facilitators who may feel uncomfortable when dealing with a certain theme (*COMPASS* should be sufficient);
- is eminently practical and based on experiential activities;
- is attractive, reflects the concerns of young people in Europe and is a tool to develop their social skills and attitudes as much as their knowledge and competencies;
- focuses on values and on social issues rather than (just) on formal rights as laid down in conventions;
- is usable in formal and non-formal education;
- leaves "background information in the background" and not at the beginning so that users can get on with the activities but know that supporting information is available for reference.

As a result, COMPASS is organised in the following way:

Chapter 1: Familiarises the reader with what we mean by human rights education. It should motivate, inspire and introduce the reader on how to get the best out of *COMPASS* and its educational approaches,

Chapter 2: A collection of 49 activities of different levels of complexity, which cover different themes and address different types of rights,

Chapter 3: "Taking action", contains ideas and tips for those that would like to be more active in promoting human rights,

Chapter 4: Provides essential information about human rights and international standards and documents,

Chapter 5: Supplementary background information about the themes,

The appendices: Contain essential information on legal documents, because human rights are also about laws.

The choice of themes

The Reference Group originally identified sixty-three issues that should be covered in *COMPASS*. These ranged from terrorism to euthanasia. It was difficult for the Production Team to identify and decide on a way to group all the issues into a logical framework. In the end, they chose fifteen themes – Children, Citizenship, Democracy, Discrimination and Xenophobia, Education, Environment, Gender Equality, Globalisation, Health, Human Security, Media, Peace and Violence, Poverty, Social Rights and Sport. It was a difficult decision but the Team considered this the most useful way in which to organise the activities in chapter 2. Whenever questions or doubts arose, we chose to be as inclusive as possible. For the activities, a sixteenth theme was found – general human rights, referring to activities that generally develop important attitudes and awareness on all human rights.There is no background information on this general theme.

The barrier of ethnocentrism

The most serious challenge faced during the production of *COMPASS* was related to ethnocentrism. The diversity of both background and experiences of those in the Production Team was intended to ensure that most linguistic, educational and social backgrounds would be represented in the manual. *COMPASS* should be truly European and intercultural.

It is unclear to what extent this intention was ever feasible or realistic. We came to realise that sometimes we had read things in different languages but were in fact reading and referring to the same source material. The fact that the original version of *COMPASS* was drafted in English naturally encouraged all of the writers to conduct research first of all through English reference literature and on English language Internet pages. Hopefully, our awareness of the risk may have limited the damage but it was not easy to avoid it – an inevitable consequence of globalisation! Also, it would have been impossible to produce *COMPASS* with a team of 50 people writing in 50 different languages.

Pancho, the cartoonist working with us, synthesised all these dilemmas when, confronted with the request of drawing about and for a European public, he asked "but how shall I draw a European?"

About the methods

As stated earlier, it was not our intention to produce a "new" manual, but rather to produce something that can be used easily by all those working on human rights issues with young people. We came to realise that there are many excellent materials already available.

These have naturally served as inspiration to the Production Team. Whenever possible, credits and references have been given, but we apologise for any omissions. Those familiar with this kind of work will also realise that some methods have been adapted or repeated in *COMPASS*. These *recycled* methods were kept because our purpose is to provide a practical and usable tool. If a method or dynamic has proven to be effective, it would be a loss to deprive other users from using it.

Adaptation is also a key word for this entire manual. Although the activities may appear to some as ready-made solutions, the active user of *COMPASS* will need to look around and think of where they are before deciding where to go. Suggestions are given in the relevant section about how to adapt activities to meet the specific concerns of the young people, to be appropriate to the educational context, to fit the time available, etc.

COMPASS intends to provide different paths and ways that can and should be taken bearing in mind the different cultural and social values of young people in Europe. This diversity in approaches is a strength and ensures that human rights do not become a dogma imposed on anyone.

Reaching the local level

Producing *COMPASS* is only a starting point. Training courses are being organised at regional and national level that will involve youth workers and teachers. Parallel to this, *COMPASS* will be translated into other languages. For what, when and where, please consult the website of the programme at http://www.coe.int/hre.

What is out and what comes next?

Of the many activities written by the Production Team, more than twenty had to be left out because there was not enough room for everything. Entire pages of background information had to be cut drastically or reduced for the same reason.

Some of these texts find their way to users through the on-line version of COMPASS. This version, available at www.coe.int/compass , allows much better interactivity between texts and activities and benefits from suggestions and texts proposed by users. It is also inter-connected with the Education Pack 'all different-all equal'.

Also not included in this manual is the proposed *photo pack*, a series of photos on human rights issues, *filmographies* and *songs for human rights*. *COMPASS* is, indeed, about providing directions, starting points, references and orientation. Not everything can fit in. The Human Rights Education Youth Programme still has a long way to go. Indeed, there is a lot more to human rights education than just *COMPASS*.

But *COMPASS* may be your starting point. We wish you success and fun in using it.

Chapter 1

Human Rights Education and Compass, a Brief Guide for Practitioners

Table of contents of this chapter

Understanding Human Rights Education

What is Human Rights Education?

"... educational programmes and activities that focus on promoting equality in human dignity, in conjunction with other programmes such as those promoting intercultural learning, participation and empowerment of minorities"

Official definition of Human Rights Education for the Council of Europe Youth Programme

A long-term aim

There are many definitions and a number of different approaches, but human rights education is best described in terms of what it sets out to achieve. The long term aim of such programmes is to establish a culture where human rights are understood, defended and respected. Thus, anyone who works with other people may be said to engage in human rights education if they have this end in mind and take steps to achieve it – no matter how or where they go about it.

There may be slightly different views about the best or most appropriate way to move towards such an end, but that is as it should be. No two individuals, or groups of individuals, or cultures have identical requirements, and no one educational approach will suit all individuals, all groups, or all societes. This only goes to show that effective human rights education needs to be, above all, learner-centred: it has to begin from the needs, preferences, abilities and desires of each person, within each society.

"Education shall be directed to the full development of the human personality and to the strengthening of respect for human rights and fundamental freedoms. It shall promote understanding, tolerance and friendship among all nations, racial or religious groups, and shall further the activities of the United Nations for the maintenance of peace".

Article 26, UDHR

A learner-centred educational approach recognises the value of personal action and personal change and also takes account of the social context in which learners find themselves, but this need not mean that educators have to work in isolation, or that they cannot learn from others who may be working in different contexts. What draws human rights educators together from around the globe is a common enterprise – a desire to promote and inhabit a world where human rights are valued and respected. There are general guidelines, tried and tested methods, educational materials, and many people working in the field – all of which can help us to achieve this common aim. This manual is intended as another contribution.

 **What do *you* understand by human rights education?**

Breaking it down

The long view is important but for practical purposes we sometimes need a more down-to-earth picture of our aims. It can help to break these down into more concrete objectives: to look at the different components that go to make up a culture of human rights, and then to think about how we might be able to approach these individually. A human rights culture, after all, is not merely a culture where everyone knows their rights – because knowledge does not necessarily equal respect, and without respect, we shall always have violations. A human rights culture is a

"A journey of one thousand kilometres always begins with a single step."

Lao-Tse

network of interlocking attitudes, beliefs, behaviours, norms and regulations. Understanding these can give us hooks on which to hang the work we carry out within our groups.

Towards a human rights culture

The following points derive from the essential elements of such a culture. They can provide us with general objectives for human rights education:

- to strengthen respect for human rights and fundamental freedoms
- to develop a sense of individual self-respect and respect for others: a value for human dignity
- to develop attitudes and behaviour that will lead to respect for the rights of others
- to ensure genuine gender equality and equal opportunities for women in all spheres
- to promote respect, understanding and appreciation of cultural diversity, particularly towards different national, ethnic, religious, linguistic and other minorities and communities
- to empower people towards more active citizenship
- to promote democracy, development, social justice, communal harmony, solidarity and friendship among people and nations
- to further the activities of international institutions aimed at the creation of a culture of peace, based upon universal values of human rights, international understanding, tolerance and non-violence.

Outcomes of HRE

What are the aims for my group?

We have identified a global aim for human rights education, and some long-term goals. But we can move, even closer to home, and think about the needs of individual groups and communities: changing in the world, by working locally!

The world, at the moment, is a world where there are violations of human rights all around us. In an ideal case, it might be enough to instil in the members of your group a sense of respect towards other human beings, and to hope that they, at least, will not be among those who will violate the rights of others in the future. This is one important aspect of the work we do as educators for human rights.

But we can aim for more: we can aim to inspire the young people with whom we work to act not only on themselves but also on the world around them. We can try to inspire them to become, in their own right, mini-educators and mini-activists who will themselves assist in the defence of human rights – even when the issues do not appear to touch them personally. There is nothing unachievable about that aim: it does not mean that we should expect young people to devote their lives to the defence of human rights, but only that they should be aware of the issues, concerned by the issues, and capable of acting to alter the existing state of affairs where they feel that this is necessary.

With this idea in mind, existing models of human rights education sub-divide objectives into three main areas:

- Promoting awareness and understanding of human rights issues, in order that people recognise violations of human rights

- Developing the skills and abilities necessary for the defence of human rights
- Developing attitudes of respect for human rights, so that people do not willingly violate the rights of others.

What can you identify as the main concerns for the young people that you work with?

Knowledge, skills and attitudes

What type of knowledge is necessary for young people to gain a deeper understanding of human rights issues? Which skills and attitudes will be required for them to help in the defence of human rights? The lists below provide some of answers to these questions; these were the objectives that we used in putting together this manual.

Knowledge and understanding

learning *about* human rights

- Key concepts such as: freedom, justice, equality, human dignity, non-discrimination, democracy, universality, rights, responsibilities, interdependence and solidarity.
- The idea that human rights provide a framework for negotiating and agreeing standards of behaviour in the family, in school, in the community, and in the wider world;
- The role of human rights and their past and future dimension in one's own life, in the life of communities, and in the lives of other people around the world.
- The distinction between civil/political and social/economic rights;
- Different ways of viewing and experiencing human rights in different societies, different groups within the same society, and the various sources of legitimacy - including religious, moral and legal sources;
- Main social changes, historical events and reasons leading to the recognition of human rights;
- Major international instruments that exist to implement the protection of human rights - such as the United Nations Declarations of Human Rights (UDHR), the United Nations Convention of the Rights of the Child (UNCRC), the European Convention on the Protection of Human Rights and Fundamental Freedoms (ECHR);
- Local, national, international bodies, non-governmental organisations, individuals working to support and protect human rights.

Skills

learning *for* human rights

- Active listening and communication: being able to listen to different points of view, to advocate one's own rights and those of other people;
- Critical thinking: finding relevant information, appraising evidence critically, being aware of preconceptions and biases, recognising forms of manipulation, and making decisions on the basis of reasoned judgement;
- The ability to work co-operatively and to address conflict positively;
- The ability to participate in and organise social groups;
- Acting to promote and safeguard human rights both locally and globally.

Attitudes and values

learning *through* human rights

- A sense of responsibility for one's own actions, a commitment to personal development and social change;
- Curiosity, an open mind and an appreciation of diversity;
- Empathy and solidarity with others and a commitment to support those whose human rights are under threat;
- A sense of human dignity, of self-worth and of others' worth, irrespective of social, cultural, linguistic or religious differences;
- A sense of justice, the desire to work towards the ideals of freedom, equality and respect for diversity.

An inclusive approach

"The word 'education' implies the entire process of social life by means of which individuals and social groups learn to develop consciously within, and for the benefit of, the national and international communities, the whole of their personal capacities, attitudes, aptitudes and knowledge."

UNESCO Recommendations, 1974

In this manual we have taken an inclusive approach to HRE in a number of different senses. Firstly, we have tried to embrace every one of the three different dimensions – knowledge, skills and attitudes – to an equal degree. Secondly, the activities have been designed with a broad audience in mind – both in terms of age range and in adressing the formal, non-formal and informal education sectors simultaneously. Thirdly, we tried to link human rights education through participatory and active learning activities to relevant local and global issues such as development, environment, intercultural relations and peace. We do not suggest that HRE can only be approached as a separate discipline.

The use of such participatory activities has been central. Studies show that co-operatively structured small group work helps in building group cohesion, and in reducing biases between group members. Co-operative group work also helps to improve understanding of complex concepts and increases problem-solving skills, enabling participants to devise solutions that demonstrate greater creativity and practicality. All of these outcomes are important aims of human rights education. That means that we need to 'include' young people themselves at every moment of learning process. We should not fall into the trap of assuming that we, the educators, are in possession of an ultimate truth, which must be passed on to passive learners. Such an approach can easily transform human rights education into the worst type of 'ideological' education. An essential feature of the methodology contained in this manual involves the idea that young people will bring to any educational process a rich pool of experience, which must be actively drawn upon to ensure an interesting and effective development of the educational activities. Questions, often even conflicts, should be regarded as fundamental educational resources, which can be adressed in a positive manner.

HRE with young people

"I hear and I forget. I see and I remember. I do and I understand."

Confucius

It is increasingly accepted that attention should be devoted to human rights education for young people, not only because it is important for society, but also because young people themselves appreciate and benefit from the type of activities that this work involves. Contemporary societies and, in particular, the youth population are increasingly confronted by processes of social exclusion, of religious, ethnic and national differences, and by the disadvantages – and advantages – of increasing globalisation. Human rights education addresses these important issues and can help to make sense of the different perceptions, beliefs, attitudes

and values of a modern multi-cultural society. It helps individuals to find ways of using such differences in positive ways.

Perhaps more importantly, young people care about human rights, and in that sense, they provide the main resource for human rights education. Young people today are often criticised for being apathetic and uninterested in politics; but a number of studies appear to suggest that the opposite is actually the case. Research carried out for the European Commission in 2001, for example, reminded us that young people do participate in society - not least, through associations and youth clubs. On average, within the countries of the European Union, more than 50% of young people either participate in, or belong to, an association of some type[1] (although there are significant differences from one country to another).

As far as interest in political issues goes, a study of young people's attitudes to the European Union revealed that human rights issues rank among their top priorities. Beaten only by the issues of unemployment and crime, young people would most like their governments to address the protection of human rights, protection of the environment, the fight against racism, and inequality between the sexes[2].

"Active and participatory approaches are particularly valuable in assuring learning acquisition and allowing learners to reach their fullest potential"

From the 1990 Jomtien Declaration.

Is it your experience that young people are not interested in political issues? If so – why do you think this might be?

Experience from around the globe has shown the energy and commitment that young people will devote to such issues if they can themselves take joint responsibility for what they do and how they learn, and if the issues are presented in relevant and interesting ways.

As educators, we need to harness that energy. That they will take up these ideas and run with them is evident from the numerous existing programmes for young people - from the small scale activities carried out on a relatively *ad hoc* basis in individual youth clubs or schools, to the major international programmes conducted by the Council of Europe and other organisations.

Which types of issues are most likely to raise the interest of members of your group?

Formal and non-formal educational settings

The most appropriate way of involving participants and structuring an educational process depends to a large extent upon the setting in which an educator is working. You may have more or less freedom regarding content, timing and form of activity depending on whether you are operating within a formal, informal or non-formal educational context. The activities presented in this manual have been designed to be flexible enough for use in all such contexts: within youth clubs, schools, summer camps, informal meetings, and so on.

Informal education refers to the lifelong process, whereby every individual acquires attitudes, values, skills and knowledge from the educational influences and resources in his or her own environment and from daily experience (family, neighbours, marketplace, library, mass media, work, play, etc.).

Formal education refers to the structured education system that runs from primary school to university, and includes specialised programmes for technical and professional training.

Non-formal education refers to any planned programme of personal and social education for young people designed to improve a range of skills and competencies, outside the formal educational curriculum.

"Education is what survives when what has been learned has been forgotten"

B. F. Skinner

"learning [is]...a process that is not only related to the function of school or other organised educational settings. This conception of learning is based upon the idea and observation that a considerable number of our meaningful learning experiences happen outside the formal education system: in workplaces, families, different organisations and libraries..."

Dr. Pasi Sahlberg in Building Bridges for Learning - The Recognition and Value of Non-Formal Education in Youth Activity.

Non-formal education as practised by many youth organisations and groups is :

- voluntary;
- accessible to everyone (ideally);
- an organised process with educational objectives;
- participatory and learner-centred;
- about learning life skills and preparing for active citizenship;
- based on involving both individual and group learning with a collective approach;
- holistic and process-oriented;
- based on experience and action, and starts from the needs of the participants.

Formal, non-formal and informal education are complementary and mutually reinforcing elements of a lifelong learning process. This manual has not been designed as a 'course' in HRE, and the individual activities can usefully be applied in very different contexts, in formal or less formal settings, and on a regular or irregular basis.

HRE as a starting point for action

At the core of human rights education is the development of critical thinking and the ability to handle conflict and take action. We have included among the aims of this manual the encouragement of solidarity-based activities and the organisation of events in the community, both because these are important for the development of skills and abilities closely connected with HRE, and because they are in themselves a means towards the end of developing a positive human rights culture. Young people can make a direct difference to the world around them, and this has been an important theme in the manual. We have included an individual section on taking action (Chapter 3) which provides a series of simple ideas for community activities related to human rights.

In addition to this section, each of the activities in Chapter 2 has been designed with the aim of helping to develop certain key skills useful for organising and carrying out actions in the community. We have tried to adopt a pluralistic approach and a *learning-by-doing* perspective, in line with, for example, the Council of Europe's Education for Democratic Citizenship (EDC) project recommendations. Here, HRE is presented as a daily practice that should be based on experiential learning and learning-by-doing, with the aim of mobilising competencies and initiatives in a continuing and changing process.

The following recommendations for educational policies are drawn from "Education for democratic citizenship: a lifelong learning perspective", and are intended to support this spontaneous process of change:

- directly involving practitioners in designing, monitoring, implementing and evaluating their own educational innovations;
- encouraging the solving of concrete social issues, using the know-how and practical experiences of reflective practitioners;
- promoting bottom-up educational change;
- working towards greater autonomy of educational agents so that they can work out specific forms of action and linkage with the local community, civil society and social partners;
- encouraging networking, joint projects and activities, as well as communication between practitioners and decision makers.

"Never be afraid to raise your voice... against injustice and lying and greed. If people all over the world... would do this, it would change the earth."

William Faulkner

International support for HRE

The Council of Europe

For the Member States of the Council of Europe, human rights are meant to be more than just assertions: human rights are part of their legal framework, and should therefore be an integral part of young people's education. The European nations made a strong contribution to the twentieth century's most important proclamation of human rights, the Universal Declaration of Human Rights, which was adopted by the United Nations General Assembly on 10 December 1948. The European Convention on Human Rights, which has legal force for all member states of the Council of Europe, drew its principles and inspiration from the UN document, and was adopted two years later.

Recommendation No R (85) 7 to the Member States of the Council of Europe (adopted by the Committee of Ministers on 14 May 1985) is related to teaching and learning about human rights in schools. This document emphasises that all young people should learn about human rights as part of their preparation for life in a pluralistic democracy; and this approach is slowly being incorporated into different European countries and institutions.

At the level of the European Union, at a meeting in Luxembourg in December 1997, the European Council recommended that all states should work towards:

- strengthening the role of civil society in promoting and protecting human rights;
- promoting activities on the ground and developing technical assistance in the area of human rights;
- strengthening training and education programmes concerning human rights.

Youth Policy

In April 1998, the European Ministers responsible for Youth met in Bucharest, and agreed on the aims and objectives of the Council of Europe youth policy[3]:

- to encourage associative life and all other forms of action which embody democracy and pluralism, and to help all young people to participate more fully in the life of the community;
- to adapt current partnership patterns to social change and to other types of youth organisations and youth work which have so far been under-represented, and further develop the concept of active participation by young people;
- to take full advantage of the valuable contribution which young people can make as active, responsible citizens;
- to develop citizenship education projects which make it possible to involve young people more quickly and more effectively in the life of the community, while respecting differences;
- to implement, from local to European level, an inter-sectoral, integrated and coherent youth policy, based on the principles of the European Convention for the Protection of Human Rights and Fundamental Freedoms and the European Social Charter.

United Nations

In December 1994, the United Nations General Assembly officially proclaimed 1995-2004 the United Nations Decade for Human Rights Education. This followed a recommendation at the

"Human history becomes more and more a race between education and catastrophe."

H.G. Wells

1993 World Conference on Human Rights in Vienna, which stated that human rights education, training and public information were essential for the promotion and achievement of stable and harmonious relations among communities and for fostering mutual understanding, tolerance and peace. The Vienna Conference had recommended that States should "strive to eradicate illiteracy and should direct education towards the full development of the human personality and the strengthening of respect for human rights and fundamental freedoms". It had called on all States and institutions to include human rights, humanitarian law, democracy and rule of law as subjects in the curricula of all learning institutions in formal and non-formal settings. The UN Decade has taken up that challenge.

UNESCO

One other area of relevance is the increasingly multicultural and multi-faith nature of modern societies. The importance of "learning to live together" within and across different societies is central to the whole idea of education - the "necessary utopia" that was recommended by the 1996 UNESCO report about education in the twenty-first century[4]. Human rights lie at the core of the concept outlined in the UNESCO report – for example, in the ability to mediate conflict and to find common perspectives in analysing problems and planning future directions. Facilitation of non-violent change is of fundamental importance and of urgent concern both within and between societies. It should occupy a central role in educational efforts.

References

Dr. Pasi Sahlberg, Building Bridges for Learning - The Recognition and Value of Non-Formal Education in Youth Activity, *study for the National Board of Education (Finland) and for the European Youth Forum, European Youth Forum, December 1999.*

Staying Alive, *Information paper of the European Youth Forum for the General Assembly, 2000.*

Chisholm, Lynne, Towards a revitalisation of non-formal learning for a changing Europe, Report of the symposium on non-formal education, Council of Europe Directorate of Youth and Sport, 2000.

HRE and Other Education Fields

A human rights world

Human rights affect every aspect of our lives. Indeed, violations of human rights lie at the root of almost every problem in the world today: violence, poverty, globalisation, the environment, economic inequality, and lawlessness. Not to mention the wars and conflicts that are destroying parts of the globe.

Although human rights, in their original conception, were broadly confined to the civil and political spheres, it is now acknowledged that they must embrace social, cultural, and economic issues as well. Today, people even speak of a third generation of rights that takes into account collective rights and issues concerning future generations of mankind. All of this has significant implications for the work we do as educators: it means that education dealing with such issues as globalisation, the environment, peace and intercultural relations, among others, are all forms of human rights education. They deal with human rights issues and they attempt to build a culture that respects them.

What have been the main changes in your country over the last 20 years in the area of human rights?

In this manual we try to address the full spectrum of issues connected with human rights. We shall look, in this chapter, at the way in which many, if not most, of these issues are relevant to other fields of education – such as development education, peace education, environmental education, education for citizenship, and so on. Anyone who is engaged in one or other of these forms of education should find questions of relevance within these pages.

What is a "human rights issue"?

Almost any question concerning violations of rights may be termed a human rights issue. The international community now recognises three different "generations" of rights, which cover different dimensions of human activity:

First generation rights (Liberty rights)

These include the civil and political rights – such as the right to freedom of expression, freedom of association, the right to life, to a fair trial, to participation in the political life of society, and so on. These issues (though not only these issues) are traditionally addressed in the formal education sector through citizenship education, civic education, political education /education for democracy or law-related education.

Second generation rights (Equality rights)

These include the social, economic and cultural rights – such as the right to an adequate standard of living, to work, to join a trade union, to health and to education. Within the formal education

"The rights of all men are diminished when the rights of one man are threatened."

John Kennedy

sector, at least, these areas are often neglected. Economics education, for example, rarely deals with such issues - although arguably it should do. The issues are sometimes addressed by the "hidden curriculum" – that is, by many of the less formal activities carried out by schools or youth groups, or the work done in tutor groups or personal, social and health education. There is, however, increasing recognition that second generation rights are just as relevant to citizenship as the traditionally accepted first generation rights – and rightly so.

Third generation rights (Solidarity rights)

These rights are also known as "emerging" rights, because they are still in the process of being acknowledged and recognised. They refer to the *collective* rights of society or peoples – such as the right to sustainable development, to peace, or to a healthy environment. There are increasing educational areas that look specifically at these rights – for example, environmental education, peace education and development education.

(More information about the different generations of rights can be found in Chapter 4)

? **Have any of the issues that you have explored with your group been human rights issues?**

Issues covered in the manual

This manual has been structured around 16 human rights-related issues, each of which can be seen to be directly relevant to one or more of the different generations of rights.

- General human rights
- Children
- Citizenship
- Democracy
- Discrimination and Xenophobia
- Education
- Environment
- Gender equality
- Globalisation
- Health
- Human security
- Media
- Peace and Violence
- Poverty
- Social rights
- Sport

None of these themes is any more important than the others. Indeed, these themes are in fact interrelated to such an extent that addressing any one of them provides a common link with any other. This is a direct consequence of the fact that human rights are *indivisible, interdependent* and *interrelated*: they cannot be treated in isolation, because all are connected one with another, in various different and intimate ways.

The diagram on the following page provides one illustration of this interdependence. There are others that we could have shown: the circle round the outside could have been reordered almost randomly and connections still be identified. The issues in the outer circle blend into one another, just as the educational spheres in the central circle merge together. Even the distinctions between first, second and third generation rights is not clear-cut. Education, for example, is traditionally classed as a second generation right, but education is just as necessary for effective political participation (a first generation right) as it is for sustainable development (a third generation right).

Accordingly, the following analyses should be seen as just one description among many, but they help to illustrate the ways in which the various themes are relevant to many of the current educational fields, and how these educational fields overlap with one another.

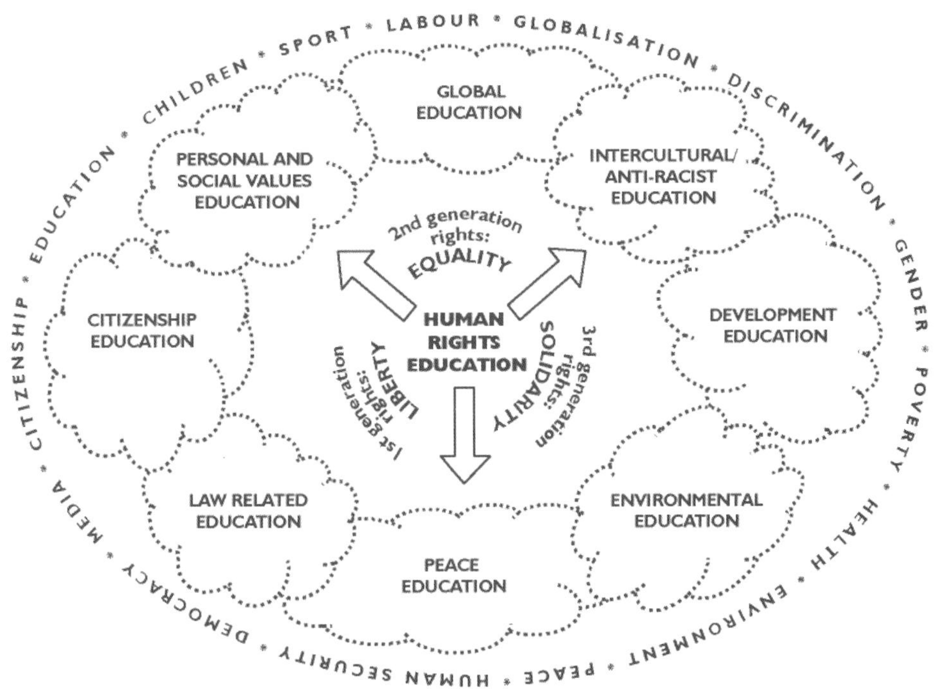

Citizenship Education

Citizenship education encourages the development of young people as active and responsible citizens. In 1997, The Council of Europe established the Education for Democratic Citizenship project (EDC), and the June 2000 report for this project emphasises the importance of *social justice* and *equality of rights* for citizenship. T.H.Marshall, in his book *Citizenship and Social Class* (Cambridge University Press, 1950), suggests that citizenship can only be effective when it ensures access to three main types of rights. In this way, he identifies three components of citizenship:

- the *civil component*, which includes the rights addressing individual freedom;
- the *political component* - e.g. the right to participate in the exercise of political power and to vote and participate in parliamentary institutions;
- The *social component* of citizenship, which relates to the right to the prevailing standard of living and equal access to education, health care, housing and a minimum level of income.

Personal and Social Education

Many countries have some form of education that considers the role of the individual in society and helps to prepare young people for some of the personal challenges that they will meet. This may overlap with citizenship issues but may also include aspects of the individual's life related to leisure – including sport, clubs and associations, music, art, or other forms of culture. Such education may also be concerned with personal relationships. Human rights enter into these questions in two central ways: firstly, because personal development and personal relations possess moral and social aspects that need to be guided by human rights values; secondly, because the right to take part in cultural life is recognised in the UDHR as well as in other international treaties. Even if the young people with whom *you* work are able to claim this right, there are young people around the globe who are not.

"Everyone has the right freely to participate in the cultural life of the community, to enjoy the arts and to share in scientific advancement and its benefits."

UDHR, Article 27

"The greatest evil today is indifference. To know and not to act is a way of consenting to these injustices. The planet has become a very small place. What happens in other countries affects us."

Elie Wiesel

Values Education / Moral Education

Values education is also a common part of the school curriculum in different countries, but it often gives rise to two fundamental concerns in people's minds: which values such education should aim to teach, and how we can be sure that these values are not merely relevant to our own particular culture? These are common problems faced by many who engage in this area of education, and human rights provide a convenient means of addressing it. Human rights are not only based on values that are common to every major religion and culture, but they are also admitted to be universal by almost every country in the world. No-one can be criticised for teaching human rights values!

Global Education

Globalisation is an issue at the front of many young people's minds, and we have included it as one of the separate themes within this manual. The general heading of global education normally covers work that looks at different forms of existence and patterns of behaviour around the globe. Such education is important because it looks at the individual's place not just in his or her own community or society, but in the world as a whole. It can be used to raise a number of questions connected with human rights and can help to open people's eyes to violations of rights being committed in different reaches of the globe. Global education enables young people to assess the impact of their own actions and to consider their individual responsibilities.

The Institute of Global Education, a non-profit United Nations Non-Governmental Organisation, was founded in 1984 as The World Peace University. The Institute declares its goal as "to help co-create a world where peace and food sufficiency are a way of life, where environmental responsibility exists, where social justice prevails and where an individual achieves the highest degree of self-realisation within a community of co-operation."

Intercultural Education

There is a natural connection between global education and intercultural education, which looks at the way we interact with other cultures, societies and social groupings. All societies today are characterised by increasing levels of multiculturalism and cultural diversity and this makes acknowledgement of, and respect for, the rights of minorities increasingly important. We are being forced to reassess old conceptions of national societies as culturally homogeneous entities: the dual processes of European integration, together with increased economic and social interdependence between different world regions have made such notions outdated. Even in those parts of the globe which are not experiencing patterns of immigration, existing conflicts can more often than not be traced back to a lack of understanding between different peoples or ways of life to be found in one common society. The conflicts in Northern Ireland, in the former Yugoslavia and in parts of the Caucasus are sad illustrations of the problems that can arise from an inability to respect and live with other cultures.

All different, but not indifferent!

Intercultural education is also an effective way of addressing the modern phenomena of racism and racial discrimination and intolerance.

The Directorate of Youth and Sport, especially through the European Youth Centres and Foundation, has devoted much effort to the field of intercultural education. The 'All Different All Equal' campaign against racism, xenophobia, anti-Semitism and intolerance was set up to address the growth of racist hostility and intolerance towards minority groups. The Campaign itself sought to "bring people together and give extra momentum to the struggle against all forms of intolerance."

The education pack, 'All Different All Equal', was produced in order to help youth workers and educators to contribute to the campaign. It identified two major directions for intercultural education:

- helping young people to gain the capacity to recognise inequality, injustice, racism, stereotypes and prejudices, and
- giving them the knowledge and the abilities which will help them to challenge and to try to change these whenever they have to face them in society.

The objectives and principles of intercultural education have also been pursued in a variety of ways through *intercultural learning* - a term that is more commonly used in non-formal education, particularly in European youth work.

"Intercultural education proposes processes to enable the discovery of mutual relationships and the dismantling of barriers."

'All Different - All Equal' Education Pack

Anti-racist education

Anti-racist education takes as its starting point the assertion that we live in a multi-cultural and democratic society, in which all citizens have a right to equity and justice. Nevertheless, it recognises the very real existence of racism and racist attitudes in every modern society, and the impact that this can have for black pupils – both in terms of giving them a negative experience of the education process and in terms of diminishing their chances in later life. Anti-racist education attempts to address racist behaviour, language and practices, both individual and institutional, and to increase general awareness of the harmful effects of racism in modern society. It aims to help in the creation of a multi-racial and interdependent society in which all citizens' rights are respected and protected.

Development Education

Development education has strong links with global education, but gives particular emphasis to third generation rights – such as sustainable development, the right to a healthy environment, and peace. It also gives high priority to issues concerning the *interaction* of different societies and methods of development, which is why we have created a link in the diagram with intercultural education. Development education is thus holistic, in the sense that it is based upon a view of the world as one interconnected whole, and it is oriented towards the future.

The Development Education Association is a British organisation that has been working for almost 10 years in this field. They define development education as lifelong learning that:

- explores the links between people living in the "developed" countries of the North with those of the "developing" South, enabling people to understand the links between their own lives and those of people throughout the world
- increases understanding of the economic, social, political and environmental forces which shape our lives
- develops the skills, attitudes and values which enable people to work together to take action to bring about change and take control of their own lives.

"Education should further the appropriate intellectual and emotional development of the individual. It should develop a sense of social responsibility and of solidarity with less privileged groups and should lead to observance of the principles of equality in everyday conduct."

UNESCO Recommendation concerning education for international understanding, co-operation and peace and education relating to human rights and fundamental freedoms

Environmental Education

The search for methods of sustainable development forms one of the key aims of development education, and leads naturally to concerns about the future state of the environment. From this perspective, questions concerning further economic development - particularly of

"There is no way to peace. Peace is the way."

M. K. Gandhi

developing countries – need to be balanced against their cost to mankind and the natural world as a whole. Environmental education aims to bring these questions to public attention, and to encourage greater care and respect for the natural resources of the world.

That also links in with human rights concerns. Since the life of mankind is dependent on a healthy and sustainable environment, consideration for the human rights of people throughout the globe, and of future generations, brings environmental issues to the forefront. Today, some people even speak of the need for official recognition of a separate environmental human right.

Peace Education

The natural resources of this world have not been equally distributed. They have been, and no doubt will continue to be, one source of violent conflict between different individuals and societies. There are, unfortunately, many others. Peace educators may be interested in more equitable or more sensible ways of sharing the earth's resources as a means of resolving some of the conflicts in the world, but their focus is likely to be primarily on the conflicts themselves and more particularly on their structural causes. Peace education is based on a concept of peace that goes beyond the mere absence of war: peace can only be addressed by means of a search for justice and by understanding structural forms of exploitation and injustice.

Few people will need to be convinced of the need for peace education - for a better understanding of conflict, for respect among peoples that makes violent conflict less likely, and for the skills to transform potentially dangerous situations into peaceful ones. The world needs that: a *genuine* right to life for everyone, and a genuine respect for *everyone* – including, even, those among us who have made mistakes. Education for tolerance, for intercultural understanding, and fundamentally, education in the inherent and universal nature of basic human rights must be an important route towards that aim.

The period 2001-2010 has been declared the International Decade for a Culture of Peace and Non-Violence for the Children of the World (UN Doc A/RES/53/25). The International Peace Research Association, which was set up with support from UNESCO, has a Peace Education Commission that brings together educators working to promote a culture of peace.

Law-related Education

This is perhaps the most "formal" of the different education fields we have discussed so far, but law-related education is not just learning about the laws that exist, it is also about developing respect for the rule of law and for the fundamental principles of justice that are laid out in the international human rights treaties.

The connection between law-related education and human rights can be made at two separate levels: firstly, in the specific 'legal' rights that protect the individual against unfair trials, but secondly at the level of international law. The UN institutions, the European Court of Human Rights and other regional structures are legal institutions that exist to protect our human rights, but we need to know about them and we need to use them, if they are to be effective in this aim. They will not hunt us out.

Using COMPASS across Europe

What and where is Europe?

Historians will remind us that at its origin, in Ancient Greece, "Europe" probably referred to what is today the Balkans. Today, Europe is far more extensive, but it is certainly no easier to define.

Political Europe covers a land mass of over 10 million square kilometres, and extends into the territory of geographical Asia. The climate over the entire continent ranges from sub-tropical in some southern regions to polar in northern ones. Europe is the source of over 200 living languages and the home of speakers of many more. It embraces some 50 states, which contain between them a total population of nearly 800 million.

Every major religion is to be found within its borders. The continent is associated with the birth of democracy and, at the same time, with some of the worst examples of fascism and totalitarianism that the world has ever seen. Europe's past is marked by the Holocaust, by colonialism and by slavery, and today it provides the location for enough nuclear weapons to wipe out all life on earth. Yet, it hosts the annual ceremony for the Nobel Peace Prize, and it has established a permanent court of human rights, which is acclaimed throughout the world.

The countries of Europe

Today, the states that make up Europe include some that are less than 10 years old, and others whose borders have barely changed over hundreds of years. Some continue to change even today, as conflicts threaten unstable borders. Thus, there are people in Europe leading lives that face violence and conflict on a daily basis, while many others, in one and the same continent, reside in conditions of peace, security, and often prosperity.

? What makes a country 'European'?

There are millionaires in every European country; and millions living below the poverty line in every country. There is diversity within each country, and diversity between them. Become a teacher in one part of Europe and you may receive more in a day than colleagues in other parts receive in a month. Become a teacher in another region and you may not receive a salary at all, for months on end.

Europe is indeed a mixed place.

One Europe? Two Europes...?

Can we say there is an Eastern Europe and a Western Europe to make things simpler? A Northern and Southern Europe? What about Central Europe?

Can we divide it into a Christian Europe and a Muslim Europe?

Or a rich Europe and a poor Europe ...a peaceful and a war-torn Europe ... a democratised Europe and one damaged by totalitarianism...a left-wing and a right-wing, an Americanised and a Sovietised Europe?

Which "part" of Europe do you belong to ? Are you "typical" of that part of Europe?

If any of these divisions seem correct, or at least helpful in identifying particular needs on different sides of the division, then consider how some of the following groups might 'fit' under such general categories. Would their *needs* correspond to the 'stereotypical' needs of the country or part of Europe in which they happen to be living?

- Businessmen in the Balkans
- Bengali communities in East London
- People suffering terrorist violence in the Basque country or Northern Ireland
- Hill farmers dependent on the climate in Spain, Italy, Romania and Georgia
- Roma populations in Hungary, Slovakia, Greece or France
- Islamophobes or anti-Semites in Germany, Russia, Lithuania, Sweden, Poland, and every other country of the continent
- Fishing communities in Scotland, Norway, Croatia or Estonia
- Immigrant workers in Belgium and Finland
- Refugees and asylum-seekers in Ukraine or Poland;
- Muslims, politicians, human rights activists, teachers, youth leaders, short people, bald men, women with children and women without.

Such examples show us that not one of the proposed divisions is clear cut or adequate to describe the multi-faceted nature of every single country, community and, indeed, individual. There are some common needs throughout the whole of Europe, but there are equally different needs within each small community in every individual state . Europe, and each single country that composes it, is a small world of cultural and social diversity.

A book for Europe?

So why create one manual for the whole of Europe? Can it be sufficient to meet the needs of all the peoples in this rich and mixed continent?

This section sets out some answers to those questions and the ways that we approached some of the difficulties that we faced. It also tries to illustrate our reasons for believing that such a task was not only realistic but even necessary. Europe, after all, not only has a very diverse culture but also many points of commonality. To find those points of commonality and thereby understand our differences can be as important as the task of preserving our very separate identities.

Have you had contact with other youth groups in different parts of Europe? What did your groups have in common?

"...they first came for the communists;
I did not speak because I was not a communist. Then they came for the Jews;
I did not speak because I was not a Jew.
Then they came to fetch the workers, members of trade unions;
I was not a trade unionist.
Afterward, they came for the Catholics;
I did not say anything because I was a Protestant. Eventually they came for me, and there was no-one left to speak."

Pastor Martin Niemoller

Human rights as a common factor

The idea of human rights lies at both the historical and the ideological foundation of the Council of Europe and is just one of those points of commonality running through the whole of Europe. It is not, of course, exclusive to Europe, but it is certainly one of the most important uniting and unifying factors, and with the increased membership of the Council of Europe, it will become ever more so.

Every country that has signed up for membership has also committed itself to observe the fundamental rights and freedoms set out in the European Convention on the Protection of

Human Rights and Fundamental Freedoms. This means, for the ordinary citizen of the different European states, that those rights and freedoms are, to some extent at least, *protected* by the entire community of European states.

But even with the existence of the European Court of Human Rights, protection of those human rights can only be real and substantial for every citizen when each individual helps to play an active role in their observance. Citizens need to know about the existence of those rights, they need to be able to defend them when they are violated, and they need to respect them in their everyday lives. This is the task of education, and it is a task for the whole of Europe.

Injustice anywhere is a threat to justice everywhere.

Martin Luther King

Citizens of the world

Knowing how to stand up for and protect our own rights is important but it cannot be the whole story. We have taken the view in this manual that human rights are a *global* issue and that the youth of Europe, as citizens of the world, need to appreciate this if human rights are to be respected not just in our part of the world but everywhere on our common earth.

Of course every country in Europe has its own work to do on improving the protection of its citizens' rights. There is not one country that has a clean record on human rights abuses, however human rights education is crucially about not only *our* rights but also the rights of other people. Thus, while one task of this manual is to promote a greater awareness of rights issues in order that young people (in Europe) be better able to improve their own immediate rights environment, another task is to encourage them to take an interest in those issues in the wider world, and to consider the actual and possible impact of their own behaviour.

Young people across the world and particularly across Europe have always given themselves generously to the cause of human rights and human rights education. In times of fascism and totalitarianism, it was often young people and students who were at the forefront of protests and actions against repression and oppression; and youth organisations and associations have always played a crucial role in bringing young people from Europe closer together, and in standing up for their rights. The work of international non-governmental youth organisations has often involved forging links and building solidarity among young people – both in Europe and outside it. Such work rests on the ideals of solidarity, co-operation, peace and human rights.

It is time to extend these experiences and this work to other young people in Europe and to build an appreciation of human rights issues both in this continent and beyond. There needs to be a greater understanding of the way in which our actions can assist the protection of human rights for fellow human beings. That, too, is a task for the whole of Europe.

A European Dream

Of course no-one wants the different countries and cultures of Europe to lose their separate identities. However in producing this manual, we were motivated by the fact that *not one* of the cultures of Europe – or indeed, of the world – is inherently opposed to, or need be altered to its detriment by, a flourishing human rights culture. In fact, these values exist in every country already, and the cultures will only thrive if they are strengthened (so that everyone can have the opportunity to contribute to them positively).

There was another hope. We hoped that common interests and a common endeavour could contribute towards the bringing together of young people on our common continent, to help them see each other as equals, sharing a common reality and being jointly responsible for

"Perseverance is more prevailing than violence; and many things which cannot be overcome when they are together yield themselves up when taken little by little."

Plutarch

the future of the continent: perhaps Siberia could link up with Portugal in protecting the rights of women; perhaps young people in Albania and Luxembourg could build a common web-site to focus the world's attention on child labour; or perhaps schools in Malta and Denmark could plan a simultaneous street action to focus on bullying in schools in different countries.

Young people care, and they can lead the way. They can refute those who criticise their individualism and their apathy – just as other generations have for centuries, and they can prove those wrong who insist that *there is no alternative*, and put new energy into the peaceful struggle for human rights around the world. Young people are not just the target groups for this manual: they are its main hope and its main resource.

Youth work and youth representation

Although the activities in this manual are intended to be appropriate for use in formal educational settings, it was our intention to produce a publication that could be used primarily by youth workers outside the formal education system. Clearly the nature and extent of such work may differ from one country to another. However, by proposing different types of methods and exploring different themes, we aimed to address the different needs of the diverse youth groups and associations existing in every European country. For after-school clubs, Scouts groups, church youth groups, university clubs, human rights groups and exchange clubs, the range of activities covered in the pack ought to provide something of relevance and use, in addition to being applicable to people working in more formal settings.

The main focus of youth work is the personal and social development of young people, and for that reason the majority of activities in the pack perhaps pay more attention to these aspects than to the traditional educational end of increasing knowledge. It was important in putting together the activities to concentrate on attracting the interest of young people in these issues, and to use experiential learning to engender feelings of respect for human rights, particularly among those who do not necessarily respond to attempts made in this direction within the formal education system.

? Do you use experiential learning in your work?

In educational settings and institutions where teaching methods are more knowledge-based than experiential or skills-based, such an approach may be less familiar. For that reason, we have provided useful starting points and essential background information on the educational approaches of this manual (see the chapter "*How to use the Manual*"). We see this as an important part of ensuring that the manual is accessible not only to young people everywhere in Europe, but also to teachers and group facilitators or youth workers who may be less familiar with certain working methods.

In a modest way, we hope that this manual may help to bridge the methodological gaps between formal and non-formal education. In both contexts, it is essential to involve the young people whose attention is sought – all the more so, in an area such as human rights where active involvement and participation are essential factors. Because of their inclusive nature, each of the activities included within the manual is intended to provide an interesting and attractive way for young people to become more aware of general human rights issues, in any type of environment.

? How do you involve young people in your activities?

One further focus has been the attempt to enable young people to make their own positive contribution to the issues that concern them, and for that reason we have also included a section on *Taking Action*. In this respect, it is worth noting that most of the suggestions in this section are not by any means exclusive to human rights 'activism', in the sense that they are mostly normal youth activities that many groups will already be undertaking in fields other than that of human rights. They are the type of activities that every young person is interested in taking part in.

"Young people are not only the future ... we are the present."

Statement of children and young people at the Europe and Central Asia consultation for the Special Session on the Rights of the Child, Budapest 2001.

The Convention on the Rights of the Child

All European countries have signed and ratified the UN Convention on the Rights of the Child, and have thereby undertaken an obligation to observe it, and to report regularly on progress being made towards fulfilling the rights completely. The Convention is relevant to this manual partly because of the age range of the target group – although the manual is also intended to appeal to people above the 18-year-old upper limit of the Convention.

However, the Convention also deserves a particular mention in terms of the methodology of the manual. At the heart of the Convention, and incorporated into several of its articles (in particular, Articles 3 and 12), is the idea that young people have the right to express their views and to have them taken into account, in all matters that affect them. This idea has reached different stages of realisation in different European countries: in some there are genuine opportunities for young people to participate in the decisions that directly affect them; in others, the process is less developed.

Is there a copy of the Convention on the Rights of the Child in your school or in your association?

Clearly, the opportunities that already exist will determine to some extent the degree to which young people are able to influence decisions, and also the advisability of undertaking certain actions rather than others. The overall objective, however, of treating young people as *people*, worthy of genuine respect and equal in that sense to other members of the adult population remains valid for every part of Europe.

The production process

The Production Team of *COMPASS* was composed of 8 people, and had to produce the background materials and design the activities for the manual. As is often the case, the team was put to test during the production phase, which was naturally challenging - not least, because the deadlines were very tight. In order to ensure the maximum exchange of different experiences, each writer produced texts that had to be checked and approved by two other writers. Similarly, each theme or chapter was always shared between at least two people.

The Production Team represented Europe, at least in its total internal diversity. Members came from North, South, East and West (and from the centre). Our histories, traditions, languages, dress and taste in music clashed and overlapped alternately. We wanted slightly different things, or to do them in a slightly different way – because each of us knew better than the rest the needs of his or her own country.

Yet none of us knew the needs of everyone – not even in their own country, and this, after all, was why each of us was necessary, and all of us were insufficient.

One member of the Reference Group, living in one of the ex-communist states, remarked early on that *countries in Western Europe are concerned with the rights of minorities; whereas countries in our part of Europe are concerned with the rights of the majority.* Some people disagreed with that as well: they felt 'their part' of Europe did not fall into either stereotype. Others felt that that was one generalisation which - like many generalisations - possibly contained an element of truth. We tried to take it into account. But the point may equally well have been made by every one of us in a slightly different way: '*People in Southern Europe / Muslim Europe / rural areas / capital cities / war-torn Europe... are concerned with...*'

The remark reminded us, however, that despite our common aims, the differences between our cultures were no less significant than the differences between *us*, their representatives. We left the process with the same hopes and aspirations that the issues which concerned all of us could – and should – concern others as well, wherever they were living, because these were indeed issues for the whole world. But we also left the process wondering about the extent to which we had managed to cover the *whole of Europe* adequately. But that,after all, would have been an impossible task.

Using the manual across cultures and languages

There are two central problems concerned with designing a manual for such a wide audience. The first is the problem of over-generality: that activities may not be specific enough to address the particular concerns of certain groups or populations. The second, conversely, is the problem of their touching too specifically certain issues that either do not appear to be relevant to all of the target countries, or are too sensitive to raise in some of them.

The issues that we have included in the manual are certainly relevant and of direct concern to all human beings, wherever their geographical location. Nevertheless, it may still be the case that the way that some issues are presented or some activities are developed are less suitable for certain groups and facilitators. The task of the facilitators or group leaders, in such cases, is not simply to reproduce or follow blindly the instruction, but to identify where there is need for improvement, adaptation or updating to the specific context. The general guidelines given bellow may be of assistance in this task.

This manual should be seen as a starting point, a living educational tool that is open to ideas, adaptation and any suggestions for improvement.

Guidelines for adaptation:

- Where issues are controversial within your society, or where they are likely to provoke resistance from people in authority, consider whether it is possible to look at the issue in the framework of a different society or in a historical setting, without necessarily drawing explicit comparisons to current practices. Conversely, if an issue is controversial or divisive, you may even wish to work with that fact: encourage participants to research different points of view, and perhaps ask someone with a minority perspective for their opinion.

- If using the activities in a formal educational setting, where there are pressures on the timetable and where content is of prime importance, you will probably want to make more use of the background information or other information that you or your students may find. You may also want to break up some activities (for example, over two days).
- If there are limited opportunities for including human rights education within your educational setting, there are plenty of ways of using some of the activities within other subjects – such as Geography, History, Citizenship, Political Studies, and so on. You may want to adapt some of the activities accordingly.
- If young people seem to think that certain issues are not of prime importance, or cannot see the relevance to their immediate situation, ask them to consider this question directly, and to draw out the ways in which such an issue could affect their own lives. *All* of the issues included within this manual are in fact of direct relevance to *all* young people!
- There may be activities where you feel that there is particular information that is relevant to your group, or your society, or a particular approach that is more suitable. Be flexible about the different activities: allow participants to make suggestions, extend or limit the timing or the background information if this is appropriate, and use the follow-up suggestions if the group is particularly interested in an issue. Sometimes, you may have to complete the information provided, or adapt it to your own context.
- Use your own judgement to assess the possible drawbacks of involving young people in any form of public action – for example, in tense social or political circumstances.
- Involve the young people in any difficulties you are encountering, wherever this is possible. They will appreciate the opportunity to express their opinions, and will be more likely to understand any restrictions or limitations to which you may be subject.

Trust them!

How to use COMPASS

There are many different ways of teaching and learning about human rights. How you approach the topic will depend on whether you are working in the formal or non-formal sector, the political, social and economic conditions of your country, the ages of the young people, and also their interests and motivation to learn about human rights. It will also certainly depend on your experience with human rights issues, on your own attitude and relation with the target groups and on your "learning style".

You may be a youth worker, a trainer, schoolteacher or adult education tutor, a workshop facilitator or a member of a church discussion group, or a young person who cares about human rights. Whoever you are and wherever you are working, we trust there will be something for you in this manual. We make no assumptions about teaching or training skills or about prior knowledge of human rights.

In this section we explain what we mean by participation and co-operative and experiential learning and why we use these educational approaches. We indicate how you might use the activities in formal and informal settings and try to give some answers to commonly asked questions. In the section of tips for facilitators we describe how the activities are presented and how to choose one. There are notes on discussions and group work, and on facilitating activities including debriefing and evaluation.

COMPASS should be seen as a flexible resource. Promoting human rights is an on-going and creative process, of which you - as a user of this book - are an integral part. We hope you will take the ideas that we have presented and use and develop them to meet your own needs and those of the young people you work with. We hope you will also review what you have learned and give us feedback on your experiences, which we can incorporate into the next edition of this manual. There is a feedback form on page 417.

How to work with the manual

We strongly suggest you begin by looking briefly through the whole manual to gain an overall picture of the contents. There is no special starting point; we intend that you should pick and choose the parts that are relevant for you.

In chapter 2 you will find 49 activities at different levels for exploring global themes and human rights. These are the tools for your work with young people. Chapter 5 contains supporting material. There is background information on the global issues, definitions of human rights and information about their evolution. In addition, there are summaries of the main declarations and conventions on human rights, references and lists of further resources.

There should be enough material to enable you to begin work on HRE with young people. It is important to remember that you do not have to be an "expert" in human rights to start; having an interest in human rights is a sufficient qualification. Neither do you have to be a qualified teacher or trainer. However, you do need to understand our educational approach in order to get the most out of the activities.

The educational approaches

It's not just what you do, but the way that you do it. That's what gets results.

Before you work with the activities it is important to understand the educational approaches we have used. Human rights education is about education for change, both personal and social. It is about developing young people's competence to be active citizens who participate in their communities to promote and protect human rights. Our focus is the educational process of developing knowledge, skills, values and attitudes. In this process we:

- start from what people already know, their opinions and experiences and from this base enable them to search for, and discover together, new ideas and experiences.
- encourage the participation of young people to contribute to discussions and to learn from each other as much as possible.
- encourage people to translate their learning into simple but effective actions that demonstrate their rejection of injustice, inequality and violations of human rights.

The knowledge, skills and attitudes of someone who is literate in human rights are described on page 19. These competencies, especially the skills and values of communication, critical thinking, advocacy, tolerance and respect cannot be taught; they have to be learned through experience. This is why the activities in this book promote co-operation, participation and learning through experience. We aim to encourage young people to think, feel and act; to engage their heads, hearts and hands. Knowing about human rights is important, but not enough. It is necessary that young people have a far deeper understanding about how human rights evolve out of people's needs and why they have to be protected. For instance, young people with no direct experience of racial discrimination may think that the issue is of no concern to them. From a human rights perspective this position is not acceptable; people everywhere have a responsibility to protect the human rights of others.

It does not matter whether you are discussing the right to life or freedom of expression; human rights are about democratic values, respect and tolerance. These are skills and attitudes which can only be learned effectively in an environment - and through a process - that promotes these values. This needs to be emphasised.

Co-operative learning

Co-operation is working together to accomplish shared goals. In co-operative learning people work together to seek outcomes that are beneficial both to themselves and to all members of the group.

Co-operative learning promotes higher achievement and greater productivity; more caring, supportive, and committed relationships; and greater psychological health, social competence, and self-esteem. This is in contrast to what happens when learning is structured in a competitive way. Competitive learning promotes self-interest, disrespect for others and arrogance in the winners who work against others to achieve a goal that only one or a few can attain, while the losers often become demotivated and lose self-respect.

The essential components of co-operation are positive interdependence, face-to-face interaction, individual and group accountability and interpersonal skills. The most effective way of promoting co-operative learning is through structured group work.

Participation

Participation in HRE means that young people make the decisions about what and how they are going to learn about human rights. Through participation young people develop various competencies including those of decision-making, listening, empathy with and respect for others, and taking responsibility for their own decisions and actions. The teacher's or trainer's role is that of a facilitator, that is to "help" or "facilitate" young people's participation in the learning process. In schools there may be timetabling and curriculum constraints that determine how nearly the ideal of participation can be achieved, and the activities will need to be adapted accordingly.

The activities in this manual demand participation. You have to be active and engaged; you cannot sit back and be a passive observer. In this respect the methodology used in this manual owes much to the work of Augusto Boal and other pioneers in non-formal awareness raising.

Possibly the single, most important task in human rights education is to find the spaces in which young people can become active participants and influence the form and outcome of the activities. By definition, human rights education cannot be imposed; it is really up to each facilitator, educator, teacher, trainer or leader to find the moment to create the spaces and opportunities for participation.

Experiential learning

Human rights education in common with, for example, education for development, peace education and education for citizenship uses a methodology of experiential learning based on a learning cycle with five phases:

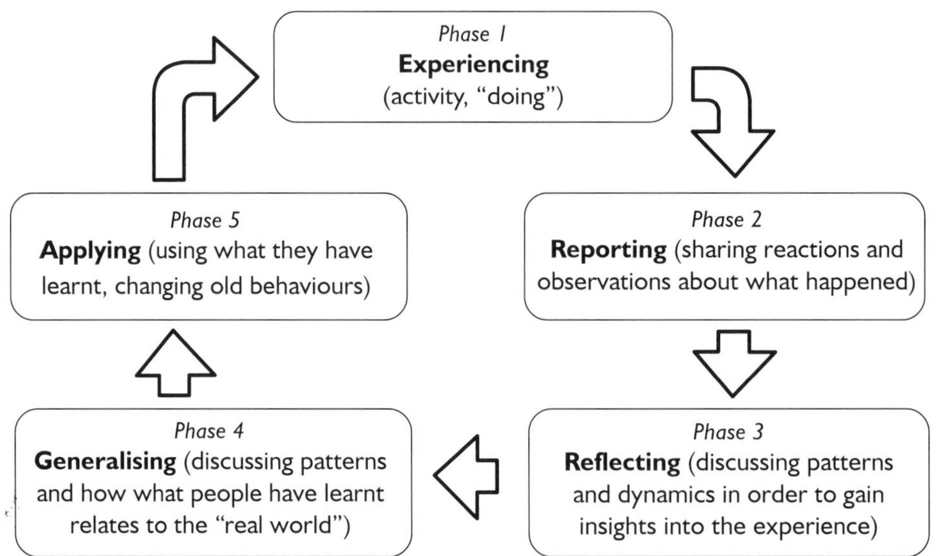

In phase 5 people explore practical actions that might address the issue in question. It is crucial that people find real opportunities for involvement. This is not only a logical outcome of the learning process but a significant means of reinforcing new knowledge, skills and attitudes which form the basis for the next round of the cycle.

Activities as tools for experiential learning

When you use the activities in the book you should bear the above learning cycle in mind.

The activities demand participation and involvement so that the people doing them gain an experience through which they learn not only with their heads but also with their hearts and hands. These sorts of activities are sometimes called "games" because they are fun and people play them with enthusiasm. You should remember, however, that the activities or games are not

"just for fun", but they are purposeful means to achieve educational aims.

You don't just "do" an activity (phase 1 of the learning cycle). It is essential to follow through with debriefing and evaluation to enable people to reflect on what happened (phase 2), to evaluate their experience (phases 3 & 4) and to go on to decide what to do next (phase 5). In this way they come round to phase 1 of the next cycle in the learning process.

In a school setting, activities can help break down artificial barriers between subjects and provide ways of extending links between subject and interest areas to promote a more holistic approach to an issue. In a non-formal educational setting, activities can awaken interest in issues and, because they promote learning in a non-didactic way, they are often intrinsically more acceptable to young people.

Activities help people to:

- *be motivated* to learn because they are fun
- *develop their knowledge, skills, attitudes and values*. Games provide a safe environment in which to do this because they allow people to experiment with new behaviour and to make errors without incurring the costs of similar mistakes in real life.
- *change*. Activities are one way of conveying the message that everyone can choose to change themselves or their relationships with others.
- *get involved*. Activities encourage the participation of the less expressive and less dominant group members.
- *take responsibility*. Because participants contribute their own experiences and skills, each group uses the game at its own level and in its own way.
- *encourage self-reliance and improve self-confidence*. Activities provide a structure that can be used to reduce dependency on the leader as the one who 'knows it all'. The participants are forced to accept some responsibility for making their part of the activities work.
- *feel solidarity with others*. Activities encourage cohesiveness in the group and a sense of group identity and solidarity.

Activities offer a framework and structure to group experiences which will allow you to work within the limits of your own and the young peoples' experience and competencies. When carefully facilitated, activities are an effective method of learning within a task-orientated setting.

Facilitation

In this manual we use the word "facilitators" for the people who prepare, present and co-ordinate the activities. A facilitator is someone who helps people discover how much knowledge they already have, who encourages them to learn more and helps them explore their own potential. Facilitation means creating an environment in which people learn, experiment, explore and grow. It is a process of sharing, of giving and taking. It is not a question of one person, who is "an expert", giving knowledge and skills to others. Everyone must grow through the sharing experience, participants and facilitators alike.

Opportunities to be a facilitator for young people and to work in an atmosphere of equality and mutuality differ across Europe, both between countries and within them. In the formal education sector we find differences in the aims and philosophy of education, techniques of classroom management and curricula. It is not common for pupils and students to decide what they want to learn within the framework of a broad curriculum nor for teachers to have a facilitating role, although there are exceptions. In the non-formal sector there are equally large variations not only in the aims and philosophies of the different organisations but also in the activities and opportunities they offer. These differences are evident both between countries and also within countries.

We all work within the educational and social norms of our own societies. It is easy to overlook or forget the fact of our own ethnocentrism and, as a result, to take the way we interact with young people for granted and normal. You may find it helpful to reflect on your own style and practice in order to develop your facilitation skills.

Thinking, learning and teaching/training styles

We are all individuals and think and learn in different ways. We all use a mixture of styles but each of has a preferred way of mentally representing the world around us (thinking style) and a preferred learning style. As facilitators we should be aware of this and use a variety of methodologies to excite the talents and interests of young people.

It must be stressed that the following are preferred styles; we all use all of the styles but each of us has a preferred style. For more information, see the references to David Kolb's work at the end of the chapter.

 **Which of the following is your preferred style?**

Summary of ***thinking styles***

- *Visual people* tend to mentally represent the world in pictures. They may use phrases like "I see what you mean".
- *Auditory people* tend to remember more of what they hear and may use phrases like "That sounds like an interesting idea".
- *Kinaesthetic* people tend to remember things through feelings, both physical and emotional. They may use terms like "I love that idea, lets go for it".

Summary of ***learning styles***

- *Activists* learn best from activities where there are new experiences, problems and opportunities from which to learn. They can engross themselves in games, teamwork tasks and role-playing exercises. They enjoy the challenge of being thrown in at the deep end. Activists react against passive learning, solitary work such as reading, writing and thinking on their own, and against the demands of attention to detail.
- *Reflectors* learn best when they are allowed to think over an activity. They enjoy carrying out detailed research, reviewing what has happened and what they have learned. They react against being forced into the limelight, being given insufficient data on which to base a conclusion and having to take short cuts or carry out a superficial job.
- *Theorists* learn best from activities where what they are learning about is part of a system, model, concept or theory. They like being in structured situations with a clear purpose and dealing with interesting ideas and concepts. They do not necessarily always like having to participate in situations emphasising emotions and feelings.
- *Pragmatists* learn best from activities where there is an obvious link between the subject matter and a real problem, and when they are able to implement what they have learned. They react against learning that seems distant from reality, learning that is "all theory and general principles", and the feeling that people are going round in circles without getting anywhere fast enough.

Teaching/training styles

Different people have different styles and approaches to teaching and taining.. Your approach as facilitator will depend on your own values, beliefs and assumptions, your personality, past experience of training and being trained, and how confident you feel both working with young people and handling human rights issues.

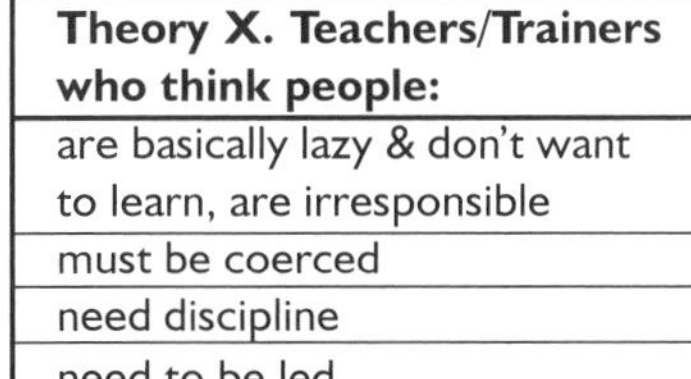

Theory X. Teachers/Trainers who think people:	Theory Y. Teachers/Trainers who think people:
are basically lazy & don't want to learn, are irresponsible	want to learn & will direct themselves
must be coerced	are creative
need discipline	want to be consulted
need to be led	want responsibility

trainer is in charge plans inflexibly	trainer seeks participation, plans flexibly
talks at people	trainer leads with consent
discipline/structure is imposed	discipline/structure is by agreement
trainees instructed, told by the expert	people responsible for their own learning
trainer gives answers to problems, others' views or solutions to problems are right or wrong	people encouraged to hold their own views and to seek their own solutions to problems.

These are obviously two extremes of training style at either end of a continuum. It should be noted that it is the theory Y assumptions that are appropriate to HRE. The aims of HRE are to develop values of respect, equality, co-operation and democracy. These values can only be promoted through a process which is itself inherently based on these values.

? Think back on your own experiences. What was it like to be taught by these two extreme types of teachers?

Using COMPASS in formal and non-formal education

The educational approach and the types of activities described in this manual may seem easier to apply in the non-formal sector than in the formal sector. The curriculum in the non-formal sector tends to be more open and focuses more on the personal and social development of young people. Also the starting point of the work is the interests of the young people. It allows for greater participation and flexibility and for young people to get involved with human rights issues in a practical way.

In a non-formal educational setting your starting point could be a question about something that is happening in your area or something that someone has seen on television. If you want to take the lead and stimulate people's interest in human rights, suggest showing a film or video. An excellent guide to useful films is "Europe on Screen: Cinema and the teaching of history" by Dominique Chancel (Council of Europe, January 2001). You can also put up posters or use pictures to stimulate spontaneous discussion, or have a music evening playing songs that call for people's freedom. You could then suggest going on to use one of the activities that explores general human rights, such as "Where do you stand?" (page 254) or "Act it out" (page 86.)

The curriculum in the formal sector is often bounded by an agreed set of knowledge, which pupils and students have to acquire and be tested on. Personal and social development, while recognised as important, is not always the main focus in the way that acquiring knowledge as a preparation for future work or further study is. This does not preclude most of the activities in this manual being adapted to fit into any curriculum subject in different classroom settings in schools and colleges throughout Europe. In fact, many have been designed with a classroom setting in mind.

Problem solving and conflict resolution as a basis for HRE

Human rights issues are often controversial because different people have different value systems and therefore see rights and responsibilities in different ways. These differences, which manifest themselves as conflicts of opinion, are the basis of our educational work.

Two important aims of HRE are first, to equip young people with the skills of appreciating - but not necessarily agreeing with - different points of view about an issue, and second, to help them develop skills of finding mutually agreeable solutions to problems.

This manual and its activities are based on an understanding that conflicts of opinion can be used constructively for the learning process, provided that the facilitator feels confident in addressing possible conflicts in a group. As in many non-formal educational activities, the purpose is not so much that everyone agrees with a given result but rather that the participants can also learn from that process (e.g. listening to each other, expressing themselves, respecting differences of opinion, etc.).

For example, the activity, "Play the Game" (page 194) specifically works with developing conflict resolution skills.

Common questions about Human Rights Education

The following answers are short, but we hope they will answer some of the questions asked by people who are beginning to incorporate HRE into their work.

? Don't young people need to learn about responsibility, rather than rights?

Answer: This manual places emphasis on both rights and responsibilities. The activities are designed to show that the relationship between an individual's rights and other people's rights is not always clear cut, and that everyone has a responsibility to respect the rights of others.

? What if the participants ask a question I can't answer?

Answer: No one should expect anyone to know all the answers to everything! It is perfectly acceptable to say that you don't know some particular facts and then involve the participants in finding the answers. You should always consider reflecting the question back to the group by asking: what do you think about this?

It is also important for everyone to remember that the answers to questions on human rights are rarely simple. Complex moral questions cannot be answered with "yes" or "no". From the educational viewpoint, raising the question is as important as finding an answer. By introducing complex issues and allowing young people to think about them, we equip young people with the knowledge, skills and attitudes to deal with such questions later in life.

What do we do if we don't have a photocopier or enough materials?

Answer: Many of the activities in this manual are designed so that they don't need expensive materials or a photocopier. However, for some activities you may have to copy role cards or fact sheets for group work by hand and make multiple copies using carbon paper. You will have to be creative and find your own solutions.

Won't parents, school heads and community leaders oppose the teaching of human rights as political indoctrination which will incite rebellious behaviour?

Answer: Human rights education develops citizens who are able to participate in society and in the development of their country. It is important to distinguish between the development of participation competencies and party politics. Human rights education through discussion and participation encourages young people to develop critical and enquiring minds and to behave rationally. In this respect, human rights education is also related to civic and political education and it also allows young people to make the connections between human rights, social issues, education and policies. As a result, it may happen that young people do engage in local or national political parties – as a result of their right to political participation and freedom of thought, association and expression. But that should remain their own choice.

Isn't it the government's responsibility to ensure that people have the opportunity to learn about human rights?

Answer: Member countries of the United Nations have an obligation to promote human rights education in all forms of learning. That is in formal, non-formal and informal education. Despite this, many governments have done very little towards the promotion of human rights education and the incorporation of human rights in the curricula. Individual educators and non-governmental organisations can do a lot to encourage the development of human rights education through their own or collaborative efforts in schools and other educational programmes, and also by lobbying and putting pressure on their governments to fulfil their obligations in this regard.

What if there are no human rights violations in my country?

Human rights education is not only about violations. It is first of all about understanding human rights as a universal asset common to all human beings and about realising the need to protect them. In addition to this, no country can claim that there are no violations of rights. One easy way to address reality is to look at the immediate social environment or community. Who is excluded? Who lives in extreme poverty? Which children do not enjoy their rights? Another way is to look at the role of your own country in the violation or promotion of human rights in other countries (e.g. the environment and the right to development, the arms trade, global poverty, etc.).

Tips for users

This manual and its activities can be used at school in a classroom or in extra-curricular activities, in a training course or a seminar, at a summer camp or in a work camp or in a youth club or with a youth group. They can also be used even if you work mostly with adults.

How to choose an activity

You should choose an activity that is at the right level for you and your group and that will fit into the time you have. Read the activity through carefully at least twice and try to imagine how the group may react and some of the things they will say. Make sure you have all the materials you will need. Check that there will be enough space, especially if the participants will be breaking up for small-group work.

Again we emphasise that the instructions for each activity are only guidelines and you should use the material in the way that suits your own needs. Indeed, it is not possible to write activities that will exactly suit every situation across Europe. We expect you to adapt the activities. For example, you might take the basic idea from one activity and use a method from another.

Each activity is presented in a standard format. Icons and headings are used to make it easy to get an overview of the whole.

Key to symbols and headings used to present the activities

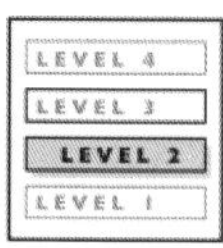

Level of complexity	Levels 1-4 indicate the general level of competencies required to participate and/or the amount of preparation involved.
Themes	The global themes that are addressed in the activity (e.g. poverty, environment, peace and violence, gender equality).
Overview	Gives brief information about the type of activity and the issues addressed.
Related rights	Rights addressed in the activity (e.g. the right to life or freedom of expression).
Group size	How many people you need to do the activity.
Time	The estimated time in minutes needed to complete the whole activity including the discussion. If the group size was "any", then the time is estimated for a group of 15 people.
Objectives	The objectives relate to the learning objectives of HRE in terms of knowledge, skills, attitudes and values.
Materials	List of equipment needed to run the activity.
Preparation	List of things the facilitator needs to do before starting.
Instructions	List of instructions for how to run the activity.
Debriefing and evaluation	Suggested questions to help the facilitator conduct the debriefing and evaluate the activity (phase 2-4 of the learning cycle, see page 40).
Tips for facilitators	Guidance notes. Things to be aware of. Where to get extra information.
Variations	Ideas for how to adapt the activity for use in a different situations.
Suggestions for follow-up	Ideas for what to do next. Links to other activities.
Ideas for action	Suggestions for the next steps to take action.
Key dates	Commemorative dates related to human rights.
Further information	Extra background information relevant to the activity.
Handouts	Role cards, action pages, background reading material, discussion cards, etc.

Complexity

The activities are coded from level 1-4 to indicate the general level of competencies required to participate in experiential activities and the amount of preparation involved. In general, the two variables go together; level 1 activities need very little preparation while those at level 4 activities need much more.

- **Level 1.** These are short, simple activities mostly useful as starters. Energisers and icebreakers fall into this category. Nonetheless, these activities are of value in the way that they make people interact and communicate with each other.
- **Level 2**. These are simple activities designed to stimulate interest in an issue. They do not require prior knowledge of human rights issues or developed personal or group work skills. Many of the activities at this level are designed to help people develop communication and group work skills while at the same time stimulating their interest in human rights.
- **Level 3.** These are longer activities designed to develop deeper understanding and insights into an issue. They demand higher levels of competency in discussion or group work skills.
- **Level 4.** These activities are longer, require good group work and discussion skills, concentration and co-operation from the participants and also take longer preparation. They are also more embracing in that they provide a wider and deeper understanding of the issues.

The global links

The activities in the manual are designed to encourage exploration of human rights and the links between rights and several global themes. Thus three "themes" are indicated in the description of each activity. The sixteen global themes are:

1. General human rights

2. Children

3. Citizenship

4. Democracy

5. Discrimination and Xenophobia

6. Education

7. Environment

8. Gender equality

9. Globalisation

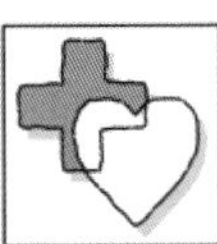

10. Health

11. Human security

12. Media

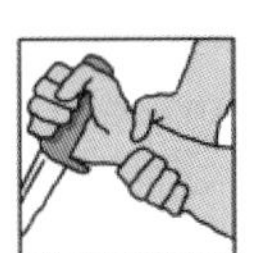

13. Peace and Violence

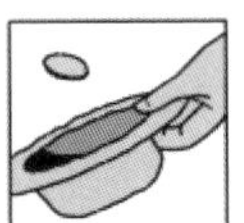

14. Poverty

15. Social rights

16. Sport

Tips for facilitation

In the manual, we use the term facilitators to describe the role of the people (trainer, teachers, youth workers, peer educators, young volunteers - or whoever) who are co-ordinating the work and running the activities. This terminology helps to emphasise that HRE requires a democratic and participative approach.

We assume that you are facilitating groups of young people, for example in a classroom, in a youth club, a training course a youth camp or at a seminar.

Group work

Group work happens when people work together, combine their different skills and talents and build on each other's strengths to complete a task. Group work:

- *encourages responsibility*. When people feel they own what they are doing, they are usually committed to the outcome and take care to ensure a good result.
- *develops communication skills*. People need to listen, to understand what others say, to be responsive to their ideas and to be able to put their own thoughts forward.
- *develops co-operation*. People soon learn that when they are working towards a common goal they do better if they co-operate than if they compete with each other.
- *involves consensual decision-making skills*. People quickly learn that the best way to make decisions is to look at all the information available and to try to find a solution that satisfies everybody. Someone who feels left out of the decision-making process may disrupt the group's work and not honour decisions which are made by the rest of the group.

Group work techniques

In Chapter 2 of the manual there are references to techniques such as "brainstorming" or "role-play". The following notes explain these terms and give some general guidelines about how to use them.

Note that successful group work must be task-orientated. There must be a clear question that needs answering or a clearly stated problem that requires solutions.

Brainstorming

Brainstorming is a way to introduce a new subject, encourage creativity and to generate a lot of ideas very quickly. It can be used for solving a specific problem or answering a question.

Instructions:

- Decide on the issue that you want to brainstorm and formulate it into a question that has many possible answers.
- Write the question where everyone can see it.
- Ask people to contribute their ideas and write down the ideas where everyone can see them, for instance, on a flipchart. These should be single words or short phrases.
- Stop the brainstorming when ideas are running out and then
- Go through the suggestions, asking for comments.

Note these points:

- Write down EVERY new suggestion. Often, the most creative suggestions are the most useful and interesting!
- No one should make any comments or judge what is written down until the end, or repeat ideas which have already been said.
- Encourage everyone to contribute.
- Only give your own ideas if it is necessary to encourage the group.
- If a suggestion is unclear, ask for clarification.

Wall writing

This is a form of brainstorming. Participants write their ideas on small pieces of paper (e.g. "Post-its") and paste them on a wall. The advantages of this method are that people can sit and think quietly for themselves before they are influenced by the others' ideas, and the pieces of paper can be repositioned to aid clustering of ideas.

Discussion

Discussions are a good way for the facilitator and the participants to discover what their attitudes to issues are. This is very important in HRE because, as well as knowing the facts, participants also need to explore and analyse issues for themselves. The news, posters and case studies are useful tools for stimulating discussion. Start people off by asking "what do you think about...?".

Buzz groups

This is a useful method if no ideas are forthcoming in a whole-group discussion. Ask people to discuss the topic in pairs for one or two minutes and then to share their ideas with the rest of the group. You will soon find the atmosphere "buzzing" with conversations and people "buzzing" with ideas!

Small-group work

Small-group work is in contrast to whole-group work. It is a method that encourages everyone to participate and helps develop co-operative teamwork. The size of a small group will depend on practical things like how many people there are all together and how much space you have. A small group may be 2 or 3 people, but they work best with 6-8. Small-group work can last for fifteen minutes, an hour or a day depending on the task in hand.

It is rarely productive to tell people simply to "discuss the issue". Whatever the topic, it is essential that the work is clearly defined and that people are focused on working towards a goal that requires them to feedback to the whole group. For example, assign a task in the form of a problem that needs solving or a question that requires answering.

Ranking

This is a useful method to use when you want to provide specific information or to stimulate a focused discussion in small groups.

You need to prepare one set of statement cards for each small group. There should be 9 cards per set. Prepare 9 short, simple statements related to the topic you wish people to discuss and write one statement on each card.

Ladder ranking

most important
least important

The groups have to discuss the statements and then rank them in order of importance. This can either be done as a ladder or as a diamond. In ladder ranking the most important statement is placed at the top, the next most important under it and so on to the least important statement at the bottom.

Diamond ranking

In diamond ranking people negotiate what the most important statement is, then the two second-most important, then the 3 statements of moderate importance and so on as shown in the diagram. Because issues are rarely clear cut, diamond ranking is often a more appropriate method. It is less contrived and therefore more acceptable to participants. It also gives better opportunities for consensus building. A variation of the ranking method is to write 8 statements and to leave one card blank for the participants to write for themselves.

Role-play

A role-play is a short drama acted out by the participants. Although people draw on their own life experiences to role-play the situation, it is mostly improvised. It aims to bring to life circumstances or events which are unfamiliar to the participants. Role-plays can improve understanding of a situation and encourage empathy towards those who are involved in it.

- Role-plays differ from simulations in that although the latter may also consist of short dramas they are usually scripted and do not involve the same degree of improvisation.
- The value of role-plays is that they imitate real life. They may raise questions to which there is no simple answer, for example about the right or wrong behaviour of a character. To gain greater insights, a useful technique is to ask people to reverse roles.

Role-plays need to be used with sensitivity. Firstly, it is essential that people have time at the end to come out of role. Secondly, everyone needs to respect the feelings of individuals and the social structure of the group. For example, a role-play about disabled people should take into account the fact that some participants may suffer from disabilities themselves (maybe not visible) or may have relatives or close friends who are disabled. They should not feel hurt, be forced to be exposed or marginalised. If that happens, take it seriously (apologise, re-address the issue as an example, etc.). Also, be very aware of stereotyping. Role-plays draw out what participants think about other people through their "ability" to play or imitate them. This is also what makes these activities great fun! It may be useful to always address the issue in the debriefing by asking, "do you think that the people you played are really like that?". It is always educational to make people aware of the need for constant, critical reviewing of information. You can therefore also ask participants where they got the information on which they based the development of the character.

Simulations

Simulations can be thought of as extended role-plays that involve everybody. They enable people to experience challenging situations but in a safe atmosphere. Simulations often demand a level of emotional involvement, which makes them very powerful tools. People learn not only with their heads and hands but also with their hearts.

Debriefing is especially important after a simulation. Players should discuss their feelings, why they chose to take the actions that they did, any injustices they perceived, and how acceptable they found any resolution that was achieved. They should be helped to draw parallels between what they have experienced and actual situations in the world.

Pictures: photographs, cartoons, drawing, collage

"A picture says a thousand words". Visual images are powerful tools both for providing information and for stimulating interest. Remember also that drawing is an important means of self-expression and communication, not only for those whose preferred thinking style is visual but also for those who are not strong in expressing themselves verbally. Ideas for activities using pictures and drawings are given with the "Picture games" on page 188.

Tips for building up a picture collection

- Pictures are such a versatile tool that it is a good idea for facilitators to build up their own stock. Images can be collected from innumerable sources, for instance, newspapers, magazines, posters, travel brochures, postcards and greetings cards.
- Trim the pictures, mount them on card and cover them with transparent, sticky-backed plastic (sold for covering books) to make them durable and easy and pleasant to handle. The collection will look more like a set if the cards are all made to one size. A4 is ideal, but A5 is a good, practical compromise.
- It can be a good idea to write a reference number on the back of each picture and to record the source, original title or other useful information elsewhere. Thus, people will have only the image to respond to and will not be distracted by other clues.
- When choosing pictures, look for variety. Be aware of gender, race, ability and disability, age, nationality and culture including sub-cultures. Try to get a selection of images from North, South, East and West, different natural and social environments and cultures. Also bear in mind the impact that individual pictures have because of their size and colour. This effect can distort people's perception of a picture, so try to trim your collection so you have a reasonably homogeneous set.

Films, videos and radio plays

Films, videos and radio plays are powerful tools for HRE and popular with young people. A discussion after watching a film should make a good starting point for further work. Things to talk about are people's initial reaction to the film, how true to "real life" it was, whether the characters were portrayed realistically, or whether they were trying to promote one particular political or moral point of view.

Newspapers, radio, television, Internet

The media are an infallible source of good discussion material. It is always interesting to discuss the content and the way it is presented and to analyse bias and stereotypes.

Taking pictures and making films

The technology of camcorders and disposable cameras now makes making films and taking pictures much more accessible for everyone. Young people's pictures and films vividly show their points of view and attitudes and make excellent display material. Video letters are a proven way to break down barriers and prejudices. They enable people who would not otherwise meet face to face to "talk" and to share insights into how they live and what is important to them.

General tips on running activities

Co-facilitating

If at all possible, always co-facilitate together with someone else. There are practical advantages in that there will then be two people to share the responsibility of helping with small-group work or dealing with individual needs. When two people run a session, it is easier to alter the pace and rhythm to keep things interesting and the participants on their toes. Two facilitators can support each other if things do not go as planned and it is also more rewarding to conduct a review with someone else than to do it alone. Better even than working with two facilitators is to develop your activities in a team, possibly involving some young people in the preparation.

Managing time

Plan carefully and not try to cram too much into the time available. If the activity is taking longer than you anticipated, try to shorten it so that you have plenty of time for discussion (see notes on the learning cycle, page 40). On the other hand, if you have lots of time in hand, do not try to drag the discussion out, have a break or do a quick energiser activity for fun.

Create a non-threatening environment

People must feel free to explore and discover, and to interact and share with each other. Be genuine, friendly, encouraging and humorous. Do not use jargon or language that participants do not understand.

Set ground rules

It is important that everyone in the group understands the ground rules for participatory, experiential activities. For example, everyone should take their share of the responsibility for the session, that everyone should have a chance to be listened to, to speak and to participate. No one should feel under pressure to say anything they do not feel comfortable with. These ground rules may be discussed and agreed when you first start working with a class or group.

Give clear instructions

Always make sure everyone has understood the instructions and knows what they have to do. The simplest way is to invite questions, and to write down what is most important. Do not be afraid of questions; they are very useful and give you (and the rest of the group) the opportunity to clarify things. No questions sometimes means a sign of general confusion ("but I am afraid to ask because everyone else seems to understand").

Facilitating discussions

Discussion is central to the HRE process. Pay special attention to ensure everyone in the group can participate if they wish to. Use words, expressions and language common to the group and explain words with which they are unfamiliar.

Invite participants to offer their opinions. Ensure that there is a balance of global and local aspects so that people see the issue as directly relevant to their own lives.

Debriefing and evaluation

Give the participants plenty of time to complete the activity and if necessary come out of

role before discussing what happened and what they learned. Spend time at the end of each activity talking over what people learnt and how they see it relating to their own lives, their community and the wider world. Without reflection, people do not learn much from their experiences.

We suggest that you try to go through the debriefing and evaluation process in sequence by asking the participants questions that relate to:

- what happened during the activity and how they felt
- what they learned about themselves
- what they learned about the issues addressed in the activity
- how they can move forward and use what they have learned

Reviewing

It is important to review the work and the learning periodically. This may be at the end of the day at a seminar or at the end of a series of two or three lessons or meetings. You may find that the group finds reviewing boring especially if there has already been a lot of discussion. Remember that reviewing doesn't have to be through discussion; you can also use other techniques including body language, drawings, sculpting, etc.

Co-facilitators should find time to relax and wind down and review how things went for them. Talk about:

- How the activity went from your point of view: preparation, timing, etc.
- What the participants learnt and if they met the learning objectives
- What the outcomes are: what the group will do now as a result of doing the activity
- What you yourselves learnt about the issues and about facilitating

When things don't go the way you expected them to

Activities rarely go exactly the way you expect them to, or the way they are presented and described in this manual! That is both the reward and the challenge of working with participatory activities. You have to be responsive to what is happening and to think on your feet.

Timing

It may be that everyone is very involved and that you are running out of time. You should consult with the participants on whether to stop immediately, in 5 minutes or how else to resolve the problem.

Flagging energy

Sometimes, especially with longer sessions, it may be necessary for you to use an energiser or to suggest a short break.

Difficult discussions

Sometimes discussions get "stuck". You will have to identify the cause. It could be many things, for example, because the topic has been exhausted or that it is too emotional. You will have to decide whether to prompt with a question, change tack or move on. You should never feel that you have to provide the answers to participants' questions or problems. The group itself must find its own answers through listening to each other and sharing. They may, of course, ask your opinion or advice, but the group must make their own decisions.

Feedback

Feedback is a comment on something someone has said or done. It may be positive or critical in a negative sense. Giving and receiving feedback is a skill and you will need to help the group members learn how to do it. Too often, feedback is received as destructive criticism even though this was not the intention of the speaker. The key words with regard to feedback are "respect" and "arguments".

When giving feedback, it is important to respect the other person, to focus on what they said or did and to give reasons for your point of view. It is better to say, "I disagree strongly with what you have just said because...." rather than "How can you be so stupid, don't you see that....?". Giving negative feedback comes readily to many people, which can be painful.

It is your role as facilitator to find ways of ensuring that people give feedback in a supportive way. For example by:

- ensuring that people start giving the feedback with a positive statement
- respecting the other person and not make any derogatory remarks
- focusing on the behaviour, not on the person
- giving a reason for what they are saying
- taking responsibility for what they say by using "I – messages"

Receiving feedback is hard, especially when there is disagreement. Your role is to help people learn from their experiences and to help them feel supported and not put down. Encourage people to listen carefully to the feedback without immediately defending themselves or their position. It is especially important that people understand exactly what the person giving the feedback means and that they take time to evaluate what has been said before accepting or rejecting it.

Resistance from the participants

Being involved in participatory activities is very demanding and while you will be using a variety of techniques, for instance, discussion, drawing, role-play or music, it is inevitable that not all activities will suit all participants all of the time. If a participant is confident and able to explain why they do not like a particular activity then you will be able to accommodate his or her needs through dialogue and negotiation.

By 'resistance', we mean behaviour that is purposefully disruptive. All facilitators experience resistance from participants at one time or another. Resistance can take several forms. An insecure young person may disturb by scraping his or her chair, humming or talking with their neighbour. More subtle ways of disrupting the session are by asking irrelevant questions or making a joke out of everything. Another "game" resisters play is "undermine the facilitator". Here they may say, "You don't understand, it's a long time since you were young", or "anything but more discussions, why can't we just do activities?" A third type of "game" is to try to avoid the learning. For example people say, "yes but....".

Obviously, it is best if you can avoid resistance. For example,

- Be aware of each person in the group and any sensitive emotions which might be triggered by a particular activity or by a particular part in a role-play or simulation.
- Make sure everyone knows that they are at no time under any pressure to say or reveal anything about themselves that they do not feel comfortable with.
- Allow participants time to warm up before any activity and to wind down afterwards.
- Remember to allow enough time for debriefing and discussion so everyone feels that their opinion and participation is valued.

You will have to decide yourself on the best way to handle a difficult situation but bear in mind that usually the best way to solve the problem is to bring it out into the open and to get the group as a whole to find a solution. Do not get into long discussions or arguments with a single group member. This can cause resentment and frustration among the other participants and cause them to lose interest.

Managing conflict within the group

Conflicts may happen in groups. This is normal and your role is to help participants deal with them. Conflicts may develop if participants feel insecure dealing with questions related to emotions and values, if they have insufficient competencies in group work or if they have completely different approaches to the issue or different values. Try to stay cool and do not become involved in conflicts with individuals.

- Remember that conflict can be helpful and creative if managed properly.
- Take enough time for the debriefing and discussion. If necessary make more time.
- Help to clarify people's positions, opinions and interests.
- Ease tensions in the group. For example, ask everyone to sit down or to talk for three minutes in small subgroups or say something to put the situation into perspective.
- Encourage everybody to listen actively to each other.
- Stress what unites people rather than what separates them.
- Search for consensus. Get people to look at their common interests rather than trying to compromise and move from their stated positions.
- Look for solutions which may resolve the problem without "recreating" the conflict.
- Offer to talk to those involved privately at another time.

If more serious and deeper conflicts arise, it may be better to postpone seeking a solution and look for another more appropriate opportunity to resolve the problem. In the meantime, you could consider how to address the conflict from another angle, for example, by playing a short game such as "Fist and Palm" (page 58). By postponing the resolution of the conflict you leave time for those involved to reflect on the situation and to come up with new approaches or solutions.

Conflicts that arise in the group and ways of resolving them can be used to develop understanding and insights into the causes and difficulties of conflicts in the wider world. The reverse is also true; discussion of international conflicts can give insights into local conflicts.

Further information on dealing with conflict can be found in the activity "Play the game!" (page 194).

Some methods and techniques for supporting effective learning groups

We have described group work and its role in experiential learning. Here we describe a few general activities at level 1 that specifically promote group-work skills. These activities make good ice-breakers and energisers and, in conjunction with other activities in the manual, are good methods for introducing human rights issues. It is often a good idea if you, the facilitator, also join in with the ice-breakers.

Taking responsibility, communication and co-operation are key skills for good group work.

Get into line

This activity is very simple, yet has all the characteristics and procedures for helping people learn to take responsibility within the group. It makes a good ice-breaker.

Complexity: Level 1 **Group size:** Any **Time:** 15 minutes +

Instructions

1. Tell the group to line up in order of height, the shortest person at the front and the tallest at the back. They should not talk but may communicate using sounds, sign language and body language.
2. When they are in line, check that the order is correct.
3. Repeat the exercise getting people to line up according to other criteria that make the game fun but not threatening, for instance, age, the month of their birthday (January to December), shoe size, etc.

Debriefing and evaluation

Try to help the group analyse how they worked together and what makes good group work. Suggested questions are:

- What problems did you have getting organised?
- What slowed the group down?
- Was a leader needed? Did anyone serve as a leader? How were they chosen?
- What responsibility did each group member have in solving the problem?
- How could the group solve the problem faster next time?

Go on, I'm listening

This activity focuses on listening skills, but it also helps develop logical thinking and confidence in expressing an opinion.

Complexity: Level 1 **Group size:** Any **Time:** 35 minutes

Instructions

1. Brainstorm with the whole group what makes a good listener.
2. Ask people to get into threes: one person to be the speaker, one to be the listener and one the watchdog.
3. Tell the speakers that they have 5 minutes to tell the listener their personal view on an issue that interests them (for example, the death penalty for crimes against humanity, limits of free speech or any other topic that requires description, analysis and an opinion).
4. The listener has to listen and make sure that they understand what the issue is about, why the speaker is interested in it and what their point of view is.
5. The watchdog observes the listener's active listening skills. They should not participate in the discussion but observe the discussion carefully, withholding any suggestions for improvement until time is called.
6. After 5 minutes, call time and ask the watchdogs to give feedback. Swap round until everyone has had a chance to be speaker, listener and watchdog.

Debriefing and evaluation

Discuss the activity. Some useful questions may be:

- Did the speakers successfully convey their ideas and feelings about the topic? Did they find it helpful to speak to someone who was using active listening skills?
- How was it to be a listener? Was it difficult to listen and not interrupt in order to make a comment or add their own opinion?

Tips for facilitators

The group may initially come up with some of the following points. Hopefully by the end of the activity, they will be able to list them all - and some more.

A good listener:

- shows respect, maintains eye contact with the speaker and doesn't fidget.
- signals that they are attentive and listening by nodding occasionally or saying "go on, I'm listening".
- does not interrupt.
- does not rush to fill silences but gives the speaker time to think and resume talking.
- does not take the focus of the conversation away from the speaker by commenting or disagreeing.
- uses open-ended questions to encourage the speaker to continue speaking or to elaborate.
- summarises or restates the speaker's remarks from time to time to show that they have understood.
- responds to the feelings that may lie behind the speaker's words, and shows that they understand how the speaker feels.

The People Machine

This is a non-verbal exercise to show how group members can respond to each other and link their individual contributions into an integrated working unit.

Complexity: Level 1 **Group size:** 6 or more **Time:** 15 minutes

Instructions

1. Ask people to stand in a circle.
2. Tell them that they have to construct one huge mechanical machine together, using only their own bodies.
3. Ask one person to start. S/he chooses a simple repetitive movement, such as moving one arm up and down rhythmically. At the same time they make a distinctive sound, for instance, a long whistle.
4. Ask a second person to come up and stand close to, or just touch the first. They choose their own action and noise. For example, they may bob up and down and make a "chkk ...chkk" sound, keeping in time and rhythm with the first person.
5. Call for more volunteers, one at a time, to join in. They can join on to any existing part of the machine. They add their own movement and sound.
6. At the end the entire group should be interconnected and moving in many inter-related ways and making many different sounds.
7. When everyone is involved and the machine is running smoothly you can "conduct" everyone to make the machine go louder or softer, faster or slower.

Debriefing and evaluation

You may like to ask the group:

- What similarities can they see between 'the machine' and an effective learning group?
- What skills did they need? Responsibility? Listening and responding skills? Co-operation? What else?

Fist and palm

This game is useful for developing co-operation.

Complexity: Level 2 **Group size:** 8+ **Time:** 40 minutes

Instructions

Score sheet

A	B	A	B
Fist	Palm	4	0
Palm	Palm	3	3
Fist	Fist	0	0
Palm	Fist	0	4

1. Write the score sheet on a flipchart.
2. Ask people to get into pairs; one is A, the other B.
3. They both put their hands behind their backs and together count 1, 2, 3.
4. On the count of 3, they must simultaneously bring their hand to the front and show either a fist or a palm.
5. Tell the pairs to keep the score.
6. Play 10 rounds.
7. At the end, list on a flipchart both the individual and combined scores of each pair.

Debriefing and evaluation

Questions to ask can include:

- Who got the highest score out of all the pairs? How did you play to win?
- Who has the lowest score? How do you feel? What happened?
- Did any pairs make any agreements about how to co-operate? If so, did anyone break the agreement? Why? How did your partner feel?
- Compare the combined scores in those groups where people competed and where they co-operated. Were there any advantages in co-operating? If so, what? (Total score? Feeling good? Still friends?)

Methods and techniques for developing discussion skills

Discussions are also an opportunity to practice listening, speaking in turn and other group skills which are important for respecting other people's rights. To allow everyone to participate, it is important that the group is of a manageable size. If your group is very large - say for example more than 15 or 20 people - it might be better to break up into smaller groups for the discussion. To encourage interaction and participation, it is preferable to seat participants in a circle or semi-circle where they can see one another. General guidelines that should be discussed and agreed by the group may include:

- Only one person should talk at a time.
- Judgmental comments or any form of ridicule are discouraged.
- Each person should talk from their own perspective and experience and not generalise on behalf of others; that is, use "I" statements.
- Remember that there is likely to be more than one 'right' answer.
- Agree to maintain confidentiality when talking about sensitive issues.

- Everyone has the right to be silent and not take part in discussion on a particular issue, if they so wish.

You may find the following strategies helpful:

Microphone

This is effective with groups that have difficulty in listening.

Instructions

The group sits in a circle. An old microphone from a tape recorder (or a similarly shaped object) is passed around the circle. Only the person holding the microphone is allowed to speak; the others are to listen to, and look at, the speaker. When the speaker is finished, the microphone is passed to the next person who wishes to speak.

The dilemma game

This is useful for encouraging people to express their opinion, listen to others and to change their opinion in the light of new understanding. It can be varied in different ways.

Instructions

1. Prepare 3 or 4 controversial statements relating to the issue you are working with, for example, "there should be no limits to freedom of speech".
2. Draw a line along the floor with chalk or tape.
3. Explain that to the right of the line represents agreement with a statement; to the left represents disagreement. The distance from the line represents the strength of agreement or disagreement; the further from the line, the greater the agreement or disagreement. The walls of the room are the limit! Standing on the line shows that that person has no opinion.
4. Read out the first statement.
5. Tell participants to stand at a point on either side of the line that represents their opinion about the statement.
6. Now invite people to explain why they are standing where they are.
7. Let everyone who wishes to, speak. Then ask if anyone wishes to change position.
8. When all who wish to move have done so, ask them their reasons for moving.
9. Ask another question.

Methods and techniques for developing collective decision-making skills

Making collective decisions by consensus is a lengthy process and requires people to have good communication skills, be sensitive to the needs of others and to show imagination and trust and to be patient. Only then can people explore issues honestly, express opinions without fear of censure or ridicule and feel free to change their minds as a result of reasonable argument.

The object of working for consensus is to make people aware of the range of opinions in the group and to consider all those opinions thoughtfully so that decisions are made based on mutually agreed common interests. Consensus decision-making is not easy to facilitate.

Decision-making processes can end up in several different ways:

- *One side persuades the other*. This, of course, is what most people think they are

doing when they take a majority vote, but it may well be that some important point of view has been overlooked. When consensus is achieved through persuasion, it means that virtually all in the group agree that the arguments in favour of one point of view are compelling and overwhelming, and they forsake their previous positions and support that point of view.

- *One side gives in*. Sometimes people decide that it is not worth the energy and decide to abandon their position. The point of view of dissenters is essential to creative decision-making; often a single person holds key information that can be decisive. People should be able to change their minds freely as new information becomes available. When working for consensus, people should be free to explore a number of positions and should not feel they are deserting their party if they change their minds.
- *Both sides find a new alternative*. Disagreement can sometimes be overcome if people stop trying to defend the positions they have taken and attempt to find a different solution that will satisfy both sides. Frequently neither group has to give up anything and both groups come out feeling that they have "won".
- *The group redefines the issue*. A sincere search for consensus frequently leads people to realise that their conflict is caused by semantic difficulties or by a misperception of the other party's position. Sometimes both sides realise that they have overstated their positions and, as they strive for consensus, they moderate their stands and find a way of viewing the issue that both can support.
- *Each side gives in a little*. Sometimes when people look at what they have in common they can come to an agreement that meets most of the needs of both sides rather than all the needs of one side and none of the other's.
- *Both sides agree to have a break*. Sometimes all involved agree that they do not yet have enough information to make a prudent decision, or that they are too upset to arrive at a workable solution. They may choose to postpone the issue until they can return with the knowledge and attitudes required to make a rational decision.

Knots

This activity makes a good ice-breaker and energiser. It involves co-operation and decision making.

Complexity: Level 1 **Group size:** 10-20 **Time:** 10 minutes

Instructions

Tell everyone to stand shoulder to shoulder in a circle with their arms stretched out in front of them.

- They should now reach out and grab hands across the circle, so that each person holds hands with two other people. No one may hold the hand of someone immediately beside them. (The result is what looks like a big knot of hands!)
- Now tell people to untangle the knot without letting go of the hands.
- Note: They will have to climb under and over each other's arms. It takes a little patience, but the surprising result will be one or two big circles.

Debriefing and evaluation

- You can ask the group how they worked together to untangle the knot.
- Was it a democratic process?
- How many ways were there of coming to a solution?

- Did everyone make suggestions or did one person assume leadership and direct the unravelling?

Points down

This is an energetic game that involves co-operation and group decision making. Also a good ice-breaker and energiser.

Complexity: Level 1 **Group size:** 6-25 **Time:** 15 minutes

Instructions

1. Explain to the group that in this game there are nine "points" of the body that can touch the floor: 2 feet, 2hands, 2 elbows, 2 knees and 1 forehead.
2. Tell people to spread out in the middle of the room. Call out a number between 1 and 9 and tell each player that they must touch the floor with that number of points. Repeat twice more.
3. Tell people to find a partner. Call out a number between 2 and 18. The pairs have to work together to put the correct number of points down. Repeat twice more.
4. Repeat the rounds with people working in groups of 4, then 8, and then 16 until everyone is working together.

Tips for the facilitator

You can allow people to talk or to communicate only with sign language.

When four people play together, the number could be as low as 2 if two people each stand on one leg while carrying the other two!

When four people play, the lowest practical number is probably 4. (The highest number will be 4 multiplied by 9 = 36).

In each round the highest number called may not be more than 9 times the number of people in the group!

Pairs to 4s

This activity involves a process of discussion and negotiation.

Complexity: Level 1 **Group size:** 4+ **Time:** 45 minutes

Instructions

1. Ask the group to get into pairs to complete a task that involves the need to discuss and make a decision, for instance, to agree on a date for a group outing, or a definition of human rights or to agree the 3 most important human rights.
2. Allow 10 minutes for this stage.
3. Then tell the pairs to get into fours and repeat the process.
4. Note: If you are using this exercise to make a collective decision about a practical matter, for example about the group trip, then you should continue the exercise and do rounds with groups of 8 and then 16 until everyone is in one big group and a consensus has been reached that best meets the needs of everyone. If you are using this method to discuss the definition of human rights, get into plenary after the groups of 4 have finished discussing. This avoids the exercise getting repetitive and boring.

Debriefing and evaluation

Suggested questions for discussing the nature of the decision-making process are:

- The method takes a long time. Was the outcome worth it?
- Does everyone feel consulted and involved in the decision-making process (even if in the end the outcome was not their preferred choice)?
- Were there any minority needs that could not be accommodated? (For example, with the date of the trip).

Activities for reviewing

During training or any teaching programme, it is important to review periodically. The following activities can be used at any time. They are fun ways to help people learn from their experiences. They include drawing, sculpting, and story-telling methods.

End game

This can be a very a quick way of getting feedback. The more rounds you do the more feedback you get.

Complexity: Level 1 **Group size:** Any **Time:** 3 or 4 minutes per round

Instructions

1. Tell people to sit in a circle.
2. Remind them briefly about what they have been doing.
3. Choose one of the pairs of statements below.
4. Go round the circle, ask each person in turn to complete their statement. No comments or discussion are allowed.
5. Do further rounds if you have time or if you want to get further feedback.

Examples of statements:

- The best thing about the activity was.... And the worst was....
- The most interesting thing was..... The most boring thing was...
- What I resented most is ... What I appreciated most is...
- The funniest thing .... The most serious thing ...
- I would have liked more of ... and less of...
- The thing I enjoyed doing most ... the thing that I least liked doing ...
- I felt most confident doing .... I felt least confident doing ...

High and low

This method is very quick and uses body language.

Complexity: Level 1 **Group size:** Any **Time:** 5 minutes

Preparation

Think of 3 or 4 questions to ask, for example, "Did you enjoy the activity?" or "Did you learn anything new?"

Instructions

1. Read out the first question.
2. Tell the group to consider their response and then to show with their whole bodies how they feel. If they strongly agree with the statement they should reach up as high as they can and may even stand on tiptoe! People who strongly disagree should crouch down low or even lie on the floor. People can also find their own in-between positions to indicate their level of response.
3. Ask people to relax and read out the second question.

Points of view

This activity combines movement with the option of discussion.

Complexity: Level 1 **Group size:** 10+ **Time:** 10 minutes

Preparation

3 or 4 questions, for example, "Did you enjoy the activity?" "Did you learn anything new?"

Instructions

1. Name the four walls of the hall 'yes', 'no', 'I don't know' and 'I want to say something', to represent four different points of view.
2. Ask the first question about the activity and tell people to go to the wall that represents their response.
3. Let those who want to say something have their say. Only people at the fourth 'I want to say something' wall may speak.

Weather report

This uses a "story-telling" method. It can be used at the end of an activity as a review. Alternatively, it works well part way through a long project to enable people to look back and then to look forward.

Complexity: Level 1 **Group size:** 6+ **Time:** 45 minutes

Preparation

Paper and pencils optional

Instructions

1. Give people 5 -10 minutes to think about the day/training/project/work you are involved in and get them to ask themselves: "Am I enjoying it so far? What am I getting out of it and is it going to be successful?"
2. Then ask them one at a time to describe how they feel in terms of a weather report.

Tips for facilitators

If people need an illustration of what you mean you could say, "My day started dull and overcast... then I had to put up my umbrella to keep me from the downpour.... but many of you helped me hold up the umbrella... showers are also forecast for tomorrow, but next week I foresee it will be bright and sunny". This could mean that you started off not too sure, then things got really bad and you were glad of people's support, you are not too sure about immediate plans but you think you will get there in the end.

The timing given is for a group of 10-12 people. Bigger groups need more time.

Variations

- People could draw their weather forecast instead of speaking it.
- You can use this basic idea to review your project as though you were doing a commentary on a football or cricket match, or any other event that is relevant.

Hit the headlines

The idea is for the group to produce a mock-up of the front page of a tabloid newspaper. The headlines summarise the group's thoughts and feelings about what they have been doing.

Complexity: Level 2 **Group size:** 8+ **Time:** 45 minutes

Preparation: You will need an A3 size sheet of paper and some felt-tip pens for each small group.

Instructions

1. Tell the participants to get into small groups of three or four.
2. Tell them to discuss what they have been doing and what they have got out of the project or activity, and to brainstorm the highlights and the disasters.
3. Each small group should agree together on 5 or 6 "stories". They should write a headline for each story together with a few sentences to give the flavour of the story if they wish. They should not write the whole story. A "photograph" is optional but a good idea.

- Display the pages.
- Presentation and discussion is optional.

Rucksack

This activity involves drawing and creativity.

Complexity: Level 1 **Group size:** Any **Time:** 40 minutes

Materials: Papers and coloured pens

Instructions

1. It is the end of a workshop or seminar. Ask people to draw themselves going home with a rucksack on their back. The rucksack contains all the items that they would like to carry home them.
2. They should consider everything that they have learnt and want to keep. Things may include items such as books or pictures, feelings, people, ideas, new ways of seeing the world, strengths they have gained from overcoming a difficulty, or values.
3. They can also show things lying on the ground - things that they want to leave behind. These might be things like bad habits, old ideas, difficult moments, bad food, no sleep - whatever!

References and further reading

Bond, Tim, Games for social and life skills, *Hutchinson, 1986, ISBN 0 09 162541 6*
Bradbury, Andrew, Develop your NLP skills, *Kogan Page, 1997, ISBN 0-7494-3260-8*
Brandes, Donna, Gamester's handbook *Hutchinson Education, 1982, ISBN 0-09-15900-9*
Boud, David, Cohen, Ruth, Walker, David, Using experience for learning, *The Society for Research into Higher Education and Open University Press, 1993, ISBN0-335-19095-2*
Claude, Richard Pierre, Methodologies for Human Rights Education, www. pdhre.org
Dearling, Alan, Armstrong, Howard, The Youth Games Book.*1980. The Intermediate Treatment Resource Centre. ISBN 1 85202 008 3*
Kolb, David, The Kolb learning cycle, www.css.edu/users/dswenson/web/PAGEMILL/Kolb.htm
Siniko, *Amnesty International,* www.afrika.amnesty.org
Stanford, Gene, Developing effective classroom groups, *Acora Books, Oak House, 1990.*
Transformative Mediation www.colorado.edu/conflict/transform
Johnson, Roger T., Johnson, David W., An overview of co-operative learning www.clcrc.com

Endnotes

[1] *Excerpts and figures from the "Study on the state of young people and youth policy in Europe", research carried out for the European Commission by IARD; Milan, January 2001.*
[2] *Source: Euro barometer 47.1, Young people's attitudes to the European Union, European Commission 1998.*
[3] *Final declaration of the 5th Conference of European Ministers Responsible for Youth, Bucharest, "Young people: active citizens in a future Europe", April 1998.*
[4] *"Learning, the Treasure Within" UNESCO report about education in the XXI Century, 1996*

Chapter 2

49 Practical Activities and Methods for Human Rights Education

Summary of activities

	Level	Children	Citizenship	Democracy	Discr. and Xenophobia	Education	Environment	Gender equality	General human rights	Globalisation	Health	Human security	Media	Peace and Violence	Poverty	Social rights	Sport	Page
A glossary of globalisation	3					✓				✓						✓		69
A tale of two cities	3		✓				✓									✓		71
Access to medicaments	4				✓					✓	✓							80
Act it out	2	✓	✓						✓									86
All equal – all different	2				✓				✓	✓								88
Ashique's story	3	✓								✓						✓		91
Beware, we are watching!	4		✓							✓						✓		95
Can I come in?	3				✓							✓		✓				98
Children's Rights	2	✓				✓			✓									103
Different Wages	2				✓			✓								✓		107
Do we have alternatives?	3	✓			✓									✓				111
Domestic Affairs	3							✓			✓			✓				114
"Draw-the-word" game	1		✓						✓				✓					120
Education for All?	2		✓			✓				✓								122
Electioneering	2		✓	✓					✓									127
Fighters for rights	2		✓						✓				✓					130
Front page	3						✓			✓			✓					135
Garden in a night	3		✓				✓				✓							139
Heroines and heroes	2		✓		✓			✓										142
Horoscope of poverty	3									✓					✓	✓		145
Just a minute	2								✓	✓							✓	150
Let every voice be heard	3	✓	✓			✓												153
Let's talk about sex!	4				✓			✓			✓							156
Living in a perfect world	3						✓				✓			✓				160
Makah whaling	4						✓		✓	✓								166
Making links	4		✓	✓					✓									173
Money to spend	2								✓			✓		✓				177
Our futures	2	✓					✓		✓									182
Path to Equality-land	3				✓	✓		✓										185
Picture games	1				✓				✓				✓					188
Play the game!	3								✓					✓			✓	194
Power Station	2		✓						✓					✓				198
Responding to racism	3				✓	✓			✓									201
Rights Bingo!	1	✓							✓			✓						206
See the ability!	3				✓											✓	✓	209
Sport for all	2				✓						✓						✓	214
Take a step forward	2				✓				✓						✓			217
The impact of the Internet	4								✓	✓			✓					222
The language barrier	2				✓	✓						✓						228
The Scramble for Wealth and Power	3									✓		✓			✓			231
The web of life	2						✓		✓	✓								235
To vote, or not to vote?	4		✓	✓					✓									238
Trade Union meeting	3		✓	✓												✓		244
Violence in my life	3								✓			✓		✓				248
When tomorrow comes	3											✓	✓	✓				250
Where do you stand?	2		✓						✓						✓			254
Who are I?	2		✓		✓			✓										257
Work and babies	2				✓			✓								✓		260
A Human Rights Calendar																		263

A glossary of globalisation

.... A smaller world – The Internet - IMF - Trade - Violent demonstrations.... What comes into your head when people use the word "Globalisation"?

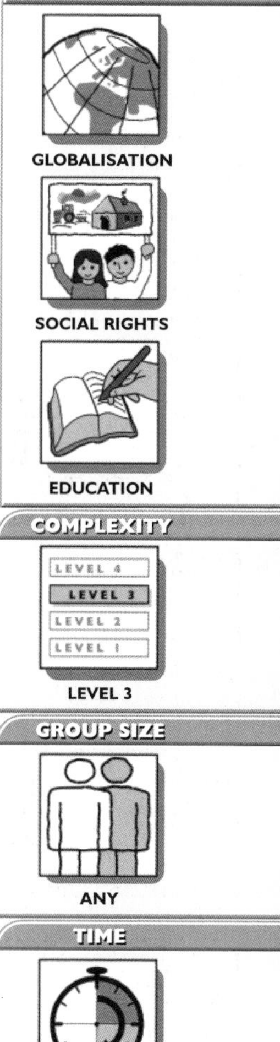

Themes Globalisation, Social rights, Education

Complexity Level 3

Group size Any

Time 90 minutes

Overview This is an information-seeking activity involving critical thinking about the manifestations, causes and consequences of globalisation.

Related rights
- The right to work
- The right to a standard of living adequate for health and well-being
- The right to education

Objectives
- To gain knowledge and understanding of the manifestations, causes and consequences of globalisation

Materials
- Dictionaries (at least 4)
- Paper, A3 and A4 size
- Tape and scissors
- Pens and markers of different colours
- Miscellaneous printed material, magazines, leaflets, for collage
- Access to sources of information (library, the Internet)
- Photocopier (optional)
- Hole punch, string, stapler for binding pages

Preparation
- Gather together as much information on globalisation as possible. If necessary, use the links and references mentioned in the background information on globalisation on page 358.
- Gather together newspapers, magazines, leaflets, brochures, calendars and postcards that may be cut up for illustrations.

Instructions

1. Explain that the aim of this activity is to create a glossary or resource-file of terms, facts and personalities associated with globalisation.
2. To warm up, do a round of the "word association" game. Ask people to say the first word that comes into their head when they think of the word "Globalisation".
3. Then do another brainstorm of possible things to put in the glossary. For example,
   - definitions of words and terms and common abbreviations such as ATTAC, IMF, CCC
   - the main globalisation issues
   - people/personalities linked to globalisation and/or the anti-globalisation movements
   - names, dates and places of events, meetings, rallies, conferences, etc.
   - transnational companies and international organisations concerned

Key date

8 September
International Literacy Day

   - illustrations - pictures and cartoons
   - quotes
4. Show people the resource materials and emphasise that they should feel free to go through the available literature and be creative. They have total liberty to design the layout as they wish. It could be in the form of a poster or booklet - anything!
5. Divide participants into small groups of three or four people to work on their glossaries.
6. When they have finished, ask each group to present its work in plenary.

Debriefing and evaluation

Start with a short review of how the activity went. Did people enjoy it? Then continue with a discussion about what people learnt.

- What was the most surprising piece of information people found? Why?
- Was all the information people found consistent? Were there contradictions or errors?
- What are the pros and cons of globalisation?
- Should/Can globalisation be avoided?
- What are the consequences of globalisation?
- Do you see any effects of globalisation in your daily lives? For good or for bad?
- How can globalisation promote human rights?
- What role can youth organisations play in a global world?

Conclude the session by referring back to the initial brainstorm, and ask the group to add the new words and concepts that they have learnt during the activity.

Tips for facilitators

It is important to provide a wide range of literature so that participants can find as much information as possible. For example, information can come from magazines and newspapers articles, Internet sources, radio, video, posters, leaflets, brochures and music.

You should not be overly concerned with the quality of the presentation of the final document. The focus of the activity should be on the interaction between the participants and the learning process of searching for, and critically analysing information. When you explain the activity, emphasise that the participants should explain the concepts as clearly and concisely as they can.

Suggestions for follow-up

If people would like to find out more about globalisation and how the Internet is used to promote human rights they could do the activity "Impact of the Internet", on page 222.

ATTAC *stands for 'Association for the Taxation of financial Transactions for the Aid of Citizens',*
IMF *stands for the International Monetary Fund*
CCC *stands for the Clean Clothes Campaign.*

Ideas for action

In a school, the class could combine their efforts and make one glossary to be kept in the school library and available to everyone as a resource. A youth group could combine their information and make a group poster.

A tale of two cities

Have you heard of Legoland? The town in Denmark made from little plastic bricks? Now's your chance to visit Equaland and Egoland!

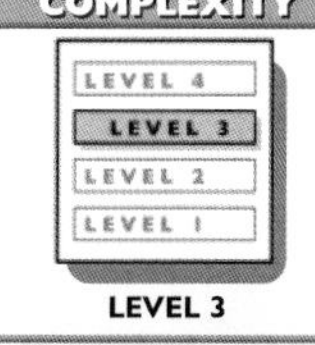

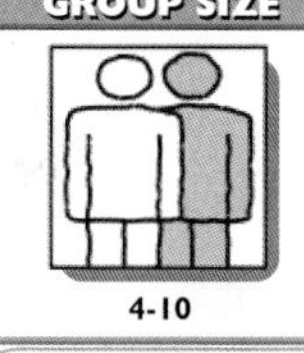

Themes Social rights, Citizenship, Environment

Complexity Level 3

Group size 4-10

Time 90 minutes

Overview This is a board game in which players vote for the kind of city they wish to live in and the amenities they wish to enjoy. The issues addressed include:
- Social solidarity
- The implications of paying taxes
- The value of local democracy

Related rights
- The right to social security
- The right to property
- The right to a healthy environment

Objectives
- To develop responsibility to the community
- To understand the importance of social welfare to community life
- To promote values of solidarity and responsibility

Materials
- 1 copy of the board game
- A3 size card or paper (optional but preferable)
- 1 die
- Paper clips of two colours (e.g. red and blue). Equal numbers of each colour. Enough clips for one per player.
- Scissors
- Removable sticky gum or "Blu-tac"
- 4 copies of replacement cards
- 2 envelopes
- Money (6 000 Ems per player) - Can be found on page 265.
- 2 copies of the City Banker's task sheet
- 1 copy of the Game Banker's task sheet
- Paper and pens
- Timer
- Overhead projector and a copy of the rules on an overhead transparency (optional)

Preparation
- Read the instructions to familiarise yourself with the board, the replacement cards and the rules.
- Take two of the sheets of replacement cards and cut them out. So the sets don't get muddled up, put each set in a different envelope clearly marked A or B! (The remaining 2 copies of the sheets will be used for reference at the city council meetings)

- Glue the photocopy of the board onto the card or stiff paper to make it strong and durable.
- Choose three people to take the special roles of bankers. Each city needs a banker and you need one Game Banker. Give the two City Bankers a copy each of the City Banker's task sheet and give the Game Banker their task sheet. Get the bankers to make labels so that they can be identified easily during the game.
- Divide the rest of the group equally into two groups. Give one group red paperclips and the other group blue ones.
- Tell each player to make their own counter by writing their name on a small piece of paper and clipping it in a paperclip of their designated colour.
- Print the money! Copy the money on page 265 and cut it up to make the bank notes. You will need one set of money for each player/citizen.

Instructions

1. Explain that this activity is a board game and show them the board. Trace out the path representing city A, and then the path representing city B. Note where the two paths cross and the squares where people collect their salary, pay their taxes and get a "chance to change", meaning a chance to move into and to play in the other city.
2. Explain how to play (see the handout below). Make sure everyone understands the rules. Decide when the game is going to end.
3. Get the bankers to make themselves simple identification labels so the players know to whom to pay their taxes!
4. Play the game! When finished, move on to the debriefing and evaluation.

Debriefing and evaluation

Start by reviewing how the game itself went and then go on to discuss what people learnt.

- Did the participants enjoy the game? What did they like and what did they dislike about it?
- In the beginning, did people think it unfair that some players had to pay more taxes than the others? Did they still feel this way after playing for a while?
- How did the City Council meetings go? How were decisions made? Democratically?
- How did people who disagreed with the city council decisions feel about it?
- Who moved from one city to the other? Why did they do it?
- Did anyone at a council meeting give money out of their own pocket to contribute to the social well-being of the community? Why did they do it?
- At the beginning of the game the social conditions in cities A and B were the same. How did they end up? Were there any differences? What were they?
- Which city would you prefer to live in? Why?
- Is it worth paying higher taxes in order to have a better community life for all? Or would you prefer to keep all your salary and buy things you need and want?
- What was the situation with respect to the two cities at the end of the game? Were they in the land of equality, that is in Equaland, or in the land where people were selfish and egoistic, that is in Egoland?

- On a scale of 1 to 10 (1 being extreme Egoland and 10 being an extreme Equaland), how would you rate your own society?

Tips for Facilitators

The game is fairly easy for anyone familiar with playing board games, but take care to explain the rules of the game and how to play. It may help the players if you write the rules on a flip chart or use an overhead transparency or hand out copies of the rules of the game.

The game works best with a maximum of 10 people playing as citizens, and there should be an equal number of citizens in each city at the start of the game. If you have say 16 participants, you could get the bankers to work in pairs. If you work with a larger group it is best to run two games. In this case, don't forget to multiply all the materials by two, and be sure to have a co-facilitator to be responsible for the second game!

A good piece of advice: before you try the game with your group, play it with friends and neighbours! You will then feel more secure about giving the instructions and getting it to run smoothly.

Note: The people responsible for collecting the taxes and managing the cities' funds have been called "bankers". In reality a banker does not perform these functions. The term is used because it is the word used in many popular board games. If you feel that the term "banker" is not the most appropriate, choose another instead, for instance, "finance administrator".

Suggestions for follow-up

Why not encourage people to explore their ideas about what the Equaland of their futures might be like? See the activity "Our futures", on page 182.

The rules of the game

Number of Players: Between 7 and 13. Three people take the roles of bankers. At the start of the game there should be an equal number of players in each city.
Objective of the game: The winner is the player who has the most money at the end of the game.

How to play

1. Have three people take the roles of bankers: one banker for city A, one for city B and one Game Banker.
2. Half of the players have red counters and half have blue counters.
3. At the start, players are divided into two equal groups. Each group has equal numbers of "red" and "blue" players. One group will travel round the path in city A, the other group will travel round the path in city B.
4. All players start from the "start and salary" square.
5. During the game a player can only change city if he/she stops in the "chance to change" square.
6. Every player starts with a salary according to their colour:
   - Blue players: 500
   - Red players: 100

Key dates

1st Monday in October
World Habitat Day - "Cities Without Slums"

7. Throw the die to decide who starts. Highest throw starts, then each player in turn, anticlockwise round the circle.
8. On their turn, each player throws the dice and moves forward the indicated number of squares along the path in their own city. When a player lands on a square, s/he reads the instruction out aloud, and complies with the instruction.
9. Note: a player who follows an instruction to move backwards stops when they have reached the target square. They do not comply with the instruction on this second square.
10. If a payment is due and the player does not have enough money to pay, s/he stays on the square and becomes a beggar.
11. Two or more players may occupy the same square at the same time.

Special Squares

Tax Contribution

Each time a player passes the "tax payment" square, s/he has to pay tax. (Players pay as they pass over the square, even if they do not land on it). The amount of tax to be paid depends on the player's salary and on the city.

City A	40% if salary of 500 or more
	10% if salary is 100 or less
City B	10% irrespective of salary

Note: An unemployed person with no unemployment benefit pays no taxes.

An unemployed person who receives benefit pays 10% of the unemployment benefit, irrespective of the city.

The tax payment is paid to the City Banker of the respective city. (Players in *Equaland* to Equaland's banker and players on *Egoland* to Egoland's banker).

Salary

Each time a player passes the "start and salary" square (you do not have to stop on the square, only pass it), s/he receives their respective salary from the Game Banker.

If the player is unemployed, and if the city has a social security system, they receive unemployment benefit from the City Banker.

Chance for Change

Any player who lands on the "chance for change" square may choose whether to change city or not (change from *Equaland* to *Egoland* or from *Egoland* to *Equaland*). In order to change, a player needs only to announce his/her decision to the rest of the players and the bankers. On their next turn, they move on round the path in the other city.

A player who changes city continues to receive the same salary as before, but they pay taxes according to the new city's tax scheme.

City Council Meetings

All players who are in the city attend city council meetings. The meeting is an opportunity to make changes (if any) in the city's policy.

The meeting can take place at every 5th payment of taxes. The City Bankers keep a record of how many people have passed the tax payment square in their city. When every fifth person has passed the square, s/he calls a meeting.

Players in the city can decide whether they want to hold a meeting or not.

The game stops during a city council meeting and the players of the other city have to wait until the meeting is finished before resuming the game.

Players have 5 minutes to decide the needs of the city and any changes in policy. Policy options are given on the replacement cards and the citizens can refer to a copy of the replacement cards sheet to know which policies are "on the agenda" (that is, the options they can choose).

To change a policy, players have to buy a replacement card out of the city's taxes. The cost is stated on each card. The City Council can only make changes that it can afford. The City Banker pays the amount due to the Game Banker. Citizens can decide to change as many policies as they wish, but they have to be able to afford them.

A city council that is in financial trouble can decide to "sell back" one or more replacement cards to the Game Banker. The "buy-back" price is 50% of the original cost.

Rich individuals may, if they wish, contribute to the city funds in order to buy replacement cards.

The banker uses a very small amount of the "Blu-tac" to stick the replacement card onto the board over the agreed square.

Replacement Cards

There are seventeen replacement cards that represent policies that the City Council can adopt at a council meeting. Replacement cards are purchased from the Game Banker at the cost printed on the card. Once purchased, the City Banker sticks the card(s) onto the board, over an existing square as decided by the citizens.

Any square may be "replaced". If, at the time of replacement, there is a player on that square, s/he does not comply with the new instructions. The new policy only comes in force when the next player lands on that square.

At a City Council meeting citizens/players decide the city policy and may purchase one or more replacement cards. All cards must be paid for.

Beggars

A player who has no money to pay their taxes or other payments stays on the square where they have just landed and becomes a "beggar". However, if there is a home for the homeless in the city, beggars may choose to sleep there, if they wish to, instead of on the square where they landed. Moving does not release a beggar from his/her debts.

S/he can beg for money from every player who lands on the square where s/he is sitting. It is up to each player whether or not they give money to the beggar. When the 'beggar' has enough money to pay their dues they wait for their next turn, pay their dues, throw the die and move on. Beggars throw the die every alternate time their turn comes round. It is a chance they take:

Throw a 6	Find 50 Ems in a rubbish bin.
Throw a 5	Collect 20 empty beer bottles and get 50 Ems for the deposits - if the city has a recycling centre!
Throw a 4	The next person who passes you gives you 10 Ems.
Throw a 3	You got drunk and sleep through your next turn.
Throw a 2	You sleep in the park and find a 10 Em note under the bench. If the city has renovated the park, you find 20 Ems.
Throw a 1	You get robbed. Hand the next donation you receive over to the City Banker.

A beggar's winnings are paid by the City Banker of the city in which the beggar lives.

When does the game end?

Players decide how to end the game before they start. They can choose one of the following options:

- when the first player completes 20 rounds
- after an agreed length of time, for example, 45 minutes.

Note: the game will automatically end if one city goes bankrupt.

The winner is the person with the most money at the end of the game.

Further information

European Code of Social Security

The Council of Europe's European Code of Social Security came into force in 1968. As of July 2001 it has been ratified by 18 member states. It provides a wide range of social protection including guarantees of

- Medical care, which includes general practitioner care, specialist care and emergency care
- Unemployment benefit
- Old-age benefit, and
- Disability benefit.

HANDOUTS

Replacement Cards

Renovation of the park, with swimming pool and children's play area. Cost: 200 Ems	Clean up the park. Cost: 100 Ems	Roads are good now. Totally reconstructed. Go 3 blocks forward. Cost: 400 Ems	Roads are OK, holes are patched. Good only until next City Council meeting. Cost: 200 Ems.	You lose your job! Unemployment fund pays 30% of salary. City must have a reserve of 1000 Ems.
School strike finished. Play again! Cost of increased salaries: 400 Ems.	A new theatre and cinema opened. Cost: 400 Ems.	Your father is retired but has a pension. To establish pension scheme costs 400 Ems.	You want to read and now there is a library! Have an extra throw. Cost of library: 200 Ems.	No more street kids. Orphanage constructed. Cost of orphanage: 200 Ems.
You get ill. Public hospital is fully subsidised. Pay only 10 Ems. Cost: 600 Ems.	You get ill. Public hospital not subsidised. Pay 30 Ems. Cost: 400 Ems.	Beach access free! Just enjoy! Cost for subsidising access: 100 Ems.	Transport problems eased with cycle path. Cost of cycle path: 150 Ems.	Recycling system reduces garbage collection. Go 3 blocks forward. Cost: 150 Ems for recycling system.
You have a legal problem. Get a legal-aid lawyer. Go 2 blocks forward. Cost: 200 Ems.	No more homeless in the city. A shelter has been opened. Cost of shelter: 200 Ems.			

HANDOUTS

City Bankers' task sheet

Neither city starts with any money. All revenue will come from taxes paid as players pass the tax payment square.

1. City Bankers use the tally sheet to keep a record of how many players pass the "tax payment" square and call a city council meeting as every 5th player passes.
2. City Bankers collect taxes from each player in their city as the player passes the tax payment square. Note: players who have changed city pay the new taxes.
   The tax scheme is as follows:
   City A 40% if salary of 500 or more
   10% if salary is 100 or less
   City B 10% irrespective of salary
   Unemployed citizens who receive no benefit pay no taxes
   Unemployed citizens receiving benefit pay 10% of their benefit.
3. City Bankers' other tasks:
   - look after the city's money
   - pay to the Game Banker any payments due for the purchase of replacement cards
   - stick replacement cards on the board over the square agreed by the citizens at a council meeting
   - administer the unemployment fund as and when the city decides to establish one
   - pay unemployment benefit to players who are entitled to receive it if the city has agreed to set up a social security system. There must be at least 1000 Ems in the bank at the time of setting up the system.
   - Keep an eye on the beggars in your city and ensure correct play when they chance a throw with the die:

Throw a 6	They find 50 Ems in a rubbish bin
Throw a 5	They collect 20 empty beer bottles and get 50 Ems for the deposits - if the city has a recycling centre!
Throw a 4	The next person who passes them gives them 10 Ems
Throw a 3	They get drunk and sleep through their next turn
Throw a 2	They sleep in the park and find a 10 Em note under the bench. If the city has renovated the park, they find 20 Ems.
Throw a 1	They get robbed and hand over the next donation - or any money they chance to find next throw.

Note: you hand over the money if they chance to find any in the park or in a rubbish bin, and you take money from them if they get robbed.

Record of tax payments

Each time a player in your city passes the "tax payment" square, collect their taxes and check off one segment in the first circle. When 5 players have been checked off, call the first city council. When play resumes start checking off segments in the second circle, and so on.

1st Meeting

2nd Meeting

3rd Meeting

4th Meeting

5th Meeting

6th Meeting

HANDOUTS

Game Banker's role card

At the start of the game the Game Banker has all the money. S/he is to:

1. Ensure the game runs smoothly
   - start the game
   - ensure the rules are followed
   - time all City Council meetings. They should last a maximum of 5 minutes and
   - stop the game after the agreed playing time or when the first player completes the agreed number of rounds, whichever was agreed.
2. Keep records
   - at the start of the game record the name, colour and city of each player
   - record how many times each player passes "start and salary"
3. Pay a salary to each player at the start of the game, and every subsequent time they pass the "start and salary" square. Salaries are paid according to the players' colour regardless of which city they are in:
   - Blue players: 500 Ems
   - Red players: 100 Ems
4. Collect all payments for replacement cards from the City Bankers.

Tally sheet

Record players' names with a red or blue pen according to their colour. It is recommended that you use the "five-bar gate" method of keeping the tally. Each of the first four rounds is recorded with a line IIII and on the fifth round you strike them through. The sixth round you start another set of five. In this way you can easily sum the rounds. Thus a count of twelve would look like this: ~~IIII~~ ~~IIII~~ II.

Players in city A at the start of the game	
Name of player	Times passed "start"

Players in city B at the start of the game	
Name of player	Times passed "start"

A tale of two cities

Gameboard

CITY B —>

CITY A —>

COMPASS

A Manual on Human Rights Education

		The roads are full of holes. Journeys take too long. Miss one turn.	Street kids rob you. Give 10 Ems away.	Free Space.	You get ill. No hospitals. Go back 3 squares	You win the lottery! Receive 50 Ems		
		The park is dirty and needs renovating. Miss one turn to help with the cleaning.				Nothing to do in the evening. You are bored. Go back 3 squares.		
Your father retires with no pension. Pay 20 Ems to help him.	Nothing to do in the evening. You are bored. Go back 3 squares.	**Start + Salary**	Street kids rob you. Give 10 Ems away	Free Space.	The roads are full of holes. Journeys take too long. Miss one turn	**Chance to Change!**	You get ill. No hospitals. Go back 3 squares	Free Space.
Free Space.		Free Space.				Nice day to go to the beach. Pay 10 Ems for beach access.		You lose your job! Sorry!
You are having a legal problem. Contract a private lawyer. Pay 50 Ems.		Nothing to read. Pay 10 for a book.				You lose your job! Sorry!		Nice day to go to the beach. Pay 10 Ems for beach access.
Nothing to read. Pay 10 Ems for a book.		Job Back! Same salary.				Free Space.		You win the lottery! Receive 50 Ems.
Job back! Same salary.	Garbage collectors on strike. Miss 1 turn to take your rubbish to the tip.	**Chance to Change!**	A homeless drunk is disturbing you. Miss 1 turn to sort it out.	The park is dirty and needs renovating. Miss one turn to help with the cleaning.	Bus service not working. Take a taxi. Pay 10 Ems.	**Tax payment.**	Free space.	Teachers are on strike for better salaries. Miss 1 turn to take care of your children.
		Your father retires with no pension. Pay 20 Ems to help him.				Bus service not working. Take a taxi. Pay 10 Ems.		
		A homeless drunk is disturbing you. Miss 1 turn to sort it out.	Free Space.	Garbage collectors on strike. Miss 1 turn to take your rubbish to the tip.	You are having a legal problem. Contract a private lawyer. Pay 50 Ems.	Teachers are on strike for better salaries. Miss 1 turn to take care of your children.		

City Council Meeting
Every 5th tax payment contribution

Access to medicaments

"A united global effort by concerned citizens can make a difference"
Zackie Achmat, Treatment Action Campaign.

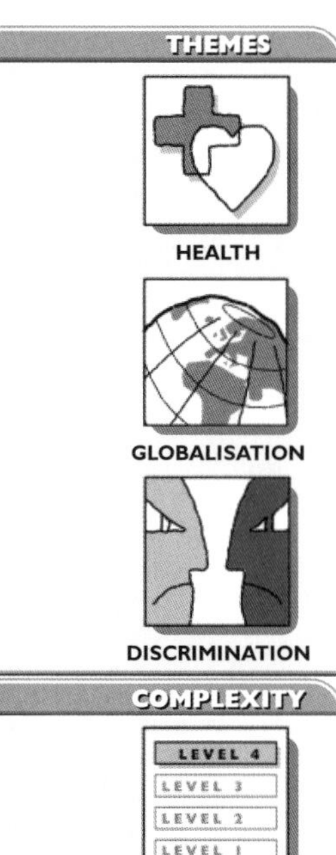

Themes Health, Globalisation, Discrimination and Xenophobia

Complexity Level 4

Group size 16 - 40

Time 190 minutes

Overview This activity is a simulation of the 2001 "AIDS drug" trial in South Africa. It addresses issues of:
- HIV/AIDS and access to medicines
- How to resolve conflicting claims to rights.

Related rights
- The rights to life and dignity
- The right to property

Objectives
- To develop an understanding of the complexity of human rights issues
- To compare different ways of decision-making (adversarial approach, consensus approach)
- To develop skills of communication and co-operation

Materials
- Flipchart paper and pens·
- Trial role cards
- Instructions for small group work, one per participant
- Small cards (10 cms by 6 cms). One red and one green card per participant
- Space for plenary and small group work

Preparation For part 1:
- Make copies of the trial role cards; you need one role card per person

For part 2:
- Make copies of the instructions for small group work, one per participant
- Make one red and one green card per participant.

Instructions

This activity is in two parts. Part 1 is a simulation of the trial and part 2 is a consensus-building phase.

Part 1. The trial (total time 65 minutes)

1. Set the scene. HIV/AIDS is a very serious epidemic throughout the world, but especially serious in Africa. It is a big issue in South Africa where millions of poor people are suffering and dying unnecessarily because they cannot afford the expensive drugs they need. Their only alternative is to use cheaper copies of the drugs. The leading pharmaceutical companies are against this. They wish to protect their property rights and so they have joined forces to prevent any State from

copying and selling their products at cheaper prices. They have started legal action against the South African Government, which is distributing and selling cheaper copies of the anti-HIV/AIDS drugs.

2. Explain that participants will be involved in simulating a trial that recently took place in South Africa over this issue. The question is: Is the right to property a valid argument to jeopardise the right to life and dignity of a group of people?
3. Divide the participants into four equal groups to represent Pharma Inc., the South African Government, members of the Treatment Action Campaign (TAC) and Judges.
4. Distribute the trial role cards to the appropriate groups.
5. Give the groups 25 minutes to read their role cards and prepare their cases and/or questions for the trial. Each group must also select a spokesperson to represent the group and one or two resource persons to back the spokesperson up and help answer questions during the trial.
6. Once each group is ready, invite people to come back into plenary. They should remain in their four groups.
7. Now Pharma Inc., the S.A. Government and TAC each have 5 minutes to present their positions and raise any questions. The judges should introduce the groups in turn.
8. The judges themselves now have 10 minutes to answer any questions raised by the groups, and to summarise the different arguments and positions.

Part 2. Consensus-building phase (total time 100 minutes)

1. Ask participants to divide themselves into small groups, each of 4 people. In each group there should be one former member of Pharma Inc., one former member of the S.A. Government, one former TAC group member and one former judge.
2. Hand out the copies of the instructions for small groups. Check that people understand what they have to do and how to use the red and green cards. The groups have 30 minutes to try to reach a consensus decision about how to resolve the conflicting claims.
3. Call everyone back into plenary and ask them to report back on the results of their discussions. Give each group 5 minutes to present their report. Note the main solutions and issues on a flipchart.
4. When all groups have reported their positions/solutions, move on to a discussion about the decision-making process. You could ask:
   - How easy was it to reach a consensus?
   - What are the strengths and weaknesses of this approach?
   - Was there a tension between trying to agree a solution and trying to include all members of the group in the decision?
   - Which were the most burning issues?
5. You may like to end this phase of the activity by reading out the following extract from the court's ruling on 19 April, 2001. "The purpose (...) to promote cheaper access to drugs (...) is a commendable purpose, and, in the context of the HIV/AIDS epidemic, a constitutional obligation of the highest order linked to the duty of the State to respect, protect, promote and fulfil a number of fundamental rights including the rights to human dignity and life (held to be the source of all other rights) (...) There is no merit to the (...) challenges to the Act made by the applicants (i.e. pharmaceutical companies)."

Key date

1 December
World AIDS Day

Debriefing and evaluation

The evaluation will already have started during the discussions in part 2. Now continue by encouraging the participants to reflect on the overall process and then go on to identify the key human rights issues behind the trial. Key questions may include:

- Had participants heard about this case before?
- What were their initial assumptions?
- Did these assumptions change during the activity?
- How do people compare the two forms of decision-making process, the adversarial and the consensus? Which produces the most satisfactory results? How do you define what is a successful result?
- What were the key human rights issues behind the trial?
- How do these issues relate to the participants' own social reality?
- What are the implications for people where you live?

Tips for facilitators

You need a long time for this activity because the issues are complex and participants need to think deeply about them. You should note that the two parts do not need to be run on the same day; they can be done in two different sessions.

The purpose of using the red and green cards is to help people be more aware of what helps and what hinders decision-making. Ideally, at the end of the discussions and negotiations in part 2, all participants will show green cards and be able to agree a shared solution.

In part 2, some groups may reach a consensus, others may not. In the discussion, you should use the opportunity to explore the strengths and weaknesses of a consensus approach to decision-making. Ask those groups that did reach a consensus to report not only their final position but also the main arguments behind it. Ask those groups that did not reach a consensus to outline what brought them closer, and what contributed to the divisions between them. Note: you will find more information on consensus-building in chapter 1 on page 59.

It is important to check the actual situation of people in the local community who live with HIV/AIDS, and to adapt/link the activity to issues that concern them.

Note: The name of the coalition of pharmaceutical companies, Pharma Inc. is made up for the purposes of this activity.

Suggestions for follow-up

Discuss aspects of the right to life and to human dignity in your country in relation to health issues.

Inform yourselves about health and human rights issues globally. Visit web sites of, or obtain publications from key NGOs (MSF, TAC, Christian Aid) and international institutions (WHO). Find out about actions that are being taken to promote health issues and list them on a flipchart.

The TAC ran a very successful campaign. Unfortunately not all campaigns achieve their goals. There may be many reasons for this, but one may be poor organisation and ineffective publicity. The group can explore these issues and develop their skills for effective campaigning through the activity "Beware, we are watching", on page 95.

Ideas for action

Find out who is promoting actions on health issues in your locality and how you can contribute.

Further information

This activity is based on a case which came before the South African high court in 2001. The Pharmaceutical Manufacturers' Association of South Africa prosecuted the president of the Republic of South Africa and others, including the Treatment Action Campaign (TAC), for disregarding their patents on HIV medicines and for importing cheaper, generic drugs to treat the millions of citizens suffering from AIDS.

The judges had to balance the different interests and rights of the two sides. On the one hand the Pharmaceutical Manufacturers' Association claimed the right to property, equality or free choice of trade, occupation and profession while, on the other hand, the government and TAC claimed that it was the duty of the state to respect, protect, promote and fulfil the fundamental rights of human dignity and lives of its citizens.

In a historic judgement the court concluded that the right to property was of a lower order than the right to human dignity and life and should therefore be limited. Subsequently the drug manufacturers dropped their case. This was widely hailed as "a real triumph of David over Goliath, not only for us here in South Africa, but for people in many other developing countries who are struggling for access to healthcare" (NGO joint press release, 19 April 2001). "This is a rare and very meaningful victory of the poor over powerful multinational companies! But our challenge now is to work together with drug producers and government to get medicines to those who need them" (Kevin Watkins of Oxfam).

AIDS and globalisation trends

In rich countries, people living with HIV/AIDS can live better and longer because of antiretroviral drugs, which are provided by states for free. In Southern countries, people affected by HIV suffer more and die earlier because they have no access to HIV treatments. On average the annual per-capita expense of their health care is around10$, whereas the triple therapy, available to people in Northern countries, costs between 10.000$ to 15.000$ a year.

Poverty, lack of education and social inequality speed up the spread of the epidemic, but the challenge is above all political, involving governments, international bodies and pharmaceutical companies. In order to be effective, the fight against AIDS needs to challenge key international mechanisms and institutions. Foremost of these are the International Monetary Fund (IMF), the World Trade Organisation (WTO), TRIPS (Trade Related aspects on Intellectual Property rights), GATS (General Agreement on Trade and Services) and the Dispute Settlement Body, which actually functions as the tribunal of the WTO.

HANDOUTS

Trial role cards

Trial role card: Pharma Inc.

You are a group of senior Pharma Inc. executives. Your company is one of the world's leading producers of pharmaceuticals. You have bought the rights for the commercialisation of key HIV- and AIDS-related medicines. You need to maintain your profit margin and to please your shareholders. Thus you wish to protect the company's right to set the selling price of your products, keeping in mind the research costs, production costs, and the wages of your work-force. To allow another company to simply copy and sell your products at a lower price would jeopardise your profit and the sustainability of your company. You have therefore joined forces with other leading pharmaceutical companies to prevent any State from allowing the copying and selling of your products at cheaper prices, and to sue them if necessary. You have started legal action against the South African Government.

You should prepare your arguments to defend your position. You will have five minutes to present them during the trial.

Trial role card: South African Government

You are senior officials in the South African Government. Your government is trying to respond to the request of the pharmaceutical companies who have started legal action against you. Pharma Inc. is trying to prevent any State from allowing the copying and selling of their products at cheaper prices, that is, below the retail price of their own products. In principle you agree with Pharma Inc's. position.

However, popular movements, led by the Treatment Action Campaign (TAC), claim that it is a constitutional obligation by the State to provide cheap access to drugs, particularly in the context of the HIV/AIDS epidemic. You have responded to popular political pressure and have started to allow the import of cheaper (copied) drugs from countries such as Indonesia.

You should prepare your arguments to defend your position. You will have five minutes to present them during the trial.

Trial role card: Treatment Action Campaign (TAC)

You are a group of activists representing the Treatment Action Campaign (TAC), South Africa. The Campaign claims that the State has the responsibility to provide cheap access to drugs, particularly in the context of the HIV/AIDS epidemic. The government has responded and has started importing cheaper drugs.

You also claim that it is the responsibility of the State to make financial provisions for patients and organisations struggling with HIV/AIDS diseases.

However, the South African Government has been brought to trial by pharmaceutical companies to prevent any copying and selling of their products at cheaper prices. Therefore, you have decided to join forces with the government to defend the role of the State in providing cheap access to drugs.

You should prepare your arguments to defend your position. You will have five minutes to present them during the trial.

HANDOUTS

Trial role card: Judges

You are the group of judges who are presiding over the attempt by leading pharmaceutical companies to prosecute the South African Government and to prevent it from allowing the copying and selling of their products at cheaper prices. Activists representing the Treatment Action Campaign (TAC) are defending the government position.

Your role is to invite the three parties in turn to present their respective positions. At the end of the presentations you should not make a judgement or come to conclusions. Your job is to help to clarify issues and to summarise the arguments in support of the conflicting claims.

The core of the problem is how to resolve conflicting claims to human rights. The defence (the government and TAC) claim the rights to life and dignity, and the prosecution (Pharma Inc.) claim the right to property. The official court records put it like this:

"The *rights to life and dignity* are the most important of all human rights, and the source of all other personal rights.By committing ourselves to a society founded on the recognition of human rights, we are required to value these two rights above all others. And this must be demonstrated by the State in everything that it does, including the way it punishes criminals."

Versus

"The *right to property* is protected by section 25 of the South African Constitution which states the following: "Property 25 (1): No one may be deprived of property except in terms of law of general application, and no law may permit arbitrary deprivation of property".

You should prepare questions to the three parties. You will have ten minutes to ask your questions and listen to the answers.

Instructions to the small groups for part 2

You are a group of four people, each one a representative of one of the four parties:

- Pharma Inc.
- the South African Government
- activists representing the Treatment Action Campaign (TAC)
- the group of the Judges in the cause initiated by the leading pharmaceutical companies.

Instructions

1. In turn, each person should identify themselves and the party they represent, that is, the role they are playing.
2. Next, each person should indicate their feelings about the situation at the end of the trial. If they think that it will be easy to find a solution, they should show a green card, and if they think it will be difficult they should show a red card.
3. Now your task is to try to come to a satisfactory decision, based on consensus among the four members. You should take the discussion in rounds. The judge chairs the discussion and presents his/her position last.
    - Round one: state your position
    - Round two: present your ideas for solution
    - Round three: negotiate different solutions
4. Listen carefully to each other. At the end of each contribution you should show your colour card to indicate how you now feel about the prospects for reaching a satisfactory solution.
5. At the end of the consensus process, choose one person to report the results back in plenary.

THEMES

GEN. HUMAN RIGHTS

CHILDREN

CITIZENSHIP

COMPLEXITY

LEVEL 2

GROUP SIZE

9 OR MORE

TIME

90 MINUTES

Act it out

Show me what you mean by "human rights"

Themes	General human rights, Children, Citizenship
Complexity	Level 2
Group size	9+
Time	90 minutes
Overview	This is a drama activity that encourages people to: ▪ Review their general perceptions of human rights ▪ Find different ways of representing these perceptions
Related rights	All
Objectives	▪ To review what participants know about human rights ▪ To develop intercultural and communication skills ▪ To develop co-operation and creativity
Materials	▪ Props: dressing-up clothes, toys, household items, etc. ▪ Paper and coloured markers, crayons ▪ Glue, string and card

Instructions

1. Explain that the purpose of the exercise is to come up with a dramatic representation of the general idea or concept of human rights that is understandable to people of different cultures, and who may speak different languages.
2. Explain that they will not be allowed to use words at all: this must be a mimed presentation. However, groups may make use of some of the materials or props, if they wish.
3. Ask people to get into small groups of between 4 and 6 people, and give each group a large sheet of paper and a set of crayons / markers.
4. Give the groups 10 minutes first to brainstorm all their ideas about human rights and then to identify two or three key ideas that they would like bring out most strongly in the mime.
5. Now give the groups 30 minutes to design and rehearse their mime. Explain that this must be a group effort and everyone should have a role in the production.
6. After 30 minutes are up, gather the groups together so that everyone can watch each other's performances.
7. Give a few minutes after each performance for feedback and discussion.
8. Ask the spectators to offer their interpretations of what they have just seen, and to try to identify the key ideas that the performance attempted to portray.
9. Then give the group itself a chance to explain briefly any points that did not emerge during the feedback. Repeat this for each of the performances.

Debriefing and evaluation

Now review the activity itself.

- How did people feel about this activity? Was it more or less difficult than they had first imagined? What were the most difficult aspects, or the most difficult things to represent?
- Did people learn anything new about human rights?
- Where were the similarities or differences among the groups? Were there any fundamental disagreements over the idea of human rights? Why?

Tips for facilitators

Unless people are entirely ignorant about the concept of human rights, it is more interesting to carry out this activity with a minimum of initial guidance from a facilitator. The main purpose is to draw out the impressions and knowledge about human rights that young people have already picked up in the course of their lives. It is worth emphasising this point to the group before they begin work, so that they do not feel constrained by not "knowing" exactly what human rights are.

Make it clear to them that their task is to portray "human rights in general", rather than to illustrate one or more specific human rights. They may decide to take one specific right to bring out general points, but they should remember that they are attempting to show what is common to the different human rights. At the end of the session spectators should be able to (or begin to!) answer the question, "what are human rights?"

Do not let those who feel they are weak at acting fail to play an active part! Explain that there are plenty of roles for all, and that this must be something that the whole group feels happy about presenting. A few unusual props may bring the performances to life and help spark creative ideas – anything from saucepans, toy cars, hats, pillows, stones, a dustbin lid...

Variations

You may want to carry this activity out as a drawing exercise: get the groups to present a poster – again without using words – to express the main ideas about human rights.

The activity could also be carried out less as an introductory one, and more in order to organise and clarify thoughts once people have already worked through some of the other activities in the manual, or carried out their own research.

Suggestions for follow-up

Look at plays or other pieces of literature with a human rights theme, and organise a dramatic performance for members of your local community.

If the group would like to move on and look at some specific human rights, why not look at the Convention of the Rights of the Child through the activity "Children's Rights", on page 103.

Ideas for action

You could develop your mimes or make a whole group production and perform it to other people outside the group. If you do the poster-making variation, make an exhibition of your posters. Both ideas could be used to celebrate Human Rights Day.

Key date

10 December
Human Rights Day

All equal – all different

"All human beings are universally equal and specifically different. Universal equality and specific differences must be respected" *

THEMES

DISCRIMINATION

GEN. HUMAN RIGHTS

GLOBALISATION

COMPLEXITY

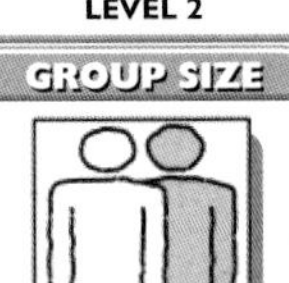

LEVEL 2

GROUP SIZE

6-60

TIME

40 MINUTES

Themes Discrimination and Xenophobia, General human rights, Globalisation

Complexity Level 2

Group size 6 – 60

Time 40 minutes

Overview This is a sort of quiz - short and provocative enough to be interesting in itself but also the basis for a great group discussion!

Related rights
- Equality in dignity
- The right to rights and freedoms without distinction of any kind, such as race, colour, religion, etc.
- The right to a nationality

Objectives
- To address the universality of human rights
- To make participants aware of ethnocentrism and prejudice in themselves and others
- To develop the ability to read information critically and independently

Materials
- Handout
- Large sheet of paper (A3) or flipchart paper and markers (optional)

Preparation Copy the handout, one per participant. Alternatively, write it on a blackboard or use an overhead projector (make sure everyone can see it).

Instructions

1. Tell the participants that the following activity is a sort of quiz, but that the purpose is not to see who has got it right and who has got it wrong; it is just a starting point.
2. Hand out or display the two quotations. Allow five minutes for the participants to read them.
3. Then ask them individually to decide:
   a) the source of the first text; which book or document is it an extract from?
   b) which country/region of the world the author of the second text comes from.
4. When everyone is ready, ask participants to get into small groups of about three people. Give them 20 minutes to discuss and analyse their individual choices. They should think about the following questions and if possible come up with a collective answer:
   - Why did they choose one answer in preference to others?
   - What do the texts say about the authors?
   - What do they think about the texts?
5. When the groups have finished, come into plenary and do a round collecting the answers to question a) from each group. Invite the groups to state the reasons that led them to their choices. Then repeat the round collecting answers to question b).

6. Reveal the author, Said al-Andalusi from Spain, and proceed to the debriefing and evaluation.

Debriefing and evaluation

Start with a brief review of the activity and then, if you feel the group is ready for it, go on to introduce the notions of prejudice and ethnocentrism. Address the following questions (either in plenary or you can have smaller groups if needed):

- Were participants surprised by the solution?
- How did people make their original individual choices? Were they based on guesswork? Intuition? Or real knowledge?
- Did people change their minds about their choices during the discussions in small groups? What made them change their minds? Peer pressure? Good arguments?
- How did people defend their choices in the small group discussions? Did they stick to their choices tentatively or strongly?
- Why did the author describe people from the North the way he did?
- What clues does the second text give us about the author, about his looks and about his culture?
- To what extent is the author's view the result of his own ethnocentric viewpoint and prejudice? Or is it fair to say that at that time the cultures in northern Europe were less "civilised" than his culture?
- Can participants think of examples when they heard of or read about other people being addressed in similar ways? How would it feel to be considered as some kind of inferior people?
- When people are not valued for what they are, what consequences often occur? Can they think of examples from history? And from the present?
- What should we do to counter the effects of prejudice? Are there people or groups in the participants' areas or countries that are also the subject of prejudice? Which ones?

Tips for facilitators

The extracts were taken from a book by a famous scholar from Cordoba, Andalusia (in what is now Spain) who was born in 1029 AD / 420 AH. Said al-Andalusi was a scholar well known for his wisdom and knowledge. For him, civilisation and science were very close to knowing the Holy Koran. He was not only learned in religion, but he also excelled in Arabic literature, medicine, mathematics, astronomy and other sciences.

It should be remembered that at this time, the Mediterranean basin, and especially the Arab Kingdoms around it, constituted the centre of 'civilisation'. Knowledge was not nearly as advanced in "the North", as Said calls northern Europe, as it was in the Arab world, Persia, China and India.

Be aware that, depending on the group, you may need to give participants insights into how to read texts more critically. You may have to point out that the second text actually reveals a lot about the author, his appearance and his culture, for example, that he must have had curly hair and dark skin. Critical reading involves not only understanding the content of the text, but also thinking about the context, who the author is and why s/he writes what s/he does. Realising this is an important step to understanding how to read all messages (history, news, poems, song texts, etc) and to be aware of the values that they transmit.

Key dates

21 June
World Peace and Prayer Day

One way of introducing the issue of ethnocentrism is to point out to participants that the author - used to people with dark skin and curly hair - provides a very good definition a "contrario" of what he considers "normal". It is also important that, through the discussion, you help participants understand that cultural differences do not make people "better" or "worse" than others. You should point out that it is hard not to judge others without prejudice because we take our own cultural perspective as being "the norm". To appreciate this - our own ethnocentrism - is an essential step towards recognising it in others, and to being able to communicate successfully with people of other cultures.

Leave extra time at the end of the activity so you have the flexibility to discuss further the issues and ideas which were raised. For example, you may wish to go into an analysis of, or discussion about, history teaching and how much (or how little) we in Europe actually learn about other cultures.

Note: the excerpts are taken from the "Book of the Categories of Nations – Science in the Medieval World", by Said al-Andalusi, translated by Sema'an I. Salem and Alok Kumar, University of Texas Press, Austin, 1991.

Suggestions for follow-up

If you wish to go further with ideas about the universality of human rights, you could use the activity "Act it out", on page 86, which involves creativity and drama.

HANDOUT

All equal – all different quiz

1. What is the source of the following text? What book or document is it an extract from?
"All people on earth from the East to the West, from the North and from the South, constitute a single group; (they) differ in three distinct traits: behaviour, physical appearance and language."

Choose one of the following answers:

❑The UNESCO declaration on racism, 1958 ❑Herodotus "History", 440 BC ❑The Vedas, India, c.a. 1.000 BC
❑Report of the "All different - all equal" youth campaign, Council of Europe, 1996 ❑Said Al-Andalusi, 1029 AD / 420 AH
❑None of the above

2. Which country/region of the world does the author of this text comes from?
"Those who live in the extreme North (of Europe...) have suffered from being too far from the sun. Their air is cold and their skies are cloudy. As a result, their temperament is cool and their behaviour is rude. Consequently, their bodies have become enormous, their colour turned white, and their hair drooped down. They have lost keenness of understanding and sharpness of perception. They have been overcome by ignorance and laziness, and infested by fatigue and stupidity."

Choose one of the following answers:

❑China ❑Europe ❑India ❑Africa ❑Persia ❑None of the above

---

* *Article 1 of the Declaration of Rights and Duties of Human Beings as Proposed by Young People. The declaration was created by 500 young people from 80 different nationalities at the Palace of Europe in Strasbourg, under the initiative of Les Humains Associés and the Association for the Declaration of 26 August 1989 (AD 89).* www.humains-associes.org

Ashique's story

Child labour creates necessary income for families and communities. Take it away and it is the children who will suffer most. Is it so?

Themes Children, Social rights, Globalisation

Complexity Level 3

Group size 5+

Time 90 minutes

Overview This activity uses small group discussions to explore the issues of:
- The reality of child labour
- The causes of child labour and how to end it

Related rights
- The right to protection against harmful forms of work and exploitation
- The right to education
- The right to play and recreation

Objectives
- To increase knowledge about the reality of child labour
- To develop critical thinking about the complexity of the problem
- To encourage the values of justice and the feeling of responsibility for finding solutions

Materials
- Copies of the facts of Ashique's life; one copy per participant
- Pens and markers
- Flipchart paper or large sheets of paper (A3)

Preparation
- Copy the design for the "ideas for solutions" sheet onto large, A3-size sheets of paper or flipchart paper: one per small group, plus one for the plenary
- Gather some of the further information below to use to introduce the activity

THEMES

CHILDREN

SOCIAL RIGHTS

GLOBALISATION

COMPLEXITY

LEVEL 3

GROUP SIZE

5 OR MORE

TIME

90 MINUTES

Instructions

1. Tell the participants that the activity is based on a case study of Ashique, a child worker in Pakistan. The aim is to try to find possible ways of changing Ashique's situation.
2. To warm up, do a round of "composed story-telling". Make up an imaginary and imaginative story about a day in Ashique's life. Go round the circle asking each person in turn to add a sentence.
3. Divide the participants into small groups with a maximum of 5 people per group. Give everyone a copy of Ashique's life facts. Allow 5 minutes for reading and sharing comments.
4. Give each group a copy of the "ideas for solutions" sheet. Explain that their task is to brainstorm solutions to the problems faced by Ashique and other child labourers. They must write down in the appropriate columns the possible steps that can be taken to

solve the problem "by tomorrow", "by next month" and "in the future". They have 30 minutes to complete this task and to nominate a spokesperson to report back.

5. In plenary, take it in rounds to get feedback on each column in turn. Summarise the ideas on the flip chart. Allow discussion on the ideas if desired, but be aware of time constraints!
6. When the table is complete, move on to a fuller discussion and debriefing.

Debriefing and evaluation

The depth of the discussion will depend on the participants' general knowledge but try to cover questions both about their views on child labour as well as on the possible solutions.

- How much did people already know about the existence of child labour before doing this activity? How do they know? Where did they get the information from?
- Is there child labour in their country/town? What work do children do and why do they work?
- Should children work? Should they be able to choose whether to work or not?
- "Child labour creates necessary income for families and communities. Take it away and it is the children who will suffer most." How do you answer this?
- In what ways do we, as consumers, benefit from child labour?
- How difficult was it to think of possible steps to solve child labour? Which of the three columns - " by tomorrow", "by next month" and " in the future" - was the most difficult to fill in? Why?
- There have been many national and international declarations and conferences about the issue of child labour. Why is it still such a large-scale problem in the world?
- Who should be responsible for the solving the problem? (Take a different colour pen and write the suggestion on the chart.)
- Can ordinary people like you and me help solve this problem? How and when?

Tips for facilitators

If participants know very little about child labour, you may want to start the activity by giving them a few facts about child labour and its consequences. A fun way to do this might be to take the statistics below and turn them into a short quiz.

It may be difficult for groups to find ideas for the first two columns (tomorrow and next month) which might create a feeling of powerlessness and frustration. You could motivate them by reading out the following statement:

" *The task is big, but not so big as to prove either unwieldy or burdensome. It is worth developing countries dealing with child labour. This shows that what has caused the problem of child labour here is really not a dearth of resources, but a lack of real zeal. Let this not continue*."

Supreme Court in the case of *M. C. Mehta v. the State of Tamil Nadu and Others*, India, 1986

Usually participants realise that, in order to find effective and lasting solutions to a problem, it is first necessary to identify the causes. Having analysed the causes, solutions often become more apparent. However, you may have to point this out to some groups, especially if they are getting bogged down with identifying solutions.

You could provoke ideas for solutions by suggesting one or more of the following:

- reduce poverty so there is less need for children to work
- increase adults' wages so there is less need for children to work

- develop education so that it is more attractive and relevant to children's needs
- develop international standards for the employment of children
- ban products made with child labour
- develop global minimum labour standards as a requirement for membership of the World Trade Organisation (WTO)

Use any current news reports about child labour - either local or global - to make the activity topical and more interesting.

Variations

If you want to develop participants' knowledge on the concept of child labour, previous to the activity, you can use a quiz. You can find numerous quizzes on the ILO web page (http://us.ilo.org/ilokidsnew/whatis.html) and on the Unicef web page (www.unicef.org/aclabour/quiz.htm).

Suggestions for follow up

Find out more about youth campaigns against child labour, for example, "Kids Can Free the Children", a children's rights foundation, which was created by a 12-year-old Canadian boy (www.icomm.ca/freechild/).

Further Information

In chapter 5, in the background information sections on children and on social rights, there are statistics about child labour, and information about what is made with child labour, about international law and about child labour and the consequences of child labour for the child.

The scale of the problem of child labour means that there is a wealth of information available on this issue. Useful Internet sites include the International Labour Organisation (www.ilo.org), Unicef (www.unicef.org) and Save the Children (www.savethechildren.org.uk).

Key date

2 December
International Day for the Abolition of Slavery

HANDOUTS

Ashique's life facts

Personal Data
Name: Ashique Hashmir
Age: 11 years old
Nationality: Pakistani
Family: Parents, 2 grandparents, 1 sister and 3 brothers
Family Income: about 70 € /month

"Professional" Data
"Profession": worker in a brick factory
Working Hours: between 12 to 16 hours a day (1/2 hour break) – 6 days a week
Working Production: about 600 bricks a day
Wage: 1.3 Euro for 1000 bricks (but 50% goes for repayment of loan made by his family)
Working since he was 5 years old

Other Information
His family has been bonded for 2 years because they took a loan of about (P)Rs. 6000 (110 €). Now, with the loan interest, the amount owed is about 280 €.
Ashique was sent to school for 3 months by his father but the factory owner removed him and put him back to work. His father was punished because of what he had done.
The family income is very low and consequently insufficient to send the children to school and to provide adequate food and health care.

Real life situation.
Information gathered from ILO and Free the Children materials.

Source
Free the Children campaigns: www.freethechildren.org

Ideas for solutions

What can be done about Ashique's situation - and that of other child labourers?

By tomorrow?	By next month?	In the future?

Beware, we are watching!

No one made a greater error than those who did nothing because they could only do a little.

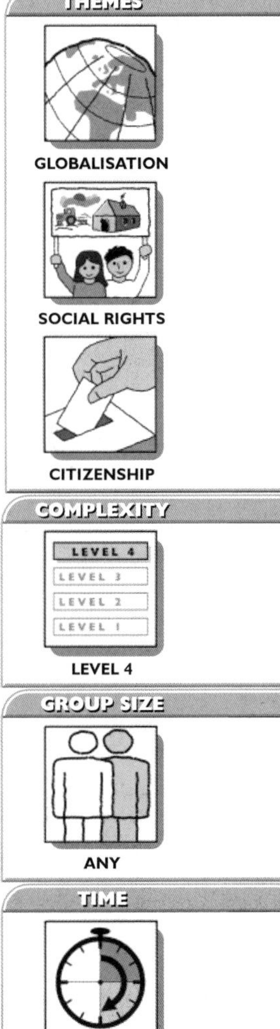

Themes Globalisation, Social rights, Citizenship

Complexity Level 4

Group size Any

Time 150 minutes

Overview In this activity, participants design a public awareness campaign about the consequences of relocation by transnational companies.

Related rights
- The right of everyone to the enjoyment of just and favourable working conditions
- The right to form trade unions
- The right to social security

Objectives
- To analyse the consequences of the relocation of transnational companies, locally and globally
- To promote human rights activism
- To encourage creativity and imagination

Materials
- Sticky labels that people can make into campaign stickers/labels
- Large sheets of paper or flipchart paper for making posters
- A4 size sheets of paper for making leaflets. (Coloured paper optional)
- Tape and glue
- Coloured markers and pencils
- Scissors
- Newspapers, magazines, brochures and any other printed material as sources of pictures.

Preparation
- Make copies of the fact sheet and the campaign objectives, one each per participant

Instructions

1. Explain that this activity is about globalisation with particular focus on the practice of relocation by transnational companies.
2. Ask people what they already know about this topic and their opinion about how it is covered in the media.
3. Brainstorm what makes a good publicity campaign.
4. Divide the group into small groups of 3 or 4 people.
5. Quote the case of the Eastern European Clean Clothes Campaign (EECCC) as an example of a campaign which is trying to inform the public about the consequences of globalisation and hand out the fact sheet.
6. Set the scene for the activity. Tell the group that they are to imagine that the NGO

(non-governmental organisation), The Eastern European Clean Clothes Campaign, has just received a grant from the Council of Europe. Whereas previously, due to funding problems, it had only been able to work on a small scale in a very few countries, the board of directors of the CCC have now decided to renew and expand the campaign Europe-wide. The organisation wishes to hire the group as consultants.

7. Distribute the campaign objectives (handout 2). Say that the EECCC has asked you to transmit this basic information for reference.
8. Each small group is to design a proposal for the expansion of the EECCC into their country. First they should draft a short, outline proposal for the whole campaign. Then they should make more detailed proposals of how to meet the first objective, that is, to inform the general public. The detailed proposal should include:
   - a timetable for activities,
   - a list of activities proposed (concerts, television and radio programmes, street theatre, leafleting, etc),
   - places where the activities will take place (schools, public buildings, etc),
   - number of staff required,
   - proofs of materials to be used (stickers, posters, etc.)
9. Emphasise that the proposal should be clear and concise. Tell the participants that the NGO is open to any kind of proposal, especially creative ones, but that they insist that the groups meet the objectives as laid out in the objectives of the campaign and justify their means of achieving them. Later, they will be expected to present their proposals to representatives from the NGO for recommendation to the EECCC board. For now, they have 60 minutes to design the proposal.
10. When the proposals are finished organise the presentations.
11. Open the plenary for discussion.

Debriefing and evaluation

Start with a brief review of how the activity went. Ask each group in turn to feedback about how they organised the tasks and how they worked together. Was everyone involved? Did every one feel that they participated? Then go on to discuss the issues of globalisation and what people learned.

- What are the positive and negative impacts of relocating a company? On local employment rates? On the national economy? On the global economy?
- Do the workers have any real choice about accepting the conditions of work they are offered, or not?
- Who is responsible for the situation?
- What can and should be done to educate the workers about their rights?
- Are campaigns like the ones proposed useful? Why?
- What makes a good campaign?
- Do you think that institutions working in the field of the protection of workers' rights, such as NGOs, Trade unions, United Nations agencies, organisations leading anti-globalisation campaigns, are making a difference?

Tips for facilitators

You will find information about the practice of relocation by transnational companies in the

background information to globalisation. Before you start this activity, check if the EECCC or a similar organisation has branches in your country.

One of the objectives of this activity is to stimulate the creativity of the participants. Thus, you should emphasise that they have complete freedom to "invent" any kind of new campaign strategies, always bearing in mind that they must meet the objectives set up by the NGO.

At point 10 in the instructions, that is, when the groups present their work, you could play the role of a member of the review panel from the EECCC. However, it is recommended that, if possible, you find other people from outside, who have not be involved in the group work. This makes the activity more exciting and it provides an opportunity to open up the discussion, especially if you can invite someone from an NGO, who works on either globalisation issues or is a campaigner.

If you can invite "experts" to visit, it is a good idea to do the activity over two sessions. Use the first session to make the campaign report and materials, and the second for the discussion.

Key date

24 October
World Development Information Day

Suggestions for follow-up

Contact the EECCC and develop the work the group has started.
If the group wants to carry on the theme of social and labour rights they could do the activity "Ashique's story", on page 91, which looks at the issue of child labour.

HANDOUT

1. Fact sheet: The Eastern European Clean Clothes Campaign

The Eastern European Clean Clothes Campaign (EECCC) is a network that started in the Netherlands in 1990, aimed at improving working conditions in the global sportswear industry. There are now CCCs in approximately 10 Eastern European countries, where each CCC is a coalition of consumer organisations, trade unions, human rights and women's rights organisations, researchers, solidarity groups and activists.

The major issues at the work place are:
- Low remuneration
- Casualisation of labour (no contracts, irregular working hours, forced and unpaid overtime, etc.)
- Denial of the right to organise (intimidation of workers' activists)

2. Campaign objectives

The objectives of the campaign are to:
- Inform the general public about what is happening in order to gain support for the campaign
- Show through concrete examples the impact of some of the consequences of globalisation which violate human rights.
- Put pressure on the companies to improve respect for the human rights of their workers by disseminating information about their rights.
- Activate a network of people, organisations and institutions that fight for the same cause.

Can I come in?

Refugee go home! He would if he could.

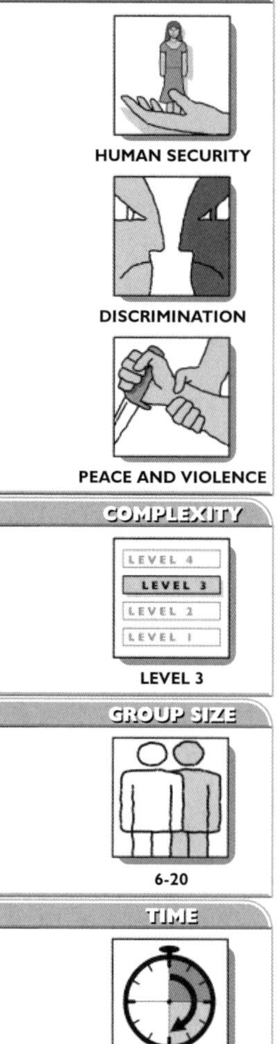

Themes Human Security, Discrimination and Xenophobia, Peace and Violence

Complexity Level 3

Group size 6 - 20

Time 60 minutes

Overview This is a role-play about a group of refugees trying to escape to another country. It addresses:
- The plight of refugees
- The social and economic arguments for giving and denying asylum

Related rights
- The right to seek and enjoy, in other countries, asylum from persecution
- The right of non-refoulement (the right of refugees not to be returned to their country where they can risk persecution or death)
- The right not to be discriminated against

Objectives
- To develop knowledge and understanding about refugees and their rights
- To understand the arguments for giving and denying refugees entry into a country
- To promote solidarity with people who are suddenly forced to flee their homes.

Materials
- Role cards
- Chalk and or furniture to create the border crossing post
- Pens
- Paper

Preparation
- Copy one information sheet per participant
- Copy the role cards, one for each immigration officer, refugee and observer
- Set the scene for the role-play. For example, draw a line on the floor to represent a border or arrange furniture to make a physical frontier with a gap for the check post. Use a table to serve as a counter in the immigration office and make signs for the immigration office about entry and customs regulations, etc.

Instructions

1. Explain that this is a role-play about a group of refugees fleeing their homeland who wish to enter another country in search of safety.
2. Start with a brainstorm to find out what people know about refugees. Write the points on a large sheet of paper or flipchart paper to refer to in the discussion later.
3. Show people the set-up in the room and read out the following text. "It is a dark, cold and wet night on the border between X and Y. A large number of refugees

have arrived, fleeing from the war in X. They want to cross into Y. They are hungry, tired and cold. They have little money, and no documents except their passports. The immigration officials from country Y have different points of view - some want to allow the refugees to cross, but others don't. The refugees are desperate, and use several arguments to try to persuade the immigration officials."

4. Divide the participants into equal groups. One group to represent the refugees from country X, the second group to represent the immigration officers in country Y and the third group to be observers.
5. Tell the "refugees" and the "immigration officers" to work out a role for each person and what their arguments will be. Distribute the handouts and give them fifteen minutes to prepare.
6. Start the role-play. Use your own judgement about when to stop, but about ten minutes should be long enough.
7. Give the observers five minutes to prepare their feedback.

Debriefing and Evaluation

Start by asking the observers to give general feedback on the role-play. Then get comments from the players about how it felt to be a refugee or an immigration officer and then move on to a general discussion about the issues and what people learnt.

- How fair was the treatment of the refugees?
- Refugees have a right to protection under Article 14 of the Universal Declaration of Human Rights and under the 1951 Convention Relating to the Status of Refugees. Were the refugees given their right to protection? Why/why not?
- Should a country have the right to turn refugees away?
- Would you do this yourself if you were an immigration officer? What if you knew they faced death in their own country?
- What sorts of problems do refugees face once inside your country?
- What should be done to solve some of the problems of acceptance faced by refugees?
- Are there any Internally Displaced Persons in your country? Or in a neighbouring country?
- What can and should be done to stop people becoming refugees in the first place?

Tips for the facilitator

Use the brainstorm to ascertain how much people already know about why there are refugees, what causes people to flee their homeland, and where they come from and the countries that they go to. This will help you decide how to guide the debriefing and evaluation, and what additional information you may need to provide at that stage.

Think about what to do if someone in the group is a refugee. Perhaps, they should not be in the group role-playing the refugees in case they have painful memories of the experience.

The three groups do not have to be equal. You may, for instance, choose to have only three or four observers and let the rest of the group be active role-players.

You may wish to give the observers copies of the further information so that they can inform themselves of the rights of refugees while the rest are preparing for the role-play.

The scene is set on a dark, cold and wet night. So why not turn off the lights and open the windows when you do the role-play? To add to the refugees' confusion, you could make the signs at the border in a foreign (or invented) language. Remember to brief the immigration officials in group 2 about what the signs say!

Note: This activity was adapted from *First Steps: A Manual for starting human rights education*, Amnesty International, London, 1997. The quote, "Refugee go home! He would if he could" was a slogan used in an UNHCR campaign.

Variations

Run the role-play again, but let immigration officers and the refugees swap parts. The observers should now have the additional task of noting any differences between the first and the second role-plays, especially those that resulted in a higher protection of the refugees' rights.

Do a follow-on role-play involving an official team sent by UNHCR to help the refugees from country X.

A school class may like to carry on with the topic by researching information about the role of UNHCR (www.unhcr.ch) and then writing an "official report" including the following points:

- Those arguments which persuaded the immigration officers to let the refugees in
- Any inappropriate behaviour by the immigration officers
- Recommendations for what country Y should do to protect the rights of the refugees.

Suggestions for follow-up

Find out more about refugees in your country, especially about the realities of their daily lives. Participants could contact a local refugee association and interview workers and refugees.

If you want to try an activity that follows the events after refugees have crossed the borders and are applying for asylum, you can run the activity "The language barrier", on page 228.

Ideas for action

Make contact with a local or national organisation that works for refugees who are sheltering in your country and see what you can do to support them. For example, they may need people to help gather essential items and deliver them to refugees.

Further Information

Every year millions of people have to leave their homes, and often their countries, because of persecution or war. These people become refugees. They nearly always have to move suddenly and leave most of their possessions behind. In the move families often get separated. Many refugees are never able to return to their homes.

Most refugees seek safety in a neighbouring country, arriving in large numbers at a time (called a mass influx). Other refugees have to travel great distances to find safety and arrive at airports and seaports far from their native land.

In 1951, the United Nations adopted the Convention Relating to the Status of Refugees to which more than half of the countries in the world have now signed up. There is a United Nations High Commission for Refugees (UNHCR), which oversees the implementation of the convention and assists refugees, mainly with humanitarian aid.

According to the Convention, a refugee is someone who has left their country and is unable to return because of a real fear of being persecuted because of their race, religion, nationality, membership of a particular social group, or political opinion. The main protection that a refugee must have is the right not to be returned to their country where they can risk persecution or death (right of non-refoulement). This also applies if a government wants to send a refugee to a third country from which the refugee might be sent home.

Governments have the duty to hear the claim of a refugee who wants to find safety (seek asylum) in their country. This principle applies to all states, whether or not they are party to the 1951 Convention. The 1951 Convention also says that refugees should be free from discrimination and should receive their full rights in the country where they go to be safe.

However, countries disagree about who a "genuine" refugee is; rich countries often say that refugees are not victims of oppression, but that they only want a better standard of living. They call them "economic migrants". Governments often argue that refugees' fears are exaggerated or untrue.

Key date

20 June
World Refugee Day

Numbers of Refugees Worldwide

Region (at 1st January 2000)	Refugees
Africa	3 523 250
Asia	4 781 750
Europe	2 608 308
Latin America & the Caribbean	61 200
North America	636 300
Oceania	64 500
Total	11 675 380

Source:
Refugees by numbers, 2000 Edition, UNHCR Publications.

Origin of Major Refugee Populations in 1999

Country of Origin	Main Countries of Asylum	Refugees
Where do they come from?	*Where do they go?*	
Afghanistan	Iran/Pakistan/India	2 562 000
Iraq	Iran/Saudi Arabia/Syria	572 500
Burundi	Tanzania/D. R. Congo	525 700
Sierra Leone	Guinea/Liberia/Gambia	487 200
Somalia	Ethiopia/Kenya/Yemen/Djibouti	451 600
Bosnia - Herzegovina	Yugoslavia/ Croatia/Slovenia	448 700
Angola	Zambia/ D. R. Congo/ Congo	350 600
Croatia	Yugoslavia/Bosnia-Herzegovina	340 400

Source:
Refugees by numbers, 2000 Edition, UNHCR Publications.

Internally Displaced Persons (IDPs)

Not every person who has been forced to flee his/her home moves to another country; these are called internally displaced persons (IDPs).The IDPs are the fastest growing group of displaced persons in the world. In Europe the number of IDPs (3 252 300) is higher than the number of refugees (2 608 380), with major concentrations in Bosnia-Herzegovina and countries of the former Soviet Union.Unlike refugees, they are not protected by international law nor are they eligible to receive many types of aid. A widespread international debate has been launched on how best to help all IDPs and who should be responsible for their well-being. The UNHCR provides assistance to some groups of IDPs upon request of the Secretary General of the United Nations.

HANDOUTS

Refugees' role card

Refugees' arguments and options

You should prepare your arguments and tactics; it is up to you to decide whether to put your argument as a group or whether each member, individually, takes responsibility for putting individual arguments.

You can use these arguments and any others you can think of:
- It is our right to receive asylum.
- Our children are hungry; you have a moral responsibility to help us.
- We will be killed if we go back.
- We have no money.
- We can't go anywhere else.
- I was a doctor in my hometown.
- We only want shelter until it is safe to return.
- Other refugees have been allowed into your country.

Before the role-play, think about the following options:
- Will you split up if the immigration officers ask you to?
- Will you go home if they try to send you back?

You are to role-play a mixed group of refugees, so in your preparations each person should decide their identity: their age, gender, family relationships, profession, wealth, religion and any possessions they have with them.

Immigration officers' role card

Immigration officers' arguments and options

You should prepare your arguments and tactics; it is up to you to decide whether to put your argument as a group or whether each member, individually, takes responsibility for putting individual arguments.

You can use these arguments and any others you can think of:
- They are desperate: we can't send them back.
- If we send them back we will be responsible if they are arrested, tortured or killed.
- We have legal obligations to accept refugees.
- They have no money, and will need state support. Our country cannot afford that.
- Can they prove that they are genuine refugees? Maybe they are just here to look for a better standard of living?
- Our country is a military and business partner of their country. We can't be seen to be protecting them.
- Maybe they have skills that we need?
- There are enough refugees in our country. We need to take care of our own people. They should go to the richer countries.
- If we let them in, others will also demand entry.
- They don't speak our language, they have a different religion and they eat different food. They won't integrate.
- They will bring political trouble.
- There may be terrorists or war criminals hiding among them

Before the role-play, think about the following options:
- Will you let all of the refugees across the border?
- Will you let some across the border?
- Will you split them up by age, profession, wealth...?
- Will you do something else instead?

Observers' role card

Your job is to observe the role-play. At the end of the role-play you will be asked to give general feedback. Choose a member to be your representative.

As you watch you should, amongst other things, be aware of:
- The different roles played by both the refugees and immigration officers
- The arguments they use and how they present them.
- Look out for any infringements of human and refugees' rights

You have to decide how you are going to take note of everything. For example, you may consider dividing into two sub-groups so one group observes the immigration officers and the other the refugees.

Children's Rights

A child without courage is like a sky without stars.

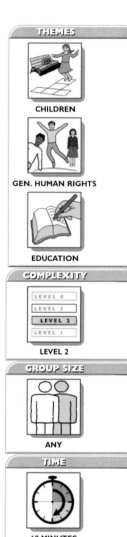

Themes Children, General human rights, Education

Complexity Level 2

Group size Any

Time 60 minutes

Overview This activity uses diamond ranking to promote discussion about the Convention on the Rights of the Child (the CRC), including the issues of:
- Fundamental human rights and the special rights of the child under the CRC
- Duties and responsibilities under the Convention
- How to claim the rights

Related rights
- The right to know and live with one's family
- The right to protection from economic exploitation
- The right to special treatment in court proceedings

Objectives
- To provide knowledge about the Convention on the Rights of the Child (CRC)
- To develop skills to review information critically and relate it to everyday experience
- To stimulate feelings of responsibility, solidarity, justice and equality

Materials
- Statement cards - one set per small group
- A large sheet of paper to make a wall chart
- Markers
- Enough space for small groups to work independently

Preparation
- Refer to the abridged version of the CRC on page 406. List the Articles on the large sheet of paper to make a wall chart.
- Review the statement cards provided below and refer to the CRC. Decide which Articles will promote the most interesting discussion with your particular group. Consider which issues are most relevant to the group members and also which will be the most controversial.
- Prepare one set of cards for each small group. Put each set in an envelope so that they don't get mixed up!

Instructions

1. Start with a brief review of the CRC. Ask what people know about it. Point out the wall chart and go over the main Articles.
2. Ask participants to get into small groups of three to four people. Hand out the envelopes with the statement cards.
3. Explain the diamond ranking procedure. Each small group is to discuss the nine

statements and consider how relevant each one is to their own lives. They should then arrange them in a diamond pattern in order of importance. They should lay the most important statement on the table. Underneath it, they should lay, side by side, the two next most important statements. Underneath these, they should lay out the next three statements of moderate importance. The fourth row should have two cards and the fifth row one card, the statement that they thought was the least important. In this way the cards will lie in the shape of a diamond.

4. Give the groups 25 minutes to discuss and decide the order of ranking.
5. When all the small groups have finished, let people walk around the room to see how each group ranked the statements. Then call everyone into plenary for a debriefing.

Debriefing and evaluation

Start by inviting each group in turn to present the results of their discussions. Then go on to review how participants enjoyed the activity and what they learned.

- How do the results of the different groups' discussions compare? What are the similarities and differences?
- Why do different people have different priorities?
- As a result of listening to others, do any of the groups wish to reconsider their own decisions about the ranking of the cards? Which arguments were the most persuasive?
- In general, which rights are not respected in your community, and why?
- Are there any rights which are not in the Convention that you think should be included?
- Do you think that children need their own Convention? Why?
- If children have their own Convention, is there not a case for a Convention for young people aged 18 to 30?
- What special rights should such a convention for young people contain?
- It is one thing for children to have rights under the CRC, but, in reality, how realistic is it for them to claim them?
- How do people in general claim their rights?
- If participation in the democratic process is one way for people to claim their rights, what can the participants do now to begin to "claim their rights" at home and in their school or club?
- To whom, in your society, can children turn, if they know of serious violations of their rights?

Tips for facilitators

There is more information about diamond ranking on page 49 of chapter 1 "How to use the manual". Point out to the groups that there are no right and wrong ways in which to order the cards. They should recognise that different people have different experiences and therefore different priorities, and these should be respected. Nonetheless, they should try, in each of their small groups, to come to a consensus about the order. After all, in real life, issues have to be prioritised and decisions made in the best interests of all!

Variations

Instead of providing nine Articles to be ranked, you can provide eight and leave one card blank for the groups to identify the ninth themselves.

Put the statement cards in a hat and ask people in turn to take one out and to talk about it for one minute. Refer to the activity "Just a minute", on page 150, for information on this method. Ask the small groups to write a short story or to present a short role-play of an incident relating to selected Articles. Alternatively, the stories/role-plays could be based on events from the media: something heard or seen in a film or theatre, or read in a book or magazine. The role-plays can be developed so that participants start with the incident and go on to improvise solutions or ways to prevent the incident in particular, or the violation in general, from happening again.

Key date

20 November

Universal Children's Day

Suggestions for follow-up

Invite someone who is familiar with the CRC, a state attorney, the head of a child help-line, a child psychologist or someone from the ombudsman's office, to talk to the group. Before the talk, conduct a brainstorm of abuses of children's human rights, for example, child abuse, sexual exploitation, neglect and bullying. Find out from the speaker who in the local community has a duty of care and responsibility, for example, parents, police, help-lines, social workers, etc. Also, get advice on how to take action if they witness a violation, especially if it is something as serious as a neighbour maltreating their children. Such issues need to be tackled with care, concern and caution.

Children and young people often feel discriminated against. If the group would like to explore issues about discrimination, they may like to do the activity "All equal, all different", on page 88.

Ideas for Action

Review the school's management, policies and curriculum to see how well the school meets its duties and responsibilities in relation to the CRC. For example, does it provide education that is directed to the development of the child's personality, talents and abilities, or is there too much emphasis on cramming for exams? Do pupils have the right to express views freely on all matters affecting them? Are the pupils' views given due weight? In other words, is there a school council and how effective is it? Is school discipline administered in a manner consistent with the child's dignity? How does the school deal with racist incidents and bullying? Discuss where there is room for improvement and what measures could and should be taken to address the issues. Look at the example on page 276 in "Taking action", and plan a project. Be careful not to rush into things or do things in ways that will (unnecessarily) upset the teachers, especially if they might resent you wresting power from them!

Further information

For the full text of the Convention, relevant UNICEF documents, published annually, on the state of the world's children, and other books and publications relating to children's rights, see the references in chapter 5 in the section on background information on children (page 317).

HANDOUTS

Statement cards

Copy the following Articles and cut them out to make the statement cards.

The child has the right to express freely views on all matters affecting him/her, and the child's views should be given due weight. The child has the right to freedom of expression.

The right of the child to freedom of thought, conscience and religion shall be respected. The child has the right to freedom of association and peaceful assembly.

No child shall be subjected to arbitrary or unlawful interference with his/her privacy, family, home or correspondence. The child should be protected from unlawful attacks on his/her honour and reputation.

Parents have the prime responsibility for the upbringing and development of the child.

The child has the right to education. The State shall make primary education compulsory and available and free to all. School discipline shall be administered in a manner consistent with the child's dignity. Education should be directed towards the development of the child's personality, talents and abilities, towards the development of respect for human rights and fundamental freedoms, towards the development of a responsible life in a free society in the spirit of peace, friendship, understanding, tolerance and equality, and towards the development of respect for the natural environment.

The child has the right to rest and leisure, to play and participate freely in cultural life and the arts.

The child shall be protected from economic exploitation and from performing work that is hazardous to his/her life and development. The child shall be protected from all forms of sexual exploitation and sexual abuse, the use of children in prostitution or other unlawful sexual practices, in pornographic performances and materials.

The State shall take all feasible measures to protect and care for children affected by armed conflict.

Every child accused of having committed an offence or crime should be guaranteed to be presumed innocent until proven guilty, to have legal assistance in the presenting of his/her case, not to be compelled to give testimony or to confess guilt, to have his/her privacy fully respected, and to be dealt with in a manner appropriate to his/her age, circumstances and well-being. Neither capital punishment nor life imprisonment without possibility of release shall be imposed for offences committed by children below the age of 18.

Different Wages

Equal pay for equal work!

Themes Social rights, Gender equality, Discrimination and Xenophobia

Complexity Level 2

Group size 4+

Time 90 minutes

Overview This is a simulation that confronts people with the realities of the labour market. It addresses issues of
- Different wages for the same job
- Discrimination in the workplace
- Policies of low pay for young workers

Related rights
- The right to fair remuneration
- The right to equal work and equal pay
- The right not to be discriminated against on the grounds of age and sex

Objectives
- To confront participants with the realities of discrimination in the workplace
- To analyse whether discrimination on the basis of age and gender should be allowed or not
- To promote solidarity, equality and justice.

Materials
- 1 copy of the "Workers' wage rates"
- Labels, one for each participant / worker
- Pens
- Money. You can use the E-money on page 265.

Preparation
- Prepare the labels. These should state the sex and age of the workers. Use the list of workers' wage rates for reference.
- Decide what work the participants will have to do. Collect together any equipment they will need.

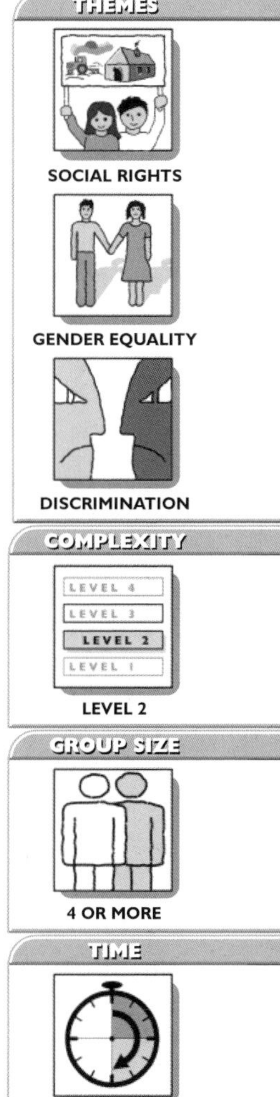

Instructions

1. Explain to the participants that they are workers and have to do some work for their employer (you!). They should not worry; everyone will be paid.
2. Hand out the labels at random, one to each participant.
3. Explain the task and make sure everyone knows what they have to do.
4. Let people get on with the work!
5. When the tasks are all completed, ask people to line up (queue up) to be paid. Pay each person according to their age and sex as laid out in the list of workers' wage rates. You should count the money out aloud so everyone can hear and all are aware of how much each of the others is getting.

6. If participants start to question or complain, give brief "reasons", but avoid being drawn into discussion.
7. You will have to use your own judgement about how far to go, but stop when you believe it is beginning to get too heated! Give everyone time to calm down and to get out of role, and then sit in a circle for the debriefing.

Debriefing and evaluation

Take the discussion in stages. Start with a review of the simulation itself:

- How did it feel to receive more (or less) than others workers even though everyone did exactly the same task?
- Why did some people receive more (or less) than others? Why did this happen?
- How did it feel to get more than others? How did it feel to get less than others?
- Does this sort of discrimination happen in workplaces in your country?

Next talk about remuneration on the basis of sex:

- Can different pay for the same job, when done by a man and a woman, be justified? Why? Why not? When?
- What if a man does the job better than a woman? Is that reason enough for paying the woman less?
- If a man is more qualified than the woman, does it follow that he should be paid more?
- Do you think that there are jobs that should be done exclusively by men? Why? Why not? If yes, which jobs?
- Do you think that there are jobs that should be done exclusively by women? Why? Whynot? If yes, which jobs?
- Do you think that the practice of affirmative action (or positive discrimination) can be justified in order to change social attitudes?

Finally, go on to talk about remuneration on the basis of age:

- Is there a policy for different wages on the basis of age in your country? If not, do you think there should be?
- What is the rationale for applying this kind of policy, especially in the case of young people?
- What is your opinion about this type of policy? Is it good? Bad? Necessary? Unnecessary? Give reasons.

Tips for facilitators

You will very probably have to adapt the activity. If you need to add or to delete some workers from the list, make sure that you still have a balance of sexes and a variety of different age groups. If the group is large or if you want to get into a deeper discussion on the two different types of discrimination, it is a good idea to sub-divide the group into two groups. Then one group can take the task of discussing discrimination on the grounds of sex and the other discrimination on the grounds of age.

What sorts of tasks are suitable for this activity? It should be exactly the same task for every worker. Also try to choose something that can be done by several people at the same time, so it does not become tedious for people to wait and watch. Think about the following:

- If you want to go outdoors, can it be done during the season of the year?
- Do you have the space?
- Can it be done equally easily and well by people of different ages and by both men and women?
- Is it safe?
- Will people feel embarrassed or refuse on ethical grounds?
- How long will it take?
- Does it require many skills?
- How can it be repeated several times over?

Examples of tasks:

- Clean the blackboard/whiteboard and neatly write a given phrase on it.
- Take books off a shelf and put them in a box. Carry the box to the other side of the room and unpack the books onto a second bookshelf.
- Make an origami aeroplane or simple hat
- Collect three different types of leaves and mount them on a piece of paper
- Look up the definition of a word and write it on a piece of paper. (If you choose different words, each relating to human rights, then at the end you may have a short glossary of terms!)

When you are paying out and have to give explanations for the different salaries, you will have to think up "reasons". They can be grounded in what actually happened or they can be ridiculous. For example:

- Someone who stumbled gets less
- Someone who smiled and looked happy gets more
- It's Tuesday!

The information below, and the background information in chapter 5 will help you to be a resource person during the discussions.

Variations

If you do not feel it appropriate to do this activity as a simulation you could adapt the information to use as a basis for discussion. You could create a 'fact sheet' for each worker with information about the work they do, their age, sex and remuneration. You could also include other details such as educational background and professional experience. Alternatively, you could develop a few in-depth case studies for different workers. However, you should be aware that discussion alone will not stimulate the strong emotional response that you get through the simulation.

Suggestions for follow-up

If the group enjoys role play and would like to explore the role of trade unions in defending workers' rights for fair pay and conditions, you may like to do the activity "Trade union meeting"on page 244.

Further Information

The issues about inequality of workers' remuneration are different in different countries and also different depending on whether the issue is age or sex discrimination. Discrimination on a

Key date

1 May
International Workers Day

Right to Fair Remuneration

International Covenant on Economic, Social and Cultural Rights, Article 7
"The States party to the present Covenant recognise the right of everyone to the enjoyment of just and favourable conditions of work, which ensure, in particular:
(a) Remuneration which provides all workers, as a minimum, with:
(i) fair wages and equal remuneration for work of equal value, without distinction of any kind, in particular women being guaranteed conditions of work not inferior to those enjoyed by men, with equal pay for equal work.".

European Social Charter Article 7 (5)
The right of children and young persons to protection of fair remuneration for young workers and apprentices.

Article 8 (3)
The right of employed women to protection for non-discrimination between men and women workers in respect of remuneration.

gender basis is nothing more than evidence of discrimination against women. Historically, women have been disadvantaged in the social, political and economic spheres. Examples of discrimination against women in the workplace include discrimination during the selection and interviewing of job applicants, discrimination in relation to promotion prospects and the fact that, on average, they get lower wages than men. It is a violation of the right to fair remuneration when women receive less than men do for doing the same job.

As workers, young people should also receive fair remuneration. However, here the situation is complex and differs from country to country. In general, the unemployment rate for young people is higher than for adults.

Although the principle of equal work for equal pay is generally upheld, youth remuneration is often held to be a special case and many countries have policies that allow young workers' to be paid less than an adult for the same job. These policies are justified on two grounds. On the one hand, there is the aim to discourage young people from entering the labour marker and to encourage them to stay at school to gain a good education. On the other hand, it should still be attractive for employers to hire inexperienced and low-skilled young workers, especially the ever-increasing numbers of school drop-outs, who otherwise would be "loose on the streets", getting into trouble and being a burden on the state. The application of this kind of policy and its success in decreasing youth unemployment varies from country to country.

The European Committee of Social Rights (the implementation body of the European Social Charter) does not view low pay for young people as incompatible with the guarantee of a fair wage so long as the difference is reasonable and the gap closes quickly. For example, a wage 30% lower than the adult starting wage is seen as acceptable for fifteen to sixteen-years-olds. However, for-sixteen to eighteen-year-olds, the difference may not exceed 20%.

Youth wages are not always low. In fact there are a lot of well educated young people who earn a lot of money - too much in the eyes of some people! For example, young people flourish in the sectors based on new technologies and receive far higher remuneration than older workers who are close to retirement age.

HANDOUT

Workers' wage rates according to sex and age.

	Sex	Age	Pay in Ems
1.	Male	35 years	100
2.	Female	16 years	30
3.	Male	22 years	70
4.	Female	32 years	90
5.	Male	16 years	50
6.	Female	19 years	60
7.	Male	26 years	100
8.	Male	20 years	70
9.	Female	24 years	80
10.	Male	37 years	100
11.	Female	17 years	30
12.	Female	23 years	80

Do we have alternatives?

"We worry about what a child will be tomorrow, yet we forget that he is someone today." Stacia Tauscher

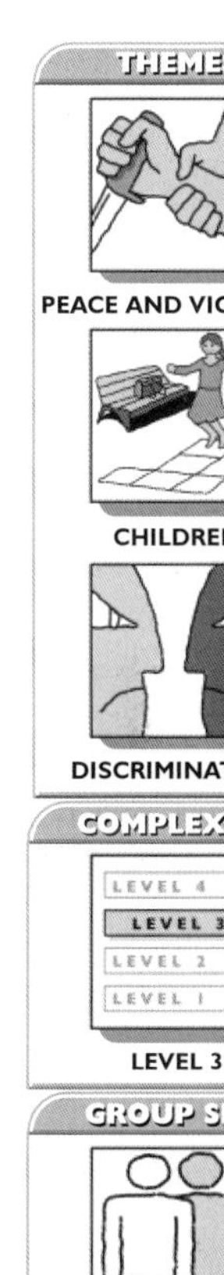

Themes Peace and Violence, Children, Discrimination and Xenophobia

Complexity Level 3

Group size 9 - 24

Time 90 minutes

Overview This is a role-play activity that addresses issues of:
- Interpersonal violence
- Bullying

Related rights
- The right to live in freedom and safety (security)
- The right to dignity and not to be discriminated against
- Children have the right to be protected and shielded from harmful acts and practices e.g. from physical and mental abuse

Objectives
- To develop knowledge and understanding about the causes and consequences of bullying
- To explore ways of confronting the problem
- To create empathy with the victims of bullying

Materials
- Copies of the scenes to be role-played (one scene per group)
- One copy of the sheet of "bullying stories"

Preparation
- Prepare the room so that the participants have space to perform their role-plays.

Instructions

1. Introduce the activity. Explain that they are going to work in small groups to make short role-plays on the theme of bullying.
2. Ensure, with a quick brainstorm, if necessary, that everyone knows what bullying is and that it can happen in any school or college, in clubs and in the workplace.
3. Divide the participants into three sub-groups and assign one of the scenes to each group. Give them 15 minutes to rehearse and prepare their role-plays.
4. Once they are ready, ask each group, in turn, to present their scene.
5. Leave any comments until all groups have presented their scenes and then come together into plenary for discussion.

Debriefing and evaluation

Start by reviewing the role-plays.

- Where did the groups get the material to develop their scenes? Was it from stories or films about bullying, or was it based on experience?

Key date

4 June
International day of Innocent Children Victims of Aggression

- Were the scenes realistic?
- In scene 1, which things that people said were constructive and helped the situation and which things hindered the situation?
- In relation to scene 2, how easy is it to talk frankly with a friend who is also a bully. In general, what techniques would tend to have a positive effect and what tactics would tend to have a negative effect?
- In relation to scene 3, how easy is it to talk frankly with a friend who is being bullied? What is the best way to find solutions that are acceptable to the victim?

Now ask three participants to read out the three "bullying stories". Ask for general comments about the "real stories" and then go on to talk about the causes of bullying and how it can be tackled.

- How do you think it feels to be bullied?
- Is the person being bullied responsible for it?
- Are bullies trying to prove something by abusing other people?
- Is bullying a form of violence?
- Is bullying about power?
- Is bullying inevitable?
- If you are friends with someone who is being bullied, should you inform an authority figure, even though your friend told you about their problem in confidence?
- What are the most common prejudices against people who are being bullied?
- Who is responsible for controlling a problem of bullying?

Tips for facilitators

Bullying may be direct or indirect. Direct bullying means behaviour such as name-calling, teasing, pushing or pulling someone about, hitting or attacking, taking bags and other possessions and throwing them around, forcing someone to hand over money or possessions, and attacking or threatening someone because of their religion, colour, disability or habit. Indirect bullying is behaviour such as spreading rumours with the intention that the victim will become socially isolated. Such behaviours are mostly initiated by one or more people against a specific victim or victims. In both direct and indirect bullying, the basic component is physical or psychological intimidation which occurs systematically over time and creates an on-going pattern of harassment and abuse.

If you are working with an outreach group or in a club, college or workplace you may want to adapt the scenes to suit your particular situation. Be aware of the young people in your group and any personal experiences of bullying. Form the groups and share out the scenes accordingly.

Suggestions for follow-up

Find out if there are any programmes locally that train peer educators (young volunteers) in conflict mediation. Ask a speaker to come to talk to the group and consider the possibility of setting up a system of peer mediators in your school, college or club.

The group may like to develop an anti-bullying policy for their school or organisation. The method described in the activity "Responding to racism", on page 201, on how to develop an anti-racist policy is also appropriate for developing an anti-bullying policy.

If the group enjoys role-playing and would like to explore issues of conflict resolution further, they could do the activity "Play the game!", on page 194.

Ideas for action

Find a group or association that works to address bullying in your country, and offer your support.

If you have a particularly creative group, suggest they script their own scenes and then perform them for others.

Members of the group could also lead or organise a debate in their own schools or communities on the topic of bullying.

Together with other friends, create a group in your own school or community to help young people who are being bullied.

HANDOUTS

Scenes for the role-plays

Scene 1

A student turns to people in authority and tries to explain that one of his/her classmates is being bullied. The headteacher is authoritarian and traditional. S/he thinks standards are slipping and has poor opinions about the general behaviour of young people these days. The class teacher does not want to assume responsibility for the situation. Other teachers underestimate the problem and do not recognise the bullies' behaviour for what it is. The representative of the local authority care service is concerned, but has too heavy a workload to be able to intervene now.

Scene 2

A group of students try to talk to a friend who is bullying a younger student.

Scene 3

Various students are gathered together talking about a friend who is being bullied by a group of older students. They would like to help their friend and analyse all the possible solutions to help him/her.

Bullying stories

Story 1

"I am 12 and I hate going to school because nobody likes me. There is a group of kids who call me names every time they can. They say that I am ugly and fat and that my parents should be ashamed of me. My best friend stopped talking to me and now she has even made friends with some of the kids in this group. I hate her. I feel so lonely and I am scared that what they say about my parents is true."

Rosanna

Story 2

"I started classes in a new college this year and from the first day I felt that some of the girls looked at me funny. Then I realized that they were jealous because most of the boys started being very friendly to me. Now I want to go to another college because I am receiving little notes threatening me. I also receive abusive phone calls at home. They have even stolen my books several times. Last week, I went to the toilet and three girls followed me inside. They shouted at me, threatened me with a knife and told me that I should go study elsewhere and called me a whore. I cannot stand this any more. I am scared and angry. I tried to talk to the principal but she did not really listen to my problem. I don't know what to do."

Lisbeth

Story 3

"My best friend told me other students were bothering him at our school. Since I wanted to help him, I decided to go and talk to them but after I did this they started doing the same to me. Now we are both being bullied: they make fun of us, play dirty tricks and have threatened to beat us up. We have both decided to keep our mouths shut because we are scared things will get worse if we tell someone."

Andrey

Domestic Affairs

" (...) the police always come late / if they come at all."
Tracy Chapman

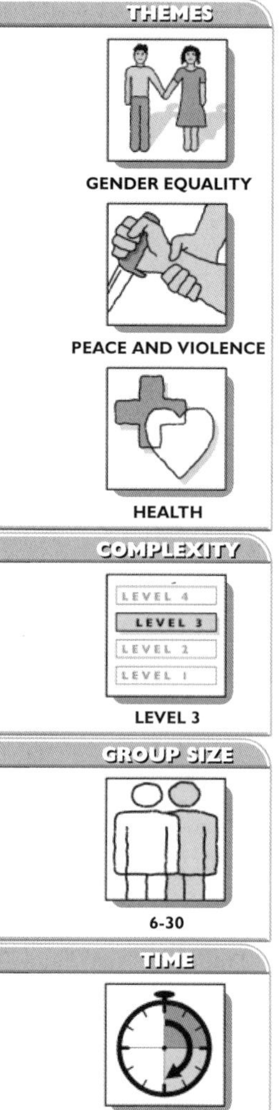

Themes Gender Equality, Peace and Violence, Health

Complexity Level 3

Group size 6 - 30

Time 120 minutes

Overview This activity looks at domestic violence as one of the most common and least spoken about forms of violence.

Related rights
- The right to protection from violence, torture and degrading treatment.
- The right to equality and non-discrimination.
- The right to equal protection by the law (or to fair treatment from the courts)

Objectives
- To raise awareness of domestic violence and knowledge about violations of women's human rights
- To develop skills of discussing and analysing human rights violations
- To promote empathy and the self-confidence to take a stand against domestic violence

Materials
- Large sheets of paper or a board and pens or markers for the brainstorm and group work.
- Choose one or more of the "Crime witness reports" below or write your own. Make enough copies for one per participant.
- Copies of the "Guidelines for group discussions" (one per small group)

Preparation
- Compile information about existing centres and organisations active in the support of victims of domestic violence and find out what the main issues are in your local community or area.
- Consider carefully the issues you wish to work on, taking into account the personal experiences of the participants.

Instructions

1. Prepare the group for the activity by conducting a brainstorm of "the most common forms of violence in our neighbourhood". Write down everything that the participants say but do not discuss anything at this stage. Leave the flipchart or board where everyone can see it. (10 minutes)
2. Ask people to get into small groups of between two and six people per group. There should be at least three groups.
3. Hand out the copies of the "Crime witness report" cards. There are three different cards/cases but the same case may be given to more than one group. Also hand out a copy of the "Guidelines for group discussions".

4. Give participants five minutes to read through the crime witness reports. Stress that their discussions should be focused on these case studies. Participants should be aware that discussions about these issues can be very personal and that no one should feel under pressure to disclose more than they want.
5. Allow the participants one hour for their group work.
6. At the end, come into plenary and move on to the evaluation and debriefing.

Debriefing and evaluation

Start with a short review of how the group work went. How realistic were the crime witness reports and how relevant were the questions? If different groups worked with different case studies, let the groups feedback on their analyses of the different crimes. Then go on to talk about the transfer to social reality:

- How prevalent is domestic violence in your community and in your country as a whole?
- Which human rights are at stake?
- What are the causes of domestic violence?
- Why is it that there are more cases of men being violent towards women than of women being violent towards men?
- How can domestic violence be stopped? What could/should be done by:
  - the public authorities?
  - the local community?
  - the people involved?
  - friends and neighbours?
- Check the output of the groups and the points raised in discussion against the list from the initial brainstorm. Was domestic violence on the list? If not, why not?
- What other forms of violence against women have come up in the course of the discussion? Add them to the list.

Ask if anyone would like to work further on any of the issues raised and discuss how they would like to follow up or take action.

Tips for facilitators

Be aware of issues of sensitivity and anonymity/privacy (some participants may have personal experiences of domestic violence at home or in the family). Make it clear to everyone that no one should feel under pressure to disclose more than they want. You should feel free to adapt the activity according to the concerns of the participants.

The activity is called "domestic affairs" because most acts of violence against women occur in the home or between people who are in a relationship. One of the most common forms of domestic violence is that of physical violence, which is why these particular "Crime witness reports" were chosen. The stories are all based on actual cases about real victims and crimes. You may want to change some of the details or to substitute other case studies in order to make the activity more relevant to your local situation and the concerns of the participants.

People's opinions will vary in what they consider constitutes an act of violence. The Declaration on the Elimination of Violence Against Women, adopted by the United Nations General Assembly in 1993, defines violence against women as "*any act of gender-based violence that results in, or is likely to result in, physical, sexual, or psychological harm or suffering to women, including threats of such acts, coercion or arbitrary deprivation of liberty, whether occurring in public or private life*". It encompasses, but is not limited to, "*physical, sexual and psychological violence occurring in the family, including battering, sexual abuse of female children in the household, dowry-related violence, marital rape, female genital mutilation and other traditional practices harmful to women; non-spousal violence and violence related to exploitation; physical, sexual and psychological violence occurring within the general community, including rape, sexual abuse, sexual harassment and intimidation at work, in educational institutions and elsewhere; trafficking in women and forced prostitution; and physical, sexual and psychological violence perpetrated or condoned by the state, wherever it occurs.*"

If you have difficulties in finding out about your local support centres, there is a database of centres at the European Information Centre Against Violence web-site: www.wave-network.org.

Male participants may react strongly to the activity or some of the discussions. It is important to bear in mind that the purpose is not to make men or boys feel guilty for what other men do; however, it is important to acknowledge, or discuss, the idea that men are part of an oppressive patriarchal system and thus play a part in it. In this context, it may also be interesting to explore the consequences of violence against women on men, directly and indirectly.

You may wish to end the session with a minute's silence for the victims of domestic violence. It is a powerful way to close the activity and promote empathy and solidarity.

Variations

There are many forms of violence against women (see below under "further information"). You can develop your own case studies to explore any of the other aspects of the issue.

Suggestions for follow-up

The group could get in touch with the local police and find out what they do when they receive calls for help in cases of domestic violence. Another possibility is to contact their nearest women's help organisation or centre and invite a speaker to present facts and figures about the situation in their local community.

Another almost taboo subject in many countries is sexuality - and homosexuality in particular. If the group would like to explore these issues, they could look at the activity "Let's talk about sex", on page 156.

Taking action

Contact a local women's refuge or information centre or an organisation working for women's rights and find out what their needs are and how you can help them.

Further information

A universal challenge to human rights

Women's and young women's rights are inalienable and indivisible and an integral part of human rights. Nonetheless, this does not imply that they are in any way sacred or secure. On the contrary, violence against women is a problem of enormous proportions. Young women in particular run a much higher risk of having their fundamental rights violated than men do.

"Violence against women and girls is a major health and human rights issue. At least one in five of the world's female population has been physically or sexually abused by a man (or men) at some time in their life. Many, including pregnant women and young girls, are subject to severe, sustained or repeated attacks.

Worldwide, it has been estimated that violence against women is as common a cause of death and incapacity among women of reproductive age as cancer, and a greater cause of ill-health than traffic accidents and malaria combined. The problem with violence against young women is a global one that does not recognise borders; trafficking, for example, is an obvious example of this. "There is not one single country in the world where women are free from violence. There is not one single area in any woman's life where she is not exposed to threats or to actual acts of violence against her. Violence against women knows no geographical boundary, no age limit, no class distinction, no race, no cultural difference and manifests itself in many different ways.[1]"

Violence against women is clearly political, in the sense that it constitutes a serious obstacle to equality between women and men and perpetuates inequality.[2] It is also clearly political in the sense that it constitutes a major threat to democracy, since, as is stated in a Council of Europe resolution, "inequality and disparities between women and men in the field of human rights are inconsistent with the principles of genuine democracy".[3]

Key date

25 November
International day for the Elimination of Violence against Women

Violence across the life span

Violence against women throughout the life cycle

Phase	*Type of violence*
Pre-birth	Sex-selective abortion; effects of battering during pregnancy on birth outcomes
Infancy	Female infanticide; physical, sexual and psychological abuse
Childhood	Child marriage; female genital mutilation; physical, sexual and psychological abuse; incest; child prostitution and pornography
Adolescence and adulthood	Dating and courtship violence (e.g. acid-throwing and date rape); economically coerced sex (e.g. school girls having sex with "sugar daddies" in return for school fees); incest; sexual abuse in the workplace; rape; sexual harassment; forced prostitution and pornography; trafficking in women; partner violence; marital rape; dowry abuse and murders; partner homicide; psychological abuse; abuse of women with disabilities; forced pregnancy
Elderly	Forced "suicide" or homicide of widows for economic reasons; sexual, physical and psychological abuse

Source: Violence Against Women Information Pack – World Health Organisation, 1997

Some figures on the size of the problem

The figures on violence against women, and specifically on domestic violence, can be astonishing, showing the extent and universality of the problem and its relative invisibility. Every day in Europe one woman in five is a victim of violence. More women in Europe die or are seriously injured every year through domestic violence than through cancer or road accidents.[4] Every year 14,500 Russian women are killed as a result of domestic violence.[5]

A study conducted by the European Women's Lobby in 1999 on domestic violence in the European Union reached the conclusion that 1 in 4 women in the EU experience some form of violence by their intimate partner. 95% of all acts of violence take place within home. A Finnish study (1998) showed that 52% of adult women had been victims of violence or physical or sexual threats from the age of 15, and 20 % had been within the past year. A Portuguese study (1997) revealed that 53.3% of women living in the suburbs of large cities, 55.4% of women living in cities and 37.9% of women living in the countryside had been subjected to violence; 43% of acts of violence were committed within the family. A Belgian study (1998) indicated that 68% of women had been the victims of physical and/or sexual violence.[6]

Additional resources on the Internet:

The site of Women Against Violence in Europe Network*:* *www.wave-network.org.*

The European Women's Lobby*: www.womenlobby.org where the report "Unveiling the hidden data on domestic violence in the European Union" can also be ordered.*

The White Ribbon Campaign *is "the largest effort of men working to end men's violence against women". www.whiteribbon.ca.*

EuroPRO-Fem, European Pro-feminist Men's Network *is a network of organisations and projects of men concerned with male domination, violence and oppression of women www.europrofem.org.*

Many of the statistics have been taken from the seminar report "Violence against young women in Europe", by Ingrid Ramberg, Council of Europe, 2001 – available at www.coe.int/hre.

Domestic violence

Violation of women's human rights of is not something that only happens in war. It is something that happens first and foremost at home. "The 'private' nature of this violence is exactly what has always made and still makes intervention and action so difficult."[7]

Research consistently demonstrates that a women is more likely to be injured, raped or killed by a current of former partner than by any other person. Domestic violence affects not only the woman but also the children, with a particularly high incidence amongst girls and young women.

Silent Witnesses exhibition

This activity was inspired by an exhibition on domestic violence and the murder of women, which was brought to the European Youth Centre Budapest by *NANE* Women's Rights Association (Budapest, Hungary), including the stories about *Eszter* and *Kati*. This exhibition was aimed at raising public awareness of the dimensions and brutality of domestic violence and murder by telling the stories of murdered women, the 'silent witnesses'.

The Silent Witnesses originated in Minnesota, USA, where it has now achieved a nationwide dimension and is part of a movement to bring an end to domestic murder by 2010. Organising a Silent Witnesses exhibition can be a very practical and effective way of addressing domestic violence in your community, in your town or in your region. There are books on how to make the witnesses and how to organise the exhibition, including a book called "Results" which tells about the first years of the campaign in the USA and lists a handful of stories which could be used as examples. The website's address is www.silentwitness.net. It also contains a long list of international contacts who already have such exhibits.

Note: The cases of Kati and Eszter are reported by Morvai Krisztina in Terror a családban – A feleségbántalmazás és a jog (Terror in the Family – Wife Battering and the Law)*, Kossuth Kiadó, Budapest 1998.*

---

1 *European Women's Lobby (www.womenlobby.org)*
2 *Fact Sheet. "Violence against women. Action undertaken by the Council of Europe". Division Equality between Women and Men, DG II, Council of Europe, 2001.*
3 *Resolution 1216 (2000) Follow-up action to the United Nations 4th World Conference on Women (Beijing 1995) Parliamentary Assembly of the Council of Europe.*
4 *Recommendation 1450 (2000) Violence against women in Europe. Parliamentary Assembly of the Council of Europe.*
5 *The Unicef Report on Women in Countries in Transition, September 1999.*
6 *European Women's Lobby.*
7 *Ending domestic violence; actions and measures. Proceedings of the Forum Bucharest (Romania), 26-28 November 1998. Steering Committee for equality between women and men. (EG/BUC (99) 1) Council of Europe 2000, p. 13.*

HANDOUTS

Crime witness report 1

Eszter

On November 1995 Eszter's husband arrived home slightly drunk. He discovered that she and her daughter were visiting a neighbour. He ordered them to come home immediately.

When they got in, he locked the door and told their daughter: "I'm gonna have a little talk with your mother now". He got out an axe, a broom and a knife.

He started an argument with his wife, accusing her of not having done any washing, cooking and other housework. All the same time he kept beating her; he hit her head and face with his bare hands. He tore out handfuls of her hair and kicked her with his boots. Then he stripped the clothes from her upper body and threw her on the bed with the intention of beating her further.

All this happened in front of their 8-year-old daughter who begged him to stop. Then he did stop. He threw Eszter out of the bed and fell asleep.

Eszter died that night.

Crime witness report 2

Kati

Kati tried to escape from her fiancé who was becoming increasingly abusive. She found a flat to rent in another city but he kept phoning and harassing her. Kati's mental state deteriorated.

One day, the fiancé went to get her after work to make her move back. He took her to a nearby forest, where he tried to strangle her with her pullover. The next day Kati told her colleagues at work that she was afraid he would one day strangle and kill her.

Four days later the fiancé had a few drinks. Again, he waited for her after work and when she came out he started to beat her. In the evening, he decided that they should visit relatives. On the way they stopped the car several times. Kati, seeing the state he was in, agreed to have sex with him but he was too drunk.

Kati told her fiancé that she was not interested in him any more. This made him very angry. He grabbed a long leather belt and strangled her.

He then pulled her dead body into a ditch and covered her with tree branches.

Crime witness report 3

Z

Z is a woman living in your neighbourhood; she is married and has two small children. Sometimes her husband gets angry and beats her, mostly with his hands and fists. However, lately he has also resorted to using a belt and broomstick. Two months ago he broke a bottle on her head. Z wants to leave home but her husband threatens to kill her if she "even thinks of it". She has two young sons to look after and she is horrified at the prospect of having to leave them.

Yesterday she reported to the local hospital with a broken nose and bruises which, she explained, were caused by falling down the stairs.

Guidelines for the group discussions

I The analysis of the crime (20 minutes)

1. What do you think of the crime as reported?
2. Where might such a crime have happened? Could it be in your neighbourhood?
3. Why has the crime happened?
4. Is there anything that could justify such a crime?
5. How could the victim have defended herself?

II – Transfer to social reality (40 minutes)

1. Do you know, or have you heard of any cases of domestic violence recently?
2. What forms does domestic violence take in our society?
3. What can the victims do if they need help?
4. Should the police intervene if they hear of violence or should such intervention be considered as interference in domestic affairs and should they "allow time for the wounds to heal"?
5. What power does the woman have in such situations? What power does the man have?
6. Do you know of cases of domestic violence in which a man is the victim?
7. How can domestic violence be prevented and stopped?
8. What could/should be done by:
   a. the public authorities?
   b. the local community?
   c. the people involved?
   d. friends and neighbours?

"Draw-the-word" game

Non-artists have rights too!

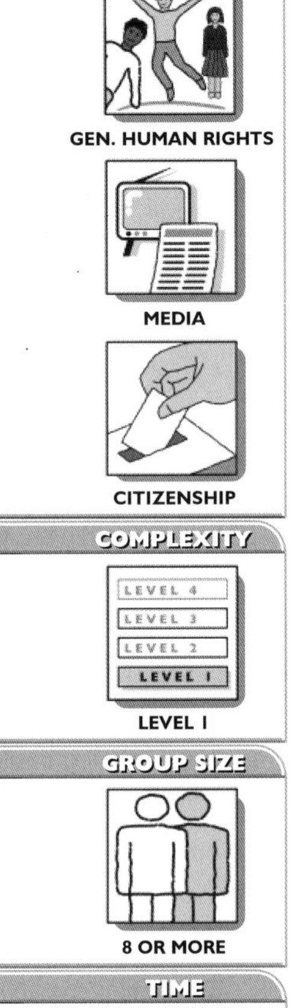

Themes	General human rights, Media, Citizenship
Complexity	Level 1
Group size	8+
Time	45 minutes
Overview	This is a team game in which people have to draw creatively to depict a word relating to human rights.
Related rights	▪ The right to freedom of opinion and expression ▪ The right to freedom of thought ▪ Equality in dignity and rights.
Objectives	▪ To develop knowledge of the UDHR ▪ To develop team-building and creative thinking, and an awareness of how we use images ▪ To promote solidarity and respect for diversity
Materials	▪ A wall chart which lists the articles of the UDHR. ▪ A large sheet of paper or flipchart paper and a marker to record the scores ▪ Sheets of paper (A4 size) and pens for the group drawings, one sheet per team per round of the game ▪ Sticky tape or pins to display the drawings
Preparation	▪ Refer to page 402 for the abridged version of the UDHR and copy it onto a large sheet of paper. ▪ Select the rights you want the group to work with and make a list for use in the game.

Instructions

1. Ask participants to get into small groups of four to five people and to choose a name for their team.
2. Explain that in the activity they will be working in teams. You will give one person in each team an Article from the UDHR to draw. The others in the team have to guess which right it is. The team that guesses first scores a point. The team with the most points at the end wins.
3. Tell the teams to collect several sheets of paper and a pencil and to find somewhere to sit around the room. The teams should be spread out so they do not overhear each other.
4. Call up one member from each team. Give them one of the rights on your list, for example, "freedom from torture" or "the right to life".
5. Tell them to return to their groups and to make a drawing to represent the right while their team mates try to guess what it is. They may only draw images; no numbers or words may be used. No speaking is allowed except to confirm the correct answer.

6. The rest of the team may only say their guesses; they may not ask questions.
7. After each round, ask all the drawers to write on their picture what the right was, whether they finished it or not, and to put the paper to one side.
8. Do a second round; call new people to be the drawers and give them a different right. Do 7 or 8 rounds. A different person should draw in each round. Try to ensure that everyone has the opportunity to draw at least once.
9. At the end, ask the groups to pin up their pictures so that the different interpretations and images of the different rights can be compared and discussed.

Key date

10 December
Human Rights Day

Debriefing and evaluation

Begin by reviewing the activity itself and then go on to talk about what people know about human rights.

- Was it easier or harder than people had expected to depict human rights?
- How did people choose how to depict a particular right? Where did they get the images from?
- How do the different images of each right compare? How many different ways were there to depict and interpret the same concept?
- After all the pictures have been reviewed, ask how much - or how little - participants discovered they knew about human rights.
- Do they think human rights have any relevance to their own lives? Which ones?

Tips for facilitators

Before you do this activity you should read through the UDHR (page 403) and be familiar with what is meant by human rights; for example, that they are internationally guaranteed, legally protected, they focus on the dignity of the human being, they protect both individuals and groups, they can not be taken away, they are equal and interdependent and they are universal.

You will need to decide how to use the wall chart. If participants have very little knowledge of the UDHR you may like to use the chart before you start the activity, so people have some clue as to what they should be guessing! If participants have more knowledge, then use the chart at the end to stimulate discussion about the rights that were not drawn.

Be aware that people who consider themselves poor artists may think this will be too difficult for them. Reassure them that you are not looking for works of art and encourage everyone to have a go. They may be surprised!

Use the abridged version of the UDHR for finding rights for drawing. Some suggestions are: the right to life, freedom from torture, the right to a fair trial, freedom from discrimination, the right to privacy, the right to education, freedom from slavery, freedom of association, freedom of expression, the right to a nationality, freedom of thought and religion, the right to vote, the right to work, the right to health, the right to own property, the right to marry and found a family and the right to choose who to marry.

Variations

If you have a small group of less than 8 people you can play as one group; ask one person to draw in the first round, and whoever guesses draws in the next round, etc.

Suggestions for follow-up

The group may like to go on to explore some of issues relating to the rights of disabled people using the activity "See the ability", on page 209.

Education for All?

Do you have a good memory? Now is the time to test it!

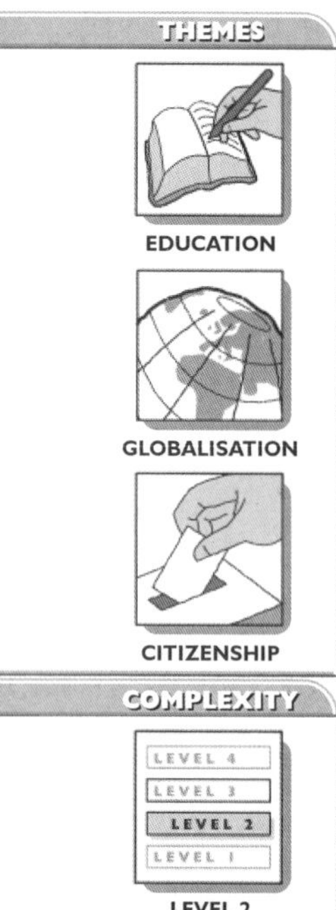

GROUP SIZE
6-30
TIME
90 MINUTES

Themes Education, Globalisation, Citizenship

Complexity Level 2

Group size 6 - 30

Time 90 minutes

Overview In this activity participants have to locate and match pairs of cards as they think out about the inequalities of educational provision world-wide and how to achieve "Education for All".

Related rights
- The right to education
- The right to full development of one's personality
- The right to equality regardless of gender and social status

Objectives
- To reflect on education as a human rights issue
- To critically analyse the level of access to quality education world-wide
- To encourage responsibility for attaining the goal of Education for All

Materials
- 1 set of the game cards for every three or four participants
- 2 sheets of stiff paper or thin card (A4 size) for every three or four participants and glue (optional but preferable)
- Scissors
- Paper and pens for notes in part 2

Preparation
- Familiarise yourself with the cards.
- Copy the sheets of game cards and back them with the stiff paper to make the cards more durable. Cut out the 40 cards.Make sure to mix them well so that matching pairs are not adjacent.

Instructions

The activity is divided into two parts: part 1, the memory game and part 2, reporting on the issues.

Part 1, the memory game (10 minutes)

1. Explain that there are twenty pairs of cards; each pair comprises a statement card and a picture card. The task is to identify the pairs and to match them. The texts on the cards relate either to the aims of the World Education Forum (WEF), to bring about "education for all", or to general issues of human rights and education.
2. Tell people how to play. The participants should form small groups of three or four. They should spread the cards face down on the floor. In turn, people turn over two cards. If one (or both) of the cards is a statement card, then the player reads out the text to the rest of the group. If the cards are a pair, then the player keeps them and has another go. If the cards do not match, then s/he turns them over so they lie face down again on the floor in exactly the same spot as they were before. The next player then has a go to turn over two cards. It is a memory game, because people

have to memorise where the different cards lie, in order to be able to pick up matching pairs.

3. The winner is the player who holds the most pairs of cards at the end of the game.

Part 2. Reporting the issues (60 minutes)

1. Summarise the issues on a flipchart. Ask people to read out the headings on their cards (not the whole statement again) while you write them down.
2. Ask the group to identify four to six issues which interest them most.
3. Divide the group into sub-groups of 4 or 5 people. Ask each sub-group to pick two of the issues they would most like to discuss. (Try to organise it so that two different groups discuss the same issue in order to generate more ideas. This will mean that the sub-groups will have to do some negotiating about which issues to discuss.)
4. When the issues have been agreed and allocated, give the groups 20 minutes to discuss their two chosen issues. The focus of the discussions will differ slightly depending on the card. If the card has a question, this should be answered. If the card has a statement, people should prepare a critical comment.
5. After 20 minutes, call people into plenary for reporting back. Take each issue in turn. Give each group just 5 minutes to feed back and allow no more than an extra 5 minutes for questions from the floor.
6. After all the groups have reported on all the issues, move to the debriefing.

Debriefing and evaluation

You will have already had a good discussion about the issues, so now go on to evaluate the game itself and what people learned.

- Did the participants enjoy the memory game?
- Was it a good way to start a discussion on the issues of education?
- How did the discussions in the groups go? Did everyone feel that they could participate?
- Are there too many challenges? Is it possible to have "education for all"?
- What can you, your group, your community do to work towards achieving the goal of education for all in your country and/or in developing countries?

Tips for facilitators

The intention in using this technique is to bring an ingredient of fun to the process of gaining information which will be needed for the discussion.

This is a fairly simple activity to facilitate. Just make sure that you have read all the cards before you do the activity. Be sure that you know which card matches with which so that during the game you can offer guidance and verify that pairs are correct. When explaining how to play the game, you may like to illustrate the instructions by showing what one of the pairs looks like.

Some of the cards contain acronyms, for instance WEF (World Education Forum). Make sure that when you introduce the game you explain what these letters stand for (see under "Further information" below).

Note that one-third of the cards contain statements relating to the goals of education for all as stated by the World Education Forum (WEF), Dakar, Senegal in April 2000. The rest of the cards

Key date

8 January
World Literacy Day

are on human rights and education issues, or on issues that have to be addressed in order to achieve good quality education for all.

Variations

If there is not enough time to do part 2, you could use the technique described in the activity "Just a minute", on page 150 instead. Ask each participant to choose one of the issues on the cards they picked up, and to speak about it for one minute without hesitation or repetition. This is also a good option if you feel that the group needs to improve their oral presentation skills.

Suggestions for follow up

Several issues which come up in the memory game can be pursued in other activities. For instance, if you want to explore the issue of budgets for education and other social needs and the budget spent on militarisation, you can do the activity "Money to spend", on page 177. Issues relating to child labour and lack of access to education can be explored in the activity "Ashique's story", on page 91.

Ideas for action

The memory cards show numerous problems which hamper the "Education for All" project. The group could choose any one of the problems on which to do research, to find ideas for solutions and finally to take action. Refer to chapter 3 on taking action for tips about how to go about this.

Why not write letters to MPs enquiring about what your country is doing in order to fulfil the goals that were set during the World Education Forum?

Further information

The right to education is one of the recognised social and economic rights. However, while there is a general acceptance and commitment by states to offer free basic education to all, the reality is that free education is not for all, but for a minority.

To face this challenge, the international community gathered in Senegal in the year 2000 for a World Education Forum (WEF). The conference aims were to review the progress made during the 1990s to provide basic education, and to reinvigorate the commitment to Education for All. Some 1100 participants from 164 countries adopted the Dakar Framework for Action, committing themselves to achieving quality basic education for all by 2015. UNESCO was entrusted with the overall responsibility for co-ordinating all the international players and for sustaining the global momentum.

It was acknowledged that different countries face different challenges. For instance, some countries face lack of resources, while others lack the political will. One of the results of the meeting was the acknowledgement that in order to reach and sustain the goals and targets of Education for All, it is necessary to establish broad-based partnerships within countries, supported by co-operation with regional and international agencies and institutions.

During this meeting the fundamental importance of education for sustainable development, peace, the effective participation of society and for sound economies in the twenty-first century was highlighted. A commendable result of the WEF was the setting of specific goals, with specific time limits, as well as the description of actions that must be taken at all levels in order to achieve Education for All. Whether these goals will be reached and the actions carried out is a question that can only be answered if everyone at every level of society is aware of and fights for Education for All.

Source: UNESCO Education for All: World Education Forum Final Report, 2000.

Money & Education
Lack of resources is the main threat to education for all. Without financial means, governments cannot meet their commitments to education for all. It is also a question of standards. Poorly paid teachers and lack of materials jeopardize the quality of education. Without resources, education is meaningless; no money, no education! Do you agree?

Globalisation & Education
Whoever thinks that globalisation only brings advantages to education through access to new technology is wrong! The effects of rapid trade liberalization, and the need for structural adjustment characteristic of globalisation, have threatened the revenue base of governments in several countries, but mainly developing countries. In these circumstances funding for education is often hit very hard.

Food & Education
In developing countries there is a strong view that food and education should come together: a hungry student cannot concentrate properly.
Food is often used as an incentive for parents to send their children to school; if the children were not fed at school, then they would send them out to work instead.

Education & the Internet
In many countries, information technology has become a core part of the education process. It is seen as essential for research and for homework. Many would agree that the Internet has opened new 'ways' for education, but it has also closed some. The gap between developed and developing countries has increased. In many countries not only are there no PCs, there is not even electricity

Education & Alcohol
In many schools/universities, alcohol abuse is a big problem. It prevents students from learning and increases violence.
Most schools have a policy that no alcohol can be brought onto the premises, but this does not seem to work.
What do you think can be done in order to solve this problem?

University (Higher and Further) Education
In terms of human rights law, nation states have the duty to provide free basic (primary) education only. Their commitments do not extend to higher or further education.
Should the State's duty be extended to university level? And if so, is it a realistic demand?

Teachers & Education
The quality of teachers/lecturers is sometimes a problem; they may lack experience or training to be top quality educators. There are calls for minimum requirements for teachers/lecturers, such as a teaching degree for school teachers and a doctorate for university lecturers. Are these demands realistic or would they only increase the problem of teacher shortages?

Education & Environment
The lifestyles of the majority of people in European countries are unsustainable. If people are to make informed choices about how to change their lifestyles they need to understand ecological relationships, economics, politics and history. They need intercultural skills and values of responsibility and concern. How would you include education for sustainability into the curriculum?

Free Education
Governments have the duty to guarantee free primary education to all. The reality is that in many countries if a family has no resources to pay for the fees and/or materials, their children cannot go to school

Discipline & Education
Schools and universities in different countries use different means to ensure discipline. Methods include corporal punishment, suspension, extra-work, expulsion and participation in a school or college council. What do you think is the best approach to guarantee discipline in an educational setting?

Women & Education
In developing countries, 78% of girls are in schools, as opposed to almost 86% of boys.
Some 60% of out-of-school children are girls.
One of the goals of the World Education Forum (WEF) is to eliminate gender disparities in primary and secondary education by 2005, and to achieve gender equality in education by 2015.

Peace & Education
"Peace starts at home"
Educational institutions are often seen as students' second homes. Education for peace should then be part of the formal education curriculum as well as being encouraged in non-formal educational settings. How would you include peace education within the formal curriculum?

Education & Equality
Extremes in pre-school enrolment figures range from close to 100% coverage in Bermuda, Malaysia, Belgium and Sweden to 2% or less in countries suffering from war and economic challenges.
One of the goals of the WEF is to ensure that the learning needs of all young people and adults are met through equal access to appropriate learning and life skills programmes

Sports & Education
A) Sports need not be compulsory during the entire school period. If time is lacking for other subjects, these should be prioritised.
B) Sports should always be present during the entire school period. It teaches many things that cannot be learnt in other subjects, such as co-operation and full development of body and mind.
Which statement do you agree with?

Education & Militarisation
Even though education and the military are seen as two separate things, they are in reality closely related. In many highly militarised countries a high proportion of the budget is allocated to military expenditure and not enough money is left for the social sector, especially education.

Social Exclusion & Education
Not everyone can be included in the State educational system. Street children, poor children, full-time child workers are usually not catered for by the school state system. In Romania, the foundation "Back to School" caters to the needs of children excluded from the state system – giving them a chance of education and better employment opportunities later in life.

Education & Minorities
The inclusion of minorities in school/universities is a common problem in multicultural societies. Besides the issue of discrimination against the person, differences of religion and language also present the system with challenges . How would you adapt the system and the curriculum to meet the needs of minorities?

Life-Long Learning
Adult illiteracy is a big problem in countries without even basic education. One of the WEF's goals is a 50 % improvement in levels of adult literacy by 2015.
Many European countries have made commitments to "life-long learning". However, they fail to deliver adequate further education to adults. What do you think a government's educational priorities should be?

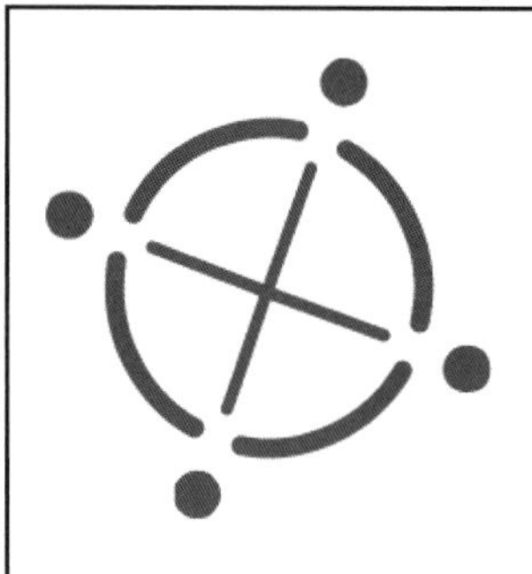

Human Rights Education
Human rights education (HRE) in formal, non-formal or informal education is considered to be a responsibility of the government. Why then in civil society should NGOs be responsible for something that is the government's duty and responsibilit?

Aids/HIV & Education
"The first battle to be won in the war against AIDS is the battle to smash the wall of silence and stigma surrounding it" (Kofi Annan). It is necessary to break the silence to end discrimination and to prevent further transmissions. The HIV/AIDS crisis should be at the centre of national educational agendas. What can be done to fight HIV/AIDS in educational institutions?

Electioneering

How persuasive are you?

Themes	Democracy, Citizenship, General human rights
Complexity	Level 2
Group size	Any
Time	45 minutes
Overview	This is a discussion-based activity that addresses: ▪ Rights and responsibilities connected with democracy ▪ Democratic discussion
Related rights	▪ The right to participate in the democratic process ▪ Freedom of opinion and expression
Objectives	▪ To consider some of the controversial aspects of a democratic society ▪ To practise and develop skills of listening, discussion and persuasion ▪ To encourage co-operation
Materials	▪ An open space ▪ Card (A4) and coloured pens to make the signs ▪ Sticky tape ▪ Small cards and pens for making notes (optional)
Preparation	▪ Make two signs, "agree" and "disagree", and tape them one at either end of a long wall. Make sure there is enough space along the wall for people to form a straight line. ▪ Place two chairs in the centre of the room, about 50cms apart, and with space around them for people to move about.

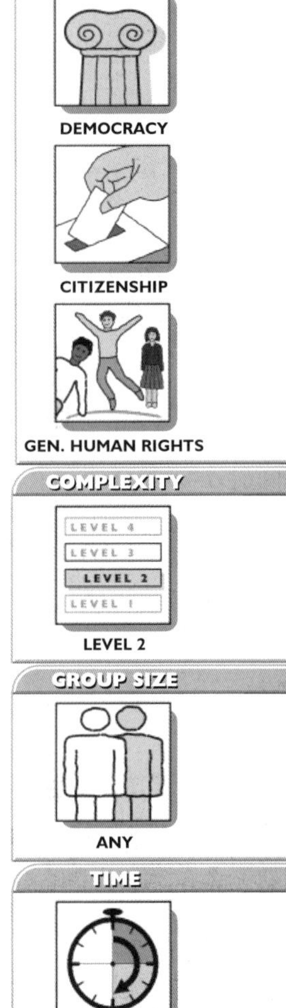

Instructions

1. Point out the two signs at either end of the wall, and explain that you are going to read out a statement, with which they may agree to a greater or lesser extent.
2. Select one statement from the list below and read it out to the group.
3. Tell people to position themselves along the wall between the two signs according to "how much" they agree or disagree: if they agree or disagree totally they should stand at one of the ends; otherwise they should stand somewhere between the two points.
4. When people have positioned themselves along the line, invite the two at the furthest extremes to occupy the two chairs in the centre of the room. Everyone else should now gather around the chairs, positioning themselves behind the person whose view they agree with "most"; or occupying a position in the centre if they are undecided.
5. Give each of the people sitting in the chairs one minute to state their reasons for agreeing or disagreeing with the original statement. No one should interrupt or assist them. Everyone should listen in silence.

6. At the end of the minute, ask the others in the group to move behind one or the other of the speakers (they cannot remain undecided), so that there is one group of people "for" the statement under discussion, and one group "against". Allow the two groups ten minutes apart from one another to prepare arguments supporting their position and to select a different speaker to present these arguments.
7. At the end of the ten minutes, call the groups back and invite the two new speakers to occupy the two chairs with their "supporters" around them.
8. Give these speakers three minutes each to deliver their arguments, at the end of which time, supporters for one or the other side may change position and move to the opposite group if the opposite side's arguments have been convincing.
9. Give the groups a further five minutes apart to work on their arguments and select a third speaker. Again, after the speeches, allow people to change position if they wish to.
10. Bring the group back together for the debriefing.

Debriefing and evaluation

Now move on to reflect on the process and purpose of discussion as a form, and on the reasons for valuing a pluralist society. Try not to get drawn back into discussion of the issue itself.

- Did anyone change their mind during the course of the discussion? If they did, what were the arguments that convinced them?
- Do people think they were influenced by things other than the actual arguments that were being put forward, for example, by peer pressure, emotional language or a feeling of rivalry?
- For those that did not change their opinion in the course of the discussion, was there any purpose in talking through these issues? Can they imagine any evidence that might persuade them to change their views?
- Why do people hold different opinions? What should be done about this in a democratic society?
- Should *all* opinions be tolerated in a democracy?

Tips for facilitators

The first part of this activity, when participants position themselves along the line, should not take more than a couple of minutes. The point of this is simply to establish people's "starting positions" and for them to see where they stand in comparison with others.

The purpose of the activity is as much to practise skills of communication and persuasion as to think through the issues themselves. Therefore, participants should be encouraged to think not only about the content and presentation of their own opinions, but also about the type or form of arguments that will be most persuasive to people on the other side. They are aiming to draw as many people as possible into their "party". They can use the breathing time between "speeches" to consider the opposition's position, and to think about ways of weakening it.

You may have other topics besides those suggested below that could equally well be used as the basis for discussion. The important thing is to select a statement that will be controversial within your group.

Note: it will take about 30 minutes to discuss one statement going through the different rounds of discussion. If you want to use more statements, you will have to allow more time accordingly.

It is advisable to be flexible about the exact order of events, depending on the strengths and weaknesses of the group and on the liveliness of the discussion. For example:

- You may want to add one or two more intervals for the groups to prepare arguments, so that different speakers have the opportunity to present their points of view.
- If you have performed this activity before with the group – or even if you have not – you can keep an element of surprise by varying the way that the first speakers are chosen – for example, you could select the two people *third from each end*.
- You may decide, in one of the intervals for preparing arguments, to ask the "supporters" of each speaker to work with the opposing speaker – in other words, to prepare arguments *against* the position that they themselves hold. This can be a good way of getting people to consider the opposite point of view, and can provide an interesting variation if people do not appear to be changing sides at all.

You may want to allow the speakers to have a postcard-sized piece of paper on which to make brief notes to remind them of the different arguments and to which they can refer while speaking.

You may want to raise the issue of whether "pluralism" or freedom of expression should be subject to any limits in a tolerant society: should fascist or nationalist demonstrations be permitted, for example?

Key date

24 October
United Nations Day

Suggestions for follow-up

If you are interested in following up the idea of how opinions are formed or changed, especially by the media you may want to look at the activity "Front page", on page 135.

Ideas for action

If you choose the statement on voting, you may want to follow up the activity with a survey of voting habits in your local community; see the activity "To vote, or not to vote", on page 238.

Statements for discussion

- We have a moral obligation to use our vote in elections.
- We should obey all laws, even unfair ones.
- The only people who have any power in a democracy are the politicians.
- "People get the leaders they deserve".
- It is the responsibility of citizens to control the day-to-day activity of the government.

Fighters for rights

"It is an ideal to live for and to achieve." Nelson Mandela

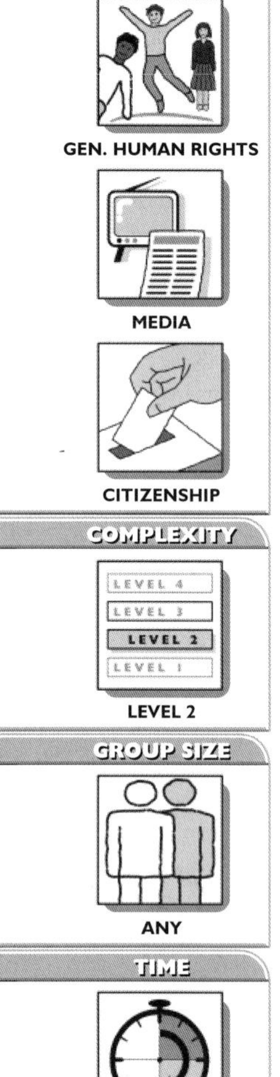

Themes General human rights, Media, Citizenship

Complexity Level 2

Group size Any

Time 60 minutes

Overview This activity uses information cards to stimulate interest in human rights heroes. The issues addressed are:

- Political repression
- Human rights activists in the twentieth century
- The struggle for rights in various countries

Related rights

- Freedom of opinion and expression
- The right to a fair trial
- The right not to be tortured.

Objectives

- To learn about some of the individuals who have fought for human rights in different countries
- To develop skills of handling and ordering information, co-operation and group work skills
- To promote respect, responsibility and curiosity about human rights.

Materials

- One set of thirty cards per small group
- Scissors
- Envelopes
- Optional: glue and pieces of stiff paper for backing the cards

Preparation

- Arrange the room so that people can work in small groups
- Make copies of the cards on the handouts, so that you have one set for each small group
- Cut up each set of thirty cards, shuffle them so that they are not in sequence, and put them in envelopes. It is important to keep the sets separate from each other!

Instructions

1. Ask people to get into small groups (3 or 4 in each group), and hand out one set of cards to each group.
2. Ask them to spread the cards out, face down on the floor.
3. Explain that the cards describe events in the life of six human rights activists. The aim for each group is to match the events with the correct character, and thereby to build up a brief description of each person.
4. Explain that each of the characters is made up of a "set of five" (i.e. one 'A', one 'B', one 'C', one 'D' and one 'E' card).
5. Tell each group to do rounds of picking up one card at a time, until the cards run out.

6. Give people a few minutes to read their own cards in silence.
7. Then let them go... Allow each group to devise their own strategies for building up the personalities. They will need about 15 - 20 minutes for this stage.
8. Gather everyone together, and ask a representative from one group to introduce, in their own words, one of the personalities. Then repeat with the other groups in turn, so each personality is presented in full, and each group can check that they put the "pieces" together correctly.

Debriefing and evaluation

1. How easy was the exercise, and which strategies did the different groups use to sort the sets of cards?
2. Which of the characters had people already heard of, and which of them were new? Why were some of the personalities better known than others?
3. Were people surprised by any of the information? What did they find most impressive?
4. Ask people to select the quotation with which they most strongly identify: how do they think they would have behaved if they had been put in the same position as this person?
5. What actions are available to people?

Tips for facilitators

There is a huge amount of information available on each of these characters and the short biographies that have been supplied offer a very shallow (and subjective) perspective on the matter. There are also hundreds of other activists who could just as well have gone onto the list - those selected here are intended only to give a "taster", and a way into the subject.

Suggestions for follow-up

It is highly recommended that you try to follow up this activity by encouraging people to find out about other human rights activists, so that they develop a feel for the characters who throughout history have contributed to the struggle for human rights. The group could start to build up its own "portrait gallery" of human rights activists. The six given in this activity can be used as a starting point: the photographs can be stuck to pieces of card together with the quotations and the short biographies, and displayed about the room. Each member of the group could be asked to find out about other personalities and to add them to the portrait gallery. The six that have been introduced here are all campaigners in the area of civil and political rights, but you may want to extend the range of rights to include social and economic ones as well. In civil society there are several channels for expressing opinion and fighting for rights. If you want to take a closer look at these you could do the activity "Making links", on page 173.

Ideas for action

Find out about some of the current political prisoners or activists – for example, those that Amnesty International has labelled a "Prisoner of Conscience". Write a letter or organise a campaign to inform people about this prisoner, and to put pressure on the relevant individuals to release him or her.

Key date

10 December
Human Rights Day

Further information

Useful web-sites giving information on human rights activists:
www.speaktruthtopower.org
www.universalrights.net/heroes
www.globalyouthconnect.org
www.hrw.org

The UK Section of Amnesty International have produced their own historical wall chart of human rights defenders, which can be ordered through their website: www.amnesty.org.uk

HANDOUTS

Discussion cards

A

"I have fought against white domination, and I have fought against black domination. I have cherished the ideal of a democratic and free society in which all persons live together in harmony and with equal opportunities. It is an ideal to live for and to achieve. But if needs be, it is an ideal for which I am prepared to die."

Nelson Mandela

A

"As a result of certain painful but at the same time comforting encounters, I saw for myself how from the depths of moral savagery there suddenly arose the cry 'it's my fault' and how, with this cry, the patient recovered the right to call himself a human being."

Evgenia Ginzburg

B

Born in a village near Umtata, and was elected President of the Republic of South Africa in the first democratic elections in that country at the age of 76. Up to that point – and beyond - his/her life was devoted to

B

Born in 1906 in Russia and died in Moscow in 1977. Worked quietly as a teacher and journalist until branded a terrorist by the Stalin regime in a fabricated trial. Spent 18 years in

C

the fight against apartheid, the racist system used by the former white government to suppress the majority black population. S/he suffered various forms of repression: was banned from meetings, forced to go into hiding, and was finally

C

Siberian prison camps under horrifying conditions because s/he refused to accuse others of crimes they did not commit. Spent the first year in solitary confinement in a damp cell, forbidden to exercise, speak, sing or lie down in the day. Later on s/he was

D

arrested, and sentenced to life imprisonment at the age of 44. S/he spent the next 28 years of his/her life behind bars, away from his/her family and children.

D

sent from one to another of the Siberian labour camps - including, as a punishment for helping a fellow prisoner, the very worst, from which few returned alive.

©MTI

©David King Collection

A

"I have a dream that one day this nation will rise up and live out the true meaning of its creed: 'We hold these truths to be self-evident: that all men are created equal.' I have a dream that my four children will one day live in a nation where they will not be judged by the colour of their skin but by the content of their character." *Martin Luther King*

A

"Non-violence is the greatest force at the disposal of mankind. It is mightier than the mightiest weapon of destruction devised by the ingenuity of man."
Mahatma Gandhi

B

Born in Atlanta, Georgia, in 1929, when the law required blacks to occupy special seats in buses, theatres and cinemas, and to drink from separate water fountains from whites. When s/he was 28, co-founded

B

Born in 1869, to Hindu parents who lived in Gujarat, when India was still held by force in the British Empire. S/he led the struggle for Independence, never straying from his/her firm belief in

C

an organisation of black churches that encouraged non-violent marches, demonstrations and boycotts against racial segregation. The organisation participated in a protest in Birmingham, Alabama, at which hundreds of singing school children

C

non-violent protest and religious tolerance, despite being arrested and imprisoned on several occasions. When Indians acted violently against one another, or against the British Raj, s/he fasted until the violence ended. S/he led a 241 mile march across India, and

D

filled the streets in support. The police were ordered in with attack dogs and firemen with high-pressure hoses. S/he was arrested and jailed.

D

persuaded followers to accept the brutality of the police and soldiers without retaliation. S/he spent a total of 2338 days in jail in a life tirelessly devoted to peace.

A

"We're not trying to destroy or annihilate the military regime; they are always threatening to annihilate us but ... the purpose of our movement is to create a society that offers security to all our people, including the military."

Daw Aung San Suu Kyi

B

Born in 1945, in Burma, s/he was the child of the assassinated national hero in the struggle for independence from colonial rule. Became a popular leader of the struggle for democracy against

C

a cruel military regime and was nearly assassinated by an army unit ordered to aim their rifles at him/her. Was placed under house arrest for 6 years without being charged with any crime, and was effectively cut off from the outside world. Even when released, the government

D

prevented him/her from seeing his/her dying spouse. In 2001 s/he is still confined to his/her residence, with access tightly controlled and the telephone lines cut.

©Gamma Press

A

"Alas, this sad song in my mind I send to those who help prisoners. These feelings in this dark season - I will never forget the horrible tortures. May this present misery in prison never be inflicted on any sentient being."

Ngawang Sangdrol

B

is a Buddhist nun who believes Tibet should be independent from China, and who was arrested for the first time at the age of 10 by Chinese authorities. His/her only crime was to participate in

C

a peaceful demonstration for the independence of Tibet. Was arrested again at the age of 15, and sentenced to 3 years imprisonment. The sentence was extended first because s/he sang an independence song in prison; and then again for 8 years because s/he

D

shouted "Free Tibet" while standing in the rain in the prison yard. Today s/he has problems with her kidneys as a result of the torture s/he has suffered.

©Tibet Information Network

Front page

To spread the news is to multiply it.
Tibetan proverb

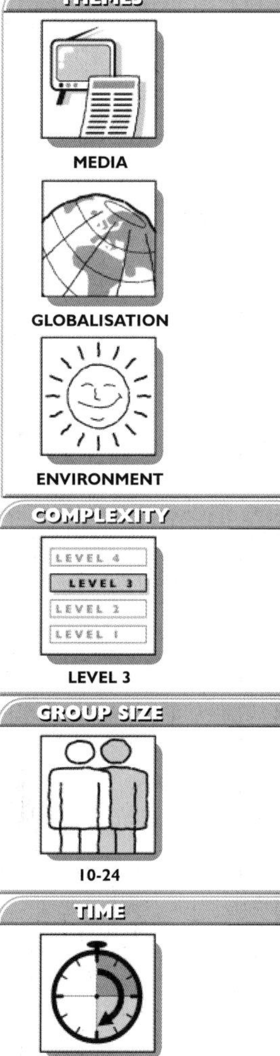

Themes Media, Globalisation, Environment

Complexity Level 3

Group size 10 - 24

Time 180 minutes

Overview This is a simulation of a group of journalists working to get the front page of their paper ready to go to press. People work in small groups as they explore issues about:
- Bias, stereotyping and objectivity in the media.
- Images and the role of media in addressing human rights issues.

Related rights
- The right to freedom of thought, opinion and expression
- The right to privacy
- The rights to development, life and health

Objectives
- To stimulate interest in human rights issues through working with images
- To reflect on the media and their approach to human rights issues
- To develop the skills to communicate and co-operate

Materials
- A large room with enough space for two or three small working groups and plenary.
- 40 photographs from newspapers
- Paper and pens for making notes
- Large sheets of paper (A3) size or flipchart paper and markers
- Scissors and glue for each small group
- Tables with a working surface large enough for the working groups to spread all their papers out

Preparation
- Select forty to forty-five pictures from a magazine or national newspapers. Note: you need copies of the same 40 pictures for each small working group. You will therefore either have to buy several copies of each newspaper from which you select photographs, or have access to a photocopier.
- Display one set of photographs on a table.

Instructions

1. Introduce the activity. Explain that this is a simulation of an evening in a newspaper office where a group of journalists are working on the front page of their paper. Although these are local papers serving the community, each has a policy to keep its readership informed about current global issues, including human rights.

2. Divide the participants into small working groups of eight people. Each group is to imagine that it is an editorial group working on a different newspaper. Their task is to design and layout the front page of tomorrow morning's edition.
3. Ask each group to choose a name for their newspaper.
4. In plenary, briefly discuss the features and layout of a typical front page.
5. Show people the display of photographs. Ask them to walk around the table in silence and not to make any comments at this stage. Explain that these are the images that they have to work with; they may use them and interpret them as they wish.
6. Now set the editorial teams to work. Hand out the paper and pencils, glue and scissors to each group - but not the photographs yet.
7. Go over the instructions. They have one hour to select four or five news stories that they wish to present, to write the headlines, choose the photos and design the layout. Explain that they do not have to write long articles: the headlines and bi-lines are really sufficient. They should focus on the impact the front page makes, rather than actually telling the full stories. Suggest they start by discussing the themes or issues they want to include in their reports. Tell them that after ten minutes they will receive the photographs from the "print department".
8. When the groups have been working for about ten minutes, make the sets of newspaper photographs available to them.
9. When the teams have completed their front pages, they should lay them out for everyone to read. Then go on to the debriefing and evaluation.

Debriefing and evaluation

Start with a review of the activity itself and then go on to discuss the media, human rights issues and commitment.

- How did the groups organise the work? How did they make decisions about how to do the work and about which stories to cover? Did everyone feel they could participate and contribute?
- How did people choose the themes or issues to work with? Which came first, the issue or the picture? That is, did they first identify an issue and then find a suitable picture to illustrate it or were they inspired by a certain picture and then create a story around it?
- What themes or issues were presented? Did any relate to human rights issues? Were there issues that anyone would have liked to have used, but which they had to drop?
- How do the different front pages of the different papers compare? Have the same themes or photographs been used?
- Have different groups used the same image, but in different ways?
- How do people follow the news? In newspapers, on the television, radio or the Internet? Why do – or don't – they follow the news?
- In this simulation did they try to imitate a real front page? Or did they want to do it differently? What were the differences?
- What sort of news dominates the media in real life?
- Is there generally good coverage of human rights issues in the news?
- One of the major points of discussion regarding the media is its "objectivity". Do participants think it is possible to present news objectively?
- Which human rights themes were included in their front pages?

- What image do participants have of young people in other parts of the world?
- Are there important themes missing from the set of pictures?

Tips for facilitators

When choosing the pictures to use in this activity, make sure that you have a good variety of images and that you avoid stereotypes. The news are often full of murders, wars and other disasters and more rarely contains positive messages. (There is more that happens in Africa than war and famine!) Let the pictures you select give the participants an opportunity to pick images of "good" news as well as the "bad" news. There should be a good geographical spread, gender balance, images of young people, and things relevant to the everyday lives of young people, including positive images of how they can make a difference. Include images relating to hot news events and personalities, as well as images relating to issues of living in a multicultural society and a global world. The following list will give you some ideas. (It is based on the list of images used in the activity, "The news factory", described below under "variations".)

TV news presenter- woman
Globe
Camera team in the Third World
Women making dam
Unemployment benefit
African miner
Pesticides
Advertising a hamburger restaurant
Dry soil
Children playing in water
Washing a car
Burning oil
Greenpeace action
Plume of industrial smoke
Advertisement for alcohol
Advertisement: for Coca Cola

Seller on the beach
Market place in Asia
Lonely woman
Slums in Brussels
Overfull bin
Sorting out cans
Black boy with guitar
Rock star
State police
Graffiti
Parliament
Drugs
Refugee camp
Children in asylum centre
Football player
Action by Amnesty International

Demonstration in the Philippines
UN troops in Yugoslavia
Fighter plane
Guerrilla
Two dead soldiers
Piled up grain bags
Women's meeting
Family planning
AIDS prevention
Crowd of people
Public transportation
Car exhibition
Traffic jam
Young man with microphone
Mobile telephone

When introducing the activity and discussing the features and layout of a typical front page you should draw the participants' attention to the way the headlines are written to be attention-grabbing and the way the stories are then presented; first there is usually a short summary of a couple of column centimetres and then the finer text with the fuller story. Discuss how pictures are used to support the story or to capture the reader's attention. Point out also what the pictures don't show! Talk about how they have been cropped to draw the viewers' eye to what the photographer - or the picture editor - wants to show. Also point out the way in which captions are written.

Variations

An alternative way of presenting this activity is to present a radio or television news programme. If you choose to work on a television broadcast it is highly recommended that you use slides (dia-positives) in a blacked-out room to give the "feel" of watching the television. There is a set of slides which have been specially prepared for such an activity, available for loan from EFIL, the European Federation for Intercultural Learning.

Key date

3 May
World Press Freedom Day

Suggestions for follow-up

Discuss aspects of the rights selected by the groups for their news. For example, how are they addressed in your country?

Participants could contact a local newspaper or radio or television station and talk to journalists about how they work and discuss issues of objectivity and the way global and human rights issues are presented in the media.

If the group enjoy activities that involve quick thinking, they could do "Just a minute", on page 150, which is about the relationship between sport and human rights.

Ideas for action

Many local radio stations have opportunities for community groups to make their own broadcasts. Work on a group project to research and produce a radio broadcast about issues of concern to them, for example, under the headline: "think globally, act locally".

Further information

Some starting points for reflection about the themes addressed in the activity:

a) Media

1. Young people, as well as adults, are continually swamped with a mass of information through all the different media. We can ask ourselves: what do we do with this information? Does it mean that we are all better informed?
2. The media are becoming more and more commercialised and the simplification of the message, stereotyping and sensationalism are alarming developments. It is becoming increasingly difficult to find quality news.
3. Finding quality news is especially true in relation to news about inequality issues, particularly where developing countries are concerned. Non-western news is often seen only through western eyes. This very often results in negative and dismal news.

b) Human rights issues

The media are obviously important for raising the public's awareness about human rights. But we should be aware of how the issues are presented and the motives. Everyone needs to be critical of what is - and is not - given to us, and the way information and facts are presented. For example, in a war, fighters may be described either as freedom fighters or as terrorists in different papers depending on different political viewpoints. People of other cultures may be presented in non-objective ways. For example, the Inuit may be presented as being exotic, hardy people fighting to preserve their traditional way of living in igloos, but when it comes to a discussion about whaling, then they are described as "murderers".

c) Commitment

Some of the images used in the simulation should picture opportunities for people, especially young people, to commit themselves in very practical ways. As teachers, youth workers, etc., we wish to motivate young people to work for a better world. We ask ourselves how best to encourage young people to become engaged, and may question whether or not the existing opportunities are in fact attractive to young people. We may get some indication to the answers from the slides which the young people choose.

Garden in a night

Would you take the challenge to build a garden overnight?

Themes Environment, Citizenship, Health

Complexity Level 3

Group size 6+

Time 180 minutes

Overview This is a creative activity using drawing and model building to explore
- The forces that drive development
- How local development does or does not meet local people's needs
- How decisions about local development are made

Related rights
- The right to participate in decision-making processes
- The right to participate in the cultural life of the community
- The right to rest and leisure

Objectives
- To understand that the outcomes of development are not inevitable
- To develop skills necessary for participating in local democracy and development
- To develop creativity, group work skills, co-operation and respect for others

Materials
- Maps and pictures of where you live (past and present)
- A large-scale map of the neighbourhood showing your chosen site
- Pens and paper for drawing up designs
- Materials for making the models. For example, small boxes, tubs, tissue paper, paints, string, wool, wine corks, cardboard tubes, aluminium foil, egg cartons and other household junk, twigs, stones, bark, shells, etc.
- Glue and tape
- Paint and paint brushes
- Stiff cardboard or plywood to use for bases for the models

Preparation **For part 1.** Development – how and why
- Collect together past and present maps and pictures of the town or area where you live.
- Identify possible sites for the group to work on. Research in the locality to find out if there are any sites, which are due to be developed

For part 2. Making development plans:
- Collect information about the site the group decided to work on for example, newspaper articles and minutes of council meetings
- If you are going to make models using "junk", make sure that you have plenty of materials. Start saving small containers, inner tubes from toilet rolls, etc., well in advance of starting this activity.

THEMES

ENVIRONMENT

CITIZENSHIP

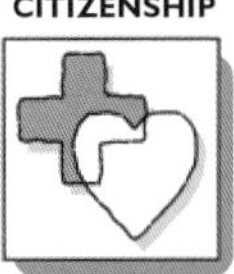

HEALTH

COMPLEXITY

LEVEL 3

GROUP SIZE

6 OR MORE

TIME

180 MINUTES

Instructions

This activity is in two parts: part 1, "Development – how and why" is a discussion about the forces that drive change; in part 2, "Making development plans" people design a development project in their own locality, and build a model of it.

Part 1. Development – how and why

1. Introduce the topic of local development. Use maps and pictures to stimulate discussion about how the local environment has developed over the last 50 to100 years. Talk about the political, economic and social forces that caused these changes. In general, have these changes been for the better? For whom and why?
2. Ask the group to name examples of developments that have happened during their life-times, such as extensions to buildings, shopping malls, housing estates, and who has benefited from these developments and how. For example, did the scheme provide much needed low-cost housing for local people or was it luxury apartments or holiday homes built as an investment by a finance company?
3. Look at the large-scale map of your locality and agree a local site that everyone wishes to work on.

Part 2. Making development plans

1. Display the large-scale map to show the site you have decided to work on. Make sure everyone is familiar with the site, and if necessary visit it.
2. Review the current plans for the site using information from local papers or minutes of council meetings. Talk about who is making the different proposals and what their interests in them are.
3. Brainstorm all the possible ways the site could be developed. Be as imaginative as possible.
4. Now break into small groups of 4 to 5 to review the brainstorm and briefly discuss the pros and cons of the different options.
5. The next task for each group is to come to a consensus about how the site should be developed, to draw up a design and then make a model of it.
6. When all the models are complete, let each group present their model and explain their plans.

Debriefing and evaluation

Start with a review of how the different groups worked. Did everyone feel involved? How were decisions made? Then go on to talk about the plans themselves.

- What were the main considerations when deciding how to develop the site? For example, cost, time, effort, profit, local needs - what?
- Were the plans people- and environment-friendly, and sustainable?
- Did the plans meet the needs of everyone in the locality? For example, the disabled, children, minorities?
- What resources would be needed to put the plan into effect?
- Were renewable resources used whenever possible?
- Were non-renewable resources used with care?
- How would the project affect the ecosystem in general? For example, was wildlife encouraged or were trees planted?
- What wastes would be produced building the project and in maintaining it? How will these wastes be disposed of?

Tips for facilitators

This activity assumes that most young people live in or near urban environments. The choice of site to work on must depend on your location and on your group. All sites have potential! Ideally, the group should research and decide. However, in some circumstances, for example, in schools, there may be curriculum constraints, so the teacher will have to choose.

Options for what to put on the site may include a shopping centre, a leisure centre, a school, housing, a car park, an open green space, a playground, a sports field, a quiet rose garden with seating for elderly people, a city farm, a wildlife sanctuary, an amusement park, a bowling green, etc. Encourage people to take the needs of different sections of the community into consideration.

Key date

5 June
Environment Day.

Variations

You could choose a fantasy scenario. For example, what would you rather see on the site where your town hall, council offices, hospital, etc. now stand? Or if you live in a rural locality, what better use could there be for a disused pit or a slag heap left over from mining operations?

Suggestions for follow-up

Find out more about the council's plans for developing the site you have been working with. Talk about what you think about the plans and write to the council or to your local paper to let others know your views. Find out how planning decisions are made in the town or village where you live. How much influence do local people have on decision-making? How can young people have more say in planning decisions that affect them? If the group are interested in exploring issues related to local decision-making, they could do the activity "To vote or not to vote", on page 238.

Ideas for action

Attend a planning meeting of your local council and contribute to the planning process.

Participate in celebrating Environment Day. Look on the web for information about Environment Day activities in your country in: www.unep.org

Further information

The idea for this activity came from the project "Have p□ en nat" (Garden in a night) that was part of the Copenhagen City of Culture Festival in 1996. A group of young people from □kologiskeigangsćttere, a local Agenda 21 organisation, worked for two years preparing to build a garden on a derelict inner city site – not quite in one night – but over a few days. The young people decided that they wanted a community garden on the 300 m^2 site. They learnt practical skills such as carpentry, plumbing, bricklaying and horticulture and prepared and grew everything off site, so that when the time came the garden could be assembled almost "overnight". There was something for everyone: little paths wound around the site by a turfed area, trees, shrubs, flowers and vegetables. The garden remained until the site was reclaimed by the council to be developed for housing in April 2001.

Heroines and heroes

If lions could talk, hunters would never be heroes

THEMES

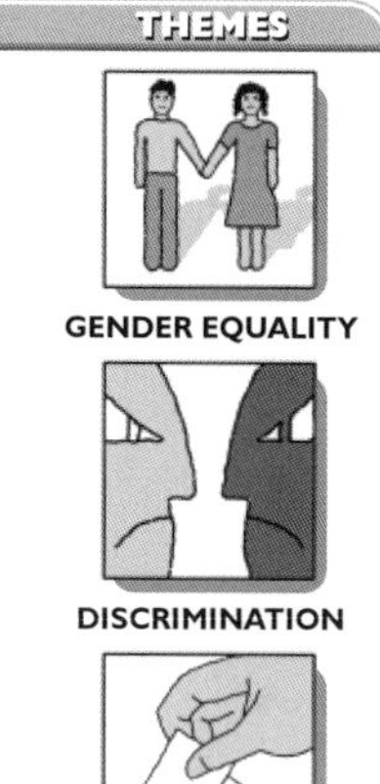
GENDER EQUALITY
DISCRIMINATION
CITIZENSHIP

COMPLEXITY

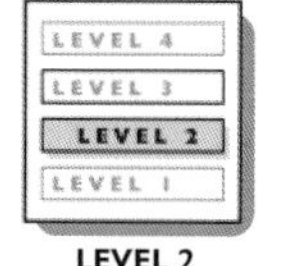
LEVEL 2

GROUP SIZE

ANY

TIME

60 MINUTES

Themes Gender equality, Discrimination and Xenophobia, Citizenship

Complexity Level 2

Group size Any

Time 60 minutes

Overview This activity involves individual, small and whole group work, brainstorming and discussion about:
- heroines and heroes as symbols of socialisation and culture
- stereotyped images of heroines and heroes

Related rights
- Equality in dignity and rights
- The right to freedoms without distinction of gender

Objectives
- To reflect on history teaching and to appreciate different perspectives on shared historical events and the heroes and heroines associated with them.
- To critically analyse the significance of heroes and heroines as role models and how gender stereotypes take their roots in our history, culture and everyday life.

Materials
- Paper and pens. (One blue and one red pen per participant; optional but preferable)
- Flipchart paper and markers

Instructions

1. Give people five minutes to think about which national heroines and heroes (historical or living) they particularly admire.
2. Hand out the paper and pens and ask each person to draw two columns. In the first column they should (using the red pen) write the names of three or four heroines plus a brief description of who they are and what they did for their country. At the bottom of the paper they should write key words to describe the heroines' personal characteristics.
3. Repeat the process (using the blue pen) for three or four heroes. Write this information in the second column.
4. Now ask the participants to get into small groups of between five and seven people to share their choices of heroines and heroes. Ask the groups to come to a consensus on the four most worthy heroines and four most worthy heroes.
5. Now come into plenary and write the names of each group's heroines and heroes in two columns on the flipchart. Add the key words that describe the personal characteristics.
6. Discuss the list of characteristics and the use of heroines and heroes as role models and the extent to which they are gender stereotypes. Then move on to the debriefing.

The following is an example of what a group in Ukraine produced at step 2.

Heroines	Heroes
Princess Olha, first Christian in Kyiv Rus	Prince Volodymyr Kyiv Rus (old name of Ukraine) was baptised.
Young woman, Roksalana, captured by the Turks. She lived in the khan's harem. She used her position to influence politics.	Hetman Mazepa, independence fighter
Poetess Lesya Ukrainka wrote about Ukrainian identity and women's emancipation	Poet Shevchenko, glorified freedom
strong cunning soft womanly powerful beautiful	strong powerful brave courageous adamant obstinate

Debriefing and evaluation

Start by reviewing the activity and what people learnt about heroes and heroines and then go on to talk about stereotypes in general and how they influence people's perceptions and actions.

- What kinds of people are heroines and heroes? (Ordinary men and women? Kings?) What did they do? (Fight? Write poems?) How did the participants learn about them?
- What were the differences and similarities between the two lists of characteristics?
- What values do the heroines and heroes stand for? Are these values the same for both, or are there differences?
- What do people understand by the word, "stereotype"? How true are stereotypes? Are stereotypes always negative?
- Do you personally, and people in your society in general, have general stereotypes and expectations of men and women?
- Do participants feel limited by these expectations? How?
- Does the list of characteristics produced in this activity reflect traits that some might describe as national characteristics?
- To what extent are social and cultural barriers in general the result of stereotyped thinking?
- In what ways does gender stereotyping deny people their human rights?
- Stereotyped expectations often act as barriers to both men and women limiting life choices and options. What gender-related barriers have participants experienced? In the home, school, club or work place?
- What can participants do about these barriers? Can they identify strategies to break away from cultural norms and values related to masculinity and femininity?

Tips for facilitators

This is a very good activity to do in a multicultural setting because the cultural element may become more apparent.

Key dates

8 March
International Women's Day

3 November
World Men's Day

At point 5 in the instructions you should accept all contributions from the small groups and write everything onto the flip chart. If someone suggests terms like "feminine" or "masculine" you should accept them at this stage and return to them in the debriefing when you should discuss the meanings of these words.

Variations

When working in youth groups it is likely that you will want to work with other types of heroines and heroes, for example, characters in comic books and films, pop, film and sports stars. You could start the session reading comics and then brainstorm the characteristics of the characters. Alternatively, you could put up posters of pop or sports stars and ask people to write speech bubbles or add drawings. If you leave the question, "who are your heroines and heroes?" completely open, you may find some interesting surprises that make for fruitful discussion.

Suggestions for follow-up

If the group would like to look at human rights heroines and heroes, then do the activity "Fighters for rights", on page 130.

Ideas for action

Make a personal pledge to be more aware of stereotyping in your daily life, especially that which leads to prejudice, both by others and (inadvertently!) by yourself.

Further information

A stereotype is a generalisation in which characteristics possessed by a part of the group are extended to the group as a whole. For example, Italians love opera, Russians love ballet, young people who wear black leather gear and ride motor bikes are dangerous and people who are black come from Africa.

There may be confusion about the words, sex and gender. *Sex* refers to the *biological* differences between men and women, which are universal and do not change. Gender refers to *social* attributes that are learned or acquired during socialisation as a member of a given community.

Gender therefore refers to the socially given attributes, roles, activities, responsibilities and needs connected with being men (masculine) and women (feminine) in a given society at a given time, and as a member of a specific community within that society.

Source: United Nations Development Program (UNDP), Gender in development programme, learning and Information pack, gender mainstreaming programme and project entry points. January, 2001

Horoscope of poverty

Can you see into the future? What will next year bring for Amina or to Misha?

Themes Poverty, Globalisation, Social rights

Complexity Level 3

Group size 15 - 21

Time 60 minutes

Overview This activity combines knowledge and creative composition to explore issues about the consequences of poverty and the opportunities in life which are denied to the poor.

Related rights
- The right to food and housing
- The right to health
- The right to work

Objectives
- To reflect on both the lack of opportunities poor people have, and the difficulties they face in taking those which are presented
- To understand the cycle of poverty
- To promote social justice, human dignity and responsibility

Materials
- 12 Horoscope cards
- 12 Life cards
- One sheet of paper and a pencil for each participant
- Large sheet of paper or flipchart or board
- Markers or chalk
- Tape

Preparation
- Copy the Horoscope and Life cards and cut them out.
- Make up three sets of cards so there are four life cards with their corresponding horoscope cards in each set. Put each set in a separate envelope so that they don't get muddled up.

Instructions

1. Introduce the activity. Talk briefly about horoscopes in general. Do participants ever read them? Do they believe them? What sorts of information do they usually give?
2. Divide the participants into three small groups and give each one a set of Life cards together with the corresponding Horoscope cards.
3. Give the groups twenty minutes to write fantasy horoscopes for the four lives on their cards. They should use their imagination, intuition and general knowledge to foretell what will happen to the people in the coming year. Stress that there are no right or wrong answers, but that they should try to make the predictions within the scope of reality.
4. When they have finished, call people into plenary. In turn, ask each group to present their work. They should first read out the information on the life cards so everyone

is introduced to the different characters, and then they should read out the horoscopes.

5. Finally tape the life cards and the predictions onto the large sheet of paper to make a wall chart.

Debriefing and evaluation

Start the discussion by asking each group to explain how they decided the futures of each of their characters. Then go on to try to define poverty and finally move on to discuss the consequences of poverty.

- What images do participants have of people who are poor? In their own country and in developing countries? Are these stereotypes? How well-founded are the images? Where do people get their information from?
- What do participants understand by the term poverty?
- Might someone be regarded as 'rich' if they lived in one country and 'poor' if they lived in another? In other words, is poverty relative?
- In your society, why are some people rich and others poor?
- What are the main passports out of poverty, both in your country and in Eritrea, one of the poorest countries in the world? Having a rich uncle? Winning the lottery? Having an education? Being healthy? Knowing the right people? Working hard? What else?
- How easy is it for people who are poor to break the circle of poverty? In other words, how hard is it for someone born into a poor family not to be poor as an adult?
- What kinds of opportunities do people have when they are rich?
- What kinds of opportunities do people have when they are poor?
- Is it people's own fault that they are poor? Is it their fate? Is it because of social, political and economic forces?
- Poverty often goes hand in hand with poor health, hunger and malnutrition, lack of education, poor work skills and unemployment. Is it a coincidence or are they connected? If so, what are the connections?
- In general how do people view/treat poor people?
- What sort of political and social policies lead to the best opportunities for life for all citizens?
- To what extent is education a key to reducing poverty in your country?
- In almost every country of the world, the gap between rich and poor is increasing. The gap is also increasing between countries. What are the consequences of this for Europe?
- Does it matter that the gap is widening? If people think it does matter, then whose responsibility is it to act to reduce the gap?
- What can individuals, groups, local communities and nations do to close the gap?

Tips for facilitators

Make it clear to participants that this is a fantasy horoscope and that it is not necessary to be an astrologer or know anything about the characteristics traditionally attributed to the signs of the zodiac. Rather, they should focus on the details given in the life stories on the cards and use their own general knowledge and knowledge of history, economics and sociology. The "love" item in the horoscope cards should be taken to refer not only to the love life of the individual, but also their relationships with family and friends.

Variations

You can adapt the life stories or replace all or some of them with others you find more interesting or appropriate. You can also replace these stories by real cases you know of, or have heard of, in your own community or country.

Suggestions for follow-up

Women are frequently the sole breadwinners in the family, either because they are single parents, or because their partners are out of work. However, women are often discriminated against in the workplace and, if social support is lacking, it is often extremely hard to both work and bring up a family. If the group are interested in exploring some of these issues, they could do the activity "Work and babies", on page 260.

Ideas for action

Offer your support to an NGO or association that is working with people who are poor and trying to create opportunities for them. You could identify a local group and find out what their needs are, then develop a project to raise funds.

Key date

17 October
International Day for the Eradication of Poverty

HANDOUTS

Life cards

Maria, a single mother with three children, lives in a very poor suburb in Madeira, Portugal. Her latest companion has just left her. She works as a maid for a wealthy family, but for how much longer? Someone recently stole an expensive ring from the lady of the house, who suspects one of the maids. They can't find out who is guilty, so all the maids are going to be sacked and replaced. Maria is **Capricorn**.

Amina is from Turkey. She lives in a small village in one of the poorest region of the country. She is 12 years old and her parents - very poor peasants - are talking about looking for a husband for her. But she does not want to get married; instead she decides to run away from home and travel to the capital where she hopes to have a brighter future. Amina is **Gemini**.

Misha is from Tomsk in Siberia. He has been unemployed for many months and he does not know what to do. His wife is very ill and has to stay in bed all day. He has four children aged 20, 18, 10 and 8 and the two youngest are disabled. Misha is **Virgo**.

Yuriy lives with his parents and three younger brothers in Tomsk in Siberia. He is twenty years old and a very promising ice-hockey player. His uncle in America has offered to try to find him a scholarship to study in an American college. Yuriy's father, Misha, has been unemployed for many months and at the moment, the only source of family income is from odd jobs that Yuriy does. Yuriy does not know what to do. His mother is ill, two of his younger brothers are disabled and the family relies on him. Yuriy is **Cancer.**

Bengt is a young Swedish skinhead. He has been arrested twice this year for violent behaviour. He has been out of work for two years now and despite this, refuses all the offers that have been made to him. He prefers to spend his time training his dog, a pit bull terrier, doing body-building and being in the streets with his mates, who have been linked to several recent racist incidents. Bengt is **Aries.**

Ricardo lives on his own in Barcelona, Spain, in a tiny apartment he can hardly afford. He has been ill for many months and lives off social security payments from the government. He used to work doing odd jobs. His wife took the children away and abandoned him when she heard that he has AIDS. He is **Libra**.

Abdoul came from Mauritania many years ago to look for work in the French capital, Paris. He spent the first years alone but was later able to bring over his wife and four sons as well as his grandparents. They all live in one apartment in a poor area of Paris. For a while things went well, especially when Abdoul's wife gave birth to twins, but it has proved a struggle to bring the children up to keep the Mauritanian traditions. The twins are now 12 years old. They are having lots of problems at school and often refuse to obey their parents. Recently, Abdoul lost his job because of the general economic downturn. Abdoul is **Leo**.

The twins, **Moktar** and **Ould**, were born in Paris in France. They are the children of Abdoul, a migrant worker, originally from Mauritania. The whole family, their parents, four older brothers as well as their grandparents all live in one apartment in a poor area of Paris. The twins are now 12 years old and have lots of problems at school. They refuse to study, skip classes very often to hang around with their friends in the suburbs of Paris and refuse to obey their parents, with whom they fight a lot, sometimes violently. Reports from school show that they are becoming increasingly aggressive. Moktar and Ould are **Aquarius.**

Krista, 20 years old, rents a tiny flat in a very poor suburb of Prague and dreams of living in Germany. She has read an advertisement offering jobs in Berlin. She called the number and met a man who promised to get her out of poverty saying that she will easily find a job in Berlin. She decides to trust the man and to take the chance to go to Germany. Krista is **Sagittarius**.

Jane is an elderly widow who lives in Scotland. Her husband was an alcoholic and hardly ever worked. She survives on the very small state pension but now needs extra care as her health is worsening. Jane is **Pisces**.

Bella lives together with her sister, Angelica, in Palermo in Italy. Their parents died when the girls were sixteen and seventeen, which meant that they had to leave school and work to support themselves. They are now twenty-two and twenty-three. Bella has two jobs; she works as a maid during the day and as a cleaning lady in a hospital at night. She also looks after Angelica, who is a drug addict. Bella refuses to let her sister down because she knows how much her sister suffered from their violent father. Bella has problems with her own hot temper, that she finds hard to control and which has caused her to lose her job on two recent occasions. Bella is **Taurus.**

Angelica lives together with her sister Bella in Palermo in Italy. Their parents died when the girls were sixteen and seventeen, which meant that they had to leave school and work to support themselves. They are now twenty-two and twenty-three. Bella has two jobs and she also looks after Angelica, who is a drug addict. Angelica often steals her sister's wages to buy drugs. She has been on and off drugs for many years but finds it very difficult to control her addiction. Angelica is **Scorpio**.

Horoscope cards for the year

Aries (Bengt) (21 March-21 April) Love Work Health	**Libra** (Ricardo) (23 Sept-22 Oct) Love Work Health
Taurus (Bella) (22 April-21 May) Love Work Health	**Scorpio** (Angelica) (23 Oct-22 Nov) Love Work Health
Gemini (Amina) (22 May-21 June Love Work Health	**Sagittarius** (Krista) (23 Nov-21 Dec) Love Work Health
Cancer (Yuriy) (22 June-22 July) Love Work Health	**Capricorn** (Maria) (22 Dec-20 Jan) Love Work Health
Leo (Abdoul) (23 July-22 August) Love Work Health	**Aquarius** (Moktar and Ould) (21 Jan-19 Feb) Love Work Health
Virgo (Misha) (23 August-22 Sept) Love Work Health	**Pisces** (Jane) (20 Feb-20 March) Love Work Health

Just a minute

Talk for 'just a minute' - no hesitations - no repetition!

Themes Sport, Globalisation, General human rights

Complexity Level 2

Group size Any

Time 40 minutes

Overview In this activity, people have to be quick and inventive to talk for one minute on the relationship between sports and human rights.

Related rights All

Objectives
- To share knowledge about sport and human rights issues.
- To understand how all human rights issues are interconnected and indivisible
- To develop self-confidence to express personal opinions

Materials
- Statements, one per participant
- A hat
- A watch with a second hand, or a timer

Preparation
- Make a copy of the sheet below, and cut out the statements.
- Fold the strips of paper over and put them into a hat.

Instructions

1. Ask people to sit in a circle.
2. Pass round the hat. Ask each person in turn, without looking, to dip into the hat and take out one slip of paper.
3. Participants then have 5 minutes to prepare to talk non-stop for one minute on the statement written on their slip of paper. The rules are no hesitations and no repetitions.
4. Go round the circle and ask each person in turn to give their "speech".
5. After each "speech", allow two or three minutes for short comments. If people have a lot to discuss, make a note of the topic and agree to return to it at the end.
6. When everyone has had their turn, go back and finish any discussions that had to be cut short.
7. Then go on to the debriefing and evaluation.

Debriefing and evaluation

Start by reviewing how the activity went and then go on to talk about the issues that were raised.
- Was it difficult to talk non-stop on the topics for one minute?
- Which were the toughest topics to talk about and why?
- Which of the statements was the most controversial and why?
- What was the most surprising piece of information people heard?

Tips for facilitators

This activity works at many different levels and the questions may be interpreted in different ways. It is important to work at the level of the young people. You may wish to say something to provoke deeper thinking, but be aware of the danger of giving the impression that you are expecting a "a certain answer".

If you think that the statements below are not of interest to your group, then compose others.

Encourage reluctant speakers to have a go. Suggest they try to talk for half a minute or even for just twenty seconds or tell them they may first confer briefly with a friend before they talk, or offer to let them have their go later.

Variations

In a small group you can do two or more rounds. People take one slip of paper in each round. If you are working with more than fifteen people, work in two sub-groups.

This technique of taking statements out of a hat can be adapted to use with any theme.

Suggestions for follow-up

If people want to continue with the theme of sport and are feeling energetic, try the activity "Sport for all", on page 214.

If one of the other themes provoked particular interest, check the index of activities at page 68 for to find an activity on that theme.

Ideas for action

Decide on one issue to tackle and agree the next stage in taking action. Develop a project to continue working on the chosen issue. Link up with a local organisation which is working in the field. Use the project as a learning opportunity and help people reflect on what they have gained in group work skills and action competencies.

Further information

"How you play the game: the contribution of sport to the promotion of human rights", Conference in Sydney 1 to 3 September 1999: www.hrca.org.au/#sport_and_human_rights.

Key date

7 April
World Health Day

HANDOUTS

Sheet of statements

Sport and general human rights

Do you think that Ronaldo makes a good special representative for the "Force for Change: World AIDS Campaign with Young People"?

Sport and general human rights

Athletes at international level have to agree a code of conduct. Those who then breach the code, for instance, by using a sporting event to make a political statement are penalised. Is this a denial of a person's right to free expression?

Sport and general human rights

The police have powers to stop football supporters whom they suspect of being troublemakers from travelling to other countries for matches. Is this a legitimate denial of their right to freedom of movement and association?

Sport and children

What would you say to ambitious parents and trainers who force children to train for hours on end? Who should have the right to decide about a young person's health and how they spend their leisure time?

Sport and citizenship

Many people are born in one country, but then make their home and become citizens in a second country. Nonetheless, they continue to support the national team of their country of birth, instead of that of the second country. Which national team should they support?

Sport and discrimination

To what extent do the Paralympics break down prejudices against disabled people?

Sport and discrimination

Is sex testing of athletes necessary to ensure fair competition or is it too great an infringement of people's human dignity and right to privacy?

Sport and education

Do you think sports lessons should be compulsory throughout formal schooling?

Sport and social rights

Do you think professional sportsmen and women should have similar rights to those of other workers, for instance, the right to form trades unions and the right not to be unfairly dismissed?

Sport and environment

Golf courses are frequently criticised for being both people and environment unfriendly because they are often developed on land that was used by local people for farming and forestry. They also require a lot of water, herbicides and pesticides for their maintenance. Does this make golf a human rights issue?

Sport and gender equality

Some people say that there are few women among the top coaches and sports administrators because of discrimination against women. Do you agree? If you do, what can be done about it?

Sport and globalisation

Sports shoes and much other sports equipment are made cheaply with exploited labour in Eastern Europe and in the Far East. The workers want to continue working and do not call for a boycott. What can we, as consumers, do to avoid being party to their exploitation?

Sport and human security

China has a poor human rights record. Should they have been chosen to host the Olympic games in 2008?

Sport and health

What can be done at a local level to combat the use of drugs in sports?

Sports and the media

Do you think that any particular television company has the right to buy exclusive coverage of any sporting event?

Sport and peace

To what extent do competitive sports promote co-operation and understanding between people?

Sport and poverty

Do you think that politicians in your country use sport, or sporting events, to distract and divert people from political and economic issues?

Sport and poverty

In many countries, sport, but especially soccer, offers individuals the possibility of a "passport out of poverty". Should poor countries, therefore, put more focus on soccer?

Let every voice be heard

"To educate is to believe in change."
Paulo Freire

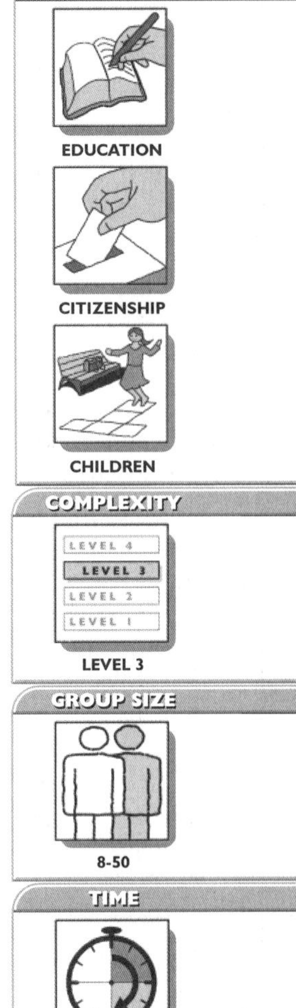

Themes Education, Citizenship, Children

Complexity Level 3

Group size 8-50

Time 115 minutes

Overview This is a discussion exercise in small groups and plenary, working with the issues of:
- What education is and how it meets, or does not meet, people's needs
- Participation in decision-making processes.

Related rights
- The right to education
- Freedom of opinion and expression
- The right to take part in the government of one's country

Objectives
- To reflect on the education system and how it meets people's needs
- To develop skills of co-operation and participation in democratic decision-making at school and club level
- To promote justice and inclusion

Materials
- 4 large sheets of paper or flipchart paper and pens per small group of four people
- Extra paper, sufficient for people to make notes on if they wish to

Instructions

This activity is in two parts: part 1 (35 minutes) is a discussion about what sort of education people want, and part 2 (60 minutes) is a discussion about how to develop democratic systems to ensure that people can have their say about the education that they get.

Part 1. What sort of education do we want? (35 minutes)

1. Start with a short general discussion about what people understand by the term "education". They should know that to receive an education is a human right.
2. Now brainstorm all the positive and negative sides of education and note the keywords on flipchart paper.
3. Ask people to get into pairs. Give them fifteen minutes to assess the value of the right to education in the context of who makes the decisions about what people are to learn and how.
4. Come back into plenary and ask people to give feedback.

Part 2. Developing democratic systems to ensure that people can have their say about the education that they get. (60 minutes)

1. Ask people to go back into their pairs and to review how decisions are made in their school, college or club. For instance, who decides what is taught or what activities will be arranged? How is the school, college or club administrated? How are budgetary and spending decisions made? How are policies developed and agreed? How much say do young people have?
2. Now ask the pairs to combine to make small groups of four people. Tell them to bear in mind that they have a human right to education, and also that they have a right to be involved in the decision-making processes in matters which concern them.
3. Ask each group to consider the positive and negative aspects of having a democratically elected body to make decisions about their education at the local level. Such a body might be a Student Council in a school or college, or a board in a youth club or youth organisation.
4. Now ask the groups to consider what would be the best form of council or board that would meet their needs to have a say in the education that they receive.
5. The next stage depends on the circumstances of the group. If there is no council in your school or club, then the groups should work to decide what sort of council they would like and how to go about establishing one. If your group already has a council or a board, then they should review how it works and develop plans for how to make it work better. Explain how to do a SWOT analysis and tell the groups that they have thirty minutes to develop an action plan written up on a large sheet of flipchart paper.
6. Come back into plenary and ask the groups to report their results.

Debriefing and evaluation

Many points will already have been made at the various stages of the previous discussions. However, take time to review the activity as a whole, to reflect on the general learning points and to plan what to do next.

- Did people enjoy the activity? Was it useful? Why? Why not?
- Why are the existing decision-making structures as they are? What are the historical precedents? Did the structures fulfil their functions in the past? Why are they not appropriate now?
- Why do decision-making structures and procedures need to be reviewed regularly?
- How did the different action plans compare?
- What did they cost in terms of time, effort and money?
- How realistic were they? (Note: it is good to have big visions, but you need to take one step at a time towards the goal!)

Tips for facilitators

Depending on the group, you will have decide what is the best way to introduce the activity with regard to the human rights aspects, that is, the right to education and the right to take part in decision-making processes. You can do this either by asking people to share their existing knowledge or by giving some initial input yourself.

The SWOT analysis is described and explained in the "Taking action" (chapter 3)

Suggestions for follow-up

Let the group work further on the ideas generated in this activity and, taking tips from the "Taking action" chapter, on page 269, strive for more say in the decision-making in their school, college or club.

If the group enjoyed thinking about the sort of education they would like to have, they may enjoy the board game "A tale of two cities", on page 71, which raises issues about what sort of city people would like to live in.

Ideas for action

The participants might consider linking and exchanging information with other student councils in their area, at the national level, or internationally.

Further information

Why have a school council?

A Student Council is intended to give students a voice in the school issues that directly affect them. There are many good reasons for establishing school councils and ensuring that they work effectively.

Pupil-centred benefits

Participation in a school council promotes the educational or personal development of pupils because:

- councils promote citizenship learning, political efficacy and democratic attitudes
- councils promote social confidence and personal values
- students are empowered to challenge authority
- students learn how to make decisions in a fair and accountable way
- students learn about the realities of life, for instance, how to work within limited budgets or with unresponsive authorities.

Pragmatic benefits

- democratic management styles work better than autocratic ones because they are ultimately more effective as they encourage pupils' responsibility
- councils encourage co-operation, harness energy and reduce alienation
- councils can improve the atmosphere of the school: teachers are trusted more, rules are shown to be more fairly based
- whatever the limitations because of outside social and political pressures, a student council is a practical way of demonstrating to students the good faith of the staff and commitment to certain values.

Key dates

5 October
World Teachers' Day

Let's talk about sex!

"Have you heard that Peter is gay?"

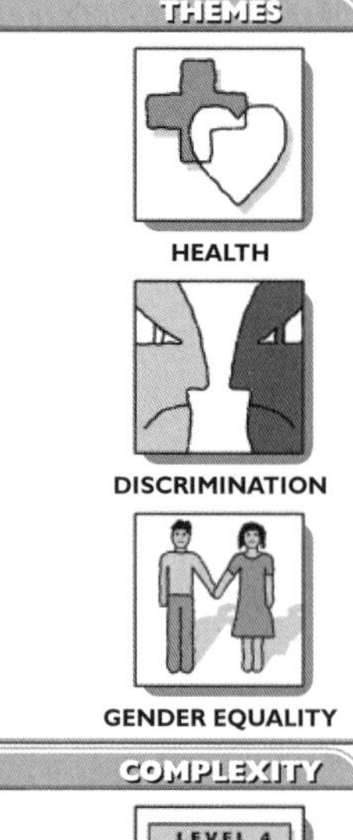

COMPLEXITY

LEVEL 4

GROUP SIZE

10 OR MORE

TIME

60 MINUTES

Themes	Health, Discrimination and Xenophobia, Gender equality
Complexity	Level 4
Group size:	10+
Time:	60
Overview	This activity uses the "fish-bowl" technique to explore attitudes to sexuality including homophobia.
Related rights	▪ The right to marry and found a family ▪ The right to freedom and discrimination and equality of treatment ▪ The rights of expression and association.
Objectives	▪ To address issues and rights related to sexuality, including homosexuality ▪ To develop self-confidence to express one's own opinion on these issues ▪ To promote tolerance and empathy
Materials	▪ 3 chairs ▪ 2 facilitators ▪ Space for participants to move about ▪ Board or flipchart and markers ▪ Small slips of paper and pens ▪ A hat
Preparation	▪ Be aware that in many communities sexuality is a sensitive issue and be prepared to adapt either the methodology or the topic – or both! ▪ Identify a few people who have been out-spoken about their sexuality including heterosexual and homosexual, bisexual and transsexual men and women.

Instructions

1. Set the scene. Explain that, although most people view sexuality as a private matter, the right not to be discriminated against because of sexual orientation is a fundamental human right and protected by legislation in most European countries. This activity is an opportunity to explore attitudes to sexuality and in particular to homosexuality. Then warm up with a brainstorm of famous people who have been out-spoken about their sexuality.
2. Hand out the slips of paper and pens and ask people to write down any questions they have about homosexuality or sexuality in general, and to put their papers in the hat. The questions should be anonymous.
3. Explain that this activity is about exploring attitudes to sexuality and in particular to homosexuality. Everyone is free to express opinions that may be conventional or unconventional, controversial or which challenge the norms of their society. People

may present points of view with which they agree, or with which they disagree with without fear of ridicule or contempt.

4. Place the three chairs in a half-circle in front of the group. These are for the three conversationalists who are in the "fish-bowl". The rest of the group are observers.
5. Explain that you will begin by inviting two volunteers to join you in a conversation in the "fish bowl". If at any point someone else would like to join you then they may do so, but as there is only room for three fish in the bowl at any one time, someone will have to swap out. Someone who wishes to join the conversation should come forward and gently tap one of the "conversationalists" on the shoulder. These two people exchange seats and the original "conversationalist becomes an observer.
6. Encourage people to come forward to express their own opinions, but also to express other opinions, which are not necessarily their own. In this way points of view that are controversial, "politically incorrect", or unthinkable can be aired and the topic thoroughly discussed from many different perspectives.
7. Offensive or hurtful comments, which are directed at individuals in the group, are not allowed.
8. Ask a volunteer to pick up a question from the hat and start discussing it. Let the discussion run until people have exhausted the topic and points are being repeated.
9. Then ask for three volunteers to discuss another question and start another round of conversations under the same rules as before.
10. Discuss as many questions as adequate in function of the time you have and the interest of the group. Before you finally go on to the debriefing and evaluation, take a short break to allow time for people to come out of the "fish-bowl". This is especially important if the discussion has been heated and controversial.

Debriefing and evaluation

Start with a brief review of how people felt being both inside and outside the "fish-bowl". Then go on to talk about the different views that were expressed, and finally discuss what people learnt from the activity:

- Was anyone shocked or surprised by some points of view expressed? Which ones? Why?
- In your community, how open-minded are people generally about sexuality?
- Are some groups more open than others? Why?
- What forces mould how our sexuality develops?
- Where do people get their values about sexuality from?
- Do participants' attitudes about sexuality differ from those of their parents and grandparents? If so, in what ways do they differ? Why?
- In some countries, laws and social pressure appear to conflict with the human rights of the individual to respect and dignity, to fall in love with the person of his/her own choice, to marry freely etc. How can such conflicts be resolved?

Tips for facilitators

Be aware of the social context in which you are working and adapt the activity accordingly. The aim of this activity is to allow participants to reflect on their own sexuality and the norms of their society and to encourage them to have the self-confidence to express their own point of view while being tolerant of people who hold different views. The aim is *not* to convince people of one point of view or another, nor to come to a consensus decision.

Before running the activity it is recommended that you prepare yourselves by reading the background information on gender and on discrimination and xenophobia. Think over what topics may come up. Some frequently asked questions and issues include:

- What is homosexuality?
- What are the differences between heterosexual, gay, lesbian, bisexual and transsexual people?
- Is homosexuality an illness?
- How do people become gay or lesbian?
- What about the risk of AIDS?
- In some countries homosexuality is accepted and gay people can get married in others it is punishable by death.
- How do homosexuals make love?

It is also important for you as facilitators to reflect on your own values and beliefs about what is right for yourselves, your families and for others and to remember that these values will be reflected in everything you do and say, and what you don't do or say. It is crucial that you acknowledge your own values and prejudice and understand the origins of those values in order that the participants may also develop insights into the origins of their own values.

The aim of the brainstorm of famous people who have been outspoken about their sexuality is to encourage the participants themselves to be open about discussing sexuality. It is also an opportunity to clarify terms such as gay and lesbian, homosexual, heterosexual, bisexual and transsexual. (See the background information on page 339).

Your role in the activity is crucial in setting the general tone. It is a good idea to start off with two facilitators as conversationalists. For example, one of you may start by saying, "Have you heard, Peter has announced that he is gay?" The other might reply, "No, I would never have thought it, I mean he doesn't *look* gay". In this way you imply that the conversation is about a mutual friend and therefore at a "local" level and not a theoretical debate. It also helps open up a discussion about what people know about homosexuality and their attitudes to it.

Hopefully one of the observers will quickly replace you, thus enabling you to leave the discussion to the participants. However, you should continue to participate as an observer so that you maintain the possibility of taking another turn as a conversationalist. This leaves open the possibility for you to discretely manipulate the discussion either to open up different avenues of debate or to tactfully remove a participant who is not keeping to the rules.

If you wish to, you can introduce a rule that any particular point of view can only be raised once. This prevents the discussion focusing on only a few aspects of the topic and helps to discourage repetition of popular prejudices.

Variations

Other topics that could be used include:

- The age of consent (to marriage or to having sex): should it be different for homosexuals?
- Adoption and marriage: should gay and lesbian couples be allowed to marry? And to adopt children? Why / Why not?
- Aids: is it true that homosexuals are more exposed?

Suggestions for follow-up

If people are interested in exploring other aspects of discrimination including those of the rights of transsexuals to compete in sports, then they may like to do the activity "Just a minute", on page 150.

Taking action

Contact gay or lesbian organisations in your country; finding about them is one way to take action! Invite one of their representatives to address your group and find out which issues of equality and rights are the most pressing in your own country.

Further information

"Human sexuality is an integral part of life. Our sexuality influences our personality and behavioural characteristics - social, personal, emotional, psychological - that are apparent in our relationships with others. Our sexuality is shaped by our sex and our gender characteristics and by a host of other complex influences, and is subject to life long dynamic change".

ASPA information technology project, www.aspa.asn.au

Sexual diversity and human rights

At a common sense level, these two issues appear not to be related. It might be argued that the one is related to private and individual choice, the other to the public domain of legal and political structures, which operate in relation to citizenship. Yet, recent historical, anthropological and sociological studies show how sexual identity and modes of expression of sexual desire are seen, both over time and across cultures, to be potentially disruptive to the maintenance of social order. In some contexts, same or ambiguous sex desire challenges or ruptures traditional or religious beliefs, in others it may be regarded as a psychological illness.

There is a hegemonic force which lies at the centre of the connection between sexual diversity and human rights, and which arguably operates to consistently marginalize equal access to human rights. That force is the institutionalised assumption that heterosexuality as 'naturally ordained' and therefore the 'normal' mode of expression of sexual desire. A constant theme in this process marginalisation is the assumption that heterosexuality is "natural" and therefore morally acceptable while other forms of sexual expression are "unnatural" and therefore morally unacceptable.

Adapted from the Gay and Lesbian Human Rights Commission, www.iglhrc.org

Key date:

17 May
International Day against Homophobia

Living in a perfect world

Si vis pacem, para pacem (If you want peace, prepare peace)

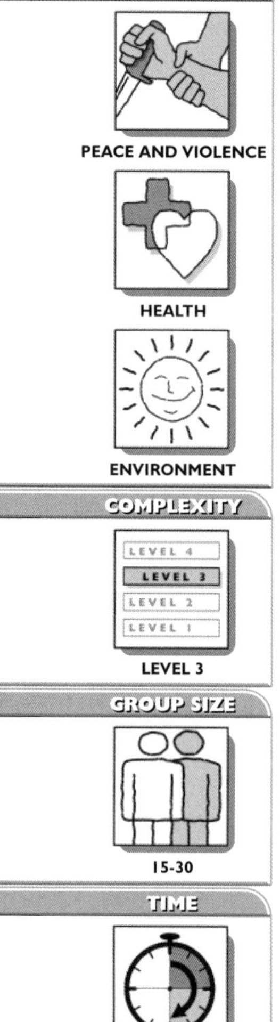

Themes Peace and Violence, Health, Environment

Complexity Level 3

Group size 15 - 30

Time 90 minutes

Overview This activity starts with a quiz on proverbs and wise sayings that reflect different aspects of being at peace, and goes on to let participants reflect on:
- The meaning of peace
- Inner peace, peace with others and peace with the environment
- Developing peaceful behaviour

Related rights
- The right to peace
- The right to life
- The right to a healthy environment

Objectives
- To sense the interdependency between the different dimensions of peace
- To discuss the different meanings of peace and how it applies to our daily lives
- To promote respect, solidarity and responsibility

Materials
- One large sheet of paper (A3) or flipchart paper
- Coloured markers
- Quiz sheets and pens, one per group
- Discussion guides, one per small group
- Copies of box 1 and box 2, one per small group

Preparation Copy the peace wheel in box 1 onto a large sheet of paper. Make it as big as possible.

Instructions

This activity is in two parts: part 1, completing the mandala (25 minutes) and part 2, talking peace (30 minutes).

Part 1, completing the mandala (25 minutes)

1. In plenary, show participants the copy you have drawn of an empty peace circle, or mandala. Point out the sections: peace with yourself, peace with others and peace with nature. Tell them that the completed mandala will represent the attainment of an ideal state of peace. To complete it people have to find the twenty-one "words of universal truth" that relate to each of the twenty-one areas of a life in peace. These missing words can be found all over the world in wise sayings or proverbs.
2. Ask people to get into three groups and hand out a pen, a copy of the empty mandala and a copy of the quiz sheet to each group. Remind them that they have to find the

missing words in each of the proverbs. These are the clues to the values that fit in the different areas of the peace circle.

3. When they have finished, call everyone together. Ask people to volunteer to read out the completed proverbs one at a time. Check they are correct and ask the reader to take a coloured pen and write the word on your large copy of the peace circle.
4. Repeat for all the proverbs until the mandala is complete and a state of peace is attained.

Part 2, talking peace (30 minutes)

1. Ask people to return to their three sub-groups. Give out the discussion guides, one to each group. Ask them to discuss the questions in their discussion guide, while at the same time keeping an eye on the values associated with the relevant area of the peace wheel. They should see if they can come to a consensus about the questions, and they should be prepared to report back on their discussions.
2. At the end, call everyone into plenary, and ask each group to report back.

Debriefing and evaluation

Start by talking about the mandala and the universality of the values represented. Then go on to review part 2 of the activity.

Part 1.

- How hard was it to find the missing words? How many of the proverbs or sayings did people already know? Are they in fact "words of wisdom" that are relevant to our lives today?
- Do the words in the innermost circle represent universal values? Are they equally important in all cultures? Which are the most important in yours?
- Are there other core values which are not represented?

Part 2. Ask someone from each group to make a very short summary of the questions on their discussion guide. Then take the following questions in rounds.

- Was it easy to reach a consensus on all the issues discussed?
- Which question was the most controversial? Why?
- What is their opinion on the controversy?
- Why do people have different views on these issues relating to peace?
- People often link discussions about inner peace with religion. Why is this?
- Do people have to be religious to have values necessary for inner peace?
- What relationships are there between what they have been discussing and human rights?
- Is peace a necessary prior condition for a culture of human rights to exist, or it is necessary to have human rights respected before people can reach a state of peace?

Tips for facilitators

There is further information about the issues raised in this activity in the background information on peace and violence on page 377. This will help you to guide the discussion in plenary. Try to bring out the interrelation between the three dimensions of peace. Do not be afraid of controversy; this is by nature a controversial topic. Rather, reflect on the arguments in favour

Key date

21 June
World Peace and Prayer Day

and against the issues and emphasise that these are not black and white issues; there are no clear answers.

If there are more than eighteen people in the group, it is best to double up on the numbers of small groups and work with six small groups rather than three large ones. Remember to make extra copies of the materials!

Variations

You could organise part one, completing the mandala, as a whole group activity. Read out the proverbs one at a time and ask for suggestions for the missing words. In this case, you will want to mark the words straight onto the large chart and you will need to make copies of the completed wheel for people to refer to in part 2.

Suggestions for follow-up

With the insights gained in this activity, the group might like to go on to discuss incidents when there has not been peace in their lives and to work out practical strategies for dealing with personal violence. See the activity "Violence in my life", on page 248.

Further information

The idea of the peace wheel used in this activity comes from Pierre Weil, "El Arte de Vivir en Paz, Hacia una nueva conciencia de Paz", Errepar, Argentina, 1995. "El arte de vivir en paz, hacia una nueva conciencia de paz" means "the art of living in peace, towards a new consciousness of peace".

There are many ways to interpret the peace circle. The following notes may help guide you in discussions about it:

- At the centre of the mandala is infinity, there is no beginning and no end.
- All the words in the innermost circle represent the values and behaviour or a state of being that *should be* in each of the corresponding areas of our lives. For example, in relation to our ability to be at peace with others and at peace with society, we need to be at peace in the areas of economy, our social life and culture.
- Mind, body and emotions are the areas of focus in our relationship with "oneself" and our inner peace. To have individual inner peace, we need wisdom, to feel love, patience, compassion, and joy and to have a healthy body.
- The third dimension of peace is environment, which coincides with peace with nature. Here we have three areas: we need to have knowledge to be informed, to have respect for life and to be in harmony with substance (things - nature, trees, flowers, animals, etc.)

HANDOUTS

The peace wheel

Quiz sheet

Can you find the words which are missing from the following proverbs and quotations? Identify the words and you have the clues to fit into the peace circle!

The words you have to match are: Beauty, Body, Compassion, Co-operation, Culture, Economy, Emotions, Environment, Patience, Harmony, Health, Individual, Information, Joy, Justice, Knowledge, Life, Love, Mind, Respect, Social life, Society, Solidarity, Substance, Truth, Welfare and Wisdom.

Area 1. Experience is the mother of ____________.

Area 2.

a) Where there is ________there is no darkness. (Burundi Proverb)

b) _________ and perseverance have a magical effect before which difficulties disappear and obstacles vanish. (John Quincy Adams)

c) Man may dismiss ___________from his heart, but God never will. (William Cowper)

d) Don't promise something when you are full of _______; don't answer letters when you are full of anger. (Chinese Proverb)

Area 3. ________ is better than wealth.

Area 4. Doubt is the key to _________. (Iranian Proverb)

Area 5. If you want to be respected, you must __________yourself. (Spanish Proverb)

Area 6. To touch the earth is to have ____________with nature. (Oglala Sioux. Native American)

Area 7. For the sake of others' _______, however great, let not one neglect one's own ________; clearly perceiving one's own __________, let one be intent on one's own goal. (Buddhist proverb)

Area 8. Government and _____________are in all things the law of life; anarchy and competition the laws of death. (John Ruskin)

Area 9.

a) _________without wisdom is like a flower in the mud. (Romanian Proverb)

b) Sooner or later the ________comes to light. (Dutch Proverb)

c) _________ forever, ________forever, _______ forever. For the union makes us strong. (Ralph Chaplin)

d) When violence comes into the house, law and _______ leave through the chimney. (Turkish Proverb)

Area 10. _______ of the mind must be subservient to the heart. (Mahatma Gandhi)

Area 11. See _________and glee sit down, / All joyous and unthinking, / Till, quite transmogrified, they're grown / Debauchery and drinking. (Robert Burns, 1759–1796).

Area 12. There can be _______ where there is no efficiency. (Beaconsfield)

Area 13. Be not deceived with the first appearance of things, for show is not________. (English Proverb)

Area 14. A moment of patience can prevent a great disaster and a moment of impatience can ruin a whole________. (Chinese Proverb)

Area 15. Where is the wisdom we have lost in knowledge? Where is the knowledge we have lost in________. (T.S. Eliot)

Area 16. Easier to bend the ________ than the will. (Chinese Proverb)

Area 17. By starving ________ we become humourless, rigid and stereotyped; by repressing them we become literal, reformatory and holier-than-thou; encouraged, they perfume life; discouraged, they poison it. (Joseph Collins)

Area 18. See with your________, hear with your heart. (Kurdish Proverb)

Area 19. Man shapes himself through decision that shapes his________. (Rene Dubos)

Area 20. Every heart is the other heart. Every soul is the other soul. Every face is the other face. The ________ is the one illusion. (Margaurite Young)

Area 21. You can tell how high a ________ is by how much of its garbage is recycled. (Tahanie)

Discussion guides

Discussion guide: Peace with oneself (group 1)

1. What does it mean to be at peace with oneself?
2. What sorts of things that we say and do everyday, show that we are at war with ourselves and do not have a quality of inner peace?
3. Is there a relationship between the body, mind and emotions? What kind of relationship?
4. How can we develop the qualities that help us to be at peace with ourselves?
5. Is it possible to have a positive relationship with others if we do not have inner peace ourselves?

Discussion guide: Peace with nature (group 3)

1. Does society value the environment?
2. What does it mean to live in harmony with nature?
3. Whose duty is it to care for the environment?
4. In the future, how many wars will be fought over basic natural resources (for example, water), compared to wars fought for other reasons (for example, ethnic, cultural or religious clashes)?
5. Do you think that the art of living in peace with nature is relevant to the achievement of a total state of peace?

Discussion guide: Peace with others (group 2)

1. Do we - as human beings - have the capacity to live at peace with others?
2. Does absence of war mean that we are at peace with others?
3. Can we learn to be more peaceful with others in our daily lives? How?
4. What grounds are there to be hopeful for a peaceful world in the future?
5. Can the scars left by wars be overcome so that people can live in peace again?

Answers to the peace wheel quiz.

Area 1. Wisdom.
Area 2. a) Love,
b) Patience,
c) Compassion,
d) Joy
Area 3. Health
Area 4. Knowledge
Area 5. Respect
Area 6. Harmony
Area 7. Welfare
Area 8. Co-operation
Area 9. a) Beauty,
b) Truth,
c) Solidarity,
d) Justice
Area 10. Culture
Area 11. Social life
Area 12. Economy
Area 13. Substance
Area 14. Life
Area 15. Information
Area 16. Body
Area 17. Emotions
Area 18. Mind
Area 19. Environment
Area 20. Individual
Area 21. Society

The completed peace wheel

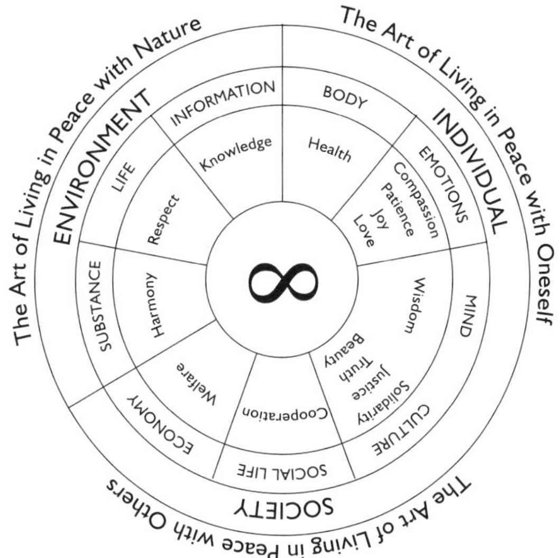

Makah whaling

"Dress it up how you like – whaling is murder and murder is wrong"
Greenpeace

THEMES

COMPLEXITY

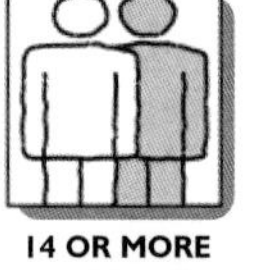

LEVEL 4

GROUP SIZE

14 OR MORE

TIME

150 MINUTES

Themes Environment, Globalisation, General human rights

Complexity Level 4

Group size 14+

Time 150 minutes

Overview This activity involves small group work, role-play, discussion and consensus building about the issues of:
- The sustainable use of marine resources
- The rights of indigenous peoples to their culture and development

Related rights
- The right to take part in cultural life
- Peoples' right to freely dispose of their natural wealth
- The right to development and utilisation of natural resources

Objectives
- To explore the conflicts between the right to development and cultural life and protection of the environment
- To develop intercultural skills and reflect on prejudice
- To develop attitudes of open-mindedness to cultural difference

Materials
- Handouts
- Pens and paper for the groups to make their own notes

Preparation
- Read through all the handouts to familiarise yourself with the information on the issues. You will then be able to act as a resource person if needed.
- Make copies of the role cards for each group. Each participant should have their own role card.

Instructions

The activity is divided into two parts: part 1 (30 minutes) is an introduction to the activity and the environmental and cultural issues involved, and part 2 (90 minutes) is a simulated meeting to discuss the Makah tribe's application to the International Whaling Commission (IWC) to resume whaling. Make sure you leave time after the activity for discussion, debriefing and evaluation.

Part 1. Introduction to the environmental and cultural issues (30 minutes)

1. Explain that this activity is about environmental and cultural rights. It centres on a request by the Makah nation to the IWC to resume whaling and the opposition to this from conservationists and others.
2. Tell the group about the Makah. (see handouts)
3. Now introduce the issues addressed in this activity. Ask people to indicate their response to the following questions by standing "high or low". (For how to use this technique, see page 62). Read out the following statements one at a time:
   "People's customs should be respected so long as they do not abuse human rights."

"We should respect people's right to be free to choose what they eat; to be vegans, vegetarians or to eat meat."

"The food we eat should be produced using environmentally friendly methods."

"Animal husbandry should not include cruel methods such as intensive rearing or cruel ways of slaughtering. "

"Cultural traditions are very important for people and should be respected."

"Whales should not be hunted, even for cultural purposes."

Part 2. A simulated meeting to discuss the Makah tribe's application to the International Whaling Commission (IWC) to resume whaling. (90 minutes)

1. Remind the group that the Makah tribe has applied to the International Whaling Commission (IWC) to resume whaling and that several environmental groups oppose this. This activity is a simulated meeting of an imaginary organisation called Crest (Culture, Rights, Environment, Sustainability and Talk). Crest is an independent organisation that works to bring a human rights perspective to environmental issues. They are committed to promoting understanding through dialogue.
   The simulation is a Crest meeting between four groups:
   a, The Makah tribe who wish to present their case for restarting whaling
   b, High North Alliance, an umbrella organisation representing whalers and sealers. The HNA is committed to working for the future of coastal cultures and the sustainable use of marine mammal resources. The HNA supports the Makah.
   c, Sea Shepherd, an organisation that investigates and documents violations of international laws, regulations and treaties protecting marine wildlife species. They oppose the Makah's request.
   d, Greenpeace, environmental activists who oppose whaling .
2. Crest's role is to mediate between the groups. The discussions will focus on four questions:
   - Should whaling be allowed?
   - Is there a special case for whaling as part of cultural tradition?
   - If whaling is to be carried out, at what level is it to be carried out?
   - What sort of management regimes are needed?
3. Ask for two volunteers to represent Crest and divide the rest into four small, equal groups. Hand out the role cards. The groups have 30 minutes to discuss the information and to prepare to defend their positions on the Makah's request.
4. When the groups are prepared, call them into plenary. Ask the pair representing Crest to organise the simulated meeting, which should last about 60 minutes. The purpose of the meeting is to share information and discuss the issues, and to come to an agreement on the four questions.
5. Crest opens the meeting with a short statement about the human rights and environmental frame of the discussions. The Makah tribe follow by stating their case. Then the discussion begins.
6. At the end of the discussion move on to the debriefing and evaluation.

Debriefing and evaluation

Ask the groups to reflect on the process of the discussion and whether it was possible to come to a consensus.

- Was it difficult to take the different roles?

- What was the most interesting thing people learnt?
- What made the best arguments? Appeals to the emotions or rational, logical arguments?
- How hard was it to see the other side of the argument? How hard was it to accept it?
- In real life, how hard is it to accept other people's cultural practices that participants find either rude, incomprehensible or unethical?
- At what point does the cultural clash become discrimination?
- How difficult is it to be open-minded about cultural differences?
- Does globalisation inevitably lead to loss of culture? Is a changed culture a lost culture?
- Should we see cultural change as a positive process in a changing world?
- Conflicting legal claims to rights are usually resolved in the courts. Is this a fair way to resolve rights issues?
- Which should be prioritised, the claims of people to food and life or environmental protection and preservation of species?

Finish the session by doing another round of "high or low" to see if people have moved in their attitudes to the issues of whaling. Repeat the same questions as you asked in part 1.

Tips for facilitators

The complexity of the issues addressed in this activity means that it is best suited to a mature group with good discussion skills. There is a lot of information to assimilate and the text on the role cards assumes a certain level of knowledge of human rights and environmental terminology. You may wish to consider doing the activity over two sessions and giving the groups time in between to read the role cards and think about the issues.

One important objective of this activity is to confront young people with the limitations of their own cultural perspectives and enable them to reconsider their attitudes to the sustainable use of wildlife. Whaling is a very emotive issue for many people and one on which they often hold very strong views. This makes it a challenging - but also difficult - topic to work with. A second objective is to develop consensus-building skills, which is why the activity has been designed to be a meeting which is mediated by an imaginary organisation, Crest (culture, rights, environment, sustainability and TALK). Before doing the activity, you may like to refer to the information about consensus building on page 59.

It may be necessary to check that participants fully understand the meaning of some of the terms and concepts introduced on the role cards. For example:

Indigenous peoples

There are no hard and fast distinctions that enable us to unambiguously define indigenous people. In general, it may be said that they are the descendants of peoples who originally occupied the land before colonisers came and before state lines were drawn. They are always marginal to their states and they are often tribal.

The precautionary principle

The precautionary principle states that "when an activity raises threats of harm to human health or the environment, precautionary measures should be taken even if some cause and effect relationships are not fully established scientifically". It includes taking action in the face of uncertainty; shifting burdens of proof to those who create risks; analysis of alternatives to potentially harmful activities; and participatory decision-making methods.

Sustainability

In 1989 the UN World Commission on Environment and Development (WCED), also called the

Brundtland Report, defined sustainable development as "development that meets the needs of the present without compromising the ability of future generations to meet their own needs". "Sustainable use" is a term that is applicable only to renewable resources: it means using the resource at rates that are within their capacity for renewal. There is a globally agreed principle of sustainable use of the world's natural resources, based on scientific evidence and objective data.

Key date

9 August
International Day of Indigenous People

Variations

If the group is small you can work with two groups, the Makah and the High North Alliance on one side and Greenpeace and Sea Shepherd on the other.

An alternative way to present this activity is as a panel debate. Have one person to represent each of the four groups, the Makah, the High North Alliance, Sea Shepherd and Greenpeace. Get them to present their cases and then proceed with questions from the floor. At the end, take a vote on each of the four questions. In this way you get people to consider the human rights, cultural and environmental aspects of the issue, but it will lack the element of consensus building.

Suggestions for follow-up

Globalisation was one of the issues touched on in this activity. If the group are interested in researching other aspects of globalisation, they may like to do the activity "A glossary of globalisation", on page 69.

Ideas for action

Support indigenous peoples by buying their products. Many handicraft items for sale in shops that sell "fair traded" products are made by indigenous peoples. Go and have a look next time you are out shopping for a present for someone.

Further information

High North Alliance web site: www.highnorth.no, The Sea Shepherd International: www.seashepherd.com, International Whaling Commission www.iwcoffice.org, Conservation Makah Nation web site: http://content.lib.washington.edu/aipnw/renker/contemporary.html, Greenpeace web site: www.greenpeace.org.

HANDOUTS

The Makah people (also called the Makah or Makah tribe) live on a reservation that sits on the most north-western tip of the Olympic Peninsula in Washington State, USA. The current reservation is approximately 27,000 acres. In July 1999 tribal census data showed that the Makah tribe has 1214 enrolled members, although only 1079 members currently live on the reservation. The average unemployment rate on the reservation is approximately 51%. Almost 49% of the reservation households have incomes classified below the federal poverty level, and 59% of the housing units are considered to be substandard.

In spite of this bleak description, the traditions are very strong and many Makahs who graduate from college come back to the reservation to work for the Makah tribe, the local clinic, and the public school.

Source: http://content.lib.washington.edu/aipnw/renker/contemporary.html

HANDOUTS

Role cards

CREST role card

Your position on the whaling issue is neutral. Your role is to provide background information on the human rights and environmental legislation and to mediate between the groups. Your job as mediators is to ensure that the discussion is focused on the task in hand and to clarify misconceptions and misunderstandings. You should help the groups move away from their differences and explore instead what they have in common in order to come to a consensus about the following questions:

- Should whaling be allowed or not?
- Is there a special case for whaling as part of cultural tradition?
- If whaling is to be allowed, at what level is it to be carried out?
- What sorts of management regimes are needed?

Start by welcoming everyone. Set the framework for the discussions. Take about two minutes to set the scene by summarising the main human rights and environmental aspects of the issue, quoting if you wish from the extracts below. You should also point out that some people have moral objections to whaling.

Then ask the Makah tribe to explain their reasons for wanting to resume whaling before opening the general discussion. After 40 minutes' discussion, start summing up.

Some background information about human rights, culture and the environment

The International Covenant on Economic, Social and Cultural Rights states in Article 1 that:

1. All peoples have the right of self-determination. By virtue of that right they freely determine their political status and freely pursue their economic, social and cultural development.
2. All peoples may, for their own ends, freely dispose of their natural wealth and resources without prejudice to any obligations arising out of international economic co-operation, based upon the principle of mutual benefit, and international law. In no case may a people be deprived of its own means of subsistence.

Article 15:

1. The States Parties to the present Covenant recognise the right of everyone:

(a) To take part in cultural life;

(b) To enjoy the benefits of scientific progress and its applications;

The preamble to the Vienna declaration of 1993 states that, "All human rights are universal, indivisible and interrelated. The international community must treat human rights globally in a fair and equal manner, on the same footing and with the same emphasis ... the significance of national and regional particularities and various historical, cultural and religious backgrounds must be borne in mind".

In 1981, the IWC decided to permit aboriginal subsistence whaling (ASW). This is defined as "whaling for purposes of local aboriginal consumption carried out by or on behalf of aboriginal, indigenous or native peoples who share strong community, familial, social and cultural ties related to a continuing traditional dependence on whaling and the use of whales".

The UN Convention of the Law of the Sea states that, "One of the general principles is the optimum sustainable utilisation of renewable marine resources."

In 1982, there was a moratorium on fishing for the endangered grey whale. In 1994 the population had recovered to an estimated 21,000 individuals and was removed from the U.S. Endangered Species List.

Makah tribe role card

Your role is to present the case of the Makah Indians who live on the north-west coast of North America. In this activity you should use your own existing knowledge of human rights and environmental issues together with the following quotes and information from the Makah web site:

"Even though it is 70 years since the last whale hunt took place, the ceremonies, the rituals, the songs and the tales have been passed down and kept alive. A whole social structure was built around the hunt. Nowadays some Makah Indians make a living fishing salmon and pacific sable fish, which is sold to a local fish plant, but the old system of sharing between family and friends is still in existence."

"It was the industrial whaling operations carried out by Europeans and Americans that depleted the whale stock. When the US government finally decided to take conservation measures, the Makahs were also forced to stop their hunt. Now, the stock is back up at what is considered a historically high level of 21 000, and was last year removed from the US Endangered Species List."

"There is a growing appreciation amongst young people of the value of having an identity based on one's own culture and history. Being part of a culture that has a long tradition is a privilege that not many young people in the US are given."

"We're not going to hunt the grey whales for commercial purposes ... even though we've heard rumours that we are going to sell them to the Japanese. Our purpose for our whaling is for ceremonial and subsistence. We've requested up to 5 grey whales but that's not to say that we'll take them all. We will be an active player to make sure the grey whale never goes back on the Endangered Species List .... The tribe is the first to recognise the need for harvest limitations ... it is built into our values."

"The Makah carry out their fishing operations in small coastal vessels. No decisions have as yet been made with regard to what technology will be used. Options include the old hand harpoon as it was used traditionally, or a modified version with a grenade on the tip like the ones used in the Alaskan bowhead hunt."

The High North Alliance role card

The High North Alliance is an umbrella organisation representing whalers and sealers from Canada, Greenland, the Faeroe Islands, Iceland and Norway, as well as a number of local communities. The HNA is committed to working for the future of coastal cultures and the sustainable use of marine mammal resources. In this activity you should use your own existing knowledge of human rights and environmental issues together with the following quotes and information from the High North Alliance web site.

"The Makahs had been whaling for 2,000 years until these white imperialists came over and were more eager to take the whales because this oil and so on was so very important to them. And then they raped that resource and the Makahs were not able to continue their tradition. The Makahs had been very patiently waiting for this resource to come back again. And that has happened now. But now the white people have changed their minds. Suddenly they want to ban all use of this resource."

"Different cultures will never be able to agree on which animals are special and which ones are best for dinner. In northern Norway people have a special relationship to the eider duck although in Denmark all reputable game merchants sell eider breast as a delicacy. Therefore, the statement 'whales are different' begs the question: different for whom?"

"Whaling, as well as sealing, is allowed only as long as it is conducted by indigenous peoples and is non-commercial. Only 'traditional' usage is allowed, and it tends to be the outsiders who define what is 'traditional'. To link whaling and sealing to a non-commercial mode of production is to deny people their obvious right to define their own future. No culture is static, but the policy of anti-whalers is de facto an attempt to "freeze" the situation, to turn an evolving culture into a static museum object. Commercialism in itself seems to be considered bad by the majority of the contracting governments at the IWC. It is ironic that this view is expressed by governments which are usually strong advocates of free trade. But apparently, some people shall be denied access to the world market. And if they want to partake in the world economy, it shall not be on their own terms but on those of the outsiders."

"The current moratorium, or 'hands off whales' policy is difficult to defend using logical arguments. There are many practices in agriculture, fishing and forestry that are clearly unsustainable, but there is no blanket ban on these industries."

"The report on Marine Mammals, Council of Europe, July 12, 1993: 'Marine mammals are part of the living resources of the ocean ecosystems. They should be protected when threatened and only hunted when there is certainty that the size of their stocks allows it. Hunting may also be necessary in order to avert over-population and imbalances in marine ecosystems."

"Whaling is a good example of how international co-operation can transform a situation of over-exploitation into one of sustainable use. International co-operation is not perfect, but it can and does work. "

Sea Shepherd and the Whale and Dolphin Conservation Society role card

The Sea Shepherd International is a non-profit, non-governmental organisation (NGO) involved with the investigation and documentation of violations of international laws, regulations and treaties protecting marine wildlife species. The Whale and Dolphin Conservation Society (WDCS) is the world's most active charity dedicated to the conservation and welfare of all whales, dolphins and porpoises.

Your role is to present the views of people concerned with protecting nature and wildlife. You should use your own existing knowledge of human rights and environmental issues together with the following quotes and information from the Sea Shepherd and Whale and Dolphin Conservation Society web pages.

"The real reason for this initiative by the Makah is because they know very well that whale meat goes for $80 per kilo in Japan, and that one of those whales is worth close to one million dollars. And that doesn't just mean the five whales that they say they want to kill. It will have implications for literally thousands of whales because Norway and Japan and those other nations that want to go whaling, like Russia and Iceland, are looking at this very closely because if the Makah are given permission to take whales it will undermine any integrity the United States has in the international marine conservation movement." Capt. Paul Watson, Sea Shepherd Society

"We are walking the tightrope of trying to respect people's historical right to carry on long-standing traditional ways of collecting necessary food and yet balance the interests of conserving and protecting whales ..., (and) attempting to understand the changing world of indigenous peoples. For instance, in 1995 there was criticism of the Russian grey whale hunt when it was alleged that whale meat was not being eaten by indigenous peoples but was actually being fed to foxes in fox fur farms."

"The Alaskan North Slope Eskimos are now economically very different to the peoples who hunted whales a century ago. Oil exploitation has brought pollution, disruption and a host of new people to Alaska. It has also brought an enormous amount of money to the local people. To the casual observer, hunting from modern skidoos and helicopters is straining the definition of what is aboriginal."

"While the International Whaling Commission (IWC) continues to debate the emotive issue of the resumption of commercial whaling, hundreds of whales, and their cousins, the smaller dolphins and porpoises, are dying every year, almost unnoticed, in aboriginal hunts."

"In the context of wildlife, the precautionary principle demands that when the impact of a proposed action upon a species is not known, the benefit of the doubt should be given to the species and the action should not be undertaken until it can be shown that the action will not impose an unacceptable cost or loss to the species".

Greenpeace role card

Greenpeace supporters around the world campaign for their visions of how to achieve a more sustainable world.

In this activity you should use your own existing knowledge of human rights and environmental issues together with the following quotes and information from the web.

"Dress it up how you like – whaling is murder and murder is wrong. To be sure, whales are not human but are they less than human? The mind set that exults in the killing of whales overlaps with the mindset that accepts genocide of 'inferior' human beings. We believe that the phrase "human rights" is only superficially species chauvinistic. In a profound sense, whales and some other sentient mammals are entitled to human rights, or at least 'humanist rights', to the most fundamental entitlements that we regard as part of the humanitarian tradition."

"Greenpeace does not support any whaling programme, but we don't oppose truly subsistence whaling. But if there's ever a commercial element, we'd be front of the line, in their face, opposing their programme."

"The undersigned groups respectfully appeal to the Makah nation to refrain from the resumption of whaling. People from many cultures world-wide hold whales to be sacred and consider each species a sovereign nation unto itself, worthy of respect and protection. Grey whales migrate vast distances each year and bring joy to many thousands of whale watchers. They only briefly pass through Makah waters. We submit that important spiritual traditions must be observed in the context of a planet whose wildlife is being destroyed." Action for Animals, Action for Animals Network and others.

"I was in complete shock when I heard that we were thinking of killing grey whales - or any whales ... We went ahead and did the homework and found out that there was a proposal to authorise 5 grey whales to be taken by one tribe, and if they got it, several other tribes on up into Canada and Alaska said 'Well, if they can hunt them, we can hunt them.' And I just think that the American people - who have a special relationship with whales - I don't think that they're ready for any kind of whale harvest at this time". U.S Rep. Jack Metcalf

"Despite the moratorium on whaling imposed by the international community in 1986, the whales are still threatened. An effective method to give further protection to the whales is the creation of sanctuaries - areas where whaling is forbidden not just temporarily, but for the indefinite future."

"It's extremely difficult to accurately determine the actual number of whales in different whale populations. The size of most populations is known no more accurately than plus or minus 50%. Since changes happen very slowly, it is impossible to tell if a population is growing or shrinking in the course of a few years' study. However, there is no doubt about the decline in whale numbers caused by commercial whaling."

Making links

What is civil society - and who does what, for whom?

Themes Citizenship, Democracy, General human rights

Complexity Level 4

Group size 8 - 20

Time 90 minutes

Overview This activity involves negotiation about the rights and responsibilities of citizens, the government, NGOs and the media in a democracy.

Related rights
- The right to vote; to serve and to participate in the running of the country
- Freedom of information and expression
- Duties to the community

Objectives
- To develop an understanding of the link between rights and responsibilities
- To develop a feeling for the complex relations between the different sectors in a democracy
- To promote co-operation and civic responsibility

Materials
- A large sheet of paper (A3) or flipchart paper for each group
- 2 markers of different colours (e.g. green and red) for each group
- A ball of string or wool (preferably green)
- A roll of sticky tape (Scotch tape or sellotape) for each group
- Scissors

Preparation
- Cut up about 24 strands of wool into 1.5m lengths.

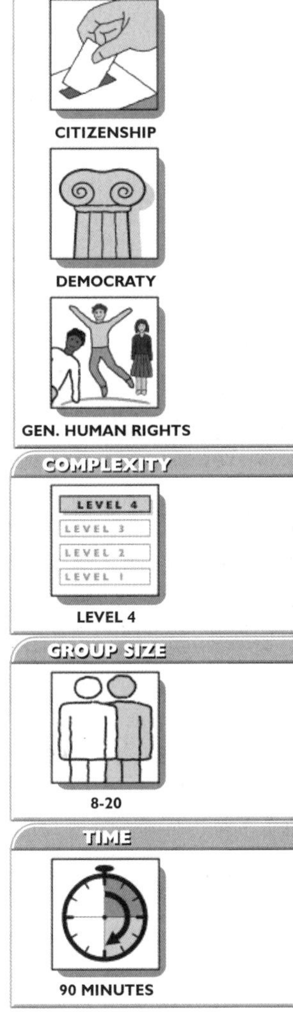

Instructions

1. Explain that the purpose of the activity is to draw a "map" of the different relations between four sectors within (an ideal) democratic society.
2. Divide the participants into four equal-sized groups to represent four "actors" in a democracy: the government, the NGO sector, the media, and citizens respectively.
3. Hand each group a large sheet of paper and markers and tell them to spend 10 minutes brainstorming the role that their "actor" plays in a democratic society, that is, what are the main *functions* it performs. They should list their five most important functions on the large sheet of paper, using the red marker.
4. Bring the groups together to present their ideas. Let the groups share their reactions. Ask them if they agree about the main functions of these four "actors". Allow the groups to amend their lists if they wish to in the light of the feedback.
5. Now separate the four groups again and ask them to brainstorm what they require from each of the other "actors", in order to carry out their own functions, that is, what demands do they make of each of the other "actors". They should list these demands under separate headings using the green marker. Give them fifteen minutes for this task.

6. When the time is almost up, ask the groups to prioritise up to six of the most important demands, and hand each group a roll of tape and strands of wool to represent these demands.
7. Hand out the copies of the "Rules of play", go through them and make sure everyone understands what they have to do next. Ask the groups to bring their sheet of paper into the middle of the room and to lay them in a square about 1m apart (see diagram). Ask members of each group to position themselves near their "corner".
8. The rounds of negotiation now begin. You should allow 10 minutes for each round. Remind people that when a demand is accepted one piece of wool should be taped between the two papers to signify acceptance of responsibility.
9. By the end of the process, the four "actors" should be linked up by a complicated web of wool. Move on to the debriefing and evaluation while people are still sitting around the chart.

Debriefing and evaluation

Ask the participants to look at the web they have created and to reflect on the activity.

- Was it hard to think of the functions that the government, NGOs, media and citizens perform in a democracy?
- Were there any disagreements within the groups about which claims should be accepted or rejected?
- Which of the claims made on other groups did they not accept as responsibilities? Why was this? Do you think that such cases would cause any problems in reality?
- Were there responsibilities that each group accepted but which they had not recognised before? How do they feel about this now?
- Did the activity show people anything new about democratic society that they did not know before? Were there any surprises?

Tips for facilitators

In step 4 of the instructions, after the groups have drawn up their list of functions, don't spend too long discussing the issues as a whole group. You should use this more as a prompt for the next small group work they will be doing. Groups may want to make a note of the other groups' functions.

When they draw up their lists of demands (step 5), tell them not to be unrealistic in their demands on the other "actors"! These responsibilities will need to be acceptable, so they should not make unfair or unreasonable claims.

When the groups start negotiating (step 8), this should not be presented as a "competition", nor should this stage occupy too much time. Emphasise to groups that they should see themselves as *co-operating* with each other: the purpose is to establish a society in which all "actors" work together for everyone's satisfaction. Therefore, the transactions should be relatively quick: tell groups to accept claims if they seem to be reasonable, and otherwise to reject them, with any controversial ones to be discussed at a later stage.

Variations

The activity may be made more or less complicated by using different numbers of "actors" within society: for example, you may want to add "businesses", "minorities", or "disadvantaged groups". However, this will make the negotiation process a lot more complicated, and you may not want all of the groups to exchange demands with each of the others. You could also use different categories with more direct relevance to young people's reality – for example, replace "citizens" by "young people" and "the government" by "school".

The activity could be simplified by removing one or more of the groups: for example, by working with only "citizens" and "the government". This may be preferable if you have a small group. You may want to try the activity without the use of the chart: during the negotiation process, someone from the first group should hold one end of the piece of wool, and offer the other end to someone in the second group. If people keep hold of their ends, the whole "society" should be physically linked up by the end of the process!

Suggestions for follow-up

The group could continue to add to the map, by including different groups within society (see Variations). They may want to transfer the map to another sheet of paper for greater clarity, and then to draw in the connections using different colours – for example, red for the government, yellow for the media, green for NGOs, etc. Think about which connections in your own society are not well developed, and what could be done to overcome this.

If the group would like to work on a more practical project that involves liaison and co-operation between local government, NGOs and media in their own community, they may enjoy the activity "Garden in a night", on page 139.

Key date

9 November 1989

The fall of the Berlin wall

HANDOUT

Rules of Play

1. The aim of the exercise is for each "actor" to get their demands accepted by each of the other "actors".
2. The negotiations are made between pairs of "actors" in three rounds as follows:
   - Round 1: citizens and NGOs negotiate, and the media and the government negotiate.
   - Round 2: citizens and the media negotiate, and NGOs and the government negotiate.
   - Round 3: citizens and the government negotiate, and the media and NGOs negotiate.
3. Pairs decide themselves who is to start and they take it in turns to make demands of each other.
4. When making a demand, people should state the demand clearly and concisely. They should also explain what it involves and why they are making this particular demand, that is, why it is important to enable them to fulfil their own functions.
5. When deciding whether or not to accept a demand, people should decide whether what is being asked is fair, and whether they would be able to carry it out.
6. If the second group rejects the demand, the piece of wool is put aside. If they accept it, then one strand of wool is taped to the charts to represent the link that has been established between the two groups. The "accepting group" should make a brief note on their chart to remind them what the demand was.
7. Repeat the process, until all demands have been discussed.
8. Repeat the process in each round until there are connections between the four actors.

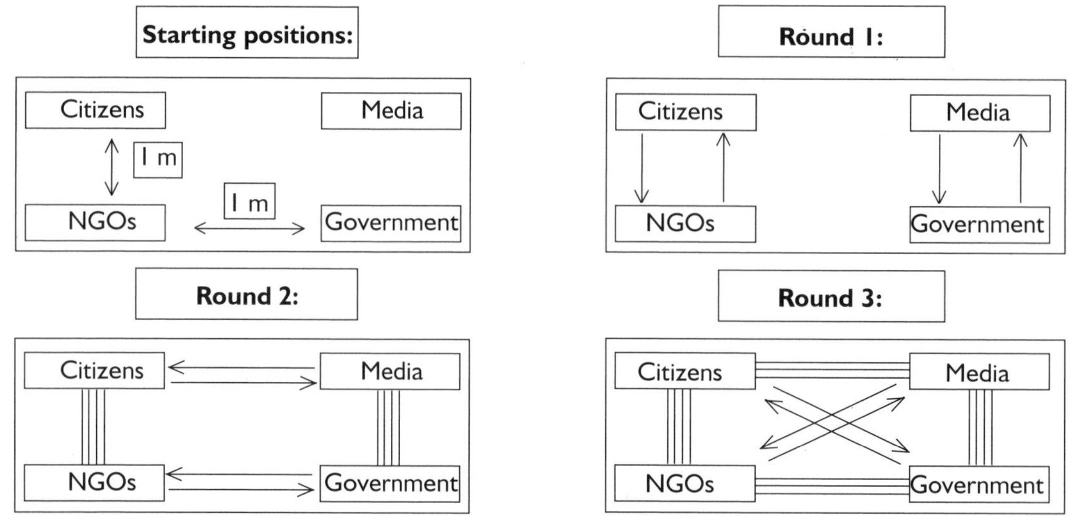

Money to spend

In the time of war, bread is better than bombs

Themes Human security, Peace and Violence, General human rights

Complexity Level 2

Group size Any

Time 90 minutes

Overview This activity uses activity cards in small group discussions to decide a family budget. There is an element of role-play. The issues addressed include:
- The distinctions between "wants" and "needs"
- State expenditure and militarisation
- The opportunities that could come from the peace dividend

Related rights
- Social and economic rights such as the right to health, food and education
- The right to live in a healthy and clean environment
- The right to security of person

Objectives
- To reflect on personal and family needs and how they should be prioritised
- To develop democratic decision-making skills
- To promote responsibility and justice

Materials
- Copies of the "Item cards" (one set per group)
- Envelopes, one per group
- Scissors
- Tape or glue for sticking cards to wall charts (one per group)
- Large sheets of paper (A3 size) or flipchart paper to make wall charts (1 sheet per group)
- 1 copy of the Parent role card
- 1 copy of Box 3.

Preparation
- Copy the items sheet. Cut it up to make the "item cards" and put the cards in an envelope. You need one set of cards per group.
- Copy the chart on world military spending and its alternatives on page 380 (in chapter 5) onto a large sheet of paper or an overhead transparency, or make one photocopy per participant
- Arrange the room so that people can work in small groups
- Prior to starting the activity, discretely choose one participant to role-play a "special parent" in one of the families. Tell them to keep their "special" role secret from everyone else and give them the copy of the "Parent role-play card". There should be only 1 "special parent" in one family/group, irrespective of the number of groups.
- Make copies or overhead transparencies of any of the data boxes you may wish to use.

Instructions

1. Explain that people will be working in small groups, each group representing a different family. The aim is for each family to draw up a budget for their expenditure in the coming month.
2. Divide the participants into small groups (preferably not more than 5 participants per group). Each group should be composed of a father, a mother and child(ren). Ask people to agree who will play the different roles, and then to decide together on a family name.
3. Give one envelope containing item cards and one large sheet of paper to each group,
4. Explain that the items cards represent those items that are to be discussed in relation to the next month's budget. Only these items may be considered. The cost is written on each card and cannot be altered.
5. Their budget is 10 000 (ten thousand) so each family will have to select what should be included, and what should be excluded from the budget.
6. Explain that the budget should preferably be agreed as the result of democratic consultation and that they should stick the item cards they have chosen onto the large sheet of paper to make a wall-chart for display.
7. Groups have 20 minutes to make their decisions and to prepare their wall-charts.
8. Allow 10 minutes for everyone to walk around and look at the different budgets and to consider which family budget is the most appropriate and which is the least appropriate.
9. Come into plenary and begin the debriefing.

Debriefing and evaluation

Ask each group in turn for their general comments on the activity. Then use the following questions as a guide for further discussion:

- How did the families decide the budget? Was it democratic?
- What criteria did they use to make the decisions?
- How did they balance their "needs" for food, shelter and clothing with the need for security and with their "wants" for leisure? What social and economic factors were important?
- How did people feel when an item, which they considered important, was out-voted by the rest of the family and not included in the budget?
- Which budgets were the most appropriate and which the least appropriate? Why?
- Are there parallels between the family budgets and the budgets of states worldwide? Can they be compared?
- Which lists most nearly reflect state budgets?
- Which lists should ideally reflect state budgets?

Now show the group the chart, "World military spending and its alternatives".

- What do people think about the actual total state budget in military equipment, armaments and other military-related things?
- Why do states worldwide spend so much on armaments?
- Has this spending been justified? Is the world a safer or more peaceful place?
- What are the consequences of this kind of budget allocation for people's enjoyment of their social and economic rights? And for the environment?

- How can we change the situation? Has anyone heard of "military conversion" or the "demilitarisation fund"? If not, why do you think that there is so little information about them in the news?

Tips for facilitators

The traditional family varies from country to country. Therefore, allow participants to include grandparents or other relatives in the families as appropriate.

The aim of having one "special parent" is twofold; first to provoke discussion, especially in countries where there are strong traditions of democracy and second to ensure that there are a variety of budgets to compare and discuss. You should be aware that the other "family members" in the role-playing group might get upset and even angry at the parent's attitude. They may also be confused because they do not know that it is a role-play! You will have to be sensitive to the fact that "problems" may arise within that group, which will require your intervention. Try to ensure that the group continues with the activity without discovering the role-played character! However, if you think the role will create too many difficulties or will not work in your situation, then omit it from the activity.

Feel free to adapt the list of items if it does not reflect the reality of families in your locality, region or country. However, be sure to include some "security" items and some very luxurious items, so participants still have to make a choice as to what are to be considered as needs and what are not.

Variations

An alternative to using cards is to simply use the sheet as a list and ask the families/groups to tick their choices. In this case, ask the families/groups to write down their budgets on a large sheet of paper that can be put up for everyone to see.

Suggestions for follow-up

The group could do some research into positive changes, for instance, into the proposal for a demilitarisation fund or into the situation in countries that do not have any army or military weapons (such as Costa Rica).

If you want to explore some of the consequences of war especially on refugees, you may like to do activity "Can I come in?", on page 98.

Ideas for action

Why not encourage discussion on the issue of demilitarisation? The more people there are who are aware of the problem, the more there will be who can bring pressure on governments to make changes. Find out what proportion of your state budget is spent on military and social needs. The group could write to their MP and ask for changes.

There are also numerous opportunities to join the many demilitarisation campaigns that are organised worldwide, such as Youth and Student Campaign for Nuclear Disarmament (http://youthstudentend.org.uk) and Pax Christi International (www.paxchristi.net/). Or start your own campaign in your group and you can use organisations like these ones as resources.

Key date

Tuesday following the second Monday of September
Peace Day

Further information

The international arms industry fundamentally undermines human security because it diverts priority attention, and therefore resources, away from basic human needs. The main argument forwarded for the allocation of resources for the military is the need to protect the state's population and territory. But are people truly protected if they do not receive education, health and food? Does military spending reflect the populations' needs or the states' interests?

An additional problem is that the state's investment in its security (and arguably the security of its people) is a vicious cycle; each state tries to have better and better weapons to overcome the military power of other states. This is called the "arms race".

During the 10-year period following the end of the cold war there was a reduction in military spending. As demilitarisation took place state policies should have been developed to ensure that the "peace dividend" - the money saved from the military budget - was used to enhance human security, for instance, by increased spending on education and health. In reality this rarely happened because most of the "peace dividend" was used to reduce national debts.

World military expenditure is now on the increase again. The rise began in 1999 and continued in 2000. This would appear to be a paradox because security is now much improved in many areas of the world. The reason seems to be that several of the major spenders have adopted or announced defence plans that include growth.

Peace activists and campaigners have argued for decades that a vigorous and creative programme of conversion from military to civilian production is vital. They give a number of reasons including:

- the immorality of the arms industry itself and its destructive capacity
- the dangers of the increasing proliferation in arms dealing
- the inability of the arms industry to police itself and the use to which its products would be put
- the inherent wastefulness of the industry and scandalous misuses of resources and human brain-power and
- the potential which conversion would unleash.

In chapter 5, in the background section on Peace and Violence on page 376, there are statistics and tables which are relevant to this activity.

HANDOUTS

Item cards

Food (2 000)	School/University fees (2 000)	Family medical insurance (1 000)
New car (4 000)	Monthly payment for sport activities (300)	Toys and games (200)
Computer (800)	Lottery (100)	House renovation(400)
Alarm system (1 500)	Clothing (400)	Pet food (100)
Water bill (200)	Trained security dog (400)	Medicines (300)
Transport (petrol, bus and train fares) (400)	Rent or mortgage repayments (2 500)	Mother's birthday present (400)
Washing machine repair (200)	School/University materials for the month (300)	Personal gun (400)
Fishing equipment (200)	New electronic equipment for the house (100)	Electricity bill (200)
New model of reclining chair (700)	Self-defence lessons for mother and daughter(s)(300)	Leisure activities (cinema, theatres, funfair, amusement parks) (200)
Car-alarm (300)	Long weekend in a beach house (400)	Personal defence equipment (for example, pepper spray and shock)(100)
Family dinner in a restaurant (100)	Telephone bill (300)	Financial help for grandparents or other relatives (200)
Youth holiday camp (200)		

Parent role card

Authoritarian parent role card

You are the family breadwinner and because of this you feel that you should have more say in money matters than your spouse or children; after all you are the one who brings home the money!

You strongly believe that there is a big problem of lack of law and order in the city where you live. It is so dangerous nowadays! Therefore, you put the highest priority on protection and the security of your family, home and property.

Our futures

The test of our progress is not whether we add more to the abundance of those who have much; it is whether we provide enough for those who have little.
Franklin D. Roosevelt

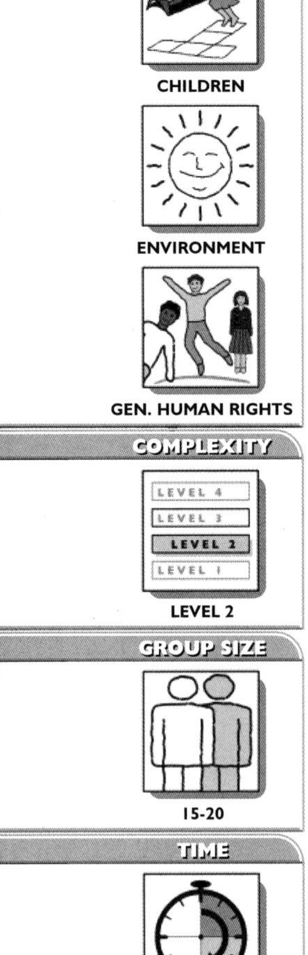

Themes Children, Environment, General human rights

Complexity Level 2

Group size 15 - 20

Time 60 minutes

Overview In this activity participants draw, contemplate and discuss their hopes and concerns for the future of their generation. Among the issues addressed are:
- Environmental issues affecting future generations
- Young people and the family
- Community life

Related rights
- The right to an opinion and access to information
- The right to be heard on all matters concerning the best interests of the child
- The right to a decent standard of living

Objectives
- To develop knowledge about community life, rights and responsibilities
- To promote skills to discuss openly, to work in a team and to have vision
- To see the world as a developing and open-ended opportunity to which every young person can make a positive or negative contribution

Materials
- Paper for drafts
- Large sheets of paper for the final design
- Paints, pens and markers
- Materials for a collage, coloured paper, magazines, twigs, rice, beans, dead leaves, shells, etc
- Glue
- Pictures or photographs of how the neighbourhood/town looked ten or twenty years ago (optional)

Instructions

1. Introduce the concept of change over time. Ask participants to think back to when they were younger and what their homes and the local streets looked like, and how they have changed. Have any of the rooms in the training centre been redecorated, or do they have any new furniture? Are there any new buildings in the neighbourhood? Ask people to think about why these things have changed and who made the decisions about what should be renewed and how it should be done.

2. Ask people to brainstorm the changes they would have made if they had been consulted.
3. Now make the links with making decisions that affect other people and human rights. Do people think that human rights make a useful framework for decision making? Will human rights be more or less important for decision-makers in the future? Why?
4. Tell the group that the opportunity is now! This is the moment for them to take the chance to start thinking about - and influencing - the futures they may inhabit.
5. Ask people to get into groups of three to four.
6. Hand out the paper and pens and ask them to draft or sketch ideas for their ideal neighbourhood/town of the future. They have a free hand. The limits are their own imaginations.
7. When each group has agreed a draft plan, they should transfer it onto a large sheet of paper and complete it with paint and collage materials.
8. When the work is done, ask each group in turn to present their plan and to say where they got their ideas and how they developed them. Allow time for short questions and answers after each presentation, but leave general discussion for the debriefing.

Debriefing and evaluation

Start with a review of how people worked together in their groups and how they made their decisions and carried out the work.

- Did everyone feel able to participate and to contribute to the work? How did the different small groups make the best use of the individual talents of their members?
- How did it feel to receive feedback about their plans?
- How did it feel to give feedback about their plans?
- Would they be prepared to compromise some of their ideals if they now had to design a single class or group plan that met the needs and aspirations of everyone in the class or group?
- Did people enjoy the feeling of being "architects of their futures"?
- Do they believe their ideals could ever come true? Why? Why not?
- Do they believe adults would be ready to discuss their plans? Why? Why not?
- What was the biggest surprise in any of the plans?
- What would be their rights as citizens in the future?
- What would be their duties as citizens in the future?
- What steps can young people take now to have influence in the democratic processes which shape their lives and their futures?

Tips for facilitators

The title of this activity is "Our futures". The intention of using the plural is to emphasise that the future is not pre-determined but, rather, that it is what we make it. Therefore, there are many possible futures and the challenge for young people is to build a future which reflects their ideals and aspirations.

To reinforce the concept of change, you may like to show old pictures of how the local area looked ten or twenty years ago. You can also ask them to think of global changes. For instance, they should think about the fact that thirty years ago the Internet was the stuff of science fiction, but that in a few years time there will be connections to the web in every school and library in the world.

Key date

12 August
International Youth Day

If the participants are not sure about what the future town may be like you could prompt them by asking:

- Who will live here? People born here, or newcomers? What ages will they be? Will they live in families?
- What will their daily lives be like? Where will they shop for food? How will they travel around?
- What sort of welfare services, such as hospitals, dentists, etc. will they need?
- What will their schools be like?
- What will their social lives be like? What will they do for leisure activities?
- Will they have pets?
- What work will people do?
- What new technological developments might there be?
- What about the environment? The natural surroundings?

Variations

An alternative method could be to use the idea of "futures wheels". Get people to work in small groups. Each group takes one issue, (for instance, education, the family, the community, employment or health) and draws the futures wheel for that topic. For example, an environment wheel would have a hub of the most important things and then other concentric circles around it. "Spokes" divide the wheel up into sections, in which people can write points such as: no smoke, electromobiles, lots of trees, clean rivers and humane farming.

Suggestions for follow-up

Find out more about the planning processes for local development and how to influence them. Get involved with decision-making in the school, club or association by attending council meetings, or even standing for election. There are other activities that can be useful to explore futures options. For instance "Path to Equality-land" looks at how to achieve gender equality, and "The impact of the Internet" looks at future scenarios for new technologies.

While we dream about our futures, we can make a start at building a more just society. If the group would like to look at the issue of bullying and explore ways to develop empathy and respect for everyone, then they could do the activity "Do we have alternatives?", on page 111.

Ideas for action

Take the plan to the local council and see if you can involve them. Your plan could be used in the town/village plan.

Path to Equality-land

"The obstacle is the path."
Zen proverb

Themes Gender equality, Discrimination and Xenophobia, Education

Complexity Level 3

Group size 4+

Time 90 minutes

Overview This activity involves small group work, imagination, and drawing to explore issues of gender equality and discrimination against women.

Related rights
- Freedom from discrimination on grounds of sex and gender
- The right to marry with the free and full consent of the intending spouses
- The right to special protection for mothers before and after childbirth

Objectives
- To develop understanding and appreciation of the goals of equality and gender balance
- To develop imagination and creativity to envision the future
- To promote justice and respect

Materials
- 1 A4 sized sheet of paper and 1 pencil per small group for the brainstorm
- Large sheets of paper (A3 size) or flipchart paper, one sheet per small group
- Marker pens of different colours, enough for all small groups
- A map, preferably a hiking map or any other sort of map that shows physical features, for instance, mountains, valleys, rivers, forests, villages, bridges, etc.

Preparation Familiarise yourself with the map and the symbols used.

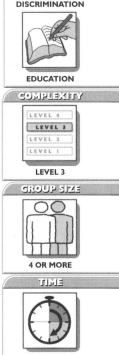

Instructions

1. Explain that in this activity participants will be drawing a fantasy map of how to travel to Equity-land, a country where there is true gender equality. It will exist in the future, but at present it only exists in people's imaginations.
2. Ask people if they know of any folk tales or other stories that use the metaphor of a person going on a journey to present moral ideals. Talk about the way a dark forest, for instance, may be used as a metaphor for evil or a red, rosy apple be used to represent temptation. The traveller may show moral strength swimming across a fast flowing river or humility helping a distressed animal.
3. Briefly review what a map looks like. Point out the ways that contours are drawn, the shading for mountains and rivers and the symbols that are used for forests, moorland, buildings, power cables, etc.

4. Ask people to get into small groups of three to five people. Hand out the small sheets of paper and pens and give them about 15 minutes to make three short brainstorms on:
   - what they imagine Equality-land might look like
   - what obstacles they might encounter on the path to Equality-land
   - how they would overcome the obstacles
5. Now hand out the large sheets of paper and the markers. Ask each group to make their own fantasy map to represent the landscapes of the present and the future together with a path that runs between the two. They should make up their own symbols for the geographical features and for the obstacles and facilities that lie along the path.
6. Give the groups 40 minutes to draw their maps. Remind them to make a key for the symbols they have used.
7. Come into plenary and ask people to present their maps.

Debriefing and evaluation

Start with a discussion about the way the different groups worked together and how they made decisions about what to represent and about the way they drew the map. Then go on to talk about what Equality-land in reality might look like and the obstacles.

- Did people enjoy the activity? Why?
- Which of three questions was the easiest to brainstorm? Which was the hardest and why?
- What were the main features of Equality-land?
- What are the main obstacles which prevent their present society from being the ideal Equality-land?
- What needs to change in order to build a society where there is gender equality?
- Are policies of positive discrimination justified as short term measures to boost gender equality?
- If you had to rate your country amongst all the countries of the world for equality of opportunity for both men and women, how would you rate it on a scale of 1 to 10? 1 is very unequal, 10 is almost ideal equality.
- Which other groups are discriminated against in your society? How is this manifested? Which human rights are being violated?
- How can disadvantaged groups be empowered to claim their rights?
- What role has education to play in empowerment?

Tips for facilitators

If participants get stuck thinking about how to picture their ideas, you could start them off by suggesting a woman uses a bridge of education to go over a river of prejudice against women who want to be lawyers. Another example could be for a man to find a jewel of satisfaction working as a nursery teacher, looking after very small children. Of course you will have to think of examples of gender stereotyping that reflect the reality in your society!

Variations

The groups could make models of the landscape using "junk". In this case, you will need to have a good collection of small boxes, tubs, tubes, paper, stones, nuts, bits of string and wool, paper clips, etc and also glue and card for the bases for the models.

The method of drawing a map from the present to the future can be adapted to most issues where you want participants to think freely and imaginatively about finding solutions to problems.

Suggestions for follow-up

Explore gender further or one of the other issues which were raised. For example, you could do research in the local library or on the Internet or ask a representative of an organisation that works to address inequality of opportunity for a particular group in society to come to talk to the group.

Alternatively, you may like to explore issues about discrimination and the right to cultural identity within the context of sustainable development in the activity "Makah whaling", on page 166.

Ideas for action

Look at your own school, club or workplace policies about equal opportunities in relation to gender and discuss how the policies are implemented and whether or not any changes or extra efforts need to be made to bring your institution to the status of Equality-land.

Further information

The concept behind this activity is that of "Empowerment". Empowerment is difficult to translate and sometimes also difficult to explain, even in English! "Empowerment" is both the means and the outcome of the pedagogy that some people call "Liberatory" education.

One definition of 'empowerment', from Oxfam, is:

"Empowerment involves challenging the forms of oppression, which compel millions of people to play a part in their society on terms that are unequal, or in ways which deny their human rights."

Key dates

25 November
International Day for the Elimination of Violence against Women

Picture games

A picture says a thousand words and the camera does not lie - or does it?

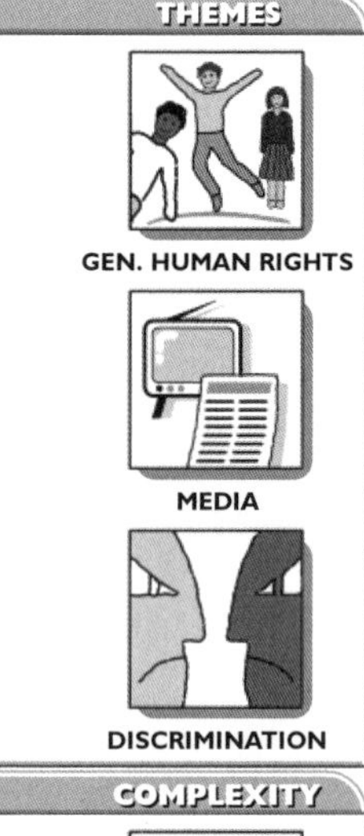

GROUP SIZE

TIME

30 MINUTES

Themes General Human Rights, Media, Discrimination and Xenophobia,

Complexity Level 1

Group size Any

Time 30 minutes

Overview Working with images is creative and fun, and these activities make good icebreakers while having value in their own right. They focus on issues about:
- Stereotypes
- How each person perceives the world in a unique way
- How images are used to inform and mis-inform

Related rights Any: depending the pictures and the issues you choose to adress

Objectives
- To raise awareness about the relevance of human rights to everyday life
- To develop "visual literacy" skills, listening and communication skills
- To promote empathy and respect for human dignity

1. What do you see?

Materials
- A set of photos
- Stiff card, glue, sticky-backed plastic (optional)
- Board, large sheets of paper or flipchart paper, and markers
- A wall chart listing the Articles of the UDHR (copied from the abridged version on page 402)

Preparation
- Collect together a set of 25 pictures showing people in different countries and different settings.
- Back the pictures with stiff card and cover with sticky-backed plastic for durability (optional)
- Number the pictures

Instructions

1. Lay the pictures out on tables round the room.
2. Tell people to work individually.
3. Read out *one* of the articles from the UDHR and write it up on the board/flip chart.
4. Ask people to look at the photographs and to choose the one that in their opinion best represents the article.
5. Then ask each person in turn to say which picture they chose and why.
6. Make a note of which pictures were chosen; write the numbers on the board.
7. Do four or five more rounds naming different articles from the UDHR. (Choose a mixture of the civil and political and social and economic rights.)

Debriefing and evaluation

Start with a review of the activity itself and then go on to talk about what people learned.

- Was it difficult to choose pictures to represent the different rights? Did individuals choose different pictures in the different rounds, or did they think that one or two pictures said it all?
- Did different people choose the same pictures in the different rounds, or did people have very different ideas about what represented the different rights? What does this tell us about how each of us sees the world?
- Review the list on the flipchart. Which photographs were chosen most often? What was special about these images? Why were they chosen often? Did the size or colour make a difference, or was it what was in the picture that was significant?
- Was any individual picture chosen to represent several different rights?
- Did anyone disagree with anyone else's interpretation of a particular picture?
- Were there any photos that were never chosen? Could they nonetheless be interpreted to represent a human right? Which rights? People should explain the reason for their choices.
- Did people know that they have all the rights that were talked about in the course of the activity? If not, which ones did they not know about?
- How do the media use and mis-use images? Pick one example of a current event and analyse how it is presented in the newspapers and on the television. How are the related human rights issues presented?

Tips for facilitators

There is no limit on the number of times a particular photograph can be chosen. One particular image may be chosen several times in one round, or it may be chosen in different rounds. In other words, it may represent one of the articles to several people, or it may represent different articles to different people.

Refer to section "How to use COMPASS", on page 38 for more information about making your own set of photos. You can collect images from colour magazines, travel brochures, old calendars and post cards. Be sure that there is no text with any of the pictures, but make a note of each picture's original caption or other information, so you can answer questions about it. The pictures should show a wide variety of aspects of "life on earth"; they should include images of individuals and groups, people of different ages, cultures and abilities. There should be pictures in rural and urban settings, of industry and agriculture, people doing different sorts of work and leisure activities. Don't try to put the pictures in any sort of order when you number them. The purpose of the numbers is just so the pictures can easily be identified.

It will depend on the group and their general skills of "visual literacy" how much you need to guide the participants to analyse the pictures. You may consider starting the activity with a joint analysis of one or two of the pictures. The questions presented in the "further information" section below can be used as a guide.

Variations

You could also ask people to pick the one that for them best represents the concept of human rights. When everyone has chosen, ask them to give their reasons.

Suggestions for follow-up

Borrow cameras, or look out for some of the disposable ones when they are on sale, and make a project to photograph "Views on human rights" in your locality.

Images do not only come from pictures; they also come from situations and events. Let the group "see" discrimination through the activity "Take a step forward", on page 217.

Ideas for action

Make an exhibition of photographs from the "Views on human rights" project. Alternatively, develop some of the ideas for posters from the "Other picture games" below and use them for an exhibition.

Further information

"Reading" pictures is a skill, which has to be learned and developed. People talk of literacy skills, meaning skills to recognise the letters of the alphabet and to read the printed word. But the term implies more than that. It also refers to skills of analysing, understanding and interpreting the text as a whole. In much the same way, some people talk about "visual literacy" to describe the skills of "reading" an image. To "read" a picture, you have to ask who made the image and why they made it in the way they did - what are their motives? You also have to be aware of the emotional impact the picture has and how it affects your attitude to the subject. You may like to ask yourself the following questions while looking at the pictures of the "Fighters for rights", on page 130:

The subject: who, what, where and when?

- Who is portrayed; what is their age, sex, health, wealth or status?
- What does their posture and facial expression tell me about them?
- Is the subject aware that they are being photographed? Was the picture posed, or is it natural?
- What are the surroundings like? Do they harmonise with the person, or do they contrast with him/her?
- What are they doing? Is it a normal activity, or something special?
- What is your overall impression of the person? Is it positive or negative, sympathetic or disinterested?

The context

- Where was the picture originally published? In a newspaper, magazine or travel brochure? In other words, was it being used for information, sales, or propaganda? Or what?
- Is there a title or any other information with the picture that seals the message which the photographer wants the viewer to receive?

Technical details

- Is the picture in black and white or in colour? Does this affect the impact it has on you? Would the picture have a bigger impact if it were larger?
- Are you impressed by the angle the picture was taken at?
- What special effects have been used, such as soft lighting or focusing? Why?
- Has the image been manipulated? Does the picture lie? Is the image actually what was in front of the photographer when they took the picture, or have they used a computer to retouch the image (to make the person look more glamorous, for example?)

Who took the picture?

- What is the relationship between the photographer and the subject?
- Are they sympathetic to their subject?
- Are they being paid, or is it an amateur snapshot?
- Why did the photographer want to take the picture? What were their motives? What were they trying to "tell us" with the picture?

To conclude, *what* visual symbols or stereotypes have you recognised? For example, Martin Luther King as the political leader standing over his people, or Ngawang Sangdrol as a Tibetan peasant? *Why* did the editors of this manual choose these photographs to be used with the activity? *What* effect do these images have on your attitude to the person portrayed? Do they add anything to your appreciation of the person over and above what you read in the texts? How? Why?

Source: Information adapted from "Focus for Change" (Class, gender and race inequality and the media in an international context.) Focus for Change, 1992. (103 London Street, Reading, Berkshire, RG1 4QA, England.)

2. What do you see in Pancho?

Materials/preparation

- Photocopy all of Pancho's illustrations in the manual (see chapter 5). Enlarge them if possible.
- Make duplicate sets of the illustrations, one set per small group

Instructions

1. Ask people to get into small groups.
2. Give one set of Pancho's illustrations to each group and ask the participants to look at all the pictures and then, individually, to choose the one that appeals to them the most - for whatever reasons.
3. When everyone has chosen, then each person in turn should share their choice saying:
   - What the cartoon says to them
   - Why they chose the picture
   - How it relates to their concerns and reality
   - How they see it relating to human rights
4. After each turn the rest of the group should share their reactions.
5. When all have finished, ask everybody to come into plenary.

Debriefing and evaluation

Get brief feedback from each group about their general impressions and continue with questions as described in the first picture game, "What do you see?", on page 189.

Tips for facilitators

You could use Pancho's illustrations in other ways. For example ask people to write captions or you could white-out the texts in the speech bubbles and ask people to write their own. Please make your participants aware of the importance to respect artists' copyrights.

3. Part of the picture

Materials/preparation

- Find pictures that tell a simple story. Cut them into two parts in such a way that separately the two images encourage the viewer to read the situation in a way which is quite different from the way they would read the situation if they read the two images together as a whole.
- Put the picture sets in separate envelopes. You need one set per participant.

Instructions

1. Ask people to get into pairs.
2. Give each pair two envelopes.
3. Tell participants to take turns to open an envelope and give their partner one part of the picture inside. Let the partner say what they think is going on in the picture, who the subject is and what they are doing.
4. Then, the first participant should hand over the second piece and ask their partner what they think is happening now that they have the full picture.
5. Go on to a short debriefing:
   - What surprises were there?
   - How often do people accept what they see and forget that it may not be the "whole story"?

Tips for facilitators

You can use this activity as an icebreaker or you can develop it further by getting the pairs to swap their pictures with another pair and repeating the activity. Do people find it easier the second time round? Or is it more challenging? Why?

4. Captions for pictures

Materials/preparation

- Numbered pictures
- Paper and pens, one per participant
- Scissors and tape
- Large sheets of paper (A3) or flipchart paper. You will need as many pieces of paper as you have pictures.

Instructions

1. Lay the pictures out on a table and ask participants either individually or in pairs to write captions for each of the pictures. They should keep their writing neat because later they will cut the captions out.
2. When everyone is finished, hold up the pictures one at a time and invite volunteers to read out their captions.
3. Glue the picture in the centre of a large sheet of paper and ask people to glue their captions around the picture to make a "poster".
4. Tape the posters to the wall.

5. Go on to a brief review of the different pictures and their captions.
   - How difficult was it to write captions?
   - What makes a good caption?
   - If a picture can say a thousand words, why do they need captions?

Tips for facilitators

Using coloured paper and pens for the captions makes the posters more attractive. Using this method to get several different captions for each picture is usually both amusing and provocative. People are engaged and prepared for a good discussion. The captions are an ideal base for making the point that each person sees the world in a unique way, which should be respected.

Key date

21 March
Word Poetry Day

5. Speech bubbles

Materials/preparation
- Pictures, one picture per pair. (Two or more pairs should get the same picture.)
- Paper and pen, one between two people
- Glue

Instructions

1. Ask people to get into pairs. Hand out the pictures, sheets of paper and pens.
2. Invite them to analyse the Who? What? Where? When? and How? of the picture.
3. Tell them to glue the picture onto the paper and to write speech bubbles for the characters in the picture.
4. Ask the pairs to share their work and go on to a short debriefing:
   - How hard was it to analyse the pictures and to write speech bubbles?
   - For the pairs who had the same picture - how do your analyses of your pictures compare?
   - What stereotypes did people find in the pictures and in the speech bubbles?

Tips for facilitators

You do not have to restrict the group to pictures of people. Why not include some pictures with animals? This can be especially fruitful if you want to get people to talk about stereotypes. You can start out by pointing out how often animals are cast as stereotypes in cartoons and then get the group to look for examples of stereotyping in their pictures and speech bubbles.

Play the game!

"Life is like a game in which God shuffles the cards, the devil deals them and we have to play the trumps."
Yugoslavian Proverb

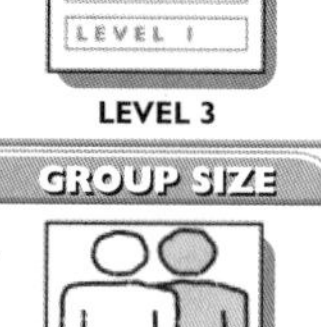

TIME
45 MINUTES

Themes Sport, Peace and Violence, General human rights

Complexity Level 3

Group size 10-15

Time 45 minutes

Overview This is a simulation. People play a well-known, but simple, well-known game, for example a card or board game, but not all the players play the game fairly. It deals with issues about conflict and conflict resolution.

Related rights
- The right to participate in decision making processes
- Equality in dignity and rights
- The right to fair treatment under the law

Objectives
- To develop insights into how to identify problem and their roots
- To develop conflict resolution skills
- To promote participation, co-operation and respect for others.

Materials
- A pack of standard playing cards, or other cards, for example for playing "happy families" or "Uno"
- Role cards

Preparation
- Read the information on conflict resolution given below and be clear about the process.
- Find a suitable game to play. It should be simple and adaptable so it can be played in about 20 minutes. It could be cards, for instance play a few rounds of "snap" or "pontoon", or a board game such as "snakes and ladders" or even a frame or two of team snooker. Choose a game that can be played by a minimum of 8 people and which gives possibilities for cheating.
- Make one copy of each role card, either by hand or with a photocopier.
- Secretly, and one at a time, choose four participants to take a special role during the activity. Give each of them one of the role cards. Tell each of them that it must be a complete secret.

Explain the simulation to them and give each of them one of the role cards. Tell each of them that it must be a complete secret.

Instructions

1. Call the participants together and ask if anyone would like to join you in a game (of cards or a board game – whatever you chose!).
2. Check that everyone knows the general rules of the game and if not, go through them briefly (you can be a bit vague...). If the group is big, split the group and organise several games at one (you will need co-facilitators).

3. Begin the game and leave it to run for as long as possible. (Let the players try to spot what is happening and develop a mediation process themselves. You should intervene only if the players don't take the initiative and if things get very heated. Then you should intervene as tactfully as possible and preferably between one round of the game and the next.)
4. After the game has finished, give people time to calm down and get out of role before going on to the debriefing.

Debriefing and evaluation

There will already have been a lot of discussion during the various attempts at reconciliation. Now let people talk about how they feel about the activity and what they learned about mediation and the process of conflict resolution.

- Did they enjoy the activity? What was going on during the game?
- Four people had special roles; who were they and what were their roles?
- What happened when someone disrupted the game the first time? Ask each player in turn to say what they noticed and what they did.
- How did the ideas given to solve the conflicts emerge? And how were they applied?
- Was it frustrating that the facilitator tried to mediate, rather than putting his/her foot down and declaring how the game was to be played?
- Can people identify the steps of the conflict resolution process?
- In real life, what are the pros and cons of trying to solve problems by negotiation rather than by decree?

Tips for facilitators

If the players are themselves trying to develop a means of conflict resolution, then allow them to do so with as little intervention from you as possible! After all, that is the objective of this activity and if participants can develop the skills by themselves, great! If that happens, then be sure to evaluate their approaches during the debriefing.

During the game, try to guide the participants to find their own procedures and solutions bearing in mind the process of conflict resolution, or principled negotiation as it is sometimes called. There are three main stages:

1. Becoming aware of the conflict
   - *Don't argue over positions*. (In this case don't argue over who is right and wrong.)
   - *Identify the problem* (Clarify what happened)
   - *Separate the person from the problem*. (Don't let players exchange insults, but focus on the behaviour that is the problem.)
2. Diagnosing what is wrong and finding possible solutions.
   - *Focus on interests, not positions*. That is, seek common ground. (Do they want to play the game or not?)
   - *Invent options for mutual gain*. Propose solutions that are seen to be fair and will satisfy everyone. (For instance, play the last round again. Ask if it would it help to clarify the rules? Should we have a discussion about this? Should we stipulate penalties? Any other ideas?)
3. Applying the appropriate solutions.

Key dates

1st Saturday in July
International Day of co-operatives

- *Insist on objective criteria.* (In this case define the rules and penalties)
- *Participation.* Ensure that the disputing parties participate and take responsibility for resolving the problems themselves. Solutions which are imposed are far less likely to work; it is much better for people to be fully involved in finding their own, mutually acceptable solutions.

Be aware that, even though there are three stages in the process of conflict resolution, in practice it is not possible to completely separate them and that it is normal for there to be overlap!

Do not be scared of the level of skills necessary to facilitate this activity: it is necessary neither to have a degree in conflict resolution nor to have been able to solve all the conflicts that you have been involved in! To help you develop your own skills, why not do a thought experiment? Think through some of your own personal experiences of conflicts. Reflect on what happened and then try to analyse them within the framework of the three stages described above. The roles work better if you re-define them specifically for the game you intend to play with the participants.

Variations

If the group that you are working with is more than fifteen people, you may split them into subgroups and run two or three games at the same time. But you can only do that if you have the assistance of several co-facilitators! You can also change the players from one round to the next, that gives more dynamic to the game and makes it more difficult to discover the "undercover" players.

You can arrange for some of the group to observe. These people can either act solely as observers and give feedback on what happened in the debriefing at the end, or they can act as mediators, in which case they will probably need some prior guidance from you on how to mediate. Make sure you do not have too many observers.

Suggestions for follow-up

If the group want to put their skills in principled negotiation into practice, they could do the activity "Let every voice be heard", on page 153, which is about setting up representative structures in an organisation, for example, a school or club council.

Ideas for Action

Focus on personal change. Encourage people to keep the three stages of conflict resolution in mind when faced with any conflict – of any scale and with anyone, parents, teachers or friends. Arrange to have occasional, meetings to share experiences and to review people's progress in developing their skills.

Further Information

Conflict is experienced at all levels of human activity from intra-personal to the international. *Conflict resolution* is a comprehensive approach based on sharing mutual problems between the conflicting parties. Resolution of a conflict implies that the deep-rooted sources of conflict are addressed, changing behaviour so it is no longer violent, attitudes so they are no longer hostile, and structures so they are no longer exploitative. The term is used to refer both to the process (or the intention) to bring about these changes, and to the completion of the process.

The conflict resolution process is designed, firstly, to diffuse the negative emotional energy that keeps the disputing parties apart and, secondly, to enable the disputing parties to understand and resolve their differences in order then to go on to find or create solutions which are mutually acceptable and which address the root causes of the conflict. In recent years, some specialists in the field have begun to use the term 'conflict transformation' as shorthand for the long-term and deeper structural, relational and cultural dimensions of conflict resolution. Thus, conflict transformation may be seen as the deepest level of change in the conflict resolution process.

A conflict is: Disagreement or incompatibility of goals by different people or groups. Derived from the Latin *conflictus*, meaning, "to strike together", it is used to denote both a process and a state of being."Conflicts involve struggles between two or more people over values, or competition for status power and scarce resources." (Moore, 1986).

Conflict resolution is based on co-operation.

It is *focused* on the subjective perceptions and long-term view *aims* at removing the causes of conflict and *improves* communication, to develop win-win situations without using coercion

You can find out more about developing conflict resolution skills at www.brad.ac.uk/acad/confres including a self-study course, which is easy, free and very good. The book, "Getting to Yes" by Roger Fisher and William Ury (Arrow books 1987) is a classic on the subject and is very easy and entertaining to read.

HANDOUTS

Role cards

The Rule-maker

You try to make up new rules for the game. These are not new rules that you discuss and agree with the other players - you just do it on your own initiative! Generally these rules, of course, are to your own advantage!

The rules that you create can be important or unimportant, but you must be insistent and keep saying that you are right and these are the official rules of the game and that you can't believe no one else knows them!

For example, depending on the game, you could make a rule that disqualifies anyone who delays in taking their turn, or a rule that anyone who plays a "6 of diamonds", or throws a 1 on the die has a second go or collects bonus points.

The Accuser

You are the kind of person who disrupts the game by accusing others of not playing by the rules. Depending on the game you can accuse people of taking too long over their turn, not shuffling the cards well enough - or whatever.

You really enjoy stirring things up. A little fight would not be bad at all, so just try to point a finger at innocent people!

The Cheater

You are always trying to cheat; taking an extra card here or there, counting more points to yourself and fewer to others.

Try to start cheating in a very discrete and secretive manner; wait a little while before you make it more obvious and provocative. In the beginning you should deny any accusations, but as time goes on you will have to decide how adapt your role, taking into account the discussions and resolutions which have been made during the conflict resolution process.

The Bad Loser

First make sure that you do not win the game; play very badly in every round! However, you should role-play the type of character who likes to win! If you don't, you are a very bad loser... you get mad, and you say and do things to make those who do win feel bad about it (like throwing cards in the air or screaming).

THEMES

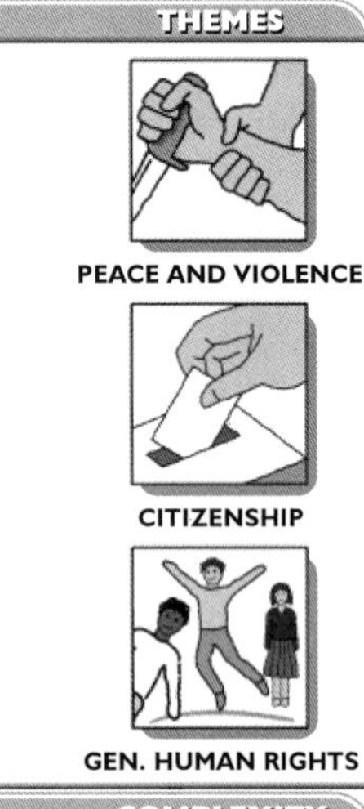

PEACE AND VIOLENCE

CITIZENSHIP

GEN. HUMAN RIGHTS

COMPLEXITY

LEVEL 3

GROUP SIZE

10 OR MORE

TIME

90 MINUTES

Power Station

Make this power station generate positive and creative energy!

Themes Peace and Violence, Citizenship, General human rights

Complexity Level 3

Group size 10+

Time 90 minutes

Overview Power is often associated with violence. This activity uses creative group work to address issues of:
- Violence in the community, and
- Ways to solve the problems of violence

Related rights
- The right to security of the person
- The right not to be discriminated against
- The right to privacy and protection of honour and reputation

Objectives
- To develop knowledge and understanding about the expressions of violence and their causes
- To develop co-operation and group work skills
- To take responsibility for seeking creative solutions to violence

Materials
- Long piece of strong wool or string equal to the length of the room.
- A pair of scissors
- A4 size sheets of paper; 6 sheets per participant should be sufficient
- Markers, one per person
- Bell (optional)
- Sticky tape
- 2 rooms (optional, but preferable)

Preparation
- Prepare one room to be the "power station". Clear a space in the middle. Stretch one strand of string across the room and anchor the ends firmly. It is to represent an electrical cable. It should hang about one meter above the floor. Do not make it too tight (you will need some slack for tying the knots when the cable has to be mended after each power failure!)
- You may wish to put a sign on the door saying Power Station.

Instructions

The activity is in two parts: part one, a brainstorm of expressions of violence (ten minutes) and part 2, working in the power station (sixty minutes).

Part 1. Brainstorm of expressions of violence

1. Ask participants to do a quick personal brainstorm of the expressions of violence in their community (school, youth club, college, neighbourhood, etc.). Explain clearly that they are not going to look at the "big issues" such as terrorism or genocide but

rather for those expressions of violence we all meet in everyday life, for instance, mobbing, bullying, verbal abuse, sarcasm, jokes in poor taste, etc.

2. Ask people to use the markers and to write in big letters. They should use key words or a short phrase and write each idea on a separate piece of paper.
3. Collect the sheets together and do a quick check to see if there are any that repeat the same expression. Discard the duplicates.
4. Give the participants a five-minute break while you prepare for the next part. Fold the sheets of paper over and hang them over the "electric cable". The papers should be spaced at about 0.5 m intervals from each other. It will be necessary to tape them onto the string so that they stay in position and do not slide.

Part 2. In the power station

1. Now invite the participants into the "power station", where they are going to work as technicians.
2. Split the participants into 2 groups.
3. Tell them that this power station generates "negative energy" and that because "negative energy" is very heavy there are often power failures. (Your job is to simulate the power failure by cutting the string at a point between two "problem" papers) Their job is to reverse the situation and to put some "positive energy" into the wires.
4. Explain that when a power failure is imminent the lights will flicker and they will hear a bell. As soon as the electricity is cut, one person from each group must run forward to the cable. They each grab a broken end, which they then hold together "to temporarily enable the electricity to flow again".
5. With their spare hand, each technician takes one of the pieces of paper, which are hanging on either side of the break, and reads the message out loud.
6. Both groups are now responsible for mending the failure. Give them five minutes to come up with a proposal for solutions for the two problems.
7. The groups then share and discuss their proposals and agree the solutions for each problem. These are then written on clean sheets of paper and handed to the technicians.
8. The technicians now knot the ends of the "cable" together and tape the "solutions" pieces of paper over the join to make a permanent repair.
9. Stick the two used "expression of violence" pieces of paper on the wall.
10. Now cut somewhere else along the "cable" and repeat the exercise. The activity finishes when all the "expression of violence" papers have been removed from the wire and are replaced by "solutions" papers.
11. Finally, collect all the "solutions papers" off the wire and stick them on the wall beside the various expressions of violence.

Debriefing and evaluation

Start the debriefing with a review of the activity itself and then go on to discuss each expression of violence and the proposed solutions:

- How did people feel during the activity? Did they enjoy it? Why (not)?
- What are the causes of the particular expressions of violence identified?
- Were the proposed solutions and actions realistic? In the short term? In the longer term?
- What challenges or resistance might people face when trying to implement these solutions?

Key date

20 February
Non-violent
Resistance Day

- How can young people prevent or fight against violence?
- Which human rights are violated by violence?

Tips for facilitators

You will need to allow about 10 minutes for part 1, the brainstorm, about 60 minutes for the work in the power station and 20 minutes for the debriefing and evaluation.

Try to do this exercise quite quickly. Do not let the young people get bored.

If people need a further explanation about how to come up with an idea or slogan that could be a solution to the problems (point 6 in the instructions), you could give the following example. If the one piece of paper reads "bullying" and the other reads "violence on television", one group might suggest that there should be workshops in schools on how to deal with bullying and that violent films should be broadcast only after 11 p.m. The other group might suggest training peer mediators for the bullying problem and that there should be a 9 p.m. watershed before which violent films should not be shown. The two groups then discuss these proposals and combine or amend them before writing them on the "solutions" pieces of paper. Each group may come with 2 or more proposals, but one is enough.

If the group is small, you can work with one group of "emergency technicians". The reason for working with two groups is that two groups very often come up with different solutions to the same problem, which widens the options.

The icebreaker "People machine", on page 57, makes a good, co-operative warm-up.

This technique can be adapted for use with any issue which involves identifying problems and finding solutions.

Suggestions for follow-up

Discrimination or gender issues might have come up in the "power station" Even if they didn't, you may be interested in exploring issues about identity and the right to equality in dignity and respect. Have a look at the activity "Who are I?", on page 257.

Ideas for action

Tackle one of the problems identified in this activity. For instance, if bullying was the chosen issue, the group could take forward the proposal to organise a workshop in their school and put it on the agenda of the next school or association council meeting.

Note: "Power station" has been developed from an activity proposed by Dariusz Grzemny, Association for Children and Young People (Chance), Glogow, Poland.

Responding to racism

Everyone in the school community has a responsibility to monitor and tackle racial harassment and racist incidents.

Themes Education, Discrimination and Xenophobia, General human rights

Complexity Level 3

Group size 4-50

Time 120 minutes

Overview This activity uses role-play and review of a critical incident to provoke participants to review their understanding of cultural difference. It also involves discussion and collective writing to address issues about:
- The difficulties of stepping outside one's own cultural perspective
- Racism, stereotypes and cultural differences
- How to deal with racism in a school or other educational organisation.

Related rights
- Equality in dignity and rights
- The right not to be discriminated against
- The right to freedom of thought, conscience and religion

Objectives
- To stimulate interest in human rights and racism
- To develop skills for democratic participation, communication and co-operation
- To promote responsibility, justice and solidarity

Materials
- Large sheets of paper or flipchart paper and markers
- 4 volunteers to present a role-play
- Critical incident role card and guidelines for facilitators, handout 1
- The school's (or organisation's) policy and guidelines on racial Incidents
- Copies of handout 2, " some practical points for consideration", or write the points up on a large sheet of paper or overhead transparency (optional)

Preparation
- Review the critical incident presented in handout 1, and if necessary adapt it to your own situation.
- Choose four volunteers and ask them to prepare to present a very short role-play based on the critical incident.

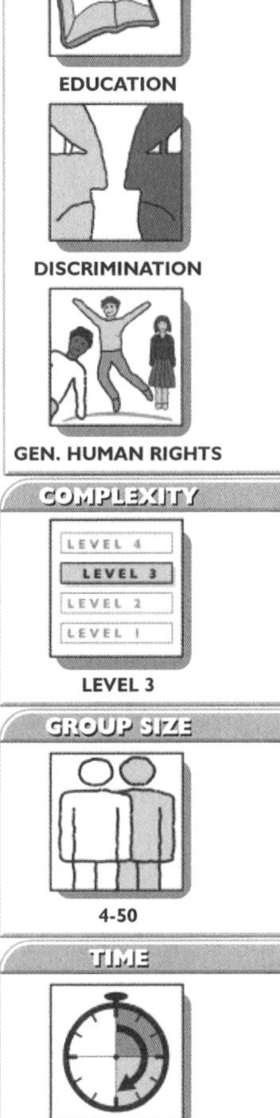

Instructions

This activity is in two parts: part 1, a review: what do we understand by the term "racism"?; part 2, drafting a policy for dealing with racist incidents in school (or in a club or organisation).

Part 1. A review: what do we understand by the term "racism"?

1. Begin the activity with a brainstorm about racism. You may consider challenging participants to react to racism by telling a racist joke and asking them what they think about it. Write their responses on the large sheet of paper or flipchart paper.
2. Racist incidents and potential intercultural misunderstandings happen every day. Go on to

brainstorm what kinds of everyday incidents and behaviour people identify as being racist.

3. Now work with the critical incident. Hand out paper and pens. Ask people to watch the role-play and to write down a couple of key words which summarise their response at each of the breaks in the presentation. Get the volunteers to act out the role-play.
4. Conduct a short debriefing of people's comments:
   - What did people write down in the first break? What led participants to their conclusions?
   - What did people write down in the second break? What led them to those conclusions?
   - What did people realise at the end? What assumptions had they been making?

Part 2. Drafting a policy for dealing with racist incidents in school (or in an organisation).

1. Introduce the next task, to draft a policy for the school, club or organisation.
2. Make a short brainstorm of the different actors in their school or club. For example, in a school there are pupils/students, teachers, a headteacher, cleaning staff, librarians, school bus drivers and supervisory staff, for instance, playground supervisors.
3. Next, ask the participants to divide themselves into small groups of four or five people to consider the duties and responsibilities of the different members of the school community with respect to racist incidents. The objective is to draft guidelines on how these people should deal with such incidents. Give the groups 30 minutes for their discussions and to prepare a report with key points on flipchart paper.
4. Ask participants to come back into plenary to report on their work. The facilitator should make a summary of the points and invite the participants to compare them with whatever policies or guidelines already exist in their school.
5. Now encourage each group to work further to develop one aspect (step or measure). For example: if a general school statement about racism and discrimination is needed, then one group should be in charge of writing it. Groups should also discuss ways to present their results in plenary, for example, using not only their writing but also images, collages and body sculptures to better convey their feelings.
6. In plenary, ask the groups to report their results and discuss how to implement their ideas.

Debriefing and evaluation

Begin with a review of the activity itself and then go on to talk about what people learned and what they should do next.

- How prevalent is racism in the school or club, and in society at large?
- Which groups suffer most? Why? Were the same groups targeted twenty or fifty years ago?
- Have people's concept of what constitutes a racist incident changed as a result of doing the activity? How? Give examples?
- Whose responsibility is it to ensure that racist incidents do not happen in your school (or organisation)?
- Think back to the critical incident. What should the teachers, Abdallah's father and the headteacher have done to ensure a just outcome?
- Having a policy on dealing with racist incidents is important, but would it not be better not to need it in the first place? What can and should be done to address the causes of racist behaviour, both in school and in society at large?

Tips for facilitators

Be aware of the background of the members of the group and adapt the activity accordingly. People will be more engaged if you deal with issues that are real for the group. On the other hand, you need to be prepared for the emotions that may be brought out as a result. It is important to pay attention to the feelings of those participants who feel that they themselves have been discriminated against at school. It may be useful, instead of focusing on one critical incident/case study, to gather insights from several examples and different perspectives. This approach will enable you to take different power relations into account; for example, the implications of racism among peers and racism coming from a teacher or headteacher.

If you want to be provocative at the beginning and to use a racist joke, you may consider choosing one that pokes fun at a group which is not represented in your class or youth group. In every country there are traditions of jokes about other nationals. You could start off the discussion by asking the group to share one or two. You could then go on to talk about the dividing line between racist and non-racist jokes. For instance, are jokes about Pakistanis or Turks nationalistic or racist? This could lead you on to the definition of a racist joke and of a racist incident (see below in "further information").

It may be that at the end of part 2 at step 4, the conclusions are not sufficiently focused for the participants to use them for the next step. In this case, you may wish to use handout 2, "some practical points for consideration" and encourage groups to develop the first four steps.

Key date

21 March
International Day for the Elimination of Racial Discrimination

Variations

The activity can be adapted to address issues such as bullying. If bullying is an issue, you may like to explore the activity "Do we have alternatives?", on page 111, before you try to develop an anti-bullying policy.

Suggestions for follow-up.

Review the issue regularly, for instance, once or twice a year. Policies need to be reviewed to ensure that they are in fact meeting the objectives. As society changes, so policies need updating to ensure that they continue to meet the challenges of the changing conditions.

The group may wish to look at how aspects of racism come into commercial decision-making. The activity "Access to medicaments", on page 80, looks at various issues, including racism, which were raised in the 1990 court case between the South African government and companies producing drugs for the treatment of AIDS.

Ideas for action

Continue to work on the policies in your own school or organisation and ensure their implementation. The group could also link up with anti-racist projects in other countries. For instance with "Schools Without Racism", a programme implemented in Belgium that requires at least 60% of the school population to sign and implement a common anti-discrimination statement (www.schoolwithoutracism-europe.org).

Further information

Definitions of racism

Racism, in general terms, consists of conduct or words or practices which advantage or disadvantage people because of their colour, culture or ethnic origin. Its more subtle forms are as damaging as its overt form.

Institutionalised racism is the collective failure of an organisation to provide an appropriate and professional service to people because of their colour, culture or ethnic origin. It can be seen or detected in processes, attitudes and behaviour which amounts to discrimination through unwitting prejudice, ignorance, thoughtlessness and racist stereotyping which disadvantages people from ethnic minorities. Racist incidents and harassment can take place in any institution, regardless of the numbers of pupils from different ethnic backgrounds within it.

A racist incident is any incident which is perceived to be racist by the victim or any other person.

What kind of incidents may be considered racist?

The following list of actions may be considered to be racist incidents.

Physical harassment: comprises the more obvious examples of violent attacks or physical intimidation of both children and adults from minority groups, as well as incidents of "minor" intimidation which may be cumulative in effect.

Verbal harassment: name-calling directed at those from minority groups and any ridicule of a person's background or culture (e.g. music, dress or diet) may be the most obvious examples. There may be other forms of verbal abuse, which are less obvious, involving teachers, pupils or other adults, such as off-the-cuff remarks of a racist nature, which cause offence.

Non co-operation and disrespect: refusal to co-operate with or show respect to minority pupils, students, teachers, trainers, youth leaders and others by people in the school/education community may constitute a racist incident if there is evidence of racist motivation or if the "victim" perceives racism to be a motive. Disrespect can also be inadvertent, for example if a teacher or trainer shows ignorance of a pupil's cultural practices in a way that makes the victim feel harassed or uncomfortable.

Other incidents: racist jokes and use of racist vocabulary, the wearing of racist insignia, badges, T shirts, etc., racist graffiti, the distribution of racist literature or posters, the presence of racist or fascist organisations in or around the school community, or stereotyping by adults which could lead to discrimination.

Many racist incidents will be of a less obvious type. Such insidious actions which occur are often the most difficult to detect and deal with. Many racist incidents involving pupils or students will not occur in the presence of teachers or adults. It is therefore important that schools develop strategies to ensure that all members of the school community are sensitive to, and take responsibility for, reporting and dealing with incidents.

Some practical points for consideration in relation to developing an anti-racist policy.

In dealing with racial harassment and racist incidents, a whole school (organisation) approach to policy development and implementation is required. It is important that approaches to racist incidents fit in with general school/organisational policy and practice. The issues should be regarded as "special but not separate". Some practical points for consideration are:

- A clear statement of policy needs to be made showing that no racist incidents or racial harassment will be tolerated.
- In the policy, the school should make a clear statement as to the procedures that should be followed when a racist incident occurs.
- The whole school approach, including processes and agreed actions for dealing with incidents, must extend to all members of the school community: governors, staff (teaching and non-teaching), parents, pupils, students and visitors.
- There must be clear understanding that everyone in the school community has a responsibility to monitor and tackle racial harassment and racist incidents.
- There should be a consistency of approach so that everyone involved is aware of what is expected of them.
- It should be understood that a response to an incident should be made at the time the incident occurs or is reported.
- Any follow up responses to an incident should be made within an agreed time-scale.

(Source: Northamptonshire Country Council)

HANDOUTS

A critical incident – Role-play card

Improvise a very short role-play based on the following incident. It should be presented in three short scenes as indicated below. In the breaks, the facilitator(s) will ask the observers to write down their thoughts about what is happening.

Scene one. Two teachers chatting in the staff room.
Over the last month there have been several incidents of pickpocketing in the school. Once again money is missing. The headteacher is determined to get to the bottom of it and involves the teachers in trying to identify the thief. Abdallah, a pupil whose family is originally from Northern Africa is suspected of being responsible, at least for the latest incident.

Scene two. The conversation between Abdallah's father and the headteacher.
The headteacher invites Abdallah's father to a meeting. As a result, Abdallah's father reimburses the full sum that was stolen to the headteacher.

Scene three. The two teachers are again chatting in the staff room.
That Abdallah's father paid is viewed by the teachers as an admission of Abdallah's guilt. Later however, they find evidence that Abdallah had nothing to do with the stealing.

A critical incident - guidelines for the facilitator

Let the volunteers perform their role-play. At the breaks, you should interject with the questions and ask the observers to write down a couple of key words which summarise their response at that stage in the presentation.

Scene one: Over the last month there have been several incidents of pickpocketing in the school. Once again money is missing. The headteacher is determined to get to the bottom of it and involves the teachers in trying to identify the thief. Abdallah, a pupil whose family is originally from Northern Africa is suspected of being responsible, at least for the latest incident.

First break. First question to the observers: If you were the headteacher, what would you do?

Scene two: The headteacher invites Abdallah's father to a meeting. As a result, Abdallah's father reimburses the full sum that was stolen to the headteacher.

Second break. Second question to the observers: Do you think the matter has been solved satisfactorily?

Scene three: The teachers view this as an admission that the thief was actually Abdallah. Later, however, they find evidence that Abdallah had nothing to do with the stealing.

Third break. Third question to the observers: What do you think now?

Rights Bingo!

What do we know about human rights?

THEMES

GEN. HUMAN RIGHTS

CHILDREN

HUMAN SECURITY

COMPLEXITY

LEVEL 1

GROUP SIZE

8 OR MORE

TIME

40 MINUTES

Themes General human rights, Children, Human Security

Complexity Level 1

Group size 8+

Time 40 minutes

Overview This is a simple quiz and variation of the game, Bingo!, in which people share their knowledge and experiences of human rights.

Related rights Any human rights

Objectives
- To know that human rights are relevant for everyone everywhere
- To develop listening skills
- To encourage respect for other people and their opinions

Materials
- One copy of the quiz sheet and pencil per person
- Flipchart paper and markers

Preparation
- Make a copy of the quiz sheet on a large sheet of paper or flipchart paper.
- Familiarise yourself with the basic rights listed in the UDHR (see page 402) and the Convention on the Rights of the Child (see page 406)

Instructions

1. Hand out the quiz sheets and pencils
2. Explain that people should find a partner and ask them one of the questions on the sheet. The key words of the answer should be noted down in the relevant box.
3. The pairs then split and find others to pair up with.
4. The aim of the game is not only to get an answer in each box but also to get a different person to answer each question.
5. Whoever gets an answer in every box first shouts out "Bingo!". They win.
6. Move on to the discussion. Take the question in the first box and ask people in turn to share the answers they received. List the key words on the flipchart. Allow short comments at this stage
7. When the chart is complete, go back and discuss the answers in each box more fully.

Debriefing and evaluation

- Were all the questions related to human rights? Which rights?
- Which questions were the hardest to answer? Why?
- Which questions were the most controversial? Why are rights controversial?
- How did people know about human rights and human rights violations? Do they trust the sources of the information?

Tips for facilitators

Feel free to change any of the questions to tailor the activity to the interests and level of your group.

When recording people's answers to each question, only put down key words. The point of the chart is to help with the discussion later. After each round, deal briefly with any questions of clarification or differences in interpretation. Highlight any points that require more in-depth discussion and agree to return to these at the end.

It is likely that people will give examples that you yourself may not know about, either because they are obscure or because they are personal. This should not matter. No one can be expected to know everything! You can ask people how they know a certain piece of information and discuss its authenticity and reliability. Indeed, it is a good opportunity to encourage people to think critically about information as a matter of principle.

Some of the answers will be controversial. For example, someone might say that abortion is a denial of the right to life. Some people in the group may hold this view very strongly; others may disagree equally strongly. The first learning point is that it is important to try to understand any issue from all perspectives: try to establish *why* people hold the view they do. There are always conflicts of interests and rights (in this case between the interests and rights of the mother and the unborn child). Whatever the difference of opinion or interpretation of rights people should always treat others whose opinion differs from their own with respect. They may disagree with their point of view, but they should respect the person.

The second learning point is that we should know about human rights because they are controversial. It is not clear-cut and decided once and for all how they should be interpreted and applied; they need to be reassessed and developed continually. It is therefore everyone's responsibility to be part of the process of promoting and protecting human rights.

Suggestions for follow-up

Take one or two of the answers that provoked controversy and discuss the real life dilemmas that there are when trying to develop a culture of respect for human rights.

Another way of exploring human rights is through images. Find out how people see human rights with the activity "What do you see?", on page 188. The activity can lead on to many discussions, for instance, about stereotypes, how we build up our images of the world and about discrimination.

Key date

8 May
World Red Cross and Red Crescent Day

HANDOUTS

Quiz sheet

The name of a document that proclaims human rights	A special right all children should have	The sister organisation of the Red Cross
A right denied to some people in your country	A human right that has been denied to you personally	An organisation that fights for human rights
A duty we all have in relation to our human rights	An example of discrimination	A right sometimes denied to women
Someone who fights for human rights	A violation of the right to life	An example of how someone's right to privacy may be violated

See the ability!

See the ability - not the disability!

Themes Discrimination and Xenophobia, Social rights, Sports

Complexity Level 3

Group size 6 - 36

Time 120 minutes

Overview A practical activity to encourage empathy with people with disabilities. Among the issues addressed are:
- The obstacles disabled people face in integrating into society
- Perceptions of the rights of the disabled as basic human rights

Related rights
- The right not to be discriminated against
- Equality in dignity and rights
- The right to social security

Objectives
- To raise awareness about some of the everyday problems faced by disabled people
- To develop insights into, and skills to respond to, the needs of disabled people
- To promote empathy and solidarity

Materials

For the introduction:
- A sheet of paper and a pen per participant

For part 2, per pair:
- A plastic bag containing a cabbage or lettuce leaf, a pencil, a stick of chalk, a leaf (from any tree), a coloured sheet of paper and a bottle or can of any soft drink
- A blindfold
- A sheet of paper and a pen

For part 3, per pair:
- 1 role card
- One sheet of paper and a pen

For part 4:
- Wheelchairs, one between eight people
- Space for creating an obstacle course. (A second room would be preferable, but not absolutely necessary.) Alternatively, access to outdoors would present a further option)
- Obstacles, for example, tables and chairs, planks of wood, piles of old newspapers, etc.
- One large sheet of paper or board and markers
- A watch or timer

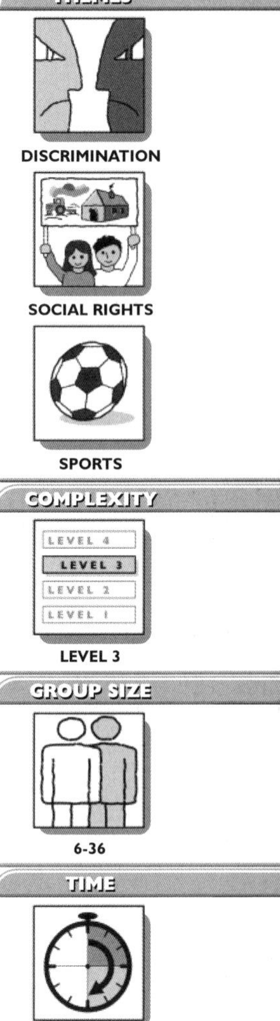

Preparation

- Make the role cards. Either choose one of the situations suggested with this activity or develop your own.
- If possible, have a second room that you can prepare in advance for the obstacle race, or better still go outdoors where you will be able to make the obstacle track over more challenging terrain. If you are setting it up indoors, then use tables and chairs to make narrow passages and planks of wood or old newspapers on the floor to substitute for naturally difficult terrain.

Instructions

This activity is organised in four parts: part 1, the introduction, part 2, the blindfold walk, part 3, signing, and part 4, the wheelchair race.

Part 1. Introduction (10 minutes)

1. Explain that the activity focuses on three particular disabilities: blindness, deafness and muteness, and paralysis.
2. Invite the participants to think for a few minutes about how they would like - and how they would not like - to be treated if they were disabled. Let them write down a few key words.
3. Now ask participants to write down what they would be most afraid of, if they were disabled.
4. When this has been done, ask the participants to turn over their papers and to get ready to "step into reality".

Part 2. The blindfold walk

1. Ask people to get into pairs. Hand out the blindfolds. One person from each pair is to be the disabled person and the other is their guide. It is the guide's responsibility to ensure the safety of their partner at all times. They may only answer simple questions related to safety with a "yes" or a "no" answer.
2. Ask the guides to take their partners for a 5-minute walk around and about, including up or down stairs or outside if possible.
3. On returning to the room let the guides lead their partners to their chairs. But there is a surprise on the chair! A bag! What is in it?
4. The blind players have to identify the contents. The guides' job is to write down their guesses.
5. Then let the "blind" people take off the blindfolds and see the objects. Invite the partners to briefly review their experiences and surprises with each other.
6. Give people a few minutes to come out of their roles and then move on to part 3.

Part 3. Signing

1. Tell the pairs that they are to swap over; the guides are now to be the disabled, this time people who are mute (can't speak), and the partners are the able-bodied helpers.
2. Hand out one of the situation cards to each disabled player. They must not show the cards to their partners. Give a piece of paper and pen to the helpers.
3. Explain that the mute players have to convey their problem to their helper. They may not speak, write or draw. The helpers must write down what they understand the message to be about.
4. When the "mute" player has communicated as much as they can, s/he should reveal the role card to their helper. Invite the pairs to briefly review their intentions, problems and frustrations.

Part 4. The wheelchair obstacle race

1. Point out the obstacle course to the participants. Explain that the winner is the person who gets round in the fastest time. There are penalties for crashing into the obstacles on the way.
2. Record the results on the large piece of paper.
3. When all who wish to have had a turn, take a short break and then go on to the debriefing and evaluation.

Debriefing and evaluation.

Take this in plenary. Start with a review of parts 2, 3 and 4 of the activity and then go on to reflect on what people knew at the beginning and about what they learned as a result of their experiences.

1. Start with the blindfold walk. Ask both those who were blindfolded and those who were the helpers to share their reactions:
   - How did each of them feel during the exercise?
   - What was most difficult? What was funny? What was scary?
   - How hard was it to trust and to be trustworthy?
   - How successful were people at identifying the objects in the bag? Which senses did they use? How many people dared to open the bottle/can to try the drink?
2. Then go on to review part 2, the signing:
   - How did each of them feel during the exercise?
   - What was most difficult? What was funny? What was scary?
   - Was it frustrating to sign and not to be understood?
   - Was it frustrating or embarrassing not to understand?
3. Next review the wheelchair obstacle race:
   - How did people feel not being so mobile?
   - What was most difficult? What was funny? What was scary?
4. Now review the fears and expectations people expressed at the beginning of the exercise. Ask people to look at the key words they wrote down:
   - Were some of their fears confirmed during the activity?
   - How did people try to help their partner?
   - How was the help received?
   - How easy is it to assess how much help to give?
5. What did people fear about being disabled? What did they base their fears on? Have people ever been afraid of becoming disabled as a result of an accident or illness?
6. What was the most surprising thing people learnt through the activity?
7. Do people know anyone who is either blind, mute or confined to a wheelchair? What is their social life like? How do other people react to them?
8. Look at the environment in the buildings and in the streets nearby, how "disability friendly" are they?
9. What can and should be done to ensure the equality and dignity of people who are disabled?
10. Are disability rights also a matter of human rights? Which rights in the UDHR are particularly relevant?
11. What can your school, association or local youth group do to promote the equality and dignity of people with disabilities?

Key dates

3 December
International Day of Disabled Persons

Tips for facilitators

Do not make the obstacle course for part 4 too long. 2-3 minutes is sufficient, especially if you only have two or three wheelchairs, because people will have to wait and they may get bored. You can try to borrow wheelchairs from a local hospital or organisation providing support for people temporarily in need of wheelchairs. Alternatively, you will have to improvise to give the participants physical disabilities. For example, by making people wear enormous rubber boots on the wrong feet!

How you run this activity will depend very much on the group. Make sure that everyone realises that they are going to go through different "simulations of reality" during which they will have the opportunity to experiment with their feelings and reactions to what it is like to be disabled. Explain that the purpose is not to make fun of anyone, or to cause undue stress or embarrassment. They should act "naturally", and not overdo things. Reassure people that at certain moments they may feel awkward and insecure, but that nothing harmful or dangerous will happen to them.

If you do not have time to do all the "simulations of reality", then do one or two. The experience of being blindfolded is perhaps the most personally challenging and touching of the experiences presented in this activity. Therefore, if you have to choose one part, it is recommended that you choose this one. Let the participants swap over so that both have the experience of disability. Remember, in this case to create a second set of objects for identification.

This activity is serious, but you should expect many funny situations. Let it be so. Feel compelled to intervene or comment only if people are doing something unsafe or making comments which ridicule people with disabilities. You may also wish to address this in the evaluation and debriefing with questions such as: when do people make fun of those with disabilities? Who does it and why? When is it all right to make jokes about people's disabilities? How does one judge the borderline between good humour and offence?

Variations

You may simulate many other kinds of disabilities, including less visible ones, such as learning disabilities or language difficulties, according to what is closest to your group's reality. One possibility is to simulate situations of disability due to age; this may contribute to raising young people's awareness towards older people and the (lack of) conditions for a life in dignity.

Suggestions for follow up

If you are working with children, you may like to look at Article 23 of the CRC, which states that disabled children have the right to special care, education and training that will help them to enjoy a full and decent life. You could ask the groups to find out about people in their own social environment (including family) who suffer from some kind of disability. They could further investigate what services and provisions those people have access to. Are there any children with disabilities in the youth group or association or in school? Can they do the same as everyone else? If not, why not?

If the group would like to look at how to respond to "everyday" problems of discrimination of another form - discrimination on the grounds of race, they could do the activity "Responding to racism", on page 201.

Ideas for action

The group may wish to identify a vulnerable group and decide what they can/should do to support them. Consult the section of the manual on "taking action" for guidance and ideas. It is important to work together with organisations that work with the disabled and to start from the needs of the disabled, as defined and identified by the disabled themselves.

Further information

The level of care and safeguarding of rights of the disabled varies greatly from country to country, ostensibly for economic reasons but in reality for reasons that have probably more to do with taking equality and social solidarity seriously than with anything else. For example, hearing aids may or may not be paid for by social security. There may or may not be special provisions for extra telecommunications equipment for deaf people and if someone needs an electric wheelchair, then sometimes the community or the state pays for it.

Information about discrimination against people with disabilities can be found in the background information on discrimination and xenophobia on page 338. Information about the Paralympic Games can be found in the background information on sports and human rights on page 392.

Note: This activity has been suggested by Dr Mónika Mádai, President of Common Fate Organisation (Közös Sors Egyesület, a Hungarian NGO working for promoting social integration of disabled and non-disabled people). She is also a member of the Hungarian National Council on Disability Affairs, which represents Hungary in Rehabilitation International, an international youth trainer and a concerned person, disabled since birth.

HANDOUTS

Situation 1.

Without words, try to explain to your friend that you have been a victim of violence. A group of young skinheads attacked you in the park, stole your bag and beat you up. Ask where the police station is.

You cannot speak, write any words or draw on paper.

Situation 2.

You are in a cafeteria; possibly at school or perhaps the cafeteria at one of the European Youth Centres. Explain to the cook that you can not eat Spaghetti Bolognese because you are a vegan: not only do you not eat meat but you are a vegetarian who doesn't eat any dairy products either (i.e. no milk, eggs or cheese).

You cannot speak, write any words or draw on paper.

Sport for all

"It is a bad game where nobody wins."
Italian proverb.

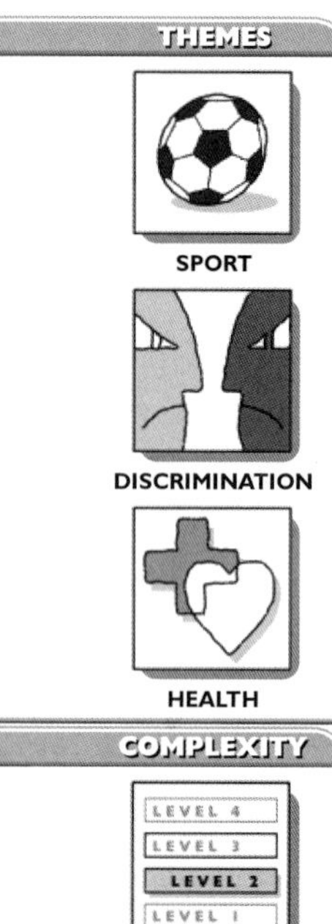

GROUP SIZE

8 OR MORE

TIME

120 MINUTES

Themes Sport, Discrimination and Xenophobia, Health

Complexity 2

Group size 8+

Time 120 minutes

Overview This is a high-energy activity. Participants use their imagination and creativity to design new games. The issues addressed include:
- Rules of games, their justification and monitoring
- The idea of human rights as rules for living
- Discrimination in sports

Related rights
- The right to health
- Equality in dignity and rights

Objectives
- To raise awareness of social and political exclusion from sporting activities
- To develop group-work and co-operative skills and creativity
- To encourage people to think about human rights as rules for fair play in life

Materials You will need one set of the following for each group of 4 people:
- 4 large buckets or waste-paper bins
- 1 ball of thick string
- 2 football-sized balls
- 2 newspapers
- One piece of chalk
- A pair of scissors

Instructions

1. Tell participants about the "Sport for all" movement. Say that, to mark the millennium, the National Sports Council has decided to hold a competition to invent a new game which can be played by all.
2. Ask people to get into groups of four.
3. Explain that each group has twenty minutes to devise a game using the equipment provided. It is up to each group to decide the aims of the new game and the rules.
4. Let the groups play each other's games.

Debriefing and evaluation

Start with a review of how people in the different groups interacted with each other and whether they enjoyed the activity. Then go on to discuss the games themselves and the rules people invented and, finally, talk about sports and games in real life.

- Was it hard to design a game?
- How did the groups work? Democratically or did one person make all the decisions?
- Did you share the jobs? I.e. was one person an ideas person, another good at putting the ideas into a practical form, someone else good at setting the game up, etc.?
- Which games did people enjoy the most? What makes a game a "good game"?
- Which groups found it necessary to change the rules once they tried the game out with others? Why did they need to change the rules and how did they do it? (Was the process carried out by the whole group, by just a few individuals or by just one person?)
- How important is it to have a clear aim and fair rules in order for everyone to feel that they can participate?
- Did everyone feel able to participate fully, or did some feel that they were at an advantage or disadvantage?
- In reality, how are certain groups excluded from sports? Which modes of exclusion are infringements of people's human rights?
- The Articles in the UDHR could be seen as rules for living in a pluralistic world. Are they good rules? For instance, are they universally acceptable to all players (everyone throughout the world)? Are there enough rules or too many? Are the rules fair? Do all players (all countries) play by the rules?

Tips for facilitators

Try to ensure that the groups are "mixed", for example, tall and short people, those with glasses and those without, a mix of genders, ages, athletic abilities, etc.

Depending on the group, you may need to begin the session with a brainstorm about games in general. For example, that games need to have clear aims or objectives and rules.

You may need to set limits, for example, that the game must be played within a certain location or not last longer than a total of twenty minutes. If they find design faults as their games are being played, let the designers of the game change the rules.

The discussion can be linked to human rights in various ways. You can consider the similarities and differences between rules and human rights. Good rules, like human rights, exist to ensure the game is fair by limiting the use of power by some players over others. The rules have to apply to all players in the same way that human rights are universal. Many rules prescribe a right together with duties. For instance, a football player has the right to kick the ball but not a fellow player. There are penalties in the case of an abuse of the rules.

The process of making decisions about changing the rules can be compared with how laws are changed in "real life". Are they changed by decree, by the legislature or by people through referenda or consultation with NGOs and others?

In the debriefing, people may say that exclusion and discrimination are not really big issues because people tend to choose sports that they are naturally good at. For example, tall people may play basketball and less energetic types may play snooker or chess. Nonetheless, there is an issue if only those young people who show promise get all the attention and opportunities to play in competitions while those who like to play for fun get less. Some sports exclude on grounds of wealth, because, for example, they need expensive equipment or coaching.

You may like to tell the group about the Street Sports project, an initiative with young people in the Balkans that is promoting tolerance and human rights (see the background information on sport and human rights on page 392).

Key date

10 October
World Mental Health Day

Variations

If you want to use this activity primarily to promote group-work skills you could ask one group to devise a co-operative game and the other a competitive one. In the debriefing you can compare how enjoyable each game was.

Suggestions for follow-up

If the group are interested in exploring other issues of equality, they may like to do the activity "Path to Equality-land", on page 185, which explores issues about gender equality.

Ideas for action

Organise a co-operative "Sports day". Invite young people from other clubs to play your new games. The group will have to decide how to make the event as inclusive as possible.

Further information

"Sport for All' is a movement promoting the Olympic ideal that sport is a human right for all individuals regardless of race, social class and sex. The movement encourages sports activities that can be practised by people of all ages, of both sexes and of different social and economic conditions.www.olympic.org/ioc/e/org/sportall

Take a step forward

"Everything flows from the rights of the others and my never-ending duty to respect them".
Emmanuel Lévinas

Themes	Discrimination and Xenophobia, Poverty, General human rights
Complexity	Level 2
Group size	10 - 30
Time	60 minutes
Overview	We are all equal, but some are more equal than others. In this activity participants experience what it is like to be someone else in their society. The issues addressed include: ▪ Social inequality being often a source of discrimination and exclusion ▪ Empathy and its limits.
Objectives	▪ To promote empathy with others who are different ▪ To raise awareness about the inequality of opportunities in society ▪ To foster an understanding of possible personal consequences of belonging to certain social minorities or cultural groups
Materials	▪ Role cards ▪ An open space (a corridor, large room or outdoors) ▪ Tape or CD player and soft/relaxing music
Preparation	▪ Read the activity carefully. Review the list of "situations and events" and adapt it to the group that you are working with. ▪ Make the role cards, one per participant. Copy the (adapted) sheet either by hand or on a photocopier, cut out the strips and fold them over.

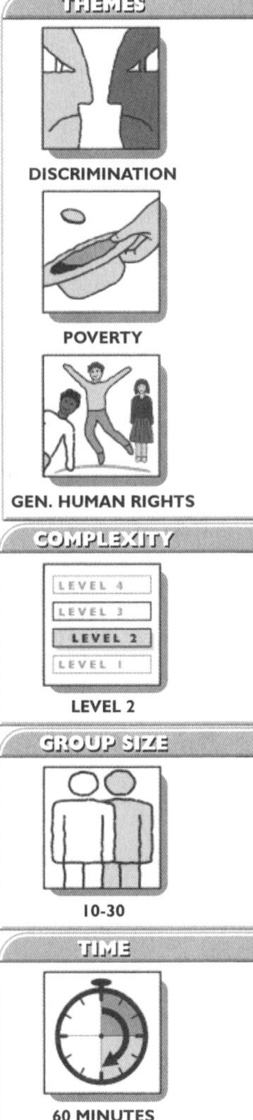

Instructions

1. Create a calm atmosphere with some soft background music. Alternatively, ask the participants for silence.
2. Hand out the role cards at random, one to each participant. Tell them to keep it to themselves and not to show it to anyone else.
3. Invite them to sit down (preferably on the floor) and to read their role card.
4. Now ask them to begin to get into role. To help, read out some of the following questions, pausing after each one, to give people time to reflect and build up a picture of themselves and their lives:
   ▪ What was your childhood like? What sort of house did you live in? What kind of games did you play? What sort of work did your parents do?
   ▪ What is your everyday life like now? Where do you socialise? What do you do in the morning, in the afternoon, in the evening?
   ▪ What sort of lifestyle do you have? Where do you live? How much money do you earn each month? What do you do in your leisure time? What you do in your holidays?
   ▪ What excites you and what are you afraid of?

5. Now ask people to remain absolutely silent as they line up beside each other (like on a starting line)
6. Tell the participants that you are going to read out a list of situations or events. Every time that they can answer "yes" to the statement, they should take a step forward. Otherwise, they should stay where they are and not move.
7. Read out the situations one at a time. Pause for a while between each statement to allow people time to step forward and to look around to take note of their positions relative to each other.
8. At the end invite everyone to take note of their final positions. Then give them a couple of minutes to come out of role before debriefing in plenary.

Debriefing and evaluation

Start by asking participants about what happened and how they feel about the activity and then go on to talk about the issues raised and what they learnt.

1. How did people feel stepping forward - or not?
2. For those who stepped forward often, at what point did they begin to notice that others were not moving as fast as they were?
3. Did anyone feel that there were moments when their basic human rights were being ignored?
4. Can people guess each other's roles? (Let people reveal their roles during this part of the discussion)
5. How easy or difficult was it to play the different roles? How did they imagine what the person they were playing was like?
6. Does the exercise mirror society in some way? How?
7. Which human rights are at stake for each of the roles? Could anyone say that their human rights were not being respected or that they did not have access to them?
8. What first steps could be taken to address the inequalities in society?

Tips for facilitators

If you do this activity outdoors, make sure that the participants can hear you, especially if you are doing it with a large group! You may need to use your co-facilitators to relay the statements.

In the imagining phase at the beginning, it is possible that some participants may say that they know little about the life of the person they have to role-play. Tell them, this does not matter especially, and that they should use their imagination and to do it as best they can.

The power of this activity lies in the impact of actually seeing the distance increasing between the participants, especially at the end when there should be a big distance between those that stepped forward often and those who did not. To enhance the impact, it is important that you adjust the roles to reflect the realities of the participants' own lives. As you do so, be sure you adapt the roles so that only a minimum of people can take steps forward (i.e. can answer "yes"). This also applies if you have a large group and have to devise more roles.

During the debriefing and evaluation it is important to explore how participants knew about the character whose role they had to play. Was it through personal experience or through other sources of information (news, books, and jokes)? Are they sure the information and the images they have of the characters are reliable? In this way you can introduce how stereotypes and prejudice work.

This activity is particularly relevant to making links between the different generations of rights (civil/political and social/economic/cultural rights) and the access to them. The problems of poverty and social exclusion are not only a problem of formal rights – although the latter also exists for refugees and asylum-seekers for example. The problem is very often a matter of effective access to those rights.

Variations

One way to get more ideas on the table and to deepen participants' understanding is to work first in small groups and then to get them to share their ideas in plenary. Having co-facilitators is almost essential if you do this. Try this method by taking the second part of the debriefing - after each role has been revealed - in smaller groups. Ask people to explore who in their society has fewer, and who has more, chances or opportunities, and what first steps can and should be taken to address the inequalities. Alternatively, ask people to take one of the characters and ask what could be done, i.e. what duties and responsibilities they themselves, the community and the government have towards this person.

Suggestions for follow-up

Depending on the social context you work in, you may want to invite representatives from advocacy groups for certain cultural or social minorities to talk to the group. Find out from them what issues they are currently fighting for and how you and young people can help. Such a face-to-face meeting would also be an opportunity to address or review some of the prejudices or stereotyping that came out during the discussion.

If the group would like to find out more about the issues relating to inequalities in education provision world-wide and the measures that are being taken to address the problems, you may wish to look at the activity "Education for all", on page 122.

Ideas for action

Take up the ideas from the follow-up. Follow through how you and young people can help groups and organisations working with cultural or social minorities, and turn the ideas into practice.

Key date

18 December
International Migrants Day

HANDOUTS

Role cards

You are an unemployed single mother.	You are the president of a party-political youth organisation (whose "mother" party is now in power).
You are the daughter of the local bank manager. You study economics at university.	You are the son of a Chinese immigrant who runs a successful fast food business.
You are an Arab Muslim girl living with your parents who are devoutly religious people.	You are the daughter of the American ambassador to the country where you are now living.
You are a soldier in the army, doing compulsory military service.	You are the owner of a successful import-export company.
You are a disabled young man who can only move in a wheelchair.	You are a retired worker from a factory that makes shoes.
You are a 17-year-old Roma (Gypsy) girl who never finished primary school.	You are the girlfriend of a young artist who is addicted to heroin.
You are an HIV positive, middle-aged prostitute.	You are a 22-year-old lesbian.
You are an unemployed schoolteacher in a country whose new official language you are not fluent in.	You are a fashion model of African origin.
You are a 24-year-old refugee from Afghanistan.	You are a homeless young man, 27 years old.
You are an illegal immigrant from Mali.	You are the 19-year-old son of a farmer in a remote village in the mountains.

Situations and events

Read the following situations out aloud. Allow time after reading out each situation for participants to step forward and also to look to see how far they have moved relative to each other.

- You have never encountered any serious financial difficulty.
- You have decent housing with a telephone line and television.
- You feel your language, religion and culture are respected in the society where you live.
- You feel that your opinion on social and political issues matters, and your views are listened to.
- Other people consult you about different issues.
- You are not afraid of being stopped by the police.
- You know where to turn for advice and help if you need it.
- You have never felt discriminated against because of your origin.
- You have adequate social and medical protection for your needs.
- You can go away on holiday once a year.
- You can invite friends for dinner at home.
- You have an interesting life and you are positive about your future.
- You feel you can study and follow the profession of your choice.
- You are not afraid of being harassed or attacked in the streets, or in the media.
- You can vote in national and local elections.
- You can celebrate the most important religious festivals with your relatives and close friends.
- You can participate in an international seminar abroad.
- You can go to the cinema or the theatre at least once a week.
- You are not afraid for the future of your children.
- You can buy new clothes at least once every three months.
- You can fall in love with the person of your choice.
- You feel that your competence is appreciated and respected in the society where you live.
- You can use and benefit from the Internet.

The impact of the Internet

In every great technology there is a political or social prejudice.

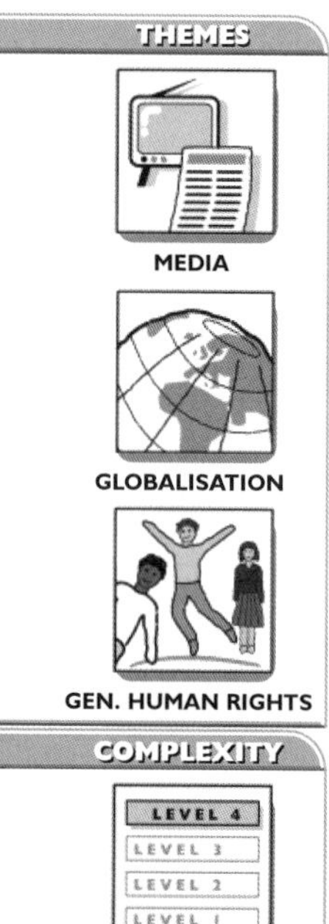

Themes Media, Globalisation, General human rights

Complexity Level 4

Group size 8-50

Time 180 minutes

Overview This activity involves both small-group and plenary discussions to analyse issues of:
- the future of the Internet and the digital divide
- the use of the Internet for the promotion of human rights.

Related rights Any human rights

Objectives
- To raise awareness about the implications of the Internet and access to information world-wide
- To develop imagination and critical thinking skills
- To promote justice and solidarity with others working to promote human rights issues.

Materials
- Copies of the handouts
- Large sheets of paper and markers for each group
- Space for plenary and small-group work

Preparation
- Make copies of handout no. 1, "Six options for predicting the impact of the Internet", enough for one copy between 2 people.
- Copy handouts 2, 3, 4, 5 and 6, enough so that each member of the five working groups will have a copy.

Instructions

This activity is in three parts: part 1, introduction (10 minutes), part 2, predicting the impact of the Internet (60 minutes) and part 3, how the Internet can be used to promote human rights (90 minutes).

Part 1. Introduction (10 minutes)

1. Introduce the activity by explaining that it will need the imagination and critical thinking skills of all participants. Their task will be to assess the impact of the Internet and new information technologies on our lives and on human rights' work.
2. As a quick warm-up and to provide some common knowledge, give the group a few basic facts about the Internet, and then ask them to talk in pairs about their own experiences with the Internet and the advantages and disadvantages of using it. Allow about ten minutes for this.

Part 2. Predicting the impact of the Internet (60minutes).

1. Distribute copies of handout no. 1, "Six options for predicting the impact of the Internet". Explain that, in order to polarise decisions, the scenarios have been written in fairly extreme terms.

2. Ask each pair to decide which scenario is the most likely to happen and which one is the least likely to happen. Give them 15 minutes to do this.
3. Ask all participants to come into plenary to give feedback on their decisions. Try to summarise the discussions about:
   - The most likely scenario(s).
   - The relevance of human rights on information technology, for example, the right to freedom of expression.
   - The digital divide.
4. Ask one or two participants to write the key points up on the flipchart.

Part 3. How the Internet can be used to promote human rights (90 minutes).

1. Divide the participants into five groups, A-E. Distribute the handouts. Each person in group A should have a copy of the "Handout for group A, the 'Future scenarios: Pessimistic view' ", those in group B should each receive a copy of the "Handout for group B, 'Future scenarios: Optimistic view' ", etc.
2. Give them 20 minutes to read the handouts and to share general comments.
3. Ask them to consider the information on the sheets in relation to the outcomes of the discussions in part 1 on the impact of the Internet. They should pay special attention to this part of the work as it provides them with relevant information for the next stage of the activity.
4. Divide the participants into new groups. There should be five people in each new group, one person originating from group A, one from group B, one from group C, and so on.
5. The task for each of these new groups is to decide which are the three most important advantages or uses of the Internet for promoting human rights.
6. Suggest that they start with a round of sharing information, beginning with the people from the C, D and E groups (that is, those who have the information about NGO work) and ending with the people from groups A and B. After that, they will be in a better position to go on to the tasks of identifying and agreeing the uses of the Internet for promoting human rights.
7. They should also appoint a rapporteur to present the results on a flipchart for the final plenary. Give them 35 minutes to complete this phase.
8. Call the participants into plenary to share the results of their work.

Debriefing and evaluation

Start with a review of the activity and how people participated. Then go on to review what they learned.

- How much do people already know about the Internet? How much do they use it? What do they use it for?
- Was there a digital divide amongst the participants? What effect did this have on peoples' ability to participate in the activity? Did some people feel excluded because they did not feel competent enough to contribute?
- Did others see this lack of experience as a handicap to the group's work?
- What are the advantages of working in a group where people have very different experiences and attitudes to an issue?
- What were the most interesting things people learnt about the work of the human rights NGOs? Were there any surprises?

▪ The Internet is a world-wide network of interconnected computers.
▪ The Internet is accessible to over 150 million people around the world.
▪ 90% of Internet-users live in North America, Europe, Japan and Australia.
▪ People talk about the digital divide, meaning this very unequal access to the new information technology.
▪ The Internet allows users to publish and access information on-line and to communicate directly with each other through electronic mail (e-mail), mailing lists, newsgroups and chat rooms.

▪ Do the overall advantages of using the Internet to promote human rights outweigh the disadvantages?
▪ What needs to be done to address the disadvantages?

Tips for facilitators

Assess how familiar the participants are with the Internet prior to the activity so that you can pitch the level and the overall approach.

In the debriefing, it is a good idea to focus on global as well as on local issues of access to new information technology, making sure that those who lack or have difficulties accessing the Internet can make their voices and feelings heard. The aim of the questions about the digital divide within the group and the advantages of working with people with very different experiences is to encourage people to consider various issues about making decisions.

Variations

You can extend the activity to include an exercise in building consensus, as follows:

1. In part 1, after step 4 (decision in pairs), ask each pair to join another pair and in groups of four compare their choices and come to a consensus concerning which scenario is most likely to happen and which one is least likely to happen. Ask each group of four to add a couple of sentences about potential human rights issues (such as freedom of expression) to the scenario they think is most likely to happen. The writing should ensure that group(s) that come to a consensus quickly are encouraged to continue to reflect together on the chosen scenario and have a greater sense of ownership about it, before going on to the next step (15').
2. Now ask each group of four to join another group of four, and in groups of eight compare their choices and come to a consensus concerning which scenario is most likely to happen and which one is least likely to happen. Ask each group to appoint a rapporteur (15 minutes) Now proceed with the activity as from step five, that is, the report of group results in plenary.
3. In the plenary, ask participants to read the additional key sentences/human rights issues and provide the main reasons for their choices. Encourage the participants (and not only the rapporteurs) to:
   ▪ reflect on the differences and similarities in the choices made by the different groups,
   ▪ the reasons motivating the choices,
   ▪ the human rights issues in relation to the Internet ,
   ▪ the actual consequences of the chosen scenario(s).
4. Also ask people to reflect on how they worked.
   ▪ Did people change their ideas during the various negotiations?
   ▪ Was it harder to work in larger groups?
   ▪ Who tended to take the lead (for example: those experienced/inexperienced with Internet)?
   ▪ Could people express themselves freely regardless of their specific Internet competence?

Suggestions for follow-up

Encourage participants to visit the web sites (and links) listed in the handouts "NGO Profiles". They could then go on to reflect about a project to:

(a) Use available Internet resources to increase awareness about human rights issues in their neighbourhood

(b) Find new ways of using the Internet for the promotion of human rights issues.

(c) Create their own web site and link to other youth groups.

If participants are interested in working with a specific example of the Internet being used to promote human rights, they could do "When tomorrow comes", on page 250. This activity, which is about the right to life, uses material from a web site created by a prisoner facing the death penalty.

Ideas for action

Take the ideas developed in the activity and follow-up, or take up one of the numerous possibilities for actions offered by the web sites (and links) listed in the handouts "NGO Profiles".

Further information

The 2001 UNDP "Human Development Report" focuses on the digital divide and is available at www.undp.org

Key date

17 May
World Telecommunications Day

HANDOUTS

Six options for predicting the impact of the Internet

1. THE WORLD WILL BE A BETTER PLACE! By 2010, everyone in the world will be on-line. The Internet will make shops, offices, and business travel entirely unnecessary. This will save so much money that everything will be free! Wars will end! Everyone will be happy!

2. THE WORLD WILL BE A WORSE PLACE. By 2010, everyone *in the West* will be on-line, but growing billions outside developed capitalist society will still live in poverty. The resulting instability will cause world-wide war, or someone will finally use the nuclear bomb recipe – available on-line. Everyone will die.

3. PEOPLE WILL TAKE OVER THE INTERNET. By 2010, the sheer volume of Internet traffic will mean that government control will be impossible. Self-governing little societies will spring up with people living in "virtual villages". Everyone will be free.

4. GOVERNMENT WILL TAKE OVER THE INTERNET. As Orwell had predicted in "*1984*", by 2010, Big Brother will really be watching you. All your e-mails, all your bank details, all your personal schedules and purchases – everything will be recorded and scrutinised. Internet computers will be equipped with cameras that will monitor you 24 hours a day. Totalitarian regimes will be in power everywhere. Everyone will be oppressed.

5. THE INTERNET IS A PASSING FAD. By 2010, the novelty of cyberspace will fade. Everyone will go about their business, just as they always did. There is no more need for discussion about new information technology being another battleground for freedom of expression. It will save you a lot of money to ignore the cyberspace – it will go away.

6. THE INTERNET IS HERE TO STAY. By 2010, everyone in the world will be connected to everyone else. You will socialise through your computer screen, go on holiday without leaving your living-room, and have arguments with thousands of people you have never met before. The Internet will be so pervasive that your only chance for economic survival is to invest heavily and re-orient your entire strategy around the Net.

Source: Adapted from "Human Rights and the Internet", by S. Hicks, E. F. Halpin and E. Hoskins (ed.), McMillan Press ltd, London, 2000

Group A. Future scenarios: Pessimistic view

Neil Postman, "Five ideas about technological change"

First, that *we always pay a price for technology*; the greater the technology, the greater the price.

Second, that *there are always winners and losers*, and that the winners always try to persuade the losers that they are really winners.

Third, that *there is embedded in every great technology an epistemological, political or social prejudice*. Sometimes that bias is greatly to our advantage. Sometimes it is not. The printing press annihilated the oral tradition; telegraphy annihilated space; television has humiliated the word; the computer, perhaps, will degrade community life. And so on.

Fourth, *technological change is not additive; it is ecological*, which means, it changes everything and is, therefore, too important to be left entirely in the hands of Bill Gates.

And **fifth,** *technology tends to become mythic*; that is, perceived as part of the natural order of things, and therefore tends to control more of our lives than is good for us.

(From a speech delivered at the Conference, "The New Technologies and the Human Person: Communicating the Faith in the New Millennium" Denver, Colorado, March 27, 1998, www.newtech.org/address10_en.htm)

Group B. Future scenarios: Optimistic view

Sean Kidney, "The Internet as a facilitator of citizen activity"

For people interested in the web, I think the scenario is optimistic. Like any kind of major upheaval and change, the web creates opportunities, but also losses. We will see some losses of print media as a result. I think this is a revolution where there is enormous scope for individuals to have an impact, because there is scope for people to actually have their say - scope to be informed. News usually disappears in revolutions, but here it doesn't.

One of my hopes for the Internet is that it will become a facilitator of citizen activity, and lead to a different kind of democracy. I think this is quite important for us if we are to make sure we don't increase social division, especially in the next 10 years or so while the revolution slowly catches up with the rest of the world. We need to work together, not just nationally, but also globally, to help craft the future of this particular revolution.

If you *can* read, the next barrier to knowledge is access to information, access to stuff to read, like a library. Think about what a revolution community libraries have been in our culture. The promise of the web, of course, is of a global library.

(From a Talk to the NSW Society of Editors, 6 April 1999, http://online.socialchange.net.au)

Group C. NGO profile: Amnesty International (www.amnesty.org)

Amnesty International , founded in 1961, campaigns to free all prisoners of conscience; ensure fair and prompt trials for political prisoners; abolish the death penalty, torture and other cruel treatment of prisoners; end political killings and "disappearances"; and oppose human rights abuses by government or opposition groups. Amnesty International has around a million members and supporters in 162 countries and territories. Activities range from public demonstrations to letter-writing, from human rights education to fundraising concerts, from individual appeals on a particular case to global campaigns on a particular issue.

It is impartial and independent of any government, political persuasion or religious creed. Amnesty International is financed largely by subscriptions and donations from its world-wide membership. Its web-site offers a campaigning manual, a fair-trial manual and opportunities to participate in campaigns, register to receive urgent appeals on your mobile phone (SMS message), and send postcards to get torture abolished.

Examples of Amnesty International's work

After some mistakes and consequent bad publicity, in the late 1960s, Amnesty International adopted the rule that people in the organisation were to work only on cases outside their own countries. Volunteers still carry out most of Amnesty International's work. They write letters to governments that abuse the human rights of those who hold opposing viewpoints, whether through imprisonment, harassment, threats, physical mistreatment, torture, "disappearances", or politically motivated murder. They staff tables at public events, passing out information to the public on prisoners of conscience and human rights issues. They organise demonstrations, write press releases, found letter-writing groups at their churches, synagogues, or mosques and exercise their intelligence and imagination in almost unlimited ways.

Amnesty International never claims credit for the release of prisoners. Releases are the result of many factors, not the least of which are the actions (often taken at considerable risk) of families and friends. However, many released prisoners have said that Amnesty International's publicity and letters were very important.

In 1977 Amnesty International was awarded the Nobel Peace Prize for its work. Its "Get up Sign up" campaign to mark the 50th anniversary of the UDHR collected 13 million pledges in support of the declaration. In 2001 the AI Stoptorture Web-site won the Revolution Award 2001 for "best use of e-mail". (www.stoptorture.org).

Group D. NGO profile: Derechos Human Rights (www.derechos.org)

Derechos Human Rights was founded in 1995, probably the first Internet-based human rights organisation. Together with Equipo Nizkor, the group's sister organisation in Spain, Derechos started with the clear realisation that the Internet has the potential of being a most efficient tool in the battle against human rights violations world-wide and to allow human rights organisations to speak to the world in their own voice. Derechos works with human rights organisations in Latin America and the world to spread accurate and timely information on the human rights situation in their countries, as well as to give opportunities to help. The organisation also co-ordinates several human rights mailing lists, publishes an internet human rights journal, and works on the preservation of memory and justice for the disappeared. The web-site offers a comprehensive list of links to other human rights organisations.

An example of Derechos' work

In 1998, Javier Vildoza (21) read the following statements on the Derechos web-site: "Vildoza, Jorge (alias) 'Gaston', Lieutenant Commander, subchief GT332 (...); currently a fugitive, he lives in England; he may have taken the son of Cecilia Vinas, born in mid-September 1977". Javier found that the man he thought to be his father was a known human rights abuser, and that this man had stolen a child born at the same time he was born at the Naval Mechanical School, a notorious concentration camp during the Argentine dictatorship. He was the son of Cecilia Vinas and Hugo Reinaldo Penino but had been taken by Jorge Vildoza, who was later indicted on over 60 charges of torture and murder. He had been registered as Javier Gonzalo Vildoza Grimaldo and raised by Vildoza and his wife as their own child and had never been told the truth about his origins.

'Surfing' through the Derechos and Project Disappeared web sites, Javier discovered that his natural parents are still on the list of the disappeared and that his natural grandparents had been searching for him for more than 20 years. In 1998, he found them. His realisation as to who he really was and what his father had done compelled him to write to an investigating court in Argentina and request a DNA test. The results were conclusive: he was the son of Cecilia Vinas and Hugo Reinaldo Penino. He has since been reunited with his natural grandparents. The story of Javier illustrates how on-line activism can bring unpredictable results and can far exceed expectations. When Project Disappeared was conceived, its purpose was to memorialise the disappeared as human beings, to denounce those responsible for their disappearances in Latin America and the world. It was never expected that the web site would help one of the disappeareds' children to learn the truth about himself.

(Adapted from "Doing Human Rights Online: the Derechos' Cyberbirth", by Michael Katz-Lacabe and Margarita Lacabe, in "Human Rights and the Internet", by S. Hicks, E. F. Halpin and E. Hoskins (ed.), McMillan Press ltd, London, 2000)

Group E. NGO profile: Human Rights Watch (www.hrw.org)

Human Rights Watch is an independent, non-governmental organisation, supported by contributions from private individuals and foundations world-wide. The organisation was founded in 1978 as Helsinki Watch (now Human Rights Watch/Helsinki), in response to a call for support from embattled local groups in Moscow, Warsaw, and Prague, which had been set up to monitor compliance with the human rights provisions of the landmark Helsinki accords. It accepts no government funds, directly or indirectly. Human Rights Watch works to end a broad range of abuses, including summary executions, torture, arbitrary detention, restrictions on the freedom of expression, association, assembly and religion, violations of due process, and discrimination on racial, gender, ethnic and religious grounds.

Human Rights Watch publicises information on abuses in order to embarrass a government before its own citizens and in the eyes of the international community. Human Rights Watch also presses for the withdrawal of military, economic and diplomatic support from governments that regularly abuse human rights.

Three examples of Human Rights Watch's work:

The International Criminal Court: Human Rights Watch has been at the forefront of efforts to create the International Criminal Court, a permanent tribunal that has been established to try the most serious human rights crimes, regardless of where they are committed. The creation of the Court is the result of public pressure and advocacy efforts with governments and civil-society groups around the world.

Chechnya: Human Rights Watch was the only international human rights group stationed continuously on the Chechnya border throughout the Russian offensive, providing information leading the United Nations Commission on Human Rights to adopt a resolution condemning Russia's conduct in Chechnya. The resolution marked the first time the commission had censured one of the five permanent members of the UN Security Council.

Kosovo: Human Rights Watch launched a significant research operation in Kosovo, well before the NATO bombing campaign. Its first book-length report on Kosovo was published in 1990, and the organisation monitored developments closely throughout the 1990s. On-site investigations of several massacres in late 1998 and early 1999 led to front-page stories around the world.

The language barrier

Can you answer these questions? Would your asylum application be acceptable?

THEMES

DISCRIMINATION

HUMAN SECURITY

EDUCATION

COMPLEXITY

LEVEL 2

GROUP SIZE

ANY

TIME

30 MINUTES

Themes Discrimination and Xenophobia, Human Security, Education

Complexity Level 2

Group size Any

Time 30 minutes

Overview This is a simulation of the difficulties that refugees face when applying for asylum. Issues raised include:

- The frustrations and emotional factors refugees have to face
- Overcoming the language barrier
- Discrimination during the application procedure

Related rights

- The right to seek and enjoy asylum
- The right not to be discriminated against on the basis of ethnicity or country of origin

Objectives

- To raise awareness about discrimination by immigration authorities in relation to asylum applications
- To demonstrate the importance of both language and intercultural education
- To develop empathy through being aware of the frustrations refugees face when applying for asylum

Materials

- Copies of the "Asylum Application" handout, one for each participant
- Pens, one per person

Preparation Arrange the room so you can sit behind a desk and role-play the formality of a bureaucratic official.

Instructions

1. Let people arrive but do not greet anyone or acknowledge their presence. Don't say anything about what is going to happen.
2. Wait a few minutes after the scheduled start time and then hand out the copies of the "Application for Asylum" and the pens, one to each participant.
3. Tell them that they have five minutes to complete the form, but don't say anything else. Ignore all questions and protests. If you have to communicate speak another language (or a made-up language) and use gestures. Keep all communication to a minimum. Remember that the refugees' problems are not your concern, your job is only to hand out the forms and collect them in again!
4. Greet any latecomers curtly (for example, "You are late. Take this form and fill it in. You have only got a few minutes left to do it.")
5. When five minutes are up, collect the forms without smiling or making any personal contact.

Note: This activity is adapted from Donahue, D., Flowers, N., The Uprooted, Hunter House Publishers, 1995

6. Call a name from the completed forms and tell that person to come forward. Look at the form and make up something about how they have filled in the form, for instance, "you didn't answer question 8" or "I see you answered 'no' to question 6. Asylum denied." Tell the person to go away. Do not enter into any discussion. Go straight on to call the next person to come forward.
7. Repeat this process several times. It is not necessary to review all the applications, only continue for as long as necessary for the participants to understand what is happening.
8. Finally break out of your role and invite participants to discuss what happened.

Debriefing and evaluation

Start by asking people how they felt during the activity and then move on to discuss what happened and what they have learned.

- How did the participants feel when they were filling out an unintelligible form?
- Was this a realistic simulation of an asylum-seeker's experience?
- Do you think that in your country asylum-seekers are treated fairly during their application for asylum? Why? Why not?
- What could be the consequences for someone whose asylum application is refused?
- Have the participants ever been in a situation where they could not speak the language and were confronted by an official, for instance, a police officer or a ticket-controller? How did it feel?

Tips for facilitators

This is a fairly easy activity to facilitate: the main thing required from you is to do be "strong" in your role and you must be serious, tough and bureaucratic. The plight of the refugees is not your concern; you are here to do your job! The point is that many people do not want refugees in their country. Immigration officers are under orders to screen the refugees and to allow entry only to those who have identification papers and who complete the application forms correctly. The refugees frequently have a poor command of the other country's language and find it very difficult to fill in the forms. Also, they are in a distressed and emotional state. It is especially hard for them to understand what is happening because their applications are frequently denied and they do not understand the reasons.

Suggestions for follow up

If you want to look at the arguments for accepting or denying refugees entry into a country, look at the activity "Can I come in?", on page 98.

You will find more ideas for activities about refugees on the UNHCR website: www.unhcr.ch

Ideas for action

The group could invite an immigration officer to come and talk about the challenges of the job. Alternatively, arrange to visit an immigration office and see how the procedure for application

Key date

26 June
UN Charter Day

21 February
International Mother Language Day

for asylum works. Group members could also interview asylum-seekers and immigration officers to find out their views on the situation and to raise any issues about injustices and/or irregularities of the procedure. The information could be used for refugee awareness campaigns, or fed back to the immigration department or to organisations such as the UNHCR.

Further information

Information and data about refugees can be found in the section of further information with the activity "Can I come in?", on page 98.

Refugee or asylum-seeker: What are the differences and similarities?

Often people do not distinguish between the term "asylum-seeker" and "refugee". They use the term refugee for any person who is seeking or who has already received asylum. Legally, the terms "refugee" and "asylum-seeker" are different and have different consequences.

An *asylum-seeker* is a person who wants to be accepted as a refugee, but who is still at the stage of having his or her application considered. During the asylum procedure immigration departments have to determine whether the asylum-seeker's situation falls within the definition of refugee and whether or not s/he meets all the criteria. For instance, they have to show a well-founded fear of persecution and that they have not committed any serious (non-political) crimes, crimes against humanity or war crimes. The main rights that asylum-seekers have are the right to have their application fairly considered and the right to remain in the country where asylum is requested until the application is reviewed.

A *refugee* can be said to be an "ex-" asylum-seeker, that is, a person who has had his/her application accepted. There are various rights associated with the status of being a refugee, for instance, the right not to be returned to a country where s/he would face a risk to his/her life and well-being, the right not to be discriminated against and the right to receive some basic material assistance from the government of the country where asylum has been granted.

In the last five decades, several million people have been granted asylum in countries around the world. Currently there are approximately 1.2 million asylum applications pending world-wide.

HANDOUT

Asylum application form

1.	Családi és utónév
2.	Дата і месца нараджэння
3.	Viimeisin osoite
4.	Անձնագրի համարը
5.	Επάγγελμα ή κύρια απασχόληση
6.	Başvuran kişiye eşlik eden refakatçı veya yakınlarının isimleri
7.	Meio e local de entrada no país
8.	Ghaliex titlob ghall-azilju?
9.	Свидетельство преследований, на основании которых составлено заявление
10.	Avez-vous déj[?] présenté une demande d'asyle auparavant? Veuillez donner des détails sur les pays, les dates et les motifs.
11.	Dali imate rodnini ili poznanici vo ovaa zemja? Ako imate, navedete gi iminjata i adresite.
12.	ما هي اللغات التي تتكلمها وما هي مستوى ثقافتك

The scramble for wealth and power

In life, some people are fighting for their dreams and some are fighting for wealth and power.

Themes Poverty, Human security, Globalisation

Complexity Level 3

Group size 8 - 25

Time 90 minutes

Overview This activity simulates the fight for wealth and power and inequality in the world. The main issues addressed are:
- Inequality in the distribution of wealth
- Power imbalance and the consequences
- The injustice of poverty

Related rights
- The right to equality in dignity and rights
- The right to education
- The right to health, food and shelter

Objectives
- To develop an understanding of the injustices that result from the unequal distribution of wealth and power
- To think critically about the causes and consequences of poverty
- To promote human dignity and justice

Materials
- 120 coins
- 3 to 4 pairs of socks
- 2 large sheets of paper and markers
- Paper and pens
- An open space

Preparation
- Read through the instructions so you have an overview of the whole activity, Note that the simulation is divided into three parts: part 1, The Scramble (10 minutes); part 2, The Donations (10 minutes); and part 3, Creating Economic Fairness (40 minutes). Discussion follows at the end.
- Take 20 of the coins and keep them to one side
- Choose three people for the role of migrants
- Make a wall chart to record players' wealth (see illustration)
- Prepare a chart headed "Honourable Donors"

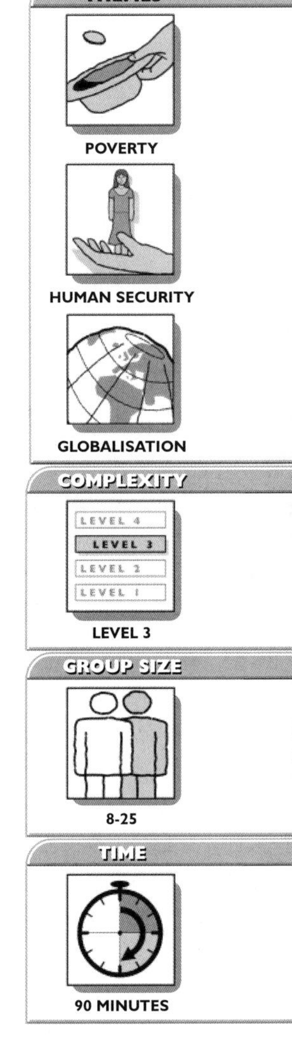

Wealth chart

Great Wealth and Power (6 or more coins)	Some Wealth and Power (3 to 5 coins)	Little Wealth and Power (2 coins or less)

Instructions

Explain that this is a simulation game. Participants will distribute the world's wealth and power among themselves.

The global divide

In developing countries, one child in 10 dies before his/her fifth birthday. By comparison, in the United States one child in 165 will die before turning five years old.

In 1998 in developing countries, about 130 million eligible children out of a total of 625 million did not attend primary school. 73 million of those children are girls. (UNICEF)

The wealthiest fifth of the world's people consume an astonishing 86 percent of all goods and services, while the poorest fifth consumes one-percent.

Life Expectancy at birth 1995-2000

The number of years a new-born infant would live if prevailing patterns of age-specific mortality rates at the time of birth were to stay the same throughout the child's life.

UNDP Report 2001

Japan:	*80.5*
Norway;	*78.1*
Ireland:	*76.1*
Greece:	*78.0*
Czech Republic:	*74.3*
Russian federation:	*66.1*
Maldives:	*65.4*
South Africa:	*56.7*
Equatorial Guinea:	*50.0*
Zimbabwe:	*42.9*
Zambia:	*40.5*
Sierra Leone:	*37.3*

From the highest life expectancy at birth to the lowest there is a difference of 43.2 years!

Part 1: The Scramble (10 minutes)

1. Explain that the aim of the game is to get as many coins as possible. There is only one rule: no participant may touch another member of the group at any time (you may stipulate a punishment for this, for example, pay 1 coin).
2. Ask everyone, except for those playing the "migrants", to sit on the floor in a large circle (so they can have enough space to play).
3. Take the reserved twenty coins and share them out between any four or five of the participants
4. Give four other participants one pair of socks each. Tell them that they must put them on their hands and keep them on during the whole game. Postpone any discussions of the reasons for sharing out the coins and socks until the debriefing.
5. Scatter 100 coins evenly in the middle of the circle.
6. On the word, "GO" participants are to gather up as many coins as possible. This will probably not take longer than 2 minutes!
7. After all the coins have been collected, ask participants to report their wealth to the rest of the group. On the wealth chart, record each participant's name and the number of coins they have.
8. Remind the group that these coins represent their wealth and power in the world. The amount they possess will affect their capacity to satisfy their needs (e.g. for basic education, adequate food and nutrition, good health care, adequate housing) and their wants (e.g. higher education, cars, computers, toys, televisions and other luxury items). The implications are as follows:
   - six or more coins - people will be able to meet all their basic "needs" and most of their "wants"
   - three to five coins - people will be able to meet their basic needs
   - two or fewer coins - people will have difficulty surviving due to disease, lack of education, malnutrition, and inadequate shelter.

Part 2: The Donations (10 minutes)

1. Tell participants that they may, if they wish, give coins away to others. However, they are not required to do so. Tell them that those who do share will be honoured as donors, with their names written on the list of "Honourable donors".
2. Allow 3-4 minutes for participants to redistribute the coins if they wish.
3. Then ask for the names of those who gave away coins and the amount that each donated. List them on the chart of "Honourable donors".
4. Ask if anyone changed category as a result of giving or receiving coins and record these shifts on the chart with an arrow.

Part 3: Creating economic fairness (40 minutes)

1. Divide the players up into three groups according to the number of coins they have (great wealth, some wealth and little wealth)
2. Place one of the "migrants" in each of the three groups. Take note of their reactions at being placed in one group rather than another, but save any discussion about their placement until the debriefing at the end.
3. Hand out the pens and paper. Give each group the task of creating a plan for the fair distribution of the coins (the world's wealth) in order to decrease the gap between

the different categories of wealth and power. Each group's plan of action should:
- explain what needs to be done (if anything),
- describe what the group plans to do and why, and
- show why their plan is fair.

4. Give the groups ten minutes to devise their plans. Explain that it is not necessary to go too deeply into the drawing-up of the plan, but rather they should highlight some of the possible actions that should be done to address the problem of poverty.
5. Ask each group to appoint a spokesperson to explain their plan to the others and answer questions. List the proposed plans on a large sheet of paper.
6. Now announce that a vote will be held to decide which plan to adopt. The distribution of votes will be as follows:
   - each participant in the group with "Great wealth and power" - five votes
   - each participant in the group with "Some wealth and power" - two votes
   - each participant in the group with "Little wealth and power" - half a vote
7. Have participants vote. Record the votes cast for each plan on the large sheet of paper. Announce which plan is to be implemented.
8. Carry out this plan, redistributing the wealth if necessary.

Debriefing and evaluation

Start with a brief feedback on the activity itself and how people enjoyed it. Then go on to discuss what happened and what people learnt. Draw on the following questions to promote the discussion:

- How did people feel about the way in which the coins were acquired and distributed? Were they treated fairly?
- Why did the people who gave coins away do so? To be honoured? Because they felt guilty? Something else?
- How did the people who received coins in part 2 feel? Grateful? Patronised?
- What about the participants with socks? What kinds of people do they represent? Which group did they end up in?
- What about the three participants, the "migrants", assigned to groups? Did they feel treated fairly? Is what happened to them similar to what happens to people around the globe? What sorts of people? Is it just chance where we end up?
- What differences were there in the recommended plans for fair distribution? Did the plans reflect the wealth of the group making the proposal?
- Why were some people given more votes than others? Was this an accurate representation of those with more or less power in the world?
- Are human rights infringed when we see such differences in wealth and power? If so, which ones?
- Who are the "haves" and the "have-nots" in the world in your country and in your community? How did they come to be in these positions?
- Should the "haves" be concerned about the situation of the "have-nots"? For what reasons? Security, economic, moral/religious or political reasons? Why might the "haves" give money or resources to the "have-nots"? Is this a way to solve the problems of poverty?
- What might the "have-nots" do to improve their situation? What are some actions that "have-nots" have taken around the world and in our country to address the inequalities of wealth and power?

Key date

17 October
International Day for the Eradication of Poverty

- Do you think there should be a redistribution of wealth and power throughout the world? Why or why not? If yes, how would you propose to accomplish this? What principles would guide your proposals for change?
- Can human rights discourse be used to support a new redistribution of wealth?

Tips for facilitators

The aim of this activity is to make people aware of the unequal distribution wealth and power in the world, yet there is a danger that it may confirm the existing inequalities. You should therefore be aware of the social and economic composition of the group and develop the discussion accordingly.

Try to bring people into the feeling of the game so they get involved and really "act" as if the coins were their wealth. You could tell them that they will be allowed to keep the coins and after the activity or during tea break, be able to "buy" drinks and/or biscuits with the money.

Emphasise that, as in real life, if they give away some of their coins they will lose some of their wealth and the privileges that wealth brings.

If it is too hot to use socks, use other means to emphasise that some players have more wealth and power than others. For example, some participants could be held back and only allowed to join in after 15 to 30 seconds. Alternatively, players could have one hand tied behind their backs - if they are right-handed they should use their left hands and vice versa.

The questions in the debriefing and evaluation are complex and may very well require deep and lengthy discussions. If the time is short or the group large, you may want to divide the questions amongst small groups. These small groups should be "mixed", that is contain people from each wealth category. Make sure that the different groups feedback in plenary so that everyone has a chance to hear and reflect on all the questions.

Note: This activity is adapted from another one in *Economic and Social Justice: A Human Rights Perspective, Human Rights Resource Center, University of Minnesota, 1999*

Suggestions for follow-up

You could debate the issues further or ask people to write a report. Suggested topics are:

- How do wealth and power affect one's ability to enjoy human rights and human dignity?
- Are there responsibilities associated with having wealth and power?

The group may like to continue with the theme poverty and explore some of its consequences through the activity "Horoscope of poverty", on page 145.

Ideas for Action

Make contact with an organisation that works with the disadvantaged in your community to ascertain the local needs. Then go on to plan a project to try to help.

Sometimes the simple fact of "spreading the word" about an issue is a good step towards making change. Thus, you could suggest that people raise the issues of wealth distribution with their parents and friends.

The web of life

People are a part of the environment – not apart from it.

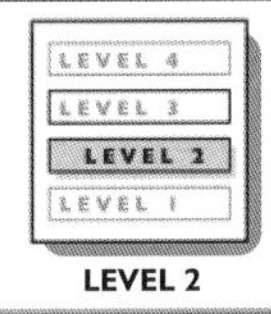

Themes Environment, Globalisation, General human rights

Complexity Level 2

Group size 10+

Time 30 minutes

Overview In this activity, people brainstorm links in a global food web. They explore:
- The interdependency of living and non-living things ~~and~~
- The inevitable impact of all human activity on the environment, and the consequences.

Related rights
- The right to own property
- The right to a healthy environment
- The right to development

Objectives
- To know about the interdependency of living and non-living things
- To appreciate the implications of human activity on ecosystems
- To develop respect for the intrinsic value of life

Materials
- A ball of thin string or strong wool
- A pair of scissors

Instructions

This activity is divided into 2 parts: 1 - building the web of life, part 2 - its destruction.

Part 1

1. Ask people to stand in a circle.
2. Explain that they are to build a model of the web of life.
3. You start. Hold the ball of string in your hand and name a green plant, for instance a cabbage.
4. Hold onto the end of the string and throw the ball to someone across the circle. They catch it! There is now a straight line of string between the two of you.
5. This person has to name an animal that eats cabbages, for instance, a caterpillar. They then hold onto the string and throw the ball to a third person across the circle.
6. This third person has to think of an animal that eats caterpillars, for instance, a bird, or if they know one, they can say a species of bird, such as a thrush. They then throw the ball to a fourth person.
7. Continue the game, so the ball of string passes back and forth across the circle until you have created a criss-cross mesh that represents the "web of life".

Part 2

1. Take the scissors and ask people to give specific examples of what is damaging this web of life, for instance, motorways being built over farmland, or over-fishing of cod.
2. For each example make one cut in the string web.

Debriefing and evaluation

Start with asking how people feel seeing the web destroyed and then go on to talk about the issues involved and what needs to be done to protect the environment

- What did you feel as you saw the web gradually being destroyed?
- Was it easy to name animals and plants in different food webs? How good is people's knowledge of natural history?
- Whose responsibility is it to protect the environment?
- The balance of nature is very complex and it is not easy to predict what the global consequences of any particular action will be. How then is it possible to make decisions about how we use the earth's resources? For example, how can people make decisions about whether to cut down a forest so the land can be used for growing crops?
- Article I of the International Covenant on Economic, Social and Cultural rights states that "all peoples may, for their own ends, freely dispose of their natural wealth and resources." Does this mean that people have a right to use the environment?
- We rely on our environment to provide us with food to eat and clean air to breathe.Without a healthy environment we could not live, it is a condition for life. Do we therefore have a paramount duty to respect the environment that limits our rights to use it? (In the same way that we have a duty to respect rights and freedoms of others, which limits our own rights as individuals.)

End with a short brainstorm of environmental success stories. It is not all hopeless! There are lots of people active all over the world, working to ensure that a sustainable environment is held in trust for future generations.

Tips for facilitators

Each food chain should illustrate actual or possible relationships. For example, grass – sheep – humans. Or plankton – whales. Or plankton – herrings – pigs (pigs are often fed fishmeal) – humans – tiger! Remember that when an animal dies, bacteria decay its body and the minerals released are taken up by other green plants. Thus the cycle of life begins over again. Billions of such cycles interlink to make the web of life.

Try to get people to think of as many different food chains as possible. Think about examples in woodland, forest, mountain, moorland, marsh, pond, river and marine habitats. You may need to intervene by saying something like, now the minerals get washed to the sea and get used by marine phytoplankton (plant plankton)." Or to move from a marine ecosystem to a terrestrial one you may have to say, now the seagull that ate the shore crab flew inland to scavenge over farmland where it died". If a player can-not think of the next link, suggest they may ask others in the group for suggestions.

In part 2, when you cut the string, make cuts at random in different parts of the web. The first few cuts will not make much difference because of the way the threads criss-cross over each other hold the web more or less together. However, as you make more cuts the web will gradually disintegrate and eventually you will be left with a heap of threads lying on the floor surrounded by a circle of people each holding a small, useless strand.

In part 2 of the activity you will have to be prepared for some controversial answers to the question "what is damaging the web?" Some people, for instance, vegetarians, may say that people eating meat damages the web. You should acknowledge the point of view and ask the

other players for their opinion. However, be careful not enter a big debate at this stage; finish the game first and then return to it at the end in the debriefing and discussion.

Try not to get bogged down in the discussion, but keep the aim of the activity, that the effect of human activity on the environment, in mind.

The destroyed web is a very powerful image. It is therefore essential that you leave time to follow on with at least a short brainstorm or discussion about the progress that is currently being made to protect the environment. You should also add points about what else can be done, including what they can do. The global situation is indeed depressing, but it is important that people do not feel helpless in the face of the task ahead.

You may want to read the background information on page 350 before asking the questions about the relationship between human rights and the environment.

This is a good activity to do with a science class.

Key dates

22 March
World Day of Water

22 April
Earth Day

Suggestions for follow-up

This activity can be used as a starter for a debate about human rights and environment. For example, would it be a good idea if there were a human right to the environment, like there are other human rights? Does the environment have value over and above its instrumental value? Does it make sense to give animals rights?

Developing the sustainable use of resources requires political will, time, effort and money. Think how much more all countries could do by way of environmental education, scientific research and practical environmental protection schemes if they did not spend so much on armaments and the military. If the group would like to explore those issues further, they could do the activity "Money to spend", on page 177.

Ideas for action

Get involved with local environmental projects. Contact Youth and Environment Europe (YEE). YEE is the umbrella organisation for over forty regional and national self-governing youth organisations involved in the study and conservation of nature and environment throughout Europe. www.ecn.cz/yee/.

Contact an local environmental organisation and ask to find out more about how to be an environmentally friendly consumer.

Further information

In nature everything is connected to everything else. All living things and non-living things are linked through cycles, for example, the carbon cycle and the water cycle. Food chains are part of these cycles. A food chain starts when a green plant uses light energy from sunshine, minerals in the soil and water to build their own food to give them energy to live and to grow. When a green plant, for instance, a cabbage gets eaten, the minerals and energy stored in the leaves are passed on and used, for instance, by the caterpillar to live and grow. As each animal in turn is eaten by another the energy and minerals get passed on through the food chain. When the animal at the top of the food chain dies, its body decays as it is "eaten" by bacteria. The minerals that were in the body are taken up by green plants and a new food chain begins.

To vote, or not to vote?

Every vote counts!

THEMES

DEMOCRACY

CITIZENSHIP

GEN. HUMAN RIGHTS

COMPLEXITY

LEVEL 4

GROUP SIZE

ANY

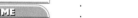

TIME

270 MINUTES

Themes Democracy, Citizenship, General human rights

Complexity Level 4

Group size Any

Time 270 minutes (in 3 parts)

Overview This activity involves a survey of people in the community to explore issues about:
- Voting in elections
- Civic participation

Related rights
- The right to take part in the government of the country
- The right to participate in democratic elections
- Freedom of expression

Objectives
- To appreciate the reasons for using your vote in elections
- To develop skills to find out and analyse information critically
- To value the personal contribution of every citizen in a democracy

Materials
- Survey sheets 1 and 2, one set per pair
- Copies of box 1, notes on how to conduct the survey, one per pair
- Pens or pencils for everyone
- Large sheets of paper (A3) or flipchart paper and markers
- Sticky tape

Preparation
- Copy box 2, the sample survey sheet, onto a large sheet of paper as an aid for giving the instructions.
- On flipchart paper, make copies of survey sheets 1 and 2 for compiling the results.
- Plan a timetable for the activity. You will need to allow 60 minutes for part 1 (introducing the survey), a minimum of 120 minutes for part 2 – (the survey) and 90 minutes for part 3 –(analysing the results and the debriefing and evaluation).

Instructions

Part 1: Introducing the survey

1. Explain that the main purpose of this first session is to prepare the group to go out into the community to survey people's reasons for voting or not voting.
2. Ask participants whether or not they are intending to vote in national or local elections, the next (first?) time they have the opportunity to do so. Take a show of hands, and then divide the group according to those who are intending to vote (A), and those who are not (B). "Don't knows" can be allocated randomly to either group, in order to balance the numbers as far as possible.

3. Ask each group to draw up a list of reasons why they do, or do not, intend to vote and to write them up on a large sheet of paper. Give them about 15 minutes to prepare their lists.
4. Bring the groups back together, and ask a representative from A and B to go through their lists. Allow time for a short discussion at the end, and add any further suggestions to the lists.
5. Hand out copies of the survey sheet. Refer to the large copy you made. Make sure people see that part 1 is for recording the non-voters' responses and part 2 for recording the voters' responses. Point out that the questions are similar except for question 2, which is different in the two parts. Go through the questions, making sure that they are clear.
6. Now explain the method of recording responses. Show the group the example (see handouts) and explain how to use the "5-bar gate" method of keeping a tally.
7. Hand out copies of the notes on how to conduct an interview, one copy to each pair. Go through it and talk about:
   - How they can ensure that interviewees are selected at random
   - How many people will each pair question? (The more the better!)
   - When and where the survey will be carried out
   - When the survey will be done
   - The time to come back and discuss the results
8. If everyone is clear about their tasks, go ahead with part 2 - the survey!

Part 2. Analysing the results

The survey is now complete. The groups meet to collate, analyse and discuss the results. You should allow 60 minutes for this.

1. Ask the pairs to add up their totals in each box and to incorporate these onto the two large charts. In this way, the information from each group is collated and the totals for the whole group can be calculated. They should also record the "reasons" that interviewees gave. If the same reason was given several times, record how often, again using the "five-bar gate" method.
2. When all the information is compiled, ask people to calculate the following statistics:
   - The total number of people questioned
   - The proportion of voters in the total sample and the proportion of non-voters in the total sample
   - The proportion of male and female respondents
   - The proportion of the people questioned in each age group
   - The age group with the smallest number of voters
   - The age group with the greatest number of voters
   - The most commonly given reasons for not-voting
   - The most commonly given reasons for voting
   - Whether more people gave reasons (of either sort) connected with people, or parties.
3. Now move on to discuss how people enjoyed doing the survey, their experiences and what they learnt.

Debriefing and evaluation

In the general discussion of results you may want to touch on a number of different issues, for example:

- What were the groups' feelings when carrying out the survey? Were people generally prepared to answer the survey questions?
- Was it difficult to do the survey? Did they enjoy it?
- Did the group manage to get a "representative" sample of the population as a whole? What were the difficulties in doing this?
- What are the problems in drawing conclusions from the groups' results? How could these be avoided?
- Were there any statistics that particularly surprised the group?
- Were the results of the survey in any way unexpected?
- Did the answers given by people tend to correspond with the feelings within your group? Do you think your group is "representative" of the population as a whole?
- Would they do anything differently if they were to do the survey again?
- Do the results of your survey give a realistic picture of voting patterns in your community? Why? Why not?
- Statistics are often presented as facts to support an argument. How wary should people be of statistics?
- What is the perception now in the group about the need, or otherwise, to use your vote?

Has anyone's opinion changed (in either direction!)? If so, which were the most compelling arguments?

Tips for facilitators

Part 1, planning the survey, is intended to lay the ground for the actual survey, part 2. At the very start, you may want to say explicitly that the purpose of the activity is to give young people a sense of their own value in contributing to the democratic process. It is advisable to emphasise this aspect of it, rather than speaking about "persuading" them to use their vote. Explain that you want each member of the group to reach their own decision at the end of the sessions, but that in order to do so it will be important for them to appreciate the many different reasons for voting that exist.

Try to make the discussion about whether or not people voted (point 4) as "objective" as possible, rather than encouraging the "voters" to try to sway the "non-voters". Do not spend too long on this discussion; it is intended to set the scene for the survey.

When discussing how to conduct an interview (point 7), you will need to take into account the difficulties that the group may face in conducting such a survey. In some communities, people may be uneasy about being questioned on the street by people they do not know. In this case, it may then be better to get group members to question their friends and acquaintances.

It is extremely important that you estimate how much information the group can handle in the analysis. Don't collect so much that people get bogged down in the calculations. If it is a large group, then each pair should interview fewer people than if you have a small group.

Suggestions for follow-up

Look at the information in the background material on democracy on page 326 and find out which day it was in your country that women first got the vote. You could also find out which groups in your society do not have the vote today (for example - children, immigrants, prisoners, etc.). Discuss the reasons behind this, and whether you think it is fair.

In a democratic society, there are many opportunities for people to take action about issues that concern them. The activity "Power Station", on page 198, gives participants a chance to think about ways to promote social change.

Key date

The day on which universal Suffrage became law in your country

Ideas for action

Organise a celebration of the day on which women were granted the right to vote in your country.

If you found groups in your society without the right to vote and you felt that this was unjust, write a letter to your members of parliement expressing the concern of your group. Try to get other signatures as well.

Notes on how to conduct the survey

Finding interviewees

1. Approach prospective interviewees at *random:* in other words, you should not "select" people to be included or excluded from the survey because they are *young, old, nice-looking, female, etc.* Try to avoid bias.
2. Ask the person you want to interview whether they would mind answering a couple of questions for a survey, explain who you are and say that answers will be anonymous and that the results of the survey will not be made public; they are only for the use of this particular group.

Recording the interview

1. If the person being approached agrees to take part in the survey, then ask them whether they used their vote in the last elections. If the answer is "no", then fill out sheet 1, the "non-voter" sheet. If the answer is "yes" then fill out sheet 2, the "voter" sheet.
2. Question 1: People should only give their age if they are happy about doing so. Otherwise, a tick should be put in the last column.
3. Question 2: Show the interviewees the options and ask them to choose one. If they have a different reason, write it down in column E. Note: the difference between B and C is that B is a reason involving a *particular person* and C is a reason involving a *party.*
4. The marks should be clear, so that they can be counted later on. As many people as possible should be registered on one sheet. Only one mark should be made against each question for each person.

HANDOUTS

Survey sheet

1: non-voters

Question 1. In which age group are you? (Optional)

	Under 25	25 – 40	40 – 60	Over 60	Would rather not say
MALE					
FEMALE					

Question 2. What was your main reason for not voting the last time there were elections?

A. I thought it wouldn't make any difference to the result
B. There wasn't anyone I wanted to vote for
C. I didn't agree with any of the policies being proposed
D. I couldn't be bothered
E. Other reason (give details):

A	B	C	D	E

2: voters

Question 1. In which age group are you? (Optional)

	Under 25	25 – 40	40 – 60	Over 60	Would rather not say
MALE					
FEMALE					

Question 2. What was your main reason for voting the last time you did so?

A. I felt it was my democratic responsibility
B. I wanted to vote for [a person]
C. I wanted to vote for [a party]
D. I didn't want [a different person / party] to win
E. Other reason (give details):

A	B	C	D	E

Example of how to fill in the survey sheet

Survey sheet 1: Non-voters

Question 1. In which age group are you? (Optional)

	Under 25	25 – 40	40 – 60	Over 60	Would rather not say
MALE	𝍸 𝍸 II	𝍸 𝍸 II	𝍸 𝍸 II	𝍸 𝍸 II	II
FEMALE	𝍸 𝍸 II	𝍸 𝍸 II	𝍸 𝍸 II	𝍸 𝍸 II	II

Question 2. What was your main reason for not voting the last time there were elections?

A. I thought it wouldn't make any difference to the result

B. There wasn't anyone I wanted to vote for

C. I didn't agree with any of the policies being proposed

D. I couldn't be bothered

E. Other reason (give details):

A	B	C	D	E
𝍸 𝍸 II 𝍸 𝍸 II	𝍸 𝍸 II 𝍸 𝍸 II	𝍸 𝍸 II 𝍸 𝍸 II	𝍸 𝍸 II 𝍸 𝍸 II	▪ I wasn't in the area at the time ▪ I don't trust politicians ▪ Someone asked me not to

Trade Union meeting

A fair day's work deserves a fair day's pay.

Themes Social rights, Democracy, Citizenship

Complexity Level 4

Group Size 10 - 15

Time 120

Overview This is a simulation of a meeting between an employer and employees together with their trade union representatives to negotiate wages and conditions. The issues addressed include:
- The role of trade unions
- Collective bargaining in the workplace
- Workers' rights

Related rights
- The right to collective bargaining
- The right of assembly and association, specifically to join and form a trade union
- The right not to be unfairly dismissed.

Objectives
- To understand the role of trade unions
- To develop consensus decision-making skills
- To promote participation, responsibility and solidarity

Materials
- Copies of handout 1 "The situation", one per participant
- Copies of handout 2 "A short glossary of some labour terms", one per participant
- Labels for identification purposes (optional)
- Paper, coloured markers and pens (optional)
- Two rooms (preferable but optional)

Preparation
- Read the activity through, including the handouts so that you will be well prepared to act as a resource person to any of the players during the activity.
- Arrange the room. Put six chairs in a circle. These chairs are for the representatives of the different parties and the person who is going to chair the meeting. Behind them, arrange other chairs for the rest of participants.

Instructions

1. Introduce the activity. Explain that it is a simulation of a meeting between employers on one side and employees' and trade union representatives on the other. The aim is to get an agreement on workers' wages and conditions using collective bargaining.
2. As a warm-up, ask the group to decide the name and business of the company they want the scene to be set in. It can be a real or imaginary company, manufacturing real or imaginary products. Let them also give the trade union a name.
3. Now divide the participants into two groups in a ratio of 2:1. The smaller group are the employers and the larger group are the employees and their trade union representatives.

4. Hand out copies of handout 1 "The situation" and handout 2 "A short glossary of some labour terms". Give people ten minutes to read the papers, and then check that everyone understands the information.
5. Outline briefly how the simulation will be: The employers are the convenors and one of them chairs the meeting. They will put their proposal on the table first. Then the TU and employees' representatives will put their proposal forward. After that all parties will negotiate to try to reach an agreement.
6. Ask the participants to agree the procedures for the meeting, for example, when the negotiations are underway, should there be a time limit on how long each person can talk - a maximum of 2 minutes perhaps? The total time for the meeting? The procedures for taking short breaks so the representatives can consult their constituencies etc. Who else can talk, or will it only be the representatives?
7. Now ask people to get into their two groups to prepare (30 minutes). The employers should choose two representatives and someone to chair the meeting. The workers/ TU should choose two representatives. Both groups should then:
   - Elaborate a new proposal to be presented at the meeting.
   - Decide what negotiating powers the representatives should have.
   - What their bottom line is, that is what is the worst case scenario and the lowest acceptable agreement?
8. When the groups are ready, invite the representatives to sit on the five chairs in the inner circle and the others to sit behind them. Invite the chairperson to open the meeting.
9. When the meeting is over, take a short break for people to get out of role and then move on to the debriefing and evaluation.

Debriefing and evaluation

Start with a short review of how people enjoyed the activity and then go on to discuss what happened and what they learnt:

- How did the two groups work together to decide their initial proposals? Was it easy or was it difficult?
- When developing their initial proposals, did the groups consider their own interests or those of the company as a whole?
- Did the groups develop tactics for the negotiation?
- How did the meeting go? Did everyone who wanted to talk get the chance to do so?
- Could the parties get to a mutually acceptable agreement?
- The right to belong to a trade union is a recognised human right. How important a right is it? What would be the consequences of not having that right?
- How much do people know about trade unions, what they are and what they do?
- How strong are trade unions in your country? What about employers, are there also employers' organisations?
- Do any of the participants belong to trade unions? Why? What are the advantages and disadvantages?

Tips for facilitators

Before starting this activity you should take into account the climate of opinion and general

Key date

1 May
Labour Day

attitudes towards trade unions in your country. For example, in post-communist societies, there may be resistance to this activity because of the legacy from the times when trade unions were seen as 'schools of communism'. In these circumstances you may like to start by exploring the images and stereotypes people have of trade unions. You could also ask participants to contact local trade unions for information and do other research on labour issues in their country. You might also wish to point out the relevance and importance of trade unions in safeguarding workers' rights irrespective of the political system that they were identified with.

Depending on the group, you may need to give more guidance about the bargaining process. You may want to give participants some tips about what to consider when developing their positions and proposals, for example:

- Would it be acceptable for employees to forego their wage rise in order to retain all the workers?
- Which category of workers should be dismissed, if dismissals are eventually carried out?
- Is the proposal realistic? Could the company sustain the economic burden?

Let the meeting and negotiations meet their destiny! If, during the discussions, employees and the trade union are thinking of backing up their proposal with a strike, you could supply them with paper and pens to make posters for the picket. If the employers want to shut the workers out, i.e. organise a lockout, make sure you have another room for the workers to go to!

Most countries in Europe have laws regulating collective bargaining. You may wish to identify such legislation and copy some of the important articles to help participants develop this activity to its full potential.

Variations

Another example of a situation involving negotiations about rights might be a meeting at a school to resolve a dispute with a "problem" student. The meeting could be between the student and his or her parents on one side and the head teacher and parent-teacher body on the other.

Suggestions for follow-up

Invite a member of a trade union to come to give a talk. You will find the phone numbers of trade unions in the local telephone directory. Generally trade unions are willing to get closer to young people and that can be a good opportunity for you!

If the group enjoys discussing ideas then they may enjoy the activity " Where do you stand?", in which people have to have defend their opinions about a range of human rights issues.

Taking Action

Develop a project together with a local trade union to promote trade unionism among young people.

Note: this activity was developed in co-operation with GMO Trade Union in United Kingdom, European Trade Union College (ETUCO) and Association for European Training of Workers on the Impact of New Technology (AFETT).

Further Information

There is information about youth and trade union membership in the background information on social rights, page 387.

HANDOUTS

The situation

The scene is a company meeting, between employers and employees and the trade union (TU), who are deadlocked in an attempt to come to an agreement over a wage claim.

The factory operates 24 hours a day, 365 days a year. It has a total workforce of one thousand, from production to the management. All workers are members of the trade union.

The company is currently experiencing financial and economic difficulties, but it is not actually facing bankruptcy. Profits have remained high but they declined last year as the sector as a whole is facing a downturn. Over the past three years wages have fallen by 3% in real terms and staff numbers have declined by 10%.

The workers are demanding a wage rise in line with rises in other sectors of industry.

Management has indicated that staff reductions will be necessary in order to pay for any wage rise. Their proposal is:

- a 4% wage rise in ordinary wage rates over 12 months on individuals contracts (inflation is currently 2% per annum).
- Payment on the basis of hours worked annually, rather than daily or weekly hours and the abolition of overtime working.
- Staff cuts (10% of staff – mainly part-time, temporary positions and apprenticeships - following the rule ' last in, first out') and voluntary redundancies.

The management proposal was rejected by the general assembly of workers who were concerned that the proposals would leave them far worse off (at the moment 40% of employees receive a significant part of their pay in overtime payments). The TU and the employees made a counter-proposal to the management:

- Increase of 9% in wages over two years
- Overtime and bonuses be kept in place
- Current staff numbers be retained and any employee who is forced into redundancy be retrained at the company's expense.
- If demands are not met, strike action will be taken.

The counter-proposal was refused by the management, who claimed that the TU and employees' suggestions would not solve the problems that the company is facing.

The negotiations have been going on for two months now.

It is company policy that when agreement can not be reached within a two-month period, then a special meeting should be called involving all parties concerned. It is this meeting that is the basis of the simulation. Both sides are required to come with a new proposal that is a realistic basis for coming to a mutually satisfactory agreement.

There should be a total of seven people around the negotiating table: two management representatives, one chair of the meeting (appointed by the employers) and four TU representatives. Because it is a special general meeting, all employees are welcome to attend.

A short glossary of some labour terms

Collective bargaining: This is a process of negotiation in which employers and employees' representatives collectively seek to agree and resolve issues, such as salaries and work conditions.

Lock-outs: A lock-out is one of an employer's most radical means of exerting power. The employer refuses to allow the employees entry to their place of work, that is s/he literally locks them out in an attempt to compel them to accept management's demands.

Redundancy: Workers are made redundant when they are dismissed because the employer decides to close down the business. The employees may be entitled to redundancy payments as compensation.

Severance pay: If a permanent employee is unfairly dismissed or is dismissed on the basis of the company being re-structured, then s/he is entitled to receive compensation, which is called severance pay. The value of the severance pay is often based on the salary that the employee was receiving, for example, one week's salary for every year of work.

Strike: The right to strike is a basic, social, human right which is seen as a necessary element for successful collective bargaining and as a tool to mitigate the inherent inequality in the employer – employee relationship. A strike is the refusal to work, or the obstruction of work, by employees. Workers can not just go on strike when they feel like it! Certain conditions have to be met which are usually laid down in legislation and differ from country to country.

Trade Union: A trade union is an association that exists to defend workers' interests, including pay and working conditions. The trade union generally represents workers in negotiations with the employers. In many countries TUs are organised into confederations.

Violence in my life

"Follow the three Rs: Respect for self / Respect for others and / Responsibility for all your actions." The Dalai Lama

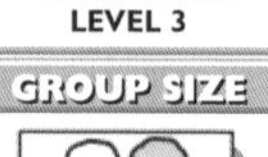

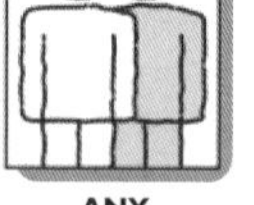

Themes	Peace and Violence, Human security, General human rights
Complexity	Level 3
Group size	Any
Time	60 minutes
Overview	This is a discussion activity in which people explore their experiences of inter-personal violence.
Related rights	▪ The right to life, liberty and security of person ▪ The right to freedom of thought, conscience and religion
Objectives	▪ To be able to identify oneself not only as an object of violence but also as someone who could be a source of violence ▪ To encourage the development of skills to deal with violence in positive ways ▪ To develop values of tolerance and responsibility.

Instructions

1. Explain that this is an opportunity for the participants to share thoughts and feelings about personal experiences of inter-personal violence, both when people were violent to them and when they were violent to others.
2. Make sure that everyone knows and understands the rules for participatory group work: that everyone should be treated with respect, that what anyone says is held in confidence and that no one is to feel under pressure to say anything which makes them feel uncomfortable.
3. Conduct a brainstorm of the word "violence" and ask them to give examples of everyday violence, for instance, verbal abuse, insults, sarcasm, queue-jumping, barging in front of someone, smacking a child or hitting/being hit, burglary, petty theft or pickpocketing, vandalism, etc.
4. Ask everyone to take five minutes to reflect about personal incidents when:
   a) someone acted violently towards them
   b) when they acted violently towards someone else
   c) when they saw someone else being violent but did not intervene.

Debriefing and evaluation

Start with a short discussion about the activity itself and whether or not it was difficult, and, if so, why. Then go on to analyse the causes and effects of the different situations a), b), and c) above. Ask for volunteers to offer their experiences for general discussion. Let them say what happened and how they feel about it and then open the discussion to everyone.

1. Why did the violent situation happen?
2. How would other members of the group have behaved in similar circumstances?
3. Why did you behave the way you did?
4. How could you have behaved differently? Has the rest of the group any suggestions?
5. What could anyone have done to prevent the incident from happening?
6. In the case of c), why didn't they intervene?
7. What were the causes of the incident?
8. How many incidents were the result of misunderstandings, how many the result of bitterness, spite or jealousy and how many the result of differences of culture and custom, opinion or belief?
9. What do people understand by the word "tolerance"? How would they define it?
10. Is it right that people should be completely tolerant of everything other people do or say?
11. Why is tolerance a key value for the promotion of human rights?

Key dates

16 November
International Day for Tolerance

Tips for facilitators

Be prepared for surprises and to support anyone who find this activity difficult or upsetting. You cannot know everyone's background nor what is happening or what has happened in their families. It might be that some participants have had bad experiences with violence of different forms. Stress that the purpose of this activity is to develop skills for dealing with violence, by recognising the causes, acknowledging feelings and emotions, and developing skills for acting assertively in order to control the situation and to find non-violent means of responding to violent situations. Tell people to remember Article 1 of the Universal Declaration of Human Rights: "all human beings are born free and equal in dignity and rights". If we expect others to follow this Article, then we too have to follow it. If you have more than ten people in the group you could divide them up into small groups to share their stories.

Variations

This makes a good drama activity. Ask two, three or four people to develop a short role-play of an incident. The rest of the group observe. You can then stop the role-play at intervals and ask the audience to comment or to make suggestions as to how the role-play should continue. Alternatively, members of the audience can intervene directly to take over from the actors and develop alternative outcomes.

Suggestions for follow-up

Find out about organisations that provide support for victims of violence, for example, telephone help-lines or victims' support networks. Find out about other organisations that promote understanding and tolerance in the community. If you would like to continue working with the theme of peace and violence you could look at the activity "Living in a perfect world", on page 160. Find the answers to the clues to complete a peace mandala!

Ideas for action

Get in touch with an organisation that works to promote peace and non-violence in the community and find out how you can get involved.

When tomorrow comes

"If you judge others how this system has judged you, it will make you no better than those who have condemned you to death." Dwight Adanandus

Themes	Human Security, Media, Peace and Violence
Complexity	Level 3
Group size	Any
Time	60 minutes
Overview	This activity uses information sheets and discussion to explore issues about: ▪ The rights of criminals ▪ The death penalty ▪ The protection of society from criminals
Related rights	▪ The right to life ▪ The right not to be subjected to cruel, inhuman or degrading treatment
Objectives	▪ To examine our preconceptions about criminals and reflect on some of the implications of the death penalty ▪ To be aware of our own listening skills and how we "interpret" information we are given ▪ To promote a sense of human dignity and justice.
Materials	▪ Copies of the handout "When tomorrow comes"; one per participant. ▪ A sheet of paper and pencil for each member of the group.

Instructions

Step 1.

1. Read part 1 of *When tomorrow comes* out loud to the group. When you have finished, give people about 5 minutes to recall all the main points and to write them down in their own words. Then ask them to exchange sheets of paper with their neighbour, to read each other's accounts and give feedback.
2. Invite some volunteers to read out their accounts. Then discuss the differences between the versions: did some people remember more details than others did? Did some people invent details that had not been mentioned in the original story?
3. Ask people for their reaction to the story: who do they think the narrator is? What has happened?

Step 2.

1. Read out the newspaper cutting and part 2 of Dwight's narration.
2. Now allow the pairs 10-15 minutes to discuss the new information with their partners. Supply them with copies of "When tomorrow comes" in case they want to refer back to points in the text.

3. Then ask them to think about the following two issues:
   - Did they find their opinion of either Dwight or Nanon changed when they learnt that they were on Death Row? How? Why?
   - What do they think Dwight meant by saying 'If you judge others how this system has judged you, it will make you no better than those who have condemned you to death!" Do they agree with him?
4. Open the issue up for general discussion, obtaining feedback from the various pairs on these questions.

Debriefing and evaluation

This activity can be used to spark off a number of important and interesting issues which can form the subject of further activities or discussion. However, it is recommended that in the debriefing you stick fairly closely to the topics that the groups have already considered rather than opening up entirely new themes (see below, under notes for facilitators).

- Has this activity taught you anything about yourself? Has it made you reconsider any of your previous opinions or beliefs?
- What do you think the activity was intended to illustrate? Did it succeed in this aim, and if not, why not?
- What, if anything, did the activity have to say to you about the right to life? Were there any other rights issues that were raised in the discussion?

Make a note of these issues on a large sheet of paper or flipchart paper for future use.

Tips for facilitators

In the first discussion (after reading part 1) it is important not to give people any hint of the two men's situation: try to draw out people's impressions of the characters, but without suggesting you have any particular reason for doing so. The purpose is for people to examine the two men's human sides, without knowing anything of their circumstances or past history.

The point of people swapping accounts at the end of step 1 is to give them an idea of the different ways that people may perceive and remember exactly the same piece of information. It is worth emphasising that this should not be seen as a "test", so that people do not feel shy about their accounts; but rather as a way of showing up different viewpoints. Try to ask for comments from people whose account has differed radically from their neighbour's. Ask why this may have been the case – why, for example, some people remembered certain pieces of information that were omitted by others.

The activity itself will most probably raise too many issues for a single session, so you should try to keep the discussion along the lines suggested, rather than allowing people to get carried away by debating – for example – the death penalty itself. Try to keep the discussion focused on the two key issues of:

1. The extent to which we, the State, everyone, are inclined to "judge" people on the basis of something (we believe) they have done. This is probably what Dwight has in mind when he talks about not "judging" others as the State has judged him (and Nanon). The State has effectively written them off as human beings on the basis of something (it believes) they have done in the past.
2. Even so-called "hardened criminals" possess and retain their inherently human

Key date

26 June
International Day in Support of Victims of Torture

characteristics - not only the “caring and compassion” of which Dwight speaks, but also the “frustration and depression” that Nanon describes as a result of the confinement.

When discussing the “right to life” issue, guide the discussion around the issues of whether these two people can be said still to *possess* the right to life – and if not, how someone can “lose” such a right. Does anyone, for example, have the authority to remove that right from other citizens, even if they have committed a crime?

Suggestions for follow-up

Pursue the issues raised at the end of the activity. Organise a formal debate or use the method “Electioneering”, on page 127. Topics may include:

- Punishment issues: what is the purpose of locking criminals up and/or of executing them? Is it primarily to protect society, to alter the behaviour of the criminals, or is it revenge/retribution?
- The death penalty: what are the arguments for and against the death penalty?
- The security of the nation vs. security of the individual: what are the limits to the way a government may treat its worst criminals or terrorists? For example - can torture of an individual justified on the grounds of “security of the nation”?

Take a take a look at Nanon’s own website, http://home4.inet.tele.dk/lepan/lene/nanon.htm Songs have always been a powerful tool in people’s fight for rights.

Ideas for action

Visit the web site of the Canadian Coalition Against the Death Penalty (CCADP) and read more of the prisoners’ writings (www.ccadp.org). Then write to someone on Death Row (the ccadp website contains information on how to become a pen-pal or contact your local association of Amnesty International).

Note: the full piece (*When tomorrow comes)* can be found at the CCADP web site.

HANDOUTS

When tomorrow comes, by Nanon Williams

Part 1

"It was a day after Dwight Adanandus died when I truly looked at life completely differently than what it was, or shall I say, what I wished it to be. This was the beginning of winter, and as I lay still thinking of a friend that always presented a smile when the days seemed so redundant, I felt tormented. As I gently moved, picking up the newspaper under the door, the paper told his story.

Reading about it and knowing I would never see him again felt like someone was sticking pincushions in my heart over and over again. Sometimes he would come swinging into the yard yelling, 'What's up youngster?' And I would look around me, stare back, and say, 'Man, who you calling a youngster,' and we would both start laughing because I was the youngest person on our block. And when I think of those moments now, well, it deeply saddens me, because I'll never look forward to being in the yard without Dwight being around to break the creases that riddled my face with anger.

As the years have gone by, my methods of passing time has changed, but I like to think these new methods will hopefully make me become a better man one day like Dwight became. During my moments of weakness, I always find myself wondering what Dwight would have done.

'Remember,' he would say to me, 'The system can only get to you if you let them. Make your peace with whoever your God is and start to live life the best you can and appreciate it.' Then he would continue, 'Youngster, I don't know why you're here, but I know you don't belong here…'

Part 2

'....... In fact, no one belongs here, not on death row. You have rapists, kidnappers, robbers, child molesters and sadistic people who don't give a damn about you. However, you also have caring and compassionate people who have done those very same things, but have found a way to change and I want you to always remember that,' he said to me weeks before he was executed. 'Remember this if nothing else. If you judge others how this system has judged you, it will make you no better than those who have condemned you to death!' And as those words ring in my ears now, I wonder why it has taken me so long to understand what he meant. Of course I heard what he said and it made sense, but making sense and fully grasping the meaning of those words was something totally different. I guess then I was the youngster he called me, but the truth hurts when you finally take the time to see it.

I know the confinement is all a psychological weapon of torture that builds frustration until depression sets in, but somehow the spirit and the will to continue remains in a few. For Dwight, he had that spirit no matter what he did that placed him on death row and with that spirit he changed other's lives who rot like living corpse in the system's graveyard. 'I know it's not easy Youngster,' he would say. 'But nobody said life was easy. Take each day for what it's worth and as long as you can see a light at the end of the road, let that be the strength that guides you,' were the last words he ever said to me tearfully as he said his final good-byes. I dare not to explain what that means to me, as I guess he said it to me so I can find my own strength that sustains me through the years that have passed and probably the years to come. I have never forsaken my principles or the things that I value most in life — like my family, so more than likely that love and one day entering heavens gates, is what tomorrow really is when it comes."

Nanon Williams was sentenced to death by the State of Texas when he was 17 years old, under the charge of capital murder. He denies the charge and has spent the last nine years on Death Row.

Source: www.ccadp.org.

Newspaper cutting

Huntsville - October 2, 1997. A convicted robber was executed Wednesday night for gunning down a San Antonio businessman who tried to stop him from fleeing a bank hold-up nine years ago. Adanandus, 41, went to death row for killing Vernon Hanan, who was shot in the chest January 28, 1988, as he wrestled with Adanandus in the foyer of a bank on San Antonio's north side.

Where do you stand?

Are social and economic rights luxuries, only for citizens of rich countries?

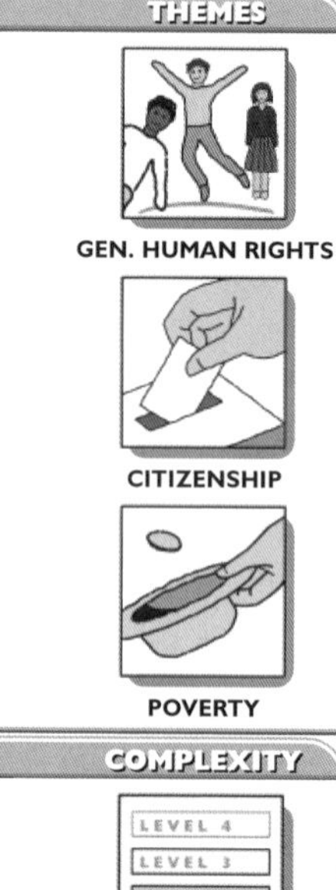

Themes General human rights, Citizenship, Poverty

Complexity Level 2

Group size Any

Time 50 minutes

Overview This is a discussion activity that addresses:
- The basic essentials necessary for human dignity
- The relative importance of civil and political rights and social and economic rights
- Governments' obligations concerning social and economic rights

Related rights All

Objectives
- To gain an understanding of the difference between civil and political rights and social and economic rights
- To think about some of the complex issues associated with protecting rights
- To use and develop skills of discussion and argumentation

Materials
- One copy of the sheet of statements
- Large sheets of paper or flipchart paper, pens
- String or chalk (optional)
- copies of the simplified UDHR on page 402 (optional)

Preparation
- Prepare 2 posters – one saying, "I agree" and the other saying, "I disagree" – and stick them at opposite ends of the room, so that people can form a straight line between them. (You may want to draw a chalk line between them, or use a piece of string)

Instructions

1. Start with a very brief introduction to the differences between civil and political rights, and social and economic rights.
2. Spend 5 minutes brainstorming the different rights that would fall under each category. List the rights on the flipchart under the headings, civil and political rights, and social and economic rights.
3. Explain that you are now going to read out a series of statements with which people may agree to a greater or lesser extent.
4. Point out the two extreme positions – the posters stating "I Agree" and "I Disagree". Explain that people may occupy any point along the (imaginary) line, but that they should try to position themselves, as far as possible, next to people whose views almost coincide with their own. Brief discussion is permitted while people are finding their places!

5. Read out the statements in turn. Vary the rhythm: some statements should be read out in quick succession, while for others you may want to take a little time between statements to allow for discussion.
6. Stimulate reflection and discussion. Ask those at the end-points to explain why they have occupied these extreme positions. Ask someone near the centre whether their position indicates the lack of a strong opinion or lack of knowledge .
7. Allow people to move position as they listen to each others' comments.
8. When you have gone through the statements, bring the group back together for the debriefing.

Debriefing and evaluation

Begin with reviewing the activity itself and then go on to discuss what people learnt.

- Were there any questions that people found impossible to answer – either because it was difficult to make up their own mind, or because the question was badly phrased?
- Why did people change position during the discussions?
- Were people surprised by the extent of disagreement on the issues?
- Does it matter if we disagree about human rights?
- Do you think there are "right" and "wrong" answers to the different statements, or is it just a matter of personal opinion?
- Might it ever be possible for everyone to reach agreement about human rights?
- Is there a fundamental difference between the (first) two "generations" of human rights: civil and political rights and social and economic rights? Is it possible to say which of these are more important?
- Do we need any more rights? Could there be a third generation of rights?

Tips for facilitators

This activity embraces all human rights, but social and economic rights in particular; for example, the rights to work and leisure, to health care, and to a basic standard of living. (Articles 16, 22-29 of the UDHR)

The statements given below are designed to address some of the debates that take place concerning the difference between civil and political rights on the one hand, and social and economic rights on the other. There is no need to go into a great deal of detail at the beginning of the activity, since many of the points should emerge in the course of discussion.

However, two points are perhaps worth drawing out by way of an introduction. First, the simple distinction that civil and political rights are those moral demands that we make on governments concerning civil and political issues, such as the right to a fair trial, to vote, to express one's opinion, etc; and social and economic rights are those demands that are connected with social and economic issues – such as homelessness, inadequate health care, poverty, etc. The first type of rights are also referred to as *first generation* rights, and the second type as *second generation* rights, because of the historical order in which they came to be recognised by people as universal human rights.

The second point is that some people have drawn a fundamental distinction between the different types of rights. Social and economic rights have been claimed by many to be either less important, and/or more difficult to guarantee than civil and political rights. Others dispute this. You can find more information about the debate in chapter 4.

Key date

5 December
International Volunteer Day for Economic and Social Development

During the brainstorming, you may want to give people copies of the simplified UDHR to jog their memories; or you yourself could read out some of the articles and ask people to put them into the correct category. Articles 16 and 22-29 are generally regarded as referring to social-economic rights.

You may want to run the lining-up part of the activity relatively quickly, without giving much time for discussion between the various points, and then to select two or three of the statements and discuss them in more detail with the whole group. But it is worth stopping the activity at certain points in order to give people the opportunity to reflect both on some of the points and on their position relative to that of others.

Variations

Compose other statements, or ask members of the group to make up their own.

Suggestions for follow-up

Organise a formal debate on one of the issues, asking people to prepare their arguments in advance, and then take a vote at the end of the debate. You could invite other young people or members of the public to attend.

Knowing about human rights is important, but being an active citizen is also essential if rights are to be safeguarded. You may like to try the activity "Electioneering", on page 127. This looks at the question of persuading others over to your opinion.

Ideas for action

Get in touch with a local organisation that works for human rights or social welfare and find out how you can contribute.

Further information

Chapter 4 of the manual contains background information on the different generations of rights, including an introduction to "third generation" rights.

HANDOUTS

Sheet of statements

- It's more important to have a roof over your head than to be able to say what you like.
- People have a duty to work, but not a right.
- The most basic responsibility of any government is to make sure that all citizens have enough to eat.
- The right to "rest and leisure" is a luxury that only rich countries can afford.
- It's not the government's job to make sure that people don't starve – but the people's!
- The way we choose to treat our citizens is no business of the international community.
- Poor countries should concentrate on a basic standard of living for all before worrying about the civil and political rights of citizens.
- Extreme economic inequality is an infringement of basic rights.
- Social and economic rights express an ideal for the future, but the world is not ready to guarantee them today.
- If rights can't be guaranteed, there is no point in having them.

Who are I?

I am what I am, you are what you are, she is what she is...but together we have a lot in common!

Themes Gender equality, Discrimination and Xenophobia, Citizenship

Complexity Level 2

Group size 8+

Time 25 minutes

Overview This activity involves buzz groups, brainstorming, drawing and group discussion to explore issues of identity.

Related rights
- Equality in dignity and respect
- The right not to be discriminated against
- The right to life, liberty and security of person

Objectives
- To be aware of our own individuality and that of others
- To identify what we have in common with others
- To promote solidarity and respect

Materials
- Coloured pens and markers, if possible a different colour for each participant
- Enough paper for one sheet per person
- Flipchart paper and markers

Instructions

1. To warm up, ask people to get into pairs to form buzz groups. Ask them to pretend that they are strangers and to introduce themselves to each other.
2. Now ask people to reflect what is interesting or important to know about someone else when you first meet, and brainstorm the general categories of information. For example, name, age, sex, nationality, family role, religion, age, gender, ethnicity, job/study, taste in music, hobbies, sports, general likes and dislikes and more.
3. Now explain that participants are going to find out how much each of them has in common with others in the group. Hand out the paper and pens and explain that the first step is for each of them to draw a representation of their identity. They should think of themselves like stars; aspects of their identity radiate out into their society. Ask people to consider the eight to ten most important aspects of their identity and to draw their personal star.
4. Tell people to go around and compare their stars. When they find someone else with whom they share a beam or ray, they should write that person's name near the beam. (For example, if Jan and Parvez both have a "rapper" beam, they should write each other's names along that beam). Allow 15 minutes for this.
5. Now come back into plenary and ask people to talk about how individual each of them was. You could ask:

- Which aspects of identity do people have in common and which are unique?
- How similar and how different are people in the group? Do people have more in common with each other than they have aspects that are different?

6. Finally, do a group brainstorm of the aspects of identity that people choose and those that they are born with. Write these up in two columns on the flip chart.

Debriefing and evaluation

Now move on to discuss what people have discovered about themselves and about each other and the implications for human rights.

- What did people learn about themselves? Was it hard to decide which were the most significant aspects of their identity?
- Were people surprised at the results of comparing stars? Did they have more or less in common than they expected?
- How did people feel about the diversity in the group? Did they feel it made the group more interesting to be in or does it make it more difficult to work together?
- Were there any aspects of other people's identity that participants felt strongly inclined to react to and say, "I am not."? For example, I am not a football fan, not a fan of techno music, not a dog lover, not homosexual or not Christian.
- How does identity develop? Which aspects are social constructs and which are inherent and fixed?
- In relation to gender issues in particular, which aspects are social constructs and which are inherent and fixed? Did participants write "girl" or "boy"? What do people associate with the words "boy" and "girl"? Are the associations the same for both sexes and for all boys and all girls?
- How much are people judged by their individual identity and how much by the group that they belong to?
- How do participants feel about having the freedom to be able to choose their own identity? What are the implications for themselves and their society, and especially for the human rights of equality and respect?

Tips for facilitators

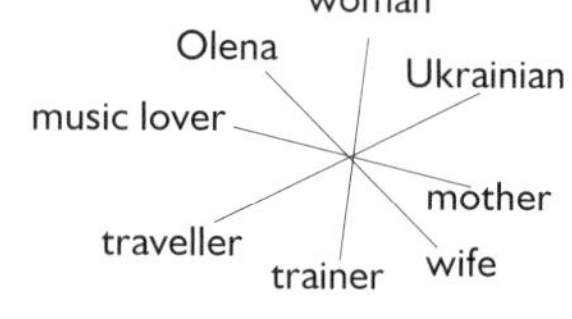

The name of this activity is not wrong! It is intended to puzzle participants.

In the warm up you may want to give some participants a tip to get them thinking on the right lines. You could give yourself as an example or use an imaginary person like: Olena, woman, Ukrainian, mother, wife, trainer, traveller, music lover.

The purpose of giving each participant a different colour is to give people the idea that everyone is unique and that the group is composed of a rainbow of identities. (The analogy is with South Africa, which calls itself the "rainbow nation", that is a nation made up of people of all colours.) If you have a large group and two or more people have to share the same colour pen, ask them to use different styles of writing.

If you wish, you can make the activity a little more sophisticated by suggesting that people draw their personal stars with longer or shorter beams or rays according to how public or private they feel a particular aspect of their identity is. Longer beams reach further out into society and are therefore more public.

Some of the following points could come up in the final brainstorm (at step 6):

- Aspects of identity I can choose: name, friend, job, membership of a political party, favourite music, style of clothes, the football team you support, where you live,
- Aspects of identity I am born with: sex, age, height, eye colour,
- There will be some aspects of identity that may cause controversy, for example nationality, gender and sexuality, religion, being member of a minority.

The discussion about how identity develops and which aspects of identity are social constructs and which are inherent and fixed will also be controversial, especially those relating to religion and gender. It is worth asking participants to consider their own process of growing up and how certain aspects of their identity have changed over the years, perhaps even those aspects of their identity that they think are fixed.

You may wish to draw some conclusions from the discussions, for example, that we are all human beings who have rights which cannot be gifted or taken away regardless of race, colour, property, birth or other status.

Suggestions for follow-up

This activity can serve as an opener for many other discussions, for instance, questions about the universality of human rights, discrimination and xenophobia, children's rights, and citizenship.

If the group want to look further at identity and gender issues they may enjoy the activity "Heroines and heroes", on page 142.

Key date

7 August
Transgender International Rights and Education Day

Work and babies

Are you planning to have a job? Then don't plan to have children!

THEMES

SOCIAL RIGHTS

GENDER EQUALITY

DISCRIMINATION

COMPLEXITY

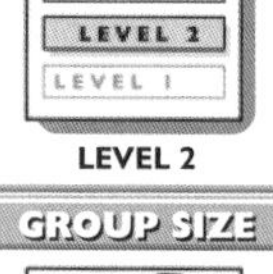

LEVEL 2

GROUP SIZE

10-25

TIME

90 MINUTES

Themes Social rights, Gender equality, Discrimination and Xenophobia

Complexity Level 2

Group size 10 - 25

Time 90 minutes

Overview This is a role-play dealing with issues of
- Reproductive rights in the workplace
- Discrimination against women in the workplace

Related rights
- A woman's right to reproductive choice
- The right not to be dismissed on the grounds of pregnancy, maternity leave and marital status
- The right to equal employment opportunities and remuneration

Objectives
- To develop knowledge about women's reproductive rights
- To attempt to make participants appreciate what it feels like to be discriminated against
- To promote equality, justice and responsibility

Materials
- A large sheet of paper, flipchart paper or board
- Space for small group work and role-play
- Props for the role-play, table and chairs, pen and paper

Preparation Copy the scenario onto a board or a large piece of paper or flipchart paper.

Instructions

1. Explain that the activity involves a role-play about the issues of women's reproductive rights at the workplace. Conduct a short brainstorm about women's reproductive rights so participants understand the term.
2. Divide the participants into small groups (maximum five people per group).
3. Read out the following, which is the background scenario for the role-play:

"Maria has been unemployed for almost a year and is looking hard for a job. Ten days ago she went for an interview for her dream job - it was exactly what she was looking for! Everything went well and she was offered the position. The company asked her to have a meeting with Mr. Wladstock, the personnel officer in order to sign her contract.

She had already discussed her duties and other job-related issues at the interview. Just as Maria was about to sign the contract, Mr. Wladstock said that a condition of the job was that she signs a declaration that she will not have a baby for the next two years."

4. In their small groups, give participants twenty minutes to decide on an ending for the story and to develop it into a role-play. The role-play should start with the meeting between Maria and Mr. Wladstock and should not last more than five minutes.
5. Invite each small group to present their role play. Keep comments for the debriefing.

Debriefing and Evaluation

Begin with a round of feedback from each of the small groups about how they developed their role-plays together with comments from the others. Then go on to talk about the implications and what should be done about discrimination of this sort.

- Was anyone surprised at the situation? Does it happen in your country?
- How did the groups decide what the outcome should be?
- Were the endings realistic? What were the good points - and weaker points - about the ways the Marias handled the situation? How hard is it to be assertive in such situations rather than aggressive or submissive?
- In your country, what rights do women have in the workplace when they get pregnant?
- Why would the company want to impose such a condition on Maria? Is it fair? Why? Why not?
- Were any human right being violated? If so, which ones?
- If Maria were a man, would the same thing happen? Why? Why not?
- In what ways do men see this issue differently from the way women do?
- What do you think can be done to promote and protect women's reproductive rights?

Tips for facilitators

Depending on the group, you may wish to divide the participants into small groups that are either mixed or single-sex (that is groups of only males and groups of only females). Choosing single-sex groups often leads to more provocative endings and richer discussion. Participants may not be familiar with the term "reproductive rights" and you may need to help them with some ideas in order to get the broad picture. Try to draw people out on the following points:

Reproductive rights include the right to:

- An enjoyable and fulfilling sexual relationship without fear of infection and disease.
- A choice whether or not to have children.
- A caring family planning service backed by a safe and empathetic abortion service that treats women with dignity and respect, and ensures privacy.
- Sex education

Bear in mind that the debriefing question about if human rights were being violated may bring up the controversial issues about abortion and a woman's right to choose, as opposed to the right of the foetus to life. This is a very important topic. It is also especially relevant to HRE, because it requires participants to be open-minded, to put aside stereotypes and pre-conceived opinions and to use their skills of critical thinking. It is a very good illustration of the inherent complexity of human rights. If the issue arises, you may like to consider taking it up at another time as a discussion in its own right.

Variations

Instead of dividing the participants into small groups, you can start with two volunteers to play Maria and Mr. Wladstock with the rest of the group as observers. Then you can stop the presentation at intervals and ask the observers to comment and to say what should happen next. Alternatively, observers can simply exchange places with the actors to develop a different angle and change the course of the role-play. See page 50, in chapter 1, for more information about role-playing techniques.

Key date

15 May
International Day of Families

Why not add other characters to the situation? You could include Maria's husband, who could be a trade union representative, and the role-play could go beyond the meeting with the human resources department.

Feel free to adapt the names of the characters to reflect common names in your country.

Suggestions for follow up

The group could do some research into reproductive rights in your country. Following that, they could hold interviews with both women and employers to find out how the legislation works in practice. They could also find out the impact of European law in this area on their own national law.

The group could also review the sex education that is taught in their country. Does it cover all aspects of reproductive rights?

If you want to explore other types of discrimination in the workplace you may like to develop the activity "Different wages", on page 107.

Ideas for Action

Take up issues about reproductive rights at your school or association council.

Further information

The role of the Convention on the elimination of all forms of discrimination against women.

Aside from civil rights issues, the Convention also devotes major attention to a most vital concern of women, namely their reproductive rights. The preamble sets the tone by stating that "the role of women in procreation should not be a basis for discrimination". The link between discrimination and women's reproductive role is a matter of recurrent concern in the Convention. For example, it advocates, in article 5, "a proper understanding of maternity as a social function", demanding fully shared responsibility for child-rearing by both sexes. Accordingly, provisions for maternity protection and child-care are proclaimed as essential rights and are incorporated into all areas of the Convention, whether dealing with employment, family law, health care or education. Society's obligation extends to offering social services, especially child-care facilities, that allow individuals to combine family responsibilities with work and participation in public life. Special measures for maternity protection are recommended and "shall not be considered discriminatory". (article 4). "The Convention also affirms women's right to reproductive choice. Notably, it is the only human rights treaty to mention family planning. It states that parties are obliged to include advice on family planning in the education process (article l0.h) and to develop family codes that guarantee women's rights "to decide freely and responsibly on the number and spacing of their children and to have access to the information, education and means to enable them to exercise these rights" (article 16.e).

A human rights calendar

The following calendar is a first attempt to compile a list of days on which people worldwide celebrate human rights. The key dates have been gathered from official UN International Days, World Days recognised by NGOs, anniversaries of historical events and birthdays of some prominent human rights activists. It is not to be taken as a complete or definitive list but as a starting point for work with young people. The activities in chapter three are listed for cross-referencing.

The calendar can be copied and made into a poster to hang on the wall to stimulate initial interest in human rights issues, especially as it gives a good indication of their range and variety. People can be invited to discuss selected issues and also to research their own local and national key dates. These can then be added to the calendar to make a resource which is personal to the group.

Each activity in chapter three has been assigned a key date. Thus it is possible to use the calendar as a tool for developing a year's human rights education programme. The starting point of each week or month could be a "topical" activity. For example on 3 May, World Press Freedom Day you could do the activity "Front page" (page 135) or on 25 November, International Day for the Elimination of Violence against Women, you could do the activity "Domestic affairs" (page 114). Alternatively, the group may wish to "take action" by getting involved with events or activities being organised by other organisations on those dates, for example with an environmental group to celebrate Earth Day on 22 April.

Just as the understanding of human rights changes and develops every year, so should this calendar. The challenge for you - the users of this manual - is to find new ways of celebrating human rights every single day of the year.

Date	Celebration	Activity
8 Jan	World Literacy Day	*Education for all?*
20 February	Non-violent Resistance Day	*Power station*
21 February	International Mother Language Day (UNESCO)	*The language barrier*
8 March	International Women's Day	*Heroines and heroes*
21 March	World Poetry Day (UNESCO)	*Picture games*
21 March	International Day for the Elimination of Racial Discrimination	*Responding to racism*
22 March	World Day for Water	*The web of life*
23 March	World Meteorological Day (WMO)	
24 March	World Tuberculosis Day (WHO)	
7 April	World Health Day (WHO)	*Just a minute*
8 April	World Roma Day	*Take a step forward*
22 April	Earth Day	*The web of life*
23 April	World Book and Copyright Day (UNESCO)	
30 April	Holocaust Memorial Day (Yom ha Shoah)	
1 May	International Workers Day	*Different Wages, Trade union meeting*
3 May	World Press Freedom Day (UNESCO)	*Front page*
8 May	World Red cross and Red Crescent Day	*Right's bingo*
15 May	International Day of Families	*Work and babies*
17 May	International Day against Homophobia	*Let's talk about sex!*
17 May	World Telecommunication Day (ITU)	*Impact of the Internet*
31 May	World No-Tobacco Day (WHO)	
4 June	International Day of Innocent Children Victims of Aggression	*Do we have alternatives?*

Date	Celebration	Activity
5 June	World Environment Day (UNEP)	*Garden in a night*
15 June	World Food Day	*Rich meal poor meal*
17 June	World Day to Combat Desertification and Drought	
20 June	World Refugee Day	*Can I come in?*
21 June	World Peace and Prayer Day	*All equal all different*
26 June	International Day against Drug Abuse and Illicit Trafficking	
26 June	United Nations International Day in Support of Victims of Torture	*When tomorrow comes*
26 June	UN Charter Day	*The language barrier*
1st Saturday July	International Day of Co-operatives	*Play the game*
11 July	World Population Day (UNFPA)	
6 August	Hiroshima Day (remembers victims of the first atomic bombing in Hiroshima, Japan, 1945)	
7 August	Transgender International Rights and Education Day	*Who are I?*
9 August	International Day of Indigenous People	*Makah whaling*
12 August	International Youth Day	*Our futures*
23 August	International Day for the Remembrance of the Slave Trade and Its Abolition (UNESCO)	
Tuesday following second Monday September	Peace Day	*Money to spend*
8 September	International Literacy Day (UNESCO)	*Glossary of globalisation*
16 September	International Day for the Preservation of the Ozone Layer	
1st Monday October	World Habitat Day (Cities without slums)	*A tale of two cities*
2nd Wednesday October	International Day for Natural Disaster Reduction	
1 October	International Day of Older Persons	
1 October	International Music Day	*One world of song*
5 October	World Teachers' Day (UNESCO)	*Let every voice be heard*
10 October	World Mental Health Day	*Sport for all*
16 October	World Food Day (FAO)	
17 October	International Day for the Eradication of Poverty	*Scramble for wealth and power*
24 October	World Development Information Day	*Beware we are watching*
24 October	United Nations Day	*Electioneering, Fighters for rights*
3 November	Men's World Day	*Heroines and heroes*
9 November	Kristallnacht, International Day Against Fascism and Anti-Semitism	
9 November	1989 Berlin Wall came down	*Making links*
11 November	International Day of Science and Peace	*Horoscope of poverty*
16 November	International Day for Tolerance (UNESCO)	*Violence in my life*
20 November	Universal Children's Day	*Children's rights*
21 November	World Television Day	*Picture games*
25 November	International Day for the Elimination of Violence against Women	*Path to Equality-land*
29 November	International Day of Solidarity with the Palestinian People	
1 December	World AIDS Day (WHO)	*Access to medicaments*
2 December	International Day for the Abolition of Slavery	*Ashique's story*
3 December	International Day of Disabled Persons	*See the ability*
5 December	International Volunteer Day for Economic and Social Development	*Where do you stand?*
10 December	Human Rights Day (1948)	*"Draw the word" game, Act it out*
18 December	International Migrants Day	*Take a step forward*
?	The day on which universal suffrage became law in *your* country	*To vote or not to vote*

500 500
COMPASS Manual on Human Rights Education Council of Europe
500Ems

500 500
COMPASS Manual on Human Rights Education Council of Europe
500Ems

500 500
COMPASS Manual on Human Rights Education Council of Europe
500Ems

100 100
COMPASS Manual on Human Rights Education Council of Europe
100Ems

100 100
COMPASS Manual on Human Rights Education Council of Europe
100Ems

100 100
COMPASS Manual on Human Rights Education Council of Europe
100Ems

100 100
COMPASS Manual on Human Rights Education Council of Europe
100Ems

100 100
COMPASS Manual on Human Rights Education Council of Europe
100Ems

100 100
COMPASS Manual on Human Rights Education Council of Europe
100Ems

50 50
COMPASS Manual on Human Rights Education Council of Europe
50Ems

50 50
COMPASS Manual on Human Rights Education Council of Europe
50Ems

50 50
COMPASS Manual on Human Rights Education Council of Europe
50Ems

50 50
COMPASS Manual on Human Rights Education Council of Europe
50Ems

50 50
COMPASS Manual on Human Rights Education Council of Europe
50Ems

50 50
COMPASS Manual on Human Rights Education Council of Europe
50Ems

50 50
COMPASS Manual on Human Rights Education Council of Europe
50Ems

10 10
COMPASS Manual on Human Rights Education Council of Europe
10Ems

10 10
COMPASS Manual on Human Rights Education Council of Europe
10Ems

10 10
COMPASS Manual on Human Rights Education Council of Europe
10Ems

10 10
COMPASS Manual on Human Rights Education Council of Europe
10Ems

10 10
COMPASS Manual on Human Rights Education Council of Europe
10Ems

10 10
COMPASS Manual on Human Rights Education Council of Europe
10Ems

10 10
COMPASS Manual on Human Rights Education Council of Europe
10Ems

10 10
COMPASS Manual on Human Rights Education Council of Europe
10Ems

10 10
COMPASS Manual on Human Rights Education Council of Europe
10Ems

10 10
COMPASS Manual on Human Rights Education Council of Europe
10Ems

10 10
COMPASS Manual on Human Rights Education Council of Europe
10Ems

Chapter 3

Taking Action

Table of contents of this chapter

Taking Action

The need for activism

Human rights education is partly about developing attitudes of respect for human rights. However, it is also about more than that because, no matter how respectful of human rights we and our colleagues or friends may be, we live in a world where violations of human rights are all around us. We cannot, unfortunately, stop those violations merely by education – or not in the short term, anyway.

Young people see this too, which can sometimes even undermine our educational efforts. After all - what use is it to know about the UDHR, if no one pays any attention to it in the real world? What use is there in recognising violations when we see them - if there is nothing we can do to stop them? And what value is there in our empathising with the suffering of victims - if that is only an addition to the pain caused by those violations?

Encouraging young people to take action against human rights abuses is important not just because they really can make a difference in the world. It is important also because that is something that young people want to see. It can be empowering, encouraging, and motivating for them to realise that their actions can make a difference; and it can bring to life the reality of human rights in a way that no activity or lesson could do for them.

"What you do may seem terribly insignificant but it's terribly important that you do it anyway."

Mahatma Ghandi

Which methods can we use?

The second part of this chapter is devoted to concrete steps that you may undertake with your group. Following this introduction, we consider some *simple steps to activism*: a series of small activities that can be used to send a powerful message. These are listed under 4 sub-headings:

1. Being informed
2. Publicising issues
3. Linking up with existing organisations
4. Getting results!

These categories are intended more for organisational purposes than in order to signify any particular sequence or order of events, but there is some progression of greater involvement from one category to the next. However, this should not be interpreted too rigidly, since many of the proposed actions will actually fall under more than one of the categories. The important point is that they are able to be conducted in isolation from one another, and they involve relatively little preparation.

The suggestions for action are not in themselves radical, and you are quite likely to be already undertaking many of them in your existing work – designing posters, debating issues, organising cultural events, meeting with different organisations, writing letters etc., but such apparently simple methods are in fact the very same ones that are used by professional activists, and they are effective.

In fact, almost any methods go! What will make your work with the group qualify as *activism* are the aims you set yourself, and the extent to which you take your work out into the community.

"He who accepts evil without protesting against it is really co-operating with it."

Martin Luther King

> "If you cry 'Forward' you must without fail make a plan in what direction to go. Don't you see that if, without doing so, you call out the word to both a monk and a revolutionary, they will go in directions precisely opposite?"
>
> *Anton Chekhov*

Planning

The third section of the chapter is concerned with effective planning. Of course, planning normally comes first, and whatever you do will require careful planning beforehand. However, this section has been included not so much to help you with one-off activities but rather with developing a more strategic approach to your activism, once people have gained a deeper understanding of the issues. If and when the group seems ready to implement a more systematic approach, then it will probably be helpful to look at the planning exercises, and to work through some of them. The exercises will help the group to define and formulate more precisely the aims they are trying to achieve, and the better they are able to do this, the more likely are their chances of success.

Allow the group to propose their own suggestions, and they will probably come up with ideas that are better fitted to their own skills, and are therefore more likely to have a better impact.

Some simple steps to activism

Find out; keep up to date

No-one can do anything unless they know what is going on. Being informed is one of the most important steps for effective activism and it will help to spark ideas for different things that you can do. But don't regard the search for information as necessarily a dry or static affair: information is all around us, and we need to be imaginative about making use of different sources.

Find out what's happening locally

- Look in the local and national papers for stories about rights violations.
- Contact the people concerned for those stories that particularly interest or trouble you: is anyone already doing something about it?
- Make a wall collage of the different cases, connecting those that deal with the same rights; and follow up what happens to them.
- Discuss with your group the possible ways of tackling the issue.
- Talk with members of minority or disadvantaged groups, and find out what their concerns are.

? What's going on? Where?

What is your country like compared with others?

- Find out which international treaties your government has signed up to, and what these treaties say.
- Find out whether international human rights NGOs (such as Amnesty International, the International Federation of Human Rights Leagues or Human Rights Watch) have any current concerns about your country.
- Find out what the government is doing about this.
- Find out which NGOs exist in your country to work against human rights violations.

Find out what's happening in the world

- Decide which human rights issues concern you most, and find out in which parts of the world these rights are particularly under threat.
- Mark the violations of these rights on a map of the world.
- Take a particular country or region (not your own) and look at the main sources of violations in this region.
- Find out which organisations are doing something about this – and contact them for more information.
- Look at the web-sites or publications of international NGOs and intergovernmental organisations (Council of Europe, UN, UNDP, UNHCR, etc).

Action

Example: Carry out a survey in your neighbourhood

A survey can be an important way of making contact with your local community if you are seeking to undertake effective action. You can test the water by seeing how people respond to particular issues; and that will help you to decide on paths of action that are particularly necessary and that will be viable in your community. Talking to people in the community is also a good way of publicising the work you may be doing, of informing others, and of drawing in additional support. Any surveying can also be combined with more concrete action.

 **How well do you know the views of people in your community?**

Who can we ask?

A survey could be carried out…

- among people you know – your friends and family;
- in your school – with pupils or teachers (or both);
- on the street;
- with minority groups, or other disadvantaged communities;
- among other youth groups;
- among businesses;
- by dropping forms through letterboxes (and returning to collect them at a later date).

What can we investigate?

You could take some of the following areas to draw up your survey. Look at the activity "To vote or not to vote", on page 238, for further details on how to carry out a specific survey.

- Find out what other people know about human rights:
  Are they aware of their rights if they are apprehended by the law?
  Are they aware of anti-discrimination legislation?
  Are they aware of [e.g.] a particular law currently under consideration?
  Are they aware of what recourse they may have if their rights are violated?
- Find out what they think is important:
  Which rights issues concern them most in their everyday lives?
  Where do they think there are the most serious violations?

Are they concerned by [e.g.] a particular issue or violation?
Have they ever acted on a particular concern?

- Find out whether people would be prepared to act on any of their concerns:
  Would they do anything to express their dissatisfaction with an issue?
  Would they be prepared to take part in a street action?
  Would they be prepared to sign a petition about …?
  Would they be prepared to write (or sign) a letter to a government official?

? Which issues concern you? Would you be prepared to do anything about these concerns?

Publicise the issues

Any publicity is good publicity

Activism works, in general, through the power of numbers. Politicians the world over have to take notice of large numbers - because no one individual is more powerful than a large enough mass of population. So the more people you can attract to your cause, the more likely are the chances of achieving a positive result.

However, people lead busy lives, and they will not always willingly give up time and energy to a cause that seems to have no connection with their immediate lives. So you may need, first of all, to *inform* and *interest* them; and to think of ways of doing so in an original and lively manner that will make them sit up and take notice. Make people laugh, make them stop and stare – and even try to shock them. You want to draw attention to yourselves!

- Design a poster, or a series of posters, to attract attention to a particular issue. Organise an exhibition and invite friends and family to come along.
- Build a web-site to publicise the work your group is doing in the area of human rights.
- Set up an Internet discussion group – and tell your friends about it. Try to get people involved from different countries.
- Make your own video or organise a theatrical production on a human rights theme (see the activity "Act it out", on page 86).
- Write a song, or a musical, or your own play, and perform it!
- Organise a public debate on a topical issue of human rights: invite friends to come along.
- Design an informational leaflet raising concerns about a human rights issue; hand them out on the street, or put them through letter boxes.
- Write an article for the local (or national) paper.
- Engage in human rights education yourself! Contact other youth groups or local schools and see if they would like you to talk about your work.

Action

Example: Try to get the press interested

? Will the event you are organising be of interest to other people? How can you make them want to read about it?

If you are planning an event, try to use the local papers and radio and TV to publicise your activities. It is always best to write down what you want to say, because this saves journalists time. It is more likely that they will use your item if it is on the desk in front of them than if they have to come to interview you. There is also a greater chance that it will be accurate.

Remember:

- Keep it short and simple, avoiding jargon and abbreviations.
- Write a short, punchy but summarising heading.
- The first paragraph should cover the basic details: who, what, when, where and why.
- In the second paragraph, explain what you are doing in more detail.
- Any additional or background information can go in the third paragraph.
- Make sure you put "for further information, contact..." at the end of the press release.
- Type it on one side of the paper only, using double spacing.

"For me, Human Rights Education is when I work with young gays and lesbians, talking about their life, about their feelings, about questions of normality."

Martin Krajcik, volunteer, participant at the Forum on Human Rights Education.

Join forces with another organisation

Do a survey of the NGOs working in your country (or region)

- You can normally find out about these by obtaining a list of the non-profit organisations registered with your local authority or with the relevant Government Ministry. Try a web-search or a trip to the local library. If you know of an organisation that is working in the area, they will often be able to point you towards others.
- Don't forget to find out which international NGOs are working in your country, or which take a particular interest in your country.
- Remember to look at organisations that may not necessarily call themselves 'human rights organisations'. Take a broad view of human rights, and include groups that may be working with the disabled, with low-income families, with victims of domestic violence, or on environmental issues.

See if you can arrange to go and talk to someone at the NGOs and find out about their work; or invite them to come and speak to your group.

- Make a chart of the different NGOs working in your region: record the rights that they are working on, the methods they use, their geographical scope and the number of employees and volunteers.

Organisation	*No. of employees (volunteers)*	*Types of rights*	*Methods*	*Area Covered*	*Volunteers required for...*
'Greenia'	5 (6)	Environmental	Campaigning, education	Local	Mass protests
Amnesty International	2 (12)	Civil and political	Lobbying, campaigning, letters	International	Writing letters
'Women are Right!'	10 (8)	Women's rights	Education, women's refuges	National	Distributing leaflets

Offer to volunteer for a local organisation

Many organisations will have a team of volunteers, and may be able to offer hands-on experience in return for some part-time voluntary assistance. Young people may be given the opportunity of working with professional activists in the field and gaining useful work experience, as well as insights into the work of the third sector.

However, you should remember that some organisations may be cautious about taking on new volunteers, at least in the beginning, where the time of regular staff may be required. So before approaching them, prospective volunteers should think hard about the following issues:

- Can you spare the time to give voluntary assistance?
- What commitment can you give to the work? Can you provide the organisation with any guarantee that you will be a reliable volunteer?
- Which skills do you have? What would you be able to offer an organisation such as this?
- What does the organisation do? Are you interested in the issues?
- What do you want to get out of it? Have you discussed this with the organisation?

Join a local human rights group, or set up your own

"Amnesty inspires us to play. The music cuts through to people, and the message is clear: you can write a letter or send a postcard. And the more you give, the more you get back."

Bono of U2

Amnesty International is a membership organisation, which relies on the work of thousands of volunteers throughout the world. Individuals in your group may be interested in joining, or you may want to consider setting up your own initiative group. You would receive some materials and support from the organisation, and in return would be expected to assist them in their campaigning and lobbying actions.

Contact the Amnesty Section in your country, if there is one, for more information. Or contact the International Secretariat at 1 Easton Street, London, WC1X , UK; or see their web-site: www.amnesty.org

The International Federation of Human Rights Leagues (FIDH) was the first international human rights organisation to be created (in 1922) and its purpose is to advance the implementation of all the rights defined by the Universal Declaration of Human Rights and the other international instruments protecting human rights. With more than 105 organisations from 86 countries, it is mostly a network of expertise and solidarity, producing credible reports on violations in many countries.

You may start by finding out if there is a human rights society in your country affiliated to the FIDH, and ask them for materials or for particular concerns about your country. At www.fidh.org you can get the addresses of the national societies and look at reports published.

Fund-raise for one of the NGOs

One way of providing assistance to a human rights organisation – which they probably won't turn down! - is to offer to raise money for their activities. Before organising any fund-raising activity, you should contact the NGO and make sure that they know what you are intending to do and how you are going to do it. Ask their advice. Some organisations have strict rules about fund-raising and may not accept finance that has been raised in certain ways.

Think about the capacities of your group and about the most effective way of raising money within your community. Brainstorm the possibilities, and discuss with members of the group what they would feel happiest about doing.

? Could you use these methods to raise money for your own group's activities?

- Running a sponsored event (run, swim, etc.)
- Making and selling your own products or artefacts
- Organising a disco or other cultural event for which people buy tickets
- A car-boot sale, jumble sale, f□te, summer fair, etc.
- Approaching people on an individual basis on behalf of a charity
- Organising a raffle
- Suggesting to a charity that you participate in one of their fund-raising events

Getting results!

> "Do not wait for leaders; do it alone, person to person."
>
> *Mother Teresa*

This section looks at a number of actions that have specific targets, and where, in general, immediate results are anticipated. They are mostly "one-off" actions and, for that reason, you will need to be particularly careful to plan them with the group. An action that does not achieve the specific results that were desired can be very dispiriting, so you need to make sure that each step has been thought through beforehand. Look at the section "Getting organised" in order to help you draw up an action plan.

It will often be sensible to combine your efforts with some form of publicity, since this will be likely to increase the impact.

Examples:

- Organise a street action – to draw attention to a human rights issue. People may be concerned about a specific new law, plans to build a factory in a conservation area, unethical business practices by a well-known company, particular infringements concerning a minority group, a local council decision to close down a public building – and so on. Think about the way you want to get your message across and who your target audience will be.
- Organise a "hearing". One way to bring about change is to make sure other people listen to what you say. At a hearing, influential local people such as councillors, business people, school governors and community leaders sit on a panel and answer questions from a panel of young people. Think about who you would like to invite to sit on the adults' panel, and write to ask them. Discuss who you want to be on the young persons' panel, and brainstorm a list of questions that you would like them to ask.
- Improve your local environment. Think about the type of environment you want, and discuss ways that you could contribute to this aim. Cleaning up communal areas, planting trees and flowers, clearing ditches and ponds are obvious places to start, and you can achieve satisfying results with minimal resources. But you may have more ambitious aims: think about including other members of the community in your project, or putting your proposals to the local council.
- Offer assistance to groups or members of the population in need – this may be help for the elderly, for disabled groups, low-income groups, minority groups, etc. You may want to raise money for a specific purpose, to assist them with clothing or provisions; to help them raise the profile of the group; to help with lobbying the government for their interests; or simply to offer them companionship and moral support.
- Write a letter - to government officials, your MP, the Head of State, the business community, the press, or other interested parties, expressing your position on a human rights issue. This is a favourite campaigning technique of Amnesty International, and is an effective way of letting those responsible know that there is public concern about an issue.
  - Make sure you find out how to address the person properly.
  - Start with a statement of your key message.
  - Explain who you are, and who you are representing.
  - Indicate how your addressee is accountable.
  - Make a maximum of three points, and support each one with a clear argument.
  - Repeat your message at the end of the letter.
  - Indicate what action you would like your addressee to take.

> "Happiness depends on being free, and freedom depends on being courageous."
>
> *Thucydides*

Devising a plan of action

> "Chi Wen Tze always thought three times before acting. Twice would have been enough."
>
> *Confucius*

In general, good activism requires good planning. That doesn't mean you *have* to start by drawing up a general plan - as long as you are clear about your aims, you could try any of the suggestions in this chapter, with relatively little preparation. However, a planning session in the group will help you to focus on exactly what you want and are able to do, and what is the best way of achieving your results. For more ambitious aims, this is probably an advisable first move, since an action that doesn't achieve its desired results can be discouraging. You need to make the first thing you do *effective*.

Try working through the four stages below within your group:

1. Find out where you stand: do a SWOT analysis for your group.
2. Decide on the problem you want to address, and the results you want to achieve.
3. Think of the best way you can to address it, given the resources in your group.
4. ACT!

Where do you stand?

> "Real knowledge is to know the extent of our ignorance."
>
> *Confucius*

A SWOT analysis is an effective way of drawing out the characteristics of your group, and of looking at the particular circumstances outside the group which might influence what you are able to do.

A SWOT analysis (example)

What are the *strengths* of our group?

- It's big!
- We have time on our hands – and we're keen to do something
- Misha's father is a politician
- We have a meeting place in the centre of town
- Gabriela is good at public speaking
- Bojka has a computer

What are the *weaknesses* of our group?

- Too many leaders!
- We haven't got any money
- Very few girls
- We've never done anything like this before
- Some of us live a long way from the centre of town
- We don't always work well as a group

What *opportunities* exist outside the group?

- There's been a lot in the news about human rights
- There are elections coming up
- There are some grants available for projects with refugees
- There's an Amnesty International group in the neighbouring town
- We have a new town hall that would be good for a theatrical event

What external *threats* exist to our activities?

- The economic situation is precarious
- Some of us have exams coming up
- The council is threatening to ban public meetings
- There's a lot of hard feeling about refugees taking local jobs
- It's too cold to do anything outside

The acronym SWOT stands for:

***S**trengths:* the things your group is good at doing

***W**eaknesses:* the things your group is not so good at doing

***O**pportunities:* the possibilities outside the group that you might use to your advantage

***T**hreats:* things outside the group that might get in the way of what you are trying to do

Divide the group into four smaller working groups, and allocate the tasks of drawing up Strengths, Weaknesses, Opportunities and Threats among them. Then bring the group back together and see if people agree with their colleagues' analyses.

The diagram above is one example of a completed analysis, and may be useful in prompting you with ideas. But don't stick to it rigidly! Your group is unique, and you will have other strengths (and weaknesses) that you need to identify for yourselves.

"How wonderful it is that nobody need to wait a single moment before starting to improve the world."

Anne Frank

Where do you want to get to?

Which issue do you want to address? Are there any obvious and pressing injustices that you want to take on or is this going to be a general protest against human rights violations?

Brainstorming Issues

If the group has already worked through some of the exercises in this manual, they may already have a number of ideas. If you are just starting work, you may want to prompt them with some of the following suggestions (or others of your own). Try to give them some information about each of the issues, and then ask them to go away and do their own research before you meet again to decide on priorities.

A sample problem list:

- The death penalty in my country
- AIDS on the African continent
- An ageing nuclear power station
- Negative attitudes towards refugees
- Child labour
- Freedom of the press in another country / my country
- The rights of minorities to education in their own language
- Domestic violence

? Which groups in your society suffer the most serious violations of human rights?

If the group is ready, and you have already looked at some of the issues in detail, you could begin by drawing up a list of their concerns in a general brainstorming session. Which issues do people feel strongly about?

See if you can narrow the list down to about 3 or 4 issues – perhaps those that are most keenly felt, and which are realistic for the group to tackle. You will need to talk through the different choices, but could make the final decision by taking a vote, if the group finds it hard to reach agreement. Give them 3 votes each, which they can use as they wish: they can vote for one issue 3 times; for three issues, giving one vote to each; or for two issues. Then add up which of the issues received the most votes.

"The clever man is not he who provides the right answers; it is he who poses the right questions."

Claude Lévi-Strauss

> "Trees and stones will teach you that which you can never learn from masters."
>
> *St Bernard of Clairvaux (c. 1100)*

Refining your objectives

It may be helpful at this stage to draw up a 'problem tree' for the issue you have decided to address. This can help to focus attention on the roots of your problem, and can help you to understand all the components that are contributing to a specific issue. You may then decide that it would be more effective to look at one of the 'root' problems, rather than approaching your original problem directly.

- Start by writing down the problem that you wish to tackle in the middle of a large sheet of paper.
- Underneath this, write in all the factors that contribute to the problem, and link them up to form the roots of your original problem.
- Take each root at a time and think about its causes, drawing in the factors that contribute to the problem.
- Keep tackling each root until you can take the exercise no further: the tree may have deeper roots than you think.
- You may also want to extend the 'branches' of the tree in the same manner: these will be the *symptoms* of your original problem. You may find that what you began with as your main concern is actually the root or branch of a different tree.
- When you have finished, take a look at your tree. Should you tackle the task you originally set yourself or one of its contributing factors first? Has the tree helped you to think of ways to go about tackling this problem?

How do we get there?

Designing a strategy

Once you have a clear picture of the possibilities of your group and have decided on the problem area that you would like to tackle, you will be ready to move on to think about the best means of approaching your problem.

You need to think about :

1. the specific problem you are going to address: *what was the outcome of the Problem Tree exercise?*
2. your target audience: *who are you trying to influence?*
3. which changes you would like to come about within your target group: *think about what you want them to do or think as a result of your action.*
4. how these changes are supposed to come about: *think about the type of thing that is likely to influence your target group.*
5. what methods you can use to effect these changes: *think about the different forms of action outlined in Part 1, plus any other ideas of your own. Which is the most appropriate method to use in the circumstances?*

Work through the different stages of the plan on page 280 (Diagram 2), discussing each stage in the group as a whole. You need to have agreement in the group over each component of your plan: if some members are unhappy about the enterprise, you are likely to be losing some valuable resources in your group.

> "The goal is not always set in order to be achieved, but in order to serve as a point at which to aim."
>
> *Joseph Joubert*

Getting organised

Finally, before the practical business can get underway, you will need to draw up an action plan

to decide the organisational questions. If you fail to do this, you may find that some of the important tasks were not done, and that can have a serious impact on the aims you have so carefully worked through.

You need to decide:

- What tasks need to be done?
- Who is going to undertake the different task(s)?
- When are they going to be done?

1. You should write everything down to keep a check on how your plans are going. You will need two large sheets of paper and a felt tip pen.
2. Make sure everyone is clear what the topic is that you are discussing. Choose one person to be the scribe. Write a heading at the top of the paper. Brainstorm a list *of all* the jobs that need to be done and write them on one of the large pieces of paper so that everyone can see.
3. If you are organising an event, think it through, imagine what is going to happen on the day and double-check that you have thought of all the jobs.
4. Now go through the list deciding whether jobs need to be done now, soon or later. Put either N, S, or L by each job.
5. Use the second sheet of paper as a "decision sheet". List all the tasks to be done in order down the left-hand side, then in the next column write down who is going to do each one. Finally, in the third column note the deadlines for getting the jobs done.
6. Share out the jobs among you: do not leave it all to one or two people. Think what would happen if they were ill or got overloaded with other work!

Here is an example of what a decision sheet might look like.

"He is able who thinks he is able."

Buddha

Decision sheet

Event: Street action on minority rights		
Task	**Who does it**	**When**
Design leaflets to hand out	Sally, John, Natalie, Ben	Meetings on Sept 10th, 17th
Organise publishing	Rumen, Ben	After 20th Sept
Make banners / placards	All	Week beginning 24th Sept
Buy materials for banners, etc.	Shila, Karen, Ivan	Week beginning 17th
Get other people interested	Shila, Moca, Tania	Week beginning 17th
Contact local council	Damien, Sue	When date is confirmed
Tell police	Damien, Sue	
Try to get influential local figure to attend		
Inform minority groups		
Draft speeches		
Organise refreshments		
Clearing up afterwards		

Diagram 2

PLANNING A PROGRAMME

Which *problem* do you want to address?

- that people do not demand their rights
- that torture exists
- that x is a prisoner of conscience in …
- that y holds illegitimate power
- that an ethnic minority is suffering discrimination
- that the government is trading weapons of mass destruction

What is your *target audience*?

- young people
- residents of our local community
- mothers
- politicians
- the business community
- the international community

Which *changes* do you hope to see?

- a change of consciousness in the target group
- a change in public opinion
- newly acquired skills
- more active involvement by other actors
- press coverage
- new legislation
- institution of ombudsman
- the righting of an injustice
- debate of the issue

***How* is change expected to come about?**

- argument / persuasion
- shocking people into action; frightening them
- through legal channels
- elections / referenda
- increased alertness
- a feeling of empowerment among the target group
- information about particular cases
- public pressure; lobbying
- international pressure

What *means* will you use to influence your audience?

- message to the press
- on the internet
- campaigns; public rallies
- mail-shots, leaflets, posters
- advertisements or infomercials
- articles, statistics
- a street demonstration
- training courses; debate programmes; seminars/ workshops
- letters to the government

Chapter 4

Background Information on Human Rights

Table of contents of this chapter

Understanding Human Rights

What are human rights?

A riddle

Human rights are like armour: they protect you; they are like rules, because they tell you how you can behave; and they are like judges, because you can appeal to them. They are abstract – like emotions; and like emotions, they belong to everyone and they exist no matter what happens.

They are like nature because they can be violated; and like the spirit because they cannot be destroyed. Like time, they treat us all in the same way - rich and poor, old and young, white and black, tall and short. They offer us respect, and they charge us to treat others with respect. Like goodness, truth and justice, we disagree about their definition, but we recognise them when we see them.

Can you define human rights? How do you explain what they are?

Where do human rights come from?

A right is a claim that we are justified in making. I have a right to the goods in my shopping basket if I have paid for them. Citizens have a right to elect a president, if the constitution of their country guarantees it, and a child has a right to be taken to the zoo, if her parents have promised that they will take her. These are all things that people can be entitled to expect, given the promises or guarantees that have been undertaken by another party.

"Human rights are what no one can take away from you."

René Cassin

But human rights are claims with a slight difference, in that they depend on no promises or guarantees by another party. Someone's right to life is not dependent on someone else promising not to kill him or her: their *life* may be, but their *right to life* is not. Their right to life is dependent on only one thing: that they are human.

An acceptance of human rights means accepting that everyone is entitled to make the claim: *I have these rights, no matter what you say or do, because I am a human being, just like you.* Human rights are inherent to all human beings.

Why should that claim not need anything to back it up? What does it rest on? And why should we believe it?

The claim is ultimately a moral claim, and rests on moral values. What my right to life really means is that *no one ought to take my life away from me; it would be wrong to do so.* Put like that, the claim needs little backing up. Every reader is probably in agreement with it because we all recognise, in our own cases, that there are certain aspects of our life, our being, that ought to be inviolable, and that no one else ought to be able to touch, because they are essential to our being, who we are and what we are; they are essential to our humanity and our human dignity. Human rights simply extend this understanding on an individual level to every human being on the planet. If I can make these claims, then so can everyone else as well.

Why is it wrong to infringe someone else's right to life? Why is it wrong to take their life away? Are these the same questions?

"What man wants is simply independent choice, whatever that independence may cost and wherever it may lead."

Fyodor Dostoevsky

Key values

There are thus two key values that lie at the core of the idea of human rights. The first is human *dignity* and the second is *equality*. Human rights can be understood as defining those basic standards which are necessary for a life of dignity; and their *universality* is derived from the fact that in this respect, at least, all humans are equal. We should not, and cannot, discriminate between them.

These two beliefs, or values, are really all that is required to subscribe to the idea of human rights, and these beliefs are hardly controversial. That is why the idea receives support from every different culture in the world, every civilised government and every major religion. It is recognised almost universally that state power cannot be unlimited or arbitrary; it needs to be limited at least to the extent that all individuals within its jurisdiction can live with certain minimum requirements for human dignity.

Many other values can be derived from these two fundamental ones and can help to define more precisely how in practice people and societies should co-exist. For example:

Freedom: because the human will is an important part of human dignity. To be forced to do something against our will demeans the human spirit.

Respect for others: because a lack of respect for someone fails to appreciate their individuality and essential dignity.

Non-discrimination: because equality in human dignity means we should not judge people on the basis of non-relevant physical (or other) characteristics.

Tolerance: because intolerance indicates a lack of respect for difference; and equality does not signify *identity or uniformity.*

Justice: because people equal in their humanity deserve fair treatment.

Responsibility: because respecting the rights of others entails responsibility for one's actions.

Characteristics of human rights

Philosophers may continue to argue about the nature of human rights, but the international community has established a set of key principles that states have agreed to and have to abide by. According to these principles:

1. **Human rights are inalienable**. This means that you can not lose them, because they are linked to the very fact of human existence. In particular circumstances some – though not all - may be suspended or restricted. For example, if a someone is found guilty of a crime, his or her liberty can be taken away; or in times of civil unrest, a government may impose a curfew restricting freedom of movement.
2. **They are indivisible, interdependent and interrelated**. This means that different human rights are intrinsically connected and cannot be viewed in isolation from each other. The enjoyment of one right depends on the enjoyment of many other rights and no one right is more important than the rest.
3. **They are universal**, which means that they apply equally to all people everywhere in the world, and with no time limit. Every individual is entitled to enjoy his or her human rights without distinction of race, colour, sex, language, religion, political or other opinion, national or social origin, birth or other status.

"Values are invisible like the wind. From the flutter of leaves you know there is wind. And you realize values through the actions of people."

Éva Ancsel

We should note that the *universality* of human rights does not in any way threaten the rich diversity of individuals or of different cultures. Diversity can still exist in a world where everyone is equal, and equally deserving of respect.

A historical outline

> "By three things is the world sustained: by truth, by judgement and by peace."
>
> *The Talmud*

The idea that people have inherent rights has its roots in many cultures and ancient traditions. We can see from numerous examples of revered leaders and influential codes of practice that the values embodied in human rights are neither a 'Western invention' nor a twentieth-century invention.

Ancient History

- The Code of Hammurabi in Babylonia (Iraq, c 2000 B.C.) was the first written legal code, established by the king of Babylon. It vowed to 'make justice reign in the kingdom, to destroy the wicked and violent, to prevent the strong from oppressing the weak, ... to enlighten the country and promote the good of the people'
- A Pharaoh of Ancient Egypt (c 2000 BC) was quoted as giving instructions to subordinates that 'When a petitioner arrives from Upper or Lower Egypt, ... make sure that all is done according to the law, that custom is observed and the right of each man respected.'
- The Charter of Cyrus (Iran, c 570 BC) was drawn up by the king of Persia for the people of his kingdom, and recognised rights to liberty, security, freedom of movement and some social and economic rights.

Which figures in your country's history have championed or fought for human rights values?

The English Magna Carta and Bill of Rights

In 1215, English nobles and members of the clergy rallied against King John I's abuse of power, and made the King agree to abide by the law by drawing up a Great Charter of liberties (Magna Carta). Although the King did not respect it, the Magna Carta became a widely cited document in defence of liberties. It enumerates a series of rights, such as the right of all free citizens to own and inherit property and to be free from excessive taxes. It establishes principles of due process and equality before the law. Following King James II's abuse of the law, his subjects overthrew him in 1688. In 1689, Parliament passed a bill declaring that it would no longer tolerate royal interference in its affairs. This bill, known as the Bill of Rights, forbade the monarch to suspend the law without Parliament's consent, specified free elections for members of Parliament and declared that freedom of speech in Parliament was not to be questioned, in the courts or elsewhere.

The birth of natural rights

During the seventeenth and eighteenth centuries in Europe, a number of philosophers proposed the concept of "natural rights". These were rights that belonged to a person because he or she was a human being, rather than because, for example, a citizen of a particular country or a member of a particular religion or ethnic group. The idea that these natural rights should entitle people to certain legal rights became more widely accepted and began to be reflected in the constitutions of some countries.

> "Man being... by nature all free, equal and independent, no one can be ... subjected to the political power of another, without his consent."
>
> *John Locke*

The French Declaration on the Rights of Man and the Citizen (1789)

In 1789, the French overthrew their monarchy and established the first French Republic. The Declaration came out of the revolution and was written by representatives of the clergy, nobility

"Thou shalt not kill."

The Bible

and commoners, who wrote it to embody the thoughts of Enlightenment figures such as Voltaire, Montesquieu, the Encyclopedists and Rousseau. The Declaration attacked the political and legal system of the monarchy and defined the natural rights of man as "liberty, property, security and the right to resist oppression". It replaced the system of aristocratic privileges that had existed under the monarchy with the principle of equality before the law.

The United States Declaration of Independence, Constitution and Bill of Rights (1791)

In 1776, most of the British colonies in North America proclaimed their independence from the British Empire in the United States Declaration of Independence. This was largely based on the "natural right" theories of Locke and Montesquieu, and inspired the French revolution and rebellions against Spanish rule in South America. Later on, the United States Constitution was amended, and the government was centralised but with powers limited enough to guarantee individual liberty. Twenty amendments to the constitution form the American Bill of Rights.

Early international agreements

In the nineteenth and twentieth centuries, a number of human rights issues came to the fore and began to be questioned at an international level, beginning with such issues as slavery, serfdom, brutal working conditions and child labour. It was at around this time that the first international treaties concerning human rights were adopted.

- Slavery became illegal in England and France around the turn of the nineteenth century and, in 1814, the British and French governments signed the Treaty of Paris, with the aim of co-operating in suppressing the traffic in slaves. At the Brussels Conference of 1890, an anti-slavery Act was signed, which was later ratified by eighteen states.
- The first Geneva Conventions (1864 and 1929) marked another field of early co-operation among nations in setting out the elaboration of the rules of war. In particular, the Conventions laid down standards for caring for sick and wounded soldiers.

Why do you think that the need for *international* agreements arose, rather than individual countries simply drawing up their own standards?

The twentieth century

The idea of protecting the rights of human beings against the governing powers began to receive ever wider acceptance. The importance of codifying these rights in written form had already been recognised by some individual states and, in this way, the documents described above became the precursors to many of today's human rights treaties. However, it was the events of World War II that really propelled human rights onto the international stage.

The International League of Nations was an intergovernmental organisation created after the First World War, which tried to protect basic human rights standards but it was only after the terrible atrocities committed in the Second World War, and largely as a result of them, that a body of international law emerged. These events made it both possible and necessary for an international consensus to emerge on the need for international regulation to protect and codify human rights.

"And fight in the way of God with those who fight with you, but aggress not: God loves not the aggressors."

The Koran

The Charter of the United Nations, signed on 26 June 1945, reflected this belief. The Charter states that the fundamental objective of the United Nations is "to save succeeding generations from the scourge of war" and "to reaffirm faith in fundamental human rights, in the dignity and worth of the human person and in the equal rights of men and women".

The Universal Declaration of Human Rights (UDHR) was drawn up by the Commission on Human Rights, one of the organs of the United Nations, and was adopted by the General Assembly on the 10 December 1948. Since then, a series of key instruments to safeguard its principles have also been drawn up and agreed by the international community. More information on some of these international treaties can be found below in this chapter, including information on the European Convention for Human Rights and Fundamental Freedoms.

"Wars will continue to be waged for as long as mankind fails to notice that human nature is identical, no matter where on earth we find ourselves."

Pierre Daco, psychologist.

Human rights around the world

Several regions of the world have established their own systems for protecting human rights, which exist alongside that of the UN. To date, there are regional institutions in Europe, the Americas, Africa and the Arab states, but not yet in the Asia-Pacific region. However, most countries in this part of the world have also ratified the major UN treaties and conventions – thereby signifying their agreement with the general principles, and expressing themselves subject to international human rights law.

The African Charter on Human and Peoples' Rights came into force in October 1985 and has been ratified by more than 40 states. The Charter is interesting for a number of differences in emphasis between the treaties that have been adopted in other parts of the world:

- Unlike the European or American Conventions, the African Charter covers social, economic and cultural rights as well as civil and political rights.
- The African Charter goes beyond individual rights, and also provides for *collective* rights of peoples.
- The Charter also recognises that individuals have duties as well as rights, and even lists specific duties that the individual has towards his or her family, society, the State and the international community.

Why do you think that duties are listed in a charter on human rights? Do you think they should be listed in all human rights documents?

In the Arab world, there currently exists a regional Commission on Human Rights, with only limited powers. However, they have also approved an Arab Charter on Human Rights that will establish a regional system. This document, like the African Charter, includes social-economic rights as well as civil-political rights, and also a list of 'Collective Rights of the Arab People'.

There have been calls for such a system to be set up in the Asian-Pacific region, but no formal agreements have yet been adopted. A meeting of NGOs in the region in 1993 resulted in the Bangkok NGO Declaration on Human Rights, which stated:

"We can learn from different cultures from a pluralistic perspective. ... Universal human rights are rooted in many cultures. We affirm the basis of universality of human rights which afford protection to all of humanity. ... While advocating cultural pluralism, those cultural practices which derogate from universally accepted human rights, including women's rights, must not be tolerated. As human rights are of universal concern and are universal in value, the advocacy of human rights cannot be considered to be an encroachment upon national sovereignty".

"While the significance of national and regional particularities and various historical, cultural and religious backgrounds must be borne in mind, it is the duty of States, regardless of their political, economic and cultural systems, to promote and protect all human rights and fundamental freedoms".

The Vienna Declaration (1993)

"We are all, and me especially, responsible for everything and for everyone."

Fyodor Dostoevsky

How can we use our rights?

Human rights exist for *us*. So how can we make use of them? It is clear that their mere existence is not enough to put an end to human rights violations, since we all know that these are committed every day, in every part of the globe. So can they really make a difference? *How can we use them?*

Do you know which rights you have?

A number of sections in this manual look at various aspects of this problem.

Recognising your rights

In the next section we look at the different types of rights that are protected under international law. If we know which areas of human existence are relevant to human rights law and we are aware of the obligations of governments under this body of law, then we can begin to apply pressure in different ways. That section illustrates that almost *every* area of injustice is relevant to human rights: from small-scale poverty, through environmental damage, health, working conditions, political repression, voting rights, genetic engineering, minority issues, terrorism, genocide ... and beyond. And the number of issues is increasing even today.

Some of the issues concerning the application of human rights legislation are addressed directly in the section "Questions and Answers". These provide brief responses to some of the more common questions often asked about human rights.

In addition, every section of Chapter 5 deals in more detail with the manual's themes. If you are concerned to find out how a particular issue - for example, the right to health, to education, or fair working conditions - can be better protected, you will find it helpful to look at the background information relevant to that issue.

Using legal mechanisms

We shall look at the legal mechanisms that exist for protecting the different areas of people's interests. In Europe, we are particularly fortunate, at least as far as some rights are concerned, in having a permanent court to deal with complaints about violations – the European Court of Human Rights. Even where complaints do not fall under the jurisdiction of the European Court, we shall see that there are other mechanisms of holding states accountable for their actions and forcing them to comply with their obligations under human rights law. It helps that the law is there, even if there are not always legal means of enforcing compliance by states.

Lobbying, campaigning and activism

Have you ever been involved in any campaigning or human rights activism?

One important role in exerting pressure on states is played by associations, non-governmental organisations, charities, and other civic initiative groups. This forms the subject matter of the section on activism and the role of NGO's. The role of such associations is particularly relevant to the man – and woman – on the street, not only because such associations frequently take up individual cases, but also because they provide a means for the ordinary person to become involved in the protection of human rights. After all, such associations are made up of ordinary people! We shall also look at how they act to improve human rights and at some examples of successful action.

"I regard the death penalty as a savage and immoral institution that undermines the moral and legal foundations of a society. I am convinced ... that savagery begets only savagery."

Andrei Sakharov

Becoming involved

Chapter 3, Taking Action, brings these types of actions down to an everyday level, and offers a number of examples of action in which *you* could become involved. Youth groups have enormous potential for putting pressure on states or international bodies and ensuring that cases of human rights violation are brought to the public eye. The examples in this section should provide you with concrete measures that could be undertaken by your group and will also give a greater insight into the way that non-governmental organisations work at an everyday level.

"Every soul is a hostage to its own actions."

The Koran

Dilemmas and misuses of human rights

What should we do when protecting the rights of one group of people involves restricting those of others? Sometimes human rights are used as an excuse to carry out actions that are themselves of questionable morality. People, even governments, may claim to be acting to protect human rights, but in fact the actions they employ themselves violate fundamental rights.

It is not always easy to judge such cases. Consider the following examples.

Conflicts of rights

In the wake of the terrorist attacks of September 11th 2001 in the United States of America, many governments are restricting certain basic liberties in order to combat the threat of terrorism. In the UK, there is a new law withdrawing from Article 5 of the European Convention on Human Rights, the article that protects people from arbitrary detention and imprisonment. This makes it possible for the government to lock people up without any charge or trial, on the basis of mere suspicion.

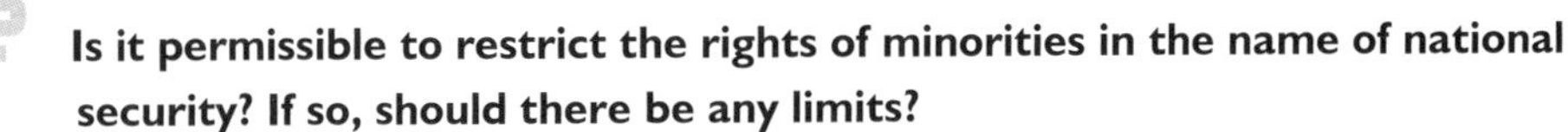

Is it permissible to restrict the rights of minorities in the name of national security? If so, should there be any limits?

The United States Supreme Court has declared that demonstrations by nazi groups in Jewish suburbs are legal forms of freedom of expression. Should such groups in fact be prevented from promoting a doctrine that would lead to the destruction of a whole people? Or is that an unacceptable restriction of the right to freedom of expression?

Cultural traditions

Arranged marriages are common practice in many cultures, where a girl is obliged to marry a man who has been chosen by her family, often at a very young age. Should such a practice be banned in order to protect the young girls? Or would that be failing to respect a different cultural tradition?

Other examples can be found in the continued practice of female circumcision in many countries, or the "honour killings" of girls and women. Thousands of people suffer the consequences of such practices and most people would certainly regard them as a serious violation of rights. Is the acceptance of female circumcision an inter-cultural difference that should be 'tolerated'?

Should cultural values ever be able to 'override' the universality of human rights?

"Every time justice dies, it is as if it had never existed."

José Saramago

In the name of a good cause

In 1995, a UN Food and Agriculture Organisation compared 1995 child and infant mortality levels in Baghdad to 1989 levels. On the basis of the data they collected, two team members published a letter, which concluded that some 567,000 Iraqi children had died as a result of the sanctions to that date. In April, 1998 Unicef claimed that some 90,000 children were dying annually as a result of the sanctions

Sanctions are sometimes used by the international community to penalise regimes that are considered to be systematically violating human rights. Sanctions forbid trade with the violator country, in order to put pressure on the government to modify their actions. Some countries have been completely isolated by the international community: South Africa was isolated for years because of its system of apartheid, and today Cuba and Iraq are unable to trade with most of the world. There is no doubt that the effects of such sanctions are felt by normal people, but they are felt particularly by the most vulnerable sectors of society. *Is this an acceptable means of putting an end to human rights violations by another government?*

Although not officially sanctioned by the UN, the Nato-led bombings in Kosovo were justified by many in terms of protecting the ethnic Albanians and bringing a perpetrator of genocide to justice. The military action led to the exodus of hundreds of thousands of refugees, to an estimated 500 directly caused civilian casualties and to the devastation of Serbian infrastructure. It also led to the capture of President Milosevic and his trial before an international tribunal. Similar action has been undertaken in Afghanistan in order to destroy the terrorist network thought to be responsible for the 11th September 2001 events. Can such actions be justified in terms of their end results if they cause large numbers of casualties?

Can the defence of human rights be used to justify a military campaign?

In April 2001, a resolution of the United Nations Commission on Human Rights rejected the notion that fighting terrorism could ever justify sacrificing human rights protections. Resolution 2001/24 condemned terrorist attacks related to the Chechnya conflict and breaches of humanitarian law perpetrated by Chechen forces, as well as certain methods often used by Russian federal forces in Chechnya. It called for a national commission of inquiry into Russian abuses.

More riddles

The questions raised in the previous section do not all have clear-cut answers: they remain the subject of fierce debate, even today. Such debates are, to a certain extent, important. They are an indication both of the pluralistic approach that is fundamental to the notion of human rights and of the fact that human rights are not a science, not a fixed 'ideology', but are a developing area of moral and legal thought. We should not always expect black and white answers – partly because the issues are complex, but also because there are no experts on the subject who are qualified to have the final word and settle all arguments.

However, that does not mean that there are no answers and no areas of agreement. There are many, and they increase almost daily. The issue of slavery is one which used to be debated, but where tolerance is no longer regarded as acceptable: the right to be free from slavery is now universally accepted as a fundamental human right. Female circumcision, although defended under some cultures, is broadly condemned as a violation of human rights. And the death penalty is, arguably, becoming such an issue – at least in Europe, where members of the Council of Europe are required to move towards abolition.

So we should be confident that many of these questions will also reach their resolution. In the meantime, we can help the debate and make our own judgements on the more controversial issues by referring back to the two fundamental values: equality and human dignity. *If any action treats any individual as lacking in human dignity, then it violates the spirit of human rights.*

References

Europe, Youth, Human Rights, *Report of the* Human Rights Week, *by Yael Ohana (ed.), European Youth Centre, Budapest, 2000.*

Garzón Valdés, E., "Confusiones acerca de la relevancia moral de la diversidad cultural", CLAVES de Razón Práctica, *No.74, Madrid, Julio/Agosto, 1997.*

Human Rights, a basic handbook for UN staff, *Office of the High Commission of Human Rights, United Nations, Geneva.*

Levin, L., Human Rights, Questions and Answers, *Unesco, Paris, 1996.*

The evolution of human rights

Promises, promises

Our leaders have made a huge number of commitments on our behalf! If every guarantee that they had signed up to were to be met, our lives would be peaceful, secure, healthy and comfortable; our legal systems would be fair and would offer everyone the same protection; and our political processes would be transparent and democratic and would serve the interests of the people.

So what is going wrong? One of the small things that is going wrong is that politicians are like the rest of us and will often take short cuts if they can get away with it! So we need to know exactly what promises have been made on our behalf and to start making sure that they are kept.

"All rights are universal, indivisible and interdependent and interrelated."

Vienna Declaration

Do you always do what you have said you will do? Even if no-one reminds you?

Which rights do we possess?

We know that we are entitled to have all human rights respected. The UDHR, the ECHR and other international treaties cover a wide range of different rights, so we shall look at them in the order in which they were developed and were recognised by the international community. The 'normal' way of classifying these rights is into 'first, second and third generation' rights, so we shall follow this for the time being but, as we shall see, such a classification has limited use and can even be misleading at times.

First generation rights (civil and political rights)

These rights began to emerge as a theory during the seventeenth and eighteenth centuries and were based mostly on political concerns. It had begun to be recognised that there were certain things that the all-powerful state should not be able to do and that people should have some influence over the policies that affected them.

The two central ideas were those of **personal liberty**, and of **protecting the individual against violations by the state**.

- **Civil** rights provide minimal guarantees of physical and moral integrity and allow individuals their own sphere of conscience and belief: for example, the rights to equality and liberty, freedom to practise religion or to express one's opinion, and the rights not be tortured or killed.
- **Legal** rights are normally also classified as 'civil' rights. They provide procedural protection for people in dealing with the legal and political system: for example protection against arbitrary arrest and detention, the right to be presumed innocent until found guilty in a court of law and the right to appeal.
- **Political** rights are necessary in order to participate in the life of the community and society: for example, the right to vote, to join political parties, to assemble freely and attend meetings, to express one's opinion and to have access to information.

"Being imprisoned is not the problem. The problem is to avoid surrender."

Nazim Hikmet

> "The shocking reality... is that states and the international community as a whole continue to tolerate all too often breaches of economic, social and cultural rights which, if they occurred in relation to civil and political rights, would provoke expressions of horror and outrage and would lead to concerted calls for immediate remedial action."
>
> *Statement to the Vienna Conference by the UN Committee on Economic, Social and Cultural Rights.*

The categories are not clear-cut, but are simply one way – among many – of classifying the different rights. Most rights fall under more than one category. The right to express one's opinion, for example, is both a civil and a political right. It is essential to participation in political life as well as being fundamental to our personal liberty.

Are all political rights also civil rights?

The civil and political rights today are set out in detail in the International Covenant on Civil and Political Rights (ICCPR) and in the European Convention for the Protection of Human Rights and Fundamental Freedoms (ECHR). These rights have traditionally been regarded by many – at least in the 'West' – as the most important, if not the only real human rights. We shall see in the next section that this is a false view.

During the Cold War, the countries of the Soviet block were severely criticised for their disregard of civil and political rights. These countries responded by criticising the western democracies, in turn, for ignoring key social and economic rights, which we shall look at next. There was at least an element of truth in both criticisms.

Second generation rights (social, economic and cultural rights)

These rights concern how people live and work together and the basic necessities of life. They are based on the ideas of **equality** and **guaranteed access to essential social and economic goods, services, and opportunities**. They became increasingly a subject of international recognition with the effects of early industrialisation and the rise of a working class. These led to new demands and new ideas about the meaning of a life of dignity. People realised that human dignity required more than the minimal lack of interference proposed by the civil and political rights.

- **Social rights** are those that are necessary for full participation in the life of society. They include, at least, the right to education and the right to found and maintain a family but also many of the rights often regarded as 'civil' rights: for example, the rights to recreation, health care and privacy and freedom from discrimination.
- **Economic rights** are normally thought to include the right to work, to an adequate standard of living, to housing and the right to a pension if you are old or disabled. The economic rights reflect the fact that a certain minimal level of material security is necessary for human dignity, and also the fact that, for example, a lack of meaningful employment or housing can be psychologically demeaning.
- **Cultural Rights** refer to a community's cultural "way of life" and are often given less attention than many of the other types of rights. They include the right freely to participate in the cultural life of the community and, possibly, also the right to education. However, many other rights, not officially classed as 'cultural' will be essential for minority communities within a society to preserve their distinctive culture: for example, the right to non-discrimination and equal protection of the laws.

Are different cultural groups in your society restricted in their rights? Which religious holidays are given national significance?

> "The right to development is an inalienable human right by virtue of which every human person and all peoples are entitled to participate in, contribute to, and enjoy economic, social, cultural and political development, in which all human rights and fundamental freedoms can be fully realised."
>
> *Article 1, UN Declaration on the Right to Development*

The social, economic and cultural rights are outlined in the International Covenant on Economic, Social and Cultural Rights (ICESCR) and also in the European Social Charter.

Are some rights more important than others?

> "Human rights start with breakfast."
>
> *Léopold Senghor*

Social and economic rights have had a difficult time being accepted on an equal level with civil and political rights, for reasons which are both ideological and political. Although it seems evident to the ordinary citizen that such things as a minimum standard of living, housing, and reasonable conditions of employment are all essential to human dignity, politicians have not been so ready to acknowledge this. One reason is undoubtedly that ensuring basic social and economic rights for everyone worldwide would require a massive redistribution of resources. Politicians are well aware that that is not the type of policy that wins votes.

Accordingly, they offer a number of justifications for why the second generation rights are of a different order. The first claim often made is that social and economic rights are neither realistic or realisable, at least in the short term, and that we should move towards them only gradually. This is the approach that has been taken in the ICESCR: governments only need to show that they are taking measures towards meeting these aims at some point in the future. The claim, however, is certainly open to dispute and appears to be based more on political considerations than anything else. Many independent studies show that there are sufficient resources in the world, and sufficient expertise, to ensure that everyone's basic needs could be met if a concerted effort was made.

A second claim is that there is a fundamental theoretical difference between first and second generation rights: that the first type of rights require governments only to refrain from certain activities (these are so-called "negative" rights); while the second require positive intervention from governments (these are "positive" rights). The argument goes that it is not realistic to expect governments to take positive steps, at least in the short term, and that they are therefore not obliged to do so. Without any obligation on anyone's part, there can be no right in any meaningful sense of the word.

However, there are two basic misunderstandings in this line of reasoning.

Firstly, civil and political rights are by no means purely negative. In order, for example, for a government to guarantee freedom from torture, it is not enough just for government officials to refrain from torturing people! Genuine freedom in this area would require a complicated system of checks and controls to be put in place: policing systems, legal mechanisms, freedom of information and access to places of detention – and more besides. The same goes for securing the right to vote and for all other civil and political rights. In other words, these rights require positive action by the government in addition to refraining from negative action.

? What positive action does a government need to authorise in order to ensure genuinely free and fair elections?

Secondly, social and economic rights, just like civil and political rights, also require that governments *refrain* from certain activities: for example, from giving large tax breaks to companies, or encouraging development in regions that already possess a relative advantage, or imposing trade tariffs which penalise developing countries – and so on.

In actual fact, the different types of rights are far more closely connected with each other than their labels suggest. Economic rights merge into political rights; civil rights are often undistinguishable from social rights. The labels can be useful in giving a broad picture but they can also be very misleading. Almost any right can fall into almost any category under different conditions.

> "First comes the grub then the morals."
>
> *Bertold Brecht*

"Culture is what lives on in man when he has forgotten everything."

Emile Henriot

Third generation rights (collective rights)

The list of internationally recognised human rights has not remained constant. Although none of the rights listed in the UDHR has been brought into question in the 50 or so years of its existence, new treaties and documents have clarified and further developed some of the basic concepts that were laid down in that original document.

These additions have been a result of a number of factors: they have partly come about as a response to changing ideas about human dignity, partly as a result of technological changes and often as a result of new threats emerging. In the case of the specific new category of rights that have been proposed as a **third generation**, these have been the consequence of a deeper understanding of the different types of obstacles that may stand in the way of realising the first and second generation rights. Increasing globalisation has also revealed the possibility for resources to be diverted towards the removal of these obstacles.

What are the main obstacles to people's rights being fully respected in developing countries? Which rights are under most threat?

The idea at the basis of the third generation of rights is that of **solidarity**; and the rights embrace **collective rights of society or peoples** – such as the right to sustainable development, to peace or to a healthy environment. In much of the world, conditions such as extreme poverty, war, ecological and natural disasters have meant that there has been only very limited progress in respect for human rights. For that reason, many people have felt that the recognition of a new category of human rights is necessary: these rights would ensure the appropriate conditions for societies, particularly in the developing world, to be able to provide the first and second generation rights that have already been recognised.

The specific rights that are most commonly included within the category of third generation rights are the rights to development, to peace, to a healthy environment, to share in the exploitation of the common heritage of mankind, to communication and to humanitarian assistance.

There is, however, a debate concerning this new category of rights. Some experts object to the idea that collective rights can be termed 'human' rights. Human rights are, by definition, held by individuals, and define the area of individual interest that is to be given priority over any interests of society or social groups. In contrast, collective rights are held by communities or even whole states.

The debate is not so much over whether these rights exist but whether or not they are to be classed as human rights. The argument is more than merely verbal, because some people fear such a change in terminology could provide a 'justification' for certain repressive regimes to deny (individual) human rights in the name of these collective human rights; for example, severely curtailing civil rights in order to secure 'economic development'. There is another concern which is sometimes expressed: since it is not the state but the international community that is meant to safeguard third generation rights, accountability is impossible to guarantee. Who, or what, is supposed to be responsible for making sure that there is peace in the Caucasus or Palestine?

Nevertheless, whatever we decide to call them, there is general agreement that these areas require further exploration and further attention from the international community. Some collective rights have already been recognised, in particular under the African Charter on Human and Peoples' Rights. The UDHR itself includes the right to self-determination and a human right to development was codified in a 1986 UN General Assembly Declaration.

"Everyone has the right [...] to share in scientific advancement and its benefits".

Article 27, UDHR

The advance of science

Another area where new rights are being acknowledged is in medical science. New scientific discoveries have opened up a number of questions relating to human rights, in particular, in the fields of genetic engineering and concerning the transplant of organs and tissues. Questions on the very nature of life have had to be addressed as a result of technical advances in each of these fields. The Council of Europe has responded to these challenges with a new international treaty: The Convention for the Protection of Human Rights and Dignity of the Human Being with regard to the Application of Biology and Medicine (from now on, referred to as the Oviedo Convention). This treaty entered into force in December 1999.

This convention has been signed by 30 member states of the Council of Europe and ratified by ten. It sets out guidelines for some of the problematic issues raised in the previous section.

Summary of most relevant articles:

- Any form of discrimination against a person on grounds of their genetic heritage is prohibited.
- Predictive genetic tests can be carried out only for health purposes and not, for example, in order to determine the physical characteristics that a child will develop in later life.
- Intervention which aims to modify the human genome may only be undertaken for preventative, diagnostic or therapeutic purposes.
- Medically assisted procreation is not permitted where this is designed to determine a future child's sex.
- Removal of organs or tissue from a living person for transplantation purposes can be carried out solely for the therapeutic benefit of the recipient. (Article 21 – Prohibition of financial gain.)

"Any intervention seeking to create a human being genetically identical to another human being, whether living or dead, is prohibited."

Additional Protocol to the Convention for the Protection of Human Rights and Dignity of the Human Being, Paris 1998

Unesco

Unesco has also attached special attention to the human genome and, on 10 November 1997, the Unesco General Conference adopted a Universal Declaration on the Human Genome and Human Rights. This Declaration establishes similar limits on medical intervention in the genetic heritage of humanity and in individuals.

Biotechnology

Genetic engineering is the method of changing the inherited characteristics of an organism in a predetermined way by altering its genetic material. Progress in this area has led to an intense debate on a number of different ethical and human rights questions; for example, whether the alteration of germ cells should be allowed when this results in a permanent genetic change for the whole organism and for subsequent generations; or whether the reproduction of a clone organism from an individual gene should be allowed in the case of human beings if it is permitted in the case of mice and sheep.

The progress of biomedical technology has also led to the possibility of transplanting adult and foetal organs or tissues from one body to another. Like genetic engineering, this offers huge potential for improving the quality of some people's lives and even for saving lives – but consider some of the problematic issues that are raised by these advances:

- If a life can be saved or improved by using an organ from a dead body, should this always be attempted? Or do dead bodies also deserve respect?
- How can we ensure that everyone in need has an equal chance of receiving a transplant if there is a limited supply of organs?
- Should there be laws concerning the conservation of organs and tissues?
- If medical intervention affects an individual's genome and this results in a threat to the individual's life or quality of life, is compensation appropriate? Would a murder charge be appropriate if the individual dies?

References

Symonides, Janusz ed., *Human Rights: New Dimensions and Challenges*, Manual on Human Rights, Unesco/Dartmouth Publishing, Paris, 1998.

Donnelly, Jack, *Universal Human Rights in theory and practice*, Cornell University Press, 1989.

Robertson A. and Merrills J, *Human rights in the world*, Manchester University Press, 1996.

Council of Europe website on bioethics: www.legal.coe.int/bioethics/.

Legal Protection of human rights

"The law does not change the heart, but it does restrain the heartless."

Martin Luther King

We already know that human rights are inalienable rights possessed by every human being, but how can we access these rights? Where can we find evidence that these rights have been formally recognised by states? And how are these rights implemented?

Human rights are recognised by agreements

At international level, states have come together to draw up certain agreements on the subject of human rights. These agreements establish objective standards of behaviour for states, imposing on them certain duties towards individuals. They can be of two kinds: legally binding or non-binding.

A binding document, often called a Treaty, Convention or Covenant, represents a commitment by states to implement rights at national level. States must individually show their willingness to be bound and this can be done through ratification or accession. (Simply signing the document does not make it binding.) States are generally allowed to make reservations or declarations which exempt them from certain provisions in the document, the idea being to get as many of them as possible to sign. After all, it is better to have a state promising to comply with some human rights provisions than with none! This mechanism, however, can sometimes be abused and used as a pretext for denying basic human rights, allowing a state to 'escape' international scrutiny in certain areas.

Why do you think that even states with a very poor record on human rights are ready to sign international human rights treaties?

By contrast, a non-binding instrument is basically just a declaration or political agreement by states to the effect that all attempts will be made to meet a set of rights but without any legal obligation to do so. This usually means, in practice, that there are no official (or legal) implementation mechanisms.

What is the value in a mere 'promise' to abide by human rights standards, when this is not backed up by legal mechanisms? Is it better than nothing?

A United Nations declaration or non-binding document is usually the result of a meeting of the United Nations General Assembly or a conference held on a specific issue. All states, by simply being members of the United Nations or by taking part in the conference, are considered to be in agreement with the declaration issued.The recognition of human rights can also be, at national level, the result of an agreement between a state and its people. When human rights are recognised at national level, they become primarily a commitment of a state towards its people.

Key international documents

The importance of Human rights is increasingly acknowledged, and are receiving ever wider protection. This should be seen as a victory not only for human rights activists, but for all people in general. A corollary of such success is the development of a large and complex body of human rights texts (instruments) and implementation procedures.

Human rights instruments are usually classified under 3 main categories: the geographical scope (regional or universal), the category of rights provided for and the specific category of persons or groups to whom protection is given.

At UN level alone, there are more than a hundred human rights related documents, and if we add in those at different regional levels, the number increases further. We can not consider all these instruments here, so this section will only deal with those that are most relevant:

- documents which have been widely accepted and have laid the ground for the development of other human rights instruments
- the major European documents
- documents which touch on the global issues explored in the manual.

The International Bill of Rights

The most important global human rights instrument is the Universal Declaration of Human Rights (UDHR), adopted in 1948 by the General Assembly of the UN. This is so widely accepted that its initial non-binding character has altered, and it is now frequently referred to as legally binding on the basis of customary international law.

The UDHR consists of a preface and 30 articles setting forth the human rights and fundamental freedoms to which all men and women everywhere in the world are entitled, without any discrimination. It guarantees both civil and political as well as social, economic and cultural rights.

The International Covenant on Civil and Political Rights (ICCPR) and the International Covenant on Economic, Social and Cultural Rights (ICESCR) both came into force in 1976 and are the main legally binding instruments of worldwide application. Together with the UDHR, they form the International Bill of Rights. Each of them, as their names indicate, provides for a different category of rights.

Whereas the rights included in the ICCPR apply as soon as a state has agreed to be bound by it, the rights of the ICESCR may be implemented gradually. (This puts states under an obligation to develop policies and legislation that will assist the full realisation of the rights). The covenants are treated differently because, generally speaking, economic, social and cultural rights cannot be realised instantly.

Do you think it is right that civil and political rights are supposed to be implemented straight away, and social and economic rights only gradually?

European instruments

Four of the five world regions have established human rights systems for the protection of human rights. In the Americas, there is the Organization of American States, and the main binding document is the American Convention on Human Rights of 1969. In Africa, we find the African Charter on Human and Peoples' Rights, adopted in 1986 within the African Union (formerly known as the Organisation of African Unity). On the Asian continent, no real system

Charter of Fundamental Rights

This is the first human rights document of the European Union. It combines in a single text the civil, political, economic, social and societal rights already laid down in a variety of international, European and national sources. It was jointly proclaimed by the European Council, together with the European Parliament and the European Commission in Nice, between December 7 and 9, 2000. Unlike the Council of Europe's conventions, it is not legally binding and it covers only the European Union.

has been developed to date and the only regional human rights instrument is a non-binding declaration - the Asian Declaration on human rights. And Europe? Europe, of course, has a well-established system within the Council of Europe for the protection of human rights.

Why do you think different regions have found it necessary to establish their own human rights systems?

The main human rights instrument is the European Convention on the Protection of Human Rights and Fundamental Freedoms (also known as the European Convention on Human Rights - ECHR). This has been accepted by all the member states in the Council of Europe, since it is a requirement for membership. It was adopted in 1950 but only came into force three years later. It provides for civil and political rights and its main strength is its implementation machinery - the European Court of Human Rights. This court and its jurisprudence are admired throughout the world and are often referred to by the UN and by constitutional courts of numerous countries and other regional systems.

Just as at the UN level, social and economic rights in Europe are provided for in a separate document. The (Revised) European Social Charter is a binding document that covers rights to safeguard people's standard of living in Europe. The charter has been signed by 32 member states and, by the end of 2001, it had been ratified by 12 of them.

Main human rights instruments and implementation mechanisms of the Council of Europe

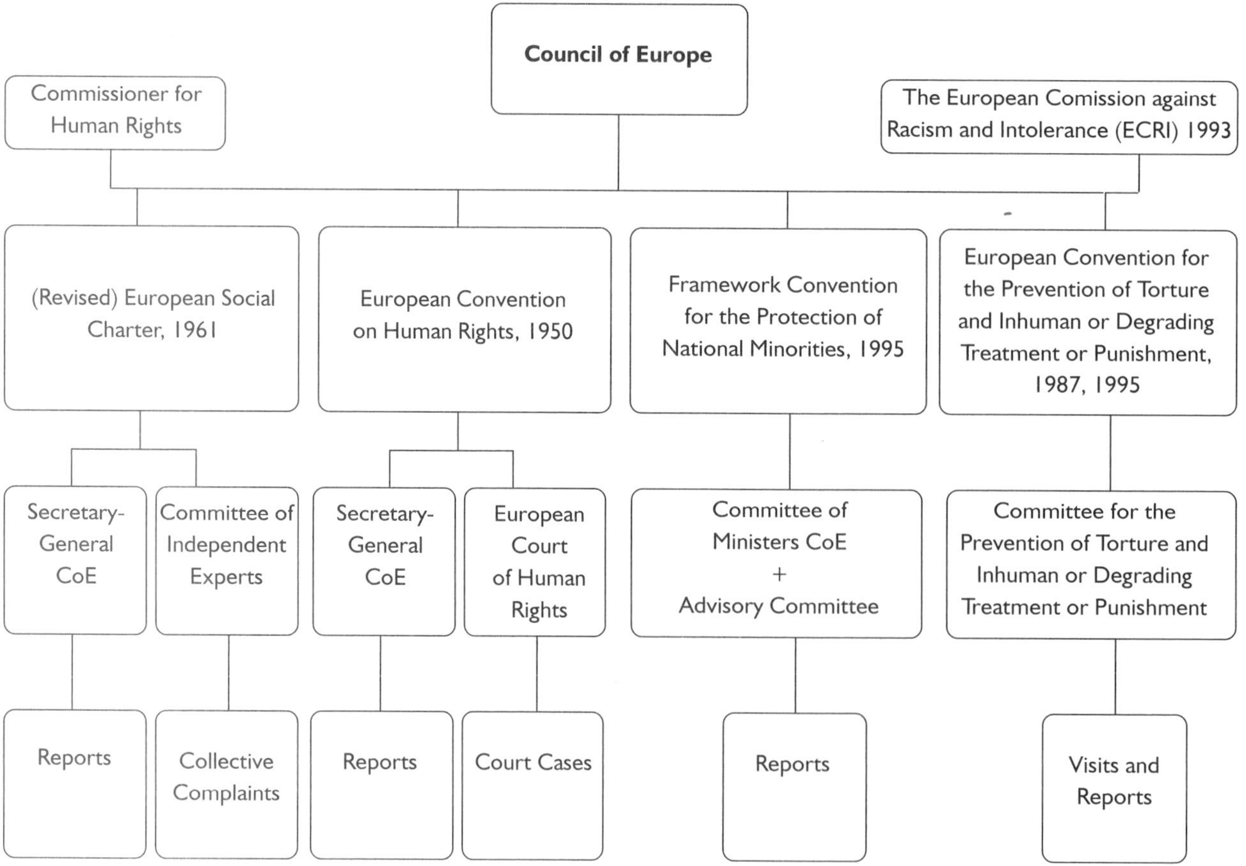

Protection of specific groups

As well as recognising the fundamental rights of individuals, some human rights instruments recognize the rights of specific groups. These special protections are in place because of previous cases of discrimination against groups and because of the disadvantaged and vulnerable position that some groups occupy in society. Examples of groups that have received special protection are:

"I see myself in every stranger's eyes."

Roger Waters

Minorities

These are protected:

- at UN level by a Declaration on the Rights of Persons Belonging to National or Ethnic, Religious and Linguistic Minorities adopted in 1992 and a Sub-Commission on the Prevention of Discrimination and the Protection of Minorities
- at European level by a binding instrument - the Framework Convention for the Protection of National Minorities, which created a monitoring body of independent experts: the Advisory Committee on the Framework Convention.
- by having a special place in the Organization on Security and Co-operation in Europe (OSCE) by the High Commissioner on National Minorities, and by relevant OSCE documents.

Children

Their main protection is given at UN level with the Convention on the Rights of the Child (CRC) of 1990, the most widely ratified convention (not ratified only by the United States and Somalia). At the African level, the African Charter on the Rights and Welfare of the Child provides basic children's rights, taking into account the unique factors of the continent's situation. It came into force in 1999.

Refugees

The rights of refugees are specially guaranteed in the Convention relating to the Status of Refugees of 1951 and by the United Nations High Commissioner on Refugees (UNHCR). The only regional system with a specific instrument on refugee protection has been Africa with the adoption, in 1969, of the Convention Governing the Specific Aspects of Refugees, but in Europe the ECHR also offers some additional protection.

Women

In an attempt to promote worldwide equality between the sexes, the rights of women are specifically protected by the UN Convention on the Elimination of All Forms of Discrimination against Women (CEDAW), 1979.

Others

Groups such as workers and detained persons are also given special protection because of their vulnerable positions, which are easily open to abuse. Other groups, for example indigenous peoples, have not been lucky enough to receive specific protection and have been fighting for years for their rights as groups.

Can you think of groups in your society that are in need of special protection?

Fighting racism and intolerance

Protocol 12 of the ECHR

A new protocol to the ECHR was adopted in 2000: Protocol 12. At the moment it has been signed by 27 states and ratified by one. It will enter into force after 10 ratifications. Its main focus is the prohibition of discrimination. The ECHR already guarantees the right not to be discriminated against (Article 14) but this is thought to be inadequate in comparison with those provisions of other international instruments such as the UDHR and the ICCPR. The main reason is that article 14, unlike the others, does not contain an independent prohibition of discrimination; that is, it prohibits discrimination only with regard to the 'enjoyment of the rights and freedoms' set forth in the Convention. When this protocol comes into force, the prohibition of discrimination will have an 'independent life' from other provisions of the ECHR.

The European Commission Against Racism and Intolerance (ECRI) is a mechanism which was established by the first Summit of Heads of State and Government of the member States of the Council of Europe in 1993. ECRI's task is to combat racism, xenophobia, antisemitism and intolerance at the level of Europe as a whole and from the perspective of the protection of human rights. ECRI's action covers all necessary measures to combat violence, discrimination and prejudice faced by persons or groups of persons, notably on grounds of race, colour, language, religion, nationality and national or ethnic origin.

ECRI's members are designated by their governments on the basis of their in-depth knowledge in the field of combating intolerance. They are nominated in their personal capacity and act as independent members.

ECRI's main programme of activities comprises:

- a country-by-country approach consisting of carrying out in-depth analyses of the situation in each of the member countries in order to develop specific, concrete proposals, matched by follow-up.
- work on general themes (the collection and circulation of examples of good practice on specific subjects to illustrate ECRI's recommendations, and the adoption of general policy recommendations).
- activities in liaison with the community, including awareness-raising and information sessions in the member states, co-ordination with national and local NGOs, communicating an anti-racist message and producing educational material.

Enforcing human rights

How can we ensure that these protection mechanisms work? Who, or what compels states to carry out their obligations? The main supervisory bodies are commissions or committees and courts, all of which are composed of independent members - experts or judges – which do not represent a single state. The main mechanisms used by these bodies are:

1. Complaints (brought by individuals, groups or states)
2. Court cases
3. Reporting procedures.

Since not all human rights instruments or regional systems use the same procedures for implementing human rights, a few examples will help to clarify.

Complaints

Complaints against a state are brought before a commission or committee in what is usually referred to as a quasi-judicial procedure. The supervisory body then takes a decision and States are expected to comply with it, though no legal enforcement procedure exists. Often a state needs to give an additional declaration or ratification of an optional protocol to signify its acceptance of the complaints system.The Human Rights Committe and the Committee on the Elimination of Racial Discrimination (within the United Nations system), and the Inter-American Commission on Human Rights (within the Organisation of American States) are examples of bodies dealing with complaints.

? **Should there be a legal mechanism for enforcing compliance with human rights standards? What sanctions could exist?**

Legal cases

There are only two permanent courts which exist as supervisory bodies specifically for the implementation of human rights: the European Court of Human Rights and the Inter-American Court of Human Rights. A new international court has been established, the International Criminal Court (ICC) was created by the Rome Statute of the International Criminal Court of 1998 which became effective in 2002. Based in The Hague, the court exists to try individuals accused of crimes against humanity, genocide and war crimes. In this respect, it is different from, and complementary to, the European and Inter-American Courts, which consider complaints against states.

Reports and reviews

The majority of human rights instruments require states to submit reports. These are compiled by states themselves, following the directions of the supervisory body, and contain general information on how rights operate at national level. The reports are publicly examined and NGOs usually play an active role at this stage, developing shadow reports alongside the states' reports. The ICCPR, ICESCR, and the Convention on the Elimination of All Forms of Discrimination against Women (CEDAW) are examples of instruments requiring the submission of reports.

Most of these enforcement mechanisms are there to remedy the violation of a particular human right. The European Convention for the Prevention of Torture and Inhuman or Degrading Treatment or Punishment (1987) is of a different kind. It is based on a system of visits by members of the European Committee for the Prevention of Torture and Inhuman or Degrading Treatment or Punishment (CPT) to places of detention - for example, prisons and places of youth detention, police stations, army barracks and psychiatric hospitals. Members of the CPT observe how detainees are treated and, if necessary, recommend improvements in order to comply with the right not to be tortured or to be inhumanly treated.

The European Court of Human Rights

The European Court in Strasbourg is famous for a number of reasons, but perhaps above all, because it gave life and meaning to the text of the ECHR. One of its main advantages is the system of compulsory jurisdiction, which means that as soon as a state ratifies or accedes to the ECHR, it automatically puts itself under the jurisdiction of the European Court. A human rights case can thus be brought against the state party from the moment of ratification.

Another reason for its success is the force of the Court's judgement. States have to comply with the final judgement. Their compliance is supervised by the Committee of Ministers of the Council of Europe.

In every case brought before the European Court, the procedure also includes the possibility of having a friendly settlement based on mediation between the parties.

The Court has also been able to develop over time. When it was initially set up in 1959, it was only a part-time court working together with the European Commission of Human Rights. With the increase of cases, a full-time court became necessary and one was set up in November 1998. This increase in the number of cases is clear evidence of the Court's success. People know that the Court is there and able to step in when they feel their fundamental rights are being infringed.

The European Committee for the Prevention of Torture (CPT)

CPT delegations periodically visit states that are party to the Convention but may organise additional ad hoc visits if necessary. During 2001, the CPT conducted 18 visits, including visits to Switzerland, the Russian Federation (Chechen Republic), Malta and Spain.

An important function of the CPT's work was seen in the case of the hunger strikes in Turkish prisons. When the Turkish government was drawing up changes to the prison system, a number of prisoners used hunger strikes to protest against some of the reforms. Their demonstrations became violent. The CPT became actively involved in negotiations with government and hunger strikers, investigating the events surrounding the hunger strikes and looking at how the draft laws could reform the Turkish prison system. The CPT visited Turkey 3 times in 2001 in connection with hunger strikes in Turkish prisons.

The reports of the CPT are usually public: www.humanrights.coe.int

"Neither in men's hearts
nor in the ways of society
will there be peace
until death has been outlawed"

Albert Camus

Important cases of the European Court of Human Rights

Below are some important cases, which have been consulted by the European Court.

- Soering v. the UK (June 1989): This was a case involving a man who was to be extradited to US to face charges of murder, where the crime was punishable by the death penalty. The Court took the view that to send him back to the US would be against the prohibition of torture, inhuman or other degrading treatment or punishment (Article 3, ECHR). One consequence of this decision was that the protection of individuals within a member state of the Council of Europe went beyond European borders. This principle has already been followed in other cases, such as Jabari v. Turkey (July 2000), and has protected asylum seekers from being sent back to a country where they would have their lives endangered.
- Tyrer v. the UK (March 1978): In this case, the Court considered that corporal punishment as a punishment for juvenile offenders was against the ECHR because it violated the right not to be tortured or to have degrading and inhuman treatment or punishment, as guaranteed under article 3. In the Court's words: "his punishment - whereby he was treated as an object in the power of the authorities - constituted an assault on precisely that which it is one of the main purposes of Article 3 (Art. 3) to

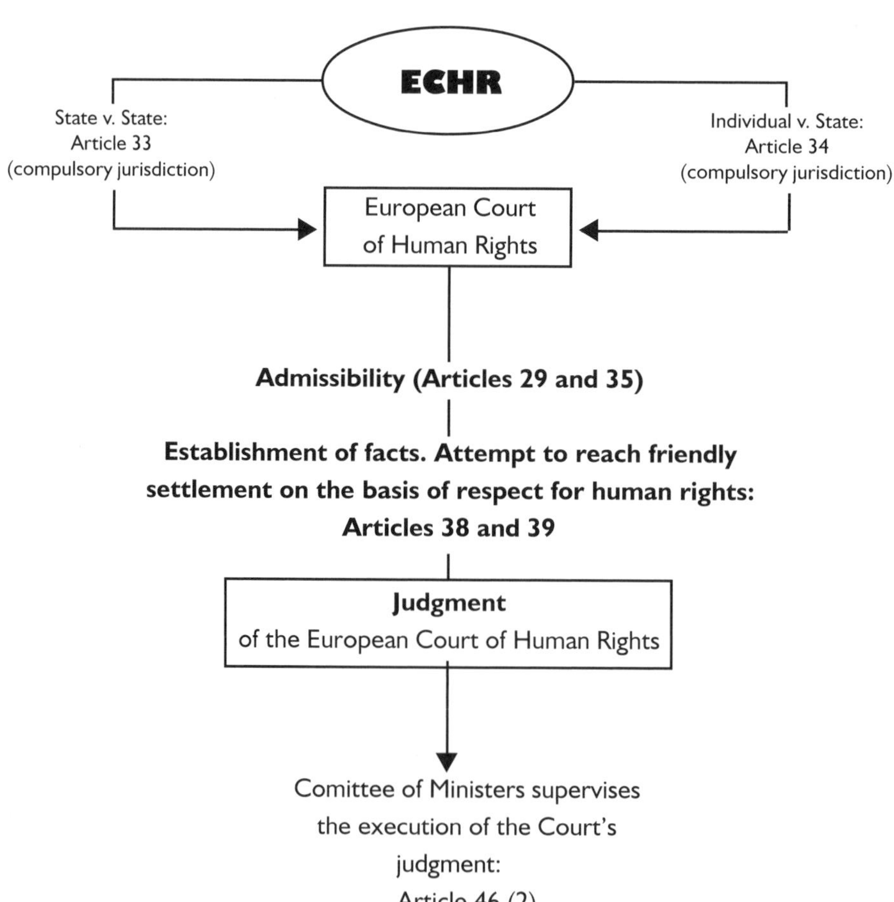

Concept and design: P. Drzemczewski, Graphic: Publication unit, Directorate General of Human Rights

protect, namely a person's dignity and physical integrity". This case is a good example of the living nature of the ECHR, where the Court keeps pace with the changing values of our society.

- Kokkinakis v. Greece (April 1993): This was an interesting case, which dealt with the conflict between the rights of different people. It was based on the issue of proselytising and whether the teaching of a religion (guaranteed under article 9 of ECHR) violates another person's right to freedom of religion. The court thought it necessary to make a clear distinction between teaching, preaching or discussing with immoral and deceitful means to convince a person to change his/her religion (such as offering material or social advantages, using violence or brainwashing).

The European Court hears cases concerning any of the rights guaranteed in the ECHR, such as the right to life, a fair trial and freedom of expression. However, since it stems from the period immediately after the Second World War, it focuses exclusively on civil and political rights, and as a result, it lacks the capacity to consider cases concerning economic, social and minority rights. In spite of these limitations, it is widely revered for its registry record.

Have there been any cases against your country at the European Court?

The European Court of Human Rights in numbers

- There are 43 judges.
An average of 180 phone calls and 800 letters were received daily in 2001.
- 19 815 cases were waiting to be considered by early January 2002 ('pending applications').
- Applications have increased by 523% per year from 1990 to 2000; in 1990 the Court received 1657 applications, in 2000 it received 10 486.
- There were 889 judgements delivered by the court in 2000, which means means more than 2 cases per day (including weekends and holidays!).

ECJ, ECHR, ICJ: What's the difference?

There is often confusion surrounding the roles of the European Court of Human Rights (ECHR), the European Court of Justice (ECJ) and the International Court of Justice (ICJ). In actual fact, the three bodies are very different in terms of their geographical jurisdiction and the types of cases they examine. The ECJ is a body of the European Union. This is a court whose main duty is to ensure that Community law is not interpreted and applied differently in each member state. It is based on Community law and not human rights law; but sometimes Community law may involve human rights issues. A famous case decided by the ECJ was the Bosman case, which concerned transfer rules between football teams. These were judged to be incompatible with the Treaty of Rome rules on competition and the free movement of workers.

The International Court of Justice (ICJ) is the principle judicial organ of the United Nations. It has a dual role: to settle in accordance with international law the legal disputes submitted to it by states, and to give advisory opinions on legal questions. Only states can bring a case against another state and usually the cases are to do with treaties between states. These treaties may concern basic relations between states, (for example commercial or territorial) or may relate to human rights issues.

How do these different legal mechanisms help the ordinary citizen?

The Commissioner for Human Rights

The office of the Council of Europe Commissioner for Human Rights was first approved at the Summit of Heads of State and Government held in Strasbourg in October 1997. The purpose of this independent institution is both to promote the concept of human rights and to ensure effective respect for and full enjoyment of these rights in Council of Europe member States. The Commissioner is elected by the Parliamentary Assembly for a non-renewable term of office of six years.

The Commissioner is a non-judicial institution whose action is to be seen as complementary to the other institutions of the Council of Europe which are active in the promotion of human rights. The Commissioner is to carry out its responsibilities with complete independence and impartiality, while respecting the competence of the various supervisory bodies set up under the European Convention on Human Rights or under other Council of Europe human rights instruments.

The fundamental objectives of the Commissioner for Human Rights are:

- to promote education in and awareness of human rights in the member States;
- to identify possible shortcomings in the law and practice of member States with regard to compliance with human rights;
- to help promote the effective observance and full enjoyment of human rights, as embodied in the various Council of Europe instruments.

The Commissioner can deal ex officio with any issue within its competence. Although it may not take up individual complaints, the Commissioner may act, within the context of its function of promoting human rights, on any relevant information concerning general aspects of the protection of human rights, as enshrined in Council of Europe instruments.

Such information and requests to deal with it may be addressed to the Commissioner by governments, national parliaments, national ombudsmen or similar institutions, as well as by individuals and organisations.

Is this sufficient?

Many people would argue that the poor human rights record in the world is a result of the lack of proper enforcement mechanisms. It is often left up to individual states to decide whether they carry out recommendations. In many cases, whether an individual or group right will in fact be guaranteed depends on pressure from the international community and, to a large extent, on the work of NGOs. This is a less than satisfactory state of affairs, since it can be a long, wait before a human rights violation actually reaches the ears of the UN or the Council of Europe.

Can anything be done to change this? Firstly, it is essential to ensure that states guarantee human rights at national level and that they develop a proper mechanism for remedying any violation. At the same time, pressure must be put on states to commit themselves to those mechanisms that have enforcement procedures.

References

Hanski, R., Suksi, M. (eds.), An introduction to the international protection of human rights: a textbook, *Åbo Akademi University Institute for Human Rights, 1999.*

Fact Sheet No. 2 (Rev. 1), The International Bill of Human Rights, Office of the High Commissioner for Human Rights, www.unhchr.ch/html/menu6/2/fs2.htm.

United Nations High Commissioner for Human Rights, www.unhchr.ch.

Short Guide to the European Convention on Human Rights, Council of Europe Publishing.

European Court of Human Rights, www.echr.coe.int.

The Committee for Prevention of Torture and Inhuman or Degrading Treatment or Punishment, www.cpt.coe.int.

The European Social Charter, www.humanrights.coe.int/cseweb.

The Framework Convention on Protection of National Minorities, www.humanrights.coe.int/minorities.

The site of the European Commission against Racism and Intolerance, www.ecri.coe.int.

The Council of Europe's Commissioner for Human Rights, www.commissioner.coe.int.

Activism and the Role of NGOs

"We had to do a lot to make [it] happen. It took several demonstrations by our organization and getting arrested, throwing myself on the table in Congress, before we got an invitation to speak ... I had five minutes."
Cheri Honkala, the first welfare recipient in the US to testify before Congress; Kensington Welfare Rights Union)

What are NGOs?

The term *non-governmental,* or, more accurately *non-profit* is normally used to cover the range of organisations which go to make up civil society. Such organisations are characterised, in general, by having as the purpose of their existence something other than financial profit. However, this leaves a huge multitude of reasons for existence and a wide variety of enterprises and activities. NGOs range from small pressure groups on, for example, specific environmental concerns or specific human rights violations, through educational charities, women's refuges, cultural associations, religious organisations, legal foundations, humanitarian assistance programmes – and the list could continue – all the way to the huge international organisations with hundreds or even thousands of branches or members in different parts of the world.

"Get up, stand up, stand up for your rights."

Bob Marley

In this section, we look briefly at the significant role that such organisations have had, and continue to have, in the protection of human rights throughout the world. At nearly every level of the different attempts to preserve the dignity of individual citizens when this is threatened by the power of the state, NGOs play a crucial role in:

- fighting individual violations of HR
- offering direct assistance to those whose rights have been violated
- lobbying for changes to national or international law
- helping to develop the substance of those laws
- promoting knowledge of, and respect for, human rights among the population.

The contribution of NGOs is important not only in terms of the results that are achieved, and therefore for the optimism that people may feel about the defence of human rights in the world, but also because NGOs are, in a very direct sense, tools that are available to be used by individuals throughout the world. They are managed and co-ordinated – as many organisations are – by private individuals, but they also draw a large part of their strength from other members of the community offering voluntary support to their cause. This fact gives them great significance for those individuals who would like to contribute to the improvement of human rights in the world.

Types of human rights NGOs

The 1993 UN Conference on Human Rights – known as the Vienna Conference - was attended by 841 NGOs from throughout the world, all of which described themselves as working with a human rights mission. Though an impressive figure in itself, this actually represented only a tiny fraction of the total number of human rights NGOs active in the world.

"The world is a dangerous place to live! Not so much because of those who make evil, but because of those who look on and allow them to do it."

Albert Einstein

"God gives us hands, but He does not build bridges."

Arab proverb

Most self-professed "human rights organisations" tend to be engaged in the protection of *civil and political rights*. The best known of such organisations, at least on the international stage, are probably Amnesty International and Human Rights Watch, both of which operate across the globe. However, as we have seen, civil and political rights are just one category of the many different human rights recognised by the international community, and new rights are continuing to emerge, even today. When we take this into account and consider the NGOs active in countering poverty, violence, racism, health problems, homelessness and environmental concerns, to name just a few, the actual number of NGOs engaged in human rights protection, in one form or another, runs into the hundreds of thousands throughout the world.

At its General Assembly in 2001, Amnesty International reformed its mandate to include economical and social rights and the right to development within its aims and areas of concern for action.

? **Do you know of any NGOs fighting for human rights in your country?**

How do they influence the process?

NGOs may attempt to engage in the protection of human rights at various different stages or levels, and the strategies they employ will vary according to the nature of their objectives – their specificity or generality; their long-term or short-term nature; their local, national or international scope, and so on.

a. Direct assistance

It is particularly common for NGOs working on social and economic rights to offer some form of direct service to those who have been victims of human rights violations. Such services may include forms of humanitarian assistance, protection or training to develop new skills. Alternatively, where the right is protected by law, they may include legal advocacy or advice on how to present claims.

In many cases, however, direct assistance to the victim of a violation is either not possible or does not represent the best use of an organisation's resources. On such occasions, and this probably represents the majority of cases, NGOs need to take a longer view and to think of other ways either of rectifying the violation or of preventing similar occurrences from happening in the future.

b. Collecting accurate information

If there is a fundamental strategy lying at the base of the different forms of NGO activism, it is perhaps the idea of attempting to 'show up' the perpetrators of injustice. Governments are very often able to shirk their obligations under the international treaties that they have signed up to because the impact of their policies is simply not known to the general public. Collecting such information and using it to 'show up' governments is an essential element in holding them to account and is frequently used by NGOs. They attempt to put pressure on people or governments by identifying a cause that will appeal to people's sense of injustice and then making it public.

Two of the best known examples of organisations that are reputed for their accurate monitoring and reporting are Amnesty International (see p xx for more information) and the International Committee of the Red Cross. Both of these organisations possess authority not only among the general public but also at the level of the UN, where their reports are taken into account as part of the official process of monitoring governments that have agreed to be bound by the terms of international treaties.

c. *Campaigning and lobbying.*

Lobbying is the general name given to the various ways of putting pressure on national or international actors in order to bring about a policy change. Again, there are numerous forms, and an NGO will try to adopt the most appropriate one given the objectives it has in mind, the nature of its 'target', and of course, its own available resources. Some common practices are outlined below.

- Letter-writing campaigns are a method that has been used to great effect by Amnesty International and other NGOs. People and organisations 'bombard' government officials with letters from thousands of its members all over the world.
- Street actions or demonstrations, with the media coverage that these normally attract, may be used when organisations want to enlist the support of the public or to bring something to the public eye in order to 'shame' a government.
- The media will frequently play an important part in lobbying practices, and the Internet is now assuming an increasingly significant role.
- In addition to demonstrations of support or public outrage, NGOs may also engage in private meetings or briefings with officials. Sometimes the mere threat of bringing something to the public eye may be enough to change a policy or practice, as in the story below.

In general, the greater the backing from the public or from other influential actors (for example, other governments), the more likely is it that a campaign will achieve its objectives. Even if they do not always use this support directly, NGOs can ensure that their message is heard simply by indicating that a large popular movement could be mobilised against a government.

"It can be fun to write to people who lead authoritarian or repressive regimes, have a dictator as a pen-pal, and be a complete nuisance to him by sending him these letters."

Sting

Have there been any high profile campaigns in your country? What was the outcome?

d. Long-term education

Many human rights NGOs also include, at least as part of their activities, some type of public awareness or educational work. Realising that the essence of their support lies with the general public, NGOs will often try to bring greater knowledge of human rights issues to members of the public. A greater knowledge of these issues and of the methods of defending them is likely to engender a greater respect and this, in turn, will increase the likelihood of being able to mobilise support in particular instances of human rights violations. It is that support, or potential support, that lies at the base of the success of the NGO community in improving the human rights environment.

Examples of successful activism

Domestic violence in Russia

There are different estimates of levels of domestic violence in Russia, but some figures suggest that between 30 and 40 percent of families have experienced it. In 1995, after the Beijing Women's Conference, the first reliable statistics were published. These suggested that 14,500 women a year had been killed by their husbands and about fifty thousand had been hospitalised. It has taken a great deal of effort for this problem even to be recognised in Russia but most of the success is a result of the efforts of an NGO called ANNA, a founding member of the Russian Association for Crisis Centres for Women.

The organisation was set up by Marina Pisklakova, a leading women's rights activist. In July 1993, she worked alone to run a hotline for women in distress and then expanded the work to

"Human Rights Education is a way of living. We've been doing it over the past few years without knowing that all our activities were about Human Rights Education."

Alexandra Vidanovic, Open Club Nis, Federal Republic of Yugoslavia, participant at the Forum on Human Rights Education.

"I couldn't say no; there were so many women."

Marina Pisklakova

establish the first women's crisis centre in the country. She lobbied for legislation banning abuse and worked with a hostile law enforcement establishment to bring aid to victims and to bring criminal prosecutions. She began a media campaign to expose the violence against women and to educate women about their rights and now regularly appears on radio and television promoting respect for women's rights.

The organisation succeeded in expanding the definition of domestic violence to include marital rape, sexual violence in the marriage or partnership, psychological violence, isolation and economic control. By the summer of 1994, they had trained a first group of women to work as telephone counsellors and, in 1995, began work in other Russian cities for local women's groups that were starting to emerge and wanted to start up hotlines or crisis centres. ANNA helped to develop programmes to provide psychological and legal counselling for the victims of domestic violence and, in April 1997, lawyers working for the organisation brought the first domestic violence case to court and won, setting a legal precedent for all of Russia. By the start of the new millennium, they had over forty women's crisis centres operating throughout Russia. Website for the organisation: www.owl.ru/anna.

Environmental concerns in Switzerland

"I am not an extraordinary person. Any woman in my position would do the same. I feel that … I was at the beginning of something new, a great development in Russia, a new attitude. Now, everybody is talking about domestic violence. And many are doing something about it."

Marina Pisklakova

Between 1961 and 1976, several large chemical giants dumped more than 114,000 tons of toxic industrial chemical waste in the former clay pit of Bonfol in Switzerland. Although it would be illegal to dump the waste today, in 1961, when the landfill site was started, the law did not prohibit such landfills. The toxic waste remained at the site and continued to contaminate surrounding communities and the environment with a mixture of organic and inorganic pollutants.

On May 14 2000, around 100 Greenpeace activists occupied the Bonfol chemical landfill site, near Basel, Switzerland, demanding that the chemical companies that dumped toxic waste at the site take full responsibility for cleaning it up. The activists declared that they would occupy the site until the chemical companies committed themselves to cleaning it up in a manner that would not pose any further risk to human health or the environment.

Occupation of the landfill forced the chemical industry to meet with community representatives and with Greenpeace and, as a result, the chemical industry finally signed an agreement to complete a clean-up study by February 2001 and to start the clean-up process in 2001. The industry also agreed to involve the local communities and environmental organisations fully in the clean-up and to inform the local communities about the ground water and drinking water pollution resulting from the dump. On July 7th 2001, Greenpeace ended their occupation of the chemical dumpsite. See the Greenpeace website: www.greenpeace.org.

Doing your sums

Development Initiatives for Social and Human Action (DISHA)

DISHA was established in the early 1990s in the Indian State of Gujarat as the representatives of groups of tribal and forest workers that have some 80,000 members between them. It has been using the right to information to analyse state budgets and the extent to which allocations match public statements and declarations to alleviate poverty.

"The chemical industry's toxic legacy should not become the burden of future generations."

Stefan Weber, Greenpeace campaigner.

The organisation began by dealing with the issue of enforcing the minimum wage for people working in forest areas. The director of DISHA explained the organisation's approach: "As part of this work, we began to look at why the area had not developed and why employment

opportunities had not been created. We looked at the money spent by the state, and that's how we began to look at the state budget."

In 1994, DISHA members decided to distribute their analysis to all parliamentarians, the press and leading citizens. This ensured that the information was widely used and discussed.

Since the organisation started work, state allocations to tribal areas have increased substantially: at the start, the allocation was 12% of the budget but is now 18%. Because their research was so solid, DISHA soon earned respect as an institution "that was not just shouting slogans and marching, but presenting very sound arguments on the basis of facts and figures. People now come to us for information on the budget - we are the only institution in the country that classifies and analyses the budget".

"The conditions were like slavery. There was hardly any human dignity or observance of the law."

M. D. Mistry, Director of DISHA.

"Seldom can campaigners have achieved so much in so little time."

The Independent Newspaper

The diamond wars

Global Witness, UK is an organisation that works to expose the link between environmental exploitation and human rights abuses. It is a London-based environmental group, which began work in 1993 in a rented office equipped only with a computer retrieved from a skip.

Today, the organisation is still tiny, with just nine members of staff, but for four years its founders, Charmain Gooch, Simon Taylor and Patrick Alley, led a campaign against the diamond industry.

During that time, Global Witness successfully linked the trade in illicit diamonds with bloody African wars. It collected evidence to convince governments, the United Nations and the public that illegally mined diamonds in African war zones were being used to bankroll conflicts in which children lose their limbs and tens of thousands die. The organisation lobbied ferociously to "make decision-makers see sense", forging alliances with other non-governmental organisations (NGOs) working in Angola, and cultivating powerful political sympathisers such as the Canadian ambassador Robert Fowler, who heads the UN sanctions committee on Angola. Very quickly a global campaign force capable of taking on a global industry emerged.

When Robert Fowler, Canada's ambassador to the United Nations, issued the warning of a fur-style boycott at the World Diamond Congress in Antwerp, the diamond industry took fright. In July 2000, the US$ 7bn-a-year global diamond industry, apparently persuaded that it was on the edge of an abyss, capitulated to the campaigners' demands for fundamental changes to the trade in diamonds.

See their web-site http://www.globalwitness.org.

Wheelchair ramps in Tuzla

In 1996, a disability NGO in Tuzla, Boznia Herzegovina, decided to run a campaign for traffic awareness. Lotos, the organisation, aimed to raise awareness about disabled people and traffic issues, and identified several concrete objectives, including special parking spaces for disabled people, better access on public transport, and accessible pavements and roads. They held events over the course of a week, just before the election campaign began. At the end of that time, public awareness had been increased and all pavements in Tuzla were rebuilt with ramps!

"I am completely confident in saying that Tuzla is the most accessible town for wheelchair users in the whole of Boznia and Herzegovina."

Campaigner, Tuzla.

References

Risse T., Ropp S., Sikkink K., The Power of human rights, *Cambridge University Press, 1999.*
Forsythe, D., Human rights in International Relations, *Cambridge University Press, 2000.* www.speaktruth.org.
Hijab, Nadia, Human Rights and Human Development: Learning from Those Who Act, *HDRO Background paper, 2000.*

Questions and answers

What are human rights?

Human rights are moral entitlements that every individual in the world possesses simply in virtue of the fact that he or she is a human being. In claiming our human rights, we are making a *moral* claim, normally on our own government, that *you cannot do that, because it is a violation of my moral sphere and my personal dignity.* No-one – no individual, no government – can ever take away our human rights.

Where do they come from?

They come from the fact that we are not only physical beings, but also moral and spiritual *human* beings. Human rights are needed to protect and preserve every individual's *humanity*, to ensure that every individual can live a life of *dignity* and a life that is worthy of a human being.

Why 'should' anyone respect them?

Fundamentally, because everyone is a human being and therefore a moral being. The majority of individuals, if shown that they are violating someone else's personal dignity, will try to refrain. In general, people do not *want* to hurt other people. However, in addition to the moral sanctions of one's own conscience or that of others, there is now legislation in most countries of the world which *obliges* governments to respect the basic human rights of their citizens, even when they may be unwilling to do so.

Who has human rights?

Absolutely everyone. Criminals, heads of state, children, men, women, Africans, Americans, Europeans, refugees, the unemployed, those in employment, bankers, charity workers, teachers, dancers, astronauts…

Even criminals and heads of state?

Absolutely *everyone*. Criminals and heads of state are humans too. The power of human rights lies in the very fact that they treat *everyone as equal* in terms of possessing human dignity. Some people may have violated the rights of others or may pose a threat to society and may therefore need to have their rights *limited* in some way in order to protect others, but only within certain limits. These limits are defined as being the minimum which is necessary for a life of human dignity.

Who looks after human rights?

We all need to. There is legislation both at national and at international levels which imposes restrictions on what governments are able to do to their citizens but, if no-one points out that their actions are violating international norms, governments can continue to violate them with impunity. As individuals, we need not only to respect the rights of others in our everyday lives but also to keep watch on our governments and on others. The protective systems are there for all of us if we use them.

How can I defend my rights?

Try pointing out that they have been violated; claim your rights. Let the other person know that *you*

know they are not entitled to treat you in this way. Point to the relevant articles in the UDHR, in the ECHR or the other international documents. If there is legislation in your own country, point to that as well. Tell others about it: tell the press, write to your parliamentary representative and head of state, inform any NGOs that are engaged in human rights activism. Ask their advice. Speak to a lawyer, if you have the opportunity. Make sure that your government knows what action you are taking. Make them realise that you are not going to give up. Show them the support you can draw on. In the final analysis, and if everything else has failed, you may want to resort to the courts.

How do I go to the European Court?

The European Convention for the Protection of Human Rights and Fundamental Freedoms does contain a procedure for individual complaints and also for complaints brought by one State against another. However, there are strong admissibility requirements before a case can even be considered. For example, you need to ensure that your complaint has already been raised in the national courts of your country (up to the highest court!) before you can bring a case to the European Court. If you wish to try, and you believe that you satisfy the admissability requirements, then you can bring a complaint using the official application form (available from the Secretariat). However, you are strongly advised to seek legal advice or the advice of NGOs working in the field in order to be sure that your claim has a real chance of success. Be aware that it can be a long and complicated process before a final judgement is given!

From whom can I claim my rights?

Nearly all the basic human rights that are listed in the international documents are claims against *your government*, or state officials. Human rights protect your interests against the state, so you need to claim them from the state or from their representatives. If you feel that your rights are being violated by, for example, your employer or your neighbour, you cannot resort directly to international human rights legislation unless there is also something the government of the country ought to have done to prevent employers or neighbours from behaving in this way.

Does anyone have a *duty* to protect my rights?

Yes. A right is meaningless without a corresponding responsibility or duty on someone else's part. Every individual has a *moral* duty not to violate your personal dignity but your government, in signing up to international agreements, has not just a moral duty but also a legal duty.

Are human rights only a problem in non-democratic countries?

There is no country in the world that has a completely clean record on human rights, even today. There may be more frequent violations in some countries than others or they may affect a larger proportion of the population, but every single violation is a problem that ought not to have happened and that needs to be dealt with. An individual whose rights are violated in one of the established democracies is hardly likely to be comforted by the fact that, in general, their country has a 'better' record on human rights than other countries in the world!

Have we made any progress in reducing human rights violations?

Great progress – even if it sometimes seems a mere drop in the ocean. Consider the abolition of slavery, the vote for women, the countries that have abolished the death penalty, the freeing of prisoners of conscience as a result of international pressure, the collapse of the apartheid regime in South Africa, the cases that have been tried before the European Court and the laws

that have had to be changed as a result. Consider the fact that the gradual change in international culture means that even the most authoritarian regimes now have to take human rights into consideration in order to be accepted on the international stage. There have been many positive results, particularly over the past 50 years, but a great deal more remains to be done.

Puzzlers

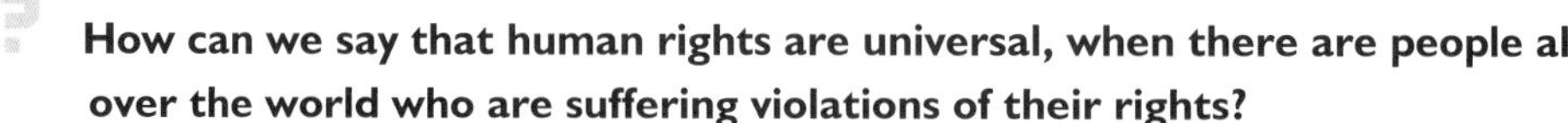

How can we say that human rights are universal, when there are people all over the world who are suffering violations of their rights?

These people still *have* their rights. The fact that they are being treated in such a way contravenes not only moral norms but also internationally agreed norms. Their state representatives are culpable under international law, and some countries are indeed 'punished' by the international community, in the form of sanctions, or even by military means. However, such processes are often arbitrary, depending on other nations' interests rather than the degree of violation. There is now a permanent International Criminal Court before which perpetrators can be brought and tried, set up by the Rome Statute of the International Criminal Court. This is a permanent court for trying individuals accused of committing genocide, war crimes and crimes against humanity. This has been an important step towards recognising that universal human rights need to be enforceable in order to be of practical assistance.

What use is the UDHR if it is not legally enforceable?

Even if there is not (yet) an international court before which governments can be tried under articles in the UDHR, this document has had enormous historical significance and continues even today to operate as a benchmark against which governments are judged internationally. Governments today know that if they wilfully infringe rights listed in the document, they face the possibility of condemnation by other governments and even some form of sanctions. The process is not always entirely objective (!) but it is certainly a start. The UDHR also formed the basis for nearly all of the international treaties that have been drawn up and which are (to a greater or lesser extent) enforceable.

What use are 'human rights' to *me*, when my government violates the rights of ordinary people on a daily basis and has no concern for the disapproval of the international community?

Again - they are a start; they are better than having nothing at all and they will, under the right circumstances and with the right approach, be able to influence the government to change some, if not all, of its practices. This can sometimes seem a very distant hope, when violations by the government are particularly severe or particularly frequent, but history has shown, time and again, that it is possible. Also, opportunities today are probably better than they have been up until now. Promoting change can be a slow process, but the fact that individuals have these rights and that they are increasingly recognised throughout the world - and are therefore at least of *some* concern to governments - provides us with a powerful weapon and a valuable head start.

If I respect the human rights of others, does that mean allowing them to do whatever they want?

Not if their desire involves violating your or anyone else's rights. But you may need to be careful not to be too demanding over the extent of your own rights: you might find someone's behaviour annoying or misguided, but that need not necessarily be an infringement of your *rights*. Therefore, if you want others to allow you to behave as you wish, you may need to cultivate a more tolerant attitude towards the behaviour of others!

Can I do *anything*, including using violence against someone, to defend my rights?

In general, no. But if it is a genuine case of self-defence, then a *legitimate use of force, appropriate to the threat against you,* may be admissible. It is not permissible as 'retribution' for the wrong you have suffered but only in order to protect yourself from further harm. Torture is never admissible.

Why should I respect the rights of others if others do not respect my rights?

Partly because if you don't respect others' rights, you may get into trouble yourself; partly because others deserve your respect, simply because they are human; and partly because you can set an example to others that will make it more likely for them to respect you. In the end, though, it is probably down to you and the type of person you want to be or the kind of world you want to live in. So you could reflect on what it would say about *you* if you were to behave in the manner that you dislike in others. Or think about the type of world it would be if everyone violated everyone else's rights in a tit-for-tat manner.

Why should those who violate the rights of others in the most inhumane way be regarded as subjects of 'human' rights?

This is perhaps the most difficult but also the most essential part of human rights theory to accept. It can sometimes seem that certain individuals are so lacking in humane characteristics that only blind faith could enable us to see them as human. The important points are perhaps the following:

- **Firstly,** despite some people's apparent inhumanity, every individual possesses some humanity. Villains love their mothers, their children, their husbands and wives – or *someone*. Villains feel pain, rejection, despair and jealousy; they desire to be appreciated, valued, supported, loved and understood. They *all*, every one of them, possess some, if not most, of these exclusively human emotions. That makes them human and deserving of our respect.
- **Secondly,** we do ourselves no good in desiring to hurt villains in the same way that they have hurt others: such feelings only make us less worthy of respect as well.
- **Thirdly,** even if, perchance, a villain were ever to emerge with 'human' form but without any human characteristics (and there has never been one yet), who among us could say with absolute certainty that he or she is Not A Human? On what criteria? On the basis, perhaps, that they are incapable of loving or being loved? But what if we turn out to be mistaken in that belief?

The third point reminds us that we need to consider the risks for humanity as a whole in setting up some people to judge others where the consequences of that judgement are terrible and irreversible. Do we really want a world where such judgements are made and where some people are simply designated as not possessing human rights and therefore as non-human? Without the absolute universality of all human rights, that is the type of world that we would have.

Chapter 5

Background Information on the Global Themes

Table of contents of this chapter

Children

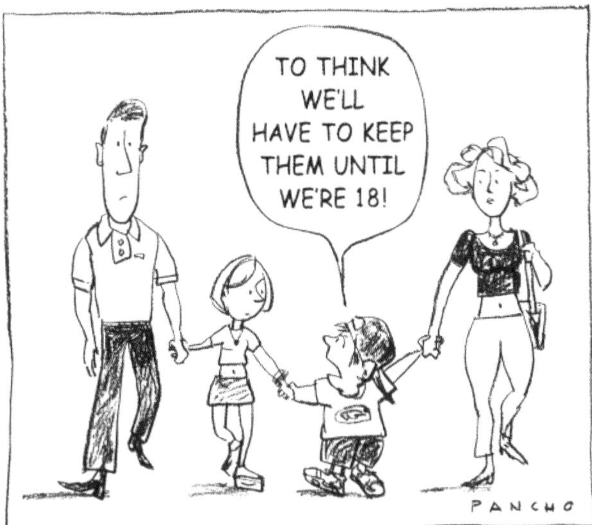

At a rough estimate, there are two thousand million children in the world today, 79 million in the European Union, and 25 million in the countries that are candidates to join the EU.

In 1989, the United Nations adopted the Convention on the Rights of the Child (CRC), which has been ratified by all the countries except the United States of America and Somalia. This convention is a landmark in the history of the rights of the children since it is the first compulsory international instrument adopted in this field.

"Your children are not your children.
They are the sons and daughters of Life's longing for itself...
You may house their bodies but not their souls,
for their souls dwell in the house of tomorrow,
which you cannot visit, not even in your dreams."

Kahlil Gilbran

Why is the Convention on the Rights of the Child so important?

The convention has brought a lot of changes in the field of the protection of the rights of children.

1. It is the most widely ratified human rights instrument in the world.
2. The convention promotes the "3p's". Firstly, it promotes the *participation* - according to their age condition and maturity - of children in matters that affect their destiny, such as judicial processes or processes of adoption, with regard to their families and to society as a whole. It also states rights for their *protection* against all forms of abuses, violence and practices that can violate their rights. Finally, similar to any other convention, it *provides* for rights which are meant as safeguards against potential violations.
3. It considers the children as subject of law instead of object of law. Traditionally, the vast majority of adults have been educated to perceive children as objects that have to obey adults unconditionally - teachers, priests, parents, doctors, etc. Instead, the convention promotes the idea of children as people with rights that have to be respected by adults, society and all the institutions that deal with children's affairs. Children are entitled to be respected and treated with dignity simply because they are human, whatever their age.
4. The best interests of the child should guide all decisions taken - judicial, administrative, etc. - involving a child. It is a hard concept to define and there is a lot of controversy about its exact meaning. In practice, it implies that if, for example, a judge has to decide who will have the custody of a child, they have to examine several aspects of the child' life and the adults concerned. In all cases, the best interests of the child are

Related activities

- Act it out, page 86.
- Ashique's story, page 91.
- Children's Rights, page 103.
- Do we have alternatives?, page 111.
- Let every voice be heard, page 153.
- Our futures, page 182.
- Rights Bingo, page 206.

Child participation

1. "Participation is essential for bringing the UN Convention on the Rights of the Child into life;
2. [it] is a decisive factor for securing social cohesion and for living in a democracy
3. [it] is a necessary process in the development of the child...[1]"

more important than the best interests of the adults concerned.

5. The content of the CRC refers to a wide range of fields - administrative, judicial, educational, legal, etc., where the rights of children have to be respected. For example, a child that has not been properly registered at birth does not exist in the eyes of the law. Thus they do not exist for the school authorities that refuse to accept them as a student and, as a result, they cannot attend school. This is a common problem affecting thousands of children in many countries. The refusal of the school authorities to accept the child as a student because they "do not exist administratively and legally" clearly violates the child's right to education.

The convention has had a practical impact in many countries, which have been obliged, by ratifying the CRC, to amend and/or reform part of their existing legislation.

Do you think children should always obey adults unconditionally for their own good?

The state of children: facts and figures

Even if the convention is a giant step in favour of the cause of children, the facts prove that the rights of children are being violated in most regions of the world.

Children in Europe...

- There is a striking increase in the number of women and children being trafficked. Estimates suggest that up to 120000 women and children being trafficked into western Europe from central and eastern European countries each year.
- In Bulgaria, there are reports that prostitution has become a principal source of income for a substantial number of 14- to 18-year-old girls and that very often they may be part of an organised network. What is also worrying is the growth in the numbers of young male prostitutes.
- In Estonia, prostitution involving very young girls has been noted in the wider context of a growing foreign market for sex tourism. In Latvia, very young girls have also been identified as prostitutes (as young as between 8 and 10 years old).
- In the UK, research indicates that there are many thousands of street children, primarily, though not exclusively, in the major cities and towns. The population of street children is split evenly between males and females. It is estimated that approximately 40000 children run away from home every year.
- In France, the phenomenon of street children began to constitute a significant problem in the 1980s. Some authorities consider that there might be as many as 10000 street children, although others estimate that the number is much lower.
- In general, there is a growing population of young people living homeless on the streets in eastern and central Europe. In Bucharest alone, there are an estimated 1500 children and young people living out on the streets
- In Poland and Hungary over a third of children under the age of fifteen live in poverty. A recent study in Poland (UNDP, 1999) found that 60% of children suffer from some form of malnutrition with 10% permanently malnourished. In the Russian Federation, the prevalence of stunted growth among children under two years old increased from 9.4% in 1992 to 15.2% in 1994.

Who is a child?

As defined by Article 1 of the convention, "a child means every human being below the age of eighteen years unless, under the law applicable to the child, majority is attained earlier."
This means that every person under 18 years old, including adolescents, is covered by the convention.

Child poverty rates in Europe[2]

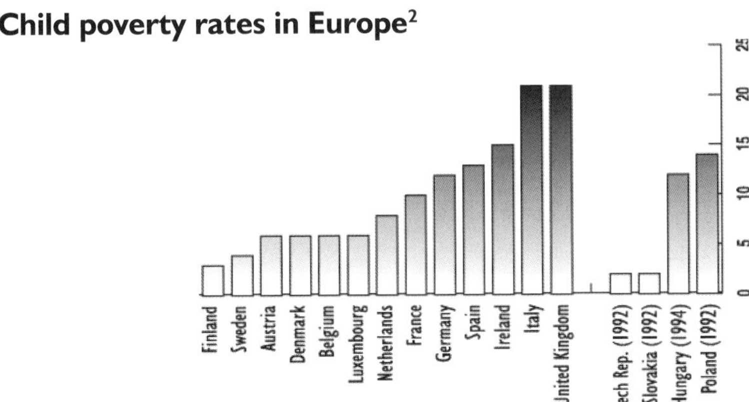

Children in the world...

- More than 10 million children under the age of five still die each year from preventable causes.
- More than 100 million children are still not in primary school, the majority being girls.
- There are an estimated 300000 children engaged in combat.
- 149 million children are malnourished, two thirds of them in Asia.
- Last year alone, some 31 million refugees and displaced persons, mostly women and children, were caught up in war conflicts and were forced to flee from their homes and become refugees.

European issues related to children and adolescents

There are specific issues related to the rights of the children that are particularly relevant to European institutions as well as to European governments. As a result, there is a clear will to promote measures aimed at protecting children against practices and phenomena that clearly violate their rights.

In the light of the statistics above cited on *sexual trafficking, prostitution and pornography* in Europe, the Council of Europe and its members have become increasingly concerned and, as a result, they have adopted several recommendations, including:

- Recommendation 1065 (1987) on the traffic in children and other forms of child exploitation;
- Recommendation No. R (91) 11 on sexual exploitation, pornography and prostitution of, and trafficking in, children and young adults;
- Resolution 1099 (1996) on the sexual exploitation of children.

Once these recommendations are adopted, states have to take practical measures to ensure their implementation. Examples of such measures are[3]:

1. At the initiative of the Belgium Minister for the Interior, on 23 November 1992, a unit specialising in countering such traffic was set up within the Gendarmerie's Central Office for Missing Persons. On 11 September 1995, the Minister for Justice ordered the creation of a Missing Children Unit within the same office. This unit is responsible for the co-ordination and provision of support and expertise relating to the disappearance of minors in circumstances giving cause for concern.
2. In Luxembourg, a special juvenile protection section has been formed in the police force. Police headquarters in Luxembourg City has a juvenile protection section in its research division. There is a telephone help-line for children (KannerJugendtelefon).

? Why is it difficult to eradicate this kind of trafficking?

Key dates

4 June
International Day of Innocent Child Victims of Aggression

12 August
International Youth Day

20 November
Universal Children's Day

"The soul is healed by being with children."

Fyodor Dostoevsky

Child labour is...

... work done by children full-time under the age of 15
... work that prevents children from attending school
... work that is dangerous for children and hazardous to their physical, mental or emotional health.

The reasons behind this practice are sometimes very complex and range from cultural practices to situations of poverty where the parents and family need the wages brought home by the child.

In terms of consequences, in addition to depriving children of a proper education and impairing their physical and mental development, child labour can lead to severe health problems such as muscular-skeletal deformation, chemical poisoning, cuts and other bodily injuries, respiratory diseases, serious burns, etc.

Examples of goods made by children include carpets, bricks, matches, sugar, clothing, shoes, cigarettes (beedis), fireworks, houses and other buildings, pencils, leather goods. They are also employed in crop picking, factory work, carrying heavy things, fishing and basic domestic services.

The Internet and pornography

Children can be exposed to a wide range of risks when they use the Internet. Some of them are exposure to inappropriate material (violent pictures, racist and xenophobic propaganda, etc.), harassment and paedophile activity. There is growing evidence that there are networks dedicated to the exchange of information (names, pictures, etc) of child pornography. In recent years, individuals have been arrested in Europe and other continents for being implicated and/or promoting this kind of illegal and immoral activities.

Some suggested solutions for individuals involved with matters relating to children, such as social workers, teachers, psychologists, etc., and parents are:

- taking *individual actions* such as reporting, complaining or asking when they become aware of a child being exposed to such risks or when they discover illegal or dangerous Internet material;
- *empowering children* through informing them and discussing the matter with them;
- *empowering parents,* who need to become aware of the dangers of the use of the Internet and to inform themselves about the issues.

The World Summit for Children

In September 1990, the World Summit for Children adopted the Declaration on the Survival, Protection and Development of Children and a Plan of Action for Implementing the Declaration. A series of goals was set up relating to child mortality, malnutrition, children's access to basic education worldwide, etc. to be met by the year 2000.

? None of the goals have been achieved, but does this mean that this summit was useless?

Many NGOs are organising themselves through a network of concerned people who monitor and report websites containing illegal materials[4].

The Council of Europe Convention on Cybercrime was adopted on 8 November 2001. When in force, this convention will be the first international treaty on crimes committed via the Internet and other computer networks, dealing particularly with computer- and Internet-related crimes including *child pornography*. Its main objective is to pursue a common criminal policy aimed at the protection of society against cybercrime, especially by adopting appropriate legislation and fostering international co-operation. Article 9 of the Convention is devoted to combating paedophilia and child pornography over the Internet.

Can we take measures to control the use of the Internet by children without violating their freedom to seek, receive and impart information and ideas of all kinds? (art.13 , CRC)

In Europe, the *European Network of Ombudsmen for Children* (ENOC) was set up in 1997. This includes representatives from Austria, Belgium, Denmark, Finland, France, Hungary, Iceland, Lithuania, the former Yugoslav Republic of Macedonia, Norway, Portugal, the Russian Federation, Spain, Sweden and Wales.

The Russian Ministry of Labour and Social Development has initiated a pilot project, establishing Commissioners for Children in 5 "oblasts" (states). The Commissioners have all been established by decree and are mandated to improve the protection and promotion of children's rights.

The Ombudsman for Children

The word 'ombudsman' comes from the Scandinavian word "ombud", which means ambassador, delegate or messenger. It has come to mean a person who deals with complaints from a defined group (in this case. children), who speaks on behalf of that group and who tries to improve conditions for individuals from that group as well as for the group as a whole.

The first ombudsman for children was established in Norway in 1981. The ombudsman is an independent, non-partisan agent, spokesperson, arbitrator or referee, ensuring that ministries and others fulfil their legislative duties by suggesting measures for improvements in issues related to children. The ombudsman protects the needs, rights and interests of minors, works for the application of the Convention on the Rights of the Child and supports its dissemination. The ombudsman has the power to investigate, criticise and publicise but not to reverse administrative action or revoke administrative decisions. The ombudsman intervenes separately from legal representatives, parents or guardians to represent the child's rights in all sorts of civil or criminal cases where children are directly or indirectly involved.

In some countries, the ombudsman is responsible for adopting assessment methods, such as the "child impact assessment" in order to evaluate and identify all possible consequences on children of various legislative proposals, regulations and any other measures. According to the Swedish NGO *Radda Barnen*, twenty countries have so far set up ombudsman for Children.

International and regional instruments and children

1. The Convention on the Rights of the Child, 1989
2. The World Declaration on the Survival, Protection and Development of Children
3. The Plan of Action for Implementing the World Declaration, 1990
4. The Parliamentary Assembly Recommendation 1460(2000) on Setting up a European Ombudsman for Children, Council of Europe, Strasbourg 2001.
5. The Council of Europe Parliamentary Assembly Recommendation 1286, 1996, on a European Strategy for Children
6. The European Convention on the Exercise of Children's Rights, Council of Europe, Strasbourg 1996

References

Asquith, S., Juvenile Justice and Juvenile Delinquency in Central and Eastern Europe - A Review - *Centre for the Child and Society, University of Glasgow.* *http://eurochild.gla.ac.uk*

Final report of the study group on street children, *Council of Europe, Strasbourg, April 1994.*

Flekkoy, M., A Voice for Children – Speaking as their Ombudsman, *UNICEF, 1991.*

The Global Movement for Children, www.gmfc.org.

Human Rights Education Newsletter, *No.29, Centre for Global Education, University of York, UK, 2001.*

Setting up a European Ombudsman for Children, *doc.8552, Council of Europe Parliamentary Assembly, 1999.*

The State of the World's Children, *UNICEF,* 2000.

"Trafficking in women, a comprehensive European strategy", information sheets, *European Commission.*

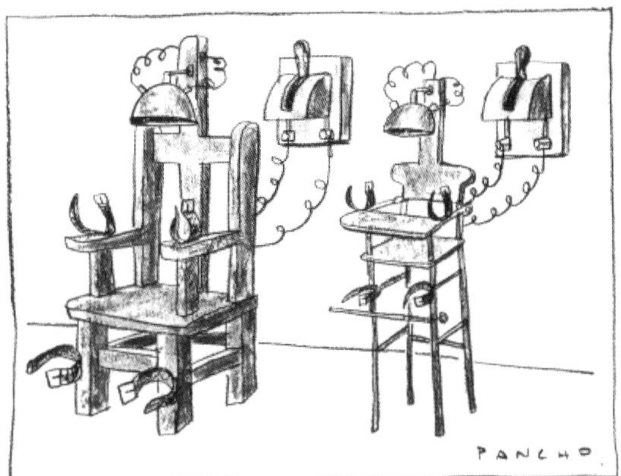

Citizenship

The simple view…

Most people in the world are legal citizens of one or another nation state, and this entitles them to certain privileges or rights. Being a citizen also imposes certain duties in terms of what the state expects from individuals under its jurisdiction. Thus, citizens fulfil certain obligations to their state and in return they may expect protection of their vital interests. Or that is the way it should be.

The complications…

There are two main questions that complicate this simple equation:

1. Which rights are states *obliged* to guarantee their citizens and on what terms?
2. What happens to those citizens that do not, for one reason or another, have the protection of the country in which they are resident?

To answer the first of these questions, we need to have a clearer idea of what being a citizen or what *citizenship* really means, and we shall look at that below. To answer the second question, we would need to look at why some people in the world do not possess citizenship of the country where they are resident and what can be done about it. This debate is really just beginning and in this section we shall raise only some of the questions.

Related activities

- A tale of two cities, page 71.
- Act it out, page 86.
- Beware, we are watching, page 95.
- "Draw the word" game, page 120.
- Education for all, page 122.
- Electioneering, page 127.
- Fighters for rights, page 130.
- Garden in a night, page 139.
- Heroines and heroes, page 142.
- Let every voice be heard, page 153.
- Making links, page 173.
- Power station, page 198.
- To vote or not to vote?, page 238.
- Trade union meeting, page 244.
- Where do you stand?, page 254.
- Who are I?, page 257.

What is citizenship?

People have been discussing the idea of citizenship for thousands of years and even today there is no absolute agreement on exactly what it means. The concept of *legal* citizenship appears to be relatively simple: this is normally linked to a nation state and is defined in terms of the laws of that nation. This is perhaps why, for many people, the idea of citizenship has an immediate connection with the idea of patriotism: a "good citizen" is often thought to be a "good patriot".

However, the concept of citizenship has far more layers of meaning than mere patriotism, as we can see from the historical origins of the idea, set out in the next section. A helpful distinction to bear in mind is that between a citizen, on the one hand, and a subject, on the other.

? Should citizens always obey the law?

Historical conceptions of citizenship

It is useful to look at some of the more important developments in the idea of citizenship, since this helps to bring out the various strands of meaning that are discussed today.

- The origin of citizenship can be traced back to Ancient Greece, when "citizens" were those who had a legal right to participate in the affairs of the state. But by no means everyone was a citizen: slaves and women, in particular, were mere subjects. For those who did have the privileged status of being citizens, the idea of "civic virtue" or being a "good" citizen was an important part of the concept. This tradition led to an emphasis on the *duties* that citizens were supposed to perform.
- The association of citizenship with national identity arose naturally from the fact that the legal status of a "citizen" was always tied to a nation state, hence the link between citizenship and patriotism.
- The liberal view of citizenship, which was developed in the nineteenth century, emphasised the importance of *rights* for all citizens. As the franchise began to be gradually extended, so justice and political rights became a reality for an increasing proportion of the population.
- In the twentieth century, the supporters of "social citizenship" went further, in recognising that civil and political rights are only part of what citizens ought to be able to expect from the state. The rise of the welfare state in the last century owed a great deal to thinkers who argued that rights of citizens ought to cover their own living and working conditions, rather than just their participation in "high" politics.
- The concept of "multiple citizenship" has been in existence for a while and allows that individuals may simultaneously be citizens of more than one state or organising body. For example, with the development of the European Union, citizens of the member states increasingly possess some rights from and duties to the Union as a whole, and not only to their own nation state.
- A final strand in the concept of citizenship, but one that is gaining increasing importance, involves the idea of *education*. If citizenship in the traditional sense involves *enjoying* rights and also *performing* duties, then there is a sense in which citizens may be said to be *not born, but created.* Loyalty and responsibility, for example, are qualities that need to be learned and cultivated. So, if these are qualities that are essential to being a citizen in the full meaning of the term, then "real" citizens need to be educated – in the broadest sense of the word.

Today, most people's notion of citizenship will include elements of each of the six concepts outlined above, although in different proportions. Some people will emphasise the "duties" element, while others will give more importance to "rights" or "patriotism", or to the qualities that should be possessed by "real" citizens.

"Citizenship is a complex and multi-dimensional reality which needs to be set in its political and historical context. One cannot speak of citizenship in isolation, since the idea only has any meaning in relation to the real needs of society or a political system. Democratic citizenship, specifically, refers to the active participation by individuals in the system of rights and responsibilities which is the lot of citizens in democratic societies.[5]".

The link with human rights

We can see that both rights and responsibilities have been an important part of the notion of citizenship from the earliest days: citizens are expected to possess certain fundamental rights, and they are also required to perform certain duties. It is these "duties", or responsibilities, that people have in mind when they speak of *what citizens ought to be like* or *how they ought to behave.*

"Everyone is as God made him, and often a great deal worse."

Miguel de Cervantes

> "Put simply, a subject obeys the laws and a citizen plays a part in making and changing them."
>
> *B. Crick.*

However, if such a notion strikes us as too directorial or as limiting too much the inherent freedom and dignity of every individual citizen, then it is important to remember that these limits arise as a direct consequence of human rights theory. It is only the desire to build societies which respect the human rights of all citizens that imposes responsibilities on us all as citizens.

There are two immediate links between the responsibilities of citizenship and human rights theory:

1. The fact that every individual possesses basic human rights does not give anyone licence to behave exactly as he or she wishes. It only gives them licence to do so in so far as this does not impinge upon the human rights of other individuals. So one thing we can certainly say about good citizenship is that *it requires citizens to have respect for the human rights of others.*
2. The second close link with human rights concerns the way in which the concept of citizenship is essentially tied in with *membership of society.* We do not speak, for example, of citizens of desert islands, because a citizen is much more than just an *inhabitant* of a particular country or region. A citizen is essentially a member of the society which inhabits that region; so, if we are concerned to build societies which respect human rights, then this imposes another restriction on the way that individuals inhabiting that society should behave.

Thus, another thing that we could say about good citizenship would be that *it requires the type of behaviour that would lead society to be more respectful of human rights.*

What should the citizen do when society is failing to respect the rights of certain sections of the community?

Problems with citizenship

Most of the debate today concerning citizenship is focused on the problem of increasing citizens' involvement and participation in the processes of democratic society. It is being increasingly realised that periodic voting by citizens is insufficient, either in terms of making those who govern in the interim period fully accountable or in promoting feelings of empowerment among ordinary citizens. Furthermore, even voting patterns themselves indicate levels of political apathy among the population that seriously undermine the effective functioning of democracy. It is with problems such as these in mind that programmes like the Council of Europe's Education for Democratic Citizenship have been initiated.

What forms of involvement or participation, other than voting in elections, are possible for the ordinary citizen?

A second set of issues which has possibly deserved less attention to date, but which is increasing in importance, concerns the question of those individuals who do not, for one reason or another, receive the full benefits of citizenship. One aspect of this is a result of continuing patterns of discrimination within societies: minority groups may very often have formal citizenship of the country in which they are living but may still be prevented from full participation in that society.

A second aspect of the problem is a consequence of increasing globalisation, including new patterns of work and migration, which leads to a significant number of people throughout the world being resident abroad but unable to apply for formal citizenship. Such people may include immigrant workers, refugees, temporary residents or even those who have decided to set up permanent residence in another country.

What should be the criteria for citizenship in an increasingly multicultural world? Should immigrant workers be entitled to some of the benefits of citizenship, if not to formal citizenship?

Education for democratic citizenship: the Council of Europe and youth

The Council of Europe's programme under this name has attempted to provide a European framework for the strengthening of education for democratic citizenship. The Council calls on member states to include such programmes within their educational, training, cultural and youth policies and practices, and it has itself worked actively to identify new strategies and approaches and to disseminate these.

The Draft Declaration and Programme on Education For Democratic Citizenship (April 1999) identified the following essential characteristics:

Education For Democratic Citizenship:

- constitutes a lifelong learning experience and a participative process developed in various contexts;
- equips men and women to play an active part in public life and to shape in a responsible way their own destiny and that of their society;
- aims to instil a culture of human rights which will ensure full respect for those rights and understanding of responsibilities that flow from them;
- prepares people to live in a multicultural society and to deal with difference knowledgeably, sensibly, tolerantly and morally;
- strengthens social cohesion, mutual understanding and solidarity;
- must be inclusive of all age groups and sectors of society.

One important aspect of the Programme on Education for Democratic Citizenship is that it is aimed at supporting various youth networks, partnerships, model initiatives, etc., in order to encourage young people to participate in civil society. Young people form an important part of the target population.

"I am impressed by the high number of young human rights activists here. Their knowledge and experience gives me confidence to continue our human rights education programme with schools and develop more out-of-school activities on learning citizenship[6]"

Ms Marina Kovinena, Youth Human Rights Education Forum, 2000.

References

Crick, B., Essays on citizenship, *Continuum, 2000.*
Education for Democratic Citizenship *(Council of Europe)* www.coe.int/T/E
Journal of Citizenship Studies, www.tandf.co.uk/journals/arfax/13621025.html.
Kennedy, K. (Ed), Citizenship education and the modern state, *Falmer Press, 1997.*
Oliver, D., Heater, D., The foundations of citizenship, *Harvester Wheatsheaf, 1994.*

Democracy

VOTE FOR ME
AS SOON AS YOU HAVE A POLITICAL IDEA, LET ME KNOW
ALRIGHT! YOU TOO
PANCHO

"No one is born a good citizen, no nation is born a democracy. Rather, both are processes that continue to evolve over a lifetime. Young people must be included from birth.[7]"

Kofi Annan

Democracy describes a system of making rules for a group of people. It comes from the Greek words *demos* - meaning people - and *kratos* meaning power. Accordingly, democracy is often defined as "the rule of the people"; in other words, a system of making rules which is put together by the people who are to obey those rules.

Could such a system exist and could it possibly be a good way of making decisions? Why did such an idea originally arise and why is it today considered, at least by most people and most countries in the world, *the only* system that is worth our attention? Does it really make sense for everyone to rule?

Why Democracy?

There are two fundamental principles that lie at the base of the idea of democracy and which help to explain its appeal:

1. the principle of *individual autonomy*: that no one should be subject to rules that have been imposed by others.
2. the principle of *equality*: that everyone should have the same opportunity to influence the decisions that affect people in society.

Both of these principles are intuitively appealing to everyone, and a democratic system of government is the only one that, at least in theory, accepts both as fundamental. Other systems, such as oligarchy, plutocracy or dictatorship, normally violate both principles: they give power to a certain (constant) sector of society and these people then take decisions on behalf of the rest of the population. Neither equality nor individual autonomy is respected in such cases.

The two principles above provide the moral justification for democracy, and we can see that both are in fact key human rights principles, but there are also pragmatic reasons that are often given as justification for a democratic system of government, rather than any other.

1. It is often claimed that a democratic system provides for a more efficient form of government, because the decisions that are taken are more likely to be respected by the people. People do not usually break their "own" rules.

Related activities

- Electioneering, page 127.
- Making links, page 173.
- To vote or not to vote, page 238.
- Trade union meeting, page 244.

2. Acceptance by the population is also more likely because decisions have been reached as a result of building a consensus among different factions; the rules would not be realistic if they were unacceptable to large sections of the population. Thus, there is a form of internal control on the type of laws that a democratically accepted government ought to consider.
3. A democratic system is also supposed to foster more initiative and therefore to be more responsive to changing conditions, on the "two heads are better than one" principle.

Do you feel any 'ownership' of the rules in your country? What might be the reasons for this?

"One ballot is stronger than the bullet."

Abraham Lincoln

A good theory...

In practice, it is not of course reasonable to expect everyone in society to contribute to the rule-making process and nor would everyone want to, so many countries use a system whereby citizens appoint representatives to make decisions on their behalf: *representative* rather than *direct* democracy. Every citizen, in theory, has an equal possibility to select the person they think will best represent their interests. In this way, the principle of equality is observed.

This was not always the case: at the birth of democracy, in Ancient Greece, women and slaves were not allowed to vote and neither, of course, were children. Today, in most countries of the world, women do have the vote but the struggle was won only relatively recently.

There are other sections of society, which commonly include immigrants, prisoners, children, who are not entitled to vote, even though they are obliged to obey the laws of the land.

Could excluding certain sectors of society from the democratic process ever be justifiable?

Control over the law-making process

If the principle of *equality* is more or less respected today, at least as far as voting is concerned, how does the first principle, of *autonomy* stand in the existing democracies? To what extent do individuals in these societies feel any "ownership" of the laws that are made by their representatives? The answer here is a great deal less encouraging. Indeed, most people, in most democracies of the world, would claim that the laws of the land *are* "imposed" on them by rulers who do not represent their interests. So has the first principle gone astray?

Is it possible, under a representative democracy, for people to have real power over those decisions that are made on their behalf?

There are a number of senses in which people can be said to have some control over the law-making process in a representative democracy. Again, we shall consider the ideal model, even if it does not seem to represent accurately the political situation in many countries. At least it assists us in identifying the problem areas and suggests ways in which these may be overcome.

1. Citizens influence the law-making process because they select the people who will make the laws: in theory, at elections, citizens choose between different possible representatives of their interests. Thus, they can choose the individual that offers the platform that is closest to their own interests.

"Two cheers for democracy: one because it admits variety and two because it permits criticism. Two cheers are quite enough: there is no occasion to give three."

E.M. Forster

2. Politicians have to stand for re-election. In the time period between elections, lawmakers will be aware that they will be judged at the next election on their performance and therefore should not be inclined to pass laws that will be obviously unacceptable to the populace. This is a form of tacit control.
3. There are, in principle, ample opportunities for citizens to indicate actively their displeasure with particular policies or laws, and thus to send a message back to their representatives that this is an area of concern.
4. There are also, in theory, opportunities for citizens to have a more positive influence on the legislative process by engaging in consultation with political representatives, either through NGOs, or other pressure groups and consultative bodies.
5. Ultimately, any individual is free to stand for election if they feel that none of the candidates is able to represent their interests.

Free and fair elections – a means to an end

"The will of the people shall be the basis of the authority of government; this will shall be expressed in periodic and genuine elections which shall be by universal and equal suffrage and shall be held by secret vote or by equivalent free voting procedures."

Article 21, paragraph iii, UDHR.

Elections are a method of exerting control over the lawmakers, and they exert that control, in theory at least, through invoking a desire, or need, for politicians to take their electorate into account in everything they do. Such a method clearly requires the elections to be free and fair but it also requires something that is perhaps more fundamental: that politicians *believe* that they will be held to account by the electorate if they fail to represent their interests. No politician has any need to represent interests that are different from his or her own unless he or she *fears* the punishment of the electorate. The system depends on that belief to operate effectively; and it therefore depends, ultimately, on the electorate applying that sanction from time to time or at least appearing to be ready to do so.

Thus "elections" may be quite easily introduced into a political system without necessarily having the effect of making that system genuinely democratic. Structural elections only contribute to a democratic system where the electorate uses them to call its representatives to account. High voter apathy in most democratic countries at the beginning of the twenty-first century threatens the effectiveness of this system of control.

It also calls into question the legitimacy of so-called democratically elected governments, which are, in some cases, actually elected by a *minority* of the total electorate.

Elections and apathy

"Stockholm, May 17 (IPS) - Apathy among voters muted celebrations after the first-ever elections to a national parliament for Sweden's indigenous reindeer-herding people, the Saami … the turnout in Sunday's inaugural election was low, with less than 50% of 12000 eligible voters going to the polls." *InterPress Third World News Agency (IPS), 1993*

"The Vladivostok City Duma's elections set for December 17 are already facing major setbacks when 12 candidates withdrew their nominations over the absence of voters in previous elections." *Vladivostok Daily, 29 November 2000*

"Although the election results represent a swing to the left, what is more indicative of the political atmosphere in Romania is the number of voters who failed to vote. Turnout was registered at an all-time low with a mere 44.5% participating in the election as compared to 56.4% in 1996." *Central Europe Review, 12 June 2000*

"Turnout at the general election in the UK dropped to an 80-year low with around 60% of the electorate bothering to cast their vote. Among the lowest was Liverpool Riverside where it stood at 34.1% of the electorate. Across the country 18-25 year olds were most apathetic, poll evidence suggests." *BBC, 9 June 2001*

"While turnout in the 1994 Slovak parliamentary elections was more than 70% overall, it is estimated that turnout among voters aged 18-25 was as low as 20%." *Rock volieb, 1998*

Democracy in the real world

There are as many different forms of democracy as there are democratic nations in the world. No two systems are exactly the same and no one system can be taken as a "model" of democracy. There are presidential and parliamentary democracies; democracies that are federal or confederal or unitary in nature; democracies that make constant use of referenda; ones that involve more consultation, or less, with outside organisations; democracies that use a proportional voting system, and ones that use a majoritarian system – or combinations of the two; and so on.

Each of these systems can lay some claim to being "democratic" in virtue of the fact that they are, nominally at least, based on the two principles above: equality of all citizens, and the right of every individual to some degree of personal autonomy. It is clearly not realistic to regard "autonomy" as meaning that every individual can *do what he or she likes,* but at the least the system, in allocating equal votes to all citizens, recognises that each individual is capable of independent choice and is entitled to have that choice taken into account. After that, a great deal depends on the individual citizens.

Nevertheless, despite the claims of almost every nation in the world to be "democratic", there is no doubt that every democratic system currently in existence is quite capable of being *more democratic* than it is at present, something that each of them is arguably in need of.

Key date

10 December
Human Rights Day

Problems with democracy

There is fairly universal concern about the status of democracy at the beginning of the twenty-first century. Much of this is based on the low levels of citizen participation at elections, which appear to indicate a lack of interest and involvement on the part of citizens and which undermine the democratic process in some of the ways that have been discussed.

Although this is undoubtedly a problem, there are other studies which indicate that participation in different forms is actually on the increase – for example, pressure groups, civic initiatives, consultative organs, and so on. These forms of participation are just as essential to the effective functioning of democracy as voter turnout at elections, if not more so. Elections, after all, are a crude way of ensuring that people's interests are accurately represented, and four or five years, which is the normal gap between elections, is a long time to wait to hold the government to account. People have short memories!

"In Northern Ireland we are discussing a new Bill of Rights. I want to link the rights in this bill to the lives of the youngsters in our youth club."

Tara Kinney, Northern Ireland Youth Forum, participant at the Forum on Human Rights Education, 2000.

There are two further problems that are more intricately connected to the notion of representative democracy, and these concern minority interests. The first problem is that minority interests are often not represented through the electoral system: this may happen if their numbers are too few to reach the minimum level necessary for any representation, or it may more commonly happen because electoral systems often use a "winner-takes-all" system. The second problem is that even if their numbers are represented in the legislative body, they will have a minority of representatives and these may not therefore be able to summon up the necessary votes to defeat the majority representatives. For these reasons, democracy is often referred to as "rule of the majority".

Democracy itself cannot be relied upon to solve the second of these issues. It is perfectly conceivable - and has happened innumerable times - that the majority authorise decisions that are detrimental to the minority. That it is the "will of the people" is no justification for such decisions. The basic interests of minorities as well as majorities can only be safeguarded through adherence to human rights principles, reinforced by an effective legal mechanism – whatever the will of the majority may be.

"Democracy is the theory that the common people know what they want and deserve to get it good and hard."

H.L. Mencken

We fight for:

freedom and human rights, so that every individual, woman and man, can have full political rights without being discriminated against on the basis of class, caste, gender, religion or race.

equality, and against any form of discrimination among individuals; for social justice; for equality between the genders; for equal opportunities and equal access to knowledge.

democracy, based on the principles of freedom and equality, and against authoritarianism, populism and dictatorship; for the right to self-determination, to liberty and freedom of expression for all peoples.

universal solidarity, because we believe in the possibility of collective action for the liberation of individuals.

political solutions to problems, because we believe in the ability of human beings to change the world.

References

Beetham, D., Democracy and human rights, *Polity Press, 1999.*

International Institute for Democracy, www.iidemocracy.coe.int/.

Inter-Parliamentary Union, www.ipu.org/.

Lijphart, A., Patterns of democracy, *Yale University Press, 1999.*

Politeia Network for Citizenship and Democracy in Europe, www.politeia.net.

Rock Volieb, Slovakia, www.rockvolieb.sk/.

Discrimination and Xenophobia

WELL THERE YOU ARE: HE'S NOT LIKE US...
WHICH ONE?
PANCHO

"Civilisation should be judged by its treatment of minorities"

Mahatma Gandhi

Related activities

- Access to medicaments, page 80.
- Act it out, page 86.
- All equal, all different, page 88.
- Can I come in?, page 98.
- Different wages, page 107.
- Do we have alternatives?, page 111.
- Heroines and heroes, page 142.
- Let's talk about sex, page 156.
- Path to Equality-land, page 185.
- Picture games, page 188.
- Responding to racism, page 201.
- See the ability, page 209.
- Sport for all, page 214.
- Take a step forward, page 217.
- The language barrier, page 228.
- Who are I?, page 257.
- Work and babies, page 260.

What is discrimination?

Neither the Universal Declaration of Human Rights nor other international agreements have a generic definition of *"discrimination"* , although they refer to it several times. International and regional human rights instruments dealing with specific forms of discrimination differ in their definitions depending on the type of discrimination involved.

"Racial discrimination" is defined by the International Convention on the Elimination of All Forms of Racial Discrimination as "any distinction, exclusion, restriction or preference based on race, colour, descent, or national or ethnic origin which has the purpose or effect of nullifying or impairing the recognition, enjoyment or exercise, on a equal footing, of human rights and fundamental freedoms in the political, economic, social, cultural or any other field of public life."

"Discrimination against women" is defined by the Convention on the Elimination of All Forms of Discrimination against Women (CEDAW) as "any distinction, exclusion or restriction made on the basis of sex which has the effect or purpose of impairing or nullifying the recognition, enjoyment or exercise by women, of human rights and fundamental freedoms in the political, economic, social, cultural, civil or any other field."

We can identify the following elements in both definitions:

There is a *cause* based, for example, on "race", on gender or on ethnic origin – she is black, she is a woman, he is Roma - of the person or group discriminated against. The person or groups that discriminate perceive the above-mentioned characteristics as a problem. There are *actions* that are qualified as discrimination; these can be rejection (not wanting to have a black person as a friend), restriction (prohibiting the entrance of gay people to a discotheque),

> "During my lifetime I have dedicated myself to this struggle of the African people, I have fought against white domination, and I have fought against black domination. I have cherished the ideal of a democratic and free society in which all persons live together in harmony and with equal opportunities. It is an idea, which I hope to live for and to achieve. But if needs be it is an ideal for which I am prepared to die."
>
> *Nelson Mandela*

exclusion of a person or a group of people (not hiring women), etc. There are *consequences* that can also be the *purpose* of the discriminatory action. All of these can prevent the victim from exercising and/or enjoying their human rights and fundamental freedoms.

Discrimination may be practiced in a direct or indirect way. *Direct* discrimination is characterised by the *intent* to discriminate against a person or a group, such as an employment office which rejects a Roma job applicant or a housing company which does not let flats to immigrants. "Direct discrimination shall be taken to occur where one person is treated less favourably than another is, has been or would be treated in a comparable situation on grounds of racial or ethnic origin." [8]

Indirect discrimination focuses on the *effect* of a policy or measure. It occurs when an apparently neutral provision, criterion or practice puts *de facto* a person or persons of a particular minority at a disadvantage compared with others. Examples may range from a minimum height criterion for firefighters (which may exclude many more female than male applicants), to the department store which does not hire persons with long skirts, or the government office or school regulation which prohibits entry or attendance by persons with covered heads. These rules, apparently neutral with regard to ethnicity or religion, may de facto disproportionately disadvantage members of certain minority or religious groups who wear long skirts or headscarves.

? Have you ever felt unfairly discriminated against?

Discrimination against persons and groups on the grounds of race, religion, sex, ethnic origin, descent, nationality or sexual orientation is forbidden by many international human rights instruments and by most national legislations.

However, minorities are traditionally discriminated against, regardless of whether they are national, religious, cultural, ethnic or social minorities.

Discrimination at work

"A staff member of the French branch of Ikea, a furniture company, has been sentenced to a 4 572 Euro fine for providing guidelines to the managers of the company not to hire "coloured people". The convicted woman, as well as Ikea France, will have to pay compensation of a total of 15 240 Euros following the complaint presented by four trade unions together with "SOS Racisme" and the "Mouvement contre le Racisme et pour l´Amitié entre les Peuples." The employee had written and sent out an e-mail which recommended not hiring "coloured people" for the work of supervising the correct distribution of the advertisement catalogues." *EFE Press release, April 2001*

The negative consequences of widespread forms of overt or covert discrimination have led some societies to adopt practices of *positive discrimination*. Positive discrimination, also known as *affirmative action*, deliberately favours or gives preference to a certain group or groups such as women, disabled people or specific ethnic groups. The main purpose of such policies is to overcome structural forms of discrimination which otherwise would prevail against specific social groups, usually minorities, and to redress balances in representation.

Non-discrimination in the ECHR.

In June 2000, the adoption by the Committee of Ministers of the Council of Europe of Protocol No.12 to the European Convention on Human Rights broadens the scope of the Convention

regarding discrimination. At present, non-discrimination is addressed in article 14, which prohibits discrimination only in the enjoyment of the rights already enshrined in the Convention. Protocol 12 marks a significant development since it provides opportunities for enhanced action in the field of racism and discrimination as a general non-discrimination clause. This Protocol will enter into force only after ten states have ratified it.

Discrimination, xenophobia and racism are also widespread in other parts of the world: there are around 160 million Dalits (Untouchables) in India. In the United States of America, studies have shown that race is a key factor in determining who is sentenced to death. In Rwanda almost one million people were killed, mostly Tutsi, over a short period of three months in 1994.

Xenophobia

The Oxford English Dictionary definition of xenophobia is "a morbid fear of foreigners or foreign countries". In other words, it means an aversion to strangers or foreigners.

Xenophobia is a feeling or a perception based on socially constructed images and ideas and not on rational or objective facts.

A xenophobic perception of the world reduces complex social and cultural phenomena to simplistic good and bad scenarios.

"*We*" (the locals) = the model, the good and normal ones, the reference who everyone should look, feel, think like – versus "*Them*" (the strangers) = the delinquents, the threat, the disturbance, the vagrants, the violent ones, the burglars, the invasive ones, etc. "*We*" (the locals) are the good ones versus "*Them*" (the others), the bad ones. It is obvious that we attach value to the perceptions we have of others and ourselves, such as

"*We*" = positive and "*They*" = negative.

To build our identities as individuals and members of a group, an ethnic group, a nation, etc. implies becoming aware of the diversity in society and one's difference from others, which is not negative in itself as long as diversity is not perceived as threatening and the recognition of these differences is not used for political manipulation. The other should be perceived first of all as a brother or sister, as a fellow human, not as a foreigner, enemy or rival.

It should be noted that while in eastern Europe the main targets of xenophobia are likely to be members of minority groups, in many Western countries the targets tend to be immigrants and refugees, including those coming from Eastern European countries.

? Can you think of recent examples of xenophobia in your country?

Even though the fear of foreigners – xenophobia - is considered morally unacceptable and goes against what would constitute a culture of human rights, it is not illegal and thus it cannot be legally punished as such. Consequently, it is only the manifestations of xenophobia, (which can derive from xenophobic perceptions and which can take attitudinal or physically violent forms, such as acts of racist attacks, discrimination at work, verbal attacks or abuse, ethnic cleansing, genocide, etc.) that are subject to sanction in so far as there are laws qualifying these actions as crimes.

Racism

Racism can be defined in many ways. One definition considers racism as a conscious or unconscious belief in the inherent superiority of one race over another. The implication of this definition is that, in the first place, the "superior" race has the right to exercise power over and dominate those that are considered "inferior"; and that, in the second place, racism conditions both the attitudes and behaviour of individuals and groups. However, there is a problem in that the term 'racism' presupposes the existence of different "races". In recent

Key date

23 August
International Day for the Remembrance of the Slave Trade and its Abolition

years, it has been established that "race" is, in fact, a social construct and that it is impossible to classify people according to any other category than that of "human being". Therefore, racism exists even though "race" does not.

Europe has a long history of racism. Historically, the existence of "superior" and "inferior" races has been argued on the grounds of biological differences. Darwinian theories of evolution were applied to human beings in order to classify them according to "race". Colonialism, when European nations subjugated others to their exploitation, was possible due to the widespread acceptance of social Darwinism and other similarly "racist" theories. The "white man's burden" implied the "duty" of colonial Europeans to "civilize" other peoples. Slavery, another common practice among European entrepreneurs and governments until the 19th century, was also based on the belief that slaves belonged to "inferior races".

Nowadays, racists put emphasis on cultural differences rather than on biological inferiority. *Cultural racism* is based on the belief that there is a hierarchy of cultures or that certain cultures, traditions, customs, and histories are incompatible. The exclusion and discrimination of foreigners or minorities is justified in the name of allegedly "incompatible cultures" , religions or "civilisations".

Power and its use and misuse are heavily bound up with racism. Racism is at one and the same time defined by those who have power and it defines power relations between perpetrators and victims. The victims of racism find themselves in a powerless position. Prejudice, or the negative judgement of other persons or groups (without significant knowledge or experience of those persons or groups), is also bound up with racism. Hence, racism can be understood as the practical translation of prejudices into actions or forms of treatment of others by those who hold power and who are therefore in a position to carry those actions out.

Racism can exist at different levels:

- a *personal level*: this refers to personal attitudes, values and beliefs about the superiority of one's "race" and the inferiority of other "races".
- an *interpersonal level:* this refers to behaviour towards others that reflects the belief of the superiority of one's "race".
- an *institutional level*: this refers to the established laws, customs, traditions and practices which systematically result in racial inequalities and discrimination in a society, organisations or institutions.
- a *cultural level*: this refers to the values and norms of social conduct that promote one's native cultural practices as the norm and the measuring standard and judge other cultural practices to be inferior.

The different levels at which racism manifests itself are highly interdependent and actively feed each other. Racism also manifests itself in overt and covert ways. In its subtlest and most covert forms, racism is as damaging as in its overt forms.

The consequences of racism, both historically and contemporarily, are devastating for both the victims and the societies where this injustice has been perpetrated. Racism has been at the origin of mass extermination, genocide and oppression. It has ensured the subjugation of majorities to the whims of tiny minorities who have a stranglehold on both wealth and power. While much progress has been made to remedy these injustices, today hidden and less hidden forms of isolation, discrimination and segregation still exist and continue to be practised. Those perceived as "different" or "foreign" face restrictions in their freedom of movement, outright aggression, humiliation or social exclusion.

It is estimated that nearly 12 million Native American Indians in North America were exterminated between 1600 and 1850. Between 10 and 20 million black Africans are presumed to have died during the 200 years of the international slave trade.

Racism and youth violence

Youth violence motivated by racial hatred is a reality in most European countries. There are numerous reported cases of young people and/or adults being attacked, beaten up, threatened and, in the most extreme cases, killed, because of their nationality, appearance, religion, the colour of their skin, their hair or even their beard.

Racist violence has other subtle, but more diffuse, means of expression. It includes multiple forms of scapegoating, segregation and discrimination. Being singled out for police controls and checks because one looks different – darker skinned or darker haired – is also a form of oppression.

Key date

21 March
International Day for the Elimination of Racial Discrimination

The United Nations World Conference against Racism, Racial Discrimination, Xenophobia and Related Intolerance (WCAR)

The third WCAR was held in Durban, South Africa between the 31 August and 7 September 2001. This conference generated a very important international movement and many expectations. Nearly 160 states and more than 1500 NGO participants took part. The conference was dominated by two issues: the plight of Palestinians (including attempts to re-label Zionism as a racist practice) and recognition of slavery as a crime against humanity and the right for compensation. The final text ended up recognising the two issues with a wording that was acceptable to most:

> *"We are concerned about the plight of the Palestinian people under foreign occupation. We recognise the inalienable right of the Palestinian people to self-determination and to the establishment of an independent state. We also recognise the right to security for all states in the region, including Israel, and call upon all states to support the peace process and bring it to an early conclusion."*

An apology for slavery was also inserted although the text did not go as far as to offer any compensation. The recognition of the slave trade and of slavery as crimes against humanity was, for many, a historical moment in the restoration of dignity to a large part of humanity.

? Do you think that the governments from countries who benefited from slavery in the past should now pay for compensation?

In addition to the official conference, an NGO forum and an international youth forum were held in the days preceding the WCAR. Youth organisations, representatives and youth delegates on government delegations were invited to participate. Some 200 young adults representing all geographical regions gathered to discuss key issues related to the struggle against racism and xenophobia.

? Why should racist propaganda on the Internet be controlled or forbidden?

Immigrants, refugees and asylum-seekers

In Europe today, many immigrants, asylum-seekers and refugees face very difficult situations and see their basic rights and dignity violated every day. Refugees and asylum-seekers have often been forced to leave their homes, countries and families to save themselves from war, persecution or a complete lack of security. Although the vast majority of refugees in the world do not seek asylum in Europe, some people and groups do. The growing or persisting feelings of nationalism and xenophobia, or simply the concerns of xenophobe politicians, have led many governments to adopt very strict measures towards asylum-seekers, aimed mostly at ensuring that they do not reach their territory.

In the city of Frankfurt-am-Oder, located on the Polish-German border, a group of young German skinheads frequently threaten and attack foreign students from the university and foreign workers. On the Polish side, in the suburbs of Frankfurt-am-Oder, there is a city called Slubice where another group of young neo-nazis hunt foreigners. An incident was reported stating how they had started to beat up a student but apologised to him when they realised he was Spanish. They had thought he was German.[9]

Key dates

20 June
World Refugee Day

18 December
International Migrants Day.

Asylum-seekers and refugees form a particularly vulnerable target group, whose status is defined and protected by the Geneva Refugee Convention of 1951. Most European countries now have legislation that allows them to be detained at airports and border police stations, often without any consideration of their rights. Deportation of illegal immigrants or asylum-seekers who see their application rejected is a common practice and sometimes a form of degrading treatment.

? **What happens if a refugee seeks asylum in your country? Do you know what they have to do?**

The Schengen agreements (1990) provide for free movement and unrestricted travel to persons across all borders of 14 of the European Union member states. However, while abolishing the former existing borders, the EU has built a larger "border" to protect the European area.

The development of a common European policy towards refugees and migrants has often been described as a "fortress Europe" policy partly because of its emphasis on exclusion and the deflection of refugees, and partly because it is an example of how the fear of economic migration can block out consideration for the reality and needs of asylum-seekers.

? **Where do refugees in your country come from? Why are they refugees?**

The very restrictive and xenophobic policies held by many European countries force many immigrants to turn to illegal methods of getting into Europe. They often fall prey to organised traffickers. Most never reach Europe, while some die on the way: on the sea and coasts of Spain, in abandoned ships and boats in the Mediterranean or in trains and trucks where they suffocate to death.

Illegal immigration also means cheap labour for many industries and entrepreneurs. Poverty in countries like Moldova and Ukraine has resulted in many men seeking work in western European countries. Because they are "illegal", they are forced to work in very bad conditions and for very low salaries. They are often blackmailed by having their passports retained or they are threatened with denunciation to the police. Young women often face similar situations of human trafficking for domestic work and forced prostitution.

In most countries, there is a *utilitarian* view of the immigrant. The immigrant is not welcomed for their intrinsic value as a person who can contribute to the development of society, but rather they are welcomed and accepted only in so far as the labour potential that they he represent is needed.

? **Do you think that only people with money should be allowed to enter your country?**

Many young people from immigrant backgrounds or of immigrant descent, so-called second or third generation immigrants, experience different forms of discrimination on a daily basis, sometimes resulting in violence, social exclusion and criminalisation. One of the most common manifestations of covert racist discrimination is asking those young people to "make a choice" between so-to-say their parents' "culture" and that of their "host" country. The same type of suspicion regarding identity, allegiance and patriotism is applied to other social and ethnic minorities.

"The value of human dignity is at the centre of my work with immigrants. We encourage those young immigrants coming to us to share their story with their peers."

Ms Giulia Sanolla, Italian volunteer at Sud

Anti-Semitism and Romaphobia

All across Europe, the Jews and the Roma have historically been the two minorities that have suffered most from discrimination on grounds of their supposed *"inferiority"* and the subsequent negative stereotyping attached to this alleged status of inferiority.

Both minorities originated from outside Europe, the Jews from the area of what is now Israel and Palestine and from the southern shores of the Black Sea, and the Roma from India. Both migrated due to persecution, both have suffered down the ages at the hands of the majorities in Europe and both were considered inferior and many of both groups were exterminated by the nazis during the second world war. Both suffered under the communist regimes in Europe and both still experience discrimination, hatred and prejudice today, even though their social realities are very different.

 **What happened to Jewish people in your country during second world war?**

Key dates

9 November
The anniversary of the Kristallnacht
International Day against Fascism and Anti-Semitism.

30 April
Holocaust Memorial Day (Yom ha Shoah)

Anti-Semitism

Anti-Semitism can be defined as "hostility towards Jews as a religious or minority group often accompanied by social, economic, and political discrimination"[10], and this has been widespread in European history up to the present. Anti-Semites have fabricated stories about Jewish conspiracies, fuelling the anti-Semitic attitude of non-Jewish people against them, the most infamous being the "Protocols of the wise men of Zion" (a fictitious slanderous document inciting violence against Jews and which still circulates today in some European countries).

By the end of the nineteen century, Jewish communities in Russia regularly became victims of *pogroms* (a Russian word meaning devastation), which were organised systematic discriminatory acts of violence against Jewish communities by the local population, often with the passive consent or active participation of the police, encouraged by the anti-Semitic policies of the government. Attacks on Jewish communities were also common in other European countries including, for example, France and Austria.

The rise of fascism in the first part of the 20th century brought further hardship for many Jews in Europe, as anti-Semitism became part of the ideology in power. Fascist regimes and parties also collaborated directly or indirectly with the German nazi regime during the Holocaust.

During the Holocaust perpetrated by the nazi Germany and its allies during the second world war, known also as the Shoah (a Hebrew work meaning desolation), an estimated six million Jews were systematically exterminated for no other reason than that they were Jews. The Holocaust was the culmination of the racist and anti-Semitic policies that characterised Hitler's government, whose savagery had commenced with the "Kristallnacht", a massive pogrom throughout Germany on 9 November 1938.

With the success of the Bolshevik Revolution, pogroms ceased in the Soviet Union but anti-Semitism continued in different forms, including forced displacements, confiscation of property and show trials. Under communist regimes, anti-Semitism was often also disguised under official anti-Zionist policies.

Today, anti-Semitism is as alive as ever, even if in an often covert manner. Groups claiming their superiority desecrate Jewish cemeteries, networks of neo-nazi groups, often including young people, openly shout their anti-Semitism, and there are many Internet websites and literature circulating and glorifying nazi propaganda.

Romaphobia

Roma people (wrongly named as Gypsies, including the Sinti), have always been viewed as different by other Europeans. For much of history, they have been nomads, moving from one place to another as tinkers, craftsmen, musicians and traders. Throughout their history they have been submitted to forced assimilation; the Roma language has been prohibited in some countries and their children have been forcibly taken away from the parents. Roma people

Key date

8 April
World Roma Day

were slaves in many countries, the last having been Romania, where their slavery was abolished in 1856. The Roma have never had a state and they have never fought wars against other people. Throughout the twentieth century they continued to be considered as *vagrants* and in many countries laws were passed to force them to settle down.

Today, Roma communities continue to be directly and indirectly discriminated, persecuted and unwanted across all European countries.

What is the size of the Roma community in your country?

Porajmos refers to the Genocide of European Roma and Sinti perpetrated by German nazis and their allies between 1933 and 1945. The estimated number of victims varies according to different sources between 500000 and 2000000. As the result of *Porajmos*, Roma in Europe lost up to 70% of their pre-war population.

The communist regimes of eastern Europe, under the banner of "emancipating the Roma", broke the Roma traditional way of life. The Roma family disintegrated even further with the advent of capitalism – the Roma are generally not qualified for high-tech work and they are thus condemned to manual labour, unemployment and social exclusion.

Today, the Roma population in Europe totals an estimated eight to twelve million people, across literally all European states. The vast majority are sedentary but in some Western countries nomadism is still practised, fully or partially. While Roma in Spain and Portugal have practically lost Romany as a language (because it was forbidden and repressed) in most other countries' Roma communities, the Romany language is still a unifying cultural factor.

Romaphobia, discrimination and hostility towards Roma people, is a widespread common reality all over Europe. The Roma are among the first to suffer in armed conflict, as in the wars in the former Yugoslavia where the plight of Roma, caught in the crossfire, was mostly ignored. Other recent examples, include Roma families being de facto illegally stripped of their right to property on the grounds of "fighting crime" (Portugal); discrimination regarding access to education for Roma children and provision of basic community services (in the United Kingdom and France, for example, for travelling communities) or simply having their recognised rights respected. In many countries, Roma have been victims of violent fascist and racist groups, resulting in murders; Roma children are sometimes put together in the same school as mentally handicapped children. Roma villages are often segregated and isolated.

"Gypsies should be hunted down with fire and sword."

Spanish law, eighteenth century.

What can you find in your local news about Roma?

Many young Roma people and children grow up in hostile social environments where the only support and recognition they have is in their own community or family. They are denied many basic rights or have limited access to them, such as education or health.

A greater awareness and concern about the Roma is slowly emerging. At the international level, the International Romany Union is the most representative political Roma organisation, with consultative status at different United Nations bodies. The European Roma Rights Centre, based in Budapest, is the main international Roma human rights organisation, active in raising public awareness, monitoring and defence of Roma human rights.

The disabled and handicapped

Disability is defined as a condition that disables, as a result of an illness, injury or physical handicap; the expression is also used as a term of legal disqualification or incapacity.

"Persons with disabilities have the right to independence, social integration and participation in the life of the community."

Article 15 of the revised European Social Charter

The term *"disability"* encapsulates a great number of different functional limitations occurring in any population in any country of the world. People may be disabled by physical, intellectual or sensory impairment, medical conditions or mental illness. Such impairments, conditions or illnesses may be permanent or temporary in nature.

The term *"handicap"* means the loss or limitation of opportunities to take part in the life of the community on an equal level with others. It describes the encounter between the person with a disability and the environment. Both terms are indeed adequate, but the emphasis carried by each of them is slightly and significantly different.

? How can people with disabilities participate in the activities of your organisation?

It has been estimated that, on average, 10% of the world population has a disability. For the nearly 800 million population of the 43 Council of Europe member states, that would mean some 80 million persons with disabilities. Despite the progress made in recent years in numerous areas, many people with disabilities in Europe today are still faced with barriers to equal opportunities and full participation in the life of the community, such as low levels of education and vocational training; high unemployment rates; low income; obstacles in the physical environment; social exclusion; intolerance, clichés and stereotypes; direct or indirect discrimination; violence, ill-treatment and abuse.[11] According to a Eurobarometer survey in 2001, 97% of the people interviewed think that something should be done to ensure better integration of people with disabilities into society.[12]

Key dates

10 October
World Mental Health Day

3 December
International Day of Disabled Persons

Within the European Union, most organisations active in promoting the rights of the disabled are part of the European Disability Forum (EDF). Within the Council of Europe, actions and policies are co-ordinated by the Directorate General of Social Affairs.

The European Union declared 2003 to be the European Year of the Disabled Citizen.

What do people with disabilities want?

"Nothing special, nothing unusual. We want to be able to attend our neighbourhood school, to use the public library, to go to the movies, to get on a bus to go shopping downtown or to visit friends and family across town or across the country. We want to be able to get into our neighbourhood polling station to vote with everyone else on election day. We want to be able to get married. We want to be able to work. We want to be able to provide for our children. We want high quality, affordable medical care. We want to be seen as real people, as a part of society, not something to be hidden away, pitied or given charity." Adrienne Rubin Barhydt, April 10, 1996[13].

Source: www.disrights.org

Homophobia or discrimination because of sexual orientation

Homophobia may be defined as aversion or hatred to gay or homosexual people or their lifestyle or culture, or generally of people with a different sexual orientation.

Key date

17 May
International Day against Homophobia

7 August
Transgender International Rights and Education Day

In many parts of the world, individuals that have a different sexual orientation (different from the majority) are subjected to discrimination that ranges from being insulted to being murdered. In many countries, the practice of homosexuality is still a crime and in some of them it is punishable by the death penalty. Within Europe, although progress has been achieved, in changing legislation, many people still see homosexuality as a disease, a psychological disorder or unnatural behaviour.

Homosexuality means different things to different people. Some basic definitions:

- *Bisexual* refers to somebody attracted to person(s) of the same and the opposite gender.
- *Gay* is a term used for homosexual men. In some circles it also includes homosexual women (Lesbians).
- *Homosexual* refers to a person attracted to persons of the same gender only.
- *Heterosexual* refers to persons attracted to persons of the opposite gender only.
- *Lesbian* is used to refer to female homosexuals, i.e. women attracted to other women.
- *Transgender* is used to refer to a person who has a different gender from what their biological sex indicates (i.e. a man in a female body or the other way round).
- *LGBT* is an abbreviation of Lesbian, Gay, Bisexual and Transgender.

Living as an LGBT person in Europe today varies from being very easy (in the larger towns in western Europe, with a well-developed subculture, bars, clubs and organisations), to being relatively difficult (in small-town western Europe, and large parts of central Europe where views about homosexuality are slowly changing) all the way to being outright dangerous (harassment by the police as well as "normal" people as well as discriminatory laws and hate-crimes are the order of the day in some eastern European Countries such as, for example, Bulgaria, Albania, Romania and Moldova).

In a report presented in June 2001 to the European Parliament on sexual discrimination in Poland, 22% of LGBT people stated that they have experienced physical abuse and 77% of them have never reported these incidents to the police for fear of the reactions of their families and the police .[14]

Lesbian and Gay couples across all of Europe are also victims of legal discrimination, in areas such as the right to marry, to constitute a family or to adopt children (in other words, they can not benefit from the same status as heterosexual couples).

 **Do you know any famous gay or lesbian person from your country?**

The pink triangle

Tens of thousands of homosexuals died in the nazi concentration camps. The pink triangle and the pink colour are commonly associated with homosexual movements and culture, derived from the pink badge that homosexuals had to wear in the nazi concentration camps on the grounds of "sexual deviance".

"In the case of gays, history and experience teach us that the scarring comes not from poverty or powerlessness, but from invisibility. It is the tainting of desire, it is the attribution of perversity and shame to spontaneous bodily affection, it is the prohibition of expression of love, it is the denial of full moral citizenship in society because you are what you are (...)"
Justice Albie Sachs, Constitutional Court of South Africa, 1998.[15]

The biggest problems LGBT young people face are, on the one hand, discrimination by strangers, meaning violence, harassment and denial of services (getting kicked out of a restaurant is a common occurrence). On the other hand, there are often problems with family and friends once somebody comes out to them. For a lot of people, these are very serious problems, and a lot of LGBT young people postpone their coming-out for fear of rejection. At school, peer pressure can be very strong and make life difficult for LGBT students.

 **Should gay and lesbian couples be allowed to marry?**

Young people are also particularly vulnerable targets of homophobic violence and discrimination. Often they have to cope with feelings of guilt and deep questions about their sexual identity

and they fear rejection or being misunderstood. The negative "feedback" they receive puts them at odds with themselves and society. On top of this, violence and abuse force many into depression and sometimes leads to suicide.

Religious discrimination

Diversity within Europe is often most visible as religious diversity. The majority of Europeans are Christians, even if they don't "practise" their religion, but this majority often "hides" a lot of diversity. Europe has been deeply torn by wars between Catholics and Protestants, as it was previously by wars between Catholics and Eastern Orthodox Christians. Within each denomination there are many branches with differences that are often indiscernible to the layperson but are crucial to those who believe in them.

Although Christian religious minorities exist across the whole of Europe, historically they have been (and in some countries are still) discriminated against. Their religion or church is not "recognised" or does not have the same status or rights (for example, in education) as the "official" or dominant church.

Partly due to the process of European integration and co-operation, differences between Christian denominations have become less important in socio-political terms. For some thinkers and politicians, Christianity should be a basis of European identity, a dangerous move that ignores the millions of Europeans who are not religious and, of course, also those who are not Christian.

Which minority religions exist in your town or community? Where do they gather and worship?

Among non-Christian religions, Judaism is perhaps the one that, throughout history, has been the most widely discriminated against across the continent. After the expulsions from Spain and Portugal in the 15th century, for example, those who remained were converted by force or had to practise their religion secretly and at great risk to their lives. Prejudice and misconceptions about the Jewish faith has certainly contributed to fuelling anti-Semitic attitudes. It has also been historically used to justify discrimination and segregation against Jews and probably contributed to the passive tolerance of the Holocaust in some predominantly Christian societies.

During second world war, Jehovah's Witnesses were sent to concentration camps because they refused to serve in the German army.

Other important religious minority communities in Europe include Hindus, Buddhists, Baha'is, Rastafarians and Sikhs. Depending on the country, they may experience different forms of discrimination. In many cases, religious discrimination is combined with racism.

Islamophobia

Among non-Christian religions, Islam is the most followed in Europe. It is the majority religion in some countries and regions in the Balkans and in the Caucasus and is the second largest religion in France, Germany and in many other countries, both western and eastern.

The spotlight that has been focused on Muslims across the world in the aftermath of the horrific attacks on the United States in 2001 show how fragile community relations and our sense of tolerance really are. Muslims living in the West were surprised that people whom they thought to be friends, neighbours and co-citizens could suddenly turn and blame them for the attack on the World Trade Centre and even carry out revenge attacks on innocent men, women and young children. Of particular concern is that fact that in the United States and across Europe a number of women who wear the headscarf have been attacked.

"Everyone has the right to freedom of thought, conscience and religion; this right includes freedom to change their religion or belief, and freedom, either alone or in community with others and in public or private, to manifest their religion or belief, in worship, teaching, practice and observance."

European Convention on Human Rights, article 9, 1.

 **What images do you have of Islam?**

Islamophobia, literally meaning a fear of Islam, Muslims and matters pertaining to them, is not a new phenomenon. It is in fact an ancient form of prejudice that has recently become a topical issue due to the devastating effect it is having on the lives of Muslims, especially those Muslims who live in minority communities.

The present situation feeds on strong and deep-rooted prejudice in most European societies regarding Islam. Some of the most common forms are the lack of official recognition as a religion, the non-granting of permission to build mosques or the non-provision of facilities or support to Muslim religious groups or communities.

Ignorance about Islam is the main reason for Islamophobia. Islam is often associated only with terrorism and extremism. In fact, Islam is a religion that preaches tolerance, solidarity and love for each other, like many religions do.

What can be done in your organisation or school to increase knowledge and understanding of other religions?

One of the most common prejudices about Islam is its so-called *"incompatibility"* with human rights. This prejudice often stems from the reality of countries where Islam is the majority religion, mostly Arab countries. The absence of democracy and widespread violations of human rights are given as examples of this *"incompatibility"*. The prejudice lies in considering Islam as the only contributing factor for these situations, when in fact most of the regimes in question are simply undemocratic. Applied to Christian countries, this would be the equivalent of making Christian religions responsible for the previous dictatorships in Portugal, Spain or Greece, for example, and then to conclude that Christianity is incompatible with human rights and with democracy.

Young people are often harassed for displaying their allegiance to Islam. In some countries, Muslim girls have been forbidden to attend school wearing the veil on their head.

Legal framework

Numerous international and regional instruments either refer to discrimination generally speaking or deal with specific forms of discrimination. Some examples, at the level of the United Nations, include:

- The Universal Declaration of Human Rights (1948)
- The International Convention on the Elimination of All Forms of Racial Discrimination (1965)
- The Convention on the Elimination of All Forms of Discrimination against Women (1979)
- The Declaration on the Rights of Disabled Persons (1975)
- The ILO Convention (No.169) Concerning Indigenous and Tribal Peoples in Independent Countries (1989).

Within the Council of Europe, in addition to the European Convention on Human Rights, important achievements have been made in recent years, especially through:

- The European Charter on Minority Languages (1992)
- The Convention on the Participation of Foreigners in Public Life at Local Level (1992)
- The Framework Convention for the Protection of Minorities (1995)

Further information

On racism and discrimination

- The European Commission against Racism and Intolerance of the Council of Europe, www.ecri.coe.int
- La Ligue Internationale contre le Racisme et l'Antisémitisme (LICRA), France, www.licra.com
- SOS Racisme (France), www.sos-racisme.org
- UNITED for Intercultural Action - the European Network against nationalism, racism, fascism and in support of migrants and refugees, www.xs4all.nl/~united
- The European network against racism, www.enar-eu.org/
- The Internet Anti-racism Centre in Europe, www.icare.to/
- The European Monitoring Centre on Racism and Xenophobia (EUMC), www.eumc.eu.int
- Minorities of Europe (MoE), www.moe-online.com
- Young Women from Minorities (WFM), www.wfmonline.org

On Roma

- The European Roma Rights Centre (ERRC), www.errc.org
- The International Romani Union, www.romaniunion.org
- Union Romani (Spain), www.unionromani.org
- Patrin Web Journal, www.geocities.com/Paris/5121/patrin.htm

On People with Disabilities

- The World Institute on Disability (WID), www.wid.org
- The European Disability Forum, www.edf-feph.org

On Immigrants and Refugees

- The United Nations High Commissioner for Refugees: www.unhcr.org
- The portal for the promotion and protection of the rights of migrants, www.december18.net
- Asssociation des Travailleurs Magrébins en France, www.atmf.org
- SOLIDAR, www.solidar.org
- The European Council on Refugees and Exiles, www.ecre.org

On religion

- The United Religions Initiative, www.uri.org
- Bahá'í Faith (site of Bahá'í World), www.bahai.org
- On Islam – site of the Islam 21 Project, www.islam21.net
- The Forum against Islamophobia and Racism (UK), www.fairuk.org
- The Sikhism home page, www.sikhs.org
- Hindu Resources on-line, www.hindu.org
- The World Council of Churches, www.wcc-coe.org
- Catholic Church – The Holy See website, www.vatican.va
- Eastern Orthodox Churches, www.orthodoxinfo.com
- Russian Orthodox Church, www.russian-orthodox-church.org.ru

- Shamash: Jewish Network information and discussion on the Internet, http://shamash.org/about.shtml

On anti-Semitism

- Antisemitism and Xenophobia Today, www.axt.org.uk
- The Anti-Defamation League, www.adl.org
- The World Jewish Congress: www.wjc.org.il

On Gay and Lesbian issues

- The International Lesbian and Gay Association, www.ilga.org
- The Institute for Lesbian and Gay Strategic Studies, www.iglss.org
- "Facts on sexual orientation and sexual prejudice", http://psychology.ucdavis.edu/rainbow
- The International Lesbian and Gay Youth Organisation (IGLYO), www.iglyo.org

References

Alaux, J.P., Bach, J., Benot, Y., et Al., Égalité sans frontičre:les immigrés ne sont pas une marchandise, *Les notes de la Fondation Copernic, Haut Conseil de la Coopération Internationale, Éditions Syllepses, Paris, 2001.*

Brander, P., Cardenas, C., Gomes, R., Vicente Abad, J, Taylor, M., Education pack "all different – all equal", *Council of Europe European Youth Centre Strasbourg, 1995.*

Crimes of Hate, Conspiracy of silence, *Amnesty International, London 2001.*

Liégeois, J-P, Roma, Gypsies, travellers, *Council of Europe Press, Strasbourg, 1994.*

Ohana, Y., Participation and citizenship – Training for minority youth projects in Europe, *(ed.), Council of Europe Publishing, 1998.*

Patrin Web Journal (www.geocities.com/Paris/5121/).

Symonides, J., Ed., "The struggle against discrimination", *A collection of international instruments adopted by the United Nations System, Unesco, Paris, 1996.*

Taguieff, P.-A., La force du préjugé, *Gallimard, Paris, 1987.*

"Xenophobia in a European context", Mind and human interaction, *Vol. 9, No.1, University of Virginia, 2001.*

Education

The right to education as a human right

In a case from the European Court of Human Rights, the right to education was defined as "a right of access to educational institutions 'existing at a given time' and the right to draw benefit from the education received, which means the right to obtain official recognition of the studies completed"[16].

"Education is not merely a means for earning a living or an instrument for the acquisition of wealth. It is an initiation into a life of spirit, a training of the human soul in the pursuit of truth and the practice of virtue."

Vijaya Lakshmi Pandit

Education

"...is both a human right in itself and an indispensable means of realising other human rights. As an empowerment right, education is the primary vehicle by which economically and socially marginalised adults and children can lift themselves out of poverty and obtain the means to participate fully in their communities. Education has a vital role in empowering women, safeguarding children from exploitative and hazardous labour and sexual exploitation, promoting human rights and democracy, protecting the environment and controlling population growth. Increasingly, education is recognised as one of the best financial investments States can make. But the importance of education is not just practical: a well-educated, enlightened and active mind, able to wander freely and widely, is one of the joys and rewards of human existence[17]."

The right to education is referred to in the following human rights instruments:

- The Universal Declaration on Human Rights (art. 26)
- The European Convention on Human Rights and Fundamental Freedoms (art. 2 of Protocol No.1)
- The Convention on the Elimination of All Forms of Discrimination against Women (art. 10)
- The Convention on the Rights of the Child (arts. 28 and 29)
- The African Charter on Human Rights and Peoples' Rights (art. 17)
- The Protocol of San Salvador to the American Convention on Human Rights (art. 13).
- The International Covenant on Economic, Social and Cultural Rights (arts. 13 and 14). It is interesting to note that Article 13 is the longest provision in the Covenant and the most wide-ranging and comprehensive article on the right to education in international human rights law.

Related activities

- A glossary of globalisation, page 69.
- Children's rights, page 103.
- Education for all, page 122.
- Let every voice be heard, page 153.
- Path to Equality-land, page 185.
- Responding to racism, page 201.
- The language barrier, page 228.

Key dates

September 8
International Literacy Day

5 October
World Teachers' Day

What are the present educational challenges?

In 1996, a Unesco commission provided an outline of the seven main tensions facing the world and affecting education:

1. The tension between the global and the local;
2. The tension between the universal and the individual;
3. The tension between tradition and modernity;
4. The tension between the spiritual and the material;
5. The tension between long-term and short-term considerations;
6. The tension between competition and equality of opportunity;
7. The tension between the extraordinary expansion of knowledge and the capacity of human beings to assimilate it.

Unesco has highlighted what they have called the four 'pillars' of learning, as a strategy that could help face and deal with these challenges:

1. *Learning to live together*: Specifically, this means that education should strengthen in students the skills and abilities necessary for them to accept their interdependence with other people; to manage conflict; to work and plan with others common objectives and a common future; to respect pluralism and diversity (for example in gender, ethnicity, religion and culture); and to participate actively in the life of the community.
2. *Learning to know*: This means that education should help students to acquire the instruments of knowledge: the essential learning tools of communication and oral expression, literacy, numeracy and problem-solving; to gain both a broad general knowledge and an in-depth knowledge of a few areas; to understand rights and responsibilities; and most importantly, to learn how to learn.
3. *Learning to do*: Education should help students to acquire occupational skills and social and psychological competencies that will enable them to make informed decisions about diverse life situations, to function in social and work relationships, to participate in local and global markets, to use technological tools, to meet basic needs and to improve the quality of their own and others' lives;
4. *Learning to be*: Education should contribute to developing the personality and enable people to act with greater autonomy, judgement, critical thinking and personal responsibility. It should aim to develop all aspects of potential, for example, memory, reasoning, an aesthetic sense, spiritual values, physical capacities and communication skills; a healthy lifestyle, and enjoyment of sports and recreation; an appreciation of one's own culture; possession of an ethical and moral code; an ability to speak for and defend oneself; resilience.

The complementary roles of formal and non-formal education

There are two key concepts that are being integrated in European educational policies: the vision of *lifelong learning* in a *learning society*. The idea is of a community where people are offered different opportunities to develop their competencies throughout their lives. It is important to note that there is increased recognition not only of the role of formal education but also of the opportunities offered by non-formal education, that is, the programmes outside the formal education system. Such programmes are often managed by non-governmental

"If you think education is expensive, try ignorance".

Anonymous

organisations, including youth organisations. They are able to address a wide range of topics and different methodologies, using flexible approaches, and may include ways of providing literacy and other skills to the millions of children and adults who are denied access to the formal education system or who are functional illiterates.

"as one of the principal means available to foster a deeper and more harmonious form of human development and thereby to reduce poverty, exclusion, ignorance, oppression and war[18]"

Can you think of examples of non-formal education programmes in your own community?

In the twentieth century, in Europe, public or state schools have also become the major institution for mass education, and formal education is widely accepted.

In recent decades, this tendency has resulted in increased budgetary allocations for basic education, in legislation making schooling compulsory, and in widespread media coverage of education and development issues.

Experts in education speak of the importance of "crossing boundaries" between formal and non-formal education, promoting communication and co-operation that will help with synchronising educational activities and learning environments in order to provide learners with a coherent set of opportunities.

The role of European youth organisations

At the European level, youth organisations have found ways of making their voice heard on educational issues. So too have student organisations such as the National Union of Students in Europe (ESIB) and the Organising Bureau of European School Student Unions (OBESSU), which is the largest European platform of national school student organisations and unions, and is active in general secondary and secondary vocational education. These organisations work to facilitate the exchange of information, experience and knowledge between national school student organisations, and they play a seminal role in promoting discussion on new trends within the formal education systems in Europe.

To what extent are education systems generally keeping up with current challenges?

As the world has become more complex, school systems have expanded both in size and complexity. The sheer number of children in these systems has grown probably at a rate even faster than the growth of population: total primary enrolment in developing countries grew from 50% in 1970 to 76% in 1990 and to 82% in 1995. Most systems have stretched themselves to cover children of pre-school age, adolescents and adults more systematically than before.

Literacy rates in developing countries have also grown - from 43% in 1970 to 65% in 1990 and to more than 70% in 1995. Such expansion is largely the result of improvements in the quality of education, in more attention to schooling by governments and the international community and in the continued value attached to schooling by families. Education is valued for its own sake and it is also seen as a panacea to the everyday challenges faced by families.

However, in contrast to this picture, some evidence to the contrary can be seen in the stagnation of enrolments in a number of countries. Some experts have pointed out that in the past twenty years

> *"the rate of growth of primary, secondary, and tertiary (post-secondary) school enrolment was slower for most groups of countries. The rate of growth of public spending on education, as a share of Gross Domestic Product (GDP), also slowed across all groups of countries"*[19]

These patterns have had particularly negative consequences for educational achievements, including literacy rates, in countries that have seen less rapid improvement in the past twenty years compared to that in the previous two decades.

Globalisation

Key elements of globalisation, such as selective trade liberalisation, companies' ability to shift operations around the globe and tax evasion are threatening long-term funding for education. Tax problems have affected government funding for education. In the case of Ghana, the government is able to collect 12% of Gross National Product (GNP) in taxation. If it were to lose just 10% of tax revenue – i.e. 1.2% of GNP - then this would be equivalent to about half the primary-education budget. Protecting revenue-collection capacity is therefore of vital importance to achieving progress towards the goal of universal primary education.[20]

In many central and east European countries, economic recovery is still not a reality. What are the consequences for education?

> *"The decentralisation of social expenditures has had a substantial effect on available resources for education (Poland, 1999; Russian Federation, 1999; Romania, 1999). Several central European countries had introduced greater decentralisation of educational finance and governance prior to 1990, but in the rest of the region there have been new efforts to devolve responsibilities from central governments to local levels.*
>
> *Thus, local governments have been given increasing responsibility for education provision from pre-primary to secondary schooling. In many cases, schools themselves have been assigned considerable authority. Measured in terms of expenditure responsibilities, regions are often responsible for a majority of spending on education and in some countries there are growing disparities in the ability of different regions of a country to finance educational programmes (Poland, 1999).*
>
> *In some cases, local authorities, particularly in rural areas, are not allocated the financial resources to meet these new responsibilities and have few means to raise additional funds. Often, teachers' wages (representing the largest share of the educational budget) are still fixed by central authorities, which leaves schools with little autonomy over budgetary decisions.*
>
> *However, the share of resources going to education is coming from a public budget that has been greatly diminished. Faced by large falls in national income and by reduced tax revenues, state support for education has been sharply reduced in real terms.*
>
> *In spite of the difficulties associated with the transition process, countries have taken many concrete steps towards education reform. These reforms have focused on the areas of education legislation, democratisation of curricula and decentralisation of governance and finance. However, in some countries, the actual implementation of these reforms has been slow and often difficult"*[21].

"The roots of education are bitter, but the fruit is sweet."

Aristotle

Unfortunately, the available indicators on the condition of education worldwide make it evident that far too limited resources are being invested in this sector. In a world that is characterised by accelerating change, parents and young people are questioning the relevance of what schools teach. In addition, too many schools throughout the world are characterised by high teacher absenteeism, poor use of available instructional time and negligible attention to the interests and abilities of individual learners. It comes as no surprise that in such schools, where children may be getting little useful knowledge and much of their time is spent in rote learning, many children reject what education systems offer. Among those students who continue in school, many do not acquire elementary skills in analysing and applying their school learning to life-relevant tasks.

Experts from the Council of Europe have highlighted three main groups of young people who are particularly vulnerable within education systems:

1. those who come from economically disadvantaged families;
2. those whose parents have limited educational experience;
3. ethnic minorities, immigrants and travellers.

> "We are born weak, we need strength; helpless, we need aid; foolish, we need reason. All that we lack at birth, all that we need when we come to man's estate, is the gift of education."
>
> *Jean-Jacques Rousseau*

Can you identify any other groups, not mentioned in this list, that are particularly vulnerable in your community?

In many parts of the world there is increasing scepticism concerning formal, uniform systems of education. People see growing disparities and gaps - in cost, quality, achievements, and certification - and this has led to a "crisis of confidence" in public schooling throughout much of the world.

If all children of primary school age were to receive a good quality basic education lasting for a minimum of four years, the problem of illiteracy would be resolved in the space of a single generation. Yet today:

1. 125 million children of primary school age are not in school; most of these are girls.
2. Another 150 million children start primary school but drop out before they have completed four years of education. The vast majority leave before they have acquired basic literacy skills.
3. In much of sub-Saharan Africa and South Asia, children can expect to receive about 4 to 7 years of education. In the industrialised countries they can expect 15 to17 years.
4. Today 870 million people are illiterate; 70% of these are women.

Can you think of reasons why such a large percentage of illiterate people are women?

Fifty years ago, the Universal Declaration of Human Rights proclaimed free and compulsory education to be a basic human right. In 1990, the Convention on the Rights of the Child, signed by all but two of the world's governments, reaffirmed this right as a legally binding obligation.

Since then, there have been many high-level international commitments to this fundamental human right.

> "Education is a better safeguard of liberty than a standing army."
>
> *Edward Everett*

Developed countries have repeatedly committed themselves to greater development co-operation, in order to achieve the goals that were set at international summits during the 1990s. The world's governments met in 1990 at the World Conference on Education for All, held in Jomtien, Thailand. Here they set goals so that, within a decade, all of the world's children would be provided with the opportunity to develop their full capacities. That commitment covered universal access to good-quality primary education, and an end to gender inequalities.

The most recent commitment by states and heads of governments for universal primary education aims to achieve this by 2015. On current trends, even this less ambitious target will be unattainable. If the world's governments fail to act now, 75 million children will be deprived of basic education in 2015.

Yet the most recent world summit on education (Dakar, 2000) stressed that

> *"Education is a fundamental human right. It is the key to sustainable development and peace and stability within and among countries and thus an indispensable means for effective participation in the societies and economies of the twenty-first century."*

References

Building Bridges for Learning, Youth Forum, Brussels, 1999.
Education for All - country reports, 2000. http://www2.unesco.org
Education Now Campaign, Oxfam www.caa.org.au/oxfam/advocacy/education.
European Youth Trends 2000, Council of Europe, 2001.
Learning: The treasure within, Unesco, Paris, 1996.
orld Education Report www.unesco.org

Environment

"If the desert is growing, forests disappearing, malnutrition increasing, and people in urban areas living in very bad conditions, it is not because we are lacking in resources but because of the kind of policy implemented by our rulers, by the elite group. Denying people's rights and people's interests is pushing us to a situation where it is only poverty that has a prosperous future in Africa ... It is only free people, people who have rights, who are mature and responsible citizens, who can then participate in the development and in the protection of the environment."

Speaker from the floor, WECD Public hearing, Nairobi, 23 September 1986

It is not possible to separate the environment - the deserts, forests or urban sprawl - from people and human rights issues, especially those of social justice and development. This is not only true in Africa, but also everywhere, including Europe. The environment and people have a two-way relationship: all human activity impacts on the environment and the environment impacts on human life. One example is the "greenhouse effect". 300 years of using oil, coal and gas to fuel industrial development worldwide has contributed significantly to global warming. The consequent catastrophic climatic events we have witnessed in the last four years affect people all over the globe. However, people in the rich countries of the North, which are largely to blame for the carbon dioxide emissions, are better able to protect themselves against "natural disasters" than those living in developing countries of the South. These are questions of justice and therefore also questions of human rights.

Some other examples of links between the environment and human rights are:

- agricultural land that has been poisoned with landmines during wars and which becomes a threat to human security;
- people being forced by poverty to grow crops on marginal land, which leads to desertification and more poverty;
- the Baia Mare accident, which caused cyanide pollution first in the Szamos river, then in the Tisza and ultimately in the Danube.

Related activities

- A tale of 2 cities, page 71
- Front page, page 135.
- Garden in a night, page 139.
- Living in a perfect world, page 160.
- Makah whaling, page 166.
- Our futures, page 182.
- The web of life, page 235.

Our environmental base

We use the environment to provide us with the raw materials for development and we also use it as a dustbin for our waste. Yet at the same time, to sustain life, it must provide us with stable temperatures, oxygen in the air and clean water. We live on a finite globe where everything is connected to everything else, for example through food chains and the water and rock cycles. There is some natural resilience, but serious disruption of these cycles, for example by pollution,

unsuitable farming practices, irrigation projects or over-fishing, destabilises the natural balance. The Chernobyl disaster in Ukraine, the death of the trees in the Black Forest in Germany, desertification in southern Spain, mad cow disease in Britain, the drying up of the Aral Sea in Uzbekistan and the Ilisu dam project in Turkey are all examples of how humans in the process of development are damaging the environmental base for all economic activity and life itself.

Can you identify local examples? For example, what impact are road building projects or industrial mining or other developments having on the environment near where you live?

World disasters[22]

Catastrophic events	1996	2000
Hurricanes	62	99
Floods	69	153
Droughts	9	46

The idea of sustainable development

In 1989, the United Nations World Commission on Environment and Development (WCED), also called the Brundtland Report, promoted the principle of "sustainable development", which it defined as "development that meets the needs of the present without compromising the ability of future generations to meet their own needs". This was followed in 1992 by the Rio Declaration, which stated: "Human beings are at the centre of concerns for sustainable development. They are entitled to a healthy and productive life in harmony with nature".

The real and urgent problem is how to address the human rights issues of poverty, globalisation and the right to development within a framework that does not destroy the environment that supports us.

One approach is through international agreements about specific issues. For example, at the 1997 United Nations Climate Change conference in Kyoto, industrialised countries made specific commitments to reduce their emissions of greenhouse gasses. There was much bargaining about exemptions for developing countries and many criticisms about both the ultimate effectiveness and fairness of the final agreement.

An alternative approach is to take a human rights approach, which would ensure that principles of justice and equality are central to all agreements. Some people argue that environmental questions are already sufficiently covered through existing human rights legislation, for example through rights to property, health and life. Others talk in different ways about new or "emerging" environmental rights.

One idea is that there should be an environmental human right added to the list of existing human rights. For example, the 1994 draft Declaration of Principles on Human Rights and the Environment declares: "All persons have the right to a secure, healthy and ecologically sound environment. This right and other human rights, including civil, cultural, economic, political and social rights, are universal, interdependent and indivisible".

Some people, especially ecologists, criticise such a demand for an environmental human right. They fear that if human life and health are the aims of environmental protection, then the environment will only be protected as a consequence of, and to the extent needed to protect, human well-being. Instead, they argue for a more holistic human rights approach. They say that people are part of the biosphere (the web of life on earth) and therefore their duty to humanity is inseparable from their duty to environmental protection. Within a broader framework, human rights claims should take into account intrinsic values and the needs of future generations as well as the competing interests of states and peoples.

Some people argue that other species should have "animal rights" in the same way that people have human rights.

"The environmental movement can only survive if it becomes a justice movement. As a pure environmental movement, it will either die or it will survive as a corporate "greenwash". Anyone who's a sincere environmentalist can't stand that role. But it has limitless possibilities as both an ecological and justice-based movement."

Vandana Shiva

In law, animals do not have rights as such. However, they are often protected by legislation. For example, there are laws in most European countries to safeguard the welfare and conditions of farm animals.

Ecological human rights

Ecological human rights can be seen as a response to the global environmental situation. They are a product of our time, in the same way that political and civil rights were a product of historical events in earlier times.

Another way forward being discussed by some people is the concept of ecological human rights. This approach attempts to reconcile the philosophy of human rights with ecological principles. Human rights (such as human dignity, liberty, property and development) need to respond to the fact that individuals operate not only in a political and social environment, but also in a natural environment. Just as each individual has to respect the intrinsic value of fellow *human* beings, the individual also has to respect the intrinsic value of *other* fellow beings (animal, plants and ecosystems).

One of the biggest challenges facing teachers and youth workers today is educating people to understand the dual concepts of respect for human dignity and for the intrinsic value of life and how to live accordingly. In other words, to "think globally and act locally" and to find new lifestyles which can be sustained into the future.

Participation by young people and youth organisations

Schools, environmental non-governmental organisations and other institutions in every country provide opportunities for young people to become actively involved in environmental issues. At the local level, they can make their homes, schools and youth clubs more environmentally friendly and they can participate in local decision-making processes. At the regional and national level, they can influence public discussion and political debate by, for example, writing letters, presenting plays and (peacefully) demonstrating about issues that concern them. At the international and global level, they can have influence through declarations such as the Earth Charter and through international campaigning organisations such as Greenpeace.

At all levels, young people can participate through Internet correspondence, campaigns and global celebrations such as World Environment Day and Earth Day. World Environment Day, June 5, was established by the United Nations General Assembly in 1972. It can be celebrated in many ways, including street rallies, bicycle parades, green concerts, essay and poster competitions in schools, tree planting, recycling efforts and clean-up campaigns. Each

The Goldman Environmental Prize

The Goldman Environmental Prize is the world's largest prize programme honouring grassroots environmentalists work

In 2000, Oral Ataniyazova won the prize for her work with Uzbekistani communities affected by the Aral Sea crisis. She focused on education, medical and family welfare issues and human rights of women and children.

The 2001 award was won by Myrsini Malakou and Giorgios Catsadorakis who worked to save the endangered wetland ecology of Préspa in north-western Greece. One of their achievements was the signing of an agreement between Albania, the Former Yugoslav Republic of Macedonia and Greece to establish the first transboundary protected area in the Balkans, a model of peaceful collaboration between these countries.

year there is a theme for people to focus on. Examples of previous themes include "For Life on Earth - Save Our Seas", "Poverty and the Environment - Breaking the Vicious Circle" and "Children and the Environment" (www.unep.org). Earth Day, April 22, is co-ordinated by the Earth Day Network, which works together with other environmental and human rights organisations, for example, the Sierra Club and Amnesty International, to generate public action through celebrations and activities in protest against human rights and environmental abuses. www.earthday.net/events/events-europe.stm

Key date

5 June
Word Environment Day

22 April
Earth Day

Council of Europe's work

The Council of Europe launched its environment programme in 1961. Its activities in this field focus on the conservation of nature and landscapes. The programme is now integrated within the Culture and Cultural and Natural Heritage Department of the Council of Europe. It has three main directions: the Pan-European Biological and Landscape Diversity Strategy, the Convention on the Conservation of European Wildlife and Natural Habitats (Bern Convention, 1979) and the Promotion of Awareness on Biological and Landscape Diversity.

Information and awareness on environmental protection is carried out through the Council of Europe's publications. Its network of national agencies also contributes to the promotion of the conservation of biological and landscape diversity.

International instruments and declarations

A few of the many treaties and other instruments that address both environment and human rights and that may be useful are:

1. The 1989 European Charter on Environment and Health
2. The 1992 United Nations Declaration on Environment and Development
3. The 1994 draft Declaration of Principles on Human Rights and the Environment
4. The 1999 Declaration of Bizkaia on the Right to Environment
5. The 2000 Earth Charter

"The salvation of the world lies in the human heart, in the human power to reflect, in human meekness and in human responsibility. We are still under the sway of the destructive and vain belief that man is the pinnacle of creation and not just a part of it, and therefore, everything is permitted. We still don't know how to put morality ahead of politics, science and economics. We are still incapable of understanding that the only genuine backbone of all our actions - if they are to be moral - is responsibility. Responsibility is something higher than my family, my country, my firm, my success. Responsibility to the order of Being, where, and only where, they will be properly judged."

Vaclav Havel

References

Boyle, A, Anderson, M.R., Human rights approaches to environmental protection: An overview, *Clarendon Press, Oxford, 1996.*

Bosselmann, K., Human rights and the environment: redefining fundamental principles, *www.arbld.unimelb.edu.au*

Caring for the Earth, *The World Conservation Union (IUCN), United Nations Environment Programme (UNEP), World Wide Fund for Nature (WWF-UK), www.ciesin.org/IC/iucn*

The Council of Europe environment programme, www.nature.coe.int

The 1994 draft Declaration of Principle on Human Rights and the Environment www1.umn.edu/humanrts/instree/1994-dec.htm.

The Earth Charter initiative, www.earthcharter.org

Worldwatch, www.worldwatch.org.

Gender equality

FOR WOMEN'S RIGHTS!!
WHY DON'T WE DEMAND HUMAN RIGHTS STRAIGHTAWAY?
PANCHO

Some basic concepts

"It ought to be a beautiful position in life: to be young and to have a life ahead for which you can plan and dream. It ought, furthermore, to be equally beautiful whether you are a young woman or a young man. In reality, however, many young people are deprived of their rights to make plans and have dreams, as well as of their rights to security and dignity in life. In reality, it also makes a substantial difference if you are born a girl or a boy. Young women run a much higher risk of having their fundamental rights as human beings violated."[23]

While in the 1970s and 1980s women activists talked about "integrating women into development", in the 1990s the emphasis was on the integration of gender issues as part of development policy and planning.

Today, both the terms "women's rights" and "gender equality" are used. What do the terms mean and what is the difference between them? The phrase "women's human rights" is used to emphasise the point that women's rights are human rights, rights to which women are entitled simply because they are human. This idea integrates the topic of women into the human rights movement, and integrates human rights principles into the women's movement at the same time.

Gender equality means an equal level of empowerment, participation and visibility of both sexes in all spheres of public and private life. Gender equality is not to be thought of as the opposite of gender difference but rather of gender inequality. It aims to promote the full participation of women and men in society. Gender equality, like human rights, must be constantly fought for, protected and encouraged.

The term 'gender' refers to the socially-constructed roles of women and men which are attributed to them on the basis of their sex. Gender roles therefore depend on a particular socio-economic, political and cultural context and are affected by other factors including race, ethnicity, class, sexual orientation and age. Gender roles are learned and vary widely within and between cultures. Unlike a person's biological sex, gender roles can change.

"The discussion about socialisation and stereotypes revealed the 'old' forms of socialisation created spaces for new forms of identity and individuality. 'New' forms of socialisation are taking their place but they may be replicating similar stereotypical expectations and producing similar consequences as before. The influences of the family, school and the workplace may no longer be so powerful, but new information technologies and burgeoning cultural practices (in music, media and television) may be stepping into the breach, strengthening the social power of men and maintaining the subordination of women."[24]

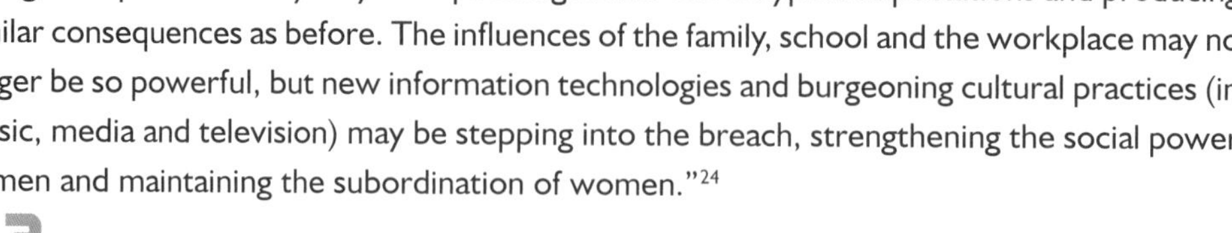

How easy is it for men to adapt to the changes that have come about as a result of the recognition of women's rights?

Related activities

- Different wages, page 107.
- Domestic affairs, page 114.
- Heroines and heroes, page 142.
- Let's talk about sex, page 156.
- Path to Equality-land, page 185.
- Who are I?, page 257.
- Work and babies, page 260.

Examples of violations of women's rights

Domestic violence

The most common form of violence against women is domestic violence. Domestic violence has for many years been considered a private affair, in which the state and the judicial system has no business interfering. Yet domestic violence is not only a violation of the physical and psychological well-being of the women concerned, and therefore a direct attack on their human rights, it is also a criminal offence.

Statistics show that a woman is more likely to be beaten, attacked and even killed by her partner or former partner than by any other person.

- Depending on the European country concerned, between 20% and 50% of women are victims of domestic violence.
- Domestic violence affects all sectors of society and all ages.
- Domestic violence takes many forms: physical, sexual, psychological and structural.
- One woman in five is subjected to sexual assault at some stage in her life. The age of the victims ranges from two months to 90 years.
- 98% of aggressors are male, and 50% are married men or living in a *de facto* marriage or as a couple.
- 70% of rapes are premeditated and only 3% of aggressors are mentally unbalanced.
- There is an increase in the phenomenon of multiple rape.
- Figures show an increasing number of cases of assault against very young girls.

"Statistics are grim, no matter which part of the world one focuses on ... No country or region is exempt from domestic abuse". So says a UNICEF report on domestic violence against women and girls, published in 2000, in a first attempt to establish the global dimensions of this phenomenon.

Trafficking of women and girls

Every year, millions of men, women and children are the victims of trafficking worldwide in conditions amounting to slavery. Among these numbers, many thousands are young women and girls who have been lured, abducted or sold into forced prostitution and other forms of sexual servitude. The process is made even easier by globalisation and modern technologies. The underlying causes of trafficking include poverty, unemployment and a lack of education, all of which force people to take risks to improve their quality of life. One worrying trend in industrial countries is "the use of cheap and undeclared labour forces as well as the exploitation of women and children in prostitution and pornography."[25]

Trafficking in human beings is hardly a new phenomenon, but selling na□ve and desperate young women into sexual bondage has become one of the fastest-growing criminal activities in the global economy. "The trafficking flow between certain developing countries (Northern and Central Africa, Latin America and Asia) and Western destination countries continues. However, the most striking factor ... is the increase in the number of women and children trafficked into the European Union from central and eastern European countries. Estimates of up to 120000 women and children being trafficked into western Europe each year are made."[26] For several years now, the trafficking of women and children - and of people in general - has been a priority issue on the working agenda of the Council of Europe.

Female genital mutilation

The practice of female genital mutilation (FGM) affects an estimated 130 million girls and women and is most prevalent in Africa. FGM is a cultural practice harmful to women, which violates

Key dates

8 March
International Women's Day.

25 November
International Day against Violence against Women.

Every year in the world, two million little girls are circumcised in this way, and that is in addition to the 130 million circumcised women.[27]

women's human rights to life, body integrity, health and sexuality. Because it is practised mostly on young girls, female genital mutilation also raises serious questions about children's rights.

In conflict areas...

In recent years, episodes of violence against women were reported in Bosnia, Cambodia, Chechnya, Haiti, Peru, Somalia, Sierra Leone, East and West Timor, and in other conflict zones of the world. At some point, the international community will have to find alternative responses to the small number of *ad hoc* international criminal tribunals - such as the ones for Yugoslavia and Rwanda. While these are useful and necessary, they are clearly inadequate and insufficient for protecting women's rights.

The Parliamentary Assembly of the Council of Europe

"regrets that despite the fact that rape has been recognised as a war crime, it continues to be systematically used - and has been so in recent conflicts (Kosovo and Chechnya) - as a war weapon inflicting not only psychological trauma but also forced pregnancy."[28]

 **What can be done to put an end to violence against women and girls?**

Existing international human rights instruments

Since the United Nations held the first world conference on women (Mexico City, Mexico, 1975), important progress has been made towards achieving equality between women and men.

The United Nations Development Fund for Women (UNIFEM) was set up in 1976 to fund innovation and change in this area. Since then, it has supported numerous projects and initiatives throughout the developing world, promoting the political, economic and social empowerment of women.

The first legally binding international document prohibiting discrimination against women and forcing governments to take steps in favour of equality for women is the Convention on the Elimination of All Forms of Discrimination Against Women ("Women's Convention" or CEDAW). This was adopted in 1979 and came into force in 1981.

The convention aims to eliminate all forms of discrimination against women. This is defined in Article 1 as "any distinction, exclusion or restriction made on the basis of sex which has the purpose or effect of impairing or nullifying the recognition of enjoyment or exercise by women, irrespective of their marital status, on a basis of equality of men and women, of human rights and fundamental freedoms in the political, social, cultural, civil or any other field". States Parties are obliged to submit periodic reports on their compliance with the convention.

Over the past decade, a global movement has emerged to challenge the limited notions of human rights that see the rights of women as secondary to other human rights questions.

"Inequality and disparities between women and men in the field of human rights are inconsistent with the principles of genuine democracy."

Parliamentary Assembly of the Council of Europe, Resolution 1216 (2000).

In 1999, the General Assembly of the United Nations added an optional protocol to the CEDAW that had been elaborated by the United Nations Committee on the Elimination of Discrimination Against Women. The Optional Protocol entered into force in 2000. It marks an important step in the protection of women's rights, in so far as it allows individual women or groups of women to submit allegations of human rights violations directly to the Committee on the Elimination of Discrimination Against Women. It also provides the Committee with the ability to initiate inquiries into cases of grave or systematic violations of women's rights around the world. However, the

force of the protocol is limited, since ratifying states have the option of rejecting a request from the Committee to investigate violations of women's rights on their territory.

Within the Council of Europe, the issue of equality between women and men is seen as a fundamental human right and is the responsibility of the Steering Committee for Equality between Women and Men (CDEG). This is an intergovernmental body within the Council, which carries out analyses, studies and evaluations, defines strategies and political measures and, where necessary, decides on the appropriate legal instruments.

The 1995 Fourth World Conference of Women, held in Beijing, China, drew together almost 47000 women and men, and to date it remains the largest gathering of government and NGOs representatives at any United Nations conference. At this historic event, 189 countries unanimously adopted the Beijing Declaration and the Platform for Action. National governments committed themselves to promoting gender equality in the formulation of all government policies and programmes. They identified the following twelve common critical areas of concern: poverty, education and training, health, violence against women, armed conflict, economy, power and decision-making, institutional mechanisms for gender equality, human rights, media, the environment and young girls.

The main problem is that the definition of equality used is a very narrow one of *de jure* equality and this does not always provide protection against discrimination. A second problem lies in the fact that women have traditionally had to work on these questions outside the "mainstream" of society. A third problem is that women occupy a weak position in decision-making structures in most countries.[29]

Education ... the solution.

A very important step would be to move from rights recognition to rights empowerment. All human rights educators need to appreciate the sensitive nature of the human rights vision and to honour the differences among individual women's needs and responses. Without such sensitivity, human rights education could become just another form of manipulation or oppression of women. *Education* is a key target for gender equality, since it involves the ways in which societies transfer norms, knowledge and skills.

"Combating gender-based violence and promoting gender equality requires education and active involvement of all sectors of society, especially young women and men and members of minority groups, from the beginning"[30]

As an educator or youth leader, do you use a gender focus in your work with young people?

References

Connell, R. W., Gender and power, *Stanford University Press.*

Mertus, J., Flowers, N., Dutt, M., Local action, global change, *UNIFEM and the Center for Women's Global Leadership, 1999.*

Williams, S., and others, The Oxfam gender training manual, *Oxfam Publication, 1994.*

Ramberg, I. Violence against young women in Europe, *seminar report, Council of Europe, 2001.*

Some useful websites on women's issues

OECD-DAC Gender, www.oecd.org/dac/gender

United Nations Educational, Scientific and Cultural Organisation (Unesco), www.unesco.org/gender

United Nations Statistics Division Gender Statistics, www.un.org/depts/unsd/gender

United Nations Development Fund for Women (UNIFEM), www.undp.org/unifem

Women Watch, www.un.org/womenwatch

European Women's Lobby (EWL), www.womenlobby.org

Women Against Violence Europe (Wave Network): www.wave-network.org

Men Against Violence Against Women (MAVAW), http://menagainstviolence.tripod.com

Young Women from Minorities (WFM), www.wfmonline.org

Globalisation

Our world is gradually becoming one single huge market. Some people have said that the world has become a village.

We all talk about globalisation but do we know what it is exactly?

Globalisation refers to a process that is characterised by:

1. the expansion of telecommunications and information technologies;
2. the reduction of national barriers to trade and investment;
3. Increasing capital flows and the interdependency of financial markets.

Indeed, globalisation promotes an increasing mobility of people although the control over migrations is greater then ever (air traffic has never been so important in the world's history), global alliances among companies are more and more common (see the examples of the telecommunication and food industries), and it is possible to chat through computers with people from virtually any country in the world. Finally, the recent financial crashes in Asia and Latin America have demonstrated the increasing financial and economic interdependency.

Related activities

- A glossary of globalisation, page 69.
- Access to medicaments, page 80.
- All equal all different, page 88.
- Ashique's story, page 91.
- Beware, we are watching, page 95.
- Education for all?, page 122.
- Front page, page 135.
- Horoscope of poverty, page 145.
- Just a minute, page 150.
- Makah whaling, page 166.
- The impact of the Internet, page 222.
- The scramble for wealth and power, page 231.
- The web of life, page 235.

And what are the key challenges of globalisation?

There is a lot of controversy about the current and potential consequences of globalisation. We can identify many dilemmas and in many cases there are no clear-cut answers. Numerous sectors and individuals such as human rights activists, scholars, economists, researchers and sociologists concerned by its negative impact have identified some of the following issues as key challenges:

1. *Reduction of state sovereignty*: Where governments have less and less control over key decisions that can affect their economies and consequently the well-being of their people, the most powerful transnational companies, intergovernmental structures and private financial institutions have a growing influence and tend to act in the same way as governments. This is why it is said that the sovereignty of states has been strongly reduced. Their traditional roles are being redefined.

2. *"Economically focused"*: Economical considerations are taking over political and social considerations. Since private companies and intergovernmental international and regional organisations are increasingly assuming a predominant role in running states and world affairs, there is a risk that the economic and financial dimensions will prevail as the sole concerns of these institutions ignoring other fundamental issues related to social, health or environmental aspects.

3. *Lack of transparency and responsibility:* Governments, public institutions, national banking authorities, etc., traditionally in charge of deciding the future of their countries and people, have seen this responsibility in some cases being gradually taken away from them. Many of their actions and decisions are controlled since they are democratically accountable, but this is not the case for transnational corporations or international and regional institutions. In the case of human rights violations, for example, is it almost impossible to hold them responsible and to monitor their actions. Furthermore, in many of these instances, concern has been expressed over the lack of transparency of the existing decision-making mechanisms. For instance, in some cases in the World Trade Organisation, decisions are taken behind closed doors after complex processes of multilateral informal or formal negotiations.

4. *"Race to the bottom":* One particular characteristic of the liberalisation of trade is that transnational companies tend to relocate in countries offering better comparative advantages, which in practical terms means lower salaries for workers, less strict labour legislation, more flexible working conditions, non-existing or non-applied environmental legislation, lower taxes and cuts in social expenses such as unemployment insurance, health care, etc. In these circumstances, it is easy to come to the conclusion that human rights are strongly being affected by such practices, especially but not exclusively with regard to the economic and social rights of the workers in the host countries that are facing difficult social and economic conditions and are in need of foreign investments to help reactivate their already fragile economies.

5. *Homogenisation*: Some argue that the threat of living in a single integrated society with standardised social and cultural patterns of behaviour would condition us to eat the same food, listen to the same music or watch the same movies wherever we live and whatever our nationality. This situation would deny the specificity of each country and would violate our rights to enjoy our own cultures.

In this context, consumer boycotts have sometimes been successful in rectifying unethical and unlawful business practices. Additionally, some companies and organisations are trying to develop business strategies that would transcend the problems of globalisation.

More specifically, as far as trade liberalisation is concerned, some of the main intergovernmental international and regional institutions that have been promoting it are:

- The World Trade Organisation
- The International Monetary Fund
- The World Bank
- The World Economic Forum. A private organisation gathering the most powerful 2000 companies in the world. They meet every year in Davos, Switzerland.
- Regional trading blocs such as the European Union, the North American Free Trade Agreement (NAFTA) and the Asia Pacific Economic Co-operation (APEC).

Do you know where the clothes you are wearing or the food you are eating come from?

The Universal Declaration of Human Rights, the International Covenant on Economic, Social and Cultural Rights and the revised European Social Charter, as well as the Community Charter

The Fair Trade Movement

intends to label goods and products that are produced in conformity with social practices and with human rights. This way the consumers who are aware of such issues have the opportunity to make a difference by using their purchasing power.

"The Sub-Commission on the Promotion and Protection of Human Rights … requests all governments and economic policy forums to take international human rights obligations and principles fully into account in international economic policy formulation." [31]

of Fundamental Social Rights of Workers and the European Union Charter of Fundamental Rights (although this last is not yet legally binding) are some of the international and regional instruments that are particularly relevant to the issue of globalisation. It is worth mentioning that the United Nations Sub-Commission on the Promotion and Protection of Human Rights, as well as the Sub-Commission on the Prevention of Discrimination and Protection of Minorities have both adopted resolutions on human rights and globalisation, the first one on trade liberalisation and its impact on human rights (Resolution 1999/30) and the second one on human rights as the primary objective of trade, investment and financial policy (Resolution 1998/12).

Some of the assumed positive aspects of globalisation

1. Redefining citizenship: There is a new dimension of citizenship that is emerging and which is called global citizenship. It combines with the traditional concept of citizenship linked to the exercise of political and legal rights and obligations such as voting. Indeed, to be a global citizen nowadays means to be more critical of what we consume and in which conditions products have been produced, and to be more aware of global issues such as poverty affecting the world, environmental problems or violence. Additionally, some people argue that social and cultural globalisation means the opposite of homogeneity; that, on the contrary, new practices and identities are created as a result of the processes of interaction.

2. Increasing mobility and faster communications: Despite the obvious increasing technological gap between the haves and the have-nots which is one of the major downsides of this trend, one of the positive consequences of the opening up of borders and the development of the Internet and other technologies is that it has become increasingly easier to travel from one country to another or to communicate with people from all over the world. This gives us the opportunity to share and learn from one another and from other cultures, hopefully by teaching us to be more tolerant and respectful.

3. The gradual opening up of borders: Should facilitate the development and implementation of transnational and regional judicial systems of protection of human rights that can rectify human rights violations. The European Court of Human Rights is an example of quite an efficient regional system of protection of human rights.

The anti-globalisation movement

As a response to financial and economic globalisation, important sectors of civil society concerned by its negative impact have started to organise a world movement to promote what they call a humanisation of globalisation. This international movement commonly called 'the anti-globalisation movement', gathers trade-unions, environmental non-governmental organisations, politicians, human rights activists, scholars, women's institutions, etc., in short, a wide range of institutions and individuals interested in building a more equitable world which, according to them, cannot exist as long as neo-liberalism, deregulation and privatisation are the main engines of economic globalisation. They call for globalisation with a human face. Some of these groups have chosen to demonstrate their disagreement by participating in large protests during meetings organised by the G7+1 and other institutions that promote such phenomena. Unfortunately, the most highly visible aspect during such events has been the violent incidents which have caused a lot of material damage. This movement is also gradually organising itself. The Word Social Forum has met in Porto Alegre, in Brazil "parallel" to the World Economic Forum meeting

in Davos, Switzerland, and gave the opportunity to thousands of delegates from civil society organisations to analyse issues related to globalisation and its consequences and to study alternatives. Under the slogan "Another world is possible" some of the numerous key issues discussed were the process of reforming the World Trade Organisation, the defence of human rights (especially economic, social and environmental rights) and debt relief for the Third World.

In conclusion, we could quote Xavier Godinot of ATD Quart Monde: *"Globalisation is a collective challenge as well as an invitation for each of us to reinvent new ways of being citizens of the world."*

"Solidarity is the tenderness of peoples."

Ernesto Cardenal

Some NGOs and institutions dealing with globalisation:

Oxfam, www.oxfam.org
Fédération Internationale des Droits de l´Homme, www.fidh.org
International Forum on Globalisation, www.ifg.org
Third World Network, www.townside.org.sg
L´Observatoire de la Mondialisation, http://terresacree.org/obsmondi.htm
ATTAC, www.attac.org
World Social Forum: www.forumsocialmundial.org.br

? Do you know any other institution or individual from your own country that can be added to this list?

References

Bîrzéa, C., Education for democratic citizenship: A lifelong learning perspective, *Council for Cultural Co-operation, Strasbourg, June 2000, pp. 8-11.*

Leary, V., "Globalisation and human rights", Human Rights, New Dimensions and Challenges, *Unesco, Paris, 1998, pp.265-276.*

"Mondialisation et droits de l´homme", La Lettre, *No.28,* Fédération Internationale des Droits de l´Homme, *Paris, 1999.*

"Mondialisation et pauvreté", Revue QUART MONDE, *No.175, Éditions Quart Monde, Paris, 2000.*

Oloka-Onyango, J., Udagama, D., "Human rights as the primary objective of international trade, investment and finance policy and practice. Working paper submitted in accordance with Sub-Commission resolution 1998/12". United Nations, E/CN.4/Sub.2/1999/11, 1999.

Health

IT'S THE WORST TYPE:
H.I.V. POSITIVE,
DOLLAR NEGATIVE...
LABO INC.
PANCHO

"Health is a state of complete physical, mental and social well-being, and not merely the absence of disease or infirmity."

Heave

Health is a social, economic and political issue as well as an issue concerning human rights. Inequality and poverty lie at the root of ill health, as well as the deaths of poor and marginalised people. The World Health Report classifies sicknesses and causes of death with number codes. The first cause of death around the world, according to the World Health Report, is that corresponding to number 259.5: extreme poverty. It has become a vicious circle: poverty causes illness, which in turn leads to greater poverty.

In recent decades, economic changes worldwide have profoundly affected people's health and their access to health care and social services. World resources are increasingly concentrated in the hands of a few economic players who strive to maximise their private profits. Economic and financial policy is increasingly made by a small group of governments and international bodies, such as the World Bank, the International Monetary Fund and the World Trade Organisation. The policies of these organisations, together with the activities of multinational companies, have severe effects on the lives, livelihoods, health and well-being of people in both the Southern and the Northern hemispheres.

As never before, the figures of deaths and illnesses have the face of injustice and inequality: 75% of the world population live in developing countries and represent only 8% of the world's pharmaceutical market. Furthermore, one third of the world population has no access at all to essential drugs.

Related activities

- Access to medicaments, page 80.
- Domestic affairs, page 114.
- Garden in a night, page 139.
- Let's talk about sex, page 156.
- Living in a perfect world, page 160.
- Sports for all, page 214.

Aids and human rights

A paradigmatic example is Aids. While in rich countries, people who have HIV/Aids can live better and longer because of anti-retroviral drugs, which are provided by some states for free or at reasonable prices, in southern countries people affected by HIV die because they have no access to treatment. In most cases, the annual per-capita expenses in health amount to about US$10.

The United Nations Commission on Human Rights in a report issued on Aids and human rights has identified the following human rights, among others, as tightly linked to the spread of Aids all over the world: [32]

- *The right to marry and found a family*. A report by the UN Commission on Human Rights states that "it is clear that the right of people living with HIV/Aids is infringed by mandatory pre-marital testing and/or the requirement of "Aids-free certificates" as a precondition for the grant of marriage licences under state laws. Secondly, forced abortions or sterilisation of women living with HIV violates the human right to found a family, as well the right to liberty and integrity of the person."
- *The human rights of children and young people* may also be under threat. "Many of these rights, such as freedom from trafficking, prostitution, sexual exploitation and sexual abuse, are relevant to HIV/Aids prevention, care and support for children, since sexual violence against children, among other things, increases their vulnerability to HIV/Aids. The freedom to seek, receive and impart information and ideas of all kinds and the right to education both provide children with the right to give and receive all the HIV-related information they need to avoid infection and to cope with their status if infected."
- "*The right to privacy* covers obligations to respect physical privacy, including the obligation to seek informed consent to HIV testing, and also privacy of information, including the need to respect confidentiality of all information relating to a person's HIV status. The individual's interest in his/her privacy is particularly compelling in the context of HIV/Aids, firstly because of the invasive character of a mandatory HIV test, and secondly because of the stigma and discrimination attached to the loss of privacy and confidentiality, if HIV status is disclosed. The community has an interest in maintaining privacy so that people will feel safe and comfortable in using public health measures."
- *The right to education:* "This right includes three broad components which apply in the context of HIV/Aids. Firstly, both children and adults have the right to receive HIV-related education, particularly regarding prevention and care. Access to education concerning HIV/Aids is an essential life-saving component of effective prevention and care programmes. It is the state's obligation to ensure, in every cultural and religious tradition, that appropriate means are found so that effective HIV/Aids information is included in educational programmes inside and outside schools. Secondly, states should ensure that both children and adults living with HIV/Aids are not discriminated against by being denied access to education, including access to schools, universities, scholarships and international education or subjected to restrictions because of their HIV status. There is no public health rationale for such measures since there is no risk of transmitting HIV casually in educational settings. Thirdly, states should, through education, promote understanding, respect, tolerance and non-discrimination in relation to persons living with HIV/Aids."
- "*The right to work* entails the right of every person to access to employment without any precondition except the necessary occupational qualifications. This right is violated when an applicant or employee is required to undergo mandatory testing for HIV and is refused employment or dismissed or refused access to employee benefits on the grounds of a positive result."

Key dates

1 December
World Aids Day

7 April
World Health Day

In which way do people in your country who suffer from Aids or are HIV positive see their rights violated? How can it be avoided?

Health and environment in Europe

Some health issues are also linked to environmental problems. In October 2001, a conference was organised to analyse the consequences on health of climate change and ozone depletion. Experts in the field believe that "the potentially damaging impacts of the interaction between climate change and ozone depletion are very significant" and that "urgent action is required to reduce both environmental damage and its impact on health".[33]

Health and youth

In recent years, a worrying trend in many European Member States has been the rise in the consumption of alcohol by young people at increasingly younger ages. The harm they experience as a result is considerable. A comparative risk analysis shows, for instance, that one in four deaths in males aged 15-29 years in the European region is attributable to alcohol. These considerations led to the decision to make "Young people and alcohol" the theme of the WHO Ministerial Conference (Stockholm, 19-21 February 2001), and the overall goal of the conference was to boost implementation of the European Alcohol Action Plan.

The conference adopted a declaration containing the following main elements:

1. identification of alcohol as an important issue in young people's health;
2. confirmation of the need to have public health/alcohol policy developed, without any interference from commercial or economic interests;
3. the opportunity to have young people themselves involved in the policy-making process;
4. the need to determine targets, at national and local levels, to reduce the impact of alcohol on young people's health.

Several steps were recommended for approval by the Regional Committee for Europe of the World Health Organisation. These included:

- strengthening *international partnerships*, especially with the European Commission, the Council of Europe, the United Nations Children's Fund and the European Forum of Medical Associations and World Health Organisation (WHO);
- maintenance of contact with *young people* and their organisations throughout the region;
- the establishment of a system for *monitoring the promotion of alcoholic beverages* to young people.

Can you make a list of concrete and practical actions that could be developed to help implement these recommendations in your own community and country?

As is emphasised in the above recommendations, young people can and should be strategic partners in activities or programmes that deal with health problems, either through prevention or intervention. There are youth organisations that are active in this field of health, such as the International Federation of Red Cross and Red Crescent Societies, which have youth sections all over the world. The European Network of Health Promoting Schools is a tripartite project launched by the World Health Organisation Regional Office for Europe, the European Commission and the Council of Europe. It emphasises the importance of health promotion in the education

system by means of collaboration between health and education professionals and members of the community.

The right to health

The right to health is mentioned in several international human rights instruments such as in Article 12 of the International Covenant on Economic, Social and Cultural Rights, and Article 24 of the Convention on the Rights of the Child. As far as Europe is concerned, Article 13 of the European Social Charter refers to it extensively:

"With a view to ensuring the effective exercise of the right to social and medical assistance, the Contracting Parties undertake:

1. To ensure that any person who is without adequate resources and who is unable to secure such resources either by his own efforts or from other sources, in particular by benefits under a social security scheme, be granted adequate assistance, and, in case of sickness, the care necessitated by this condition;
2. To ensure that persons receiving such assistance shall not, for that reason, suffer from a diminution of their political or social rights;
3. To provide that everyone may receive by appropriate public or private services such advice and personal help as may be required to prevent, to remove, or to alleviate personal or family want;
4. To apply the provisions referred to in paragraphs 1, 2 and 3 of this Article on an equal footing with their nationals to nationals of other Contracting Parties lawfully within their territories, in accordance with their obligations under the European Convention on Social and Medical Assistance, signed at Paris on 11th, December 1953."

The 1999 World Health Report identified the following four main challenges for national governments, the international community, and civil society:

1. *directing health systems towards delivering a minimum number of interventions, which would have the greatest impact in reducing the excessive disease burden suffered by the poor.* This includes a renewed commitment to malaria control, extended efforts to control tuberculosis, a focus on maternal and child health and nutrition, and the revitalisation and extended coverage of immunisation programmes.
2. *enabling health systems to counter proactively the potential threats to health resulting from economic crises, unhealthy environments or risky behaviour. One of the most important threats is tobacco addiction.* A global commitment to tobacco control could avert millions of premature deaths. Other priorities include combating the spread of resistance to anti-microbials and mounting an effective response to the threat of emerging diseases. Also critical are the global eradication of polio and the promotion of healthy lifestyles (including cleaner air and water, adequate sanitation, healthy diets and safer transportation).
3. *developing health systems that provide universal access to clinical services with no fees (or only small fees) at the point of delivery. This will require public finance, government-mandated social insurance, or both.* However, it is recognised that if services are to be provided for all, then not all services can be provided. The most cost-effective services should be provided first. Even the wealthiest countries cannot provide entire populations with every intervention where the medical value outweighs the risks.

4. *encouraging health systems to invest in expanding the knowledge base that made the twentieth-century revolution in health possible and that will provide the tools for continued gains in the twenty first century.* The most critical need is for research and development on infectious diseases that disproportionately affect the poor and the establishment of an information base to help countries develop their own health systems.

References

The World Health Report, *World Health Organisation*, www.who.int/whr/.

Human security

The concept of human security emerged on the world scene only towards the end of the twentieth century. Before that, for over three hundred years, the idea of *state* security was a familiar and accepted concept. States were entitled, indeed expected, to defend their territorial integrity against external threats, and special measures were even permissible towards such an end, but the notion of security, at least at the international level, stopped at the borders of the state.

The discourse on security changed in the 1990s, and the international community began to accept the importance of special measures to defend not just states but *people* from threats to their security, even where this went against the wishes of the government in question. Of course, even before that, there was a common use of the word "security" which applied to people, but the radical change in the 1990s lay in international discourse: for the first time, the defence of *a people*, which had formerly been regarded as the sovereign business of individual nation states, became potentially the business of the international community.

"The meaning of human security is synonymous with that of 'the security of people' ... The objective of human security is the safety and survival of people."

Dr. Sverre Lodgaard

The language changed, and so did the actions

Collective security actions, involving coalitions of nations and under the guidance of the United Nations, were taken not necessarily with the aim of enhancing the security of states, but primarily in the name of the security of people(s). Events that had previously been referred to only in such terms as *humanitarian disasters* came to be redefined in terms of peace and security. This was used to justify international enforcement measures, one of the first examples of which was the humanitarian enforcement programme in Somalia (1992-93), where the United Nations Security Council determined that

> *"the magnitude of the human tragedy ... constitutes a threat to international peace and security".*

Related activities

- Can I come in?, page 98.
- Money to spend, page 177.
- Rights bingo, page 206.
- The language barrier, page 228.
- The scramble for wealth and power, page 231.
- Violence in my life, page 248.
- When tomorrow comes, page 250.

The United Nations Operation in Somalia (UNOSOM) was established in 1992 to monitor the cease-fire in Mogadishu and escort deliveries of humanitarian supplies to distribution centres in the city. The mission's mandate and strength were later enlarged to enable it to protect humanitarian convoys and distribution centres throughout Somalia.

"The Security Council,

Bearing in mind the purposes and principles of the Charter of the United Nations, and the primary responsibility of the Security Council for the maintenance of international peace and security,

Determined to resolve the grave humanitarian situation in Kosovo, Federal Republic of Yugoslavia, and to provide for the safe and free return of all refugees and displaced persons to their homes,

Determining that the situation in the region continues to constitute a threat to international peace and security … and *acting* for these purposes under Chapter VII of the Charter of the United Nations,

…*Decides* that the responsibilities of the international security presence to be deployed and acting in Kosovo will include:

1. Deterring renewed hostilities … ;
2. Demilitarising the Kosovo Liberation Army (KLA) … ;
3. Establishing a secure environment in which refugees and displaced persons can return home in safety … and humanitarian aid can be delivered;

Ensuring public safety and order …"

Extracts from Resolution 1244 (1999). Adopted by the UN Security Council at its 4011th meeting, on 10 June 1999.

Two aspects of change:

The above extract from the United Nations resolution on Kosovo illustrates the two fundamental changes that had come about in the classification of issues as posing a threat to international security:

1. the types of events that came to be seen as a threat to security;
2. the extension of security concerns to cover intra-state events as well as conflicts between nation states.

What led to the change?

There were a number of influences which prompted this movement away from a definition of security that focused on states to one that focused on people. One such influence was undoubtedly the end of the cold war, which allowed the interests of governments and peoples that had previously been hidden to come to the surface. One result was an outburst of complex and vicious conflicts, often intra-state, where the cost in terms of civilian casualties required a new type of response.

However, there was perhaps a more important influence than merely the realisation that the defence of peoples sometimes required an international response. This realisation had, after all, been there for many years, but "interfering" in what were seen as purely domestic affairs had not been considered a possible or acceptable course of action. Now, however, the increasing profile of human rights concerns in the world led to a form of justification which was, if not universally, then at least very widely acceptable: human rights, after all, are concerned precisely with people rather than states, and all countries in the world express their agreement at least in principle with these norms.

To what extent should the domestic policies of nations be subject to scrutiny by the international community?

Individual or state interests?

"Security is a condition in which other things become possible."

Emma Rothschild

The central idea behind human rights is that there is a certain level of human dignity which cannot be infringed by any government or individual. Thus, it is an inevitable consequence of embracing human rights that states relinquish some of their sovereignty, in the old sense of that term. In signing up to internationally agreed human rights norms, they have thereby agreed to put the individual at the forefront of all their actions, and they therefore relinquish their ability to do absolutely *anything* in the name of the interests of the state.

It is this idea that has gained ground in the last ten years in the field of international relations. It has resulted not only in an increasing number of United Nations missions with a much broader mandate than previously but also in the pressure to set up a permanent international criminal court, where violators of human rights can be tried outside the borders of any particular state.

The International Criminal Court

The international community met in Rome, Italy, from 15 June to 17 July 1998 to finalise a statute which, after ratified by a minimum of 60 countries, has established the International Criminal Court (ICC). This is a permanent court for trying individuals accused of committing genocide, war crimes and crimes against humanity.

Continuing debates: freedom from "want"

The origins of the new focus on human security are often traced to the publication of an Agenda for Peace by United Nations Secretary-General Boutros Boutros-Ghali in 1992. This document suggested that threats to global security were not only military in nature:

> *"A porous ozone shield could pose a greater threat to an exposed population than a hostile army. Drought and disease can decimate no less mercilessly than the weapons of war."*

It was suggested that not only were environmental instability, poverty, famine and oppression critical security issues in and of themselves, they were also both sources and consequences of conflict.

The United Nations Development Programme Human Development Report of 1994 followed up this idea of a broader interpretation of the concept of security, suggesting that the concept of human security can be broken down into two component factors:

1. "protection from sudden and hurtful disruptions in the pattern of our daily lives," (known as *freedom from fear*); and
2. "safety from the constant threats of hunger, disease, crime and repression," (known as *freedom from want*).

The report elaborated these concepts further and went on to identify seven separate components of human security:

- *economic security* (assured basic income);
- *food security* (physical and economic access to food);
- *health security* (relative freedom from disease and infection);
- *environmental security* (access to sanitary water supply, clean air and a non-degraded land system);
- *personal security* (security from physical violence and threats);
- *community security* (security of cultural identity);
- *political security* (protection of basic human rights and freedoms).

Youth and human security

Youth organisations working in programmes and activities that promote peace, human rights education, environmental issues or hunger relief, for example, can all be said to be working for greater human security: they are aiming to develop conditions where people can have more freedom from want and freedom from fear.

However, this very broad conception of human security has been criticised by many who believe that the more components we include within the concept, the less useful it becomes as a policy tool. In particular, one of the founding members of the international "Human Security Partnership", the Canadian Department for Foreign Affairs and International Trade (DFAIT), proposes a much narrower definition: "Human security means safety for people from both violent and non-violent threats. It is a condition or state of being characterised by freedom from pervasive threats to people's rights, their safety, or even their lives ... The litmus test for determining if it is useful to frame an issue in human security terms is the degree to which the safety of people is at risk."

What are the advantages and disadvantages of extending the concept of security to include freedom from 'want' as well as freedom from fear?

The Human Security Agenda

Despite the different interpretations, definitions and emphases, the different concepts of human security do have common elements. The following characteristics are emerging as central to a human security agenda.

- There is a shift of emphasis from the security of states to the security of people. This is considered one of the primary contributions of the concept of human security. As mentioned previously, for centuries, security has been seen primarily as national or state security; now, the notion of human security brings people into international discussions and raises concerns around the security and safety of people, not just States.
- This implies and re-emphasises the obligations of states to ensure the security of their citizens. The focus on people's security raises the profile of states to provide for and protect their citizens.
- It recognises the inter-relatedness of people and the fact that many issues cross state borders and other boundaries. A human security position highlights the inter-dependent nature of people in today's world, reminding us that many problems do not have "passports" and cannot be stopped at political borders. Women and men in industrialised countries, for example, are not isolated from poverty in developing countries, as is evidenced by migration patterns and diseases that do not respect borders; and people in developing countries are at risk from the industrial pollution produced by northern factories.
- It recognises the importance of non-state actors. The international campaign against landmines is often cited as an effective initiative spearheaded by non-governmental organisations. "Civil society organisations are seeking greater opportunity and greater responsibility in promoting human security. In many cases, non-governmental organisations have proven to be extremely effective partners in advocating the security of people."[34]
- It requires that those responsible for violations of human rights and humanitarian law are held accountable. The creation of the International Criminal Court as well as the International Criminal Tribunals for the former Yugoslavia and Rwanda are seen as important advances in the pursuit of a human security agenda.
- It highlights the complexity of security issues reinforcing the need for multi-faceted responses. Among the different uses of human security, there is agreement that it is a multi-faceted concept that requires co-ordination and collaboration among a wide range of actors. One response given prominence is an increased reliance on "soft power" or persuasion rather total focus on military might and hardware ("powerful ideas rather than powerful weapons").[35]

"... decent people cannot sit back and watch systematic, state-directed massacres of other people. Decent people simply cannot tolerate this and cannot fail to come to the rescue, if a rescue action is within their power."

Vaclav Havel

Personal security and the ECHR

The right to liberty and security of person is protected under Article 5 of the European Convention on Human Rights, and the importance of Article 5 was soon apparent in some of the early cases coming to Strasbourg. Of the first 10000 cases, nearly a third came from individuals deprived of their liberty.

This article concerns the protection of physical liberty and in particular freedom from arbitrary arrest or detention. It guarantees certain basic procedural rights such as the right to be informed promptly of the reason for arrest, the right to be brought promptly before a judicial officer and the right to take proceedings by which the lawfulness of the detention, or continuing detention, may be decided speedily by a court.

Examples of cases under Article 5 that have been tried before the European Court of Human Rights include:

1. *Bozano v. France, 1986*
   The Court found that the circumstances surrounding the arrest and deportation of the applicant from France to Switzerland were neither lawful nor compatible with the right to security of person.
2. *Brogan and Others v. the United Kingdom, 1988*
   The Court found that the holding of the applicants under prevention of terrorism legislation for periods exceeding four days, without having the legality of their detention decided upon, violated their right to be brought promptly before a judicial officer.
3. *De Wilde, Ooms and Versyp v. Belgium, 1970/71*
   The Court held that the procedures open to the applicants to challenge the lawfulness of their detention under vagrancy legislation did not give them access to a remedy with the necessary guarantees to contest their long deprivation of liberty, ranging from seven months to one year and nine months.

References

Annan, K., "Two concepts of sovereignty", The Economist, *18 September 1999.*
Charter of the United Nations, www.un.org/peace
www.humansecuritynetwork.org
Lodgaard, S., "Human security: concept and operationalization", Norwegian Institute of International Affairs, unpublished, 2000.
Rothschild, E., "What is security?", DAEDALUS, the Journal of the American Academy of Arts and Sciences, *Vol. 124, No. 3, Summer 1995.*
Human Development Report 1994, *United Nations Development Programme, www.undp.org.*
The Canadian Department for Foreign Affairs and International Trade (DFAIT), www.dfait-maeci.gc.ca/foreignp/humansecurity

Media

AND THE WINNER
IN THE CATEGORY
OF TORTURE IS...
PANCHO

In his autobiography, President Mandela recounts a stopover he made north of the Arctic Circle at Goose Bay where a group of young Inuit had come to him:

> "... in talking with these bright young people, I learned that they had watched my release on television and were familiar with events in South Africa. 'Viva ANC!'one of them said. The Inuit are an aboriginal people historically mistreated by a white settler population; there were parallels between the plights of black South Africans and the Inuit people. What struck me so forcefully was how small the planet had become during my decades in prison; it was amazing to me that a teenage Inuit living at the roof of the world could watch the release of a political prisoner on the southern tip of Africa. Television had shrunk the world, and had in the process become a great weapon for eradicating ignorance and promoting democracy."[36]

The process skilfully described with one single image by President Mandela is that of an exponential acceleration in the diffusion of the various media. A little over a century ago, in 1895, Marconi sent the first wireless message; two decades earlier Edison had invented the phonograph. Recent decades have seen technical progress accelerating after the invention of radio and television and subsequently broadcasting in both media. How this broadcasting is currently taking place was difficult to foresee when in October 1957, the Soviet scientists launched the Sputnik, the first spacecraft to go into orbit, a metallic sphere two feet in diameter that was designed to determine the density of Earth's upper atmosphere. In this case, the event was broadcast through radio and the satellite circled Earth for only three months. Twelve years later the United States of America would broadcast by television the images of our planet as one single body and of the first man to set foot on the moon.

Today, the idea of "one world" and of satellite/parabolic communication has acquired a central role in addressing key global as well as local issues. The first international satellite system, Intelsat, was put in place in 1965. Since then, space-age telecommunications, information technology, and optical electronics have converged with conventionally understood "mass media" to give people an unprecedented array of tools - from the simple cellular telephone to

Related activities

- "Draw the word" game, page 120
- Fighters for rights, page 130.
- Front page, page 135.
- Picture games, page 188.
- The impact of the Internet, page 222.
- When tomorrow comes, page 250.

the Internet - to diversify their perceptions, to express their opinions, to interact with others and to understand and react to change.

In the media sphere the simple perception of change is undergoing a radical transition. It took the radio 38 years to reach 50 million users, 13 for television and 16 for personal computers, but only 4 years for the world wide web, the dominant browsing mode on the Internet.

Key dates

21 November
World Television Day

17 May
World Telecommunication Day

Challenges of a media-rich world

The Unesco Commission on Culture and Development that helps to analyse modern communication trends and the central role of Western culture within the globalisation process describes new technologies as offering unheard-of scope for the media. Traditional forms of censorship have become increasingly difficult, the media can reinforce a sense of global solidarity and multi-media technologies are creating new artistic and intellectual challenges. The ease of reproduction and transmission has made it much more difficult for any government to control - let alone censor - the information people receive or send. The media of today are helping to sustain people's movements as well as to create a better-informed citizenry. They are also strengthening the sense of global solidarity, without which no global ethics could begin to crystallise. "Media images of human suffering have motivated people to express their concern and their solidarity with those in distant places by contributing to relief efforts and by demanding explanations and action from governments."

Negative aspects have to be stressed as well. It is probably an underestimate to say that at this moment over 100 journalists are being held in prisons in over 20 countries for exercising their ostensibly guaranteed right to freedom of expression, not to mention those who have paid with their lives for exercising their profession.

The availability of means is another problem that has to be mentioned. How can the communications revolution reach the billions of people without electricity in hundreds of thousands of human settlements in the developing world? They are still the *have-nots* of the information revolution. The *haves* are a minority, mostly citizens of developed countries and urban residents elsewhere, who can hope to be connected to satellite television or the international information networks.

Did you know that...

For developing countries, the weak link in the infrastructure chain is often the "last mile" from the local exchange to the household. Some African countries are indeed so poor in telecommunications that there is less than a single telephone line per 1000 people. Or, to put it more starkly still, there are more phones in Tokyo or Manhattan than in the whole of Africa. The 1999 Human Development Report provides a comprehensive comparison of the availability of telephone lines, TV sets, faxes, PC and Internet hosts world-wide. Developed countries have an average of 502 telephone lines, 595 TV sets, 45 faxes, 204 PC and 35 Internet hosts for every 1000 people, while poorer countries, for every 1000 people, have an average of 4 telephone lines, 36 TV sets, 0.2 faxes and no significant presence of PCs or Internet access. Presently, the radio remains the only medium which is sufficiently wide-spread across the globe and responds to the need of oral cultures as well.

What effects do these rapid changes have on our perception of world events?

Three crucial dimensions in the changing nature of media can be highlighted:[37]

1. The rapid development of telecommunications and media technologies has changed the very nature of the media. In terms of both space and time they are becoming an integral part of events taking place. Live coverage itself has been transformed into a new event. Examples of this are the landing of United States marines in Somalia and

"Everyone has the right to freedom of opinion and expression; this right includes freedom to hold opinions without interference and to seek, receive and impart information and ideas through any media and regardless of frontiers."

Article 19, Universal Declaration of Human Rights

Haiti and the assault on the Beli Dom and the Ostankino television station in Moscow.

2. Politicians have a powerful and crucial influence on the media in non-democratic regimes and unconsolidated democracies. In democratic societies, politicians endeavour to influence the media as much as possible by spin-doctoring. On the other hand, the media themselves are able to exert an increasingly decisive influence on the behaviour and decisions of politicians.
3. Commercialisation suppresses the diversity of programming, as well of programmes relating to minorities, alternative culture and subcultures. The pursuit of higher audience ratings is reflected in the reporting of news and current affairs. News presentation, the selection of excerpts from reality presented by media to their audiences is now characterised by the trivial, the bizarre and the scandalous. As a consequence of this, hard news now occupies less space in the media. There is less willingness to cover the expenses of public service broadcasters which are now being forced into commercialisation. In the process, the public has the most to lose – it loses its sources of information.

Article 11 of the European charter for regional or minority languages (1992) on Media

The Parties undertake, for the users of the regional or minority languages within the territories in which those languages are spoken, according to the situation of each language, to the extent that the public authorities, directly or indirectly, are competent, have power or play a role in this field, and respecting the principle of the independence and autonomy of the media:

A. to the extent that radio and television carry out a public service mission:
   - i. to ensure the creation of at least one radio station and one television channel in the regional or minority languages; or
   - ii. to encourage and/or facilitate the creation of at least one radio station and one television channel in the regional or minority languages; or
   - iii. to make adequate provision so that broadcasters offer programmes in the regional or minority languages.

A need for alternatives

Especially at the time of tensions and violent conflicts such as those affecting, for example, the Balkan region, "new channels for the free flow of information could and should contribute to pluralism, economic and social development, democracy and peace ... Training programmes on journalistic ethics should sensitise journalists to prejudices and discrimination".[38]

One of the leading Internet portals promoting information about human rights, One World (www.oneworld.net), has summarised in the following way the present four main challenges to democracy in the media:

1. *Freedom of speech.* Traditionally, many discussions of media democracy have focused on the right to freedom of expression. Particularly during the Cold War years, Western governments made much of state censorship in the Soviet bloc as a useful contrast to the supposed freedom of their own press. Yet, although free speech is still a right denied in many instances across the world, concentrating exclusively on that aspect has obscured issues even more fundamental to media democracy in many countries today.
2. *Voice projection*. In the media, democracy is much more than just "being able to say what you like". Media democracy is about voice projection - making yourself heard. While technology has made it easier than ever to publish your own magazine (or record your own video news), it has become ever more difficult to reach even the smallest audience with that material. Even if you can find a distributor to take it round to the tiny number

of independent outlets still open and willing to stock it, the fact that you can't spend millions on advertising each year means only a hardened few will ever pick it up.

3. *Concentration of ownership.* In its more sophisticated form, censorship is achieved not through legal repression but through capitalist institutions working together to maintain the hegemony of their beliefs. Control of the most powerful new media tools is still concentrated in the hands of a few (nationally or internationally), in private ownership or under governmental monopoly. This means that the majority of media businesses are owned by a tiny number of industry giants. Whether in individual countries or - increasingly - on a global scale, these cartels effectively control the images and stories through which we understand the world. Instead of a true democratic diversity, we are offered infinite versions of the same product (with slight variations in the packaging).
4. *Keep it safe.* This lack of variety has serious consequences, as it becomes increasingly difficult to voice alternatives to the mainstream media's orthodoxy. How much coverage was given to the hundreds of thousands in North America and Western Europe campaigning against their countries' assault on Iraq in the Gulf War? Restricted media democracy leads to restricted political democracy, as alternative ideas are deliberately kept away from public attention (especially if they might offend the advertisers).

Freedom of expression - much remains to be done

"Many journalists around the world, including Europe, are still harassed, prosecuted and sometimes even murdered when trying to report on matters of public concern, said Council of Europe Secretary General Walter Schwimmer in a statement to mark World Press Freedom Day (3 May 2001)."[39]

Concentration of ownership

"Two nuclear power plant manufacturers own two of the USA national TV networks – General Electric owns NBC and Westinghouse owns CBS. The other network is owned by a cartoon company: Disney owns ABC", alerted USA presidential candidate Ralph Nader. One advertising group is able to corner today 40% of the market. The concentration of power as witnessed with the fusion of American On Line (AOL), Time Warner and the Turner group raises the spectre of cultural hegemony.

Do you think that being subjected to the continuous commercial propaganda through mass media takes away from us our capacity to make free choices?

Do you think that youth exposure to inappropriate material with violent or racist content, for example, on television has an influence on its thinking and attitudes?

NGOs and media

1. The Baltic Media Centre is an independent, non-profit foundation (NGO) promoting democracy, social development, and a peaceful international co-operation through the active participation of the media, www.bmc.dk
2. AIM (Alternativna Informativna Mre•a / Alternative Information Network) is a network of independent journalists in former Yugoslavia and the southern Balkans, which provides a service of in-depth information in the local languages and in English. www.aimpress.org
3. *Reporters sans Frontičres* is an organisation that provides information on reporters who wrote freely and are in jeopardy worldwide. It organises petitions and letter writing campaigns in defense of threatened journalists. For more information, see www.rsf.fr

References

Human Development Report 1999, *United Nations Development Programme, www.undp.org*
Human Development Report 2001, *United Nations Development Programme, www.undp.org*
www.humanrights.coe.int/media
Our creative diversity, *report of the World Commission on Culture and Development, Unesco, 1995*
World Communication and Information Report, *Unesco publishing, 1999*

Peace and Violence

WATCH OUT,
THERE MIGHT BE SOME
HUMAN RIGHTS LEFT
UNDER THE RUBBLE...
PANCHO

"Bread in times of peace is better then cake in times of war."

Slovak proverb

What is the relationship between peace and human rights? Is peace a human right?

The massive violations of human rights during world war II and the desire and need for peace were at the origin of the Council of Europe.

A culture of human rights is a pre-condition to achieve a state of peace in any country of the world. The right to peace belongs to the third generation of human rights or so-called solidarity rights.

The United Nations Educational, Scientific and Cultural Organisation (Unesco) is the leading institution that has been active in promoting this right. Indeed, in 1994, Federico Mayor, the then Director-General of Unesco, launched an international appeal for the establishment of a right to peace. In 1997, a proposal for a declaration presenting peace as a human right was submitted to the Unesco General Conference . The proposal was rejected, but the right to peace is still on the United Nations agenda. The Commission on Human Rights in early 2001 adopted a Resolution on the Promotion of the Right of Peoples to Peace.

Do you think there should be a specific right to peace, or is it part of existing human rights already?

Related activities

- Can I come in?, page 98.
- Do we have alternatives?, page 111.
- Domestic affairs, page 114.
- Living in a perfect world, page 160.
- Money to spend, page 177.
- Play the game!, page 194.
- Power station, page 198.
- Violence in my life, page 248.
- When tomorrow comes, page 250.

Then what is peace?

The concept of peace has an important cultural dimension. Traditionally in oriental cultures, peace has to do more with inner peace (peace in our minds or hearts) while in the western world, peace is understood to be outside the individuals (absence of war or violent conflict). For example, in India the word peace is "shanti" and implies a perfect order of the mind or peace of mind. Gandhi based his philosophy and strategy on a concept called Ahimsa, which means broadly to refrain from anything at all harmful. He said, "literally speaking, Ahimsa means non-violence. But to me it has a much higher, an infinitely higher meaning. It means that you may not offend anybody; you may not harbour uncharitable thoughts, even in connection with those who you consider your enemies. To one who follows this doctrine, there are no enemies". In the Maya tradition, peace refers to the concept of welfare; it is linked to the idea of a perfect balance between the different areas of our lives.

They are many definitions of peace. One of them that has had a strong influence is the distinction that has been made between positive and negative peace by Johan Galtung, an internationally renowned Norwegian scholar and researcher in this field.

Negative peace means that there is no war, no violent conflict between states or within states such as the wars in the Balkans.

On the other hand, *positive peace* means no war or violent conflict combined with a situation where there is equity, justice and development.

We could summarise these two concepts the following way:

no war = negative peace

no war + social justice/development = positive peace

A high level of social justice and a minimum level of violence therefore characterise positive peace.

While some people think that all the problems have been fixed when a war has stopped, in reality a great deal of work remains to be done, namely, to rebuild the country and develop structures that will lead to more social justice and development for all the people living in the countries affected.

We can therefore say that peace is *not only* a matter of disarmament but it *also* has to do with the way people live.

Who should be responsible for implementing strategies preventing violence of any kind in your own community?

Peace Conference

In May 1999, 10000 peace activists of all ages met in The Hague in the Netherlands in pursuit of new strategies for a peaceful twenty-first century. Participants in the historic Hague Appeal conference included 1 500 young people from one hundred different countries. At the end of the conference, the Hague Agenda for Peace and Justice for the 21st Century was presented to the United Nations Secretary General, Kofi Annan. It is now an official United Nations document, with a 50-point plan for global action by governments and civil society.

But can we talk about peace without speaking of violence?

There are many definitions of violence, one of which is that violence is the use of strength - overt or hidden - with the objective of obtaining from an individual or a group something they do not want to consent to freely.

There are different kinds of violence. We can distinguish between direct and indirect (or structural) violence:

- *Direct violence* = physical violence
- *Indirect or structural violence* = poverty, exploitation, social injustice, no democracy, etc.

Therefore, there is peace when there is no direct *and no* indirect violence.

What is the cost of violence?

In a situation of non-peace, the parties involved in the conflict see their economic and social rights being violated (economy of the country disrupted, black market, loss of jobs or homes, etc.) as well

Key date

The third Tuesday of September each year
International Day of Peace

as their civil and political rights (the right to life is threatened, as well as the right not to be tortured or the right to physical integrity, etc.). The short- and long-term consequences of a violent conflict in terms of human rights violations are devastating and leave deep scars in societies.

The statistics and information below illustrate the cost of violence in human and monetary terms.

Direct violence:

1. In Bosnia and Herzegovina, despite the 1995 General Framework Peace Agreements, between 850000 and 1.2 million people are still displaced internally or living as refugees; around 17000 people are still reported as having disappeared.
2. 800000 people died in three months during the 1994 war in Rwanda.
3. The total number of people who died during the first world war was 8538315
4. In the 1990s, civil wars killed 5 million people worldwide.
5. 500 million small arms are in circulation around the world.
6. In the 1990s, wars and internal conflicts forced 50 million people to flee from their homes.
7. 800 deaths a month are due to anti-personnel mines (landmines).
8. In 1995, 53 million people - one out of every 115 people on earth - were uprooted from their homes, either being displaced within their countries or becoming refugees abroad.

Indirect violence:

1. Around 17 million people die every year from lack of medicine.
2. About 24000 people die from the effects of hunger each day. That is about one person every 3.5 seconds.
3. More than 30000 children a day die from mainly preventable diseases.

Violence in general not only leaves physical scars but also emotional scars on any person that has participated either directly or indirectly in conflict situations such as wars or situations of interpersonal violence such as family violence. These scars can provoke long-term traumas that are not visible in people. They are impossible to estimate in terms of monetary costs but nevertheless have a high human cost.

The International Campaign to Ban Landmines is co-laureate of the 1997 Nobel Peace Prize. www.icbl.org

Do you think that there should be rules limiting the levels of violence in TV programmes?

Priorities in Public Spending (as % of GDP) [41]

Country	Public Expenditure in Education 1995-1997	Public Expenditure on Health 1998	Military Expenditure 1999
Angola	6.2 (1985-1987)	5.8	23.5
Costa Rica	5.4	5.2	...
Eritrea	1.8	...	22.9
Ethiopia	4.0	1.7	9.0
Norway	7.7	7.4	2.2
Russian Federation	3.5	2.5 (1990)	3.8
Saudi Arabia	7.5	12.8	13.2
Turkey	2.2	2.2 (1990)	5.0
Ukraine	5.6	3.6	3.1
United Kingdom	5.3	5.9	2.5

The six major military spenders in 2000[40] (in billions of US Dollars)

Rank 2000 (1999)	Country	2000	Share of world military expenditure (%)
1 (1)	USA	280.6	37
2 (7)	RUSSIA	43.9	6
3 (3)	FRANCE	40.4	5
4 (2)	JAPAN	37.8	5
5 (5)	UK	36.3	5
6 (4)	GERMANY	33	4

World military spending and its alternatives.[42]

Total Chart = Total Annual World Military Expenditure in 2001 (US$ 756 billion) ☐ =US$1 billion

Amount Necessary to...

A) STABILIZE POPULATION
US$10.5 billion

B) STOP DEFORESTATION
US$7 billion

C) PREVENT GLOBAL WARMING
US$8 billion

D) PREVENT ACID RAIN
US$8 billion

E) PROVIDE HEALTH CARE
US$15 billion

F) ELIMINATE STARVATION AND MALNOURISHMENT
US$19 billion

G) STOP OZONE DEPLETION
US$5 billion

H) PREVENT SOIL EROSION
US$24 billion

I) PROVIDE CLEAN SAFE ENERGY
Renewable Energy: US$17 billion
Energy Efficiency: US$33 billion

J) ELIMINATE ILLITERACY
US$5 billion

K) END DEVELOPING NATIONS' DEBTS
US$30 billion

L) PROVIDE SHELTER
US$21 billion

M) PROVIDE SAFE CLEAN WATER
US$58 billion

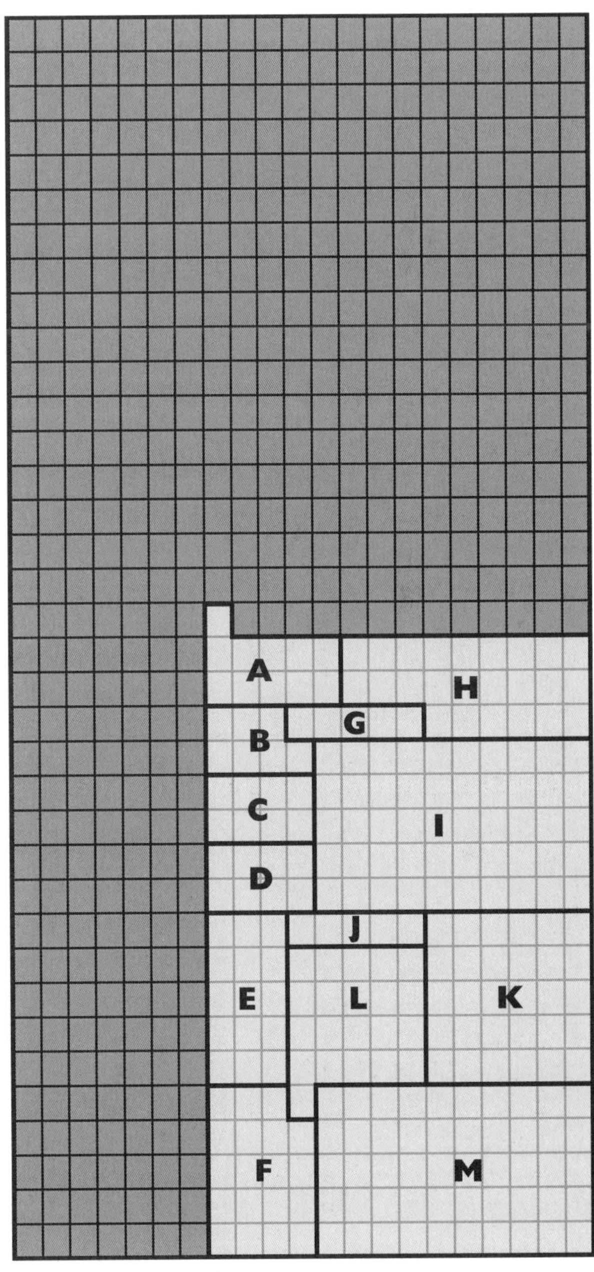

Key date

25 November
International Day for the Elimination of Violence against Women

Is violence natural?

Many people are convinced that human beings are naturally violent and that consequently we cannot avoid wars, conflicts and general violence in our lives and our societies. Other specialists in this field claim that we *can* avoid thinking, feeling and acting violently. The Seville Statement on Violence elaborated in 1986 by a group of scholars and scientists from many countries, North and South, East and West, confirms this by stating that:

1. "It is scientifically incorrect *to say that we have inherited a tendency to make war from our animal ancestors.... Warfare is a solely human phenomenon and does not occur in other animals....*
2. *There are cultures that have not engaged in war for centuries and there are cultures which have engaged in war frequently at some times and not at others....*
3. It is scientifically incorrect *to say that war or any other violent behaviour is genetically programmed into our human nature....*
4. It is scientifically incorrect *to say that humans have a "violent brain"... how we act is shaped by how we have been conditioned and socialised...*".

Most of us are conditioned to react aggressively and violently by our environments. We learn to think, feel and act aggressively and in some cases violently. Wherever we live, we are submitted to a social and cultural pressure that conditions us to read about violence, watch violence, and hear about violence almost constantly. Television programmes, advertisements, newspapers, video games and the movie and music industries contribute largely to this situation. Before reaching adolescence, a child has seen thousands of murders and violent acts just by watching television. Our modern societies, whether consciously or not, make an apology for violence. Violence is seen as being of positive value. In most cultures, saying no to violence and avoiding physical violence or confrontation is perceived as a sign of weakness especially for men, who are put under a lot of pressure by their peers from a very young age.

? Do you agree with the statement that violence is never justified, even against the most violent people?

Bullying is a form of interpersonal violence among young people and illustrates how violence is used as a means to feeling more powerful while damaging others. In a 2001 survey, almost half of the students interviewed from a sample of Spanish secondary school students admitted knowing cases of fellow students who were being intimidated by fellow students.

Apart from bullying, there are many forms of interpersonal violence: alcohol- and drug-related violence, gang violence, forced prostitution, slavery, violence in schools, and violence related to racism are all manifestations of interpersonal violence that affect our lives or the lives of many others. Some of these forms of violence affect young people more specifically - gang violence, school violence and racist violence, for example.

? Do you agree with the belief that a "real man" should not be afraid of violence?

"Just as 'wars begins in the minds of men', peace also begins in our minds. The same species that invented war is capable of inventing peace. The responsibility lies with each of us."

Seville Statement on Violence

Sexual abuse and sexual violence against children or women (or even men), are widespread phenomena in our societies. Most of the cases take place in homes and private places and not on the streets, contrary to what is often believed. The offenders are very often known by their victims, and they abuse the trust and confidence they receive to commit their crimes. Most of the victims do not report the crime that has been committed or wait many years

before they do. There are many reasons for this, most of the time interrelated, and , linked to the situation, the identity of the offender, the nature (duration and frequency) of the abuse, the personality of the victim, etc.. It can happen that the victim is too young and does not understand what is going on until much later; and/or they need assistance and have no one to trust; and/or they tell the story to someone who refuses to believe them, which happens quite often especially in the case of children; and/or they feel too ashamed, guilty and betrayed; and/or they are threatened and manipulated by the offender. In the majority of the cases, the offender is a family member.

References

Declaration on the Rights of Peoples to Peace, *A/RES/39/11, United Nations General Assembly, 12 November 1984.*

Human Development Report 2000, *United Nations Development Programme, Oxford University Press, USA, 2000.*

Report 2000, *Amnesty International, Amnesty International Publications, UK, 2000.*

The Seville Statement on Violence, www.unesco.org/human_rights/hrfv.htm , *Spain, 1986.*

Tyler, J., Berry A. (Comp.), Time to abolish war, a youth agenda for peace and justice, *Hague Appeal for Peace, European Youth Foundation, 2001.*

United Nations Commission on Human Rights, Resolution on the Promotion of the Right of Peoples to Peace, *E/CN.4/RES/2001/69, 25 April 2001.*

Fisas, V., Introducción al estudio de la paz y del conflicto, *Lerna, Barcelona, 1987.*

Voices of youth explore children and war, www.unicef.org/voy/meeting/war/war-exp2.html, *Unicef.*

World Report 2001, *Human Rights Watch, USA, 2000.*

Poverty

DON'T WORRY,
WE ARE GLOBALISING
POVERTY TOO.
PANCHO

"We must not hand down to future generations a selfish Europe which is blind and deaf to the needs of others."

Vaclav Havel

Poverty is a worldwide problem and it is increasing. We tend to connect it with places like Sub-Saharan Africa, Asia and Latin America, but in Europe poverty affects millions of people, too. Of the European Union's 400 million inhabitants, 60 million live below the poverty line (which is defined as 50% of a country's average income), and 2.7 million are homeless. In Spain, 20% of the population live under this poverty line and 4.5 % live in extreme poverty. In the United Kingdom, one third of children grow up in poverty.

Poverty in transition

" (...) almost all the former socialist countries have experienced an important increase in poverty during the transition period. Nevertheless, poverty is not an absolutely new phenomenon and it is not due solely to the transition process; poverty existed before in the Soviet Union and the region, although for political and ideological reasons it was not recognised. One social group that was not previously affected by poverty is public sector workers, who have seen their salaries and living standards decrease dramatically. Unemployment is one of the main causes of poverty in the region." *UNDP, 2001*

Poverty in the world

"In rich countries, fewer than one child in one hundred fails to reach its fifth birthday, while in the poorest countries as many as a fifth of children do not. Also, while in rich countries fewer than 5% of all children under five are malnourished, in poor countries, as many as 50% are." The *World Bank, 2000*

Related activities

- Horoscope of poverty, page 145.
- Take a step forward, page 217.
- The scramble for wealth and power, page 231.
- Where do you stand?, page 254.

Defining poverty

Absolute poverty is based on what is considered to be a minimum requirement for survival. By this definition, it is assumed that there are minimum standards below which people fall into the category of "poor". One of the most frequently used measurements is level of income: where the income of a person or a family falls below a certain level, considered to

be the minimum required for a reasonable standard of living, then this person or family is considered poor.

In *relative poverty*, the status of a specific group is defined and measured in relation to others in the same environment, community or country. Consequently, someone who is considered poor in the developed world may actually have a higher income than someone in a less developed country who is considered well-off. The meaning of poverty depends on the customs, standards and values of each country and region of the world. In this way, there is also a cultural dimension in the perception of what constitutes poverty.

Nowadays, many people recognise that poverty is not necessarily reduced by a country's economic growth. In countries that have experienced economic growth, poverty has not disappeared. Poland, for example, has achieved significant success in the economic sphere, but poverty has still increased. It is widely accepted that "poverty is a multi-dimensional phenomenon consisting of mental, political, communal and other aspects", together with a material dimension (normally expressed in terms of monetary value). The factors underpinning it may be economic, social, political or environmental. Poverty has many faces: it can be rural or urban, a permanent or temporary state of affairs. Some people may be poor throughout their lifetime, while others may move in and out of poverty. It is not a static condition.

A further important dimension of poverty concerns what is often called the "feminisation of poverty". This means that is there is a prevalence of women among the poor, which is linked, among other things, to gender-biased consequences of poverty.

"Economic growth broadens the material base for satisfaction of human needs, but the degree to which they are satisfied depends on the distribution of resources among the people and the use and distribution of opportunities, particularly employment."

Moreira

Poverty and human rights

The Vienna Declaration and the Programme of Action adopted during the World Conference on Human Rights in Vienna, Austria, (June 1993) states that "the existence of widespread extreme poverty inhibits the full and effective enjoyment of human rights…especially the economic, social and cultural rights." (Article 14).

It is important to realise that the denial of adequate health care, education, equality, shelter, etc., which are some of the consequences of poverty and social exclusion, impedes access to civil and political rights, which in turn prevents people from claiming their economic, social and cultural rights. This is a clear example of the indivisibility and interdependence of human rights.

The Fourth World Youth Movement

is part of the Fourth World Movement, an organisation dedicated to the fight against poverty.
www.atd-fourthworld.org

Amnesty International and economic, social and cultural rights

The International Council Meeting of Amnesty International which took place in August 2001 agreed to expand the organisation's mandate to enable it to work on a wide range of human rights. From now on, the organisation will work not only against torture or for prisoners of conscience, but also against all forms of discrimination, whether they affect political and civil rights or economic, social and cultural rights.

The Declaration on the Right to Development, adopted by the UN General Assembly on 4 December 1986, is the first international instrument that refers exclusively to the right to development. It is closely connected with the second generation of human rights, as described in the International Covenant on Economic, Social and Cultural rights. Development is defined in Article 1 as "A global economic, social, cultural and political process that tends to improve the well-being of all the people and all the individuals based on their free, active and significant

Key dates

17 October
International Day for the Eradication of Poverty.

5 December
International Volunteer Day for Economic and Social Development.

participation in the development and the fair distribution that derives from it". Article 2 of the same declaration emphasises that "The human person is the main subject of development and should be an active participant and beneficiary of the right to development."

Do you think all the documents that have been agreed by governments can make a difference to the fight against poverty throughout the world?

At the 1995 World Summit for Social Development, known as the Copenhagen Summit, 185 countries, through their representatives, committed themselves to eradicating absolute poverty and adopted concrete plans and proposals to that end. The heads of governments and states adopted a declaration and a plan of action, known as "Copenhagen + 6", but as of September 2001, none of the stated objectives has been achieved completely.

The existing international and regional instruments have had a limited impact on the fight against poverty. One reason is that many of these instruments do not include mechanisms to enforce these rights. Another is that, although progress has been made over the last 50 years to develop a human rights framework and the international community has accepted that sustainable human development is not possible without respect for human rights, there is still no express link being made between poverty and human rights. The Universal Declaration of Human Rights and the two International Covenants on Human Rights do refer in their preambles to freedom from want, and the human rights treaties do provide for the right to an adequate standard of living, including sufficient food, clothing and housing.

The European Social Charter

With a view to ensuring the effective exercise of the right to protection against poverty and social exclusion, the Parties undertake:

(a) to take measures within the framework of an overall and co-ordinated approach to promote the effective access of persons who live or risk living in a situation of social exclusion or poverty, as well as their families, to, in particular, employment, housing, training, education, culture and social and medical assistance;

(b) to review these measures with a view to their adaptation if necessary.

The revised European Social Charter, Article 30

Final considerations

One of the most common prejudices held about poor people is that they find themselves in this situation because they want to or because they do not work hard enough - implying that they are lazy and irresponsible. This is a way of making the poor bear sole responsibility for their situation; it suggests that society should not be responsible for them and can do nothing about them. This approach runs contrary to a culture of human rights, because it denies those people who find themselves excluded the opportunity to live with dignity and to be a subject of rights. In addition, it conflates the consequences of poverty (altered patterns of behaviour, drug abuse, refusal to work, use of alcohol, etc.) with complex root causes.

To eradicate poverty we should be addressing its roots, not just the immediate needs, and this will require a major political effort especially from states and international organisations: poverty thus has a strong political dimension.

In the Millennium Declaration (September 2000), the world community committed itself to eradicating poverty, with a target of halving those whose income was less than US $1 a day by the year 2015.

> "The fight against poverty is a deeply political issue. Poverty in most societies is about disparities in the distribution of power, wealth and opportunity." *UNDP, 2001.*

Do you agree with this statement?

Examples of social indicators associated with poverty: unemployment and youth in eastern Europe

As in the West, young people suffer higher unemployment rates than other adults. In 1999, there were 65 million young people aged 15 to 24 in central and east European countries and the Commonwealth of Independent States (27 countries). Of the total youth population, 27% (18 million) were neither in education nor in employment. The average youth unemployment rate for 18 countries stood at 30%, double the overall unemployment rate. Youth unemployment is particularly high in south-eastern Europe (71% in "the former Yugoslav Republic of Macedonia", 61% in the former Yugoslavia, 35% in Bulgaria), in the Caucasus (46% in Azerbaijan, 27% in Georgia), and in Central Asia (37% in Kyrgyzstan, 33% in Tajikistan).[43]

Example of a national plan to combat poverty

The plight of children in Moldova is disturbing. In many families, the main source of income is a modest child allowance. Recent years have seen a deterioration of nutritional standards among children from poor families, with adverse consequences for their health and cognitive development. Consequently, the government has decided to develop a special programme to combat child poverty as part of the country's Short-Term Poverty Alleviation Programme. This initiative offers a wide range of measures aimed at instituting a social care system for orphaned and disabled children as well as for children from poor families.[44]

References

Bilan économique et social 2000, *le Monde, France, Édition 2001.*
Choices for the poor, *United Nations Development Programme, New York, 2001.*
Human Development Report 2001, *United Nations Development Programme, New York, 2001.*
Moreira, C, Eradication of poverty in the world: an assessment on the threshold of the year 2000, *Social Watch, www.socwatch.org.uy/, Uruguay, 2000.*
Pettiti, L, Meyer-Bisch, P., "Human rights and extreme poverty", Human Rights, New Dimensions and Challenges, *Ed. J. Symonides, Unesco, Paris, 1998, pp. 157-176.*
Report of the expert seminar on human rights and extreme poverty, 7-10 February 2001, *E/CN.4/2001/54/Add.1, United Nations Commission on Human Rights, Geneva, March 2001.*
The dimensions of poverty, *Social Watch, www.socwatch.org.uy/, Uruguay, 1997.*
"Young people in changing societies", Regional Monitoring Reports, No 7, Florence: Unicef Innocenti Research Center, 2000.

Social rights

A glimpse of the European Social Charter

"When I think of work, it's mostly about having control over your destiny, as opposed to being at the mercy of what's out there."

Gary Sinise

While the European Convention on Human Rights guarantees civil and political rights, the European Social Charter guarantees the economic and social rights of the citizens of its state parties.

The Social Charter was adopted in 1961 by the Council of Europe and three Protocols were added to it in 1988, 1991 and 1995. The Charter and its 1988 Protocol guarantee a series of rights that we can classify into two categories:

- *working conditions*, which include the prohibition of forced labour, non-discrimination in work environments, trade union rights, prohibition of child labour under the age of 15 and protection of the 15- to 18-year-old workers, equal treatment for migrant workers, etc.; and
- *social cohesion*, which includes the right to health, social security, medical assistance, the right of older people to be protected, etc..

The revised Social Charter was adopted in 1996. It entered into force on the 1 July 1999 and will progressively replace the 1961 Charter. This new document guarantees: equality between men and women, protection in case of dismissal, dignity of the workers in the work place, protection against poverty and social exclusion, the right to housing, and the enlargement of the right not to be discriminated against, etc..

The Charter has a mechanism of control based on the presentation of national reports by state parties (1991 Protocol) as well as a system of collective complaint (1995 Protocol) which allows, "*inter alia*", trade unions and non-governmental organisations to present collective claims.

Do you think that social security systems should be private or public?

Related activities

- A glossary of globalisation, page 69.
- A tale of two cities, page 71.
- Ashique's story, page 91.
- Beware, we are watching, page 95.
- Different wages, page 107.
- Horoscope, page 145.
- See the ability, page 209.
- Trade union meeting, page 244.
- Work and babies, page 260.

The right to work

The right to work is guaranteed, as one of the social and economic rights, in international instruments such as the Universal Declaration of Human Rights (UDHR) (Article 23), the International Covenant on Economic, Social and Cultural Rights (Article 6) and the revised European Social Charter (ESC).

"The workers have nothing to lose in this but their chains. They have the world to gain."

Karl Marx

When it recognises the right to work, a state is not committing itself *to guaranteeing a job for everyone who wants one*; such an obligation could be "unworkable" in practice. Rather, it implies that the state has an obligation to develop economic and social conditions where jobs can be created.

The right to work is important in itself but also insofar as it is a basic condition to secure human dignity. Unless the right to work is guaranteed first, the actual exercise of several other basic rights may be inconceivable.

As a corollary of the right to work comes the right to just (or fair) conditions of work. This right specifically includes the guarantees not to be discriminated against, to receive a fair remuneration and paid holidays as well as to have reasonable working hours and a safe and healthy working environment that safeguards a person's physical and mental well-being. These guarantees are given in an attempt to make sure that workers begin and continue their working life in decent conditions. Work should not become an intolerable burden or an end to itself; it should be a means to ensure that at least primary needs such as food, clothing, housing and education, are met.

 **Do you think that unemployed people should receive support from the state?**

Employment: a youth perspective

Having a job implies a lot more than having means to support oneself. It is also a tool for life experience. Through employment, individuals (particularly young people) develop many skills, ranging from basic technical skills to personal skills.

Unemployment and bad working conditions are part of the complex interrelated issues creating obstacles to people's full development and to their maintaining their inherent dignity. Some examples of these consequences include the inability of the unemployed to afford adequate living conditions for themselves and their dependants, the potential creation of a large number of black market jobs decreasing workers' security and ability to protect their rights, and the need for a large social security scheme to be created in order to provide assistance to the unemployed.

The transition from school to work is a crucial stage for young people in their personal and professional development throughout adult life. The consequences of being unemployed at young ages can be serious. Youth unemployment is often associated with social problems such as violence, crime, suicide and abuse of alcohol and drugs.

Unemployment rates amongst young people are often higher than amongst adults. This difference can be wide or narrow, depending on the specific context of the country.

Unemployment rates in some European countries[45]

Country	Youth Unemployment (%)	Overall Unemployment (%)
Croatia	31.4	9.9
Germany	10.7	9.9
Latvia	25.5	13.8
Russia	26.8	13.3
Slovakia	20.4	11.1
Spain	39.2	20.9
Sweden	11.2	5.3
The Netherlands	5.1	3.8
UK	13.6	7.1

"No one can arrive from being talented alone. God gives talent; work transforms talent into genius."

Anna Pavlova

Various reasons explain the high incidence of unemployment among young people: segmentation of the labour market; technical and organisational changes that have created a demand for higher qualifications; and the labour market crisis which has meant tougher conditions for unemployed workers.

Trade unions, working for the workers

The history of trade unions is a very long one. The rights of workers have undoubtedly improved even if only gradually and trade unions have played a crucial role in this process.

Labour Day: 1st May

May 1st, International Workers' Day, commemorates the historical struggle of working people throughout the world.

May Day was born from the struggle for the eight-hour day. With workers being forced to work ten, twelve and fourteen hours a day, support for the eight-hour movement grew rapidly. The first days of May of 1886 were marked by strikes and demonstrations in the United States. As many as half a million workers took part in the May 1st demonstrations all over the country. In Chicago, for example, around 90000 people took part in a march.

The 1st of May quickly became an annual event. Around the world workers in more and more countries marked labour's day on May Day. May Day was celebrated for the first time in Russia, Brazil and Ireland in 1891.

Trade unions are associations of employees (there are also associations of employers) and their main objective is to represent the employees' interests to the employers. The right to form and join a trade union is a fundamental human right. A well functioning and respected trade union movement is often a good indicator of democracy and standards of human rights.

Besides playing a role in the fight for better working conditions, trade unions have had (and continue to have) a key role in the building of social movements and the developing of social changes. The role of trade unions has been very varied across Europe. In some countries, where fascist and communist regimes were in place, trade unions were overtaken or created by state authorities and the political elite and turned into a tool for their oppressive regimes. As a result of this historical reality, many people are sceptical of the role that trade unions can play, and only lately have the workers from these countries started to recognize the positive role of trade unions in the fight for protecting their rights. Other differences exist across Europe, especially regarding the role and organization of trade unions. In most countries, trade unions are organised in confederations.

Solidarność (Solidarity) was a new national union movement which swept across Poland during the 1980s.

The movement officially started with the signing of the Gdansk Accords on August 31 1980, which called for the right to form independent trade unions and the right to strike among other things. In reality, it started when the workers of the ship-building industry decided to protest on December 14 1970, on a march from the shipyards towards downtown Gdansk which was brutally repressed by the police. Many strikes in the summer of 1980 showed that the Solidarity movement had taken root as a force of social and democratic change. Solidarity membership grew to over nine million members. The repressive policy of the communist government became evident in the banning of Solidarity, which was thus obliged to work in secret for several years.

Youth and trade union membership

Over recent years, trade unions in many countries have seen a decrease in youth membership. Many trade unions have been slow to respond to the changes experienced by young people and have sometimes failed to formulate an agenda that attracts them in sufficient numbers to replace the traditional membership that has been lost. Consequently, many unions are now

developing a work agenda that takes into account the needs and the reality of young workers as well as appropriate structures to deal with this sector. Some have established youth committees, which is the case of the ETUC and the ICFTU - the International Confederation of Free Trade Unions.

"The work will teach you how to do it."

Estonian proverb

Are you member of a trade union? Have you ever been?

- Between 1988 and 1997, unions affiliated to the *Deutscher Gewerkschaftsbund* (DGB) lost no fewer than 609 407 young members or 55.2% of youth membership.
- Between 1987 and 1999, in Sweden the membership of youth in trade unions aged between 16 and 24 decreased from 62.7% to 46.7%.
- In Greece, 70.1% of young people expressed no trust in trade unions compared to only 22.9% who did not trust the army and 40.6% who did not trust the judiciary.[46]

Child labour

The issue of child labour today is receiving great attention. Children are engaged in numerous kinds of work, from domestic service to heavy industrial production. The number of children involved is alarming.

It is hard to gather statistics on child labour because of its illegal nature in most cases. It is estimated that some 250 million children between the ages of 5 and 14 are working; 120 million full-time, 130 million part-time.

Some 61% of this total (nearly 153 million) are found in Asia; 32%, (80 million) are in Africa, and 7% (17.5 million) live in Latin America.

Child labour also exists in many industrialised countries and is emerging in eastern European countries

The revised European Social Charter has reinforced the guarantee for the protection of children and young people in the work environment compared to the guarantees that were included in the 1961 Charter. Article 7(1) provides that "with a view to ensuring the effective exercise of the right of children and young persons to protection, the Parties undertake: to provide that the minimum age of admission to employment shall be 15 years, subject to exceptions for children employed in prescribed light work without harm to their health, morals or education". The International Labour Organisation (ILO), the major labour standard-setting organisation, has long dedicated its activities to eradicate child labour and to that end, it has adopted recommendations and conventions. Two main conventions deal specifically with child labour.

1. The ILO Worst Forms of Child Labour Convention (1999) came into force in 2000. Previous attempts to end child labour have failed and the general situation for working children continues to worsen. Therefore, the international community, within the idea of taking "one step at a time", decided to abolish completely the worst forms of child labour. As of November 2001, 108 countries have ratified this convention.
2. The ILO Minimum Age Convention (1973) is another example. Article 1 states "each Member (...) undertakes to pursue a national policy designed to ensure the effective abolition of child labour and to raise progressively the minimum age for admission to employment or work to a level consistent with the fullest physical and mental development of young persons".

The International Labour Organisation (ILO)

has played a major role in the development of and the fight for guaranteeing workers' rights and has contributed to the training and promotion of proper structures to promote workers' rights. www.ilo.org

The percentages of children between the ages of ten and fourteen who work are: 30.1% in Bangladesh, 11.6% in China, 14.4% in India, 17.7% in Pakistan, 24% in Turkey, 20.5% in Ivory Coast, 11.2% in Egypt, 41.3% in Kenya, 25.8% in Nigeria, 31.4% in Senegal, 4.5% in Argentina, 16.1% in Brazil, 6.7% in Mexico, 0.4% in Italy and 1.8% in Portugal.

One of it's the ILO's major programmes dedicated to the eradication of child labour is called the International Programme on the Elimination of Child Labour. The Convention on the Rights of the Child in Article 32(1) provides that "State Parties recognise the right of the child to be protected from economic exploitation and from performing any work that is likely to be hazardous or to interfere with the child's education, or to be harmful to the child's health or physical, mental, spiritual, moral or social development".

Globalisation has started to impact heavily on social rights.[47] Indeed, this process promotes practices that challenge social guarantees that are generally considered to be minimum safeguards of basic working conditions. With the establishment of a free market economy, many companies consider the lack of social protection as an "attractive" feature for investments and for low-cost production of goods. Relocation of industries from countries where labour guarantees are compulsory to other countries that do not provide such guarantees to the workers is seen as a viable option for lucrative ends.

In a context where the priority of most companies is to increase their profits even at the cost of the social and labour rights of their workers, the international and regional human rights instruments that provide for social and economic rights are fundamental to the protection workers' rights.

References

La Charte, ses protocoles, la Charte revisée, Editions du Conseil de l´Europe, 1998.

Conditions of employment in the European Social Charter. *Study compiled on the basis of the case law of the European Committee of Social Rights, Council of Europe Publishing, 2000.*

Pascual, S., Waddington, J., Young people: the labour market and trade unions. A report prepared for the Youth Committee of the European Trade Union Confederation, *European Trade Union Confederation Publication, May 2000.*

Solidarnosc, www.solidarnosc.org.pl

Taking steps; young people and social protection in the European Union, *European Youth Forum.*

Unicef (2000), "Young people in changing societies", *Regional Monitoring Reports, No 7, Florence Innocenti Research Centre.*

United Nations, World Bank, ILO Policy, A global alliance for youth employment: recommendations of the High Level Panel of the United Nations Secretary-General's Youth Employment Network, www.un.org/esa/socdev/youthemployment/index.html

Sport

Is sport a human right? In the strict sense, the answer is no! None of the human rights declarations or covenants contain specific provisions formulating the human right to the practice or to access to sport. However, sport can be seen as an essential element of the rights both to education and to culture.

The right to education is given in Article 26 of the Universal Declaration of Human Rights and Article 13 of the International Covenant on Economic, Social and Cultural Rights. It states "education shall be directed to the full development of the human personality and the sense of

"The practice of sport is a human right. Every individual must have the possibility of practising sport in accordance with his or her needs."

The Olympic Charter, Principle 8.

The Paralympic Games

The Paralympic Games are an athletic competition for people with disabilities, including amputees, people with impaired vision, paraplegics and people with cerebral palsy. "The Paralympic Games originated in 1948 at Stoke Mandeville Hospital in Aylesbury, England. (...) Beginning in 1952 the Paralympics were staged in Olympic years. The Winter Paralympics were first held in 1976. In 1992 in Barcelona, Spain, 3 500 athletes from 82 nations competed at the Summer Paralympics. The first true parallel with the Olympic Games took place in 1988 in Seoul, South Korea, where the athletes had a Paralympic village and used Olympic sites for competition. (...) The Paralympics are recognised and supported by the International Olympic Committee (IOC) and governed by the International Paralympic Committee (IPC)." [48]

its dignity and shall strengthen the respect for human rights and fundamental freedoms". Through sport people develop physically and intellectually. Participation in sports raises self-esteem; it provides opportunities for self-realisation and respect from others. This is especially so for disabled people through events like the paralympics.

As for children, the Convention on the Rights of the Child stipulates that the education of the child shall be directed to "... the development of the child's personality, talents and mental and

Related activities

- Just a minute, page 150.
- Play the game, page 194.
- See the ability, page 209.
- Sport for all, page 214.

physical abilities to their fullest potential" and Article 31 refers to the right to rest and leisure, to engage in play and recreational activities appropriate to the age of the child.

The right of everyone to take part in cultural life is given in Article 27 of the Universal Declaration of Human Rights (UDHR) and in Article 15 of the International Covenant on Economic Social and Cultural Rights (ICESCR). Sports of all kinds are enjoyed everywhere - soccer, swimming, darts, chess, tossing the caber, sumo wrestling, American football - whatever! Sport is undoubtedly an important part of cultural life in all countries and it can therefore be argued that everyone has a right to enjoy sport as a spectator, competitor or player.

Although sport is not generally recognised as a human right, the practice of sport and the way it is supported do have implications for human rights. In different circumstances, it may be used as a tool to promote human rights or even to abuse them.

Sports promote human rights

Participation in sport generates shared interests and values and teaches social skills that are necessary for democratic citizenship. Sport enhances social and cultural life by bringing together individuals and communities. Local or national teams are often multinational or multi-religious, and spectators also come from various backgrounds. Thus, sport helps to overcome difference and encourages dialogue, and thereby helps to breakdown prejudice, stereotypes, cultural differences, ignorance, intolerance and discrimination.

Open Fun Football Schools

Open Fun Football Schools is a humanitarian and non-profit consortium founded by two Danish NGOs, the Cross Cultures Project Association (CCPA) and the Danish Refugee Council (DRC). The context is a public sport culture characterised by a strong local focus, democratic principles, volunteerism, parental support and the basic principle of "sports for all". The wish is to empower the clubs by distributing sport equipment to all football clubs participating in the programme. It is also an incentive to the schools to open up their clubs to all children and young people regardless of skill, gender or ethnic or social background.

During the past two years, Open Fun Football Schools have implemented 15 Open Street Events. These are little 'playsports' festivals open to all children. They last three to five hours and are mainly used as an "opener" or "appetiser" in very difficult locations. For example, in 1999 a Street Sports programme in Kosovo established a network of 140 so-called streetmasters - youngsters aged between 14 and 18 - who organise street sports on a day-to-day basis for the children living in their neighbourhood. They estimate that approximately 6000 children of all ages took part in their programme, most of them on a daily basis.[49]

In relation to discrimination against women, the very fact that women can practice so-called "men's sports" like football or weight-lifting, encourages the elimination of various stereotypes about women's roles and the differences between men and women.

The status of sports personalities is such that they are often chosen to be "goodwill ambassadors" to promote humanitarian work through informal education. For example, Ronaldo, the Brazilian football star, is a special representative for the "Force for Change: World AIDS Campaign with Young People".

Human rights can also be abused through sports

The use of performance enhancing drugs is probably the most well known abuse of human dignity and health. There are also controversial issues of hormone treatment and sex-testing of women athletes that have to do with respect, human dignity and the right to privacy.

Sponsors can exploit sportsmen and women, and ambitious parents can exploit children who demonstrate precocious ability. Intensive training and pressure to compete can lead to sports injuries and be a risk to mental well-being. Everyone has the right to know the potential risks and attractions of reaching high levels of performance.

"Gymnastics: just a sport or child abuse?"

Until recently Alexandra Huci, aged 12, was just one of many talented young girls who spend their young lives in training camps and dream of becoming world champions when they grow up. One day while training, she suddenly collapsed, fell into a coma and died five days later. Her tiny body could simply take no more.

Diets and physical exertion have very often caused young gymnasts more suffering than joy. "Pain has been part of my life ever since I started training", said 10-year-old Wang Shuo in a recent interview for CNN at the Beijing training camp, where children start their "careers" at the age of three. Maria Pardo, a Spanish gymnast weighed 43 kilograms and is 170 cm tall..[50]

Sporting opportunities are not always inclusive and there may be elements of discrimination against religious or cultural minorities in access to sports facilities. Commercial pressures and interests may be linked with human rights abuses that undermine dignity and respect for others. For instance, some players accept bribes to commit "professional fouls" in soccer and to fix matches in cricket. There are other issues of human rights abuses associated with the globalisation of the sporting goods industry. In many countries, both national and local sports associations have developed policies about the labour standards demanded of producers of the equipment and clothes they use. There are campaigns, for example, the Clean Clothes Campaign in Europe, which aim to get manufacturers to respect the human rights of their workers. The Sports Shoes Campaign in North America campaigns, amongst other things, to get sports people such as Tiger Woods and André Agassi to stop promoting products made with exploited labour.[51]

Sport and politics

Sport has long been used as a peaceful means of political action against injustice. In the 1968 Olympic games in Mexico City, John Carlos and Tommie Smith gave the Black Panther salute during the victory ceremony to protest against discrimination against black people in the United States of America. During the apartheid era, many countries refused to have sporting relations with South Africa, which made a significant contribution to political change in that country.

"Capoeira"

In the sixteenth century, Angolan slaves in Brazil kept alive their traditional dances and rituals and developed them into "capoeira", an art of self-defence. The slave-masters forbade any kind of martial art, but the slaves were able to train using the guise of an innocent-looking recreational dance. In the seventeenth century the art of "capoeira" was further perfected and then used in a decade-long fight for freedom against the colonial oppressors.

Sport may also be misused for nationalistic or political purposes. For instance, at the 1972 Munich Olympic games, eight Arab terrorists invaded the Israeli team headquarters, killing two people. A further nine hostages were murdered after a failed rescue attempt by German police.

The Olympic games have long been used as a forum for nations to make political statements. For example, the United States of America together with 65 other non-communist nations boycotted the Moscow games of 1980 because of the Soviet invasion of Afghanistan. The Soviet Union and fifteen of its allies then boycotted the next games in Los Angeles in 1984 for security reasons and fears of political asylum being sought and given.

Should sport and politics be mixed?

Whether it was right that China was chosen to host the Olympic games in 2008 is debatable. China has long been criticised for its lack of democracy and for human rights abuses. Some of the arguments given for not blocking Beijing's bid were that China's handling of dissidents and other human rights abuses would anyway continue to be criticised in fora such as the annual gathering of the United Nations Commission on Human Rights. Indeed, allowing the Olympic bid to go ahead might even make Beijing take more note of such condemnation.

Sport and racism

Racism in sport is not a phenomenon confined to football grounds, nor is it confined just to players of colour. It can affect all sports and can manifest itself at several levels; in amateur sport and at institutional and international levels, as well as in the media. It can occur at local level particularly, but not exclusively, in the interaction (for real or imagined reasons of colour, religion, nationality or ethnic origin) between or against players, teams, coaches and spectators and also against referees. It can include the abuse of teams or even whole groups.

The responsibility for combating racism in sport falls on everyone, to public authorities (the legislative authority, the courts, the police, governmental bodies responsible for sport and local authorities) and non-governmental organisations (professional and amateur national sports associations, clubs, local sports associations, supporters' clubs, players' organisations, anti-racist associations and so on).

What can you in your school or club do to ensure that the sports you play are socially inclusive and promote human rights?

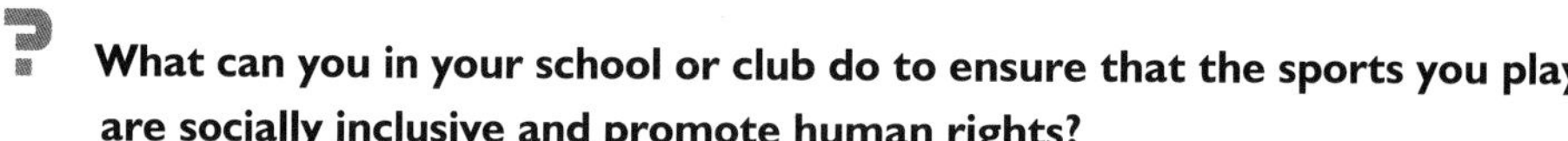

Reported incidents

21 September 2001. SK Rapid Vienna striker Gaston Taument sustained continuous racist chanting during yesterday's UEFA cup match against FK Partizan in Belgrade. Gaston Taument, who earned 15 caps for the Dutch national team and is of Surinamese origin - said earlier in an interview: "If racist incidents occur..., it is wrong to remain silent on racism."[52]

Racist behaviour at football matches provides an excellent topic for debate about the dilemmas in implementing human rights.

Should a suspected hooligan be banned from travelling to another country to attend a match? Is this an infringement of their right to freedom of movement?

Youth and sport

One example of how young people are working for human rights is through "Football against Racism in Europe". FARE fights *through* football all forms of discrimination *in* football: in the stadium, on the pitch, in the changing-room, at the training ground, in the office and classroom; by fans, players, managers, coaches, administrators or educators.

In relation to the Sports Shoes Campaign described above, student groups across the United States of America are turning sports sponsorship on its head and demanding that companies adhere to a Code of Conduct or lose the contract to kit out their college athletic teams.

The work of the Council of Europe

The Directorate of Youth and Sport is a part of the Directorate General for Education, Culture, Youth and Sport and Environment. It elaborates guidelines, programmes and legal instruments for the development of coherent and effective youth policies at local, national and European levels. It provides funding and educational support for international youth activities aimed at the promotion of youth citizenship, youth mobility and the value of human rights, democracy and cultural pluralism.

The Council of Europe Committee for the Development of Sport (CDDS) has initiated various activities to promote healthy lifestyles and participation in sport, for example, EUROFIT, (personal fitness tests for both children and adults). There is the Anti-Doping Convention of 1989 and the "Clean Sports Guide", an education and information pack for schools and sports organisations produced in co-operation with the European Union[53]. In 1986 The European Convention on Spectator Violence and Misbehaviour at Sports Events was developed.

International instruments and international days related to sports

1. The 1975 European Charter of Sport for All. Article 1 proclaims the right of everyone to practice sport.
2. The 1975 European Charter of Sport and Code of Ethics provides that access to sports installations and to sports activities be assured without any discrimination.
3. The 1978 International Charter of Physical Education and Sport, Article 1: "Every human being has a fundamental right of access to physical education and sport, which are essential for the full development of their personality".
4. The 1979 United Nations Convention on the Elimination of All Forms of Discrimination against Women. The importance of non-discrimination against women in sport is strongly emphasised. States have the obligation to ensure women's right to participate in recreational activities, sport and all aspects of cultural life.
5. The 1985 International Convention against Apartheid in Sports.

Key dates

3 December
The International Day of Disabled Persons.

31 May
World No-Tobacco Day.

7 April
World Health Day.

References

The Council of Europe, Directorate of Youth and Sport, www.coe.fr/youth/home.htm.

How you play the game: the contribution of sport to the promotion of human rights. *Conference in Sydney 1 to 3 September 1999, http://members.ozemail.com.au/~hrca/Sport_and_human_rights.htm.*

Symonides, J., Sport in the service of human rights, *World Conference on Education and Sports for a Culture of Peace, Unesco, Paris, France, 5 to 7 July 1999.*

Sports Shoes Campaign, www.heartland-cafe.com/aup/aup.html

Endnotes

1 *Recommendation No.8 of the Committee of Ministers of the Council of Europe to the member States, adopted on 18 September 1998.*

2 *The EU figures in general relate to the early 1990s. The rates displayed are the percentage of children living in households with income below 50% of the national median.* Source: *Bradbury and Jäntti (1999, Table 3.3) in Micklewright, J., Stewart, K.,* Child Well-Being in the EU and Enlargement to the East*, Working Papers, UNICEF, Innocenti Centre, 2000.*

3 *Implementation of recommendation No. R (91) 11 on Sexual Exploitation, Pornography and Prostitution of, and Trafficking in, Children and Young Adults; Strasbourg, 8 April 1998.*

4 *Bilson, A.,* Child safety on the Internet, a child rights approach, *Centre for Europe's Child, http://eurochild.gla.ac.uk*

5 *Consultation Meeting for the Education for Democratic Citizenship Programme of the Council of Europe, 1996.*

6 *Marina Kovinena, Centre for Civic and Legal Education, Rostov-on-Don, the Russian Federation, Youth Human Rights Education Forum, Budapest, 2000.*

7 *Annan, K., 1st World Conference of Ministers Responsible for Youth, Lisbon, Portugal, 1998.*

8 *European Union, Council Directive 2000/43/EC of 29 June 2000 implementing the principle of equal treatment between persons irrespective of racial or ethnic origin.*

9 *El País digital, 5 November 2000.*

10 *Webster's Third New International Dictionary*

11 *Council of Europe, Directorate of Social Affairs.*

12 *Eurobarometer report (54.2/2001) based on interviews of more than 16000 citizens between 2 January and 6 February 2001.*

13 www.disrights.org

14 *Biedron, R., Situation of sexual minorities in Poland, Campaign against homophobia, Riga, August 2001.*

15 *Amnesty International,Crimes of hate, conspiracy of silence, 2001.*

16 Belgian Linguistic Case, *relating to certain aspects of the laws on the use of languages in education in Belgium. Judgement of the European Court of Human Rights, 23 July 1968, Publications of the Court, Series A, vol. 6, p. 31.*

17 *The right to education (art.13), 08/12/99. E/C.12/1999/10, CESCR.*

18 Learning: The treasure within, *Unesco, Paris, 1996.*

19 *Weisbrot, M., Baker, D., Kraev, E., and Chen, J.,* The scorecard on globalisation 1980-2000: twenty years of diminished progress, *Centre for Economic and Policy Research, www.cepr.net/.*

20 *Watkins, K.,* Education now - Break the cycle of poverty, *Oxfam International, 2000.*

21 *Extracted from Motivans, A.,* Education for all, central and eastern Europe - Synthesis report, *Unesco Institute for Statistics, UNICEF Innocenti Research Centre, February 2000.*

22 World Disasters Report *2001, International Federation of Red Cross and Red Crescent Society.*

23 *Ingrid Ramberg, in "Violence against young women in Europe", Council of Europe, 2001.*

24 *Radicova I., "Human Rights of girls and young women in Europe: questions and challenges for the 21st Century",* General Conclusions, *Council of Europe, Strasbourg, 1994.*

25 *Extract from "Trafficking in women, a comprehensive European strategy", information sheets, European Commission*

26 *Ibidem*

27 *Lori, H., German, A., Pitanguy, J.,* Violence against women: the hidden health burden, *the World Bank, Washington, D.C, 1994.*

28 *Resolution 1212 (2000), Parliamentary Assembly, Council of Europe*

29 Gender mainstreaming conceptual framework, methodology and presentation of good practices. *Final report of activities of the group of specialists on mainstreaming (EG-S-MS), Strasbourg, May 1998.*

30 *Statement by the participants at the seminar "Violence against young women in Europe", European Youth Centre Budapest, 2001.*

31 *Resolution of the Sub-Commission on the Promotion and Protection of Human Rights (of the United Nations Human Right Commission) E/CN 4/SUB 2/RES/1999/30.*

32 Second international consultation on HIV/Aids and human rights. *E/CN.4/1997/37, United Nations Commission on Human Rights, 20/01/97.*

33 *Conference organised by the* WHO's European Centre for Environment and Health *in collaboration with the Italian Ministry for the Environment and the European Environment Agency, Orvieto, Italy, on 5–6 October 2001. Press release EURO 12/2001, www.who.dk/cpa/backgrounders_2001/pback_2001.htm.*

34 *Canadian Department for Foreign Affairs and International Trade (DFAIT), www.dfait-maeci.gc.ca/foreignp/humansecurity.*

35 *Hay, R.,* Peace building during peace support operations: a survey and analysis of recent missions, *1999.*

36 *Mandela, N.,* Long Walk to Freedom, *Little Brown and Company, London, 1994.*

37 *Veran Matic, Chairman of the Association of Independent Electronic Media (ANEM).*

38 *Stated on 13 September 1997 in the Declaration of Sofia (later adopted as Resolution 35 by the Unesco General Conference at its XXIX session in November 1997).*

39 *For more information, see www.humanrights.coe.int/media*

40 *Stockholm International Peace Research Institute (SIPRI), www.sipri.se*

41 *Human Development Report 2001, UNDP.*

42 *Instituto del Tercer Mundo (1992), Third World Guide, Uruguay.*

43 *From Unicef, "Young people in changing societies",* Regional Monitoring Reports, No7, *Florence: Innocenti Research Centre, 2000.*

44 Choices for the poor, *UNDP, March 2001.*

45 Extract *from Pascual, S., Waddington, J.,* Young people: the labour market and trade unions. A report prepared for the Youth Committee of the European Trade Union Confederation, *European Trade Union Confederation Publication, May 2000 and Unicef (2000),* "Young people in changing societies", *Regional Monitoring Reports, No 7, Florence Innocenti Research Centre.*

46 *Extracts from* Young people: the labour market and trade unions. *Report for the Youth Committee of the European Trade Union Confederation, May 2000.*

47 *See the background information on globalisation (page 358).*

48 *Extract from www.encarta.msn.com. For more information see the International Paralympic Committee, www.paralympic.org.*

49 *www.openfunfootballschools.org.mk/status.htm.*

50 *Extract from Tomek, L.,* Lidové Noviny, *23 August 2001. Translated by Jana Ondrackova.*

51 *For further information, see* New Internationalist *330, December 2000, www.oneworld.org/ni/issues330/factfile.htm. Also, see the background information on globalisation (page 358).*

52 *Football against Racism in Europe, www.farenet.org*

53 *For more information, see http://culture.coe.fr/sp/splist.html.*

Appendices

– International legal human rights instruments

– Evaluation form

Table of contents of this chapter

Status of ratification of major international human rights instruments

COUNTRIES	UNITED NATIONS			COUNCIL OF EUROPE					
	International Covenant on Economic, Social and Cultural Rights - CESCR	International Covenant on Civil and Political Rights - CCPR	Convention on the Rights of the Child - CRC	European Convention on Human Rights - ECHR	European Social Charter -ESC	European Social Charter Revised -ESC	Framework Convention For the Protection of National Minorities	European Convention for the Prevention of Torture and Inhuman or Degrading Treatment or Punishment	European Charter for Regional or Minority Languages
Status at	03.06.2005	03.06.2005	03.06.2005	27.02.06	27.02.06	27.02.06	27.02.06	27.02.06	27.02.06
Entry into force	03.01.1976	23.03.1976	02.09.1990	03.09.53	26.02.65	01.07.99	01.02.98	01.02.89	01.03.98
Albania	✓	✓	✓	✓		✓	✓	✓	
Andorra		✓	✓	✓		✓		✓	
Armenia	✓	✓	✓	✓		✓	✓	✓	✓
Austria	✓	✓	✓	✓	✓		✓	✓	✓
Azerbaijan	✓	✓	✓	✓		✓	✓	✓	
Belarus	✓	✓	✓						
Belgium	✓	✓	✓	✓	✓	✓		✓	
Bosnia and Herzegovina	✓	✓	✓	✓			✓	✓	
Bulgaria	✓	✓	✓	✓		✓	✓	✓	
Croatia	✓	✓	✓	✓	✓		✓	✓	✓
Cyprus	✓	✓	✓	✓	✓	✓	✓	✓	✓
Czech Republic	✓	✓	✓	✓	✓		✓	✓	
Denmark	✓	✓	✓	✓	✓		✓	✓	✓
Estonia	✓	✓	✓	✓		✓	✓	✓	
Finland	✓	✓	✓	✓	✓	✓	✓	✓	✓
France	✓	✓	✓	✓	✓	✓		✓	
Georgia	✓	✓	✓	✓		✓	✓	✓	
Germany	✓	✓	✓	✓	✓		✓	✓	✓
Greece	✓	✓	✓	✓	✓			✓	
Hungary	✓	✓	✓	✓	✓		✓	✓	✓
Iceland	✓	✓	✓	✓	✓			✓	
Ireland	✓	✓	✓	✓	✓	✓	✓	✓	
Italy	✓	✓	✓	✓	✓	✓	✓	✓	
Latvia	✓	✓	✓	✓	✓		✓	✓	
Liechtenstein	✓	✓	✓	✓			✓	✓	✓
Lithuania	✓	✓	✓	✓		✓	✓	✓	
Luxembourg	✓	✓	✓	✓	✓			✓	✓
Malta	✓	✓	✓	✓	✓		✓	✓	
Moldova	✓	✓	✓	✓		✓	✓	✓	
Monaco	✓	✓	✓	✓				✓	
Netherlands	✓	✓	✓	✓	✓		✓	✓	✓
Norway	✓	✓	✓	✓	✓	✓	✓	✓	✓
Poland	✓	✓	✓	✓	✓		✓	✓	
Portugal	✓	✓	✓	✓	✓	✓	✓	✓	
Romania	✓	✓	✓	✓		✓	✓	✓	
Russian Federation	✓	✓	✓	✓			✓	✓	
San Marino	✓	✓	✓	✓			✓	✓	
Serbia and Montenegro	✓	✓	✓	✓			✓	✓	✓
Slovakia	✓	✓	✓	✓	✓		✓	✓	✓
Slovenia	✓	✓	✓	✓		✓	✓	✓	✓
Spain	✓	✓	✓	✓	✓		✓	✓	✓
Sweden	✓	✓	✓	✓	✓	✓	✓	✓	✓
Switzerland	✓	✓	✓	✓			✓	✓	✓
"the former Yugoslav Republic of Macedonia "	✓	✓	✓	✓	✓		✓	✓	
Turkey	✓	✓	✓	✓	✓			✓	
Ukraine	✓	✓	✓	✓			✓	✓	
United Kingdom	✓	✓	✓	✓	✓		✓	✓	✓

Sources: ▪ United Nations Office of the High Commissioner for Human Rights ▪ Council of Europe's Directorate of Legal Affairs

The Universal Declaration of Human Rights

(Summary)

Article 1
Right to Equality

Article 2
Freedom from Discrimination

Article 3
Right to Life, Liberty, Personal Security

Article 4
Freedom from Slavery

Article 5
Freedom from Torture and Degrading Treatment

Article 6
Right to Recognition as a Person before the Law

Article 7
Right to Equality before the Law

Article 8
Right to Remedy by Competent Tribunal

Article 9
Freedom from Arbitrary Arrest and Exile

Article 10
Right to Fair Public Hearing

Article 11
Right to be Considered Innocent until Proven Guilty

Article 12
Freedom from Interference with Privacy, Family, Home and Correspondence

Article 13
Right to Free Movement in and out of the Country

Article 14
Right to Asylum in other Countries from Persecution

Article 15
Right to a Nationality and the Freedom to Change It

Article 16
Right to Marriage and Family

Article 17
Right to Own Property

Article 18
Freedom of Belief and Religion

Article 19
Freedom of Opinion and Information

Article 20
Right of Peaceful Assembly and Association

Article 21
Right to Participate in Government and in Free Elections

Article 22
Right to Social Security

Article 23
Right to Desirable Work and to Join Trade Unions

Article 24
Right to Rest and Leisure

Article 25
Right to Adequate Living Standard

Article 26
Right to Education

Article 27
Right to Participate in the Cultural Life of Community

Article 28
Right to a Social Order that Articulates this Document

Article 29
Community Duties Essential to Free and Full Development

Article 30
Freedom from State or Personal Interference in the above Rights

Universal Declaration of Human Rights

Adopted and proclaimed by the United Nations General Assembly resolution 217 A (III) of 10 December 1948

Preamble

Whereas recognition of the inherent dignity and of the equal and inalienable rights of all members of the human family is the foundation of freedom, justice and peace in the world,

Whereas disregard and contempt for human rights have resulted in barbarous acts which have outraged the conscience of mankind, and the advent of a world in which human beings shall enjoy freedom of speech and belief and freedom from fear and want has been proclaimed as the highest aspiration of the common people,

Whereas it is essential, if man is not to be compelled to have recourse, as a last resort, to rebellion against tyranny and oppression, that human rights should be protected by the rule of law,

Whereas it is essential to promote the development of friendly relations between nations,

Whereas the peoples of the United Nations have in the Charter reaffirmed their faith in fundamental human rights, in the dignity and worth of the human person and in the equal rights of men and women and have determined to promote social progress and better standards of life in larger freedom,

Whereas Member States have pledged themselves to achieve, in co-operation with the United Nations, the promotion of universal respect for and observance of human rights and fundamental freedoms,

Whereas a common understanding of these rights and freedoms is of the greatest importance for the full realization of this pledge,

Now, Therefore THE GENERAL ASSEMBLY proclaims THIS UNIVERSAL DECLARATION OF HUMAN RIGHTS as a common standard of achievement for all peoples and all nations, to the end that every individual and every organ of society, keeping this Declaration constantly in mind, shall strive by teaching and education to promote respect for these rights and freedoms and by progressive measures, national and international, to secure their universal and effective recognition and observance, both among the peoples of Member States themselves and among the peoples of territories under their jurisdiction.

Article 1.
All human beings are born free and equal in dignity and rights.They are endowed with reason and conscience and should act towards one another in a spirit of brotherhood.

Article 2.
Everyone is entitled to all the rights and freedoms set forth in this Declaration, without distinction of any kind, such as race, colour, sex, language, religion, political or other opinion, national or social origin, property, birth or other status. Furthermore, no distinction shall be made on the basis of the political, jurisdictional or international status of the country or territory to which a person belongs, whether it be independent, trust, non-self-governing or under any other limitation of sovereignty.

Article 3.
Everyone has the right to life, liberty and security of person.

Article 4.
No one shall be held in slavery or servitude; slavery and the slave trade shall be prohibited in all their forms.

Article 5.
No one shall be subjected to torture or to cruel, inhuman or degrading treatment or punishment.

Article 6.
Everyone has the right to recognition everywhere as a person before the law.

Article 7.
All are equal before the law and are entitled without any discrimination to equal protection of the law. All are entitled to equal protection against any discrimination in violation of this Declaration and against any incitement to such discrimination.

Article 8.
Everyone has the right to an effective remedy by the competent national tribunals for acts violating the fundamental rights granted him by the constitution or by law.

Article 9.
No one shall be subjected to arbitrary arrest, detention or exile.

Article 10.
Everyone is entitled in full equality to a fair and public hearing by an independent and impartial tribunal, in the determination of his rights and obligations and of any criminal charge against him.

Article 11.

(1) Everyone charged with a penal offence has the right to be presumed innocent until proved guilty according to law in a public trial at which he has had all the guarantees necessary for his defence.

(2) No one shall be held guilty of any penal offence on account of any act or omission which did not constitute a penal offence, under national or international law, at the time when it was committed. Nor shall a heavier penalty be imposed than the one that was applicable at the time the penal offence was committed.

Article 12.
No one shall be subjected to arbitrary interference with his privacy, family, home or correspondence, nor to attacks upon his honour and reputation. Everyone has the right to the protection of the law against such interference or attacks.

Article 13.

(1) Everyone has the right to freedom of movement and residence within the borders of each state.

(2) Everyone has the right to leave any country, including his own, and to return to his country.

Article 14.

(1) Everyone has the right to seek and to enjoy in other countries asylum from persecution.

(2) This right may not be invoked in the case of prosecutions genuinely arising from non-political crimes or from acts contrary to the purposes and principles of the United Nations.

Article 15.

(1) Everyone has the right to a nationality.

(2) No one shall be arbitrarily deprived of his nationality nor denied the right to change his nationality.

Article 16.

(1) Men and women of full age, without any limitation due to race, nationality or religion, have the right to marry and to found a family. They are entitled to equal rights as to marriage, during marriage and at its dissolution.

(2) Marriage shall be entered into only with the free and full consent of the intending spouses.

(3) The family is the natural and fundamental group unit of society and is entitled to protection by society and the State.

Article 17.

(1) Everyone has the right to own property alone as well as in association with others.

(2) No one shall be arbitrarily deprived of his property.

Article 18.

Everyone has the right to freedom of thought, conscience and religion; this right includes freedom to change his religion or belief, and freedom, either alone or in community with others and in public or private, to manifest his religion or belief in teaching, practice, worship and observance.

Article 19.

Everyone has the right to freedom of opinion and expression; this right includes freedom to hold opinions without interference and to seek, receive and impart information and ideas through any media and regardless of frontiers.

Article 20.

(1) Everyone has the right to freedom of peaceful assembly and association.

(2) No one may be compelled to belong to an association.

Article 21.

(1) Everyone has the right to take part in the government of his country, directly or through freely chosen representatives.

(2) Everyone has the right of equal access to public service in his country.

(3) The will of the people shall be the basis of the authority of government; this will shall be expressed in periodic and genuine elections which shall be by universal and equal suffrage and shall be held by secret vote or by equivalent free voting procedures.

Article 22.

Everyone, as a member of society, has the right to social security and is entitled to realization, through national effort and international co-operation and in accordance with the organization and resources of each State, of the economic, social and cultural rights indispensable for his dignity and the free development of his personality.

Article 23.

(1) Everyone has the right to work, to free choice of employment, to just and favourable conditions of work and to protection against unemployment.

(2) Everyone, without any discrimination, has the right to equal pay for equal work.

(3) Everyone who works has the right to just and favourable remuneration ensuring for himself and his family an existence worthy of human dignity, and supplemented, if necessary, by other means of social protection.

(4) Everyone has the right to form and to join trade unions for the protection of his interests.

Article 24.

Everyone has the right to rest and leisure, including reasonable limitation of working hours and periodic holidays with pay.

Article 25.

(1) Everyone has the right to a standard of living adequate for the health and well-being of himself and of his family, including food, clothing, housing and medical care and necessary social services, and the right to security in the event of unemployment, sickness, disability, widowhood, old age or other lack of livelihood in circumstances beyond his control.

(2) Motherhood and childhood are entitled to special care and assistance. All children, whether born in or out of wedlock, shall enjoy the same social protection.

Article 26.

(1) Everyone has the right to education. Education shall be free, at least in the elementary and fundamental stages. Elementary education shall be compulsory. Technical and professional education shall be made generally available and higher education shall be equally accessible to all on the basis of merit.

(2) Education shall be directed to the full development of the human personality and to the strengthening of respect for human rights and fundamental freedoms. It shall promote understanding, tolerance and friendship among all nations, racial or religious groups, and shall further the activities of the United Nations for the maintenance of peace.

(3) Parents have a prior right to choose the kind of education that shall be given to their children.

Article 27.

(1) Everyone has the right freely to participate in the cultural life of the community, to enjoy the arts and to share in scientific advancement and its benefits.

(2) Everyone has the right to the protection of the moral and material interests resulting from any scientific, literary or artistic production of which he is the author.

Article 28.

Everyone is entitled to a social and international order in which the rights and freedoms set forth in this Declaration can be fully realized.

Article 29.

(1) Everyone has duties to the community in which alone the free and full development of his personality is possible.

(2) In the exercise of his rights and freedoms, everyone shall be subject only to such limitations as are determined by law solely for the purpose of securing due recognition and respect for the rights and freedoms of others and of meeting the just requirements of morality, public order and the general welfare in a democratic society.

(3) These rights and freedoms may in no case be exercised contrary to the purposes and principles of the United Nations.

Article 30.

Nothing in this Declaration may be interpreted as implying for any State, group or person any right to engage in any activity or to perform any act aimed at the destruction of any of the rights and freedoms set forth herein.

The International Covenant on Civil and Political Rights (ICCPR)

(Unofficial summary)

- *This Covenant was adopted by the United Nations General Assembly on 16 December 1966 and entered into force on 23 March 1976. By the end of 2001, the Covenant had been ratified by 147 states.*
- *The Covenant elaborates further the civil and political rights and freedoms listed in the Universal Declaration of Human Rights.*
- *Under Article 1 of the Covenant, the states commit themselves to promote the right to self-determination and to respect that right. It also recognises the rights of peoples to freely own, trade and dispose of their natural wealth and resources.*

Among the rights of individuals guaranteed by the Covenant are:

Article 2
The right to legal recourse when their rights have been violated, even if the violator was acting in an official capacity.

Article 3
The right to equality between men and women in the enjoyment of their civil and political rights.

Article 6
The right to life and survival.

Article 7
The freedom from inhuman or degrading treatment or punishment.

Article 8
The freedom from slavery and servitude.

Article 9
The right to liberty and security of the person and freedom from arbitrary arrest or detention.

Article 11
The freedom from prison due to debt.

Article 12
The right to liberty and freedom of movement

Article 14
The right to equality before the law; the right to be presumed innocent until proven guilty and to have a fair and public hearing by an impartial tribunal.

Article 16
The right to be recognised as a person before the law.

Article 17
The right privacy and its protection by the law.

Article 18
The freedom of thought, conscience and religion.

Article 19
The freedom of opinion and expression.

Article 20
Prohibition of propaganda advocating war or national, racial or religious hatred.

Article 21
The right to peaceful assembly.

Article 22
The right to freedom of association.

Article 23
The right to marry and found a family

Article 24
The rights for children (status as minors, nationality, registration and name).

Article 25
The right to participate in the conduct of public affairs, to vote and to be elected and access to public service.

Article 26
The right to equality before the law and equal protection

Article 27
The right, for members of religious, ethnic or linguistic minorities, to enjoy their culture, practice their religion and use their language.

The Covenant is legally binding; the Human Rights Committee established under Article 28, monitors its implementation.

International Covenant on Economic, Social and Cultural Rights (ICESCR)

(Unofficial summary)

Cultural Rights (1966), together with the Universal Declaration of Human Rights (1948) and the International Covenant on Civil and Political Rights (1966), make up the International Bill of Human Rights. In accordance with the Universal Declaration, the Covenants recognize that "... the ideal of free human beings enjoying civil and political freedom and freedom from fear and want can be achieved only if conditions are created whereby everyone may enjoy his civil and political rights, as well as his economic, social and cultural rights."

Article 1
All peoples have the right of self-determination, including the right to determine their political status and freely pursue their economic, social and cultural development.

Article 2
Each State Party undertakes to take steps to the maximum of its available resources to achieve progressively the full realization of the rights in this treaty. Everyone is entitled to the same rights without discrimination of any kind.

Article 3
The States undertake to ensure the equal right of men and women to the enjoyment of all rights in this treaty.

Article 4
Limitations may be placed on these rights only if compatible with the nature of these rights and solely for the purpose of promoting the general welfare in a democratic society.

Article 5
No person, group or government has the right to destroy any of these rights.

Article 6
Everyone has the right to work, including the right to gain one's living at work that is freely chosen and accepted.

Article 7
Everyone has the right to just conditions of work; fair wages ensuring a decent living for himself and his family; equal pay for equal work; safe and healthy working conditions; equal opportunity for everyone to be promoted; rest and leisure.

Article 8
Everyone has the right to form and join trade unions, the right to strike.

Article 9
Everyone has the right to social security, including social insurance.

Article 10
Protection and assistance should be accorded to the family. Marriage must be entered into with the free consent of both spouses. Special protection should be provided to mothers. Special measures should be taken on behalf of children, without discrimination. Children and youth should be protected from economic exploitation. Their employment in dangerous or harmful work should be prohibited. There should be age limits below which child labor should be prohibited.

Article 11
Everyone has the right to an adequate standard of living for himself and his family, including adequate food, clothing and housing. Everyone has the right to be free from hunger.

Article 12
Everyone has the right to the enjoyment of the highest attainable standard of physical and mental health.

Article 13
Everyone has the right to education. Primary education should be compulsory and free to all.

Article 14
Those States where compulsory, free primary education is not available to all should work out a plan to provide such education.

Article 15
Everyone has the right to take part in cultural life; enjoy the benefits of scientific progress.

Source: The Minnesota Human Rights Resource Center, based on based on UN Centre on Human Rights, The International Bill of Rights, Fact Sheet #2.

The Convention on the Rights of the Child

(Unofficial summary)

- The Convention on the Rights of the Child (CRC) is the most universally accepted human rights instrument, ratified by every country in the world except two. The Convention incorporates the full range of human rights - civil, political, economic, social and cultural rights – of children into one single document. The Convention was adopted by the UN.
- General Assembly on 20 November 1989 and entered into force in September 1990.
- The Convention outlines in 41 articles the human rights to be respected and protected for every child under the age of eighteen years.

Article 1
Definition of child as "every human being below the age of eighteen years", unless the national law considers majority attained at an earlier age.

Article 2
The rights safeguarded in the Convention shall be ensured *without any discrimination* of any kind.

Article 3
In all actions concerning children *the best interest of the child* shall be of primary consideration.

Article 5
The state shall respect the responsibility, *rights and duties of the parents* or extended family.

Article 6
Every child has the inherent right to *life*

Article 7
The child has the right to *a name*, to acquire *a nationality* and to know and be cared for by *its parents*

Article 8
The child has the right to *identity and nationality*.

Article 9
The child has the right *not to be separated from its parents*, except in its best interests and by a judicial procedure.

Article 12
The child has the right to express views on all matters affecting him/her and the *child's views* should be given due weight.

Article 13
The child has the right to *freedom of expression*, including the right to seek, receive and impart *information* and ideas of all kind.

Article 14
The right of the child to *freedom of thought, conscience and religion* shall be respected.

Article 15
The child has the right to freedom of *association and peaceful assembly.*

Article 16
No child shall be subjected to arbitrary or unlawful interference with his/her *privacy*, family, home or correspondence; the child should be protected from unlawful attacks on his/her honour and reputation.

Article 17
The State shall ensure the right of the child to *access to information* and material from national and international sources

Article 18
Parents have the prime responsibility for the *upbringing* and development of the child.

Article 19
The State shall take all legislative, administrative, social and educational measures for the protection of the child from all forms of physical or mental violence, injury, abuse, neglect, maltreatment or exploitation.

Article 24
The child has the right to the highest attainable standard of *health care*, with emphasis on primary health care, the development of preventive health care.

Article 26
The child has the right to benefit from *social security*.

Article 27
The child has the right to a *standard of living* which will allow physical, mental, spiritual, moral and social development.

Article 28
The child has the right to *education*. The State shall make primary education compulsory and available and free to all and encourage the development of different forms of secondary education, make them available to every child. School discipline shall be administered in a manner consistent with the child's dignity. Education should be directed to the development of the child's personality, talents and abilities, the respect for human rights and fundamental freedoms, responsible life in a free society in the spirit of peace, friendship, understanding, tolerance and equality, the development of respect for the natural environment.

Article 30
The child has the right to enjoy his/her own *culture*.

Article 31
The child has the right to *rest and leisure*, to play and freely participate in cultural life and the arts.

Article 32
The child shall be protected from economic *exploitation* and from performing work that is hazardous to his/her life and development.

Article 33
The child shall be protected from illicit use of narcotic *drugs*.

Article 34
The child shall be protected from all forms of *sexual exploitation and sexual abuse*, the use of children in prostitution or other unlawful sexual practices, in pornographic performances and materials.

Article 38
The State shall take all feasible measures to protect and care for children affected by *armed conflict*.

Article 40
Every child accused of having committed an *offence or crime* should be guaranteed to be presumed innocent until proven guilty, to have *legal assistance* in presenting his/her case, not to be compelled to give testimony or to confess guilt, to have his/her privacy fully respected, to be dealt with in a manner appropriate to their age, circumstances and well-being. Neither capital punishment nor life imprisonment without possibility of release shall be imposed for offences committed by children below the age of 18.

The full text of the Convention and Optional Protocols can be consulted and downloaded from many Internet sites, such as UNICEF's (www.unicef.org/crc)

The European Convention on Human Rights

(Summary)

Under the Convention, which was signed in Rome on 4 November 1950 and came into force in 1953, the States Parties guarantee the basic civil and political rights of a state governed by the rule of law, not only to their own citizens but to all persons "within their jurisdiction". States or individuals can bring a complaint before the Court set up by the Convention. However, the Convention is not necessarily incorporated into each state's national legal system. The theory of international law whereby human rights have a fundamental character placing them above the legislation and practices of sovereign states is thus brought into practice.

The rights guaranteed

The right to life (Article 2)

Article 2 protects the individual against death inflicted arbitrarily by the State; but it does not exclude the use of the death penalty if carried out in accordance with the law. Protocol No. 6, abolishing the death penalty in time of peace, was adopted in 1985. A new protocol, abolishing death penalty is being prepared.

The right to liberty and security of person (Article 5)

Article 5 guarantees people physical liberty by protecting them from arbitrary arrest and detention and according them certain basic procedural rights. Its provisions are extended by Article 1 of Protocol No. 4 which prohibits imprisonment for debt.

The right to a fair trial in civil and criminal matters (Article 6)

This right is complemented by Article 13, which ensures the right to an effective remedy before a national authority. Article 6 includes the condition that the proceedings must take place within a "reasonable time". Complaints of violations of this provision are those most frequently brought by applicants. The notion of a fair trial is completed by the principle that criminal law should not be retroactive (Article 7), the right of appeal in criminal cases, the right to compensation for wrongful conviction, and the right not to be tried or punished twice for the same offence (Articles 2, 3 and 4 of Protocol No. 7).

Respect for private and family life, home and correspondence (Article 8),

which may be linked to the right to marry and found a family (Article 12).

The equality of rights and responsibilities of spouses during marriage (Article 5 of Protocol No. 7).

The right to freedom of expression (including freedom of the press) (Article 10)

The requirements of this basic right are a logical development of the rights guaranteed by Article 9 (freedom of thought, conscience and religion).

Freedom of peaceful assembly and association (Article 11).

The right to peaceful enjoyment of possessions (Article 1 of Protocol No. 1).

The right to education (Article 2 of Protocol No. 1).

The right to free elections (Article 3 of Protocol No. 1).

The Council of Europe and the protection of human rights

Liberty of movement and freedom to choose where to live (Article 2 of Protocol No. 4).

What is prohibited

Torture and inhuman or degrading treatment and punishment (Article 3).

Slavery, servitude and forced labour (Article 4).

Discrimination in the enjoyment of rights and freedoms guaranteed by the Convention (Article 14).

Expulsion of a state's own nationals or denying them entry, and the collective expulsion of aliens. (Articles 3 and 4 of Protocol No. 4)

Procedural safeguards also protect foreigners under threat of expulsion from a country (Article 1 of Protocol No. 7).

The Convention provides for a European Court of Human Rights to deal with individuals' petitions and inter-state cases. The Judges are entirely independent and are elected by the Parliamentary Assembly.

The Committee of Ministers of the Council of Europe supervises the execution of the judgment where a violation has been found, ensuring that the state takes appropriate remedial action, for example by means of new administrative procedures or by legislation

Source: Council of Europe Directorate General of Human Rights www.humanrights.coe.int

Convention for the Protection of Human Rights and Fundamental Freedoms, as amended by Protocol No. 11

Rome, 4.XI.1950

The text of the Convention had been amended according to the provisions of Protocol No. 3 (ETS No. 45), which entered into force on 21 September 1970, of Protocol No. 5 (ETS No. 55), which entered into force on 20 December 1971 and of Protocol No. 8 (ETS No. 118), which entered into force on 1 January 1990, and comprised also the text of Protocol No. 2 (ETS No. 44) which, in accordance with Article 5, paragraph 3 thereof, had been an integral part of the Convention since its entry into force on 21 September 1970. All provisions which had been amended or added by these Protocols are replaced by Protocol No. 11 (ETS No. 155), as from the date of its entry into force on 1 November 1998. As from that date, Protocol No. 9 (ETS No. 140), which entered into force on 1 October 1994, is repealed and Protocol No. 10 (ETS no. 146) has lost its purpose.

- The governments signatory hereto, being members of the Council of Europe, Considering the Universal Declaration of Human
- Rights proclaimed by the General Assembly of the United Nations on 10th December 1948;
- Considering that this Declaration aims at securing the universal and effective recognition and observance of the Rights therein declared;
- Considering that the aim of the Council of Europe is the achievement of greater unity between its members and that one of the methods by which that aim is to be pursued is the maintenance and further realisation of human rights and fundamental freedoms;
- Reaffirming their profound belief in those fundamental freedoms which are the foundation of justice and peace in the world and are best maintained on the one hand by an effective political democracy and on the other by a common understanding and observance of the human rights upon which they depend;
- Being resolved, as the governments of European countries which are like-minded and have a common heritage of political traditions, ideals, freedom and the rule of law, to take the first steps for the collective enforcement of certain of the rights stated in the Universal Declaration,

Have agreed as follows:

Article 1[1] – Obligation to respect human rights
The High Contracting Parties shall secure to everyone within their jurisdiction the rights and freedoms defined in Section I of this Convention.

Section I[1] – Rights and freedoms

Article 2[1] – Right to life

1 Everyone's right to life shall be protected by law. No one shall be deprived of his life intentionally save in the execution of a sentence of a court following his conviction of a crime for which this penalty is provided by law.

2 Deprivation of life shall not be regarded as inflicted in contravention of this article when it results from the use of force which is no more than absolutely necessary:
   a in defence of any person from unlawful violence;
   b in order to effect a lawful arrest or to prevent the escape of a person lawfully detained;
   c in action lawfully taken for the purpose of quelling a riot or insurrection.

Article 3[2] – Prohibition of torture
No one shall be subjected to torture or to inhuman or degrading treatment or punishment.

Article 4[1] – Prohibition of slavery and forced labour

1 No one shall be held in slavery or servitude.

2 No one shall be required to perform forced or compulsory labour.

3 For the purpose of this article the term "forced or compulsory labour" shall not include:
   a any work required to be done in the ordinary course of detention imposed according to the provisions of Article 5 of this Convention or during conditional release from such detention;
   b any service of a military character or, in case of conscientious objectors in countries where they are recognised, service exacted instead of compulsory military service;
   c any service exacted in case of an emergency or calamity threatening the life or well-being of the community;
   d any work or service which forms part of normal civic obligations.

Article 5[1] – Right to liberty and security

1 Everyone has the right to liberty and security of person. No one shall be deprived of his liberty save in the following cases and in accordance with a procedure prescribed by law:
   a the lawful detention of a person after conviction by a competent court;
   b the lawful arrest or detention of a person for non-compliance with the lawful order of a court or in order to secure the fulfilment of any obligation prescribed by law;
   c the lawful arrest or detention of a person effected for the purpose of bringing him before the competent legal authority on reasonable suspicion of having committed an offence or when it is reasonably considered necessary to prevent his committing an offence or fleeing after having done so;
   d the detention of a minor by lawful order for the purpose of educational supervision or his lawful detention for the purpose of bringing him before the competent legal authority;
   e the lawful detention of persons for the prevention of the spreading of infectious diseases, of persons of unsound mind, alcoholics or drug addicts or vagrants;
   f the lawful arrest or detention of a person to prevent his effecting an unauthorised entry into the country or of a person against whom action is being taken with a view to deportation or extradition.

2 Everyone who is arrested shall be informed promptly, in a language which he understands, of the reasons for his arrest and of any charge against him.

3 Everyone arrested or detained in accordance with the provisions of paragraph 1.c of this article shall be brought promptly before a judge or other officer authorised by law to exercise judicial power and shall be entitled to trial within a reasonable time or to release pending trial. Release may be conditioned by guarantees to appear for trial.

4 Everyone who is deprived of his liberty by arrest or detention shall be entitled to take proceedings by which the lawfulness of his detention shall be decided speedily by a court and his release ordered if the detention is not lawful.

5 Everyone who has been the victim of arrest or detention in contravention of the provisions of this article shall have an enforceable right to compensation.

Article 6[3] – Right to a fair trial

1 In the determination of his civil rights and obligations or of any criminal charge against him, everyone is entitled to a fair and public hearing within a reasonable time by an independent and impartial tribunal established by law. Judgment shall be pronounced publicly but the press and public may be excluded from all or part of the trial in the interests of morals, public order or national security in a democratic society, where the interests of juveniles or the protection of the private life of the parties so require, or to the extent strictly necessary in the opinion of the court in special circumstances where publicity would prejudice the interests of justice.

2 Everyone charged with a criminal offence shall be presumed innocent until proved guilty according to law.

3 Everyone charged with a criminal offence has the following minimum rights:

a to be informed promptly, in a language which he understands and in detail, of the nature and cause of the accusation against him;

b to have adequate time and facilities for the preparation of his defence;

c to defend himself in person or through legal assistance of his own choosing or, if he has not sufficient means to pay for legal assistance, to be given it free when the interests of justice so require;

d to examine or have examined witnesses against him and to obtain the attendance and examination of witnesses on his behalf under the same conditions as witnesses against him;

e to have the free assistance of an interpreter if he cannot understand or speak the language used in court.

Article 7[4] – No punishment without law

1 No one shall be held guilty of any criminal offence on account of any act or omission which did not constitute a criminal offence under national or international law at the time when it was committed. Nor shall a heavier penalty be imposed than the one that was applicable at the time the criminal offence was committed.

2 This article shall not prejudice the trial and punishment of any person for any act or omission which, at the time when it was committed, was criminal according to the general principles of law recognised by civilised nations.

Article 8[1] – Right to respect for private and family life

1 Everyone has the right to respect for his private and family life, his home and his correspondence.

2 There shall be no interference by a public authority with the exercise of this right except such as is in accordance with the law and is necessary in a democratic society in the interests of national security, public safety or the economic well-being of the country, for the prevention of disorder or crime, for the protection of health or morals, or for the protection of the rights and freedoms of others.

Article 9[1] – Freedom of thought, conscience and religion

1 Everyone has the right to freedom of thought, conscience and religion; this right includes freedom to change his religion or belief and freedom, either alone or in community with others and in public or private, to manifest his religion or belief, in worship, teaching, practice and observance.

2 Freedom to manifest one's religion or beliefs shall be subject only to such limitations as are prescribed by law and are necessary in a democratic society in the interests of public safety, for the protection of public order, health or morals, or for the protection of the rights and freedoms of others.

Article 10[1] – Freedom of expression

1 Everyone has the right to freedom of expression. This right shall include freedom to hold opinions and to receive and impart information and ideas without interference by public authority and regardless of frontiers. This article shall not prevent States from requiring the licensing of broadcasting, television or cinema enterprises.

2 The exercise of these freedoms, since it carries with it duties and responsibilities, may be subject to such formalities, conditions, restrictions or penalties as are prescribed by law and are necessary in a democratic society, in the interests of national security, territorial integrity or public safety, for the prevention of disorder or crime, for the protection of health or morals, for the protection of the reputation or rights of others, for preventing the disclosure of information received in confidence, or for maintaining the authority and impartiality of the judiciary.

Article 11[5] – Freedom of assembly and association

1 Everyone has the right to freedom of peaceful assembly and to freedom of association with others, including the right to form and to join trade unions for the protection of his interests.

2 No restrictions shall be placed on the exercise of these rights other than such as are prescribed by law and are necessary in a democratic society in the interests of national security or public safety, for the prevention of disorder or crime, for the protection of health or morals or for the protection of the rights and freedoms of others. This article shall not prevent the imposition of lawful restrictions on the exercise of these rights by members of the armed forces, of the police or of the administration of the State.

Article 12[1] – Right to marry
Men and women of marriageable age have the right to marry and to found a family, according to the national laws governing the exercise of this right.

Article 13[1] – Right to an effective remedy
Everyone whose rights and freedoms as set forth in this Convention are violated shall have an effective remedy before a national authority notwithstanding that the violation has been committed by persons acting in an official capacity.

Article 14[1] – Prohibition of discrimination
The enjoyment of the rights and freedoms set forth in this Convention shall be secured without discrimination on any ground such as sex, race, colour, language, religion, political or other opinion, national or social origin, association with a national minority, property, birth or other status.

Article 15[1] – Derogation in time of emergency

1 In time of war or other public emergency threatening the life of the nation any High Contracting Party may take measures derogating from its obligations under this Convention to the extent strictly required by the exigencies of the situation, provided that such measures are not inconsistent with its other obligations under international law.
2 No derogation from Article 2, except in respect of deaths resulting from lawful acts of war, or from Articles 3, 4 (paragraph 1) and 7 shall be made under this provision.
3 Any High Contracting Party availing itself of this right of derogation shall keep the Secretary General of the Council of Europe fully informed of the measures which it has taken and the reasons therefor. It shall also inform the Secretary General of the Council of Europe when such measures have ceased to operate and the provisions of the Convention are again being fully executed.

Article 16[1] – Restrictions on political activity of aliens
Nothing in Articles 10, 11 and 14 shall be regarded as preventing the High Contracting Parties from imposing restrictions on the political activity of aliens.

Article 17[6] – Prohibition of abuse of rights
Nothing in this Convention may be interpreted as implying for any State, group or person any right to engage in any activity or perform any act aimed at the destruction of any of the rights and freedoms set forth herein or at their limitation to a greater extent than is provided for in the Convention.

Article 18[1] – Limitation on use of restrictions on rights
The restrictions permitted under this Convention to the said rights and freedoms shall not be applied for any purpose other than those for which they have been prescribed

Section II[7] – European Court of Human Rights

Article 19 – Establishment of the Court
To ensure the observance of the engagements undertaken by the High Contracting Parties in the Convention and the Protocols thereto, there shall be set up a European Court of Human Rights, hereinafter referred to as "the Court". It shall function on a permanent basis.

Article 20 – Number of judges
The Court shall consist of a number of judges equal to that of the High Contracting Parties.

Article 21 – Criteria for office

1 The judges shall be of high moral character and must either possess the qualifications required for appointment to high judicial office or be jurisconsults of recognised competence.
2 The judges shall sit on the Court in their individual capacity.
3 During their term of office the judges shall not engage in any activity which is incompatible with their independence, impartiality or with the demands of a full-time office; all questions arising from the application of this paragraph shall be decided by the Court.

Article 22 – Election of judges

1 The judges shall be elected by the Parliamentary Assembly with respect to each High Contracting Party by a majority of votes cast from a list of three candidates nominated by the High Contracting Party.
2 The same procedure shall be followed to complete the Court in the event of the accession of new High Contracting Parties and in filling casual vacancies.

Article 23 – Terms of office

1 The judges shall be elected for a period of six years. They may be re-elected. However, the terms of office of one-half of the judges elected at the first election shall expire at the end of three years.
2 The judges whose terms of office are to expire at the end of the initial period of three years shall be chosen by lot by the Secretary General of the Council of Europe immediately after their election.
3 In order to ensure that, as far as possible, the terms of office of one-half of the judges are renewed every three years, the Parliamentary Assembly may decide, before proceeding to any subsequent election, that the term or terms of office of one or more judges to be elected shall be for a period other than six years but not more than nine and not less than three years.
4 In cases where more than one term of office is involved and where the Parliamentary Assembly applies the preceding paragraph, the allocation of the terms of office shall be effected by a drawing of lots by the Secretary General of the Council of Europe immediately after the election.
5 A judge elected to replace a judge whose term of office has not expired shall hold office for the remainder of his predecessor's term.
6 The terms of office of judges shall expire when they reach the age of 70.
7 The judges shall hold office until replaced. They shall, however, continue to deal with such cases as they already have under consideration.

Article 24 – Dismissal
No judge may be dismissed from his office unless the other judges decide by a majority of two-thirds that he has ceased to fulfil the required conditions.

Article 25 – Registry and legal secretaries
The Court shall have a registry, the functions and organisation of which shall be laid down in the rules of the Court. The Court shall be assisted by legal secretaries.

Article 26 – Plenary Court

The plenary Court shall

- a elect its President and one or two Vice-Presidents for a period of three years; they may be re-elected;
- b set up Chambers, constituted for a fixed period of time;
- c elect the Presidents of the Chambers of the Court; they may be re-elected;
- d adopt the rules of the Court, and
- e elect the Registrar and one or more Deputy Registrars.

Article 27 – Committees, Chambers and Grand Chamber

1 To consider cases brought before it, the Court shall sit in committees of three judges, in Chambers of seven judges and in a Grand Chamber of seventeen judges. The Court's Chambers shall set up committees for a fixed period of time.

2 There shall sit as an *ex officio* member of the Chamber and the Grand Chamber the judge elected in respect of the State Party concerned or, if there is none or if he is unable to sit, a person of its choice who shall sit in the capacity of judge.

3 The Grand Chamber shall also include the President of the Court, the Vice-Presidents, the Presidents of the Chambers and other judges chosen in accordance with the rules of the Court. When a case is referred to the Grand Chamber under Article 43, no judge from the Chamber which rendered the judgment shall sit in the Grand Chamber, with the exception of the President of the Chamber and the judge who sat in respect of the State Party concerned.

Article 28 – Declarations of inadmissibility by committees

A committee may, by a unanimous vote, declare inadmissible or strike out of its list of cases an application submitted under Article 34 where such a decision can be taken without further examination. The decision shall be final.

Article 29 – Decisions by Chambers on admissibility and merits

1 If no decision is taken under Article 28, a Chamber shall decide on the admissibility and merits of individual applications submitted under Article 34.

2 A Chamber shall decide on the admissibility and merits of inter-State applications submitted under Article 33.

3 The decision on admissibility shall be taken separately unless the Court, in exceptional cases, decides otherwise.

Article 30 – Relinquishment of jurisdiction to the Grand Chamber

Where a case pending before a Chamber raises a serious question affecting the interpretation of the Convention or the protocols thereto, or where the resolution of a question before the Chamber might have a result inconsistent with a judgment previously delivered by the Court, the Chamber may, at any time before it has rendered its judgment, relinquish jurisdiction in favour of the Grand Chamber, unless one of the parties to the case objects.

Article 31 – Powers of the Grand Chamber

The Grand Chamber shall

1 a determine applications submitted either under Article 33 or Article 34 when a Chamber has relinquished jurisdiction under Article 30 or when the case has been referred to it under Article 43; and

b consider requests for advisory opinions submitted under Article 47.

Article 32 – Jurisdiction of the Court

1 The jurisdiction of the Court shall extend to all matters concerning the interpretation and application of the Convention and the protocols thereto which are referred to it as provided in Articles 33, 34 and 47.

2 In the event of dispute as to whether the Court has jurisdiction, the Court shall decide.

Article 33 – Inter-State cases

Any High Contracting Party may refer to the Court any alleged breach of the provisions of the Convention and the protocols thereto by another High Contracting Party.

Article 34 – Individual applications

The Court may receive applications from any person, non-governmental organisation or group of individuals claiming to be the victim of a violation by one of the High Contracting Parties of the rights set forth in the Convention or the protocols thereto. The High Contracting Parties undertake not to hinder in any way the effective exercise of this right.

Article 35 – Admissibility criteria

1 The Court may only deal with the matter after all domestic remedies have been exhausted, according to the generally recognised rules of international law, and within a period of six months from the date on which the final decision was taken.

2 The Court shall not deal with any application submitted under Article 34 that

- a is anonymous; or
- b is substantially the same as a matter that has already been examined by the Court or has already been submitted to another procedure of international investigation or settlement and contains no relevant new information.

3 The Court shall declare inadmissible any individual application submitted under Article 34 which it considers incompatible with the provisions of the Convention or the protocols thereto, manifestly ill-founded, or an abuse of the right of application.

4 The Court shall reject any application which it considers inadmissible under this Article. It may do so at any stage of the proceedings.

Article 36 – Third party intervention

1 In all cases before a Chamber or the Grand Chamber, a High Contracting Party one of whose nationals is an applicant shall have the right to submit written comments and to take part in hearings.

2 The President of the Court may, in the interest of the proper administration of justice, invite any High Contracting Party which is not a party to the proceedings or any person concerned who is not the applicant to submit written comments or take part in hearings.

Article 37 – Striking out applications

1 The Court may at any stage of the proceedings decide to strike an application out of its list of cases where the circumstances lead to the conclusion that

a the applicant does not intend to pursue his application; or
b the matter has been resolved; or
c for any other reason established by the Court, it is no longer justified to continue the examination of the application. However, the Court shall continue the examination of the application if respect for human rights as defined in the Convention and the protocols thereto so requires.

2 The Court may decide to restore an application to its list of cases if it considers that the circumstances justify such a course.

Article 38 – Examination of the case and friendly settlement proceedings

1 If the Court declares the application admissible, it shall
a pursue the examination of the case, together with the representatives of the parties, and if need be, undertake an investigation, for the effective conduct of which the States concerned shall furnish all necessary facilities;
b place itself at the disposal of the parties concerned with a view to securing a friendly settlement of the matter on the basis of respect for human rights as defined in the Convention and the protocols thereto.

2 Proceedings conducted under paragraph 1.b shall be confidential.

Article 39 – Finding of a friendly settlement

If a friendly settlement is effected, the Court shall strike the case out of its list by means of a decision which shall be confined to a brief statement of the facts and of the solution reached.

Article 40 – Public hearings and access to documents

1 Hearings shall be in public unless the Court in exceptional circumstances decides otherwise.
2 Documents deposited with the Registrar shall be accessible to the public unless the President of the Court decides otherwise.

Article 41 – Just satisfaction

If the Court finds that there has been a violation of the Convention or the protocols thereto, and if the internal law of the High Contracting Party concerned allows only partial reparation to be made, the Court shall, if necessary, afford just satisfaction to the injured party.

Article 42 – Judgments of Chambers

Judgments of Chambers shall become final in accordance with the provisions of Article 44, paragraph 2.

Article 43 – Referral to the Grand Chamber

1 Within a period of three months from the date of the judgment of the Chamber, any party to the case may, in exceptional cases, request that the case be referred to the Grand Chamber.
2 A panel of five judges of the Grand Chamber shall accept the request if the case raises a serious question affecting the interpretation or application of the Convention or the protocols thereto, or a serious issue of general importance.
3 If the panel accepts the request, the Grand Chamber shall decide the case by means of a judgment.

Article 44 – Final judgments

1 The judgment of the Grand Chamber shall be final.
2 The judgment of a Chamber shall become final
a when the parties declare that they will not request that the case be referred to the Grand Chamber; or
b three months after the date of the judgment, if reference of the case to the Grand Chamber has not been requested; or
c when the panel of the Grand Chamber rejects the request to refer under Article 43.
3 The final judgment shall be published.

Article 45 – Reasons for judgments and decisions

1 Reasons shall be given for judgments as well as for decisions declaring applications admissible or inadmissible.
2 If a judgment does not represent, in whole or in part, the unanimous opinion of the judges, any judge shall be entitled to deliver a separate opinion.

Article 46 – Binding force and execution of judgments

1 The High Contracting Parties undertake to abide by the final judgment of the Court in any case to which they are parties.
2 The final judgment of the Court shall be transmitted to the Committee of Ministers, which shall supervise its execution.

Article 47 – Advisory opinions

1 The Court may, at the request of the Committee of Ministers, give advisory opinions on legal questions concerning the interpretation of the Convention and the protocols thereto.
2 Such opinions shall not deal with any question relating to the content or scope of the rights or freedoms defined in Section I of the Convention and the protocols thereto, or with any other question which the Court or the Committee of Ministers might have to consider in consequence of any such proceedings as could be instituted in accordance with the Convention.
3 Decisions of the Committee of Ministers to request an advisory opinion of the Court shall require a majority vote of the representatives entitled to sit on the Committee.

Article 48 – Advisory jurisdiction of the Court

The Court shall decide whether a request for an advisory opinion submitted by the Committee of Ministers is within its competence as defined in Article 47.

Article 49 – Reasons for advisory opinions

1 Reasons shall be given for advisory opinions of the Court.
2 If the advisory opinion does not represent, in whole or in part, the unanimous opinion of the judges, any judge shall be entitled to deliver a separate opinion.
3 Advisory opinions of the Court shall be communicated to the Committee of Ministers.

Article 50 – Expenditure on the Court

The expenditure on the Court shall be borne by the Council of Europe.

Article 51 – Privileges and immunities of judges

The judges shall be entitled, during the exercise of their functions, to the privileges and immunities provided for in Article 40 of the Statute of the Council of Europe and in the agreements made thereunder.

Section III[8,9] – Miscellaneous provisions

Article 52[1] – Inquiries by the Secretary General

On receipt of a request from the Secretary General of the Council of Europe any High Contracting Party shall furnish an explanation of the manner in which its internal law ensures the effective implementation of any of the provisions of the Convention.

Article 53[1] – Safeguard for existing human rights

Nothing in this Convention shall be construed as limiting or derogating from any of the human rights and fundamental freedoms which may be ensured under the laws of any High Contracting Party or under any other agreement to which it is a Party.

Article 54[1] – Powers of the Committee of Ministers

Nothing in this Convention shall prejudice the powers conferred on the Committee of Ministers by the Statute of the Council of Europe.

Article 55[1] – Exclusion of other means of dispute settlement

The High Contracting Parties agree that, except by special agreement, they will not avail themselves of treaties, conventions or declarations in force between them for the purpose of submitting, by way of petition, a dispute arising out of the interpretation or application of this Convention to a means of settlement other than those provided for in this Convention.

Article 56[10] – Territorial application

1[11] Any State may at the time of its ratification or at any time thereafter declare by notification addressed to the Secretary General of the Council of Europe that the present Convention shall, subject to paragraph 4 of this Article, extend to all or any of the territories for whose international relations it is responsible.

2 The Convention shall extend to the territory or territories named in the notification as from the thirtieth day after the receipt of this notification by the Secretary General of the Council of Europe.

3 The provisions of this Convention shall be applied in such territories with due regard, however, to local requirements.

4[2] Any State which has made a declaration in accordance with paragraph 1 of this article may at any time thereafter declare on behalf of one or more of the territories to which the declaration relates that it accepts the competence of the Court to receive applications from individuals, non-governmental organisations or groups of individuals as provided by Article 34 of the Convention.

Article 57[1] – Reservations

1 Any State may, when signing this Convention or when depositing its instrument of ratification, make a reservation in respect of any particular provision of the Convention to the extent that any law then in force in its territory is not in conformity with the provision. Reservations of a general character shall not be permitted under this article.

2 Any reservation made under this article shall contain a brief statement of the law concerned.

Article 58[1] – Denunciation

1 A High Contracting Party may denounce the present Convention only after the expiry of five years from the date on which it became a party to it and after six months' notice contained in a notification addressed to the Secretary General of the Council of Europe, who shall inform the other High Contracting Parties.

2 Such a denunciation shall not have the effect of releasing the High Contracting Party concerned from its obligations under this Convention in respect of any act which, being capable of constituting a violation of such obligations, may have been performed by it before the date at which the denunciation became effective.

3 Any High Contracting Party which shall cease to be a member of the Council of Europe shall cease to be a Party to this Convention under the same conditions.

4[12] The Convention may be denounced in accordance with the provisions of the preceding paragraphs in respect of any territory to which it has been declared to extend under the terms of Article 56.

Article 59[13] – Signature and ratification

1 This Convention shall be open to the signature of the members of the Council of Europe. It shall be ratified. Ratifications shall be deposited with the Secretary General of the Council of Europe.

2 The present Convention shall come into force after the deposit of ten instruments of ratification.

3 As regards any signatory ratifying subsequently, the Convention shall come into force at the date of the deposit of its instrument of ratification.

4 The Secretary General of the Council of Europe shall notify all the members of the Council of Europe of the entry into force of the Convention, the names of the High Contracting Parties who have ratified it, and the deposit of all instruments of ratification which may be effected subsequently.

Done at Rome this 4th day of November 1950, in English and French, both texts being equally authentic, in a single copy which shall remain deposited in the archives of the Council of Europe. The Secretary General shall transmit certified copies to each of the signatories.

References

1 Heading added according to the provisions of Protocol No. 11 (ETS No. 155).
2 Heading added according to the provisions of Protocol No. 11 (ETS No. 155).
3 Heading added according to the provisions of Protocol No. 11 (ETS No. 155).
4 Heading added according to the provisions of Protocol No. 11 (ETS No. 155).
5 Heading added according to the provisions of Protocol No. 11 (ETS No. 155).
6 Heading added according to the provisions of Protocol No. 11 (ETS No. 155).
7 New Section II according to the provisions of Protocol No. 11 (ETS No. 155).
8 Heading added according to the provisions of Protocol No. 11 (ETS No. 155).
9 The articles of this Section are renumbered according to the provisions of Protocol No. 11 (ETS No. 155).
10 Heading added according to the provisions of Protocol No. 11 (ETS No. 155).
11 Text amended according to the provisions of Protocol No. 11 (ETS No. 155).
12 Text amended according to the provisions of Protocol No. 11 (ETS No. 155).
13 Heading added according to the provisions of Protocol No. 11 (ETS No. 155).

The European Social Charter
(brief presentation)

A Council of Europe Treaty safeguarding Human Rights

The **European Social Charter** (referred to below to as "the Charter") sets out rights and freedoms and establishes a supervisory mechanism guaranteeing their respect by the States Parties. It was recently revised, and the 1996 revised European Social Charter, which came into force in 1999, is gradually replacing the initial 1961 treaty.

The appended table shows **which countries have currently signed and ratified the Charter**.

Rights guaranteed by the Charter

The rights guaranteed by the Charter concern all individuals in their daily lives:

Housing:
- construction of housing in accordance with families' needs;
- reduction in the number of homeless persons;
- universally assured access to decent, affordable housing;
- equal access to social housing for foreigners;

Health:
- accessible, effective health care facilities for the entire population;
- policy for preventing illness with, in particular, the guarantee of a healthy environment;
- elimination of occupational hazards so as to ensure that health and safety at work are provided for by law and guaranteed in practice;

Education:
- a ban on work by children under the age of 15;
- free primary and secondary education;
- free vocational guidance services;
- initial and further vocational training;
- access to university and other forms of higher education solely on the basis of personal merit;

Employment:
- a social and economic policy designed to ensure full employment;
- the right to earn one's living in an occupation freely entered upon;
- fair working conditions as regards pay and working hours;
- action to combat sexual and psychological harassment;
- prohibition of forced labour;
- freedom to form trade unions and employers' organisations to defend economic and social interests; individual freedom to decide whether or not to join them;
- promotion of joint consultation, collective bargaining, conciliation and voluntary arbitration;
- the right to strike;

Social protection:
- the right to social security, social welfare and social services;
- the right to be protected against poverty and social exclusion;
- special measures catering for families and the elderly;

Movement of persons:
- simplification of immigration formalities for European workers;
- the right to family reunion;
- the right of non-resident foreigners to emergency assistance up until repatriation;
- procedural safeguards in the event of expulsion;

Non-discrimination:
- the right of women and men to equal treatment and equal opportunities in employment;
- a guarantee that all the rights set out in the Charter apply regardless of race, sex, age, colour, language, religion, opinions, national origin, social background, state of health or association with a national minority.

European Committee of Social Rights

The European Committee of Social Rights (referred to below as "the Committee") ascertains whether countries have honoured the undertakings set out in the Charter. Its twelve independent, impartial members are elected by the Council of Europe *Committee of Ministers* for a period of six years, renewable once. The Committee determines whether or not national law and practice in the States Parties are in conformity with the Charter (Article 24 of the Charter, as amended by the 1991 *Turin Protocol*).

A monitoring procedure based on national reports

Every year the states parties submit a *report* indicating how they implement the Charter in law and in practice. Each report concerns some of the *accepted provisions* of the Charter.

The Committee examines the reports and decides whether or not the situations in the countries concerned are in conformity with the Charter. Its decisions, known as "*conclusions*", are published every year.

If a state takes no action on a Committee decision to the effect that it does not comply with the Charter, the Committee of Ministers addresses a *recommendation* to that state, asking it to change the situation in law or in practice. The Committee of Ministers' work is prepared by a *Governmental Committee* comprising representatives of the governments of the States Parties to the Charter, assisted by observers representing European employers' organisations and trade unions[1].

A collective complaints procedure

Under a *protocol* opened for signature in 1995, which came into force in 1998, *complaints* of violations of the Charter may be lodged with the European Committee of Social Rights.

Organisations entitled to lodge complaints with the Committee

– In the case of all states that have accepted the procedure:
1. the ETUC, UNICE and the IOE[1];
2. *Non-governmental organisations (NGOs) with consultative status* with the Council of Europe which are on a *list* drawn up for this purpose by the Governmental Committee;
3. Employers' organisations and trade unions in the country concerned;

– In the case of states which have also agreed to this:

4. National NGOs.

The complaint file must contain the following information:

a. the name and contact details of the organisation submitting the complaint;
b. proof that the person submitting and signing the complaint is entitled to represent the organisation lodging the complaint;
c. the state against which the complaint is directed;
d. an indication of the provisions of the Charter that have allegedly been violated;
e. the subject matter of the complaint, i.e. the point(s) in respect